P · O ·

# THESAURUS
# WORDFINDER

COVENT
GARDEN
BOOKS

## A DORLING KINDERSLEY BOOK

Produced for Dorling Kindersley by
PAGE*One*, Cairn House, Elgiva Lane, Chesham,
Buckinghamshire HP5 2JD

**PAGE*One* team**   Chris Clark, Helen Parker

**DK Managing editor**   Jane Yorke

**Dictionary editor**   Sheila Dignen

**Dictionary compilers**   Roz Combley
Jessica Feinstein
Fred McDonald
Elaine Pollard
Laura Wedgeworth
John Williams

Published in Great Britain by
Dorling Kindersley Limited, 9 Henrietta Street,
London WC2E 8PS

2 4 6 8 10 9 7 5 3 1
Copyright © 1998 Dorling Kindersley Limited, London

This edition published in 1999 for Covent Garden Books

A CIP catalogue record for this book is available from
the British Library.

ISBN 1-85605-502-7

Printed and bound in Italy by LegoPrint

# THE AIM OF THIS BOOK

The aim of a thesaurus wordfinder is to provide lists of useful synonyms or near synonyms. If you have a particular word in mind, but feel that it is not quite the word that you want to use – for example, because you have already used it once in a piece of writing, or because it does not convey the exact meaning that you wish to convey – you can look the word up in this thesaurus and find a list of other words with the same, or nearly the same meaning. You can then select the one most appropriate for your needs. The thesaurus includes phrases as well as single words where it is felt that these may be useful. For example, the entry at dance (verb) includes not only verbs such as "jive", "twirl", and "waltz", but also phrases such as "do a jig", "leap about", and "shake a leg".

## ARRANGEMENT OF ENTRIES

1 This thesaurus is arranged in strict alphabetical order. The main entries are listed in alphabetical order, and individual synonyms within the entries are also arranged in alphabetical order.

2 Different parts of speech are included as separate headwords. For example, **fence** (noun) is listed as a separate entry from **fence** (verb). They are listed next to each other in the thesaurus:

**fence** n barricade, barrier, defence, fencing, hedge, hurdle, paling, palisade, railings, rampart, stockade, wall, wire

**fence** v bound, circumscribe, confine, coop, encircle, enclose, hedge, pen, surround

3 Plural and singular nouns are listed separately. For example, **arms** (weapons) is listed as a separate entry from **arm**.

**4** Parts of speech are given immediately after the headword. The following abbreviations are used throughout the wordfinder:

| | |
|---|---|
| *n* | noun |
| *v* | verb |
| *adj* | adjective |
| *adv* | adverb |
| *prep* | preposition |
| *conj* | conjunction |

**5** Where a word has more than one meaning, each meaning is numbered and, where there is a possibility of confusion, a brief definition or example is given to make it clear which meaning is being dealt with. The following abbreviations are used throughout the book:

| | |
|---|---|
| sb | somebody |
| sth | something |

**6** Where a particular synonym is an informal or technical word, this is indicated immediately after the synonym in question. The following labels are used throughout the book:

| | |
|---|---|
| *Am* | American |
| *inf* | informal |
| *sl* | slang |
| *tech* | technical |

For example, at the entry for **abnormal**, the synonym "kinky" is labelled as informal and "wacko" is labelled as slang.

**abnormal** *adj* aberrant, anomalous, atypical, bizarre, deviant, eccentric, erratic, exceptional, extraordinary, idiosyncratic, irregular, kinky *inf*, odd, peculiar, perverse, perverted, queer, singular, strange, unexpected, unnatural, unorthodox, unusual, wacko *sl*, weird; *opp* normal

**7** Where a word has a clear or useful opposite, this is given at the end of the list of synonyms. Sometimes more than one opposite may be given if it is useful. For example:

**noisy** *adj* blaring, blasting, boisterous, deafening, ear-splitting, loud, piercing, raucous, riotous, rowdy; *opp* quiet, silent

# THESAURUS
# WORDFINDER

**abandon** v 1 (leave sb) desert, ditch *inf*, dump *inf*, forsake, jilt, leave, leave behind, maroon, run out on *inf*, strand, throw over *inf*. 2 (leave a place) depart from, evacuate, go away from, quit, vacate, withdraw. 3 (give sth away) cede, deliver, forfeit, give up, renounce, relinquish, resign, surrender, waive, yield. 4 **abandon yourself to** give yourself up to, give way to, indulge in, lose yourself in, lose yourself to

**abashed** *adj* ashamed, discomfited, disconcerted, embarrassed, humiliated, mortified, shamefaced; *opp* unabashed

**abate** v die down, diminish, ease, fade, lessen, let up, subside

**abbreviate** v abridge, clip, compress, condense, crop, curtail, cut, cut down, précis, prune, reduce, shorten, summarize, trim, truncate; *opp* lengthen

**abbreviation** n contraction, shortened form

**abdicate** v 1 (give up throne) cede, give up, quit, renounce, resign, retire, stand down, step down *inf*, vacate, waive, yield. 2 (give up responsibility) cast aside, disown, give up, refuse, relinquish, renounce, repudiate, surrender, turn your back on, wash your hands of

**abduct** v carry off, hold to ransom, kidnap, make off with, run away with, run off with, seize, snatch *inf*

**abhor** v abominate, detest, dislike, hate, loathe, recoil from, shrink from, shudder at

**abhorrent** *adj* abominable, detestable, disgusting, distasteful, execrable, hated, hateful, horrible, horrid, loathsome, nauseating, obnoxious, odious, offensive, repellent, repugnant, repulsive, revolting

**abide** v 1 accept, bear, endure, put up with, stand, stomach, suffer, tolerate. 2 **abide by** adhere to, agree to, comply with, conform to, follow, keep to, obey, observe, stand by, stick to, submit to

**ability** n adeptness, adroitness, aptitude, bent, capability, capacity, cleverness, competence, competency, expertise, expertness, facility, faculty, flair, gift, knack, know-how *inf*, power, proficiency, prowess, skill, talent

**abject** *adj* 1 (of conditions) deplorable, hopeless, miserable, pathetic, pitiable, piteous, wretched. 2 (of people) base, contemptible, cringing, despicable, grovelling, ignominious, ingratiating, low, mean, obsequious, servile, slavish, snivelling, submissive, sycophantic, toadying, vile, worthless, wretched

**ablaze** *adj* 1 (on fire) afire, alight, blazing, burning, fiery, flaming, ignited, lighted,

on fire, raging. 2 (full of light) aglow,
bright, brilliant, flashing, gleaming,
glowing, illuminated, incandescent, lit
up, luminous, radiant, shimmering,
sparkling

**able** *adj* accomplished, adept, capable,
clever, competent, experienced, expert,
gifted, masterly, proficient, qualified,
skilled, strong, talented

**abnormal** *adj* aberrant, anomalous,
atypical, bizarre, deviant, eccentric,
erratic, exceptional, extraordinary,
idiosyncratic, irregular, kinky *inf*, odd,
peculiar, perverse, perverted, queer,
singular, strange, unexpected, unnatural,
unorthodox, unusual, wacko *sl*, weird;
*opp* normal

**abolish** *v* annul, axe, cancel, destroy, do
away with, eliminate, end, eradicate,
extinguish, get rid of, nullify, put an end
to, quash, rescind, revoke, stamp out,
stop, terminate, wipe out

**abominable** *adj* abhorrent, contemptible,
despicable, detestable, disgusting, foul,
hateful, horrible, horrid, loathsome,
nasty, obnoxious, odious, offensive,
repellent, revolting, terrible, vile,
wretched

**abort** *v* 1 (end pregnancy) have a
miscarriage, miscarry, terminate. 2 (end
mission) call off, come to a halt, end,
fail, halt, stop, terminate

**abortion** *n* miscarriage, termination

**abortive** *adj* failed, fruitless, futile,
ineffective, ineffectual, pointless,
unproductive, unsuccessful, useless,
vain, worthless; *opp* successful

**abound** *v* 1 (be full of) be alive with, be
crawling with *inf*, be full of, overflow

with, swarm with, teem with. 2 (be
plentiful) be plentiful, flourish, thrive

**abrasive** *adj* 1 (rubbing a surface) caustic,
chafing, coarse, corrosive, eroding,
harsh, rough, sharp. 2 (of people)
aggressive, biting, cutting, grating,
harsh, hurtful, nasty, rough, sharp,
unpleasant

**abridge** *v* abbreviate, compress, condense,
cut, cut down, précis, prune, reduce,
shorten, summarize, trim, truncate

**abrupt** *adj* 1 (rude) blunt, brisk, brusque,
curt, direct, gruff, impolite, rough, rude,
short, snappish, terse, uncivil,
ungracious. 2 (sudden) hasty, hurried,
instantaneous, quick, rapid, sharp,
sudden, swift, unexpected, unforeseen

**abscond** *v* bolt, decamp, disappear, do a
bunk *inf*, do a runner, escape, flee, make
a quick getaway, make off, run away, run
for it, slip away, sneak away, steal away,
take flight, take to your heels

**absence** *n* 1 (person missing)
absenteeism, non-attendance, non-
appearance, truancy; *opp* presence.
2 (thing missing) deficiency, lack, need,
omission, privation, want

**absent** *adj* 1 (not present) away,
elsewhere, gone, lacking, missing, not
present, off, out, skiving *inf*, unavailable,
wanting; *opp* present. 2 (not paying
attention) absent-minded, blank, day-
dreaming, distracted, dreaming, dreamy,
empty, far-away, inattentive, oblivious,
preoccupied, unaware, unconscious,
vacant, vague

**absent-minded** *adj* absorbed, abstracted,
bemused, distracted, dreaming,
engrossed, forgetful, preoccupied,

unaware, vague

**absolute** *adj* **1** (complete) complete, downright, entire, out-and-out, outright, perfect, pure, sheer, thorough, total, unmitigated, unqualified, utter. **2** (definite) categorical, certain, conclusive, decided, definite, positive, sure, undoubted, unequivocal, unquestionable. **3** (absolute power) authoritarian, autocratic, despotic, dictatorial, full, sovereign, supreme, unbounded, unconditional, unlimited, unqualified, unrestrained

**absolutely** *adv* **1** (completely) completely, entirely, fully, perfectly, totally, utterly, wholly. **2** (definitely) certainly, definitely, positively, surely, truly, undoubtedly, unequivocally, unquestionably, unreservedly, without a doubt

**absolve** *v* acquit, clear, discharge, exempt, excuse, exonerate, forgive, free, liberate, let off, pardon, release, reprieve, set free, vindicate

**absorb** *v* **1** (take in substance) assimilate, digest, draw in, draw up, mop up, soak up, sop up, suck up, take in. **2** (engross) captivate, engage, engross, enthral, fascinate, immerse, involve, occupy, preoccupy, rivet. **3** (take over) appropriate, incorporate, swallow, take over

**absorbed** *adj* captivated, engrossed, fascinated, fixed, held, immersed, involved, lost, occupied, preoccupied, rapt, riveted, spellbound

**absorbing** *adj* captivating, fascinating, gripping, intriguing, riveting, spellbinding

**abstain** *v* **1** avoid, decline, deny yourself, desist, forbear, forgo, give up, go without, hold back, refrain, refuse, renounce, shun. **2** (not drink) be on the wagon *inf*, be teetotal, take the pledge

**abstemious** *adj* abstinent, austere, frugal, moderate, puritanical, self-denying, sober, sparing, temperate

**abstract** *adj* **1** abstruse, complex, conceptual, deep, general, intellectual, metaphysical, obscure, philosophical, theoretical. **2** (art) non-representational, non-realistic, symbolic, unrealistic

**abstract** *n* digest, outline, précis, résumé, summary, synopsis

**abstract** *v* detach, extract, isolate, remove, separate, take away, take out, withdraw

**absurd** *adj* crazy, daft *inf*, farcical, foolish, idiotic, illogical, inane, hare-brained, laughable, ludicrous, nonsensical, paradoxical, preposterous, ridiculous, risible, silly, stupid, surreal, zany

**abundance** *n* affluence, bountifulness, copiousness, heaps *inf*, loads *inf*, plentifulness, plenty, profusion, stacks *inf*, tons *inf*

**abundant** *adj* ample, bounteous, bountiful, copious, flourishing, full, generous, great, huge, large, lavish, liberal, luxuriant, overflowing, plentiful, profuse, rampant, rich, teeming

**abuse** *n* **1** (wrong use) corruption, misapplication, mishandling, misuse. **2** (cruel behaviour) beating, cruelty, exploitation, harm, ill-treatment, maltreatment, mistreatment, oppression, torture, wrongdoing.

**3** (insults) blame, censure, curses, cursing, defamation, expletives, insults, invective, obscenity, rebuke, reproach, revilement, slander, swearing, swear-words, upbraiding, vilification, vituperation

**abuse** *v* **1** (use sth wrongly) misapply, mishandle, misuse. **2** (behave cruelly to sb) batter, beat, harm, hurt, ill-treat, ill-use, injure, maltreat, manhandle, mistreat, molest, oppress, torture. **3** (insult) blame, call sb names *inf*, castigate, censure, criticize, curse, denigrate, disparage, insult, malign, rebuke, revile, scold, smear, swear, upbraid, vilify

**abusive** *adj* acrimonious, angry, censorious, critical, cruel, disparaging, hurtful, insulting, libellous, obscene, offensive, rude, scornful, slanderous

**abysmal** *adj* appalling, awful *inf*, bad, deplorable, dreadful, dire, lousy, poor, terrible

**abyss** *n* bottomless pit, chasm, depths, gulf, hole, pit, void

**academic** *adj* **1** (to do with education) educational, instructional, pedagogical, scholastic. **2** (of a person) bookish, brainy *inf*, cerebral, cultured, erudite, high-brow, intellectual, learned, literary, scholarly, studious, well-read. **3** (theoretical) abstract, conjectural, hypothetical, impractical, speculative, theoretical

**academic** *n* don, fellow, lecturer, pedagogue, professor, pupil, scholar, student, teacher, thinker, tutor

**accelerate** *v* **1** go faster, hurry, pick up speed, speed up; *opp* slow down. **2** (make

sth go faster) advance, expedite, hasten, precipitate, speed up, spur on, stimulate

**accent** *n* **1** (way of talking) articulation, brogue, cadence, dialect, enunciation, inflection, intonation, modulation, pronunciation, tone. **2** (stress) accentuation, emphasis, force, stress. **3** (written mark) acute accent, cedilla, circumflex, diacritic, grave accent, mark, sign, tilde, umlaut

**accept** *v* **1** accede, acknowledge, acquiesce, admit, agree, approve, assume, buy *sl*, comply, concur, consent, co-operate, go along with, take on, undertake. **2** (receive) acquire, come by, gain, get, obtain, receive, secure, take. **3** (tolerate) put up with, stand, submit to, suffer, take, tolerate. **4** (believe) be convinced, believe, credit, have faith, trust

**acceptable** *adj* **1** (welcome) agreeable, delightful, desirable, gratifying, pleasing, welcome. **2** (satisfactory) adequate, admissible, all right, fair, moderate, OK, okay, passable, satisfactory, so-so *inf*, tolerable. **3** (of risks) admissible, allowable, bearable, supportable, tolerable

**accepted** *adj* acknowledged, admitted, agreed, approved, authorized, conventional, customary, normal, recognized, standard, time-honoured, traditional, usual

**access** *n* accessibility, admission, admittance, entrance, entrée, entry, right of entry, way in

**accessible** *adj* **1** (able to be reached) available, exposed, get-at-able *inf*, handy, near, nearby, obtainable, on

hand, open, reachable, within reach. 2
(able to be understood) comprehensible,
fathomable, intelligible, understandable.
3 (of a person) affable, agreeable,
approachable, available, cordial, easy-
going, friendly, informal, obliging

**accessory** n 1 addition, add-on, adjunct,
appendage, attachment, component,
extra, supplement. 2 (crime)
accomplice, assistant, associate,
confederate, helper, partner

**accident** n 1 blunder, calamity,
catastrophe, disaster, mishap,
misfortune, tragedy. 2 (road accident)
collision, crash, pile-up, smash.
3 (chance) chance, coincidence, fate,
fluke inf, fortune, hazard, luck,
serendipity, twist of fate

**accidental** adj arbitrary, chance,
coincidental, fortuitous, fortunate,
inadvertent, lucky, random, unexpected,
unforeseen, unintentional, unplanned,
unpremeditated, unwitting

**accidentally** adv by accident, by chance,
by mistake, inadvertently,
unintentionally, unwittingly

**acclaim** v announce, applaud, approve,
celebrate, cheer, clap, commend,
declare, exalt, extol, hail, honour, praise,
proclaim, salute, welcome

**acclimatize** v accommodate, accustom,
adapt, adjust, become seasoned,
familiarize yourself, get used to,
habituate yourself

**accommodate** v 1 (give a room to)
board, cater for, entertain, house, lodge,
put up, shelter, take in. 2 (help) aid,
assist, help, lend a hand, meet sb's needs,
oblige, do sb a favour. 3 (give sth to sb)

equip, furnish, grant, oblige, provide,
serve, supply. 4 (adapt) accustom, adapt,
adjust, conform

**accommodating** adj agreeable,
complaisant, compliant, considerate,
co-operative, helpful, hospitable, kind,
obliging, polite, unselfish, willing

**accommodation** n board, digs inf, home,
housing, lodging, pied-à-terre, premises,
quarters, shelter

**accompany** v 1 attend, chaperon,
conduct, escort, go with, guide, tag
along with inf, travel with. 2 (musically)
provide backing for, play for, support

**accomplice** n accessory, ally, assistant,
collaborator, colleague, confederate,
conspirator, friend, helper, henchman,
mate, right-hand man, sidekick inf

**accomplish** v achieve, attain, bring
about, bring off, carry off, do, effect,
execute, finish, fulfil, perform, produce,
realize, succeed

**accomplished** adj able, adept, capable,
competent, consummate, deft, expert,
gifted, masterly, polished, practised,
proficient, skilful, skilled, talented

**accomplishment** n 1 (talent) ability,
achievement, attainment, capability,
proficiency, skill, talent. 2 (thing done)
achievement, act, attainment, coup,
deed, exploit, feat, success, triumph

**accost** v address, buttonhole inf, confront,
grab, greet, hail, nab inf, salute, speak to

**account** n 1 (report) chronicle,
description, explanation, history,
portrayal, record, report, statement,
story, tale. 2 **accounts** balance, balance
sheet, books, reckoning, tally

**account for** v explain, give reasons

for, justify

**accountable** *adj* answerable, liable, responsible

**accrue** *v* accumulate, amass, build up, collect, gather, grow, increase, mount up

**accumulate** *v* accrue, amass, assemble, build up, collect, gather, grow, hoard, increase, pile up, stash away *inf*, stockpile

**accumulation** *n* buildup, collection, heap, hoard, mass, pile, stack, stock, stockpile, store, supply

**accuracy** *n* authenticity, carefulness, correctness, exactness, faithfulness, meticulousness, precision, rightness, truth, truthfulness, validity, veracity; *opp* inaccuracy

**accurate** *adj* bang on *inf*, careful, correct, exact, faithful, literal, meticulous, precise, reliable, right, scrupulous, sound, spot on *inf*, strict, sure, true, truthful, valid; *opp* inaccurate

**accusation** *n* allegation, blame, charge, complaint, denouncement, indictment, recrimination, summons

**accuse** *v* arraign, blame, censure, charge, condemn, denounce, hold sb responsible, point the finger at *inf*

**accustomed** *adj* 1 (usual) common, customary, established, fixed, general, habitual, normal, ordinary, regular, routine, set, typical, usual. 2 accustomed to given to, in the habit of, seasoned, trained, used to

**ache** *n* discomfort, hurt, pain, pang, smarting, soreness, throb, twinge

**ache** *v* be painful, be sore, hurt, pound, smart, sting, throb

**achieve** *v* accomplish, acquire, arrive at, attain, bring about, carry out, do, earn, effect, engineer, execute, finish, fulfil, gain, get, manage, obtain, perform, procure, reach, realize, win

**achievement** *n* accomplishment, act, action, attainment, deed, exploit, feat

**acid** *adj* 1 (taste) acrid, biting, bitter, pungent, sharp, sour, tangy, tart, vinegary. 2 (remarks) acerbic, caustic, cutting, sarcastic, sharp, vitriolic

**acknowledge** *v* 1 (notice sb) address, greet, hail, notice, recognize, respond, say hello to *inf*. 2 (answer a letter) answer, reply, respond. 3 (admit sth) accept, admit, allow, concede, own, recognize

**acknowledgment** *n* acceptance, admission, agreement, answer, appreciation, notice, reaction, recognition, reply, response

**acquaintance** *n* 1 (person) associate, colleague, contact. 2 (knowledge) awareness, familiarity, knowledge, understanding

**acquainted** *adj* aware, conscious, familiar, informed, privy to

**acquiesce** *v* accept, agree, assent, bow, comply, concur, consent, go along with, submit, yield

**acquire** *v* amass, appropriate, buy, collect, come by, gain, gather, get, earn, obtain, pick up, procure, purchase, receive, win

**acquisition** *n* addition, buy, gain, possession, prize, property, purchase

**acquit** *v* absolve, clear, discharge, exonerate, find innocent, free, let off *inf*, liberate, reprieve, set free, vindicate

**acrimonious** *adj* acerbic, bad-tempered, bitter, caustic, cutting, harsh, hostile, hot-tempered, petulant, quarrelsome, rancorous, sarcastic, spiteful, unpleasant, vitriolic

**act** n 1 (thing done) accomplishment, achievement, action, deed, exploit, feat, move. 2 (law) bill, decree, edict, judgement, law, measure, ruling, statute. 3 (piece of entertainment) item, performance, routine, sketch, skit, show, turn. 4 (pretending) affectation, fake, feigning, front, pose, pretence, sham, show

**act** v 1 (do sth) be active, do sth, function, get involved, move, react, strike, take action, take steps. 2 (behave) behave, carry on. 3 (perform on stage) act out, appear as, be an actor, be an actress, dramatize, enact, mime, perform, play, play a part, portray, represent, take a part, tread the boards inf. 4 (have an effect) operate, take effect, work. 5 (pretend) affect, dissemble, fake, feign, pose, pretend, put on

**acting** adj deputy, fill-in inf, interim, pro tem, provisional, stopgap, substitute, surrogate, temporary, vice-

**action** n 1 accomplishment, achievement, act, deed, effort, endeavour, initiative, manoeuvre, measure, move, operation, step. 2 activity, energy, force, forcefulness, get-up-and-go inf, liveliness, spirit, vigour, vim, vitality. 3 **the action** activity, bustle, drama, events, excitement, goings-on inf, happenings, incidents. 4 (war) battle, combat, conflict, fighting, warfare. 5 (legal) case, lawsuit, litigation, proceedings

**activate** v arouse, energize, excite, fire, galvanize, initiate, kick-start, mobilize, motivate, prod, prompt, rouse, set going, set off, start, stimulate, switch on, trigger, turn on

**active** adj 1 animated, bustling, busy, dynamic, energetic, enthusiastic, hyperactive, industrious, lively, mobile, nimble, on the go inf, on the move inf, quick, sprightly, spry, vibrant, vigorous, vivacious. 2 effective, effectual, functioning, in force, live, moving, operating, operative, potent, powerful, running, working

**activist** n campaigner, lobbyist, man of action, militant, woman of action

**activity** n 1 (things happening) action, bustle, comings and goings inf, commotion, flurry, hurly-burly, hustle and bustle, industry, life, movement, stir, toing and froing inf, tumult. 2 (sth that you do) enterprise, hobby, job, occupation, pastime, project, pursuit, scheme, task, undertaking, venture, work

**actor, actress** n artist, artiste, lead, leading man, leading woman, performer, play-actor, player, star, starlet, supporting actor, Thespian, tragedian, trouper

**actual** adj authentic, bona fide, confirmed, definite, genuine, indisputable, legitimate, physical, real, tangible, true, undeniable, verified, veritable

**actually** adv as a matter of fact, indeed, in fact, in truth, literally, really, truly

**acute** adj 1 alert, astute, canny, clever, discerning, incisive, intuitive, keen, observant, penetrating, perceptive, perspicacious, quick, sharp, smart. **2** (of senses) discerning, keen, sensitive, sharp; *opp* dull. **3** (very great) critical, dangerous, grave, great, pressing, serious, severe, urgent, vital. **4** (of pain) excruciating, fierce, intense, piercing, racking, sharp, stabbing, shooting, sudden, violent

**adamant** *adj* determined, firm, inflexible, intransigent, obdurate, resolute, stubborn, unbending, uncompromising, unyielding

**adapt** *v* **1** adjust, alter, change, convert, modify, remodel, reorganize, reshape, tailor, transform. **2** (get used to) accommodate, adjust, become conditioned, become hardened, conform, familiarize yourself, get used to, habituate yourself

**adaptable** *adj* adjustable, convertible, flexible, malleable, modifiable, pliant, resilient, variable, versatile

**add** *v* **1** attach, affix, append, combine, include, integrate, join, tack on *inf*. **2** (figures) add up, compute, count, reckon, total, tot up *inf*

**addict** *n* **1** (drug addict) abuser, dope-fiend *sl*, freak *inf*, junkie *inf*, user. **2** (sb who is keen on sth) buff *inf*, devotee, enthusiast, fan, follower, freak *inf*, nut *inf*

**addicted** *adj* dependent, hooked *inf*, obsessed

**addiction** *n* compulsion, craving, dependence, dependency, fixation, habit, obsession

**addition** *n* adjunct, appendage, appendix, attachment, augmentation, enlargement, extension, extra, gain, increase, increment, supplement

**additional** *adj* added, extra, fresh, further, more, new, other, supplementary

**address** *n* **1** (place where sb lives) abode, domicile, dwelling, home, house, location, lodging, pad *sl*, residence. **2** (speech) lecture, oration, sermon, speech, talk

**address** *v* **1** (give a speech) lecture, preach, sermonize, speak, spout *inf*, talk. **2** (talk to) buttonhole *inf*, engage sb in conversation, greet, hail, salute, speak to, talk to

**adept** *adj* able, accomplished, adroit, clever, dexterous, expert, practised, proficient, skilful, skilled

**adequate** *adj* acceptable, ample, competent, enough, fair, mediocre, middling, OK, passable, presentable, reasonable, satisfactory, sufficient, suitable

**adhere** *v* attach, bind, bond, cling, fix, stick

**adjacent** *adj* abutting, adjoining, alongside, attached, bordering, close, near, neighbouring, touching

**adjoining** *adj* abutting, adjacent, attached, bordering, connected, connecting, joining, next door, neighbouring, touching

**adjourn** *v* break off, delay, interrupt, postpone, put off, suspend

**adjournment** *n* break, delay, interruption, pause, postponement, recess

**adjudicate** *v* arbitrate, decide, determine, give a ruling, judge, referee, settle, umpire

**adjust** *v* **1** adapt, alter, change, modify,

move, position, put right, rearrange,
remodel, set, tailor, tune, vary. 2 (adjust
to a situation) acclimatize, assimilate,
become accustomed, conform, get used
to, settle

**adjustment** n alteration, change,
modification, rearrangement,
rectification, repair, setting, tuning

**ad-lib** v extemporize, improvise, make up,
speak impromptu, speak off the cuff

**administration** n 1 (managing sth)
control, management, overseeing,
running, supervision. 2 (government)
executive, governing body, government,
ministry, regime

**administrative** adj controlling,
directorial, executive, governmental,
management, managerial,
organizational, regulatory, supervisory

**admirable** adj commendable, creditable,
estimable, exemplary, fine, good, great,
honourable, laudable, marvellous,
praiseworthy, wonderful, worthy

**admiration** n adoration, appreciation,
approval, awe, esteem, praise, regard,
respect, veneration, wonder

**admire** v applaud, approve, carry a torch
for inf, esteem, have a high opinion of,
hero-worship, idolize, like, look up to,
love, praise, respect, revere, sing the
praises of, think highly of, value,
venerate, wonder at, worship

**admirer** n 1 beau, boyfriend, girlfriend,
lover, suitor, sweetheart. 2 aficionado,
devotee, disciple, enthusiast, fan,
follower, freak inf, supporter, worshipper

**admissible** adj acceptable, allowable,
allowed, permissible, permitted,
tolerated

**admission** n 1 (getting in) access,
admittance, entrance, entry, right of
entry, ticket. 2 (admitting sth)
acceptance, acknowledgement, avowal,
confession, declaration, profession,
revelation; opp denial

**admit** v 1 (let in) accept, allow in, give
access, give admission to, grant access,
let in, permit entry, receive, take in.
2 (admit that sth is true) accept,
acknowledge, allow, concede, confess,
declare, own, own up, recognize, reveal;
opp deny

**adolescent** adj boyish, childish, girlish,
immature, juvenile, pubescent, puerile,
teenage, young, youthful

**adolescent** n teenager, young man, young
person, young woman, youngster, youth

**adopt** v 1 accept, approve, assume, back,
champion, choose, endorse, espouse,
follow, ratify, sanction, select, support,
take on, take up. 2 (adopt a child)
foster, take care of, take in

**adorable** adj appealing, attractive,
captivating, charming, cute, darling,
dear, delightful, gorgeous, lovable, sweet

**adore** v cherish, dote on, idolize, love,
praise, revere, worship

**adorn** v beautify, bedeck, deck, decorate,
embellish, enhance, festoon, garnish,
ornament, trim

**adult** adj full-grown, full-size, fully
developed, fully grown, grown-up,
mature, of age; opp immature

**adulterate** v contaminate, debase,
degrade, dilute, spoil, taint,
thin, water down, weaken

**adultery** n a bit on the side, extramarital
affair, infidelity, unfaithfulness

**advance** n breakthrough, development, finding, improvement, invention, progress

**advance** v 1 (move) come forward, forge ahead, gain ground, go ahead, go forward, make headway, move along, move forward, press on, proceed, push forward, push on inf; *opp* retreat. 2 (quicken) accelerate, expedite, forward, hasten, quicken, speed up, step up. 3 (develop) develop, evolve, flourish, grow, improve, progress, thrive. 4 (lend money) give, lend, loan, provide, supply on credit. 5 (put forward a theory) offer, propose, put forward, recommend, submit, suggest. 6 (help) assist, benefit, boost, facilitate, further, promote

**advantage** n 1 asset, benefit, blessing, boon, convenience, gain, good point, help. 2 (have an advantage over sb) edge, head start inf, lead, power, superiority, supremacy, upper hand

**advantageous** adj beneficial, constructive, convenient, helpful, invaluable, positive, profitable, useful, valuable, worthwhile

**adventure** n 1 (sth exciting that happens) escapade, experience, exploit, incident, occurrence. 2 (go out looking for adventure) danger, excitement, peril, risk, uncertainty

**adventurous** adj 1 bold, brave, courageous, daredevil, daring, intrepid; *opp* cautious. 2 challenging, dangerous, difficult, exciting, hazardous, precarious, perilous, risky

**adversary** n antagonist, competitor, enemy, foe, opponent, rival

**adverse** adj 1 (bad conditions) bad, disadvantageous, dreadful, inauspicious, unfavourable, unlucky; *opp* favourable. 2 (unkind) antagonistic, critical, derogatory, hostile, hurtful, negative, unfavourable, unfriendly, unkind, unsympathetic

**adversity** n affliction, bad luck, calamity, disaster, hardship, ill luck, misfortune, sorrow, suffering, tribulation, woe

**advertise** v 1 (try to sell sth) market, plug inf, promote, publicize, push inf, tout. 2 (tell people sth) advise, announce, broadcast, make known, notify, proclaim, publish

**advertisement** n advert inf, announcement, blurb inf, commercial, notice, poster, promotion, publicity, sign, small ad inf

**advice** n counsel, counselling, guidance, help, idea, opinion, recommendation, suggestion, tip, warning

**advisable** adj appropriate, desirable, expedient, judicious, politic, prudent, recommended, seemly, sensible, wise

**advise** v advocate, argue for/against caution, counsel, encourage, exhort, give guidance, guide, help, prescribe, recommend, suggest, urge, warn

**adviser** n confidant, confidante, consultant, coach, counsellor, guide, mentor

**advocate** n backer, champion, fan inf, promoter, spokesman, spokesperson, spokeswoman, supporter

**advocate** v advise, argue for, back, campaign for, champion, endorse, plead for, promote, recommend, speak for, uphold, urge

**affair** n 1 activity, business, case, episode, happening, issue, matter, project, question, subject, thing, topic. 2 attachment, bit on the side *inf*, intrigue, involvement, liaison, love affair, relationship, romance

**affect** v 1 (have an effect on) act on, alter, change, have an effect on, have an impact on, impinge on, influence, sway, transform. 2 (upset) concern, distress, disturb, grieve, hit *inf*, move, stir, touch, trouble, upset. 3 (put on) adopt, assume, fake, feign, pretend, put on *inf*, simulate

**affectation** n airs, airs and graces, façade, insincerity, mannerism, pose, posturing, pretence, pretension, sham, show, simulation

**affected** adj 1 (not real) artificial, contrived, fake, feigned, insincere, put on *inf*, simulated, studied, unnatural; *opp* natural. 2 (of style) high-flown, ostentatious, pompous, precious, pretentious

**affection** n devotion, fondness, friendliness, friendship, liking, love, soft spot *inf*, tenderness, warmth

**affectionate** adj caring, fond, friendly, kind, loving, tender, warm, warm-hearted

**affinity** n closeness, compatibility, connection, kinship, likeness, liking, relationship, resemblance, similarity, sympathy

**affirm** v assert, attest, avow, certify, confirm, declare, say, state, swear, testify

**afflict** v bother, cause suffering to, distress, grieve, harm, hurt, plague, rack, torment, torture, trouble, try, vex, worry

**affliction** n distress, grief, hardship, misery, misfortune, ordeal, pain, scourge, sorrow, suffering, torment, trouble, woe, wretchedness

**affluent** adj 1 (people) flush *inf*, loaded *inf*, moneyed, opulent, prosperous, rich, wealthy, well-heeled *inf*, well-off, well-to-do; *opp* poor. 2 (lifestyle) comfortable, expensive, lavish, luxurious, opulent, pampered, sumptuous

**afford** v 1 (be able to buy sth) find money for, have the means for, meet the expense of, pay for, spare the price of. 2 (be able to stand sth happening) bear, sustain, stand. 3 (give) bestow, furnish, give, offer, provide, supply

**affront** n aspersion, indignity, insult, outrage, provocation, slight, slur, snub, slap in the face *inf*

**afraid** adj alarmed, anxious, apprehensive, chicken *inf*, fearful, frightened, horror-struck, nervous, panic-stricken, scared, terrified, terror-stricken, timid, worried; *opp* fearless

**age** n 1 (period of history) date, days, epoch, era, generation, period, time. 2 (old age) advancing years, declining years, dotage, maturity, old age, senescence, senility, seniority. 3 (a long time) aeon, eternity, hours on end, lifetime, long time

**age** v become obsolete, decline, degenerate, deteriorate, get older, grow older, look older, mature, mellow, ripen, wither

**aged** adj ancient, antique, decrepit, elderly, getting on *inf*, grey, in your dotage, long in the tooth *inf*, old, past it *inf*, senile

**agency** n bureau, business, company, department, office, organization

**agenda** n list, plan, programme, schedule, scheme, timetable

**agent** n 1 broker, delegate, emissary, envoy, executor, go-between, intermediary, middleman, negotiator, proxy, rep inf, representative, spokesman, spokeswoman. 2 mole inf, spook Am inf, spy

**aggravate** v 1 compound, exacerbate, heighten, inflame, intensify, make worse, worsen. 2 (inf) (annoy sb) annoy, exasperate, get on sb's nerves, hassle inf, irritate, provoke, rub sb up the wrong way

**aggression** n attack, assault, hostility, invasion, offensive, onslaught, raid

**aggressive** adj argumentative, assertive, attacking, belligerent, forceful, hostile, provocative, pugnacious, pushy inf, quarrelsome, warlike

**aggrieved** adj distressed, hurt, ill-used, injured, peeved inf, piqued, resentful, unhappy, upset, wronged

**agile** adj acrobatic, active, fit, graceful, lithe, mobile, nimble, quick, sprightly, spry, supple

**agility** n activity, fitness, sprightliness, suppleness

**agitated** adj alarmed, anxious, confused, disconcerted, disturbed, excited, fazed, flustered, nervous, nervy, unnerved, unsettled, upset, worked up, worried; *opp* calm

**agonize** v deliberate, fret, labour, struggle, suffer, worry, wrestle

**agonizing** adj distressing, excruciating, harrowing, painful, racking, tormenting

**agony** n anguish, distress, hurt, misery, pain, suffering, torment, torture, woe

**agree** v 1 accept, acknowledge, acquiesce, admit, allow, concede, consent, grant, promise. 2 (two people agree) accord, be of the same mind, concur, get on, see eye to eye inf. 3 (figures) add up, match, tally

**agreeable** adj 1 amiable, charming, congenial, delightful, friendly, lovely, nice, pleasant, satisfying, to your liking; *opp* disagreeable. 2 (willing to do sth) accommodating, amenable, compliant, consenting, well-disposed, willing; *opp* unwilling

**agreement** n 1 accord, affinity, compatibility, concord, concurrence, congruity, consensus, harmony, unanimity, union. 2 (a deal) arrangement, bargain, contract, deal inf, pact, pledge, treaty, truce, understanding

**aid** n assistance, co-operation, encouragement, guidance, help, support

**aid** v abet, assist, benefit, encourage, facilitate, help, lend a hand, relieve, support

**aim** n ambition, aspiration, desire, dream, end, focus, goal, hope, intention, objective, plan, target, wish

**aim** v 1 (aim at sth) beam, direct, focus, line up, point, take aim, train, zero in. 2 (try to do sth) aspire, attempt, endeavour, hope, intend, resolve, seek, set your sights on, strive

**air** n 1 (space above earth) atmosphere, heavens, sky, space. 2 (breeze) blast, breath of air, breeze, draught, fresh air, oxygen, puff, ventilation, waft, wind. 3 (impression) appearance, aspect, atmosphere, aura, bearing, character, characteristic, demeanour, effect, feeling, flavour, look, manner, mood, quality, tone, vibes *inf*. 4 (tune) melody, theme, tune, song

**air** *v* 1 (air an opinion) communicate, declare, disclose, divulge, express, give vent to, make known, reveal, say, state, tell, voice. 2 (air a room or clothes) dry, freshen, ventilate

**alarm** *n* 1 angst, anxiety, apprehension, consternation, dismay, fear, fright, horror, nervousness, panic, shock, terror, uneasiness, worry; *opp* calmness, composure. 2 bell, distress signal, fire alarm, flare, red alert, siren, warning

**alarm** *v* daunt, dismay, distress, frighten, make sb nervous, put the wind up sb *inf*, panic, perturb, scare, scare sb stiff *inf*, shake, terrify, trouble, unnerve, worry

**alarmed** *adj* anxious, apprehensive, concerned, dismayed, fearful, frightened, horrified, nervous, perturbed, shocked, terrified, uneasy, worried; *opp* calm, collected, composed, cool

**alarming** *adj* daunting, distressing, disturbing, dreadful, frightening, scary, shocking, startling, ominous, terrifying, unnerving, worrying; *opp* reassuring

**alcoholic** *n* alky *slang*, dipsomaniac, drunk, drunkard, hard drinker, heavy drinker, wino *slang*

**alert** *adj* 1 (ready to respond) attentive, awake, eagle-eyed, on your guard, on your toes, prepared, ready, sharp-eyed, vigilant, wary, watchful, wide-awake; *opp* off guard. 2 (with a lively mind) bright, lively, on the ball *inf*, perceptive, quick, quick off the mark, sharp-witted,

with your wits about you; *opp* slow. 3 **alert** to alive to, aware of, clued up on *inf*, conscious of, sensitive to

**alert** *n* alarm, danger signal, emergency, flare, mayday, red-alert, signal, siren, warning

**alert** *v* advise, draw sb's attention to, notify, raise the alarm, tip sb off, warn

**alibi** *n* defence, excuse, explanation, justification, pretext, reason

**alien** *adj* extraterrestrial, foreign, outlandish, strange, unfamiliar, unnatural, weird; *opp* familiar

**alight** *v* dismount, disembark, get down, get off, get out. 2 land, come down, settle, perch

**alight** *adj* 1 (burning) aflame, blazing, burning, flaming, lit, on fire; *opp* burnt out, dead, extinguished, out. 2 (lit up) bright, glowing, illuminated, lit up, radiant, shining; *opp* dark, dead, dim, dull

**alike** *adj* cast in the same mould, comparable, duplicate, equivalent, identical, like, like peas in a pod, much the same, parallel, resembling, similar, the same, twin, uniform; *opp* different, dissimilar, like chalk and cheese, unlike

**alive** *adj* 1 alive and kicking, animate, breathing, in existence, in the land of the living *inf*, living; *opp* dead, deceased, lifeless. 2 (continuing) continuing, current, in action, in existence, in operation, on-going; *opp* dead, defunct. 3 (lively, energetic) active, alert, energetic, full of life, lively, sprightly, vibrant, vigorous, vivacious; *opp* dead, dull, lifeless. 4 (alive to a problem) aware of, alert to, conscious of, sensitive to. 5 (alive with people, insects) bustling, crawling, heaving, swarming, teeming

**allay** v alleviate, assuage, calm, diminish, lessen, pacify, quell, reduce, relieve, soothe; *opp* exacerbate, make worse, inflame

**allegation** n accusation, assertion, charge, claim

**allege** v accuse, assert, aver, contend, claim, declare, insist, maintain, profess, say, state, suggest

**allergic** adj hypersensitive, sensitive, susceptible

**allergy** n allergic reaction, hypersensitivity, sensitivity, susceptibility

**alleviate** v allay, assuage, deaden, ease, lessen, mitigate, moderate, reduce, relieve, soothe; *opp* exacerbate, make worse

**alliance** n affiliation, agreement, association, coalition, confederation, federation, league, marriage, pact, partnership, relationship, treaty, union; *opp* divorce, separation

**allied** adj associated, connected, linked, related, similar

**allocate** v allot, assign, dish out *inf*, distribute, dole out *inf*, earmark, give, give out, grant, set aside, share out

**allot** v allocate, assign, dish out *inf*, distribute, dole out *inf*, earmark, give, give out, grant, set aside, share out

**all-out** adj complete, determined, full, maximum, no-holds-barred, thorough, total, unmitigated, utmost, wholehearted, wholesale

**allow** v 1 (permit) approve, authorize, give sb the go-ahead *inf*, give sb the

green light, let, permit, sanction. **2** (allocate) allocate, allot, assign, give, grant, set aside. **3** (take sth into account) bear sth in mind, make allowances for, make provision for, take into account, take into consideration, provide for. **4** (accept that) accept, acknowledge, admit, concede, confess, grant

**allowance** n **1** grant, maintenance, payment, pocket money, remittance, stipend. **2** allocation, quota, ration, share

**allude to** v hint at, imply, mention, refer to, suggest, touch upon

**allusion** n hint, implication, insinuation, intimation, mention, reference, remark, suggestion

**ally** n accomplice, associate, collaborator, colleague, co-worker, friend, helper, partner in crime, sidekick; *opp* enemy

**alone** adj, adv **1** apart, by yourself, detached, isolated, lone, separate, solitary, unaccompanied, unattended. **2** (without help) by yourself, single-handed, solo, unassisted, unaided. **3** abandoned, deserted, forsaken, lonely. **4** (you alone, this alone) exclusively, just, nothing but, purely, only, simply, solely

**aloof** adj cold, cool, distant, haughty, inaccessible, indifferent, reserved, standoffish, unapproachable, unfriendly, unsociable; *opp* friendly, sociable, warm

**aloud** adv audibly, clearly, distinctly, out loud, plainly; *opp* silently, to yourself

**alter** v adapt, adjust, amend, change, convert, do sth differently, make sth different, modify, remodel, reshape, revise, transform, vary

**alteration** *n* adaptation, adjustment, amendment, change, conversion, difference, modification, revision, transformation, variation

**alternate** *adj* alternating, every other, every second, turn and turn about

**alternate** *v* follow in turn, intersperse, rotate, swap about *inf*, take turns, vary

**alternative** *n* choice, option, other, substitute

**always** *adv* 1 (every time) consistently, every time, invariably, without exception, without fail. 2 (continually) continually, constantly, incessantly, interminably, perpetually, repeatedly. 3 (for ever) eternally, endlessly, for ever, for ever more

**amalgamate** *v* combine, fuse, incorporate, integrate, join, link, merge, mix, unify, unite; *opp* separate, split

**amalgamation** *n* combination, fusion, incorporation, integration, linking, joining, merger, unification; *opp* separation

**amass** *v* accumulate, assemble, collect, gather together, hoard, save, stash away *inf*, stockpile, store away

**amaze** *v* astonish, astound, bowl sb over *inf*, dumbfound, floor *inf*, leave sb speechless, shock, stagger, stun, surprise, take sb's breath away

**amazed** *adj* astonished, astounded, bowled over *inf*, dumbfounded, floored *inf*, left speechless, shocked, staggered, stunned, surprised, thunderstruck

**amazement** *n* astonishment, awe, surprise, shock, wonder

**amazing** *adj* 1 (very good) brill *inf*, brilliant, excellent, fabulous, fantastic, great, incredible, marvellous, superb, terrific, tremendous, wonderful. 2 (surprising) astonishing, astounding, shocking, staggering, stunning, surprising

**ambassador** *n* attaché, consul, diplomat, emissary, envoy, representative

**ambiguous** *adj* cryptic, double-edged, enigmatic, equivocal, obscure, puzzling, unclear, vague, with a double meaning; *opp* clear, plain, obvious, unequivocal

**ambition** *n* 1 determination, drive, enterprise, get-up-and-go *inf*, motivation; *opp* apathy, indifference. 2 aim, aspiration, desire, dream, goal, objective

**ambitious** *adj* 1 determined, eager, enterprising, go-ahead, keen, motivated. 2 challenging, demanding, difficult

**ambush** *n* surprise attack, trap

**ambush** *v* attack, lie in wait for, trap, waylay

**amenable** *adj* accommodating, agreeable, flexible, open to persuasion, open to suggestion, responsive

**amend** *v* adjust, alter, change, correct, improve, modify, revise

**amendment** *n* addendum, adjustment, alteration, change, correction, improvement, modification, revision

**amenity** *n* facility, feature, resource, service

**amiable** *adj* affable, agreeable, approachable, endearing, engaging, friendly, genial, good-natured, kindly, likeable, pleasant, sociable

**amicable** *adj* amiable, civil, cordial, courteous, friendly, good-humoured, good-natured, harmonious, peaceable

**ammunition** n ammo inf, armaments, bombs, bullets, cartridges, explosives, grenades, missiles, munitions, pellets, rounds, shot

**amnesty** n dispensation, forgiveness, immunity, pardon, remission, reprieve

**amorous** adj adoring, ardent, doting, enamoured, erotic, in love, lecherous, lovesick, loving, lustful, passionate, randy, sexual, sexy

**amount** n 1 degree, extent, magnitude, quantity, number, size, value, volume. 2 lot, measure, sum, sum total, total

**amount to** v 1 add up to, come to, equal, make, run to, total. 2 add up to, be equivalent to, be tantamount to, be the same as, mean

**ample** adj 1 adequate, enough, more than enough, plenty, sufficient. 2 abundant, generous, lavish, plentiful. 3 big, expansive, full, large, roomy, spacious, substantial, voluminous

**amplify** v 1 boost, intensify, increase, magnify, make louder, strengthen. 2 develop, elaborate on, enlarge on, expound, flesh out, go into details, say more about

**amputate** v chop off, cut off, lop off, remove, sever

**amuse** v 1 entertain, make sb laugh, make sb smile, regale sb with. 2 (find sth to do) entertain, keep sb happy, occupy

**amused** adj 1 entertained, tickled, tickled pink. 2 absorbed, engrossed, entertained, occupied

**amusement** n 1 delight, enjoyment, hilarity, laughter, pleasure. 2 diversion, entertainment, occupation, recreation

**amusing** adj comical, droll, funny, hilarious, humorous, ludicrous, ridiculous, witty

**analogy** n correlation, correspondence, parallel, resemblance, similarity

**analyse** v 1 evaluate, examine, investigate, study, work out. 2 (analyse a blood sample) break down, do an analysis of, separate out, test

**analysis** n 1 examination, study, investigation, evaluation. 2 (of blood sample) test, breakdown

**analytical** adj detailed, diagnostic, methodical, investigative, systematic

**anarchic** adj chaotic, disorderly, lawless, rebellious, uncontrolled, undisciplined, unpredictable; **opp** orderly

**anarchy** n anarchism, chaos, disorder, lawlessness, rebellion

**ancestor** n family, forbear, forefather, previous generation

**ancient** adj 1 (very old) aged, ageing, antiquated, elderly, old. 2 (old-fashioned) antiquated, archaic, behind the times, dated, obsolete, old-fashioned, old hat, outmoded, out-of-date, out of the ark, passé; **opp** latest, modern, up-to-date. 3 (in early history) early, prehistoric, primeval, primitive, primordial

**anecdote** n account, cautionary tale, reminiscence, story, tale

**angel** n 1 cherub, seraph, archangel. 2 dear, gem, marvel, saint, star, treasure

**anger** n annoyance, exasperation, displeasure, fury, irritation, outrage, rage, temper

**angle** n 1 bend, corner, crook, fork, point. 2 approach, aspect, direction, point of view, position, perspective, side, slant, standpoint, viewpoint

**angry** *adj* annoyed, cross, mad, fuming, furious, heated, hopping mad, hot under the collar, incensed, infuriated, irate, irritated, mad, outraged, uptight *inf*; *opp* calm, laid-back

**anguish** *n* agony, distress, grief, heartbreak, misery, pain, sorrow, suffering, torment, trauma

**animal** *n* beast, creature, mammal

**animated** *adj* 1 enthusiastic, excited, lively, impassioned, passionate, vehement, vigorous. 2 cartoon, lifelike, moving

**animosity** *n* acrimony, antagonism, bad feeling, bitterness, conflict, disapproval, distaste, hatred, hostility, loathing, rancour, resentment

**annihilate** *v* decimate, defeat, destroy, eradicate, exterminate, extinguish, liquidate, take out, wipe out

**announce** *v* declare, give out, go public on, make known, publicize, publish, release, reveal, say

**announcement** *n* bulletin, communiqué, declaration, disclosure, notice, statement, press release, pronouncement, report, revelation

**annoy** *v* aggravate, anger, bother, exasperate, get on sb's nerves, get to sb *inf*, infuriate, hassle *inf*, irritate, madden, make sb mad, pester, vex

**annoyance** *n* 1 anger, displeasure, infuriation, irritation. 2 (nuisance) bind *inf*, bother, hassle *inf*, nuisance, pain *inf*, pain in the neck *inf*, pest, pig *inf*

**annoyed** *adj* angry, cross, exasperated, fuming, furious, hopping mad, hot under

the collar, incensed, infuriated, irate, irritated, mad, outraged, uptight *inf*

**annoying** *adj* aggravating, exasperating, galling, infuriating, irritating, maddening, tiresome, troublesome

**annual** *adj* once a year, yearly

**anomaly** *n* abnormality, fluke *inf*, freak, inconsistency, irregularity, oddity, peculiarity, quirk, rarity, unusual occurrence

**anonymous** *adj* nameless, unassigned, unidentified, unknown, unsigned

**answer** *n* 1 reply, response, retort. 2 explanation, solution

**answer** *v* 1 acknowledge, react to, reply, respond to, retort. 2 find a solution to, resolve, solve. 3 (satisfy a need) fit the bill, fulfil, meet, satisfy, suit

**answerable** *adj* accountable, responsible

**antagonistic** *adj* against, aggressive, anti, disapproving, hostile, in opposition to, on the other side, opposed

**antagonize** *v* alienate, annoy, bother, estrange, infuriate, irritate, offend, pester, rub sb up the wrong way *inf*

**anthology** *n* collected works, collection, compendium, compilation, selection

**anticipate** *v* assume, count on, expect, forecast, foresee, look forward to, predict, think of in advance

**anticlimax** *n* bathos, comedown, failure, fiasco, flop, disappointment, letdown, wash-out *inf*

**antics** *n* messing about, mischief, shenanigans, silliness, skylarking, tomfoolery, tricks

**antidote** *n* antitoxin, antivenin, cure, remedy

**antiquated** *adj* 1 aged, ancient, elderly,

old. **2** (old-fashioned) ancient, archaic, behind the times, dated, obsolete, old-fashioned, old hat, out-of-date, outmoded, out of the ark, passé; *opp* latest, modern, up-to-date

**antique** *adj* antiquarian, classic, old, veteran, vintage

**antisocial** *n* **1** (of people) cold, standoffish, unapproachable, unfriendly, unsociable, withdrawn; *opp* friendly, gregarious. **2** (of behaviour) offensive, unacceptable

**anxiety** *adj* angst, apprehension, bother, concern, hang-up *inf*, misgiving, nervousness, stress, tension, trauma, uneasiness, worry

**anxious** *adj* apprehensive, bothered, concerned, nervous, on tenterhooks, stressed-out, tense, uneasy, worried; *opp* calm, cool, laid-back, relaxed

**apartment** *n* bed-sit, flat, living quarters, penthouse, pied-à-terre, room, rooms, studio flat

**apathetic** *adj* indifferent, lazy, lethargic, listless, uninterested

**apathy** *n* indifference, laziness, lethargy, listlessness

**apologetic** *adj* contrite, repentant, remorseful, sorry

**apologize** *v* eat crow *inf*, eat humble pie *inf*, eat your words, grovel *inf*, make an apology, say sorry, take back what you said

**apology** *n* confession, excuse, expression of regret

**appal** *v* disgust, dismay, horrify, outrage, shock

**appalled** *adj* disgusted, dismayed, horrified, outraged, shocked

**appalling** *adj* atrocious, awful, disgusting, dreadful, foul, ghastly, grim, hideous, horrendous, horrible, horrific, horrifying, outrageous, really bad, shocking, terrible

**apparatus** *n* contraption, device, equipment, gear, tackle

**apparent** *adj* **1** clear, evident, noticeable, obvious, plain, visible, unmistakable. **2** ostensible, outward, seeming, superficial

**apparently** *adv* evidently, rumour has it that, seemingly

**appeal** *n* **1** application, call, entreaty, petition, plea, request, suit. **2** attraction, charm, fascination, interest

**appeal** *v* **1** ask for, beg for, call for, implore, petition for, put in a request for, request. **2** (seem attractive or interesting) attract, draw, fascinate, interest, please, tempt

**appealing** *adj* attractive, fascinating, interesting, pleasing, tempting

**appear** *v* **1** arrive, come into view, come out, come to light, crop up, emerge, materialize, pop up, show up, turn up. **2** look like, seem. **3** (in a show) perform, play, star, take part

**appearance** *n* **1** arrival, emergence, materialization. **2** air, aspect, demeanour, dress, expression, impression, look. **3** (illusion) front, guise, illusion, outward appearance, pretence, show

**appease** *v* calm down, mollify, pacify, placate, soften up, soothe

**appendix** *n* addendum, addition, adjunct, codicil, supplement

**appetite** *n* craving, desire, hunger, keenness, relish, stomach, will

**appetizing** adj delicious, inviting, mouth-watering, tasty

**applaud** v 1 clap, bring the house down, give a standing ovation to, give sb a big hand, give sb a round of applause, put your hands together for, raise the roof. 2 approve, commend, have great admiration for, praise, support, welcome

**applause** n clapping, curtain call, encore, ovation

**applicable** adj apposite, appropriate, pertinent, relevant, suitable, to the point, valid

**applicant** n candidate, claimant, interviewee

**application** n claim, form, petition, request

**apply** v 1 (be relevant) appertain, be applicable, be appropriate, be relevant, be valid, concern, involve, pertain, relate. 2 (use) carry out, employ, implement, make use of, put into operation, put into practice, use, utilize. 3 (apply medication, glue) cover with, put on, rub in, spread on

**appoint** v choose, elect, employ, name, nominate, put into office, select, sign, take on

**appointment** n 1 date, engagement, meeting, rendezvous. 2 job, office, position, post, role, situation, situation vacant

**apportion** v allocate, dish out inf, dispense, distribute, divide up, dole out inf, hand out, share out

**appraise** v assess, cast your eye over, evaluate, give sth the once-over inf, judge, review, size up inf

**appreciable** adj apparent, considerable, discernible, noticeable, significant, substantial

**appreciate** v 1 (be grateful) be appreciative of, be grateful for, be thankful for, value. 2 (appreciate art, good food) like, prize, rate, rate highly, respect, think a lot of, value. 3 (realize) accept, be aware of, be conscious of, realize, recognize, understand

**appreciation** n 1 gratitude, thanks. 2 (understanding) acceptance, awareness, realization, recognition, understanding

**appreciative** adj 1 grateful, pleased, thankful. 2 admiring, enthusiastic, supportive

**apprehend** v arrest, capture, detain, nail inf, nick inf, pick up inf, run in inf, take in, take in for questioning, take into custody

**apprehension** n 1 alarm, anxiety, butterflies in the stomach, concern, disquiet, doubt, fear, foreboding, misgiving, mistrust, nervousness, presentiment, the heebie-jeebies Am, the shakes, trepidation, unease, uneasiness, worry. 2 arrest, capture, detention, seizure. 3 appreciation, awareness, comprehension, conception, discernment, grasp, perception, realization, recognition, understanding

**apprehensive** adj afraid, alarmed, anxious, concerned, fearful, frightened, mistrustful, nervous, scared, uneasy, worried

**approach** n 1 (coming nearer) advance, advancing, advent, arrival, nearing. 2 (to a place) access road, avenue, drive, driveway, entrance, entry, passage, path, road, way. 3 (to a person) advances,

appeal, application, invitation,
overtures, proposal, proposition.
4 (to doing something) attitude, course,
manner, means, method, mode,
procedure, style, technique, way

**approach** v 1 advance, arrive, catch up,
come close, come near, come to, draw
near, gain on, go towards, meet, move
towards, near, reach. 2 (talk to sb)
address, greet, hail, speak to, start
talking to. 3 (ask sb for sth) appeal,
apply, ask, broach the matter with, chat
up inf, make advances, make a proposal,
make overtures, proposition, solicit,
sound out, suggest to. 4 (do sth) begin,
commence, embark on, make a start on,
set about, tackle, undertake. 5
approximate, be close to, be like, be near
to, be comparable with, be similar to,
come close to, come near to, compare
with, resemble, suggest

**approachable** adj accessible, affable,
amicable, easy-going, friendly, informal,
kind, open, relaxed, sympathetic,
understanding, well-disposed; opp aloof,
severe, stuffy

**appropriate** adj apposite, apt, becoming,
befitting, belonging, correct, fit, fitting,
going well with, pertinent, proper,
relevant, right, suitable, to the point, to
the purpose, well-suited, well-timed

**approval** n 1 (liking) acceptance,
acclaim, acclamation, admiration,
applause, appreciation, approbation,
commendation, esteem, favour, good
opinion, high regard, liking, praise,
regard, respect. 2 (agreement)
acceptance, acquiescence, agreement,
assent, authorization, blessing,

confirmation, consent, endorsement,
leave, mandate, permission, ratification,
sanction, the go-ahead inf, the green
light inf, the okay inf

**approve** v 1 acclaim, admire, applaud,
appreciate, be pleased with, commend,
esteem, favour, have a good/high
opinion of, have a high regard for, like,
praise, regard highly, respect, think
highly of, think well of. 2 accept, agree
to, authorize, consent to, endorse, give
the go-ahead inf, give the green light to
inf, give the nod to inf, give the OK to
inf, give your backing to, give your
blessing to, go along with, pass, permit,
ratify, recommend, sanction, validate

**approximate** adj estimated, imprecise,
inexact, loose, rough

**approximately** adv 1 about, around,
close to, give or take inf, in the region
of, just about, loosely, more or less, not
far off, or so, roughly. 2 (with dates)
circa

**approximation** n conjecture, ballpark
figure inf, estimate, guess, guesstimate
inf, guesswork, rough calculation, rough
figure, rough idea

**apt** adj 1 applicable, appropriate, apposite,
correct, felicitous, fitting, pertinent,
proper, relevant, suitable, to the point.
2 able, adept, astute, bright, clever,
competent, gifted, intelligent, quick,
quick to learn, sharp, smart, talented.
3 apt to given, inclined, liable, likely, of
a mind, prone

**aptitude** n ability, faculty, flair, gift,
knack, quickness, talent

**arbitrary** adj erratic, irrational, personal,
random, subjective

**arbitrate** v adjudicate, decide, determine, judge, mediate, settle

**arbitration** n adjudication, decision, judgement, settlement

**archaic** adj ancient, behind the times, old, old-fashioned, outdated, outmoded

**ardent** adj eager, emotional, enthusiastic, fervent, intense, keen, passionate, zealous

**arduous** adj back-breaking, demanding, exhausting, gruelling, hard, strenuous, taxing, tiring, uphill, wearying; *opp* easy

**area** n 1 district, environment, neighbourhood, patch *inf*, quarter, region, sector, space, surroundings, territory, turf *sl*. 2 acreage, expanse, extent, measurements, size. 3 (of knowledge) branch, discipline, field, province, realm, sphere, world

**arena** n 1 amphitheatre, field, ground, ring, stadium. 2 battleground, domain, realm, scene, sphere

**argue** v 1 be at each other's throats, bicker, clash, disagree, fall out *inf*, feud, fight, have a bone to pick with sb, have a row, pick a fight, quarrel, squabble, wrangle. 2 debate, discuss, dispute, reason, remonstrate. 3 assert, claim, insist, put forward, say, state, suggest

**argument** n 1 clash, controversy, difference of opinion, disagreement, discussion, dispute, dust-up *inf*, fight, quarrel, row, showdown, squabble, tiff. 2 assertion, case, claim, contention, hypothesis, idea, plea, proposition, reasoning, reasons, statement, view

**argumentative** adj awkward, belligerent, combative, contrary, difficult, opinionated, quarrelsome, stroppy *inf*

**arid** adj desert, dried up, dry, parched, waterless

**arise** v 1 appear, begin, come up, come to light, crop up *inf*, emerge, happen, occur, originate. 2 be caused by, be the result of, come of, come out of, follow, proceed, result, spring from, stem from. 3 get out of bed, get to your feet, get up, stand up

**aristocrat** n grandee, lady, lord, nob *sl*, noble, nobleman, noblewoman, patrician, peer, peeress

**aristocratic** adj blue-blooded, elite, noble, posh *inf*, privileged, upper-class, titled, well-born

**arm** n 1 appendage, limb, upper limb. 2 branch, department, division, extension, offshoot, section, sector

**arm** v 1 equip, fit with, issue with, provide, supply. 2 (prepare yourself) brace, fortify, gird your loins, prepare, steel

**armed** adj 1 (carrying weapons) in arms, tooled up *slang*, under arms. 2 equipped, fortified, prepared, primed, provided, ready, strengthened,

**armoured** adj armour-plated, bombproof, bulletproof, fortified, protected, strengthened

**arms** n 1 armaments, firearms, guns, ordnance, weaponry, weapons. 2 coat of arms, crest, emblem, escutcheon, insignia, shield

**army** n 1 armed forces, forces, land force, soldiers, the military *Am*, troops. 2 crowd, horde, host, mob, multitude, pack, swarm, throng

**aroma** n bouquet, fragrance, odour, perfume, scent, smell

**aromatic** adj fragrant, perfumed, piquant, pungent, scented, sweet-smelling

**arouse** v 1 awake, rouse, waken, wake up. 2 agitate, animate, egg on, enliven, excite, goad, incense, inflame, provoke, spur on, wind up inf. 3 cause, foster, induce, kindle, provoke, set off, sow the seeds of, stimulate, stir up, trigger, whip up. 4 excite, stimulate, turn on inf

**arrange** v 1 align, classify, grade, group, lay out, line up, order, organize, put in order, rank, set out, sort, sort out, tidy. 2 agree, decide, fix up, make a date, make an appointment, make arrangements, organize, pencil in, plan, schedule, settle on , set up. 3 (music) adapt, orchestrate, score, set to music

**arrangement** n 1 alignment, array, classification, design, display, formation, grouping, layout, line-up, order, organization, pattern, ranking, set-up, structure, system. 2 agreement, appointment, date, plan, preparations. 3 adaptation, interpretation, orchestration, score, version

**array** n arrangement, collection, display, formation, group, line-up, presentation

**array** v arrange, assemble, draw up, group, line up, order, organize, place, position, range, rank

**arrival** n 1 appearance, approach, beginning, coming, dawn, entrance, entry. 2 (a person) immigrant, incomer, newcomer, visitor

**arrive** v appear, come, come along, come on the scene, enter, get here/there, make an entrance, put in an appearance, reach, roll up inf, show up inf, turn up

**arrogant** adj big-headed, boastful, brash,

cavalier, cocky inf, conceited, contemptuous, disdainful, egotistical, haughty, high-and-mighty, high-handed, lordly, overbearing, patronizing, pompous, proud, scornful, self-important, smug, superior, supercilious, vain

**arrow** n 1 bolt, dart, shaft. 2 indicator, marker, pointer

**art** n 1 knack, knowledge, method, skill, technique, trick. 2 aptitude, artistry, craft, craftsmanship, dexterity, expertise, ingenuity, proficiency, skilfulness, skill. 3 craft, culture, fine art, the arts

**article** n 1 artifact, item, object, piece, thing, unit. 2 (in a newspaper) account, essay, feature, item, piece, report, story, write up

**articulate** v enunciate, express, pronounce, say, speak, state, talk, utter, voice

**articulate** adj 1 (of a person) eloquent, expressive, fluent, having the gift of the gab inf, lucid, silver-tongued; opp inarticulate. 2 (of language) clear, coherent, comprehensible, eloquent, fluent, intelligible, lucid, understandable

**artificial** adj 1 man-made, manufactured, synthetic; opp real, natural. 2 bogus, counterfeit, ersatz, fake, false, imitation, mock, phoney, pseudo-, sham, simulated; opp real, genuine. 3 affected, assumed, fake, false, feigned, forced, insincere, put on, unnatural, unreal; opp real, genuine

**artistic** adj 1 (of people) accomplished, creative, cultured, gifted, talented. 2 aesthetic, attractive, beautiful, decorative, elegant, exquisite, graceful, ornamental, stylish, tasteful

**artistry** n 1 ability, brilliance, creativity, expertise, flair, gift, proficiency, skill, talent, virtuosity. 2 art, craftsmanship, style, workmanship

**ascend** v climb, climb up, float up, fly up, gain height, go up, lift off, mount, move up, rise, scale, soar, take off; *opp* descend

**ascent** n climb, gradient, hill, incline, ramp, rise, slope; *opp* descent

**ascertain** v 1 determine, discover, establish, ferret out *inf*, find out, get to know, learn. 2 confirm, establish, identify, make certain, make sure, settle, verify

**ascetic** *adj* abstemious, abstinent, austere, celibate, chaste, frugal, harsh, hermit-like, plain, puritanical, restrained, rigorous, self-denying, self-disciplined, severe, simple, Spartan, strict, temperate

**ascribe** v assign, attribute, blame, charge, credit sb with, give credit to, impute, put down, refer, set down

**ashamed** *adj* apologetic, chastened, conscience-stricken, contrite, embarrassed, guilty, humiliated, mortified, red-faced, remorseful, repentant, shamefaced, sheepish, sorry, unable to look sb in the face

**ask** v 1 (ask questions) ask around, canvass, enquire, inquire, make inquiries, query, question. 2 (question sb) fire questions at, give sb the third degree *inf*, grill *inf*, interrogate, interview, pick sb's brains, put sb on the spot *inf*, pump, quiz. 3 (ask for sth) appeal, apply, beg, beseech, call upon, claim, demand, implore, petition, plead, pray, request, seek, solicit. 4

invite, summon

**asleep** *adj* catnapping, comatose, dead to the world *inf*, dormant, dozing, having a nap, having a snooze, hibernating, out like a light, resting, sleeping, slumbering, snoozing; *opp* awake

**aspect** n 1 angle, face, feature, part, side, slant, standpoint, viewpoint. 2 air, appearance, attitude, bearing, demeanour, expression, look, manner, mien

**aspiration** n aim, ambition, desire, dream, goal, hankering, hope, intention, longing, objective, purpose, wish, yearning

**aspire** v aim, be ambitious, desire, dream of, hanker after *inf*, hope, long, pursue, seek, set your sights on, wish, yearn

**aspiring** *adj* ambitious, budding, eager, hopeful, potential, striving, wannabe *inf*, would-be

**assail** v 1 (attack) assault, attack, bombard, fall on, lay into, pelt, set about, set on. 2 (criticize) abuse, berate, blast, criticize, harangue, lambast, malign, pillory, put down, revile, vilify

**assassin** n contract killer, executioner, hit man *inf*, killer, murderer, slayer

**assassinate** v eliminate, execute, hit *slang*, kill, liquidate, murder, slay

**assault** n 1 act of aggression, attack, invasion, offensive, raid, strike. 2 assault and battery, GBH, mugging, rape

**assault** v 1 (a place) assail, attack, invade, storm. 2 (a person) attack, do over *inf*, fly at *inf*, hit, lay into *inf*, set about *inf*, set upon. 3 (sexually) grope, interfere with, molest, rape, sexually assault

**assemble** v 1 (of people) call together, come together, congregate, convene, flock, gather, get together, herd together, marshal, meet, muster, rally, round up. 2 (of things) amass, bring together, collect, gather, get together, pile up. 3 (put parts together) build, cobble together *inf*, connect, construct, erect, fabricate, fit together, join, make, piece together, put together, set up

**assembly** n 1 body, company, congregation, convention, council, crowd, flock, gathering, group, mass, meeting, throng. 2 accumulation, collection

**assert** v 1 affirm, allege, announce, argue, claim, contend, declare, insist, maintain, profess, say, state, stress. 2 **assert yourself** act confidently, be assertive, exert your influence, insist, make your presence felt, put your foot down, stand firm, stand up for yourself, stick up for yourself, stick to your guns

**assertion** n affirmation, allegation, argument, claim, contention, declaration, insistence, pronouncement, statement

**assertive** adj 1 confident, decided, definite, emphatic, firm, forceful, insistent, positive, self-assured, strong-willed. 2 bossy, dogmatic, domineering, not backward in coming forward *inf*, opinionated, peremptory, pushy *inf*, stubborn, uncompromising

**assess** v appraise, calculate, determine, estimate, evaluate, gauge, judge, price, rate, reckon, size up *inf*, value, weigh up

**assessment** n appraisal, estimate, estimation, gauging, judgement, rating, valuation

**asset** n advantage, benefit, blessing, boon, godsend, help, resource, support

**assets** n capital, estate, funds, goods, means, money, possessions, property, reserves, resources, wealth

**assign** v 1 (to a job) appoint, choose, commission, designate, name, nominate, select. 2 (give) allocate, allot, consign, give, share out

**assimilate** v 1 (absorb) absorb, digest, incorporate, take in. 2 (fit in) adapt, become adjusted, become like, blend in, conform with, fit in

**assist** v 1 (help) aid, collaborate, cooperate with, help, help out, lend a hand, play a part, rally round *inf*, succour, support, work; *opp* hinder. 2 (make easier) expedite, facilitate, further, help, make easier; *opp* hinder

**assistance** n 1 a hand, a helping hand, aid, benefit, collaboration, cooperation, help, support; *opp* hindrance. 2 (financial) aid, backing, back-up, help, patronage, reinforcement, sponsorship, subsidy, support

**assistant** n 1 (colleague) accessory, accomplice, ally, associate, collaborator, colleague, comrade, helper, partner. 2 (subordinate) aide, auxiliary, deputy, helper, henchman, mate, PA, personal assistant, right-hand man, right-hand woman, second in command, secretary, subordinate

**associate** n ally, colleague, companion, comrade, co-worker, follower, friend, mate, partner, workmate

**associate** v 1 (in the mind) connect, couple, link, relate, think of together,

**tie in, tie up** *inf.* **2** (of people) ally yourself, band together, be friends, fraternize, gang up *inf,* get pally with *inf,* go round with, hang out *inf,* hobnob, join up, keep company, make friends, mingle, mix, pal up, socialize. **3** (of organizations) affiliate, ally, amalgamate, attach, combine, connect, join, link up, unite, yoke

**association** *n* **1** (group) alliance, band, body, brotherhood, cartel, clique, club, coalition, company, confederacy, confederation, cooperative, corporation, federation, firm, fraternity, gang, group, league, order, organization, partnership, society, syndicate, union. **2** (joining) amalgamation, blend, combination, connection, mixture, pairing, relation, tie in, union

**assorted** *adj* different, diverse, heterogeneous, miscellaneous, mixed, motley, multifarious, sundry, varied, various

**assortment** *n* choice, collection, hotchpotch, jumble, medley, miscellany, mishmash, mixed bag *inf,* mixture, range, selection, variety

**assume** *v* **1** believe, deduce, expect, fancy, guess, have a hunch *inf,* have an idea, imagine, infer, presume, presuppose, reckon, surmise, suspect, take for granted, think, understand. **2** (assume responsibility) accept, shoulder, take on, take up, take on yourself, undertake. **3** affect, feign, pretend, put on, simulate

**assumption** *n* belief, conjecture, expectation, guess, hunch *inf,* hypothesis, inference, premise,

presumption, surmise, suspicion, theory

**assurance** *n* **1** certainty, confidence, coolness, self-assurance, self-confidence, nerve, poise. **2** guarantee, oath, pledge, promise, vow, word, word of honour. **3** insurance

**assure** *v* convince, give your word, guarantee, persuade, promise, reassure, soothe, swear, vow

**astonish** *v* amaze, astound, bewilder, daze, dazzle, shock, stagger, stun, stupefy, surprise, take your breath away

**astonished** *adj* amazed, astounded, dumbfounded, gobsmacked *inf,* shocked, speechless, staggered, surprised, taken aback

**astonishing** *adj* amazing, astounding, bewildering, breathtaking, hard to believe, mind-boggling *inf,* shocking, striking, stunning, surprising

**astonishment** *n* amazement, bewilderment, confusion, disbelief, shock, surprise, wonder

**astounding** *adj* amazing, astonishing, awe-inspiring, bewildering, impressive, staggering, striking, surprising

**astute** *adj* artful, calculating, canny, clever, crafty, cunning, discerning, having no flies on you, knowing, nobody's fool, perceptive, sharp, shrewd, wily

**asylum** *n* a haven, protection, refuge, safety, sanctuary, shelter

**atheist** *n* free-thinker, non-believer, unbeliever

**athlete** *n* **1** competitor, contender, fitness fanatic, fitness freak *inf,* gymnast, player, runner, sportsman, sportsperson, sportswoman. **2** (in particular events) decathlete, distance runner, heptathlete, high jumper, long jumper, sprinter, triple jumper

**athletic** *adj* active, brawny, energetic, fit, muscular, powerful, robust, sporty, strapping, strong, sturdy, well-built

**atmosphere** *n* 1 (around the earth) air, ionosphere, sky, stratosphere. 2 (general mood) air, ambience, aura, character, climate, feel, feeling, flavour, mood, quality, spirit, tone, vibes *inf*

**atrocious** *adj* abominable, appalling, awful, bad, dreadful, ghastly, grim, horrendous *inf*, horrible, horrific, terrible, unspeakable

**atrocity** *n* abomination, barbarity, bloodbath, brutality, crime against humanity, killing, massacre, outrage, slaughter, war crime

**attach** *v* add, add on, affix, append, connect, couple, fasten, fit, fix, hitch, hitch up, hook up, join, link, pin, secure, stick, tie; *opp* detach

**attachment** *n* 1 (thing attached) accessory, accoutrement, addition, add-on, adjunct, affix, extension. 2 (feeling) affection, affinity, bond, devotion, emotional tie, fondness, friendship, liking, love, loyalty, tenderness

**attack** *n* 1 act of aggression, assault, incursion, invasion, onslaught, raid, storming. 2 (against person) assault, beating, mugging, rape

**attack** *v* 1 invade, raid, storm. 2 (attack a person) assail, assault, beat, beat up, lay into, mug, rape

**attacker** *n* 1 aggressor, invader, raider. 2 assailant, mugger, rapist. 3 (in sport) forward, goalscorer, striker

**attain** *v* achieve, accomplish, acquire, arrive at, earn, fulfil, gain, get, obtain, reach, realize, secure, win

**attempt** *n* crack *inf*, effort, endeavour, go, shot, stab *inf*, try

**attempt** *v* aim, do your best, endeavour, give it a whirl *inf*, have a bash at *inf*, have a crack at *inf*, have a go at, have a shot at, have a stab at *inf*, make an effort, seek, set out, strive, take it upon yourself, try, undertake, venture

**attend** *v* 1 (be at a place) be present at, go to, visit. 2 (serve sb) accompany, escort, help, serve, wait on, wait on sb hand and foot. 3 **attend to** deal with, do, handle, see to, set your mind to

**attendant** *n* aide, assistant, butler, companion, equerry, escort, guard, helper, lackey, lady-in-waiting, minder *inf*, servant, squire, steward, usher, valet

**attention** *n* 1 attentiveness, awareness, concentration, consideration, heed, notice, observation, regard, scrutiny, thought. 2 (medical) care, therapy, treatment. 3 **attentions** attendance, civilities, compliments, concern, courtesies, gallantry, ministrations, respects

**attentive** *adj* 1 alert, all ears *inf*, awake, aware, heedful, listening, looking, mindful, observant, on guard, on the lookout, on your guard, vigilant, watchful, watching, wide awake; *opp* inattentive. 2 (considerate) chivalrous, concerned, conscientious, considerate, courteous, dancing attendance, gallant, gracious, kind, obliging, polite, respectful, thoughtful

**attitude** *n* 1 (mental) approach,

disposition, feeling, opinion, outlook.
2 (physical) pose, position, posture

**attract** v allure, bewitch, captivate,
charm, draw, enchant, entice, fascinate,
interest, intrigue, pull, seduce, tempt;
*opp* repel

**attractive** adj 1 (of person) alluring,
beautiful, captivating, comely,
enchanting, good-looking, gorgeous,
handsome, lovely, pretty, seductive, sexy,
striking, stunning; *opp* repulsive. 2 (of
things, qualities) agreeable, appealing,
charming, engaging, fascinating,
fetching, interesting, inviting, nice,
pleasant, pleasing, tempting

**attribute** n aspect, characteristic, facet,
feature, hallmark, mark, property,
quality, virtue

**attribute** v ascribe, assign, charge, credit,
impute, lay at the door of, put down to

**audacious** adj adventurous, bold, brave,
cheeky, intrepid, reckless, risky

**audible** adj clear, discernible, distinct,
perceptible, within earshot, within
hearing

**audience** n 1 assembly, congregation,
crowd, fans, gallery, house, listeners,
public, spectators, turnout, viewers.
2 (for particular views or publications)
aficionados, devotees, fans, following,
market, public. 3 (meeting with
important person) consultation,
reception, hearing, interview, meeting

**audit** n book-keeping, check,
examination, inspection, monitoring,
review, scrutiny

**audit** v check, examine, go through,
inspect, monitor, oversee, review,
scrutinize

**auspicious** adj bright, encouraging,
favourable, felicitous, rosy, good,
hopeful, opportune, promising,
propitious, timely; *opp* inauspicious

**austere** adj 1 (of place, conditions) hard,
harsh, plain, spare, Spartan. 2 (of
person) abstemious, ascetic, forbidding,
frugal, puritan, sober, solemn, stern,
strict

**austerity** n belt-tightening, frugality,
hardship, poverty, recession, straitened
circumstances

**authentic** adj authenticated, bona fide,
genuine, kosher inf, real, true

**author** n authoress, biographer, composer,
creator, dramatist, essayist, journalist,
librettist, lyricist, novelist, originator,
playwright, poet, poetess, songwriter,
writer

**authoritarian** adj autocratic, despotic,
dictatorial, disciplinarian, dominant,
dominating, domineering, imperious,
strict, totalitarian, tyrannical,
undemocratic

**authority** n 1 (power to command or
decide) command, competence, control,
charge, dominion, influence,
jurisdiction, power, prerogative, remit,
rule, sovereignty, supremacy. 2 (the right
to do sth) authorization, clearance,
licence, permission, right, sanction,
warrant. 3 (controlling body) board,
body, executive, institution, local
authority, regulator, regulatory body.
4 (person with special knowledge)
expert, fount of knowledge, pundit,
scholar, source, specialist, witness

**authorize** v agree to, allow, approve,
assent to, clear, countenance, empower,

enable, entitle, give the go-ahead to,
give the green light to, let, license,
permit, sanction

**autocratic** *adj* absolutist, authoritarian,
despotic, dictatorial, dominant,
dominating, domineering, imperious,
tyrannical, undemocratic

**automatic** *adj* **1** (of machines)
mechanical, electronic, remote-control;
*opp* manual. **2** (happening by itself)
instinctive, involuntary, unconscious

**autonomous** *adj* free, independent, self-
contained, self-governing, sovereign

**available** *adj* accessible, free, handy, in
plentiful supply, obtainable, on hand, on
tap *inf*, ready, to be had, to hand, vacant

**avarice** *n* acquisitiveness, greed,
meanness, miserliness, parsimony,
selfishness, stinginess *inf*

**avenge** *v* get back at, retaliate against,
take vengeance on, take revenge on

**avenue** *n* **1** boulevard, path, road, street,
thoroughfare. **2** choice, opening;
opportunity, possibility

**average** *adj* everyday, medium, middle-
sized, middling, moderate, normal,
ordinary, run-of-the-mill, standard,
typical, unexceptional, usual

**average** *n* median, mean, midpoint,
norm, standard

**averse** *adj* antipathetic, disinclined,
hostile, ill-disposed, loth; opposed,
reluctant, unfavourable, unwilling

**aversion** *n* abhorrence, animosity,
antipathy, detestation, disinclination,
dislike, disgust, distaste, hate, hatred,
horror, hostility, loathing, opposition,
reluctance, repugnance, repulsion,
revulsion, unwillingness

**avert** *v* avoid, prevent, stop, turn aside,
turn away

**avid** *adj* eager, enthusiastic, greedy,
hungry, keen, thirsty

**avoid** *v* **1** elude, escape, evade, keep away
from, shirk, shun, stay away from. **2** (not
do sth) abstain from, get out of, refrain
from

**avoidable** *adj* escapable, preventable,
unnecessary

**await** *v* anticipate, expect, wait for

**awake** *adj* alert, aware, compos mentis
*inf*, conscious, vigilant, wide awake;
*opp* asleep

**awaken** *v* rouse, wake, wake up

**award** *n* **1** (for achievement) decoration,
presentation, prize, reward, trophy.
**2** (legally or officially granted)
adjudication, compensation, damages,
grant, order

**award** *v* accord, allot, assign, bestow,
confer, endow, give, grant, hand out,
present

**aware** *adj* **1** attentive, alert, awake,
conscious. **2** aware of able to
recognize, alive to, conscious of,
conversant with, familiar with, mindful
of, wise to

**awareness** *n* cognition, cognizance,
consciousness, perception, recognition

**awe** *n* admiration, adoration, amazement,
fear, wonder

**awesome** *adj* amazing, astonishing, awe-
inspiring, incredible, magnificent,
marvellous, stupendous, unbelievable,
wonderful

**awful** *adj* abominable, appalling,
atrocious, bad, deplorable, devastating,
disgusting, dire, dreadful, frightful,

ghastly, grim, hideous, horrendous *inf*,
horrible, horrific, shocking, sickening,
terrible, unspeakable; *opp* great, terrific,
wonderful

**awfully** *adj* dreadfully, extremely,
frightfully, horrendously *inf*, incredibly,
really, terribly, unspeakably, very

**awkward** *adj* **1** (of a person) clumsy,
embarrassed, ill-at-ease, maladroit,
nervous, unco-ordinated, ungainly.
**2** (of a problem, situation) difficult,
embarrassing, thorny, tricky

**awkwardness** *n* clumsiness,
embarrassment, nervousness

**axe** *v* abolish, dismiss, do away with, fire,
get rid of, give sb the boot *inf*, kick out
*inf*, make redundant, remove, repeal,
sack

**baby** *n* babe, babe in arms, bairn *Scot*, child, infant, neonate *tech*, newborn, sprog *inf*, tiny tot, toddler, tot, young child

**back** *n* **1** end, hind quarters, rear, rear end, reverse, stern, tail; *opp* front. **2** backbone, spine

**back** *v* **1** (give or express support for) advocate, agree with, approve, approve of, back up, bet on, champion, encourage, endorse, favour, finance, invest in, sanction, second, side with, sponsor, subsidize, support, underwrite. **2** (move backwards) back away, back up, backtrack, retreat, reverse. **3 back down** back off, backpedal, backtrack, climb down, concede, give in, give way, retreat, submit, surrender, withdraw, yield. **4 back out of** abandon, back away from, cancel, chicken out of *inf*, get cold feet about, go back on, have second thoughts about, renege on, welsh on, withdraw from. **5 back up** (back up a

statement) confirm, corroborate, prove, substantiate, support

**backer** *n* advocate, benefactor, champion, investor, patron, promoter, punter, sponsor, supporter, underwriter

**backfire** *v* blow up in sb's face, boomerang, fail, go wrong, miscarry, misfire, rebound

**background** *n* **1** (of a picture) backdrop, decor, distance, hinterland, middle distance, scenery. **2** (of a person) breeding, credentials, culture, education, experience, life history, origins, past, qualifications, upbringing. **3** (of events, situation) circumstances, context, events leading up to, history

**backing** *n* agreement, aid, approval, assistance, co-operation, endorsement, finance, help, helping hand, encouragement, sponsorship, support

**backward** *adj* **1** primitive, uncivilized, underdeveloped, undeveloped, unsophisticated. **2** (of a person) educationally subnormal, ESN, mentally retarded, retarded, slow, subnormal, with special needs

**bad** *adj* **1** (of low quality) appalling, atrocious, awful, defective, deficient, dreadful, faulty, imperfect, inferior, lousy *inf*, low-quality, mediocre, poor, rotten, substandard, terrible, useless, worthless; *opp* good. **2** (not what is wanted or needed) adverse, difficult, disagreeable, distressing, grim, inadequate, inappropriate, incorrect, nasty, unacceptable, uncomfortable, undesirable, unfavourable, unfortunate, unlucky, unnecessary, unpleasant, unsuitable, unwanted, unsatisfactory, unwelcome, wrong; *opp* good. **3** (bad accident or illness) acute, chronic, critical, disastrous, dreadful, grave, serious, severe, terrible. **4** (causing damage or harm) damaging, dangerous, deleterious, destructive, detrimental, harmful, injurious, noxious, poisonous, ruinous, unhealthy; *opp* good. **5** (of a person) badly behaved, base, corrupt, criminal, crooked, delinquent, depraved, dishonest, dishonourable, evil, immoral, nasty *inf*, naughty, sinful, unruly, unscrupulous, vile, villainous, wicked; *opp* good. **6** (of food) contaminated, decaying, festering, mouldy, off, putrescent, putrid, rancid, rotten, sour, spoiled, tainted. **7 not bad** acceptable, adequate, all right, average, fair, moderate, OK *inf*, passable, satisfactory, so-so *inf*, tolerable

**baffle** *v* bamboozle, bewilder, confound, confuse, flummox, have sb scratching their head, mystify, nonplus, perplex, puzzle, stump

**bag** *n* basket, carrier bag, case, container, handbag, holdall, rucksack, sack, satchel, shopping-bag, shoulder bag

**baggage** *n* bags, belongings, cases, gear, kit, luggage, suitcases, things

**balance** *n* **1** (personal quality) composure, equanimity, even-handedness, fairness, level-headedness, objectivity, poise, stability, steadiness. **2** (between different factors or interests) balance of power, correspondence, due proportion, equality, equilibrium, equity, parity, symmetry. **3** (machine) scales, weighing machine. **4** (sum of money) difference, outstanding amount,

remainder, residue, rest; *opp* deposit. **5 in the balance** at a crisis, at a crossroads, at a turning point, critical, finely balanced, uncertain, undecided. **6 on balance** all in all, all things considered, on the whole, taking everything into account, taking everything into consideration, when all's said and done

**balance** *v* **1** (place carefully) adjust, perch, place/put carefully, stabilize, steady. **2** (balance different factors or interests) counterbalance, equalize, give equal weight to, offset, weigh, weigh up. **3** (of figures, amounts) add up, balance out, balance up, correspond, match

**balanced** *adj* even-handed, fair, objective, unbiased

**bald** *adj* bald as a coot, bald-headed, bare, hairless, receding, thin on top, with thinning hair

**ballot** *n* election, franchise, plebiscite, poll, polling, referendum, vote, voting

**ban** *n* boycott, censorship, embargo, moratorium, prohibition, suppression, taboo, veto

**ban** *v* abolish, banish, bar, criminalize, debar, end, exclude, forbid, make illegal, outlaw, prohibit, proscribe, put an end to, put a stop to, stop, suppress, veto

**banal** *adj* bland, clichéd, common, commonplace, everyday, hackneyed, humdrum, meaningless, ordinary, pedestrian, stale, tired, trite, trivial, vapid

**band** *n* **1** (of people) bevy, brigade, bunch, clique, company, crew *inf*, gang, group, mob, pack, set, troop. **2** (of musicians) brass band, combo *inf*, ensemble, group, orchestra. **3** (narrow piece) bar, line, ribbon, sash, streak, strip, stripe

**bandit** *n* brigand, highwayman, outlaw, robber, thief

**bang** *n* boom, detonation, explosion, gunshot, thud, thump

**banish** *v* **1** (banish a person) ban, bar, boot out *inf*, cast out, deport, drive away, eject, evict, exclude, exile, expel, kick out *inf*, throw out. **2** (banish a feeling) dismiss, dispel, get rid of, shake off

**bank** *n* **1** (where money is kept) building society, depository, financial institution, investment bank, merchant bank, reserve, savings and loan association *Am*, savings bank. **2** (of a river) embankment, riverside, shore, verge, waterside, waterfront, water's edge

**bank** *v* **1** (put money in an account) deposit, pay in. **2 bank on** count on, depend on, expect, rely on

**bankrupt** *adj* broke *inf*, bust, cleaned out *inf*, failed, in liquidation *tech*, insolvent *tech*, penniless, poor, ruined, without a penny to your name

**banner** *n* colours, flag, pennant, placard, standard, streamer

**banquet** *n* blow-out *inf*, dinner, dinner party, feast, formal dinner, repast

**banter** *n* chaff, gossip, idle chat, joking, joshing, patter, small talk, talk, teasing

**baptize** *v* christen, name

**bar** *n* **1** (piece of metal) barrier, bolt, ingot, rail, rod. **2** (for drinking) beer tent, club, crush bar, drinking den, lounge, lounge bar, pub, public bar, saloon. **3** (sth that prevents progress) barrier, glass ceiling, hindrance, obstacle

**bar** *v* ban, exclude, forbid, keep out, prevent, prohibit, rule out

**barbarian** *n* boor, brute, hooligan, lout, monster, ruffian, savage

**barbaric** *adj* barbarous, brutal, cruel, primitive, savage, uncivilized, uncouth, wild

**bare** *adj* **1** (without clothes) exposed, in the buff *inf*, in the nude, in your birthday suit *inf*, naked, nude, starkers *inf*, stark naked, stripped, unclothed, undressed, with nothing on; *opp* clothed, dressed. **2** (of a room) austere, empty, plain, spare, unfurnished, vacant. **3** (of landscape) austere, barren, bleak, desolate, empty, exposed, exposed to the elements, featureless, open, scanty, stark, treeless

**barefaced** *adj* audacious, blatant, bold, brash, brazen, glaring, impudent, open, patent, shameless, undisguised

**barely** *adv* by the skin of your teeth, hardly, just, only just, scarcely

**bargain** *n* **1** agreement, arrangement, contract, deal, negotiation, pact, pledge, transaction, treaty, understanding. **2** (sth cheap) discount, good buy, good deal, good value, give-away, reduction, snip *inf* . **3 into the bargain** also, as well, besides, in addition, moreover

**bargain** *v* agree, negotiate, transact

**bark** *v* bay, growl, howl, snarl, woof, yap, yelp

**barrage** *n* **1** (of gunfire) battery, bombardment, salvo, shelling, volley, wall of fire. **2** (of abuse, criticism) burst, hail, onslaught, storm, stream, torrent

**barren** *adj* **1** childless, infertile, sterile; *opp* fertile. **2** arid, desert, desolate, infertile, unfruitful, unproductive, waste; *opp* fertile

**barricade** *n* bar, barrier, blockade, bulwark, obstacle, obstruction, palisade, rampart, roadblock, stockade

**barrier** *n* 1 bar, barricade, blockade, fence, obstacle, obstruction, railing, roadblock, wall. 2 (to achieving sth) check, handicap, hurdle, impediment, limitation, obstacle, restraint, restriction, stumbling block

**base** *adj* contemptible, corrupt, debased, depraved, despicable, dishonourable, disreputable, dissolute, evil, foul, ignoble, immoral, low, reprobate, scandalous, shameful, sinful, sordid, unprincipled, vile, villainous, vulgar, wicked

**base** *n* 1 bed, bottom, foot, foundation, pedestal, rest, stand, support; *opp* top. 2 basis, core, essence, essentials, heart, key, origin, principal, root, source. 3 camp, headquarters, post, settlement, starting point, station

**base** *v* build, construct, derive, establish, fasten, form, found, ground, hinge, rest, root

**bash** *n* attempt, crack *inf*, go *inf*, shot *inf*, stab *inf*, try

**bash** *v* bang, belt *inf*, biff *inf*, crash, deck *inf*, hit, punch, smash, sock *inf*, strike, wallop *inf*, whack

**basic** *adj* central, elementary, essential, fundamental, indispensable, intrinsic, key, necessary, primary, rudimentary, underlying, vital; *opp* peripheral

**basically** *adv* at bottom, at heart, essentially, firstly, for the most part, fundamentally, inherently, in the main,

intrinsically, mainly, mostly, primarily

**basics** *n* brass tacks *inf*, core, essentials, facts, fundamentals, hard facts, nitty-gritty *inf*, nuts and bolts, practicalities, principles, realities, rudiments

**basis** *n* base, footing, foundation, grounds, reasoning, support

**bask** *v* 1 laze, lie, loll, lounge, relax, sunbathe. 2 delight, rejoice, revel, savour, take pleasure

**batch** *n* accumulation, amount, collection, crowd, group, lot, mass, pack, quantity, set

**bath** *n* dip, douche, shower, soak, soaping, wash

**bathe** *v* clean, cleanse, immerse, moisten, rinse, soak, steep, wash, wet

**batter** *v* 1 (of a person) abuse, assault, bash *inf*, beat, clobber *inf*, hit, smack, whack. 2 (of the weather) buffet, lash, pelt, pound, pummel, smash, thrash, wallop *inf*, whack *inf*

**battle** *n* action, affray, attack, campaign, clash, combat, conflict, confrontation, contest, encounter, engagement, fight, fray, hostilities, scuffle, skirmish, struggle, tussle, war, warfare

**battle** *v* contend, fight, strive, struggle. 2 (argue) argue, bicker, disagree, dispute, feud, fight, have a row, quarrel, row *inf*, squabble, wrangle

**bawdy** *adj* blue, coarse, crude, dirty, disgusting, filthy, gross, indecent, indelicate, lascivious, lecherous, lewd, licentious, naughty, near the knuckle, obscene, pornographic, prurient, racy, risqué, rude, smutty, salacious, steamy *inf*, suggestive, ribald, vulgar

**bawl** *v* 1 bellow, call, cry, howl, roar,

scream, screech, shout, yell. **2** blubber, cry, snivel, sob, squall, wail, weep

**bay** n **1** cove, gulf, harbour, inlet, sound. **2** alcove, niche, nook, opening, recess

**beach** n coast, coastline, sand, seashore, seaside, shingle, water's edge

**beacon** n beam, bonfire, flare, lighthouse, sign, signal, warning light, watchtower

**beam** n **1** board, girder, joist, plank, rafter, support, timber. **2** flash, gleam, glimmer, glint, glow, ray, shaft, streak, stream

**beam** v **1** emit, glare, gleam, glitter, glow, radiate, shine. **2** grin, smile

**bear** v **1** bring, carry, convey, fetch, move, take, tote, transport. **2** endure, put up with, stand, stomach, suffer, tolerate, undergo. **3** (bear a child, bear fruit) beget, breed, bring forth, engender, give birth to, produce, yield

**bearable** adj acceptable, endurable, manageable, passable, sufferable, sustainable, tolerable; **opp** unbearable

**bearing** n **1** (sb's bearing) air, aspect, attitude, behaviour, demeanour, manner, mien, posture. **2** (a ship's bearing) course, direction. **3** (have a bearing on) connection, pertinence, relation, relevance

**bearings** n course, direction, location, orientation, position, situation, track, way, whereabouts

**beast** n **1** (animal) animal, brute, creature, monster. **2** (person) animal, barbarian, brute, fiend, monster, ogre, sadist, savage

**beat** v **1** bang, batter, buffet, hammer, hit, knock, pound, pummel, strike, thrash. **2** (beat a person) abuse, assault, bash inf, beat up, clobber inf, do over inf, hit,

knock about inf, lay into, punch, rough up inf, slap, smack, strike, thrash, thump, wallop inf. **3** conquer, defeat, lick inf, master, outdo, overcome, quash, rout, subdue, surpass, thrash inf, vanquish, walk all over inf

**beautiful** adj alluring, appealing, attractive, becoming, charming, comely, delightful, elegant, exquisite, fair, fine, glamorous, good-looking, gorgeous, graceful, handsome, lovely, pleasant, pleasing, pretty, radiant, ravishing, seemly, stunning; **opp** ugly

**beauty** n **1** allure, appeal, attractiveness, bloom, charm, elegance, fairness, glamour, good looks, grace, handsomeness, loveliness, prettiness, seemliness; **opp** ugliness. **2** belle, charmer, femme fatale, goddess, good-looker inf, knockout inf, seductress, stunner inf

**beckon** v bid, call, gesticulate, gesture, motion, nod, signal, summon, wave

**becoming** adj attractive, comely, chic, elegant, flattering, graceful, handsome, lovely, neat, pretty, stylish, tasteful; **opp** ugly

**bedlam** n chaos, clamour, commotion, disarray, disorder, furore, hubbub, hullabaloo, pandemonium, tumult, turmoil, uproar; **opp** calm

**bedraggled** adj dirty, dishevelled, disordered, drenched, messy, muddied, muddy, soaking, sodden, soiled, stained, sullied, tatty, unkempt, untidy; **opp** tidy

**befall** v arise, chance, come about, crop up, ensue, follow, happen, materialize, occur, result, take place, transpire

**beg** v **1** ask for, beseech, entreat, implore,

importune, plead, request. **2** (for money) cadge *inf*, scrounge, sponge *inf*

**beggar** *n* down-and-out, mendicant, scrounger *inf*, sponger *inf*, tramp, vagrant

**begin** *v* commence, get going, get the ball rolling, get the show on the road, inaugurate, initiate, instigate, institute, kick off, set about, set in motion, set on foot, start; *opp* end, finish

**beginner** *n* amateur, apprentice, fledgling, fresher, freshman *Am*, learner, new recruit, novice, probationer, rookie *Am*, trainee; *opp* expert

**beginning** *n* **1** (earliest time) birth, commencement, dawn, emergence, inauguration, inception, initiation, onset, outset, start, starting point; *opp* end, finish. **2** (of a book) foreword, introduction, opening, preface, prelude, start, starting point; *opp* end

**begrudge** *v* be jealous, envy, grudge, not be happy about, resent

**behave** *v* **1** act, function, operate, perform, work. **2** acquit yourself well, be good, behave yourself, be on your best behaviour, mind your manners; *opp* misbehave

**behaviour** *n* **1** actions, conduct, demeanour, deportment, manner, manners, ways. **2** (of a machine) action, functioning, operation, performance, reaction, response

**being** *n* animal, beast, body, creature, entity, human, human being, individual, living thing, man, mortal, person

**belief** *n* **1** conviction, feeling, impression, judgement, notion, opinion, persuasion, way of thinking, theory, thinking, view, viewpoint. **2** credo, creed, doctrine,

dogma, faith, ideology, teaching

**believable** *adj* acceptable, conceivable, credible, imaginable, likely, not beyond the realms of possibility, plausible, possible, probable, reliable, trustworthy; *opp* implausible

**believe** *v* **1** accept, be certain of, be convinced of, buy *inf*, fall for *inf*, have faith in, swallow *inf*, swear by, trust. **2** assume, be of the opinion that, consider, gather, guess, have an opinion, imagine, judge, postulate, presume, reckon, speculate, suppose, think, understand

**believer** *n* adherent, devotee, disciple, follower, supporter

**bellow** *v* bawl, call, clamour, cry, holler *Am inf*, howl, roar, scream, screech, shout, shriek, yell

**belong** *v* **1** belong to be at the disposal of, be held by, be owned by, be the property of. **2** belong to be affiliated to, be allied to, be a member of, be associated with, be included in. **3** attach to, be connected with, be part of, fit, go with, relate to, relevant to

**belongings** *n* effects, gear, goods, property, possessions, stuff, things

**beloved** *adj* adored, cherished, darling, dear, dearest, idolized, loved, precious, prized, sweet, treasured, worshipped

**belt** *n* band, cummerbund, girdle, girth, sash, strap, waistband

**bench** *n* **1** form, pew, seat. **2** counter, table, workbench, worktable. **3** (in a court) bar, court, courtroom, judge, judiciary, magistrate, tribunal

**bend** *n* angle, arc, corner, crook, curve, hook, loop, spiral, turn, twist

**bend** *v* **1** arch, bow, buckle, contort,

crook, curl, curve, flex, turn, twist, warp.
**2** (a road bends) curve, deviate, diverge,
go round, swerve, turn, twist, veer.
**3** (a person bends) crouch, hunch, lean,
stoop

**beneficial** *adj* advantageous, favourable,
good, helpful, profitable, useful,
valuable; *opp* harmful

**benefit** *n* advantage, aid, asset, assistance,
blessing, boon, favour, fringe benefit,
gain, good, help, perk, profit;
*opp* disadvantage

**benefit** *v* be an advantage, advantage, aid, assist,
avail, be an advantage to, better,
contribute to, enhance, further, help,
improve, profit, promote, serve;
*opp* harm

**benevolent** *adj* altruistic, amiable,
caring, compassionate, considerate,
friendly, generous, helpful, humane,
kind, kind-hearted, magnanimous,
obliging, sympathetic, thoughtful, warm-
hearted; *opp* unkind

**benign** *adj* **1** amiable, benevolent,
cordial, friendly, generous, genial,
gentle, kind, sympathetic; *opp* unkind.
**2** (of a tumour) curable, harmless,
innocent, non-dangerous, non-
malignant, treatable; *opp* malignant

**bent** *adj* **1** angled, arched, bowed,
contorted, crooked, curved, hunched,
stooped, twisted, warped; *opp* straight.
**2** bent on determined, insistent,
resolved, set. **3** ability, aptitude,
capacity, flair, forte, gift, inclination,
knack, leaning, penchant,
predisposition, proclivity, talent

**bequeath** *v* bestow, cede, commit,
consign, endow, entrust, give, grant,

hand down, leave to, pass on, will

**bequest** *n* estate, gift, heritage,
inheritance, legacy, settlement, trust

**bereavement** *n* death, deprivation, loss,
passing

**berserk** *adj* crazed, crazy, frenzied,
hysterical, insane, mad, manic, rabid,
raging, raving, uncontrollable, violent,
wild; *opp* calm

**berth** *n* **1** bed, bunk, sleeping
accommodation. **2** anchorage, dock,
harbour, mooring, pier, port, quay, wharf

**besiege** *v* beleaguer, beset, blockade,
encircle, encompass, lay siege to,
surround

**besotted** *adj* doting, infatuated, in love,
smitten, spellbound; *opp* indifferent

**best** *adj* chief, cream, élite, finest, first,
first-class, first-rate, foremost, greatest,
highest, leading, most fitting, most
suitable, outstanding, pick, pre-eminent,
prime, right, supreme, top, unsurpassed;
*opp* worst

**bet** *n* gamble, pledge, risk, speculation,
stake, venture, wager

**bet** *v* gamble, pledge, risk, speculate,
stake, venture, wager

**betray** *v* blow the whistle on, break your
promise, double-cross *inf*, inform on, sell
out *inf*, stab sb in the back, swindle, tell
on *inf*

**betrayal** *n* back-stabbing *inf*, breach of
faith, disloyalty, double-dealing,
duplicity, falseness, treachery, treason,
subversion, trickery; *opp* loyalty

**beware** *v* avoid, be careful, be on the
alert, be on the lookout, be on your
guard, heed, look out, mind, steer clear
of, take heed, watch out

**bewildered** *adj* baffled, bemused, confused, dazed, disconcerted, flummoxed, muddled, mystified, nonplussed, perplexed, puzzled, startled, surprised, taken aback, thrown off balance

**bewildering** *adj* baffling, confusing, disconcerting, mystifying, perplexing, puzzling, startling, surprising

**bewitched** *adj* beguiled, captivated, charmed, enchanted, enraptured, entranced, fascinated, mesmerized, spellbound; *opp* indifferent

**bias** *n* 1 bigotry, favouritism, narrow-mindedness, one-sidedness, partiality, prejudice, unfairness. 2 bent, inclination, leaning, penchant, predisposition, propensity, tendency

**biased** *adj* distorted, one-sided, partial, prejudiced, slanted, weighted; *opp* impartial

**bicker** *v* argue, disagree, dispute, fall out, feud, fight, have a row, quarrel, row *inf*, squabble

**bid** *n* 1 offer, price, proposal, proposition, submission, sum, tender. 2 attempt, effort, try, venture

**bid** *v* 1 (bid money) offer, proffer, propose, put forward, submit, tender. 2 (bid sb farewell, good-day) call, greet, say, tell, wish. 3 (bid sb do sth) ask, charge, command, demand, direct, enjoin, instruct, invite, order, require, solicit, summon, tell

**big** *adj* 1 (in size) beefy, bulky, burly, colossal, enormous, extensive, gigantic, great, huge, hulking, immense, large, mammoth, massive, muscular, prodigious, sizeable, spacious, strapping,

thickset, substantial, tall, vast, voluminous; *opp* small. 2 (in importance) eminent, important, leading, main, momentous, powerful, principal, prominent, serious, significant, valuable, weighty; *opp* small. 3 (in generosity) altruistic, benevolent, generous, gracious, kind, heroic, magnanimous, unselfish; *opp* petty, selfish

**bigot** *n* chauvinist, dogmatist, fanatic, homophobic, racist, sexist

**bigoted** *adj* dogmatic, fanatical, homophobic, intolerant, narrow-minded, opinionated, prejudiced, racist, sexist

**bill** *n* 1 account, charges, check *Am*, invoice, statement, tally. 2 act, measure, piece of legislation, proposal

**bill** *v* charge, debit, invoice

**bind** *v* 1 attach, chain, fasten, fetter, glue, hitch, lash, paste, secure, stick, strap, tether, tie. 2 (make sb do sth) compel, constrain, force, impel, obligate, oblige, prescribe. 3 (make doing sth difficult) confine, detain, hamper, hinder, inhibit, restrain, restrict; *opp* help. 4 (bind a wound) bandage, cover, dress, strap

**binding** *adj* compulsory, irrevocable, mandatory, obligatory, unalterable

**biography** *n* account, life, life story, memoir, memoirs, profile

**birth** *n* 1 childbirth, confinement, delivery, nativity, parturition. 2 beginning, beginnings, commencement, emergence, genesis, origin, rise, start, source. 3 ancestry, background, blood, breeding, descent, extraction, family, genealogy, heritage, line, lineage, origin, parentage, pedigree, race, stock

**bit** *n* chip, chunk, crumb, flake, fragment, grain, iota, jot, lump, mite, morsel, part, particle, piece, scrap, shred, sliver, speck, trace, whit

**bitchy** *adj* backbiting, catty, cruel, malicious, mean, nasty, rancorous, snide, spiteful, venomous, vicious, vindictive, waspish

**bite** *n* 1 nibble, nip, puncture. 2 morsel, mouthful, snack. 3 edge, piquancy, punch, pungency, spice, spiciness

**bite** *v* chew, champ, crunch, gnaw, masticate, munch, nibble, nip, pierce, pinch, snap, tear

**biting** *adj* 1 (of wind) bitter, cold, cutting, freezing, harsh, nipping, penetrating, piercing, stinging. 2 (of remarks) acid, caustic, cutting, sarcastic, scathing, sharp, stinging, trenchant, vitriolic

**bitter** *adj* 1 (of taste) acid, acrid, astringent, pungent, sharp, sour, tart, unsweetened, vinegary. 2 acrimonious, angry, begrudging, embittered, hostile, hurt, morose, piqued, rancorous, resentful, sore, sour, sullen

**bizarre** *adj* abnormal, curious, eccentric, extraordinary, fantastic, freakish, grotesque, ludicrous, odd, oddball *inf*, off-beat, outlandish, outré, peculiar, queer, strange, unconventional, unusual, way-out *inf*, wacky *inf*, weird; *opp* normal

**black** *adj* 1 coal-black, dark, dusky, ebony, inky, jet, murky, pitch-black, raven, sable, starless, swarthy. 2 dark, depressing, dismal, distressing, doleful, foreboding, funereal, gloomy, hopeless, lugubrious, melancholy, mournful, pessimistic, ominous, sad, sombre. 3 bad, devilish, diabolic, evil, foul, heinous, iniquitous, nefarious, villainous, wicked

**blacklist** *v* ban, bar, boycott, debar, exclude, expel, ostracize, expel, proscribe, reject

**blackmail** *v* extort, exact, extract, force, hold to ransom, intimidate, threaten

**blame** *n* 1 accountability, culpability, fault, guilt, liability, onus, responsibility. 2 accusation, castigation, censure, charge, condemnation, incrimination, indictment, recrimination, reprimand, reproof

**blame** *v* accuse, censure, charge, condemn, hold accountable, hold to account, indict, find fault with, find guilty, reprehend, reprimand, reproach, reprove, take to task; *opp* absolve

**blameless** *adj* above suspicion, beyond reproach, faultless, guiltless, innocent, in the clear, irreproachable, not to blame, perfect, stainless, unblemished, unimpeachable, upright, virtuous

**bland** *adj* 1 (of flavour) boring, dull, flavourless, insipid, mild, plain, tasteless, weak. 2 (of a person, remarks) boring, dull, insipid, middle-of-the-road, mediocre, nondescript, neutral, safe, uncontroversial, uninspiring, uninteresting, vapid

**blank** *adj* 1 bare, clean, clear, empty, plain, spotless, unfilled, unmarked, vacant, void, white. 2 at a loss, baffled, bewildered, confounded, confused, expressionless, nonplussed, perplexed, puzzled, uncomprehending

**blare** *v* bellow, blast, boom, honk, hoot,

peal, resound, roar, trumpet

**blasé** *adj* apathetic, bored, casual, indifferent, jaded, laid-back, lukewarm, nonchalant, phlegmatic, offhand, relaxed, unconcerned, unenthusiastic, unimpressed, uninterested, unmoved, unperturbed, weary, world-weary

**blaspheme** *v* curse, damn, desecrate, profane, swear

**blasphemous** *adj* godless, impious, irreverent, profane, sacrilegious, ungodly, unholy

**blast** *n* 1 bang, blowing-up, boom, crash, detonation, explosion, salvo, volley. 2 blare, boom, honk, hoot, peal, trumpeting, wail

**blast** *v* 1 bomb, blow up, demolish, destroy, detonate, explode, fire, fire-bomb, raze, ruin, shatter. 2 blare, boom, honk, hoot, peal, sound, trumpet, wail

**blatant** *adj* brazen, conspicuous, flagrant, glaring, naked, obvious, open, ostentatious, outright, overt, prominent, shameless, sheer, unashamed, unconcealed

**blaze** *n* 1 bonfire, conflagration, fire, flame, flames, inferno. 2 beam, brilliance, flare, glare

**blaze** *v* 1 (of a fire) be ablaze, burn, burst into flames, catch fire, flame, glow. 2 (of light) be ablaze, burn, beam, flare, flash, glare, gleam, glow, shine

**bleach** *v* blanch, fade, pale, peroxide, lighten, take the colour out of, whiten

**bleak** *adj* 1 bare, barren, desolate, exposed, raw, unsheltered, waste, windswept. 2 cheerless, dark, depressing, dismal, drab, dreary, gloomy, grim, hopeless, joyless, miserable, sombre,

unpromising, wretched

**bleary** *adj* blurred, blurry, clouded, dim, fogged, foggy, fuzzy, hazy, indistinct, misty, unclear; *opp* clear

**blemish** *n* 1 (on skin) blotch, defect, disfigurement, fault, flaw, imperfection, mark, mole, patch, scab, scar, smudge, speck, spot, stain, taint. 2 (on character) blot, defect, disgrace, dishonour, fault, flaw, imperfection, stain, taint

**blemished** *adj* blotted, blotchy, defective, disfigured, faulty, flawed, imperfect, marked, patchy, smudged, speckled, spotted, spotty, stained, tainted; *opp* clear

**blend** *n* alloy, amalgam, amalgamation, combination, composite, compound, cross, fusion, mix, mixture, synthesis, union

**blend** *v* amalgamate, coalesce, combine, cross, fuse, merge, mingle, mix, synthesize, unite

**bless** *v* 1 consecrate, dedicate, exalt, extol, glorify, praise, sanctify, thank. 2 (bless sb with sth) bestow, endow, favour, grace, grant, provide. 3 approve, be in favour, condone, consent, endorse, sanction, support

**blessed** *adj* 1 adored, beatified, consecrated, divine, exalted, hallowed, holy, sanctified, sacred. 2 (blessed with sth) endowed, favoured, fortunate, gifted, lucky

**blessing** *n* 1 benediction, benison, consecration, dedication, grace, invocation, praise, thanksgiving. 2 approval, assent, backing, consent, endorsement, permission, sanction, support. 3 advantage, benefit, boon, endowment, gift, godsend, good fortune, favour, windfall

**blight** n 1 affliction, bane, cancer, curse, pestilence, plague, scourge, woe. 2 (in plants) canker, disease, fungus, infestation, mildew, pest, pestilence, rot

**blight** v 1 afflict, blast, crush, curse, dash, destroy, kill, ruin, wreck. 2 (blight a plant) blast, destroy, infest, kill, rot, shrivel, wither

**blind** adj 1 sightless, unseeing, visually impaired. 2 dense, heedless, ignorant, inattentive, insensitive, neglectful, oblivious, unaware, unconscious, unmindful, unobservant

**bliss** n delight, ecstasy, elation, euphoria, gladness, happiness, heaven, joy, paradise, pleasure, rapture

**blissful** adj delightful, ecstatic, euphoric, happy, heavenly, joyful, rapturous, wonderful

**blitz** n assault, attack, blitzkrieg, bombardment, bombing, offensive, onslaught, raid, strike

**bloated** adj dilated, distended, enlarged, full, inflated, puffed up, swollen

**blob** n ball, bead, dab, dollop, drop, droplet, glob, globule, lump, mass

**block** n bar, brick, cake, chunk, cube, hunk, lump, ingot, piece, rectangle, square, wedge

**block** v 1 bung up inf, choke, clog, close, obstruct, plug, stop up. 2 bar, check, hinder, impede, obstruct, prevent, stop, thwart

**blockage** n bar, barrier, bung, clog, impediment, jam, obstacle, obstruction, occlusion, plug, stoppage

**blond(e)** adj fair, fair-haired, flaxen, golden, golden-haired

**blood** n 1 gore, lifeblood, vital fluids. 2 ancestry, birth, descent, extraction, family, genealogy, heritage, kindred, kinship, line, lineage, origin, parentage, pedigree, race, relation, relative, stock, strain

**bloodshed** n blood bath, bloodletting, butchery, carnage, gore, killing, massacre, murder, slaughter, slaying, violence, war

**bloodthirsty** adj barbaric, barbarous, brutal, cruel, ferocious, murderous, ruthless, sadistic, savage, vicious, violent, warlike

**bloody** adj 1 bleeding, blood-stained, blood-soaked, blood-spattered, gory. 2 barbaric, barbarous, bloodthirsty, brutal, gory, murderous, sadistic, savage, vicious, violent

**bloom** n 1 blossom, blossoming, bud, flower. 2 blush, flush, freshness, glow, health, lustre, radiance, rosiness

**bloom** v 1 be in bloom, be in blossom, be in flower, blossom, bud, burgeon, flower, open. 2 (of a person) blossom, flourish, glow, thrive

**blossom** n bloom, blossoming, bud, flower

**blossom** v 1 be in bloom, be in blossom, be in flower, bud, burgeon, flower, open. 2 (of a person) bloom, flourish, glow, thrive

**blot** n 1 blemish, blotch, blur, dot, mark, patch, smudge, speck, spatter, speckle, spot, stain. 2 (on reputation) blemish, blur, defect, disgrace, dishonour, fault, flaw, imperfection, stain, taint

**blow** n 1 bang, bash, buffet, clout, hit,

knock, punch, rap, slap, smack, stroke, thump, thwack, wallop *inf*, whack. **2** bombshell, calamity, catastrophe, disappointment, disaster, jolt, let-down, misfortune, reverse, setback, shock, upset

**blow** *v* **1** blast, breathe, exhale, fan, huff, pant, puff. **2** (move by air, wind) buffet, flap, flutter, sweep, toss, waft, wave, whirl, whisk. **3** pipe, play, sound, toot. **4 blow up** blast, bomb, burst, detonate, fire, explode, go off, pop, rupture, shatter

**blue** *adj* **1** azure, cobalt, indigo, navy, sapphire, sky-blue, turquoise, ultramarine. **2** dejected, depressed, despondent, down *inf*, downcast, downhearted, fed up *inf*, gloomy, glum, low, melancholy, miserable, sad, unhappy; *opp* happy

**blues** *n* dejection, depression, despondency, doldrums, dumps *inf*, gloom, gloominess, glumness, low spirits, melancholy, misery, sadness, unhappiness

**bluff** *v* con, deceive, delude, fake, feign, hoax, lie, mislead, pretend, put it on, sham, take in, trick

**blunder** *n* boob *inf*, cock-up *inf*, error, faux pas, gaffe, mistake, oversight, slip

**blunt** *adj* **1** dull, rounded, unsharpened; *opp* sharp. **2** abrupt, bluff, brusque, candid, direct, forthright, frank, honest, outspoken, plain-spoken, straight, straightforward, tactless, to the point

**blur** *n* dimness, fog, haze, indistinctness, mist, obscurity, smear, smudge

**blur** *v* blotch, cloud, darken, dim, fog, mask, mist up, obscure, smear, smudge, steam up, veil

**blurred** *adj* bleary, blurry, clouded, dim, faint, fogged, foggy, fuzzy, hazy, indistinct, misty, nebulous, obscure, out of focus, smeared, smudged, unclear, vague; *opp* clear

**blurt out** *v* babble, blab, cry, disclose, exclaim, let out, let slip, reveal, say, spill the beans *inf*, tattle, tell

**blush** *v* colour, flush, go pink, go red, redden, turn pink, turn red

**board** *n* **1** beam, panel, plank, slat, timber. **2** body, committee, council, directorate, directors, panel, trustees

**board** *v* **1** embark, enter, go aboard, go on board, mount. **2** accommodate, feed, house, lodge, put up, quarter, take in

**boast** *n* **1** bluster, bragging, crowing, exaggeration, self-congratulation, showing off, swagger, swank. **2** gem, jewel, pride, pride and joy, treasure

**boast** *v* **1** blow your own trumpet *inf*, bluster, brag, crow, exaggerate, show off, strut, swagger, swank, talk big *inf*, vaunt. **2** enjoy, have, own, possess, pride yourself on

**bodily** *adj* carnal, corporal, corporeal, fleshly, material, physical

**body** *n* **1** build, figure, form, flesh, frame, physique, shape, torso, trunk. **2** cadaver, carcass, corpse, dead body, remains. **3** bulk, essence, main part, majority, mass, material, matter, substance. **4** association, authority, band, committee, company, corporation, group, organization, society

**bog** *n* fen, marsh, mire, morass, quagmire, swamp, wetland

**boggy** *adj* marshy, muddy, soft, swampy, wet

**bogus** *adj* artificial, counterfeit, dummy, ersatz, fake, false, forged, fraudulent, imitation, mock, phoney *inf*, pseudo, sham, spurious; *opp* genuine

**boil** *n* blister, carbuncle, pustule, spot, swelling

**boil** *v* bubble, come to the boil, cook, churn, foam, froth, seethe, simmer, steam, stew

**boiling** *adj* baking, blistering, hot, roasting, scorching, searing, sweltering; *opp* freezing

**boisterous** *adj* bouncy, exuberant, lively, loud, noisy, riotous, rollicking, rough, rowdy, rumbustious, spirited, unruly, uproarious, wild

**bold** *adj* **1** adventurous, audacious, brash, brave, cheeky, courageous, daring, dauntless, enterprising, fearless, intrepid, presumptuous, valiant; *opp* timid. **2** bright, colourful, conspicuous, eye-catching, flashy, loud, lurid, prominent, showy, striking, strong, vivid; *opp* muted

**bolster** *v* aid, assist, boost, brace, buoy up, buttress, help, hold up, maintain, prop up, reinforce, shore up, strengthen, support

**bolt** *n* **1** bar, catch, fastener, latch, lock. **2** peg, pin, rivet, rod

**bolt** *v* **1** abscond, bound, dart, dash, escape, flee, fly, hurtle, leap, run, rush, sprint. **2** bar, fasten, lock, secure. **3** (bolt food) cram, devour, down, gobble, gulp, guzzle, stuff, wolf

**bomb** *n* blast, booby-trap, charge, device, explosive, grenade, incendiary, mine, shell, torpedo

**bomb** *v* attack, blast, blitz, blow up, bombard, booby-trap, destroy, detonate, explode, fire, fire-bomb, shell, torpedo

**bombard** *v* **1** assault, attack, blast, blitz, bomb, fire on, open fire, pound, shell, strafe, torpedo. **2** (with questions) assail, attack, barrage, besiege, beset, bother, harass, hassle *inf*, hound, pester

**bond** *n* **1** affinity, attachment, connection, link, relation, relationship, tie, union. **2** binding, chain, cord, fastening, fetters, manacles, shackles, rope. **3** agreement, bargain, compact, commitment, contract, covenant, deal, guarantee, obligation, pledge, promise, treaty, word

**bond** *v* bind, cement, fasten, fix, fuse, glue, join, stick

**bonus** *n* benefit, boon, bounty, commission, dividend, extra, gift, gratuity, hand-out, perk *inf*, perquisite, plus, prize, reward, tip

**book** *n* leaflet, magazine, manual, publication, text, title, tome, tract, treatise, volume, work

**book** *v* arrange, charter, engage, line up, make a reservation, organize, reserve, schedule

**boom** *n* **1** bang, bellow, blast, clap, crash, explosion, reverberation, roar, roll, rumble, shout, thunder. **2** advance, burgeoning, development, expansion, gain, growth, increase, progress, success, spurt, upsurge, upturn

**boom** *v* **1** bang, bellow, blare, blast, crash, echo, explode, resound, reverberate, roar, roll, rumble, shout, thunder. **2** advance, burgeon, develop, expand, flourish, grow, increase, progress, prosper, succeed, thrive

**boost** *n* advance, assistance,

augmentation, encouragement, help, improvement, increase, inspiration, plug *inf*, praise, promotion, stimulus, rise, support

**boost** *v* advance, amplify, assist, augment, enlarge, encourage, facilitate, foster, further, heighten, help, improve, increase, inflate, inspire, plug *inf*, praise, promote, raise, stimulate, support, uplift

**border** *n* **1** boundary, brim, brink, edge, edging, fringe, hem, limit, margin, outskirts, perimeter, rim, skirt, verge. **2** (between countries) borderline, boundary, frontier

**bore** *v* be tedious, bother, exhaust, fatigue, pall, send sb to sleep, tire, vex, wear out, weary; *opp* inspire

**bored** *adj* apathetic, blasé, fatigued, fed up *inf*, indifferent, jaded, languorous, lukewarm, tired, unenthusiastic, unimpressed, uninspired, uninterested, unmoved, weary

**boredom** *n* apathy, dullness, monotony, sameness, tediousness, tedium, weariness; *opp* excitement

**boring** *adj* dead, dull, humdrum, insipid, monotonous, repetitious, routine, stale, tedious, tiresome, uneventful, unexciting, uninteresting

**borrow** *v* acquire, adopt, appropriate, cadge *inf*, commandeer, filch, help yourself to, pinch, pirate, plagiarize, scrounge *inf*, sponge *inf*, take, use; *opp* lend

**boss** *n* chief, employer, foreman, gaffer *inf*, head, master, overseer, owner, supervisor

**boss** *v* bully, domineer, order about, order around, push around, ride roughshod over, throw your weight about

**bossy** *adj* assertive, bullying, dominating, domineering, high-handed, imperious, lordly, officious, overbearing, pushy *inf*, self-assertive

**botch** *v* bungle, fumble, make a hash *inf*, make a mess, mess up *inf*, mismanage, ruin, spoil

**bother** *n* annoyance, difficulty, effort, exertion, fuss, hassle *inf*, inconvenience, irritation, nuisance, strain, trouble, worry

**bother** *v* **1** (bother sb) annoy, disturb, exasperate, give sb a hard time *inf*, harass, hassle *inf*, irritate, molest, nag, pester, provoke, torment, vex, worry. **2** (needn't bother) be concerned, care, concern yourself, go to any trouble, inconvenience yourself, make the effort, mind, put yourself out, take the time, trouble yourself. **3** (sth bothers you) alarm, concern, dismay, distress, perturb, upset, trouble, worry

**bottom** *n* **1** base, bed, depth, floor, foot, foundation, underneath, underside. **2** backside, behind, bum *inf*, butt *Am inf*, buttocks, hindquarters, rear, rear end, seat, tail. **3** basis, cause, centre, core, essence, heart, nitty-gritty, origin, root, source, substance

**bounce** *n* **1** elasticity, give, resilience, spring, springiness. **2** animation, dynamism, energy, go *inf*, life, liveliness, oomph *inf*, pep, spirit, vigour, vitality, vivacity, zip *inf*. **3** bound, leap, jump, skip, spring

**bounce** *v* bob, bound, jump, leap, rebound, recoil, ricochet, spring

**bound** *adj* **1** (bound to happen) certain, destined, doomed, fated, predestined, sure, very likely. **2** (bound with rope) fettered, lashed, roped, secured, strapped, tethered, tied, tied up, trussed. **3** (obliged to do sth) committed, compelled, constrained, duty-bound, forced, obligated, obliged, required

**bound** v bob, bounce, caper, frisk, frolic, gambol, hop, jump, leap, pounce, prance, skip, spring, vault

**boundary** n barrier, border, bounds, brink, demarcation, edge, end, extremity, fringe, frontier, limits, margin, perimeter, threshold

**boundless** adj endless, immeasurable, incalculable, infinite, never-ending, unbounded, unending, untold, vast

**bounds** n boundary, border, confines, edges, limitations, limits, periphery, perimeter

**bouquet** n **1** (flowers) arrangement, bunch, buttonhole, corsage, garland, posy, spray, wreath. **2** (wine) aroma, fragrance, odour, perfume, savour, scent, smell

**bout** n **1** (fighting) competition, contest, encounter, engagement, fight, match, set-to inf. **2** (of illness) attack, fit, spell. **3** (of activity) period, run, spell, stint, stretch, time, turn

**bow** n bob, curtsey, genuflexion, nod, obeisance

**bow** v **1** bend, bob, curtsey, genuflect, incline your head, kowtow, make obeisance, nod, prostrate yourself, salaam, stoop. **2** **bow to** capitulate, give in, give way, submit, surrender, yield

**bowels** n **1** entrails, guts, innards inf, insides inf, intestines. **2** belly, core, depths, heart, inside, interior

**bowl** n basin, container, dish, tureen, vessel

**box** n carton, case, chest, container, crate, pack, package, trunk

**boy** n fellow, kid inf, lad, schoolboy, son, youngster, youth

**boycott** n ban, embargo, prohibition

**boycott** v ban, bar, blacklist, ostracize, place an embargo on, reject, send to Coventry, spurn

**boyfriend** n date, lover, man, sweetheart, toy boy sl, young man

**brace** n **1** buttress, clamp, prop, reinforcement, stanchion, stay, strut, support, truss. **2** couple, duo, pair, two

**brace** v bolster, buttress, fortify, hold up, prop up, reinforce, secure, shore up, steady, strengthen

**braced** adj prepared, ready, rigid, set, steady, tense

**brain** n **1** brainpower, grey matter inf, intellect, intelligence, mind, nous inf, reason, sense, understanding, wit. **2** (clever person) genius, intellectual, mastermind, thinker

**brainwash** v condition, indoctrinate, influence, re-educate

**brake** v check, decelerate, reduce speed, slow, slow down, stop

**branch** n **1** (of a tree) arm, bough, limb, offshoot, prong, stem, twig. **2** (of an organization) department, division, office, part, section, subdivision, subsection, tributary, wing

**brand** n **1** class, grade, kind, line, make, quality, sort, species, trade mark, trade name, type, variety. **2** hallmark, label, marker, sign, stamp, symbol, tag

**brand** v **1** (cattle) burn, mark, scar, sear,

stamp. **2** (give sb a bad name) characterize, denounce, discredit, stigmatize, vilify. **3** (impress on sb's mind) engrave, fix, impress, imprint, print, stamp

**brandish** v flaunt, flourish, shake, swing, wave, wield

**brash** adj arrogant, bold, brazen, cocky inf, forward, impertinent, insolent, pushy inf, rude

**bravado** n arrogance, audacity, bluster, boastfulness, boldness, bombast, bragging, machismo, swagger

**brave** adj bold, courageous, daring, dauntless, fearless, gutsy inf, heroic, intrepid, tough, unafraid, undaunted, unshrinking; **opp** cowardly

**bravery** n boldness, bottle sl, courage, daring, fearlessness, gallantry, guts inf, heroism, nerve inf, pluck, spirit, valour; **opp** cowardice

**brazen** adj barefaced, blatant, brash, flagrant, immodest, insolent, rude, saucy, shameless, unashamed

**breach** n **1** aperture, break, chasm, cleft, crack, fissure, fracture, gap, hole, opening, split. **2** breaking, contravention, infringement, transgression, violation

**breach** v **1** break through, burst through, open up, rupture. **2** break, contravene, defy, disobey, infringe, violate

**breadth** n **1** (distance across) broadness, latitude, span, spread, thickness, wideness, width. **2** (wide range) comprehensiveness, extensiveness, extent, range, scale, scope, sweep

**break** n **1** breach, breakage, cleft, crack, division, hole, fissure, fracture, gap, gash, hole, opening, rent, rift, rupture, split, tear. **2** (pause) breather inf, breathing-space, halt, hiatus, interlude, interval, lull, pause, respite, rest, stop, time out inf. **3** breach, disruption, estrangement, lapse, rift, schism, separation, split, suspension

**break** v **1** (break into parts) bust inf, chip, crack, crumple, damage, demolish, destroy, fracture, fragment, part, separate, sever, shatter, shiver, smash, smash to smithereens, snap, splinter, split, tear, wreck. **2** (break a rule) contravene, defy, disobey, disregard, flout, infringe, transgress, violate. **3** (break a person) bankrupt, bring sb to their knees, cow, cripple, crush, defeat, dispirit, make bankrupt, overwhelm, ruin, subdue, tame, weaken. **4** (stop) discontinue, interrupt, knock off inf, pause, rest, stop, take a break, take five inf. **5** (break a record) beat, cap inf, exceed, go beyond, outdo, outstrip, pass, shatter, smash, surpass. **6** (of news) announce, appear, become public, be revealed, disclose, divulge, emerge, make public, reveal, tell. **7** (of waves) crash, dash, hit. **8** (break a code) decipher, decode, unravel, solve. **9 break down** collapse, come to grief, conk out inf, crack up inf, fail, fall through, go to pieces, seize up, stop, stop working. **10 break in** barge in, break and enter, burgle, burst in, butt in, interfere, interrupt, intervene, intrude, invade, push your way in, rob, thrust your way in. **11 break off** detach, divide, pull off, separate, sever, splinter. **12 break off** bring to an end, call a halt, cease, discontinue, end, finish, stop, suspend, terminate. **13 break out** abscond, bolt, break loose, escape, flee, free yourself. **14 break out** (spots) appear, emerge, occur. **15 break up** adjourn, come to an end, dismantle, disrupt, dissolve, divorce, end, part, scatter, separate, split up, stop, terminate

**breakdown** *n* 1 collapse, destruction, disintegration, failure, malfunction, nervous breakdown, ruin, stoppage. 2 analysis, categorization, classification, diagnosis, dissection, rundown *inf*

**breakthrough** *n* advance, development, discovery, innovation, invention, leap forward, progress, revolution

**breast** *n* bosom, bust, chest, front

**breath** *n* 1 air, breathing, exhalation, gasp, gulp, pant, respiration, wheeze. 2 (suggestion) hint, murmur, suggestion, suspicion, touch, trace, undertone, whisper

**breathe** *v* 1 exhale, gasp, inhale, pant, puff, respire, wheeze. 2 murmur, say, sigh, tell, whisper

**breathless** *adj* 1 exhausted, choking, gasping, gulping, out of breath, panting, puffed *inf*, puffing, spent, tired out, wheezing, winded. 2 (with excitement) agog, all agog, avid, eager, excited, on tenterhooks, open-mouthed, with bated breath

**breed** *n* class, family, kind, line, lineage, pedigree, race, stock, strain, type, variety

**breed** *v* bear, bring up, hatch, increase, multiply, nurture, procreate, produce, propagate, raise, rear, reproduce

**breeze** *n* draught, gentle wind, gust, light wind, puff of air, waft

**brew** *n* beer, beverage, blend, concoction, drink, infusion, liquor, mixture, potion, preparation, tea

**brew** *v* 1 boil, concoct, ferment, infuse, prepare, simmer, steep, stew. 2 (of trouble) contrive, cook up *inf*, devise, foment, hatch, plan, plot, scheme, stir up

**bribe** *n* backhander *sl*, bribery, carrot *inf*, enticement, hush money *sl*, inducement, kickback *inf*, pay-off *inf*, sweetener *inf*

**bribe** *v* buy off, corrupt, get at *inf*, give an inducement to, grease sb's palm *inf*, pay sb off, tempt

**bridge** *n* 1 aqueduct, arch, causeway, crossing, flyover, footbridge, overpass, span, viaduct. 2 bond, connection, link, stepping stone, tie

**bridge** *v* bind, connect, cross, join, link, span, straddle, traverse, unite

**brief** *adj* 1 compact, concise, condensed, crisp, incisive, pithy, short, succinct, terse, thumbnail, to the point; *opp* lengthy, long. 2 ephemeral, fleeting, impermanent, passing, quick, short, short-lived, swift, temporary, transient, transitory; *opp* lengthy, long

**brief** *n* advice, briefing, description, guidance, information, instructions, orders, outline, summary

**brief** *v* advise, fill sb in *inf*, give the facts to, instruct, prepare, prime, put sb in the picture *inf*

**bright** *adj* 1 (of light) beaming, blazing, brilliant, dazzling, flashing, gleaming, glittering, glowing, incandescent, intense, luminous, radiant, scintillating, shining, shiny, sparkling, twinkling, vivid; *opp* dark, dull. **2** (clever) acute, astute, clever, intelligent, inventive, quick, sharp, smart; *opp* dull. **3** (of weather) clear, cloudless, fair, sunny; *opp* dull. **4** (of prospects) encouraging, favourable, good, hopeful, optimistic, promising, propitious, rosy; *opp* gloomy. **5** (of a person) cheerful, gay, happy, jolly, joyful, light-hearted, lively, merry; *opp* miserable. **6** (of colour) bold, brilliant, colourful, fresh, gaudy, intense, rich, vivid; *opp* pale

**brighten** *v* **1** cheer up, enliven, gladden, illuminate, lighten, light up, liven up, make brighter, perk up, revitalize. **2** (of weather) clear, clear up; *opp* cloud over

**brilliance** *n* **1** (of light) brightness, dazzle, glare, intensity, luminosity, radiance, sheen, sparkle, vividness. **2** (of an occasion) glamour, glitter, grandeur, lustre, magnificence, splendour. **3** (genius) braininess, cleverness, eminence, fame, genius, giftedness, talent

**brilliant** *adj* **1** (shining) bright, dazzling, glittering, intense, radiant, scintillating, shining, sparkling, vivid. **2** (good) brill *inf*, excellent, fabulous, great, good, marvellous, superb, wonderful. **3** (clever) bright, celebrated, clever, exceptional, famous, gifted, intelligent, remarkable, smart, talented

**bring** *v* **1** (take somewhere) accompany, bear, carry, convey, deliver, escort, fetch, gather, guide, import, lead, take, transport. **2** (lead to sth happening) attract, cause, contribute to, create, draw, earn, effect, generate, give rise to, inflict, lead to, occasion, produce, prompt, provoke, result in, wreak. **3 bring about** accomplish, achieve, cause, effect, give rise to, lead to, make happen, occasion, produce, result in. **4 bring up** care for, educate, nurture, raise, rear, support. **5 bring up** (bring up a subject) allude to, broach, introduce, mention, refer to, touch on/upon

**brink** *n* border, brim, edge, fringe, limit, rim, threshold, verge

**brisk** *adj* **1** (a brisk walk) energetic, lively, quick, smart, spanking *inf*, speedy, vigorous; *opp* leisurely. **2** (of weather) bracing, crisp, exhilarating, fresh, invigorating, keen, nippy *inf*, refreshing. **3** (of business) active, bustling, busy, hectic; *opp* slow

**brittle** *adj* breakable, crisp, crumbling, delicate, easily broken, fragile, frail, hard, splintery, weak

**broach** *v* bring up, introduce, mention, propose, raise, speak about, suggest, talk about, touch on

**broad** *adj* **1** (wide) ample, boundless, capacious, extensive, large, open, spacious, sweeping, vast, wide, widespread; *opp* narrow. **2** (of knowledge) comprehensive, encyclopaedic, far-reaching, general, wide, wide-ranging. **3** (of sb's mind) liberal, open, permissive, progressive, tolerant, unbiased, unprejudiced; *opp* narrow. **4** (of a description) general, imprecise, inexact, loose, sweeping, vague; *opp* detailed. **5** (of taste) all-embracing, catholic, eclectic, varied; *opp* narrow

**broadcast** *n* programme, show, transmission

**broadcast** v advertise, air, announce, beam, circulate, disseminate, make known, make public, proclaim, publish, report, spread, televise, transmit

**broaden** v develop, enlarge, expand, make broader, make wider, open up, spread, stretch, swell, widen

**broad-minded** adj enlightened, flexible, liberal, open-minded, permissive, tolerant, unbiased, unprejudiced, unshockable; *opp* narrow-minded

**brochure** n booklet, catalogue, circular, folder, hand-out, leaflet, pamphlet, prospectus

**broken** adj 1 burst, bust *inf*, cracked, demolished, destroyed, fractured, fragmented, punctured, severed, shattered, smashed, split, torn; *opp* whole. 2 (not working) broken down, bust *inf*, damaged, defective, faulty, kaput, out of order. 3 (not continuous) discontinuous, disrupted, disturbed, erratic, fragmentary, intermittent, interrupted, spasmodic. 4 (having lost the will to fight) beaten, crippled, crushed, defeated, demoralized, discouraged, dispirited, subdued, tamed, vanquished

**brood** n chicks, children, clutch, family, litter, offspring, progeny, young

**brood** v 1 agonize, dwell upon, fret, mope, mull over, muse, ponder, sulk, think, worry. 2 hatch, incubate, sit on

**brown** adj 1 beige, buff, chocolate, cocoa, copper, coppery, dun, ecru, fawn, hazel, khaki, mahogany, maroon, ochre, russet, rust, sepia, tan, tawny, terracotta, umber. 2 (of hair) auburn, chestnut, dark, ginger. 3 (of skin) bronze, bronzed, coffee-coloured, dark, sunburnt, sun-tanned, tanned

**browse** v 1 dip into, flip through, leaf through, look through, scan, skim. 2 look round, window-shop. 3 crop, eat, feed, graze, nibble

**bruise** n black eye, blemish, bump, contusion, discoloration, mark, shiner *inf*, swelling, welt

**bruise** v blacken, blemish, crush, damage, discolour, knock, make black and blue, mark

**brush** v 1 buff, clean, comb, groom, polish, sweep, tidy, wash. 2 caress, contact, flick, glance, graze, kiss, scrape, stroke, sweep, touch. 3 **brush up** go over, polish up, read up, refresh your memory, relearn, revise, study

**brutal** adj barbaric, barbarous, bloodthirsty, bloody, callous, cold-blooded, cruel, heartless, inhuman, merciless, murderous, pitiless, remorseless, ruthless, sadistic, savage, vicious, violent; *opp* gentle

**brutality** n atrocity, barbarism, barbarity, bloodiness, bloodthirstiness, cruelty, ferocity, savageness, savagery

**brutalize** v abuse, corrupt, dehumanize, harden, inure, make brutal, toughen

**brute** n 1 animal, beast, creature, dumb animal, wild animal. 2 barbarian, beast, bully, devil, fiend, monster, ruffian, sadist, savage, swine

**bubble** v 1 effervesce, fizz, fizzle, foam, froth, gurgle, sparkle. 2 boil, percolate, simmer

**buckle** n catch, clasp, clip, fastener, fastening, hasp

**buckle** v 1 bend, bulge, cave in, crumple,

curve, dent, fold, kink, twist, warp.
2 clip, do up, fasten, hitch, hook up,
secure

**budding** adj aspiring, burgeoning,
fledgling, flowering, growing, potential,
promising, would-be inf

**budge** v 1 dislodge, give way, go, move,
push, remove, roll, shift, slide.
2 acquiesce, change, change your mind,
convince, give in, give way, persuade,
sway, yield

**budget** n accounts, allowance, cost,
finances, financial plan, funds, means,
resources

**budget** v allocate, allow, apportion, cost,
estimate, plan, provide, ration, save, set
aside

**buffer** n bulwark, bumper, cushion,
fender, guard, safeguard, screen, shield

**bug** n 1 creepy-crawly inf, flea, insect,
mite. 2 bacterium, germ, infection,
micro-organism, virus. 3 (in a computer
program) breakdown, defect, error, fault,
flaw, gremlin inf, malfunction, mistake,
virus

**bug** v 1 eavesdrop, listen to, phone-tap,
spy on, tap, wiretap. 2 anger, annoy, get
on sb's nerves inf, hassle inf, infuriate,
irk, irritate, provoke

**build** v 1 assemble, construct, erect, form,
make, manufacture, put together, put up,
raise. 2 base, begin, establish, found,
originate, set up, start

**building** n construction, edifice, premises,
structure

**build-up** n accumulation, collection,
gathering, heap, hoard, mass, stockpile,
store

**bulge** n bump, hump, lump, projection,

protuberance, rise, swelling

**bulging** adj ballooning, bloated,
distended, full, lumpy, popping,
protruding, sticking out, swelling,
swollen

**bulk** n 1 bulkiness, extent, immensity,
largeness, magnitude, mass, massiveness,
quantity, size, weight. 2 best part inf,
greater part, lion's share, main part,
majority, mass, most, nearly all

**bullet** n missile, pellet, shot, slug

**bulletin** n announcement,
communication, communiqué, message,
news-flash, notification, report,
statement

**bully** n abuser, oppressor, persecutor,
ruffian, thug, tormentor, tyrant

**bully** v browbeat, coerce, domineer,
frighten, intimidate, oppress, persecute,
pick on inf, push around inf, ride
roughshod over, terrorize, threaten,
tyrannize

**bump** n 1 bang, blow, collision, crash,
jolt, knock, smash, thud, thump.
2 (a bump on sth) bulge, hump, knob,
lump, nodule, protrusion, protuberance,
swelling, welt

**bump** v 1 (hit sth) bang, collide, crash,
hit, hurt, injure, jar, knock, ram, slam
inf, smash into, strike, thump. 2 (bump
up and down) bounce, jerk, jolt, rattle,
shake. 3 **bump into** chance upon, come
across, encounter, happen on, meet, run
into, see

**bunch** n 1 (of things) batch, bundle,
cluster, collection, group, heap, load,
mass, pack, quantity, set. 2 (of flowers)
bouquet, clump, posy, sheaf, spray.
3 (of people) band, crowd, gang, group,

knot, party

**bunch** v 1 assemble, bundle, cluster, collect, crowd, flock, gather, group, herd, huddle, mass, pack; *opp* separate. 2 bunch up, fold, gather, pleat; *opp* lie flat

**bundle** n 1 assortment, batch, bunch, collection, heap, pile. 2 bag, pack, package, parcel, roll, sheaf

**bundle** v bind, fasten, muffle, pack, package, roll, swathe, tie, truss, wrap

**bungle** n blunder, botch, error, fiasco, mess, mistake, mix-up, muddle, pig's ear *sl*, slip-up *inf*

**bungle** v blunder, botch, fudge, make a hash *inf*, make a mess *inf*, mess up *inf*, mismanage, muck up *inf*, ruin, spoil

**buoyant** adj 1 able to float, floating, light. 2 blithe, bouncy, bright, cheerful, jaunty, light-hearted, upbeat *inf*; *opp* depressed, low

**burden** n 1 anxiety, care, difficulty, duty, obligation, problem, responsibility, sorrow, stress, trial, trouble, worry 2 cargo, encumbrance, load, weight

**burden** v afflict, bother, encumber, hamper, impose, load, lumber *inf*, overload, saddle *inf*, strain, tax, trouble, weigh down, worry

**bureaucracy** n administration, civil service, government, ministry, officialdom, red tape *inf*, rules and regulations

**burglar** n cat burglar, housebreaker, intruder, robber, thief

**burglary** n break-in, breaking and entering, housebreaking, larceny, robbery, stealing, theft, thieving

**burly** adj beefy, brawny, bulky, hefty, hulking, muscular, powerful, stocky, strong, sturdy, well-built; *opp* thin, weedy

**burn** v 1 be ablaze, be on fire, blaze, consume, flame, flare, flicker, glow, go up in flames, ignite, incinerate, kindle, light, reduce to ashes, set alight, set on fire, smoke, smoulder, spark. 2 (damage) blister, char, parch, scald, sear, shrivel, singe, toast, wither

**burning** adj 1 alight, blazing, fiery, flaming, flickering, glowing, hot, incandescent, lit up, raging, scorching, smoking, smouldering. 2 ardent, eager, fervent, impassioned, intense, passionate, vehement. 3 biting, irritating, painful, prickling, searing, smarting, stinging. 4 acrid, caustic, corrosive, harsh, pungent, reeking, scorching, smoky

**burrow** n den, earth, hole, lair, sett, shelter, tunnel, warren

**burst** n bang, blast, crack, discharge, explosion, rupture

**burst** v blow up, break, crack, disintegrate, erupt, explode, fly open, force open, fragment, give way, pierce, pop, puncture, rupture, shatter, split, tear

**bury** v 1 conceal, cover, cover up, embed, enclose, engulf, enshroud, hide, immerse, plant, sink, submerge. 2 (a dead person) entomb, inter, lay to rest

**business** n 1 (a firm) company, concern, enterprise, establishment, firm, industry, organization, outfit *inf*, partnership, practice, set-up *inf*, venture. 2 (to be in business) buying and selling, commerce, dealings, marketing, merchandising, selling, trade, transactions. 3 (business to be dealt with) affair, case, issue, matter, problem, question, subject, topic. **4** (line of business) career, job, line of work, occupation, profession, trade, work

**businesslike** *adj* efficient, methodical, neat, organized, professional, systematic, thorough, well-ordered

**bustle** *n* activity, ado, agitation, commotion, excitement, flurry, fuss, haste, hurry, movement, toing and froing *inf*, tumult

**bustle** *v* dash, fuss, hurry, scamper, scramble, scurry, scuttle, tear, whirl

**busy** *adj* **1** (to be busy) active, employed, engaged, engrossed, hard at it *inf*, hard at work, industrious, occupied, on the go *inf*, rushed off your feet, slaving, up to your eyes *inf*, working; *opp* unoccupied. **2** (a busy life) chaotic, energetic, frantic, full, hectic, strenuous, tiring; *opp* quiet

**butcher** *n* killer, murderer, slaughterer, slayer

**butcher** *v* **1** (meat) carve, cut, joint, kill, prepare, slice. **2** (people) kill, murder, massacre, put to death, slaughter, slay

**butt** *n* **1** (cigarette butt) end, fag-end *inf*, stub. **2** (butt of a joke) dupe, laughing-stock, object, subject, target, victim

**buy** *v* acquire, come by, get, invest in *inf*, obtain, pay for, procure, purchase, shop for

**bypass** *v* avoid, circumvent, detour round, evade, go round, sidestep, skirt

**bystander** *n* eyewitness, observer, onlooker, passer-by, spectator, witness

**cabin** *n* **1** chalet, hut, lodge, log cabin, shack, shed, shelter. **2** (on a ship) berth, compartment, quarters, room

**café** *n* cafeteria, coffee bar, coffee shop, diner, restaurant, snack bar, tearoom, teashop

**cage** *n* aviary, birdcage, corral *Am*, enclosure, hutch, pen, pound

**cage** *v* confine, coop up, corral *Am*, fence in, imprison, incarcerate, lock up, pen, restrain, shut up

**calculate** *v* **1** assess, consider, determine, evaluate, figure out, gauge, judge, rate, reckon, weigh up, work out.
**2** (numbers) add, compute, count, estimate, find out, measure, reckon, total, weigh

**calculated** *adj* considered, deliberate, intended, intentional, on purpose, planned, premeditated

**calculating** *adj* canny, crafty, cunning, devious, manipulative, scheming, shrewd, sly; *opp* ingenuous

**calculation** *n* answer, computation, estimate, forecast, judgement, reckoning, result

**call** *n* **1** bellow, cry, exclamation, roar, shout, shriek, signal, song, whoop, yell. **2** appeal, command, demand, invitation, plea, request

**call** *v* **1** (call to sb) cry, cry out, exclaim, hail, shout, yell. **2** (using a telephone) call up, contact, give sb a buzz *inf*, give sb a ring, phone, ring, ring up *inf*, telephone. **3** (call somewhere) drop in *inf*, pay a call, pop in *inf*, stop by, visit. **4** (name sb or sth) christen, designate, dub, entitle, label, name, style, term, title. **5** (call a meeting) announce, convene, convoke, gather, order. **6** (call an ambulance) ask for, fetch, order, send for, summon. **7** **call for** demand, entail, justify, necessitate, need, require

**calling** *n* business, career, job, occupation, profession, trade, vocation, work

**callous** *adj* cold, cool, dispassionate, hardened, hard-hearted, heartless, indifferent, insensitive, ruthless, soulless, stony-hearted, thick-skinned, uncaring, unemotional, unfeeling; *opp* sensitive

**calm** *adj* **1** airless, balmy, flat, mild, motionless, peaceful, placid, quiet, restful, serene, slow-moving, smooth, still, tranquil, windless. **2** (relaxed) collected, composed, controlled, cool, laid-back *inf*, level-headed, patient, relaxed, sensible, together *inf*, unexcited, unfazed *inf*, unflappable *inf*, unmoved, unruffled, untroubled; *opp* frantic

**calm** *n* **1** peace, peacefulness, quietness,

restfulness, serenity, stillness, tranquillity. **2** composure, equanimity, impassivity, poise, sang-froid, self-control

**calm** v **1** (calm a situation) appease, compose, control, cool, mollify, smooth; *opp* inflame. **2** (calm a baby) hush, lull, pacify, placate, quieten, relax, settle, soothe, tranquillize; *opp* disturb

**camouflage** n blind, concealment, cover, disguise, façade, guise, markings, mask, mimicry, protective covering, veil

**camouflage** v cloak, conceal, cover, disguise, hide, mask, obscure, screen, veil

**campaign** n **1** action, crusade, drive, effort, fight, movement, promotion, struggle. **2** (military) attack, battle, expedition, offensive, push, war

**campaign** v agitate, battle, canvass, crusade, fight, push, struggle, work

**cancel** v **1** abandon, abolish, abort, annul, call off, declare void, invalidate, nullify, postpone, quash, repeal, rescind, revoke, scrap, scrub inf, wipe out, write off. **2** cross out, delete, erase, strike out

**cancer** n canker, carcinoma, growth, malignancy, melanoma, tumour

**candid** adj blunt, forthright, frank, honest, open, outspoken, plain, straightforward, truthful, upfront inf; *opp* cagey, deceitful

**candidate** n applicant, competitor, contender, contestant, entrant, nominee, possibility, runner inf

**canvass** v **1** (seek votes) campaign, drum up support inf, electioneer. **2** (investigate) analyse, examine, find out, inspect, investigate, scan, sift, study.

**3** (seek opinions) ask for, discuss, poll, solicit

**cap** v **1** beat, better, eclipse, exceed, excel, outdo, outstrip, surpass, top, transcend. **2** coat, cover, crown, top

**capability** n ability, aptitude, capacity, competence, faculty, means, potential, power, skill, wherewithal

**capable** adj able, adept, clever, competent, efficient, experienced, gifted, handy inf, intelligent, masterly, practised, proficient, qualified, skilful, skilled, talented, trained

**capacity** n **1** amplitude, dimensions, extent, magnitude, range, room, scope, size, space, volume. **2** ability, aptitude, cleverness, competence, intelligence, potential, power, skill, talent. **3** duty, function, job, office, position, post, responsibility, role

**capital** adj **1** (letters) big, block, initial, large, upper-case. **2** cardinal, central, chief, foremost, important, key, leading, main, major, paramount, primary, prime, principal

**capital** n **1** assets, cash, finance, funds, investments, liquid assets, money, principal, property, resources, savings, stock, wealth, wherewithal. **2** centre of government, chief city, first city, seat of government

**capitulate** v acquiesce, admit defeat, back down, be defeated, concede, give in, give up, relent, submit, succumb, surrender, throw in the towel inf, y

**capsize** v flip over, inver l ov knock over, overturn, ti over, turn turtle, tur upset

**captain** n boss, chief, commander, head, leader, master, officer, pilot, skipper

**captive** adj caged, captured, chained, confined, enslaved, fettered, gaoled, imprisoned, in captivity, incarcerated, interned, jailed, locked up, taken prisoner, under lock and key inf; **opp** free

**captive** n convict, detainee, hostage, internee, prisoner, prisoner of war, slave

**captivity** n bondage, confinement, custody, detention, imprisonment, incarceration, internment, slavery; **opp** freedom

**capture** n apprehension, arrest, imprisonment, seizure

**capture** v apprehend, arrest, catch, collar inf, corner, ensnare, nab inf, nick inf, seize, take captive, take into custody, take prisoner, trap

**car** n automobile, motor, motor car, old banger inf, vehicle, wheels sl

**carcass** n body, cadaver, corpse, dead body, meat, remains

**care** n 1 anxiety, burden, concern, difficulty, hardship, problem, sorrow, stress, trouble, woe, worry. 2 (do sth with care) attention, carefulness, caution, circumspection, concentration, consideration, diligence, forethought, heed, meticulousness, prudence, thought, vigilance, watchfulness. 3 (in sb's care) charge, control, custody, guardianship, keeping, management, protection, safekeeping, supervision

**re** v 1 be concerned, be interested, be   oubled, bother, concern yourself with,   a hoot inf, mind, worry. 2 care for   fter sb or sth) cherish, foster, look   . minister to, mother, nurse,

protect, provide for, take care of, tend, watch over. 3 care for (like sb) be fond of, be in love with, cherish, hold dear, like, love. 4 care for (want sth) desire, enjoy, fancy, want

**career** n business, calling, employment, livelihood, living, métier, occupation, profession, trade, vocation, work

**carefree** adj blasé, casual, cheerful, contented, easy-going, happy, happy-go-lucky, insouciant, laid-back inf, light-hearted, nonchalant, relaxed, unworried; **opp** anxious. 2 (a carefree time) peaceful, quiet, relaxing, restful, trouble-free; **opp** stressful

**careful** adj 1 (careful in your work) accurate, conscientious, methodical, meticulous, neat, painstaking, particular, precise, rigorous, systematic, thorough, well-organized; **opp** careless. 2 (be careful) alert, attentive, cautious, circumspect, discreet, heedful, mindful, observant, on guard, solicitous, thoughtful, vigilant, wary, watchful; **opp** careless. 3 (careful with money) canny, cautious, economical, thrifty; **opp** wasteful

**careless** adj 1 absent-minded, forgetful, hasty, inattentive, inconsiderate, indiscreet, irresponsible, negligent, rash, reckless, remiss, scatter-brained, thoughtless, unguarded, unthinking, unwary; **opp** careful. 2 (careless with your work) casual, disorganized, hasty, imprecise, inaccurate, messy, shoddy, slapdash, slipshod, sloppy inf, untidy; **opp** careful

**caress** n cuddle, embrace, hug, kiss, pat, touch

**caress** v cuddle, embrace, fondle, hug, kiss, nuzzle, pat, pet, stroke, touch

**caretaker** n curator, custodian, janitor, keeper, porter, superintendent, warden, watchman

**cargo** n baggage, consignment, contents, freight, goods, haul, load, merchandise, shipment

**caricature** n cartoon, lampoon, parody, satire, send-up inf, spoof, take-off inf, travesty

**caring** adj altruistic, charitable, compassionate, concerned, considerate, helpful, humane, interested, kind, kind-hearted, kindly, loving, solicitous, sympathetic, thoughtful, understanding, unselfish, well-meaning; opp uncaring

**carnage** n bloodbath, bloodshed, butchery, massacre, murder, slaughter

**carnival** n celebration, fair, festival, fête, fiesta, gala, jamboree, holiday, merrymaking, parade, procession, revelry

**carriage** n 1 cab, car, coach, compartment, trap. 2 bearing, comportment, demeanour, gait, manner, mien, posture, stance

**carry** v 1 (take sth somewhere) bear, bring, cart inf, conduct, convey, ferry, fetch, haul, lug inf, manhandle, move, remove, ship, shoulder, take, transfer, transmit, transport. 2 (support sth) bear, hold, support, sustain, underpin. 3 (carry a punishment) demand, entail, involve, lead to, occasion, require, result in. 4 **carry on** continue, endure, go on, keep, keep going, last, maintain, persevere, persist. 5 **carry out** accomplish, achieve, carry through, do, effect, fulfil, perform, realize

**cartoon** n animated film, animation, comic strip, drawing, sketch

**carve** v 1 cut, cut in, chisel, engrave, etch, form, hack, scratch, sculpture, shape. 2 (carve meat) cut up, do the honours, serve, slice, slice up

**case** n 1 box, carton, chest, container, crate, holder, pack. 2 bag, briefcase, hand luggage, holdall, luggage, suitcase, trunk. 3 casing, cover, covering, jacket, sheath, outer shell, wrapper. 4 (display case) cabinet, display cabinet, display case, glass case, showcase. 5 circumstances, example, illustration, instance, occasion, occurrence, position, situation. 6 (legal action) action, dispute, hearing, inquiry, investigation, lawsuit, legal action, proceedings, trial, tribunal

**cash** n change, coins, currency, dosh inf, dough sl, funds, money, notes, pennies inf, resources, small change, the readies

**cast** n 1 actors, cast list, characters, company, dramatis personae tech, performers, players, troupe. 2 casting, impression, mould, shape

**cast** v 1 chuck inf, fling, heave, hurl, lob, scatter, sling, throw, toss. 2 discard, get rid of, shed, slough off, throw off. 3 (cast a glow) direct, emit, give off, send out, shed

**castle** n citadel, chateau, fort, fortress, mansion, pile, stately home, stronghold

**casual** adj 1 blasé, carefree, careless, couldn't-care-less, cursory, easy-going, free and easy, happy-go-lucky, indifferent, informal, laid-back, nonchalant, offhand, relaxed, slap-happy, sloppy, unconcerned.

**2** accidental, chance, impromptu, occasional, random, unexpected, unintentional, unplanned

**casualty** n fatality, injured, injured person, hospital case, stretcher case, victim, wounded

**catalogue** n **1** classification, directory, inventory, record, register. **2** booklet, brochure, guide, leaflet

**catastrophe** n blow, disaster, calamity, crisis, devastation, fiasco, mishap, tragedy

**catch** n **1** clasp, clip, fastener, fastening, hook, latch, lock. **2** (disadvantage) bad news, difficulty, disadvantage, downside, drawback, fly in the ointment, problem, snag. **3** bag, haul, prize, take

**catch** v **1** apprehend, arrest, capture, collar inf, grab, grab hold of, grasp, nab inf, nobble inf, seize, snatch; **opp** drop, let go. **2** catch sb red-handed, discover, expose, surprise, take sb by surprise. **3** (catch flu) be affected by, contract, get, develop, go down with. **4** (catch a train) get, get on, go by, take, travel by; **opp** miss. **5** catch on be all the rage, be in demand, be popular. **6** catch on get it, get the picture, realize, sth dawns on you, the penny drops, twig inf, understand

**catching** adj contagious, communicable, infectious, transmissible, transmittable

**categorical** adj absolute, clear, complete, definite, explicit, express, out-and-out, total, unambiguous, unequivocal

**category** n class, classification, division, department, group, grouping, heading, kind, nature, section, sector, sort, type, variety

**cater** v look after, provide, satisfy, supply

**catty** adj bitchy, malicious, nasty, spiteful, vicious, vindictive

**cause** n **1** basis, grounds, incentive, motive, origin, reason, source; **opp** effect, result. **2** aim, campaign, end, movement, objective, purpose, struggle, undertaking

**cause** v be the cause of, bring about, bring on, create, end in, generate, give rise to, instigate, lead to, make, produce, provoke, result in, set off, spark off, trigger

**caution** n **1** care, carefulness, circumspection, discretion, prudence, vigilance, wariness; **opp** recklessness. **2** admonition, reprimand, talking-to, telling-off, warning

**caution** v **1** admonish, give sb a caution, reprimand, reprove, tell off, warn. **2** admonish, advise, counsel, urge

**cautious** adj alert, careful, chary, guarded, tentative, vigilant, wary; **opp** reckless

**cave** n cavern, chamber, grotto, pothole

**cavernous** adj deep, huge, massive, vast, yawning

**cavity** n aperture, gap, hole, hollow, opening, pit

**cease** v break off, bring sth to a halt, come to an end, die away, end, fizzle out, grind to a halt, finish, pack in inf, pack up inf, quit, stop; **opp** begin, start

**celebrate** v **1** commemorate, drink to, eulogize, honour, observe, toast. **2** enjoy yourself, have fun, let your hair down, live it up, paint the town red, party

**celebrated** adj acclaimed, distinguished, eminent, famed, famous, illustrious, legendary, renowned, revered, well-known

**celebration** *n* **1** commemoration, remembrance. **2** bash *inf*, do *inf*, event, festivity, knees-up *inf*, party, shindig *inf*

**celebrity** *n* big name, bigwig *inf*, dignitary, luminary, personality, star, VIP, worthy

**celibate** *adj* chaste, innocent, pure, virgin, virginal

**cell** *n* cubicle, dungeon, lock-up, prison, room

**censor** *v* ban, bowdlerize, blue-pencil, clean up, cut, edit, expurgate, prohibit, remove

**censure** *n* blame, castigation, criticism, condemnation, disapproval, rebuke, reproach, slating *inf*

**censure** *v* berate, blame, castigate, condemn, criticize, denounce, lambast, rebuke, reprimand, reproach, take to task, upbraid

**central** *adj* **1** mid, middle, inner, interior; *opp* outer, peripheral. **2** basic, chief, core, fundamental, important, key, main, pivotal, principal

**centralize** *v* amalgamate, centre, concentrate, consolidate, converge, focus, rationalize; *opp* decentralize, devolve

**centre** *n* central point, core, crux, focal point, heart, hub, middle, mid-point, nucleus

**ceremonial** *adj* formal, official, ritual, ritualistic

**ceremony** *n* celebration, commemoration, formal occasion, function, rite, service

**certain** *adj* **1** (sure in your mind) confident, convinced, definite, positive,

satisfied, sure. **2** beyond question, bound to happen, clear, definite, evident, inescapable, inevitable, irrevocable, in the bag *inf*, obvious, plain

**certainty** *n* **1** assurance, confidence, conviction, sureness. **2** dead cert *inf*, foregone conclusion, inevitability, open-and-shut case, safe bet

**certificate** *n* authorization, accreditation, award, degree, diploma, document, guarantee, licence, pass, qualification, voucher, warrant

**certify** *v* accredit, authenticate, authorize, confirm, declare, guarantee, license, validate, verify

**chain** *n* progression, sequence, series, string, succession, train

**chain** *v* bind, fasten, fetter, fix, shackle, secure, tether, tie

**chairman, chairwoman** *n* chair, chairperson, convenor, moderator

**challenge** *n* **1** dare, invitation, taunt. **2** hard task, hurdle, job-and-a-half *inf*, obstacle, test, uphill struggle, venture

**challenge** *v* **1** (challenge sb to do sth) dare, defy, test, throw down the gauntlet. **2** (question sth) campaign against, contest, dispute, object to, query, question, raise an objection to, stand up to

**champion** *n* **1** gold-medallist, prize-winner, title-holder, victor, winner. **2** advocate, backer, campaigner, defender, promoter, supporter

**chance** *n* **1** (fate) accident, coincidence, destiny, fate, fluke, fortune, luck, providence. **2** risk, gamble. **3** likelihood, odds, probability, prospect. **4** (opportunity) opening, opportunity, possibility, prospect

**change** *n* about-turn, alteration, difference, innovation, metamorphosis, modification, mutation, reorganization, sea change, transformation, U-turn, variation, volte-face

**change** *v* **1** alter, do an about-face *inf*, do a U-turn, modify, rearrange, reform, reorganize, restyle, shift, transform, vary. **2** exchange, replace, substitute, swap

**changeable** *adj* changing, erratic, fickle, fluctuating, fluid, irregular, mercurial, shifting, uncertain, unpredictable, unstable, vacillating, variable, volatile

**channel** *n* canal, conduit, culvert, ditch, duct, groove, gutter, strait, watercourse, waterway

**channel** *v* direct, force, guide, lead, move, send, steer

**chant** *v* chorus, intone, sing

**chaos** *n* bedlam, confusion, disorder, disarray, pandemonium, mayhem, shambles, tumult, turmoil

**chaotic** *adj* confused, disordered, disorganized, haywire, in a mess, in chaos, messy, muddled, topsy-turvy, untidy

**character** *n* **1** (nature) disposition, flavour, individuality, make-up, manner, nature, personality, quality, temperament. **2** (a person) case *inf*, eccentric, individual, oddball *inf*, oddity, person, sort

**characteristic** *adj* distinctive, distinguishing, individual, peculiar, typical

**characteristic** *n* attribute, feature, idiosyncrasy, mannerism, peculiarity, quality, quirk, trait

**charade** *n* absurdity, farce, fiasco, game, humbug, nonsense, pantomime, parody, pretence, put-up job *inf*, sham, show, travesty, whitewash

**charge** *n* **1** cost, fare, fee, levy, price, rate, rent, toll. **2** accusation, allegation, indictment. **3** care, custody, safe hands, safekeeping

**charge** *v* **1** ask, bill, debit, demand, invoice, set a price, want. **2** dash, hurtle, run, rush, stampede, storm, tear, zoom. **3** accuse, arraign, bring charges against, indict, put on trial

**charitable** *adj* **1** big-hearted, compassionate, forgiving, generous, indulgent, kind, magnanimous, sympathetic, tolerant, understanding; *opp* mean, uncharitable. **2** benevolent, humanitarian, philanthropic

**charity** *n* aid, alms, assistance, handouts, relief, welfare

**charm** *n* allure, appeal, attraction, charisma, fascination, lure, magic, magnetism, pull, seduction

**charm** *v* attract, beguile, bewitch, captivate, delight, enchant, fascinate, mesmerize

**charming** *adj* attractive, beautiful, captivating, delightful, enchanting, lovely, picturesque, pleasant, pretty, sweet; *opp* unattractive, horrid

**chart** *n* diagram, map, plan, table

**chart** *v* log, map out, mark, note, plot, record, show, sketch

**charter** *n* agreement, bill of rights, canon, code, constitution, contract, mission statement

**chase** *v* **1** follow, hound, pursue, run after, set off after, shadow, sit on sb's tail, tail, track. 2 drive away, see off, send packing, send sb away with a flea in their ear

**chaste** *adj* celibate, innocent, pure, undefiled, unsullied, virgin, virginal; *opp* immoral, licentious

**chastity** *n* celibacy, innocence, purity, virginity, virtue

**chat** *n* chinwag *inf*, chit-chat, confab *inf*, discussion, gossip, heart-to-heart, natter *inf*, one-to-one, small talk, talk

**chat** *v* chatter, chew the fat *inf*, chinwag *inf*, cosy up to *inf*, discuss, gossip, have a chat, have a heart-to-heart *inf*, natter *inf*, talk

**chatter** *v* chat, chinwag *inf*, discuss, gossip, have a chat, natter *inf*, talk

**cheap** *adj* 1 bargain-rate, budget, cut-price, dirt-cheap *inf*, discounted, economical, economy, marked-down, inexpensive, knock-down, low-cost, low-priced, reasonable, reduced, rock-bottom *inf*, sale, tourist-class; *opp* expensive, extortionate, over-priced, top-rate. 2 cheapo *inf*, second-rate, shoddy, tacky, tawdry, trashy

**cheat** *n* con man *inf*, fraud, racketeer, shark *inf*, swindler

**cheat** *v* con *inf*, deceive, defraud, do *inf*, double-cross, fleece *inf*, hoodwink, overcharge, pull a fast one *inf*, rip off *inf*, rob *inf*, sting *inf*, swindle, take sb for a ride *inf*, take sb to the cleaners *inf*, trick

**check** *n* 1 examination, inspection, test, once-over *inf*, spot-check. 2 brake, curb, delay, halt, slow-down, stoppage

**check** *v* 1 confirm, make sure, see, verify. 2 check out, check over, examine, give sth the once-over *inf*, inspect, look at,

test. 3 curb, damp down, halt, inhibit, limit, obstruct, put the brakes on, restrain, slow down, stem, stop

**cheek** *n* audacity, brass neck *inf*, effrontery, gall, impudence, nerve, temerity

**cheeky** *adj* discourteous, impertinent, impudent, insolent, rude, sassy *Am inf*; *opp* polite

**cheer** *n* cheering, hooray, hurrah, shout, whoop

**cheer up** *v* bring a smile to sb's face, buck up *inf*, buoy up, console, liven up, make sb happier, raise sb's spirits, perk up *inf*, uplift

**cheerful** *adj* bright and breezy, bright-eyed and bushy-tailed, chipper, contented, full of beans, full of the joys of spring, enthusiastic, happy, in a good mood, in high spirits, optimistic, perky, sanguine, smiling, upbeat

**cherish** *v* 1 adore, care for, hold dear, love, revere, treasure, value. 2 (cherish a hope) foster, harbour, have, maintain, nurse, nurture

**chest** *n* 1 box, case, casket, coffer, crate, trunk. 2 chest of drawers, tallboy. 3 bosom, breast

**chew** *v* champ, chomp, crunch, gnaw, masticate, munch

**chief** *adj* central, first, foremost, key, leading, main, most important, paramount, premier, primary, principal, top, uppermost, vital

**chief** *n* bigwig *inf*, boss, controller, director, gaffer *inf*, head, leader, manager, number one, person in charge, person at the top, principal, ringleader, ruler, superior, supremo, top dog *inf*

**child** n baby, boy, brat, daughter, girl, infant, juvenile, kid, kiddie, little one, minor, mite, nipper inf, offspring, son, sprog inf, teenager, toddler, tot, youngster

**childhood** n adolescence, babyhood, boyhood, early days, formative years, girlhood, infancy, minority tech, school days, teens, young days, youth

**childish** adj adolescent, babyish, boyish, girlish, immature, infantile, juvenile, naïve, puerile, silly

**childlike** adj artless, innocent, naïve, simple, youthful

**chill** adj chilly, cold, cool, fresh, icy, raw

**chill** v cool, cool down, make cold, put on ice, refrigerate; opp warm

**chip** n 1 break, nick, notch. 2 fragment, bit, shaving, shard, flake, sliver, splinter. 3 chips French fries, fries, sautéed potatoes

**chivalrous** adj courteous, courtly, gallant, gentlemanly, gracious, honourable, knightly, noble, polite, protective

**choice** adj best, desirable, exclusive, fine, first-class, first-rate, prime, quality, select, special, superior, top-quality; opp low-quality, poor, second-rate

**choice** n 1 alternative, decision, option, pick, possibility, preference, selection, vote. 2 array, assortment, range, selection, supply, variety

**choke** v 1 asphyxiate, smother, strangle, suffocate, throttle. 2 cough, gag, gasp for air, retch. 3 block, block up, clog, congest, jam, obstruct

**choose** v decide on, desire, fix on, name, opt for, pick, pick out, plump for inf, prefer, select, single out, vote for

**chore** n 1 job, daily grind, donkey-work, duty, hack work, housework, task, toil. 2 bind inf, bore, burden, drag inf, drudgery, pain inf

**chorus** n call, refrain, response, shout

**chronic** adj 1 appalling, awful, bad, boring, dire, dreadful, tedious, terrible. 2 confirmed, constant, habitual, incessant, incurable, lifelong, long-term, non-stop, persistent

**chunk** n bit, hunk, lump, part, piece, section, wedge, wodge inf

**circle** n 1 ball, band, disc, hoop, ring, round, sphere. 2 (of people) band, clique, crowd, gang, group, set

**circle** v 1 circumnavigate, draw a ring round, encircle, ring. 2 gyrate, revolve, rotate, spin, turn, wheel, whirl

**circuit** n course, journey, lap, loop, ring, round, tour, track

**circuitous** adj indirect, meandering, labyrinthine, roundabout, tortuous; opp direct

**circular** adj 1 ring-shaped, disc-shaped, round, spherical. 2 (circular argument) going nowhere, illogical, repetitive, tautologous

**circulate** v broadcast, disseminate, distribute, pass round, promulgate, send round, spread, transmit

**circumstance** n accident, event, factor, happenstance, occasion, position, situation

**circumstances** n how things stand, position, situation, state of affairs

**citizen** n civilian, man/woman in the street, member of society, person, resident, subject, taxpayer, voter

**city** n concrete jungle, conurbation,

downtown, town, metropolis, metropolitan area, urban area

**civil** *adj* **1** cordial, courteous, pleasant, polite, well-mannered; *opp* rude. **2** civic, domestic, home, internal, municipal, public, state

**civilization** *n* country, culture, life, people, society, way of life

**civilize** *v* advance, cultivate, develop, educate, improve, refine

**civilized** *adj* **1** advanced, cultivated, developed, educated, refined, social. **2** comfortable, enjoyable, luxurious, pleasant

**claim** *n* **1** allegation, assertion, protestation, statement. **2** application, call, demand, request, right

**claim** *v* **1** allege, assert, declare, maintain, profess, say, state. **2** ask for, collect, demand, get, pick up, request, send off for

**clamber** *v* climb, scrabble, scramble, shin

**clan** *n* clique, faction, family, gang, group, set, tribe

**clap** *v* applaud, give sb a round of applause, put your hands together, show your appreciation in the usual way

**clarify** *v* disambiguate, elucidate, explain, make clear, put your cards on the table, simplify, spell out what you mean, resolve

**clash** *n* brush, confrontation, disagreement, dispute, fight, quarrel, row, showdown

**clash** *v* come into conflict, come to blows, confront, cross swords, fall out, fight, quarrel, squabble, wrangle

**clasp** *v* clutch, embrace, grasp, hold, hug

**class** *n* **1** category, classification, division, grade, group, league, rank, set, sort, status, type, variety. **2** lesson, period, seminar, study group, tutorial

**class** *v* arrange, categorize, classify, grade, group, order, rank, rate

**classic** *adj* **1** brilliant, definitive, excellent, fine, first-rate, great, superlative. **2** archetypal, copybook, model, prototypical, typical. **3** (a classic style) elegant, simple, timeless, traditional

**classical** *adj* **1** Greek, Latin, Roman. **2** elegant, harmonious, simple, traditional, well-proportioned

**classification** *n* **1** arrangement, cataloguing, codification, grading, grouping, ordering, organization, taxonomy. **2** category, class, division, grade, group, rank

**classify** *v* arrange, categorize, catalogue, class, grade, group, order, rank, rate

**clause** *n* condition, item, part, passage, point, proviso, section, statement, stipulation, subsection

**clean** *adj* **1** clean as a whistle, hygienic, immaculate, laundered, polished, pristine, scrubbed, shining, spick and span, spotless, sterile, sterilized, washed; *opp* dirty. **2** (clean water) clear, fresh, pure, uncontaminated, unpolluted; *opp* contaminated, polluted

**clean** *v* dust, polish, sanitize, scrub, spring-clean, sterilize, sweep, vacuum, wash, wipe

**clear** *adj* **1** apparent, beyond doubt, beyond question, coherent, distinct, evident, lucid, obvious, plain, unambiguous, understandable, unmistakable; *opp* unclear. **2** (clear

glass, water) clean, colourless, see-through, transparent, unclouded.
**3** (clear sky) bright, cloudless, fine, moonlit, sunny, starlit; *opp* cloudy, dull, overcast. **4** empty, free, open, unblocked, unobstructed; *opp* blocked

**clear** *v* **1** clean, clean out, empty, free, get rid of, remove, unblock, unclog, tidy, tidy up. **2** (clear sb) absolve, acquit, excuse, exonerate, vindicate. **3** (the sky clears) brighten, brighten up, lighten. **4** **clear up** (solve a mystery) crack *inf*, explain, find an answer to, resolve, solve, unravel. **5** **clear up** (tidy things away) pack up, put sth in order, put things away, sort out, tidy away, tidy up. **6** **clear up** get better, improve

**clearly** *adv* distinctly, evidently, obviously, patently, plainly, visibly

**clever** *adj* astute, brainy *inf*, bright, brilliant, canny *inf*, competent, educated, intelligent, ingenious, knowledgeable, quick, sharp, shrewd, smart, streetwise, talented

**cliché** *n* adage, hackneyed phrase, maxim, old chestnut, platitude, saying, stereotype, truism, well-worn expression

**client** *n* consumer, customer, patron, regular, user

**climate** *n* **1** (weather) atmospheric conditions, microclimate, temperature, weather. **2** atmosphere, conditions, feeling, mood, spirit, setting, situation

**climax** *n* apogee, crowning point, culmination, finale, height, peak, pinnacle, zenith

**climax** *v* **1** culminate, come to a head, end, peak, result. **2** have an orgasm

**climb** *v* **1** ascend, clamber, climb up, go up, move up, mount, rise, shin up, shoot up, soar. **2** (climb a mountain) ascend, conquer, reach the summit of, reach the top of, scale

**cling** *v* adhere, attach yourself, cling on, grip, hold, hold fast, hold on, stick

**clip** *n* **1** clasp, fastener, hair slide, paper clip, pin. **2** clipping, cutting, excerpt, extract, passage, scene, snippet

**clip** *v* **1** attach, fasten, fix, pin, staple. **2** crop, cut, cut off, lop, prune, shear, shorten, snip, trim

**cloak** *n* cape, coat, overcoat, shawl, wrap

**clog** *v* block, block up, bung up *inf*, choke, clog up, congest, jam, jam up, obstruct, stop up

**close** *adj* **1** (in space) adjacent, adjoining, close by, convenient, handy, hard by, near, nearby, neighbouring, to hand; *opp* distant. **2** (in time) approaching, at hand, imminent, impending, near, nigh; *opp* distant. **3** (of friends) dear, devoted, inseparable, intimate, loving. **4** (of weather) humid, muggy, oppressive, sultry, sweaty, sweltering

**close** *n* cessation, completion, conclusion, dénouement, end, ending, finish, termination

**close** *v* **1** bolt, fasten, lock, seal, shut, slam; *opp* open. **2** (close an investigation) bring to a close, bring to an end, cease, complete, conclude, end, finish, terminate, wind up; *opp* open. **3** (get nearer) approach, catch up, chase, near, pursue

**closed** *adj* **1** bolted, fastened, locked, sealed, shut, unopened; *opp* open. **2** completed, concluded, ended, finished, over, over and done with, resolved, settled

**cloth** n 1 fabric, material, textile. 2 (piece of cloth) chamois-leather, cover, dishcloth, duster, dust sheet, napkin, serviette, tablecloth, tea towel, wipe

**clothes** n apparel, attire, clothing, costume, dress, garb, garments, gear inf, get-up inf, kit inf, outfit, raiment, togs inf, wardrobe, wear

**cloud** n 1 cloud cover, fog, haze, mist, vapour, water vapour. 2 cirrus, cumulus, nimbus, stratus

**cloudy** adj 1 (of sky, weather) dull, foggy, hazy, misty, overcast. 2 (of liquid, glass) frosted, milky, misty, muddy, murky, opaque, smoky, steamed up

**clown** n 1 (performer) comedian, comic, fool, jester, pierrot. 2 buffoon, fool, idiot, joker

**club** n 1 association, brotherhood, circle, federation, fraternity, group, guild, league, organization, society, sorority, team, union. 2 bar, cabaret, disco inf, discothèque, night club, night spot. 3 baton, blackjack Am, bludgeon, cosh, cudgel, shillelagh, stave, stick, truncheon

**clue** n hint, idea, indication, inkling, key, lead, pointer, sign

**clumsy** adj awkward, blundering, bumbling, bungling, gawky, graceless, ham-fisted, lumbering, maladroit, unco-ordinated, ungainly

**cluster** n accumulation, bunch, clump, collection, gathering, group, knot, mass

**cluster** v accumulate, bunch, coalesce, gather, group, mass, press

**clutch** v clasp, cling to, grasp, grip, hang on to, hold, hold on to

**clutter** n chaos, disorder, jumble, litter, mess, rubbish, untidiness

**clutter** v encumber, fill, fill up, litter, pack, pile high, strew, stuff

**coach** v direct, drill, exercise, guide, instruct, manage, prepare, teach, train, tutor

**coalition** n alliance, allies, amalgamation, association, bloc, compact, confederacy, confederation, league, merger, pact, union

**coarse** adj 1 crude, rough, tough, uneven, unrefined. 2 (in manners) boorish, common, crude, gross, ill-mannered, uncouth, vulgar

**coast** n coastline, littoral, shore, seaboard, seaside, shoreline

**coast** v cruise, drift, freewheel, glide, relax, slide

**coat** n 1 anorak, cloak, duffel coat, fleece, jacket, mac inf, mackintosh, overcoat, parka, raincoat, topcoat. 2 (of an animal) fleece, fur, hair, pelt. 3 (of paint) coating, covering, film, finish, glaze, layer, patina

**coat** v cover, plaster, spread, smear

**coax** v cajole, encourage, entice, induce, inveigle, persuade, talk sb into/out of sth, sweet-talk inf, wheedle

**code** n 1 (system of rules, beliefs) canon, code of conduct, convention, custom, ethics, etiquette, manners, oath, rules. 2 (for writing and understanding messages) coding system, cypher, key, notation. 3 (sequence of letters or numbers) combination, password, PIN, user ID. 4 (types of code) Morse code, semaphore, sign language

**coerce** v compel, constrain, force,

intimate, make, persuade, put the frighteners on *inf*, twist sb's arm

**coherent** *adj* articulate, clear, cogent, cohesive, consistent, intelligible, logical, lucid, organized, reasoned, sound, systematic, well-ordered, well-structured; *opp* incoherent

**coil** *v* curl, entwine, loop, snake, spiral, twine, twist, wind

**coincide** *v* accord, agree, be the same, clash, combine, come together, concur, correspond, happen at the same time, line up, match, tally

**coincidence** *n* accident, chance, fluke, stroke of luck

**cold** *adj* **1** arctic, biting, bitter, chill, chilled, chilly, cool, draughty, freezing, fresh, frigid, frosty, frozen, glacial, ice-cold, icy, nippy *inf*, parky *inf*, refrigerated, wintry; *opp* hot, warm. **2** (of a person, atmosphere) aloof, callous, chilly, cold-blooded, cold-hearted, cool, distant, forbidding, frigid, frosty, hard-hearted, heartless, indifferent, inhospitable, inhuman, insensitive, passionless, reserved, standoffish, stony, uncaring, unemotional, unfeeling, unfriendly, unsympathetic, unwelcoming; *opp* warm

**cold** *n* bug *inf*, chill, common cold, flu, influenza, sniffle *inf*, viral infection, virus

**collaborate** *v* assist, band together, collude, connive, conspire, co-operate, help, join forces, pool resources, pull together, team up, work together

**collaborator** *n* **1** accomplice, assistant, associate, co-author, confederate, colleague, fellow worker, helper,

helpmate, partner. **2** (with an enemy) Judas, quisling, traitor, turncoat, Uncle Tom

**collapse** *n* breakdown, disintegration, failure, implosion

**collapse** *v* **1** (of an object) cave in, come apart, fall apart, fall down, fall in, fall over, fall to pieces, give way, implode, subside. **2** (of a person) be taken ill, crumple, faint, fall over, keel over, pass out. **3** (of an idea) break down, disintegrate, fail, fall apart, fall through, fall to pieces, fold, founder; *opp* succeed, thrive

**colleague** *n* associate, collaborator, comrade, fellow worker, partner, peer, workmate

**collect** *v* accumulate, assemble, bring together, gather, hoard, marshal, pile up, stock, stockpile, store

**collected** *adj* **1** accumulated, assembled, assorted, complete. **2** (of a person) calm, composed, cool, focused

**collection** *n* accumulation, anthology, array, assemblage, assembly, assortment, cluster, compilation, gathering, group, heap, hoard, pile, set, stack, stock, stockpile, store

**collide** *v* bang, bump into, crash into, come into collision with, meet head-on, smash into, strike, strike against

**collision** *n* bang, bump, crash, impact, prang *inf*, smash

**colloquial** *adj* common, conversational, everyday, idiomatic, informal, popular, slang, spoken, vernacular

**colour** *n* **1** coloration, colouring, hue, pigment, pigmentation, shade, tinge, tint, tone. **2** (attractive quality) excitement, interest, spice, variety, vividness

**colour** v colour in, dye, paint, stain, tinge, tint

**colourful** adj **1** bright, brilliant, gaudy, iridescent, multi-coloured, psychedelic, vibrant, vivid; *opp* drab, dull. **2** (of a story, event) exciting, exotic, graphic, interesting, lively, stimulating, striking, vivid; *opp* dull. **3** (of a person) dashing, eccentric, distinctive, extrovert, flamboyant, glamorous, larger-than-life, unusual; *opp* dull

**column** n **1** monument, pilaster, pile, pillar, pole, post, shaft, support, strut, upright. **2** (in a newspaper) article, diary, editorial, feature, leader, leading article, section. **3** (of people) crocodile, file, line, procession, queue, trail, train

**comb** v examine, look in, rummage through, scour, search, turn inside out

**combat** n battle, battlefield, conflict, fighting, hand-to-hand combat, hostilities, struggle, war

**combat** v battle against, defeat, fight, oppose, resist, struggle against, wage war against

**combination** n alliance, amalgam, amalgamation, blend, conjunction, fusion, integration, merger, mix, mixing, union

**combine** v **1** (combine things, people) add together, ally, amalgamate, bind, blend, bring together, fuse, integrate, intertwine, interweave, join, join together, lump together, marry, merge, mingle, mix, pool, put together, synthesize, unite. **2** (people, things combine) ally, amalgamate, blend,

club together, coalesce, coincide, come together, conspire, co-occur, co-operate, form an alliance, fuse, gang up, integrate, intertwine, interweave, join, join forces, join together, merge, mingle, mix, team up, unite

**come** v **1** (move towards) advance, appear, approach, come up, draw nearer, enter, move towards, reach. **2** (come to an event or place) arrive, attend, be present, get (to), show up, turn up, visit. **3 come about** come to pass, fall out, happen, occur, take place. **4 come across** encounter, find, meet, see. **5 come back** get back, retrace your steps, return. **6 come from** be derived from, be made from, have its origin(s) in, have its source in, originate from, originate in. **7 come from** (of a person) be a native of, be born in, be from, be originally from, hail from. **8 come round** (after being unconscious) recover, recover consciousness, regain consciousness, wake up, wake. **9 come round** (to sb's home) come over, drop in *inf*, pay a visit, pop in *inf*, pop over *inf*, pop round *inf*, visit. **10 come round to** (= agree with) accede to, acquiesce in, agree, be convinced of, be converted to, be persuaded of. **11 come up with** deliver, devise, discover, find, invent, offer, produce, propose, provide, put forward, submit, suggest, turn up

**comeback** n recovery, resurrection, return, revival

**comedian** n clown, comedienne, comic, entertainer, humorist

**comedy** n **1** clowning, humour, situation comedy, slapstick, stand-up comedy;

*opp* tragedy. **2** (individual play or performance) sitcom, situation comedy, sketch, turn. **3** (of a situation) absurdity, amusement, funny side, humour, ridiculousness, silliness

**comfort** *n* ease, luxuriousness, luxury, opulence, warmth, well-being;
*opp* discomfort

**comfortable** *adj* **1** (of furniture, surroundings) comfy *inf*, cosy, de luxe, easy, homely, luxurious, opulent, padded, plush, relaxing, snug, soft, upholstered, warm. **2** (of a person) at ease, comfy *inf*, cosy, relaxed, snug

**comforting** *adj* compassionate, considerate, consoling, fatherly, gentle, kind, paternal, reassuring, supportive, sympathetic

**comic** *adj* absurd, amusing, comical, droll, facetious, funny, hilarious, humorous, joking, light, rib-tickling, side-splitting, silly, waggish, whimsical, witty;
*opp* tragic

**comical** *adj* absurd, amusing, comic, farcical, funny, laughable, ludicrous, rich, silly, ridiculous

**coming** *adj* approaching, at hand, future, imminent, impending, in store, next, upcoming

**command** *n* **1** (words to be obeyed) commandment, decree, directive, edict, injunction, instruction, order. **2** (power to command) ascendancy, authority, charge, control, direction, domination, dominion, government, leadership, mastery, power, superiority, supremacy

**command** *v* **1** (tell sb to do sth) ask, charge, decree, direct, instruct, order, tell. **2** (command an army) be in charge of, be in control of, control, dominate, have authority over, have dominion over, have power over, have superiority over, have supremacy over, have the ascendancy over, direct, govern, head, head up, lead, outrank

**commander** *n* **1** boss, chief, commandant, commanding officer, head, leader, superior, superior officer, supremo. **2** (military and police ranks) admiral, air marshal, captain, chief constable, chief superintendent, commander-in-chief, field marshal, general

**commemorate** *v* celebrate, honour, pay homage to, pay your respects to, remember, salute

**commendable** *adj* admirable, creditable, estimable, exemplary, laudable, meritorious, praiseworthy, valiant, worthy

**comment** *n* **1** allusion, mention, observation, opinion, reaction, reference, remark, response. **2** (in writing) annotation, footnote, note

**comment** *v* **1** express an opinion, interpose, note, observe, opine, react, remark, respond, say, venture.
**2 comment on** allude to, annotate, discuss, mention, refer to, talk about

**commentary 1** (spoken) comments, narration, narrative, remarks, running commentary, voice-over. **2** criticism, discussion, exegesis, interpretation, review

**commentator** *n* **1** announcer, broadcaster, DJ, narrator, presenter, pundit, reporter, speaker. **2** critic, expert, reviewer, specialist, writer

**commerce** n business, buying and selling, commercial activity, dealing, money-making, trade, trading

**commercial** adj business, capitalist, entrepreneurial, financial, mercenary, money-making, profit-making

**commiserate** v comfort, console, empathize, sympathize; *opp* congratulate

**commission** n 1 (sth to be done) brief, instruction, mandate, remit, task. 2 (official body) authority, board, committee, tribunal

**commission** v appoint, contract, employ, engage, hire, order, request

**commit** v 1 carry out, do, effect, execute, perform, perpetrate. 2 (commit sth to sb's care) assign, certify, consign, deliver, entrust, give, hand over, send. 3 **commit yourself** bind yourself, engage, give an assurance, give an undertaking, make a decision, make up your mind, pledge, promise, swear, take the plunge

**committed** adj active, ardent, card-carrying, confirmed, dedicated, determined, devoted, diehard, earnest, engaged, fervent, firm, loyal, militant, passionate, persevering, resolute, resolved, single-minded, stalwart, staunch, sworn, unswerving, unwavering, whole-hearted, zealous

**commitment** n 1 (dedication) ardour, dedication, determination, devotion, fervour, loyalty, passion, perseverance, resolution, single-mindedness, support, zeal. 2 (sth you have committed yourself to) engagement, oath, promise, undertaking

**committee** n board, executive, panel, steering group, working party

**common** adj 1 (ordinary) common-or-garden, commonplace, customary, everyday, familiar, habitual, normal, ordinary, plain, regular, routine, run-of-the-mill, standard, stock, traditional, typical, unexceptional, usual. 2 (not rare) frequent, numerous, plentiful, popular, widespread; *opp* rare. 3 collective, communal, general, in common, joint, jointly owned, mutual, reciprocal, same, shared. 4 (of a person, manners) coarse, common as muck, crude, earthy, ill-bred, lower-class, plebeian, non-U, uneducated, vulgar

**common sense** n intelligence, nous inf, level-headedness, practicality, prudence, reason, sense

**commotion** n affray, agitation, bedlam inf, chaos, confusion, din, disorder, disturbance, excitement, ferment, fray, furore, fuss, hubbub, hullabaloo inf, kerfuffle inf, palaver inf, pandemonium, racket inf, row, rumpus, sensation, stir, to-do inf, trouble, tumult, turmoil, unrest, uproar

**communal** adj collective, common, community, general, in common, joint, jointly owned, public, same, shared

**communicate** v 1 (with sb) be in communication, be in contact, be in touch, commune, contact, get through to, interact, speak to, talk to. 2 (communicate an idea) convey, express, get across, get over, impart, transmit

**communication** n 1 broadcasting, contact, correspondence, exchange, interaction, intercourse, speech, telecommunications. **2** (letter, message) announcement, bulletin, cable, card, communiqué, conversation, despatch, dialogue, directive, E-mail, fax, letter, memo, memorandum, message, note, notice, piece of news, report, signal, statement, telegram, telephone call, transmission, wire *Am*

**communicative** *adj* chatty, expressive, forthcoming, informative, open, outgoing, talkative

**community** *n* colony, commune, group, neighbourhood, settlement, society

**compact** *adj* compressed, concise, condensed, dense, miniature, neat, small, tightly packed

**companion** *n* assistant, associate, chaperone, comrade, colleague, confidant, confidante, consort, escort, fellow traveller, friend, mate, partner, servant, sidekick

**companionship** *n* company, comradeship, friendship, partnership

**company** *n* **1** business, concern, corporation, enterprise, establishment, firm, limited company, organization, plc. **2** (group of people) assembly, audience, band, crew, crowd, ensemble, gang, gathering, group, troop, troupe. **3** companionship, friends, friendship, guests, society, visitors

**comparable** *adj* alike, analogous, equal, equivalent, like, matching, parallel, related, similar

**compare** *v* **1** balance, contrast, differentiate, juxtapose, set against. **2** draw a parallel, draw/make a comparison, equate, liken, look like, match, resemble

**comparison** *n* **1** (make a comparison) analogy, contrast, difference, distinction, juxtaposition, parallel. **2** (there's no comparison) comparability, correlation, likeness, resemblance, similarity

**compartment** *n* area, bay, berth, booth, car *Am*, carriage, cell, chamber, cubby-hole *inf*, cubicle, locker, pigeonhole, section, slot, space

**compassion** *n* benevolence, concern, consideration, heart, humanitarianism, humanity, kind-heartedness, kindness, leniency, mercy, pity, soft-heartedness, sorrow, sympathy, tenderness, understanding

**compassionate** *adj* benevolent, considerate, gentle, humane, humanitarian, kind, kind-hearted, lenient, merciful, soft-hearted, sympathetic, tender, understanding

**compatible** *adj* **1** (of people) in-tune, like-minded, similar, suitable, suited, well-matched; *opp* incompatible. **2** (of claims, ideas) consistent, in keeping, reconcilable; *opp* incompatible

**compensate** *v* **1** atone, expiate, indemnify, make amends, make good, pay back, pay compensation, recompense, refund, reimburse, repay. **2** (one thing compensates for another) balance, cancel, counteract, counterbalance, even up, make up for, neutralize, nullify, offset, redress

**compensation** *adj* atonement, damages, indemnity, recompense, refund, reimbursement, reparation, repayment, redress, restitution

**compete** *v* be a contestant, be in competition, challenge, contend, contest, fight, oppose, participate, pit yourself against, rival, take part, vie

**competent** adj able, accomplished, adept, capable, clever, effective, experienced, expert, fit, good, handy inf, proficient, qualified, skilful, skilled, trained; *opp* inept

**competition** n 1 championship, contest, game, heat, match, race, rally, tournament. 2 conflict, contention, opposition, rivalry, strife, struggle

**competitive** adj aggressive, ambitious, antagonistic, combative, cutthroat, dog-eat-dog

**competitor** n adversary, antagonist, candidate, challenger, contender, contestant, entrant, opponent, opposition, participant, rival

**compile** v accumulate, amass, arrange, assemble, collate, collect, compose, draw up, gather, organize, put together

**complacent** adj at ease, pleased, satisfied, self-assured, self-satisfied, smug, unconcerned

**complain** v belly-ache inf, bemoan, carp, criticize, find fault, fuss, go on about inf, gripe inf, grouch inf, grouse, grumble, moan, nag, object, protest, remonstrate, whine, whinge inf

**complaint** n 1 accusation, charge, condemnation, criticism, grievance, gripe inf, grouch inf, grouse, grumble, moan, objection, protest, remonstrance. 2 (medical) affliction, ailment, condition, disease, disorder, illness, infection, sickness, upset

**complementary** adj corresponding, interdependent, interrelating, matching, paired, reciprocal, twin

**complete** adj 1 comprehensive, entire, exhaustive, full, in its entirety, intact, total, unabbreviated, unabridged, unbroken, uncut, unedited, whole; *opp* partial. 2 (finished) accomplished, achieved, completed, concluded, done, ended, finished, over; *opp* incomplete. 3 (total) absolute, arrant, consummate, downright, out-and-out, outright, thorough, total, unmitigated, unqualified, utter

**complete** v accomplish, achieve, clinch, close, conclude, discharge, do, effect, end, execute, finalize, finish, fulfil, realize, round off, settle, terminate, wind up inf, wrap up; *opp* begin

**completely** adv absolutely, altogether, entirely, from beginning to end, fully, perfectly, thoroughly, totally, utterly, wholly

**complex** adj complicated, convoluted, difficult, elaborate, intricate, involved, knotty, problematical, sophisticated, tangled, tortuous; *opp* simple

**complex** n fixation, hang-up, mania, neurosis, obsession, phobia, preoccupation

**complexion** n cast, colour, colouring, hue, skin, skin tone, tinge

**complicate** v compound, confound, confuse, entangle, jumble, mix up, muddle, snarl up; *opp* simplify

**complicated** adj complex, convoluted, difficult, elaborate, intricate, involved, knotty, problematical, sophisticated, tangled, tortuous; *opp* simple

**complication** n 1 difficulty, drawback, obstacle, problem, set-back, snag. 2 complexity, confusion, convolution, difficulty, dilemma, intricacy, mix-up, muddle

**compliment** n accolade, commendation, endorsement, eulogy, flattery, honour, plaudits, praise, tribute; *opp* insult

**complimentary** adj 1 admiring, appreciative, approving, commendatory, favourable, flattering, generous, laudatory; *opp* critical. 2 free, free of charge, gratis, on the house

**comply** v abide by, accede, acquiesce, adhere to, agree, assent, conform, consent, fall in, fit in, follow, fulfil, heed, keep, meet, obey, observe, respect, satisfy, submit, yield; *opp* disobey

**component** n bit, constituent, element, ingredient, part, piece, section, segment

**compose** v 1 (music, poetry) arrange, concoct, create, devise, invent, make up, produce, think up, write. 2 (compose yourself) calm down, calm yourself, collect your thoughts, relax

**composed** adj at ease, calm, confident, cool, laid-back, level-headed, poised, relaxed, sedate, self-controlled, self-possessed, serene, undisturbed, unfazed, unflappable, unperturbed, unruffled, together *inf*; *opp* disturbed, upset

**composition** n 1 arrangement, configuration, constitution, design, form, formation, layout, make-up, organization, structure. 2 creation, essay, literary work, opus, piece, study, work, work of art

**compound** n blend, combination, composite, fusion, mixture, synthesis

**compound** v 1 amalgamate, blend, combine, fuse, mix, put together, synthesize. 2 add to, aggravate, augment,

complicate, exacerbate, heighten, intensify, magnify, make worse, worsen; *opp* alleviate

**comprehend** v appreciate, apprehend, catch on *inf*, conceive, discern, fathom, follow, get *inf*, grasp, know, make out, realize, see, take in, the penny drops, twig *inf*, understand

**comprehension** n appreciation, grasp, ken, knowledge, perception, realization, sense, understanding

**comprehensive** adj all-embracing, all-inclusive, blanket, broad, complete, exhaustive, extensive, far-reaching, full, inclusive, thorough, total, umbrella, universal, wide, wide-ranging; *opp* selective, partial

**comprise** v be composed of, consist of, contain, cover, embody, embrace, encompass, include, incorporate, involve

**compromise** n agreement, bargain, concession, deal, give-and-take, happy medium, middle course, settlement, trade-off, understanding

**compromise** v 1 (compromise on sth) come to an understanding, concede, make concessions, meet halfway, negotiate a settlement, settle, strike a balance. 2 (compromise sb's reputation) bring into disrepute, damage, discredit, endanger, imperil, jeopardize, prejudice, risk, undermine, weaken

**compulsion** n 1 desire, drive, fixation, necessity, need, obsession, preoccupation, urge. 2 coercion, constraint, duress, enforcement, force, oppression, pressure, requirement

**compulsive** adj 1 (compulsive drinker,

gambler) addicted, habitual, incurable, obsessive, persistent. **2** (compulsive viewing) compelling, fascinating, gripping, irresistible

**compulsory** *adj* mandatory, necessary, obligatory, required, requisite, statutory; *opp* optional

**computer** *n* machine, mainframe, PC, personal computer, system, word-processor

**comrade** *n* ally, associate, colleague, confederate, co-worker, crony *inf*, fellow-worker, friend, mate *inf*, pal *inf*

**conceal** *v* **1** (from view) blot out, camouflage, cloak, cover, disguise, hide, keep out of sight, mask, obscure, screen, secrete, shelter. **2** (conceal a fact) cover up, gloss over, hush up, keep quiet, keep secret, keep the lid on, veil; *opp* reveal

**concede** *v* **1** accede, accept, acknowledge, admit, make a concession. **2** capitulate, cave in *inf*, cede, give in, give up, hand over, relinquish, resign, submit, surrender, yield

**conceited** *adj* arrogant, big-headed, boastful, cocky, egotistical, full of yourself, immodest, puffed up, self-important, smug, vain; *opp* modest

**conceivable** *adj* believable, not beyond the realms of possibility, credible, feasible, imaginable, likely, possible, thinkable; *opp* inconceivable

**conceive** *v* **1** (a plan, idea) conjure up, contrive, create, design, develop, devise, draw up, dream up *inf*, evolve, form, formulate, hatch, initiate, invent, make up, plan, think up. **2** (understand) apprehend, believe, comprehend, envisage, grasp, imagine, suppose, think,

understand, visualize

**concentrate** *v* **1** apply yourself, be absorbed, be attentive, consider closely, engross yourself, give your attention to, pay attention, put your mind to, rack your brains, think, work hard. **2** (in a place) accumulate, centre, cluster, collect, congregate, converge, gather, mass; *opp* scatter

**concentrated** *adj* **1** (concentrated effort) all-out *inf*, concerted, consolidated, intense, rigorous, vigorous; *opp* half-hearted . **2** rich, strong, thick, undiluted; *opp* diluted

**concentration** *n* **1** absorption, application, close attention, heed, single-mindedness. **2** (in a place) accumulation, cluster, collection, congregation, convergence, gathering, group, mass

**concept** *n* conception, hypothesis, idea, notion, theory, view

**conception** *n* **1** (biological) conceiving, fertilization, impregnation, insemination, pregnancy. **2** beginning, birth, creation, design, formation, inception, invention, origin, outset; *opp* completion. **3** plan, project, proposal, scheme. **4** (have no conception of) appreciation, clue, comprehension, concept, idea, inkling, notion, perception, understanding

**concern** *n* **1** anxiety, apprehension, disquiet, distress, disturbance, fear, malaise, solicitude, worry. **2** (that's my concern) affair, business, department, duty, field, interest, job, matter, problem, regard, responsibility, subject, task. **3** business, company, corporation, enterprise, establishment, firm, house, organization

**concern** v 1 affect, apply, be relevant to, have a bearing on, interest, involve, pertain, refer, regard, relate, touch. 2 bother, distress, disturb, perturb, preoccupy, trouble, worry

**concerned** adj 1 anxious, bothered, distressed, disturbed, fearful, perturbed, troubled, uneasy, unhappy, upset, worried; *opp* unconcerned. 2 (the people concerned) affected, connected, implicated, interested, involved, mixed up, privy to, relevant

**concerted** adj collaborative, collective, combined, co-operative, co-ordinated, joint, mutual, shared, unified, united

**concession** n 1 acknowledgement, acceptance, admission, allowance, ceding, giving in, recognition, relinquishment, settlement, surrender, yielding. 2 (make a concession) adjustment, allowance, compromise, exception, indulgence, modification, privilege

**conciliatory** adj accommodating, appeasing, mollifying, obliging, pacifying, peaceable, placatory; *opp* aggressive

**concise** adj brief, compact, compressed, condensed, pithy, pointed, short, small, succinct, summary, terse, to the point

**conclude** v 1 bring to an end, cease, close, come to an end, complete, end, finish, halt, round off, stop, terminate, wind up *inf*. 2 assume, come to the conclusion, conjecture, decide, deduce, gather, infer, judge, presume, reckon, suppose, surmise

**conclusion** n 1 close, completion, end, ending, finale, finish, rounding-off, termination; *opp* beginning. 2 consequence, culmination, issue, outcome, result, solution, upshot. 3 (belief) answer, belief, conviction, decision, deduction, inference, judgement, opinion, resolution, settlement, verdict

**conclusive** adj categorical, certain, clinching, convincing, decisive, definite, definitive, final, incontestable, irrefutable, persuasive, unambiguous, unanswerable, unequivocal, unquestionable; *opp* inconclusive

**concoct** v contrive, cook up *inf*, design, devise, formulate, hatch, invent, make up, manufacture, plan, plot, prepare, project, put together, think up

**concrete** adj actual, definite, existing, explicit, factual, firm, material, objective, palpable, physical, real, solid, specific, substantial, tangible, visible; *opp* abstract

**condemn** v 1 berate, blame, castigate, censure, chide, criticize, damn, decry, denounce, deprecate, disapprove, disparage, rebuke, reproach, reprove, slam *inf*, slate *inf*, upbraid; *opp* commend, praise. 2 convict, find guilty, judge, pass judgement, pass sentence, punish, sentence; *opp* acquit

**condemnation** n blame, censure, criticism, denunciation, deprecation, disapproval, disparagement, rebuke, reproach, reprobation, reproof, stricture; *opp* praise

**condense** v 1 (make shorter) compress, contract, curtail, cut, précis, reduce, shorten, summarize; *opp* expand, lengthen. **2** (of liquid) concentrate, distil, reduce, thicken; *opp* dilute

**condescend** *v* **1** deign, descend, humble yourself, lower yourself, stoop, submit. **2** look down your nose at, patronize, talk down to

**condescending** *adj* disdainful, haughty, high-and-mighty, imperious, patronizing, pompous, snobbish, snooty *inf*, stuck-up *inf*, supercilious, superior

**condition** *n* **1** case, circumstances, plight, position, predicament, situation, state, state of affairs. **2** demand, essential, necessity, precondition, prerequisite, provision, proviso, qualification, requirement, requisite, restriction, stipulation, terms. **3** fettle, fitness, form, health, kilter, nick *inf*, order, shape. **4** (medical) affliction, ailment, disease, disorder, illness, infection, sickness

**condition** *v* acclimatize, accustom, adapt, educate, equip, habituate, inure, make ready, prepare, train

**conditional** *adj* contingent, dependent, provisional, restricted, subject to, with conditions, with reservations, with restrictions, with strings attached *inf*; *opp* unconditional

**condone** *v* accept, allow, approve, endorse, excuse, forgive, ignore, let pass, look the other way, make allowances, overlook, pardon, put up with, tolerate, turn a blind eye

**conduct** *n* **1** actions, behaviour, manners, mien, ways. **2** administration, control, command, direction, government, handling, leadership, management, organization, regulation, running, supervision

**conduct** *v* **1** administer, be in charge, be in control, chair, command, control, direct, govern, handle, head, lead, look after, manage, organize, oversee, preside, regulate, rule, run, steer, supervise. **2** accompany, escort, guide, lead, pilot, take, usher

**confer** *v* **1** compare notes, consult, converse, debate, discuss, exchange ideas, exchange views, have discussions, put your heads together *inf*, seek advice. **2** award, bestow, give, grant, invest, present

**conference** *n* colloquium, congress, convention, forum, meeting, seminar, symposium

**confess** *v* accept blame, acknowledge, admit, come clean, concede, confide, disclose, divulge, own up, plead guilty, reveal, tell all, unburden yourself

**confession** *n* admission, disclosure, divulgence, owning-up, revelation

**confide** *v* admit, confess, disclose, divulge, open your heart, reveal, spill the beans, unburden yourself

**confidence** *n* **1** assertiveness, assurance, boldness, composure, courage, nerve, poise, self-assurance, self-confidence, self-possession; *opp* shyness. **2** belief, certainty, credence, dependence, faith, reliance, trust; *opp* doubt

**confident** *adj* **1** assertive, bold, brave, cocksure, composed, courageous, fearless, outgoing, poised, self-assured, self-confident, self-possessed; *opp* shy. **2** certain, convinced, positive, satisfied, sure; *opp* doubtful

**confidential** adj classified, hush-hush inf, intimate, off the record, personal, private, secret

**confine** v bind, cage, coop up inf, detain, enclose, hem in, imprison, incarcerate, intern, jail, limit, lock up, repress, restrain, restrict, shut up; opp liberate

**confirm** v 1 authenticate, back up, bear out, corroborate, endorse, establish, give credence to, prove, show, substantiate, verify; opp disprove. 2 (confirm a deal) authorize, clinch, establish, formalize, fix, settle, ratify, sanction. 3 (confirm sb's doubts) add to, increase, strengthen, make firmer, reinforce, fortify; opp assuage

**confirmation** n 1 corroboration, endorsement, evidence, proof, substantiation, testimony, verification. 2 acceptance, agreement, approval, assent, authorization, endorsement, ratification

**confirmed** adj chronic, compulsive, established, habitual, hardened, ingrained, inveterate, long-established, seasoned, through-and-through

**confiscate** v commandeer, expropriate, impound, remove, seize, take, take possession of

**conflict** n 1 (violent) altercation, battle, brush inf, clash, combat, confrontation, encounter, engagement, fight, strife, war, warfare. 2 antagonism, antipathy, bad blood, difference of opinion, disagreement, discord, dissension, feud, friction, hostility, opposition

**conflict** v 1 clash, contradict, contrast, differ, disagree. 2 clash, contend, contest, cross swords, fight, struggle

**conflicting** adj at odds, at variance, clashing, contradictory, contrary, contrasting, differing, discordant, incompatible, inconsistent, mutually exclusive, opposed, opposing, paradoxical; opp similar

**conform** v be good, behave conventionally, blend in, do what you are told inf, comply, fall in with, fit in, follow the crowd, keep in step, obey, run with the pack, toe the line; opp rebel

**confront** v accost, brave, challenge, defy, encounter, face, face up to, meet head on, oppose, resist, stand up to, tackle, take on; opp avoid

**confrontation** n battle, clash, conflict, contest, crisis, encounter, head-to-head, set-to inf, showdown

**confuse** v 1 (confuse sb) baffle, befuddle, bemuse, bewilder, disconcert, disorient, flummox, fluster, mystify, perplex, puzzle. 2 jumble, mess up, mingle, mix up, muddle, snarl up, tangle, throw into disarray, upset

**confused** adj 1 at a loss, at sea, baffled, bamboozled, befuddled, bemused, bewildered, dazed, disorganized, flummoxed, muddled, mystified, nonplussed, perplexed, puzzled, taken aback, thrown inf; opp clear. 2 chaotic, disordered, disorderly, disorganized, in disarray, in disorder, jumbled, messy, misunderstood, mixed up, muddled, out of order, tangled, untidy; opp tidy

**confusing** adj ambiguous, baffling, bewildering, complex, complicated, contradictory, difficult, disorganized, disorientating, disorienting, incomprehensible, jumbled, misleading, mixed up, muddled, mystifying, perplexing, puzzling, unclear; *opp* clear

**confusion** *n* 1 bafflement, befuddlement, bemusement, bewilderment, mystification, perplexity, puzzlement. 2 chaos, commotion, disarray, disorder, hodge-podge, jumble, mess, mix-up, muddle, shambles *inf*, tangle, turmoil; *opp* order

**congenital** *adj* constitutional, hereditary, inborn, inbred, inherent, inherited, innate, natural; *opp* acquired

**congested** *adj* blocked, clogged, crammed, crowded, jammed, obstructed, overcrowded, overfilled, overflowing, packed, plugged, stuffed, teeming; *opp* clear

**congratulate** *v* applaud, compliment, offer your congratulations

**congratulations** *n* best wishes, compliments, felicitations, good wishes

**congregate** *v* assemble, collect, come together, convene, converge, convoke, crowd around, flock, gather, group together, mass, meet, muster, rally, rendezvous, swarm, throng; *opp* disperse

**congregation** *n* assembly, audience, brethren, convocation, crowd, fellowship, flock, gathering, group, host, laity, listeners, mass, meeting, multitude, parish, parishioners, rally, throng

**congress** *n* assembly, chamber, conclave, conference, convention, convocation, council, delegates, gathering, house, legislature, meeting, parliament, representatives, synod

**conjugal** *adj* bridal, connubial, marital, married, matrimonial, nuptial, wedded

**conjure** *v* 1 do magic, do tricks, juggle.

2 **conjure up** bring forth, call up, create, evoke, produce, recall, recreate

**connect** *v* 1 affix, ally, attach, combine, couple, fasten, fix, join, link, relate, tie, unite; *opp* disconnect. 2 associate, bracket, equate, identify, link, relate

**connection** *n* 1 attachment, coupling, fastening, joint, junction, link, tie. 2 affinity, alliance, association, bond, correspondence, equivalence, link, relatedness, relation, relationship, relevance, tie. 3 acquaintance, ally, associate, contact, friend

**connive** *v* 1 collaborate, collude, conspire, intrigue, plot, scheme. 2 **connive at** abet, aid, allow, be an accessory to, be party to, condone, let sth pass, overlook, pass over, shut your eyes to, tolerate, turn a blind eye to

**connoisseur** *n* aficionado, authority, buff *inf*, cognoscenti, devotee, epicure, expert, fan, gourmet, savant, specialist

**conquer** *v* annex, beat, capture, crush, defeat, get the better of, invade, lick *inf*, master, occupy, overcome, overpower, overrun, overthrow, prevail, quell, rout, seize, subdue, subjugate, surmount, take, thrash *inf*, triumph, trounce, vanquish, win

**conqueror** *n* champion, hero, lord, master, vanquisher, victor, winner

**conquest** *n* annexation, appropriation, capture, coup, crushing, defeat, invasion, licking *inf*, mastery, occupation, overpowering, overrunning, overthrow, quelling, rout, seizing, subjugation, taking, thrashing *inf*, triumph, trouncing, vanquishing, victory

**conscience** n better nature, better self, compunction, ethics, morals, moral sense, principles, qualms, scruples

**conscientious** adj careful, dedicated, diligent, dutiful, faithful, hard-working, meticulous, painstaking, particular, perfectionist, punctilious, responsible, rigorous, scrupulous, thorough

**conscious** adj 1 alert, alive to, awake, aware, cognizant, knowing, responsive, sensible, sensitive to, sentient, wise to; **opp** unconscious. 2 calculated, deliberate, intended, intentional, knowing, on purpose, premeditated, studied, voluntary, wilful, willed; **opp** unconscious

**consciousness** n alertness, awareness, cognizance, knowledge, perception, realization, recognition, responsiveness, sense, sensibility, sentience; **opp** unconsciousness

**consecrate** v bless, dedicate, devote, make holy, make sacred, ordain, sanctify, set apart

**consecutive** adj continuous, following, in a row, in sequence, in turn, one after another, running, sequential, serial, succeeding, successive, unbroken, uninterrupted

**consensus** n agreement, common consent, common ground, concord, concurrence, general opinion, harmony, unanimity

**consent** n acceptance, acquiescence, agreement, approval, assent, compliance, concurrence, go-ahead inf, permission, say-so inf, sanction, seal of approval, support; **opp** refusal

**consent** v accept, acquiesce, agree, allow, approve, assent, comply, concede, concur, condone, go along with, permit, sanction, support, yield; **opp** refuse

**consequence** n 1 aftermath, by-product, effect, end, follow-up, issue, outcome, repercussion, result, reverberation, sequel, side-effect, upshot. 2 importance, moment, note, relevance, significance, value, weight

**consequent** adj ensuing, following, resultant, resulting, subsequent

**conservation** n care, charge, custody, husbandry, keeping, maintenance, preservation, preserving, protection, safeguarding, safekeeping, saving, upkeep

**conservative** adj careful, cautious, conventional, die-hard, guarded, hidebound, narrow-minded, old-fashioned, old-school, orthodox, reactionary, right-wing, stick-in-the-mud, straitlaced, Tory, traditional, traditionalist; **opp** progressive

**conserve** v be economical with, hoard, keep, maintain, preserve, protect, safeguard, save, store, take care of; **opp** waste

**consider** v 1 cogitate, contemplate, deliberate, examine, meditate, mull over, ponder, reflect, ruminate, study, think, weigh. 2 allow for, bear in mind, have regard for, make allowances for, reckon with, remember, respect, take into account, take into consideration. 3 believe, be of the opinion, deem, hold, judge, reckon, regard, think

**considerable** adj abundant, ample, appreciable, decent, enormous, goodly, great, huge, large, lavish, notable, not inconsiderable, respectable, significant, sizeable, substantial, tidy *inf*, tolerable; *opp* negligible

**considerably** *adv* a great deal, a lot, appreciably, enormously, greatly, hugely, markedly, notably, significantly, substantially, very much

**considerate** *adj* accommodating, attentive, aware, caring, compassionate, concerned, discreet, helpful, kind, mindful, obliging, sensitive, solicitous, tactful, thoughtful, unselfish; *opp* inconsiderate

**consideration** *n* 1 awareness, compassion, concern, discretion, kindness, sensitivity, solicitude, tact, thought, thoughtfulness, unselfishness. 2 attention, cogitation, contemplation, deliberation, discussion, examination, inspection, perusal, reflection, regard, review, scrutiny, study, thought

**consignment** *n* batch, cargo, delivery, goods, load, shipment

**consist of** *v* be composed of, be made up of, comprise, contain, include, incorporate, involve

**consistent** *adj* constant, dependable, predictable, reliable, regular, stable, steady, true, unchanging, undeviating, uniform, unvarying; *opp* inconsistent

**consolation** *n* cheer, comfort, ease, encouragement, help, relief, solace, soothing, succour, support, sympathy

**console** *v* assuage, calm, cheer, comfort, ease, encourage, hearten, placate, relieve, solace, soothe, succour, support, sympathize

**consolidate** *v* cement, fortify, reinforce, secure, stabilize, strengthen; *opp* weaken

**conspicuous** *adj* apparent, blatant, clear, evident, flagrant, glaring, intrusive, loud, manifest, marked, noticeable, obtrusive, obvious, ostentatious, patent, prominent, striking, unconcealed, visible; *opp* inconspicuous

**conspiracy** *n* cabal, collusion, connivance, frame-up *inf*, intrigue, machination, plot, scheme, stratagem, treason

**conspirator** *n* collaborator, plotter, schemer, traitor

**conspire** *v* be in cahoots *inf*, be in league, collaborate, collude, connive, contrive, devise, hatch a plot, intrigue, manoeuvre, plot, scheme

**constant** *adj* 1 ceaseless, continual, continuous, endless, eternal, everlasting, incessant, interminable, never-ending, non-stop, perpetual, persistent, relentless, sustained, unbroken, unceasing, unending, unrelenting, unremitting. 2 dependable, even, faithful, firm, fixed, immutable, invariable, loyal, permanent, regular, reliable, steadfast, steady, staunch, true, trusty, unchanging, uniform, unvarying; *opp* changeable

**constantly** *adv* all the time, always, ceaselessly, continually, continuously, endlessly, eternally, incessantly, interminably, non-stop, perpetually, persistently, relentlessly, unceasingly, unrelentingly, unremittingly

**constituent** *n* component, element, factor, ingredient, member, part, principle, unit

**constitute** *v* 1 compose, comprise, form, make, make up. 2 create, establish, form, found, inaugurate, institute, make, set up

**constitution** n 1 charter, code, law, rules, principles, system. 2 condition, disposition, health, make-up, nature, temperament. 3 creation, establishment, formation, forming, foundation, founding, inauguration, organization, setting up

**constitutional** adj 1 chartered, constituted, legal, legitimate, statutory, vested. 2 congenital, inborn, inbred, inherent, innate, intrinsic, natural, organic

**constrain** v 1 compel, coerce, drive, force, impel, oblige, pressure, pressurize, push. 2 bind, check, curb, hinder, hold back, impede, limit, restrain, restrict, tie

**constraint** n 1 compulsion, coercion, force, impulsion, necessity, obligation, pressure. 2 check, curb, hindrance, limit, limitation, obstacle, restraint, restriction, tie

**construct** v assemble, build, compose, create, design, devise, erect, establish, fabricate, fashion, forge, form, formulate, found, frame, make, manufacture, organize, produce, put together, put up, raise, set up, shape

**construction** n assembly, building, composition, creation, design, edifice, erection, fabric, figure, form, formation, framework, shape, structure

**constructive** v co-operative, creative, helpful, positive, practical, productive, useful, valuable; **opp** destructive

**consult** v ask, call in, compare notes, confer, debate, deliberate, discuss, interrogate, question, refer to, seek advice, turn to

**consultant** n adviser, authority, expert, specialist

**consultation** n appointment, audience, conference, council, deliberation, dialogue, discussion, examination, hearing, interview, meeting, session, talk

**consume** v absorb, burn, deplete, devour, drain, eat up, exhaust, expend, finish off, guzzle inf, polish off inf, ingest, spend, use, use up, utilize, wear out

**contact** n 1 communication, connection, contiguity, correspondence, join, juxtaposition, proximity, touch, union. 2 (sb you know) acquaintance, ally, associate, connection, friend

**contact** v approach, call, communicate, correspond, get in touch, get hold of, notify, reach, ring, speak, talk, telephone, write

**contagious** adj catching, communicable, epidemic, infectious, passed on, pestilential, spreading, transmissible, transmittable

**contain** v 1 accommodate, carry, enclose, have capacity for, have room for, hold, seat. 2 be composed of, be made up of, comprise, consist of, include, incorporate, involve

**container** n holder, receptacle, vessel

**contaminate** v adulterate, corrupt, debase, dirty, foul, infect, poison, pollute, soil, stain, sully, taint, tarnish; **opp** purify

**contemplate** v 1 brood, cogitate, consider, deliberate, examine, gaze, look, meditate, mull over, muse, ponder, reflect, ruminate, study, view. 2 (contemplate doing sth) consider, envisage, expect, foresee, have in mind, imagine, intend, plan, propose, think

**contemporary** adj 1 coeval, coexistent, coexisting, concurrent, contemporaneous, simultaneous, synchronous. 2 à la mode, current, fashionable, in fashion, latest, modern, newfangled inf, present-day, recent, trendy inf, up-to-date, with-it inf; **opp** old, outdated

**contempt** n abhorrence, derision, disdain, disregard, disrespect, distaste, loathing, mockery, ridicule, scorn, sneering; **opp** respect

**contemptible** adj abhorrent, abject, base, cheap, despicable, detestable, distasteful, hateful, ignominious, loathsome, low, mean, pathetic, ridiculous, shabby, shameful, vile, worthless

**contemptuous** adj cutting, derisive, disdainful, disrespectful, haughty, insulting, jeering, mocking, scathing, scornful, sneering, snide, snobbish, snotty inf, supercilious, superior, withering; **opp** respectful

**contend** v 1 affirm, allege, argue, assert, avow, claim, hold, maintain, put forward, say, state, testify. 2 battle, challenge, clash, compete, contest, fight, oppose, strive, struggle, vie, wrestle

**content** adj at ease, at peace, cheerful, comfortable, contented, fulfilled, gratified, happy, pleased, relaxed, replete, satisfied, tranquil, untroubled, unworried; **opp** dissatisfied, unhappy

**content** n cheer, comfort, contentment, ease, equanimity, fulfilment, gratification, happiness, peace of mind, pleasure, satisfaction, tranquillity;

**opp** unhappiness

**content** v appease, cheer, comfort, fulfil, gladden, gratify, mollify, pacify, placate, please, put at ease, relax, satisfy, soothe; **opp** anger, annoy

**contented** adj at ease, at peace, cheerful, comfortable, content, fulfilled, gratified, happy, pleased, relaxed, replete, satisfied, tranquil, untroubled, unworried; **opp** dissatisfied, unhappy

**contentious** adj 1 arguable, controversial, debatable, disputable, dubious, tendentious; **opp** uncontroversial. 2 aggressive, argumentative, bickering, combative, competitive, cross, disputatious, factious, fractious, peevish, perverse, pugnacious, quarrelsome, querulous, wrangling; **opp** conciliatory

**contentment** n cheer, cheerfulness, comfort, content, ease, equanimity, fulfilment, gladness, gratification, happiness, peace, pleasure, repletion, satisfaction, serenity, tranquillity; **opp** dissatisfaction, unhappiness

**contents** n components, constituents, ingredients, material, matter, subject matter, substance, theme

**contest** n battle, competition, fight, game, head-to-head, match, rivalry, tournament, trial

**contest** v 1 battle, compete, contend, fight, fight over, strive, struggle, tussle, vie. 2 argue, call into question, challenge, debate, disagree with, dispute, doubt, object, oppose, question

**contestant** n adversary, candidate, competitor, contender, entrant, opponent, participant, player, rival

**context** n background, circumstances, conditions, environment, frame of reference, framework, milieu, setting, situation, surroundings

**continual** adj ceaseless, constant, continuous, endless, eternal, everlasting, incessant, interminable, never-ending, non-stop, ongoing, perpetual, persistent, recurrent, regular, relentless, repeated, sustained, unbroken, unceasing, unending, unrelenting, unremitting

**continually** adv all the time, always, ceaselessly, constantly, continuously, endlessly, eternally, incessantly, interminably, non-stop, perpetually, persistently, recurrently, regularly, relentlessly, repeatedly, unceasingly, unrelentingly, unremittingly

**continue** v abide, carry on, endure, go on, keep on, last, live on, maintain, persevere, persist, proceed, remain, rest, resume, stay, subsist, survive

**continuous** adj connected, consecutive, constant, continuing, endless, extended, never-ending, non-stop, prolonged, sustained, unbroken, unceasing, unending, uninterrupted

**contract** n agreement, arrangement, bargain, bond, commitment, compact, convention, covenant, deal, lease, pact, settlement, transaction, treaty, understanding

**contract** v 1 abridge, compress, condense, constrict, curtail, dwindle, lesson, narrow, reduce, shorten, shrink, shrivel, tighten, wither, wrinkle; *opp* expand. 2 (contract to do sth) agree, arrange, bargain, pledge, stipulate, undertake. 3 (contract an illness) be/become infected with, catch, develop, get, go down with

**contradict** v argue, be at odds, be at variance, belie, challenge, clash, conflict, counter, deny, disagree, dispute, dissent from, negate, oppose, rebut, refute; *opp* agree

**contradiction** n clash, conflict, counter, denial, disagreement, dissension, incompatibility, incongruity, inconsistency, negation, opposite, paradox, rebuttal, variance; *opp* agreement

**contradictory** adj antagonistic, at odds, at variance, clashing, conflicting, contrary, dissenting, incompatible, incongruous, inconsistent, irreconcilable, opposite, paradoxical

**contrary** adj 1 clashing, conflicting, contradictory, different, discordant, hostile, incompatible, incongruous, inconsistent, inimical, irreconcilable, opposed, opposite. 2 (of a person) awkward, bloody-minded inf, bolshie inf, headstrong, intractable, intransigent, obstinate, perverse, stroppy inf, stubborn, unco-operative, wayward, wilful; *opp* amenable, obliging

**contrast** n clash, comparison, difference, disparity, dissimilarity, distinction, divergence, foil, opposition

**contrast** v 1 compare, differentiate, discriminate, distinguish, juxtapose, oppose, put side by side. 2 be at variance, clash, differ, diverge, oppose, set off

**contribute** v add, bestow, chip in inf, donate, endow, furnish, give, grant, pitch in inf, provide, subscribe, supply

**contribution** n donation, gift, grant, hand-out inf, offering, payment, present, subscription

**contrive** v concoct, construct, design, devise, engineer, improvise, invent

**contrived** adj artificial, forced, laboured, unnatural

**control** n 1 authority, charge, command, discipline, dominance, influence, leadership, management, mastery, power, rule, supervision, supremacy. 2 (lose control) direction, grip, hold, restraint, self-control

**control** v 1 administer, be at the helm inf, be in charge, direct, dominate, govern, handle, manipulate, oversee, preside, rule, run, supervise. 2 (control a vehicle) command, pilot, steer. 3 (control your temper) bridle, check, constrain, curb, hold back, master, restrain, subdue

**controversial** adj arguable, at issue, contentious, controvertible, debatable, disputable, disputed, doubtful, open to question, questionable

**controversy** n altercation, argument, debate, disagreement, discussion, dispute, dissension, quarrel, row, squabble, wrangle

**convene** v assemble, bring together, call, come together, congregate, convoke, gather, meet, summon

**convenience** n accessibility, appropriateness, availability, expedience, fitness, handiness, suitability, timeliness, usefulness

**convenient** adj 1 (easy to use) accessible, at hand, available, close at hand, handy, labour-saving, nearby, neat, useful; opp inconvenient. 2 (suitable) appropriate, favourable, helpful, opportune, suitable, timely; opp inconvenient

**convention** n 1 code, custom, etiquette, matter of form, practice, propriety, protocol, tradition. 2 conclave, conference, congress, convocation, meeting

**conventional** adj 1 accepted, commonplace, correct, customary, expected, formal, mainstream, normal, ordinary, orthodox, proper, received, standard, straight, traditional, usual; opp unconventional. 2 (of people) conformist, conservative, pedestrian, reactionary, stuffy inf, unadventurous; opp unconventional

**conversation** n chat, chinwag inf, dialogue, discussion, exchange, gossip, heart-to-heart inf, natter inf, talk, tête-à-tête

**converse** v chat, communicate, discuss, have a conversation, speak, talk

**conversion** n adaptation, alteration, change, exchange, metamorphosis, modification, rebuilding, reorganization, substitution, transfiguration, transformation

**convert** v 1 alter, change, modify, reconstruct, reshape, transform, transmute, transpose, turn, switch. 2 (convert sb) change sb's mind, convince, persuade, re-educate, reform, rehabilitate, save, win

**convey** v 1 (take sth) bear, bring, carry, cart, ferry, fetch, move, send, shift, ship, take, transfer, transport. 2 (convey meaning) communicate, disclose, impart, imply, mean, reveal, signify, transmit

**convict** v condemn, find guilty, sentence; *opp* acquit

**conviction** n 1 assurance, certainty, confidence, earnestness, firmness. 2 belief, creed, faith, persuasion, principle

**convince** v assure, persuade, prove to, reassure, satisfy, sway, talk round, win over

**convinced** adj assured, certain, confident, persuaded, positive, satisfied, sure; *opp* uncertain

**convincing** adj 1 (of a theory) believable, cogent, compelling, credible, likely, logical, plausible, probable, valid; *opp* unconvincing. 2 (of a result) conclusive, decisive, impressive, unambiguous

**convoy** n caravan, company, escort, group, line

**cool** adj 1 chilled, chilly, cold, fresh, iced, lukewarm, nippy; *opp* warm. 2 calm, collected, composed, dignified, laid-back *inf*, self-possessed, sensible, together *inf*, unflustered, unruffled; *opp* flustered. 3 aloof, distant, indifferent, offhand, reserved, stand-offish *inf*, unfriendly, unwelcoming; *opp* friendly, warm. 4 bold, brazen, cheeky, impudent, shameless. 5 streetwise *inf*, urbane; *opp* uncool. 6 brill *inf*, brilliant, excellent, good, great, marvellous, splendid, terrific, wonderful; *opp* bad

**cool** n 1 coolness, freshness, coldness. 2 calmness, composure, control, poise, self-control

**cool** v become cold, chill, cool off, freeze, refrigerate; *opp* heat. 2 assuage, calm,

dampen, diminish, lessen, reduce; *opp* inflame

**co-operate** v assist, collaborate, combine, help, join forces, pitch in *inf*, unite, work together

**co-operation** n assistance, collaboration, contribution, give-and-take, help, helpfulness, participation, support, teamwork, unity

**co-operative** adj 1 accommodating, constructive, helpful, keen, obliging, supportive, willing; *opp* unhelpful. 2 collaborative, collective, combined, communal, joint, mutual, shared; *opp* individual

**co-ordinate** v arrange, integrate, match, organize, synchronize

**cope** v carry on, get by, get through, make do, make out *inf*, manage, muddle through, survive

**copious** adj abundant, ample, bountiful, extensive, extravagant, full, generous, lavish, luxuriant, overflowing, plentiful, profuse, rich, unstinting

**copy** n carbon copy, clone, counterfeit, double, duplicate, facsimile, fake, forgery, image, imitation, likeness, model, pattern, photocopy, print, replica, representation, reproduction, transcript, twin

**copy** v 1 (make a copy of) counterfeit, duplicate, forge, photocopy, reproduce, replicate, transcribe. 2 (copy sb's work) crib, plagiarize, steal. 3 ape, echo, imitate, mimic, mirror, parrot, repeat

**cordon** n barrier, chain, fence, line, ring

**core** n centre, crux, essence, gist, heart, inside, kernel, middle, nitty-gritty *inf*, nub, nucleus

**corner** n 1 angle, bend, intersection, joint, junction, turn, turning. 2 cranny, hideaway, hole, niche, nook, recess

**corporation** n business, company, conglomerate, firm, organization, partnership, trust

**corpse** n body, cadaver, carcass, dead body, remains, skeleton, stiff inf

**correct** adj 1 (of behaviour) appropriate, conventional, proper, seemly, suitable; *opp* improper. 2 (of work) accurate, exact, faultless, flawless, perfect, right; *opp* wrong

**correct** v 1 (correct sth) adjust, alter, amend, cure, fix, improve, mark, put right, rectify, redress, remedy, repair, right. 2 (correct sb) admonish, chastise, criticize, discipline, punish, rebuke, reprimand, scold, tell off inf

**correction** n adjustment, alteration, amendment, improvement, rectification, revision

**correspond** v 1 communicate, exchange letters, keep in touch, write. 2 agree, be analogous, be consistent, be equivalent, be similar, coincide, compare, correlate, fit, match, tally

**correspondence** n 1 communication, letters, e-mail, mail, memoranda, notes, post, writing. 2 analogy, accord, conformity, correlation, resemblance, similarity

**corresponding** adj analogous, comparable, equivalent, matching, parallel, reciprocal, similar

**corroborate** v attest, authenticate, back up, bear out, confirm, endorse, establish, support, verify

**corrode** v abrade, consume, eat away, erode, gnaw, oxidize, rot, rust, tarnish, wear away

**corrosive** adj abrasive, caustic, corroding, destructive, eroding, virulent, wearing

**corrupt** adj bent inf, crooked, degenerate, depraved, dirty inf, dishonest, evil, fraudulent, immoral, perverted, rotten, sinful, unethical, unprincipled, untrustworthy, wicked; *opp* honest

**corrupt** v 1 bribe, buy off, deprave, fix inf, influence, lead astray, pervert, seduce, subvert, tempt, warp. 2 contaminate, debase, infect, taint

**corruption** n 1 bribery, dishonesty, extortion, fraud, profiteering, villainy. 2 (corruption in society) decadence, degeneration, depravity, evil, immorality, iniquity, perversion, sinfulness, vice, wickedness

**cosmopolitan** adj 1 (of people) cultured, sophisticated, urbane, well-travelled, worldly, worldly-wise. 2 (of a place) international, multiracial

**cost** n 1 amount, charge, damage inf, expenditure, expense, fare, figure, outlay, payment, price, quotation, rate, tariff, value, worth. 2 damage, detriment, harm, hurt, loss, penalty, sacrifice, suffering

**cost** v be priced at, be valued at, be worth, come to, fetch, go for, realize, sell at, sell for, set you back

**cosy** adj 1 (of a house) comfortable, comfy inf, homely, safe, secure, sheltered, snug, warm; *opp* draughty. 2 (a cosy chat) easy, friendly, intimate, reassuring; *opp* awkward

**council** n assembly, board, cabinet, chamber, committee, convocation, governing body, house, local authority, panel, parliament, synod

**counsel** n advice, direction, guidance, information, opinion, recommendation, suggestion, warning

**counsel** v advise, advocate, caution, discuss, exhort, give help, recommend, urge, warn

**count** v 1 add, add up, calculate, compute, enumerate, estimate, figure out, number, reckon, score, tally, tot up, work out. 2 be important, be of account, carry weight, have significance, matter, mean sth, signify. 3 count on bank on, believe in, depend on, put your faith in, rely on, swear by, trust

**counter** v answer, combat, come back at inf, contradict, dispute, oppose, rebut, refute, reply, resist, respond, retaliate

**counteract** v be an antidote to, cancel out, check, counterbalance, cross, defeat, foil, frustrate, hinder, invalidate, negate, neutralize, offset, resist, thwart, work against

**counterfeit** adj artificial, bogus, copied, ersatz, faked, false, feigned, forged, fraudulent, imitation, phoney inf, pretend inf, pseudo- inf, sham, simulated, spurious, synthetic; **opp** genuine

**counterfeit** v copy, fabricate, fake, falsify, forge, sham, simulate

**countless** adj endless, immeasurable, incalculable, infinite, innumerable, myriad, numerous, untold, without end, without limit

**country** n 1 empire, kingdom, nation, principality, realm, state. 2 fatherland, homeland, land of your birth, motherland, native land. 3 (people)

citizens, inhabitants, nation, people, populace, public, society, voters. 4 countryside, farmland, green belt, provinces, rural area, sticks, wilds. 5 (landscape) area, land, landscape, scenery, terrain, territory

**coup** n 1 accomplishment, achievement, deed, exploit, feat, manoeuvre, stratagem, stroke, stunt, tour de force. 2 coup d'etat, overthrow, revolt, revolution

**couple** n brace, duo, pair, twosome

**courage** n boldness, bottle sl, bravery, daring, determination, fearlessness, fortitude, gallantry, guts inf, heroism, intrepidity, nerve, pluck, resolution, spirit, valour; **opp** cowardice

**courageous** adj bold, brave, daring, fearless, gutsy sl, heroic, indomitable, intrepid, plucky, stout-hearted, tough, unafraid, undaunted, valiant; **opp** cowardly

**course** n 1 advance, continuity, development, flow, march, movement, progress, progression, sequence, succession, unfolding. 2 channel, circuit, direction, line, orbit, passage, path, road, route, tack, track, trail, trajectory, way. 3 circuit, lap, race, racecourse, round. 4 classes, curriculum, lectures, programme, studies, syllabus

**court** n 1 cloister, courtyard, piazza, plaza, quad inf, quadrangle, square, yard. 2 assizes, bar, bench, court of justice, court of law, lawcourt, magistrates' court, tribunal. 3 castle, palace, royal residence. 4 attendants, entourage, followers, retinue, royal household

**court** v 1 (court sb) date, go out with,

make advances to, run after, woo.
**2** (court sth) ask for *inf*, attract,
bring on yourself, crave, invite, provoke,
risk, seek

**courteous** *adj* attentive, chivalrous, civil,
considerate, gallant, gracious, polite,
refined, respectful, well-mannered;
*opp* rude

**courtesy** *n* **1** chivalry, civility,
courteousness, good breeding, good
manners, politeness, respect. **2** (as a
courtesy) benefit, consideration, favour,
indulgence, kindness, service

**courtyard** *n* area, court, enclosure,
forecourt, patio, quad *inf*, quadrangle,
square, yard

**cover** *n* **1** blanket, canopy, cap, case,
coating, covering, lid, roof, top, wrapper.
**2** (blow sb's cover) disguise, façade,
front, pretence, smoke-screen. **3** (seek
cover) concealment, hiding place,
protection, refuge, sanctuary.
**4** (insurance) compensation, indemnity,
insurance, protection

**cover** *v* **1** (cover sth) blanket, carpet,
bury, cloak, clothe, coat, conceal,
disguise, drape, encase, enclose, envelop,
hide, house, mask, obscure, plaster,
screen, shade, sheathe, shelter, shroud,
veil, wrap. **2** (stand in for sb) fill in,
relieve, replace, stand in, take over.
**3** (cover a story) describe, investigate,
recount, report, write up. **4** (cover a
topic) contain, deal with, encompass,
include, incorporate, involve, take in,
treat. **5** cover up conceal, hide, hush up,
keep secret, repress, suppress

**covering** *n* blanket, canopy, casing,
cladding, coat, coating, cover, film,
layer, rind, sheet, skin, surface, veneer,
wrapping

**covet** *v* crave, desire, hanker after, long
for, lust after, set your heart on, thirst
for, want, wish for, yearn for

**coward** *n* chicken *sl*, scaredy-cat *inf*,
wimp *inf*

**cowardly** *adj* faint-hearted, fearful,
gutless *inf*, lily-livered, scared, soft,
spineless, timorous, weak, wimpish
*inf*, yellow *inf*; *opp* brave

**cower** *v* cringe, crouch, draw back, flinch,
grovel, hide, quail, recoil, shrink, skulk,
tremble

**coy** *adj* bashful, demure, diffident, evasive,
flirtatious, modest, reticent, shy,
self-conscious

**crack** *n* (break in sth) break, chink, chip,
cleft, crevice, fissure, flaw, fracture, gap,
opening, rift, slit, split. **2** (sound) burst,
clap, crash, explosion, pop. **3** (have a
crack at sth) (*inf*) go *inf*, stab *inf*, try.
**4** (funny remark) (*inf*) dig *inf*, gag *inf*,
insult, joke, quip, wisecrack,
witticism

**crack** *v* **1** (be broken) break, chip, craze,
fracture, fragment, snap, splinter, split.
**2** (of thunder) boom, crackle, go bang,
resound, ring out. **3** (hit a part of your
body) bang, bash, bump, clout, hit,
knock, smack, strike, whack. **4** (of
people) break down, collapse, give way,
go to pieces, lose control, succumb, yield

**cracked** *adj* broken, chipped, crazed,
damaged, faulty, flawed, imperfect, split

**craft** *n* **1** ability, art, artistry,
craftsmanship, expertise, handiwork,
knack, skill, technique, workmanship.
**2** aircraft, boat, ship, spacecraft, vessel

*inf*, culpable, dishonest, evil, illegal, illicit, immoral, unlawful, villainous, wicked, wrong. **2** deplorable, immoral, reprehensible, scandalous, shameful, shocking, wrong

**criminal** *n* baddy *inf*, con *inf*, convict, crook *inf*, culprit, delinquent, desperado, felon, jailbird, lag *sl*, lawbreaker, miscreant, offender, outlaw, sinner, villain, wrongdoer

**cringe** *v* blench, cower, draw back, duck, flinch, quail, recoil, shrink, shy away, tremble, wince

**cripple** *v* **1** (cripple sb) disable, enfeeble, handicap, incapacitate, make sb lame, maim, paralyse, weaken. **2** (cripple sth) damage, mutilate, paralyse, put out of action, ruin, sabotage, spoil

**crisis** *n* **1** calamity, catastrophe, dilemma, dire straits, disaster, emergency, panic stations *inf*, predicament, quandary, trouble. **2** climax, critical point, crunch *inf*, crux, height, moment of truth, turning point

**crisp** *adj* **1** (of food) breakable, crispy, crumbly, crunchy, dry, firm, fresh; *opp* soggy. **2** (of the wind) bracing, brisk, cool, fresh, invigorating, refreshing

**criterion** *n* benchmark, gauge, measure, norm, principle, rule, scale, standard, test, touchstone, yardstick

**critic** *n* **1** commentator, connoisseur, expert, judge, pundit, reviewer. **2** attacker, backbiter, detractor, fault-finder, nit-picker *inf*; *opp* supporter

**critical** *adj* **1** carping, censorious, criticizing, derogatory, disapproving, disparaging, fault-finding, hypercritical, judgemental, nagging, niggling, nit-

picking *inf*, quibbling, uncomplimentary, unfavourable; *opp* complimentary. **2** (a critical moment) deciding, decisive, important, key, momentous, pivotal. **3** (a critical situation) crucial, dangerous, grave, perilous, risky, serious, touch-and-go, urgent

**criticism** *n* **1** (criticism in general) bad press, censure, character assassination, condemnation, disapproval, disparagement, fault-finding, outcry, stick *sl*; *opp* approval. **2** complaint, diatribe, rebuke, reprimand, reproach, tirade. **3** (a criticism) analysis, appraisal, appreciation, assessment, comment, critique, evaluation, judgement, review

**criticize** *v* blame, castigate, censure, complain, condemn, disapprove, disparage, find fault, give flak *inf*, knock *inf*, nag, nit-pick *inf*, pick holes, slam *inf*, slate *inf*; *opp* praise

**croak** *v* caw, gasp, grunt, speak hoarsely, speak huskily, squawk, wheeze

**crook** *n* cheat, criminal, robber, rogue, swindler, thief, villain

**crooked** *adj* **1** (not straight) bent, bowed, contorted, curved, curving, deformed, distorted, gnarled, irregular, misshapen, twisted, twisting, warped, winding, zigzag; *opp* straight. **2** (not even) askew, aslant, asymmetric, at an angle, awry, lopsided, off-centre, skew-whiff *inf*, slanted, slanting, sloping, tilted, uneven, unsymmetrical. **3** (not honest) bent *sl*, corrupt, criminal, deceitful, dishonest, dubious, fraudulent, illegal, questionable, shady *inf*, shifty, underhand; *opp* honest

**crop** *n* fruits, gathering, harvest, produce,

season's growth, sowing, vintage, yield

**crop** v 1 clip, cut, lop, mow, pare, prune, shear, shorten, snip, trim. **2 crop up** arise, come up, emerge, happen, occur, turn up

**cross** adj angry, annoyed, bad-tempered, disagreeable, fractious, fretful, grouchy, grumpy inf, ill-humoured, in a bad mood, irritable, irritated, ratty inf, short, short-tempered, sullen, surly, testy, upset, vexed; **opp** cheerful

**cross** n 1 crucifix, rood. 2 amalgam, blend, combination, cross-breed, hybrid, hybridization, mix, mixture, mongrel

**cross** v 1 (cross a river) bridge, cut across, ford, pass over, span, traverse. 2 (of lines) crisscross, intersect, intertwine, meet, zigzag. 3 (of breeds) blend, cross-breed, cross-fertilize, cross-pollinate, interbreed, mix. **4 cross out** cancel, delete, obliterate, strike out

**crossing** n 1 crossroads, intersection, junction, level crossing, pedestrian crossing, pelican crossing, subway, underpass, zebra crossing. 2 (a rough crossing) journey, passage, ride, sea crossing, trip, voyage

**crouch** v bend down, bow, duck, kneel, squat, stoop

**crowd** n 1 (group of people) army, bevy, bunch, circle, clique, company, flock, gang, group, herd, horde, host, lot, mass, mob, multitude, pack, rabble, set, swarm, throng. 2 (people watching sth) audience, gate, house, spectators, turnout

**crowd** v assemble, cluster, concentrate, congregate, cram, flock, gather, huddle, jam, pile inf, press, push, squeeze, stuff,

surge, swarm, throng

**crowded** adj busy, congested, cramped, crushed, full, jam-packed inf, packed, swarming, teeming

**crown** n 1 circlet, coronet, diadem, tiara. 2 apex, brow, head, peak, ridge, summit, top

**crown** v 1 anoint, appoint, enthrone, inaugurate, invest, install. 2 be the climax of, be the culmination of, cap, complete, consummate, finish, fulfil, put the finishing touch to, round off, top

**crucial** adj central, critical, decisive, determining, essential, high-priority, important, major, momentous, pivotal, significant

**crude** adj 1 blue inf, coarse, crass, dirty, gross, indecent, indelicate, lewd, obscene, raunchy inf, smutty, tasteless, uncouth, vulgar. 2 natural, unprocessed, unrefined. 3 awkward, clumsy, inelegant, makeshift, primitive, rough, rough-and-ready, rudimentary, sketchy, undeveloped, unfinished, unskilful; **opp** sophisticated

**cruel** adj 1 (of people) barbaric, barbarous, brutal, callous, cold-blooded, fiendish, hard-hearted, heartless, inhuman, malevolent, merciless, murderous, pitiless, ruthless, sadistic, savage, spiteful, stony-hearted, unfeeling, unkind, vengeful, vicious; **opp** kind. 2 (of conditions) atrocious, bitter, fierce, grim, hard, harsh, hellish, painful, raw, severe, unrelenting

**cruise** v coast, drift, move, sail, travel, voyage

**crumb** n bit, bite, grain, morsel, particle, scrap, shred, speck

**crumble** v 1 (of food) break into pieces, break up, crush, granulate, grind, pound, powder, pulverize. 2 (of materials) come to dust, decay, decompose, disintegrate, fall apart, fall to pieces, moulder, perish, rot

**crumple** v crease, crinkle, crush, fold, pucker, rumple, screw up, wrinkle

**crunch** v bite, chew, chomp, crush, munch, scrunch inf, smash, squash

**crusade** n campaign, cause, drive, holy war, jihad, military campaign, movement, struggle

**crush** v 1 break, bruise, compress, crumble, crunch, grind, mangle, mash, pound, press, pulp, pulverize, shatter, smash, squeeze. 2 (of fabric) crease, crinkle, crumple, rumple, wrinkle. 3 conquer, defeat, overcome, overpower, put down, quash, quell, stamp out, subdue, thrash, vanquish. 4 (crush sb's spirit) chagrin, humiliate, mortify, shame

**crust** n coating, covering, outer layer, outside, rind, scab, shell, skin, surface, topping

**crux** n core, essence, gist, heart, nub, point

**cry** n 1 bellow, howl, scream, shriek, shout, whoop, yell, yelp. 2 blub inf, howl, keening, lamentation, sob, sobbing, wail, weep, weeping

**cry** v 1 bawl, blubber, grizzle, howl, lament, shed tears, snivel, sob, wail, weep, whimper, whine, whinge inf. 2 bawl, bellow, call, call out, exclaim, roar, scream, screech, shout, shriek, sing out, yell

**cryptic** adj coded, enigmatic, hidden, mysterious, mystical, obscure, puzzling, secret, unclear, veiled; opp clear, obvious

**cuddle** v 1 clasp, embrace, fondle, hold closely, hug, kiss, neck inf, pet, smooch inf. 2 curl up, nestle, snuggle

**cue** n hint, nod, prompt, reminder, sign, signal, suggestion

**culminate** v build up to, climax, close, come to a crescendo, come to a head, conclude, end, finish, peak, terminate

**culprit** n baddy inf, bad guy inf, delinquent, guilty party, miscreant, offender, person responsible, wrongdoer

**cult** n 1 church, denomination, faction, group, order, party, religion, sect

**cultivate** v 1 dig, farm, fertilize, grow, harvest, hoe, plant, plough, prepare, produce, raise, sow, take cuttings, tend, till, turn, work. 2 court, develop, devote yourself to, encourage, foster, improve, promote, pursue, support. 3 civilize, educate, enlighten, polish, refine, train

**cultivation** n 1 agriculture, farming, gardening, growing, horticulture. 2 advancement, development, encouragement, fostering, furtherance, promotion, support

**cultural** adj 1 (cultural experiences) artistic, broadening, civilizing, edifying, educational, elevating, enriching, highbrow, improving. 2 (cultural diversity) ethnic, racial

**culture** n 1 civilization, customs, lifestyle, mores, society, way of life. 2 (person of culture) education, enlightenment, erudition, good taste, refinement, sophistication

**cultured** adj accomplished, civilized, cultivated, educated, enlightened, erudite, genteel, intellectual, knowledgeable, learned, refined, scholarly, versed, well-educated, well-read; *opp* ignorant

**cunning** *adj* artful, astute, canny, clever, crafty, devious, guileful, imaginative, ingenious, resourceful, sharp, shrewd, subtle, wily

**cup** *n* **1** beaker, chalice, glass, goblet, mug, tankard, tumbler. **2** prize, trophy

**curb** *v* bite back, bridle, check, constrain, contain, control, hinder, hold back, impede, inhibit, keep in check, limit, moderate, muzzle, put a brake on, repress, restrain, restrict, suppress

**cure** *n* **1** antidote, cure-all, medication, medicine, palliative, panacea, prescription, remedy, solution, therapy, treatment. **2** convalescence, healing, improvement, progress, recovery

**cure** *v* **1** (make sb better) heal, make better, make well, rehabilitate, restore to health, treat. **2** (put sth right) correct, fix, put right, rectify, remedy, repair, solve. **3** (preserve food) dry, kipper, preserve, salt, smoke

**curiosity** *n* **1** inquisitiveness, interest, interference, meddling, nosiness *inf*, prying, snooping. **2** (sth unusual) freak, novelty, oddity, phenomenon, rarity, spectacle

**curious** *adj* **1** (a curious mind) inquiring, inquisitive, interested, probing, puzzled, questioning. **2** (nosy) inquisitive, interfering, intrusive, meddlesome, meddling, nosy *inf*, prying, snooping. **3** (a curious object) bizarre, exotic, mysterious, novel, odd, puzzling, strange, unusual, wonderful

**curl** *v* **1** bend, coil, corkscrew, curve, entwine, loop, meander, ripple, snake, spiral, turn, twine, twirl, twist, wind, wreathe, writhe. **2** (of hair) corkscrew, crimp, crinkle, frizz, kink, perm, wave

**curly** *adj* curling, crimped, crinkly, frizzy, fuzzy, permed, wavy; *opp* straight

**current** *adj* **1** alive, contemporary, continuing, existing, fashionable, happening *inf*, in *inf*, in fashion, in vogue, living, modern, now *inf*, popular, present, present-day, prevailing, trendy *inf*, up-to-date; *opp* old, outdated

**current** *n* **1** (of water) course, drift, flow, river, stream, tide, undercurrent, undertow. **2** (of air) draught, movement, thermal, wind

**curriculum** *n* course, programme, syllabus

**curse** *n* **1** bad language, blasphemy, expletive, oath, obscenity, profanity, swearword. **2** (put a curse on sb) evil eye, imprecation, jinx. **3** affliction, bane, evil, hardship, misfortune, plague, scourge, tribulation

**curse** *v* **1** be foul-mouthed, blaspheme, cuss *Am inf*, swear, take God's name in vain, use bad language. **2** damn, jinx, put a curse on, put a jinx on, put the evil eye on

**cursory** *adj* brief, careless, casual, desultory, fleeting, hasty, hurried, perfunctory, quick, superficial

**curtail** *v* abbreviate, break off, cut short, dock, pare down, reduce, restrict, shorten, stop, terminate, trim; *opp* extend

**curve** *n* arc, arch, bend, bow, bulge, camber, circle, crescent, curvature, half-moon, loop, spiral, twist, undulation

**curve** v arc, arch, bend, bow, coil, curl, loop, meander, snake, swerve, swirl, turn, twist, wind

**curved** adj arched, bent, bowed, concave, convex, crooked, curvilinear, curvy, humped, rounded, sinuous, twisted, undulating

**custody** n 1 (in custody) arrest, detention, imprisonment, incarceration. 2 (in sb's custody) care, charge, control, guardianship, keeping, possession, protection, safe-keeping, supervision, trusteeship

**custom** n convention, etiquette, form, formality, habit, manner, observance, practice, ritual, routine, tradition, usage, way, wont

**customary** adj accepted, common, conventional, established, everyday, familiar, general, habitual, normal, ordinary, regular, routine, traditional, typical, usual

**customer** n buyer, client, consumer, patron, purchaser, regular inf, shopper

**cut** n 1 gash, graze, groove, incision, laceration, nick, opening, rent, rip, slash, slit, snip, split, tear, wound. 2 cutback, economy, fall, lowering, reduction, saving

**cut** v 1 (injure sb) gash, gouge, graze, knife, lacerate, lance, nick, open, sever, slash, snick, stab, wound. 2 (cut sth) carve, chip, chisel, chop, cleave, clip, crop, dice, dissect, divide, engrave, grate, guillotine, hack, hew, lop, mow, notch, pare, pierce, prune, saw, score, sculpt, shave, shear, shred, slice, slit, whittle. 3 (reduce) abbreviate, abridge, axe,

condense, curtail, cut back, decrease, delete, economize, edit, excise, lessen, rationalize, reduce, retrench, shorten, slash, slim down, trim, truncate; *opp* increase. 4 cut down bring down, chop down, fell, flatten, hew, level, lop, raze. 5 cut off break off, disconnect, interrupt, isolate, remove, separate, sever, suspend. 6 cut out delete, excise, extract, remove. 7 cut up carve, chop, dice, divide, mince, slice

**cutback** n cut, decrease, economy, reduction

**cutthroat** adj 1 bloodthirsty, bloody, cruel, ferocious, fierce, homicidal, murderous, savage, violent. 2 competitive, dog-eat-dog, fierce, merciless, relentless, ruthless, unprincipled

**cutting** adj acerbic, acid, barbed, biting, hurtful, incisive, malicious, sarcastic, scathing, sharp, stinging, spiteful, trenchant, wounding

**cycle** n circle, revolution, rotation, round, sequence, series, succession

**cynic** n doom and gloom merchant inf, doubting Thomas, killjoy, pessimist, sceptic

**cynical** adj doubting, full of doom and gloom, negative, pessimistic, sceptical, scornful, sneering; *opp* optimistic

**cynicism** n doubt, pessimism, scepticism, scorn, suspicion

**dagger** n blade, knife, sheath knife

**daily** adj, adv common, day-to-day, everyday, regular, routine, usual

**dainty** adj delicate, elegant, fine, graceful, neat, petite, pretty

**dam** n 1 barrage, barricade, barrier, wall, weir. 2 artificial lake, lake, reservoir

**dam** v barricade, block, check, dam up, hold back, stop

**damage** n abuse, detriment, devastation, harm, havoc, hurt, injury, loss, sabotage, vandalism

**damage** v bend, break, bruise, bump, bust inf, chip, crack, crash, deface, dent, harm, hurt, impair, injure, rip, ruin, sabotage, scrape, scratch, spoil, tear, vandalize, warp, wreck

**damaging** adj critical, detrimental, discreditable, disparaging, harmful, hurtful, injurious, prejudicial

**damp** adj clammy, dank, humid, misty, moist, muggy, soggy, steamy, sticky, wet; **opp** dry

**damp** n clamminess, dampness, humidity, moisture, mist, mugginess, steaminess, wetness

**dance** n ball, ballet, barn dance, bop inf, ceilidh, dancing, disco, hop, jig, rave

**dance** v bop inf, cavort, do a jig, jig around, jive, leap about, shake a leg inf, smooch, sway, take the floor, twirl, waltz

**danger** n hazard, jeopardy, menace, peril, pitfall, risk, threat

**dangerous** adj chancy, daredevil, foolhardy, hairy inf, hazardous, life-threatening, nasty, perilous, risky, ugly, unsafe; **opp** safe

**dare** n challenge, provocation, taunt

**dare** v 1 challenge, defy, goad, provoke, taunt, throw down the gauntlet. 2 brave, have the courage, have the guts inf, have the nerve, pluck up the courage, risk, take the plunge, take the risk, venture

**daring** adj adventurous, audacious, bold, brave, fearless, rash, wild; **opp** timid

**dark** adj 1 black, cloudy, dim, dingy, gloomy, inky, overcast, poorly lit, shadowy, unlit; **opp** bright, light. 2 (of complexion) black, brown, dark-skinned, olive, swarthy, tanned; **opp** pale. 3 (of colours) deep, dense, rich; **opp** light

**dark** n blackness, darkness, dusk, gloom, murkiness, night, nightfall, night-time, shade, shadows, twilight

**darken** v blacken, cloud over, dim, get dark, grow dim, make dark, shade

**darkness** n blackness, dark, dusk, gloom, murkiness, night, nightfall, night-time, shade, shadows, twilight

**darling** n dear, dearest, love, pet, poppet

*inf*, sweetheart, sweetie

**dart** *v* bolt, dash, fly, hop, hurtle, nip, race, run, rush, scuttle, shoot, sprint, tear

**dash** *v* 1 bolt, charge, chase, fly, hurry, hurtle, race, run, rush, speed, sprint, tear, zoom *inf*. 2 crash, fling, hurl, pitch, slam, smash, throw

**data** *n* details, facts, figures, information, statistics

**date** *n* 1 age, day, day and age, epoch, era, period, time, vintage, year. 2 appointment, assignation, engagement, meeting, rendezvous

**dated** *adj* ancient, antiquated, fuddy-duddy *inf*, fusty, obsolete, old, old-fashioned, old-hat, outmoded, out of the ark, passé, stale, unfashionable; *opp* latest, modern, up-to-date

**daunting** *adj* disconcerting, discouraging, frightening, intimidating, overwhelming, scary, terrifying, unnerving

**dawdle** *v* amble, dilly-dally, drag your feet, go slowly, hang about, lag behind, linger, loiter, potter, saunter, shilly-shally, take your time, waste time; *opp* rush

**dawn** *n* 1 cock-crow, crack of dawn, daybreak, daylight, first light, start of the day, sunrise, sun-up; *opp* dusk, sunset. 2 advent, beginning, birth, genesis, onset, start; *opp* end

**dawn** *v* 1 begin, break, come into being, emerge, start. 2 (sth dawns on you) come to you, enter your mind, flash across your mind, hit, occur to you, the penny drops, register, strike

**day** *n* 1 daytime, daylight; *opp* night.

2 age, date, day and age, epoch, era, generation, period, point in time, time

**daybreak** *n* cock-crow, crack of dawn, dawn, daylight, first light, start of the day, sunrise, sun-up; *opp* dusk, sunset

**daydream** *n* castle in the air, dream, fantasy, pipe-dream, reverie

**daydream** *v* be in your own little world, be lost in thought, dream, fantasize, imagine, let your thoughts wander, stare into space

**daze** *v* bemuse, bewilder, confuse, floor *inf*, numb, shock, stagger, stun, stupefy

**dazed** *adj* bemused, bewildered, confused, dizzy, floored *inf*, fuddled, muddled, numbed, shocked, staggered, stunned, stupefied

**dazzle** *v* 1 blind, confuse, disorientate. 2 bedazzle, bowl over *inf*, impress, overwhelm, stagger, stun, take your breath away

**dazzling** *adj* amazing, brilliant, glittering, magnificent, sensational, sparkling, splendid, terrific, stunning

**dead** *adj* 1 deceased, departed, late, lifeless, no more, out of your misery, passed away, pushing up the daisies *inf*, six feet under *inf*, stillborn; *opp* alive. 2 (obsolete) extinct, obsolete; *opp* living. 3 (unresponsive) cold, emotionless, indifferent, inert, lifeless, numb, paralyzed, unresponsive, without feeling, wooden. 4 (not working) broken, defunct, had it, kaput, out of order, worn out; *opp* working. 5 boring, dreary, dull, flat, lifeless, uninteresting; *opp* lively

**deaden** *v* blunt, dull, muffle, numb, soothe, smother, stifle, suppress

**deadlock** n checkmate, dead end, impasse, logjam, stalemate, standoff, standstill

**deadly** adj 1 fatal, lethal, malignant, noxious, poisonous, virulent. 2 (boring) awful, boring, dire, dull, tedious, terrible

**deaf** adj hard of hearing, stone deaf, with a hearing problem, with impaired hearing

**deafen** v make deaf, damage sb's hearing, hurt your ears

**deafening** adj at full blast, at full volume, blaring, ear-splitting, loud, roaring, thudding, thunderous

**deal** n agreement, arrangement, bargain, business deal, contract, pact, transaction, understanding, venture

**deal** v 1 (share out) allocate, allot, dish out, distribute, dole out, give, hand out, share out. 2 **deal in** buy and sell, do business, handle, trade, traffic. 3 **deal with** attend to, do, fix, handle, see to, sort inf, sort out, tackle, take care of, take on, take responsibility for

**dealer** n agent, broker, buyer, handler, retailer, seller, trader, vendor, wholesaler

**dear** adj 1 cost-a-fortune inf, costly, exorbitant, expensive, extortionate, high-priced, luxury, over-priced, pricey, steep inf, stiff inf, top-rate, up-market, upscale; **opp** cheap, inexpensive. 2 (much-loved) close, close to your heart, darling, intimate, loved, much-loved

**dear** n darling, dearest, love, pet, poppet inf, sweetheart, sweetie

**death** n 1 bloodshed, curtains inf, decease, demise, dying, end, fatality, killing, loss of life, massacre, slaughter. 2 (end) annihilation, destruction, downfall, end, eradication, extermination, finish, obliteration, ruin

**debase** v cheapen, degrade, demean, devalue, discredit, disgrace, lower, shame, spoil, sully

**debatable** adj arguable, borderline, controversial, doubtful, dubious, iffy inf, open to question, questionable

**debate** n argument, deliberation, disagreement, discussion, dispute

**debate** v argue, deliberate, disagree, discuss, talk about

**debris** n detritus, dross, garbage, litter, remains, rubbish, rubble, trash Am, waste

**debt** n arrears, credit, dues, hire purchase, liability, loan, money owing, mortgage, overdraft

**debut** n appearance, entrance, first appearance, inauguration, introduction, launch, première

**decadent** adj corrupt, debauched, decaying, declining, degenerate, depraved, dissipated, dissolute, immoral, licentious, permissive

**decay** n collapse, corrosion, crumbling, death, decline, decomposition, disintegration, going bad, rot, rotting, putrefaction, withering away

**decay** v corrode, crumble, decompose, die, disintegrate, go bad, moulder, rot, perish, putrefy, shrivel, waste away, wither

**deceased** adj dead, departed, late, no more, passed away, passed on

**deceit** n cheating, deception, dishonesty, disloyalty, double-dealing, duplicity, false pretences, fraud, lying, misrepresentation, pretence, subterfuge, treachery, trickery, untruthfulness

**deceitful** *adj* bogus, crooked, dishonest, disloyal, double-dealing, false, fraudulent, lying, sham, two-faced, underhand, untrustworthy, untruthful; *opp* honest

**deceive** *v* cheat, cheat on, con *inf*, double-cross, dupe, fool, have sb on, mislead, hoodwink, pull a fast one, pull the wool over sb's eyes, swindle, take for a ride, take in, trick

**decency** *n* civility, courtesy, correctness, dignity, good manners, honesty, propriety, respectability

**decent** *adj* **1** courteous, dependable, dignified, good, honest, honourable, nice, proper, respectable, suitable, trustworthy, upright, worthy. **2** (adequate) acceptable, adequate, fair, good, reasonable, sufficient

**deception** *n* **1** cheating, deceit, dishonesty, double-dealing, duplicity, false pretences, fraud, lying, misrepresentation, pretence, subterfuge, treachery, trickery, untruthfulness. **2** con *inf*, cover-up, dodge, fiddle *inf*, hoax, lie, pretence, ruse, sham, swindle, trick

**deceptive** *adj* deceiving, false, illusory, misleading, unreliable

**decide** *v* choose, come to a conclusion, conclude, determine, give your verdict, go for, make a decision, make up your mind, opt for, plump for, resolve, settle, settle for, settle on, take the plunge

**decision** *n* choice, conclusion, finding, judgement, outcome, pronouncement, resolution, result, ruling, verdict

**decisive** *adj* **1** definite, firm, forceful, positive, resolute, self-confident, strong-minded, sure of yourself, unfaltering, unwavering; *opp* hesitant, indecisive, tentative. **2** critical, crucial, deciding, definitive, determining, key, pivotal, significant

**declaration** *n* announcement, assertion, decree, disclosure, edict, notice, press release, proclamation, revelation, statement

**declare** *v* affirm, announce, assert, claim, contend, disclose, maintain, make known, proclaim, profess, reveal, say, state

**decline** *n* degeneration, deterioration, downturn, downward trend, drop, fall, reversal, slump

**decline** *v* **1** refuse, reject, say no, send your apologies, turn down; *opp* accept. **2** decrease, degenerate, deteriorate, diminish, dwindle, fade, fall, fall off, get worse, go down, go downhill, go to the dogs *inf*, peter out, sink, tail off, wane, weaken; *opp* get better, improve, increase

**decorate** *v* **1** do up *inf*, paint, paper, refurbish, smarten up, wallpaper. **2** deck, embellish, garnish, festoon, trim

**decoration** *n* **1** decor, colour scheme. **2** bauble, embellishment, fancywork, flounce, frill, garnish, ornamentation, spangle, tinsel, trimmings

**decorative** *adj* non-functional, ornamental, ornate; *opp* functional

**decoy** *n* bait, distraction, inducement, lure, trap

**decoy** *v* attract, bait, entice, induce, inveigle, lure, tempt

**decrease** *n* cutback, decline, down-sizing, downturn, drop, fall, let-up, reduction, shrinkage; **opp** increase

**decrease** v abate, cut, cut back on, decline, diminish, down-size, dwindle, drop, fall off, go down, lessen, lower, peter out, reduce, subside, taper off; **opp** increase

**decree** n announcement, command, dictum, directive, edict, injunction, judgement, law, order, policy statement, regulation, rule, ruling

**decree** v announce, dictate, direct, lay down, prescribe, ordain, order, proclaim, pronounce, rule, say, state

**decrepit** adj broken-down, derelict, dilapidated, doddering, incapacitated, on its last legs, ramshackle, rickety, run-down, tottering, worn-out, wrecked

**dedicate** v 1 assign, commit, devote, give over to, pledge. 2 bless, consecrate, sanctify

**dedicated** adj committed, devoted, enthusiastic, keen, loyal, single-minded, wholehearted, zealous

**dedication** n 1 commitment, determination, devotion, keenness, loyalty, single-mindedness, zeal. 2 address, inscription, message

**deduce** v come to a conclusion, conclude, infer, gather, realize, surmise, suss out inf, understand, work out

**deduct** v allow, cut, discount, knock off inf, subtract, take away, take off; **opp** add

**deduction** n 1 allowance, cut, discount, mark-down, rebate, reduction, stoppage, subtraction. 2 assumption, conclusion, inference, presumption, reasoning

**deed** n 1 achievement, act, action, effort, enterprise, exercise, exploit, feat, job, operation, undertaking. 2 agreement,

contract, deed of covenant, document, indenture, paper, policy, proof of ownership, record, title deed

**deep** adj 1 abyssal, bottomless, cavernous, yawning; **opp** shallow. 2 broad, large, wide. 3 (of a voice) bass, booming, low, low-pitched, rich; **opp** high. 4 (of a colour) dark, intense, rich, strong, vivid; **opp** light, pale. 4 (of an emotion) deep-rooted, deep-seated, heartfelt, intense, passionate, profound, strong; **opp** superficial

**deface** v damage, disfigure, mutilate, spoil, vandalize

**default** v backslide, be negligent, dodge, evade, fail to fulfil, fail to pay, fall into arrears, get behind, let sb down, shirk, stop payment, withhold payment

**defeat** n 1 conquest, drubbing inf, overthrow, rout, thrashing, trouncing, victory, win. 2 collapse, disappointment, downfall, failure, frustration, reverse, ruin; **opp** victory

**defeat** v annihilate, beat, conquer, foil, get the better of, hammer inf, get the upper hand, knock the socks off inf, knock the stuffing out of inf, outclass, overthrow, rout, thrash, thwart, topple, trounce, vanquish, wipe the floor with inf

**defect** n blemish, bug inf, deficiency, error, failing, fault, flaw, mistake, shortcoming, weakness, weak spot

**defect** v change sides, desert, desert the cause, go over to the other side, join the opposition, turn traitor

**defective** adj broken, damaged, faulty, flawed, malfunctioning, not working, out of order

**defence** n 1 (protection) barricade, bastion, cover, deterrent, fortification, fortress, protection, shelter, shield. 2 (military matters) armaments, armed forces, the military, weapons. 3 (justification) case, excuse, explanation, justification, vindication

**defenceless** adj exposed, helpless, impotent, powerless, unarmed, vulnerable, weak; *opp* strong

**defend** v 1 fortify, guard, protect, safeguard, secure; *opp* attack. 2 champion, espouse, justify, speak up for, stand by, stand up for, support, uphold; *opp* attack

**defendant** n accused, appellant, culprit, litigant, offender, prisoner, respondent, suspect

**defensive** adj 1 feeling got at inf, sensitive, uptight inf, wary. 2 protective

**defer** v adjourn, delay, hold, hold over, postpone, put off, put on ice, put on the back burner, shelve, table Am

**defiant** adj belligerent, challenging, disobedient, non-compliant, intransigent, rebellious, recalcitrant, scornful, stubborn, unco-operative; *opp* compliant, submissive

**deficiency** n dearth, deficit, inadequacy, lack, scarcity, shortage

**deficient** adj inadequate, lacking, meagre, scant, scarce, short, skimpy

**deficit** n arrears, deficiency, loss, shortage, shortfall

**define** v clarify, describe, elucidate, explain, give the meaning of, outline, set out, specify, spell out

**definite** adj 1 certain, confident, confirmed, guaranteed, positive, sure. 2 clear, clear-cut, explicit, marked, obvious, precise, unmistakable

**definition** n description, explanation, meaning

**definitive** adj 1 conclusive, decisive, final, unconditional. 2 authoritative, complete, exhaustive, reliable

**deflect** v bounce off, change course, divert, glance off, ricochet, shy, swerve, turn aside, veer

**deformed** adj contorted, damaged, disfigured, distorted, injured, maimed, malformed, misshapen, mutilated, twisted

**defraud** v cheat, con inf, diddle inf, do inf, embezzle, fleece, pull a fast one inf, rip off inf, rob, rook, sting inf, swindle, take sb for a ride

**defunct** adj deceased, dead, expired, extinct, gone, invalid, obsolete

**defy** v challenge, confront, disobey, disregard, flout, foil, frustrate, rebel against, resist, thumb your nose at inf, thwart, withstand

**degenerate** adj corrupt, decadent, degraded, depraved, dissolute, fallen, immoral, low, unacceptable

**degenerate** v decline, deteriorate, fall off, get worse, go downhill, go from bad to worse, go to rack and ruin, go to seed inf, go to the dogs inf, sink, slide

**degrade** v cheapen, debase, demean, devalue, discredit, disgrace, dishonour, downgrade, lower, shame

**degrading** adj demeaning, embarrassing, humiliating, mortifying, shameful, undignified

**degree** n amount, extent, intensity, level, limit, point, stage, standard

**deign** v bother, condescend, consent, lower yourself, stoop

**deity** n divinity, god, goddess, holy being, object of worship, spirit

**dejected** adj cut up inf, depressed, despairing, despondent, disappointed, discouraged, disgruntled, dispirited, down, downhearted, down in the dumps inf, gloomy, miserable, out of sorts, sad, sick as a parrot inf, with a long face

**delay** n break, hiatus, hitch, hold-up, interruption, lull, postponement, setback, suspension, time-lag, wait

**delay** v adjourn, defer, hold, hold over, postpone, put off, put on ice, put on the back burner, shelve, table Am. 2 detain, hold up, make late, slow down

**delegate** n agent, emissary, envoy, go-between, messenger, representative, spokesman, spokesperson, spokeswoman

**delegate** v 1 (a task) assign, devolve, hand over, pass on, transfer. 2 (a person) appoint, authorize, choose, empower, mandate

**delegation** n contingent, delegates, deputation, group, mission, representatives

**delete** v blue-pencil, cancel, cut out, cross out, erase, get rid of, remove, rub out, strike out, take out, wipe out

**deliberate** adj 1 calculated, cold-blooded, conscious, intentional, knowing, preconceived, premeditated, wilful; *opp* accidental, unintentional. 2 careful, determined, measured, methodical, painstaking, patient, ponderous, resolute, slow; *opp* hasty

**deliberate** v 1 (think about) consider, evaluate, mull over, ponder, reflect,

review, ruminate, think over, think, weigh. 2 (discuss) consider, debate, discuss

**deliberately** adj 1 consciously, in cold-blood, intentionally, knowingly, on purpose, wilfully, wittingly; *opp* accidentally, unintentionally. 2 carefully, determinedly, methodically, painstakingly, patiently, resolutely, slowly; *opp* hastily

**delicacy** n 1 daintiness, elegance, fineness, flimsiness, fragility, intricacy. 2 (sensitivity) care, diplomacy, discretion, sensitivity, tact. 3 (a luxury food) luxury, titbit, treat

**delicate** adj 1 dainty, elegant, fine, flimsy, fragile, graceful, intricate. 2 (pastel) muted, pale, pastel, soft, subtle, understated. 3 (sensitive) awkward, difficult, diplomatic, discreet, sensitive, tactful, tricky

**delicious** adj appetizing, gorgeous, mouth-watering, scrumptious, tasty, tempting, yummy inf

**delight** n amusement, ecstasy, elation, enjoyment, enthusiasm, excitement, happiness, joy, jubilation, pleasure, thrill

**delight** v amuse, captivate, cheer, enchant, entertain, excite, please, thrill, tickle

**delighted** adj captivated, ecstatic, enchanted, glad, happy, in raptures, jubilant, on cloud nine inf, on top of the world, overjoyed, over the moon inf, pleased, thrilled, tickled pink inf

**delightful** adj agreeable, amusing, appealing, attractive, captivating, charming, cute, enchanting, engaging, enjoyable, entertaining, fascinating, lovely, nice, pleasant, pleasurable, thrilling, wonderful; *opp* unpleasant

**delinquent** *n* hoodlum, hooligan, rowdy, ruffian, tearaway, thug, tough, troublemaker, vandal, young offender

**delirious** *adj* **1** demented, deranged, distracted, feverish, hallucinating, incoherent, light-headed, rambling, raving. **2** carried away, ecstatic, euphoric, on a high *inf*, over the moon *inf*

**deliver** *v* **1** (deliver goods) bring, dispatch, hand over, produce, send, supply, take, transfer, transport. **2** (deliver a speech or verdict) announce, declare, give, make, pronounce, read. **3** (deliver a ball or punch) administer, aim, deal, direct, hit, hurl, inflict, send, throw

**delivery** *n* **1** carriage, conveyance, dispatch, distribution, shipment, transfer, transport, transportation. **2** batch, consignment, load, shipment

**deluge** *n* **1** downpour, flash flood, flood, inundation, overflowing, rainstorm, torrent. **2** barrage, flood, rush, spate; *opp* trickle

**delusion** *n* dream, error, false impression, fancy, fantasy, hallucination, illusion, mirage, misapprehension, misbelief, misconception, mistake, misunderstanding; *opp* reality

**demand** *n* **1** appeal, claim, clamour, entreaty, insistence, pressure, request, requisition. **2** challenge, inquiry, interrogation, question. **3** (the demands of sth) exigency, necessity, need, requirement. **4 in demand** all the rage *inf*, fashionable, in vogue, popular,

sought after, trendy *inf*; *opp* unpopular

**demand** *v* **1** (ask for sth) appeal, ask, call for, claim, clamour for, cry out for, insist on, lay claim to, make a claim for, press for, request, urge. **2** (ask a question) ask, challenge, inquire, interrogate, question. **3** call for, entail, involve, necessitate, need, require, take, want

**demanding** *adj* arduous, challenging, daunting, difficult, exacting, exhausting, gruelling, hard, taxing, tiring, tough, trying, wearing; *opp* undemanding

**demeanour** *n* air, appearance, bearing, behaviour, carriage, conduct, deportment, manner, mien

**democratic** *adj* autonomous, classless, egalitarian, free, of the people, popular, populist, representative, republican, self-governing; *opp* totalitarian

**demolish** *v* bulldoze, destroy, dismantle, flatten, knock down, level, pull down, raze, ruin, tear down, trash *sl*, wreck; *opp* build

**demon** *n* devil, evil spirit, fiend, goblin, imp, monster

**demonstrate** *v* **1** (demonstrate that sth is true) confirm, establish, indicate, prove, show, testify, validate, verify; *opp* disprove. **2** (demonstrate how to do sth) describe, explain, give a demonstration, give an idea of, illustrate, make clear, show how, teach. **3** lobby, march, parade, picket, protest, rally, sit in

**demonstration** *n* **1** (of the truth of sth) confirmation, evidence, illustration, proof, testimony, validation, verification. **2** (how to do sth) description, explanation, exposition, illustration, lesson, presentation.

**3** lobby, march, parade, picket, protest, rally, sit-in

**demonstrative** *adj* affectionate, effusive, emotional, expressive, gushing, lovey-dovey *inf*, loving, open, uninhibited, unreserved, unrestrained; *opp* reticent

**demoralize** *adj* break, crush, daunt, depress, discourage, dishearten, dispirit, unnerve, weaken; *opp* encourage

**demure** *adj* bashful, coy, diffident, modest, quiet, reserved, reticent, retiring, sedate, shy, sober, staid, unassuming; *opp* wild

**den** *n* **1** cave, cavern, haunt, hideaway, hideout, hiding place, hole, lair, shelter. **2** retreat, sanctum, sanctuary

**denial** *n* backpedalling, disavowal, disclaimer, retraction, taking back; *opp* admission, confession. **2** (not allowing sb to do sth) prohibition, rebuff, refusal, rejection, thumbs-down *inf*, veto; *opp* permission

**denote** *v* be the sign for, express, indicate, mark, mean, represent, show, signal, signify, stand for, symbolize

**denounce** *v* **1** attack, castigate, condemn, criticize, damn, decry, revile, stigmatize, vilify; *opp* praise. **2** accuse, betray, blame, incriminate, report

**dense** *adj* **1** close, compact, compressed, concentrated, condensed, heavy, impenetrable, lush, opaque, solid, substantial, thick; *opp* thin. **2** bird-brained, brainless, clueless, dim *inf*, dopey, dumb, ignorant, simple, slow, stupid, thick *inf*, thick as two short planks *inf*, unintelligent; *opp* clever

**dent** *n* chip, crater, depression, dimple, dip, hollow, indentation

**dent** *v* buckle, crumple, depress, knock in, press in, push in

**deny** *v* **1** refute, retract, take back; *opp* admit, confess. **2** (deny sb sth) give the thumbs down, prohibit, rebuff, refuse, reject, revoke, turn down, veto, withhold; *opp* allow

**depart** *v* abscond, be off *inf*, be on your way *inf*, clear off *inf*, disappear, emigrate, exit, go, go away, hit the road *inf*, leave, make tracks *inf*, migrate, move away, move off, quit, retire, retreat, scarper *inf*, split *inf*, take your leave, take yourself off, vanish, withdraw; *opp* arrive

**department** *n* **1** agency, branch, bureau, division, office, section, sector, subdivision, unit. **2** (sb's department) area, concern, domain, field, function, job, line, realm, responsibility, speciality, sphere. **3** canton, county, district, province, region, state, territory

**departure** *n* **1** disappearance, emigration, exit, exodus, going, leaving, migration, retreat, withdrawal; *opp* arrival. **2** (from the norm) deviation, difference, digression, divergence, shift, variation. **3** (a new departure) branching out, change, change of direction, innovation, novelty

**depend** *v* **1** bank on, be dependent on, cling to, count on, lean on, need, put your faith in, rely on, trust in, turn to. **2** be based on, be dependent on, be determined by, be subject to, hinge on, pivot on, rest on, revolve around

**dependable** *adj* consistent, faithful, reliable, reputable, responsible, sensible, stable, staunch, steadfast, trustworthy, trusty, unfailing; *opp* unreliable

**dependent** adj 1 conditional, contingent, controlled by, determined by, liable to, relative to, subject to. 2 (dependent children) defenceless, helpless, reliant, vulnerable, weak; *opp* independent

**depict** v describe, draw, illustrate, narrate, outline, paint, picture, portray, represent, reproduce, show, sketch

**deplete** v consume, cut, decrease, diminish, drain, empty, evacuate, exhaust, expend, impoverish, lessen, lower, reduce, use up

**deplorable** adj abominable, atrocious, awful, despicable, disgraceful, disreputable, dreadful, reprehensible, scandalous, shameful, shocking

**deplore** v abhor, censure, condemn, decry, denounce, deprecate, disapprove of, object to, regret; *opp* approve

**deport** v banish, exile, expatriate, expel, extradite, oust, remove, send abroad/overseas

**depose** v dethrone, dismiss, displace, get rid of, oust, overthrow, remove, topple, unseat

**deposit** n 1 advance payment, down-payment, initial payment, instalment, part-payment, retainer, security, stake. 2 accumulation, layer, sediment, silt, sludge

**depot** n 1 arsenal, base, depository, repository, store, storehouse, warehouse. 2 bus station, garage, railway station, terminal, terminus

**depraved** adj base, corrupt, debased, debauched, degenerate, dissolute, evil, immoral, indecent, lewd, licentious, obscene, perverted, profligate, sinful, unprincipled, vicious, vile, wicked

**depress** v dampen your spirits, discourage, dishearten, dismay, dispirit, sadden, upset, weigh down; *opp* encourage

**depressed** adj blue, dejected, despondent, discouraged, disheartened, dismayed, dispirited, down, down in the dumps, downcast, fed up, gloomy, glum, low, melancholy, miserable, moody, morose, sad, saddened, unhappy, upset; *opp* cheerful

**depressing** adj black, bleak, discouraging, disheartening, dismal, dispiriting, distressing, dreary, gloomy, hopeless, melancholy, miserable, sad, sombre; *opp* encouraging

**depression** n 1 dejection, desolation, despair, despondency, dolefulness, downheartedness, gloominess, hopelessness, low spirits, melancholy, misery, sadness, the blues, weariness; *opp* cheerfulness. 2 (economic) bad times, decline, hard times, recession, slump, stagnation; *opp* boom

**deprive** v deny, dispossess, rob, starve, strip, take away, withdraw

**deprived** adj bereft, destitute, disadvantaged, forlorn, in need, lacking, needy, poor; *opp* advantaged

**depth** n 1 deepness, drop, extent, measure, profundity. 2 (of forest) bowels, middle, midst; *opp* edge. 3 (of sea) bottom, deepest part; *opp* surface

**deputy** adj assistant, proxy, representative, second in command, sidekick, understudy, vice-chairman, vice-president

**derelict** adj abandoned, crumbling, decrepit, deserted, dilapidated, falling-down, neglected, ramshackle, ruined, run-down, tumbledown

**derisory** adj 1 (a derisory amount) contemptible, inadequate, insulting, laughable, ludicrous, outrageous, preposterous, ridiculous, tiny; *opp* fair. 2 (derisory remarks) contemptuous, derisive, jeering, mocking, scornful

**derive** v acquire, collect, draw, elicit, extract, gain, gather, get, glean, infer, lift, obtain, pick up, procure, receive

**derogatory** adj damaging, defamatory, disapproving, disparaging, injurious, insulting, offensive, uncomplimentary, unfavourable, unflattering; *opp* complimentary

**descend** v 1 come down, drop, fall, go down, move down, plummet, plunge, sink, tumble; *opp* rise. 2 (the path descends) go down, dip, incline, slant, slope; *opp* rise

**descent** n 1 dip, drop, fall, plunge, slump, swoop; *opp* rise. 2 (family background) ancestry, background, blood, extraction, genealogy, heredity, lineage, origin, parentage, stock

**describe** v define, depict, detail, explain, express, give a description, give an account, give details, illustrate, narrate, outline, portray, put into words, recount, relate, report, sketch, specify, tell

**description** n account, chronicle, depiction, explanation, illustration, narrative, outline, portrayal, report, representation, sketch

**descriptive** adj colourful, detailed, explanatory, expressive, graphic, illustrative, striking, vivid; *opp* bland

**desecrate** v abuse, contaminate, corrupt, debase, defile, degrade, dishonour, infect, pervert, pollute, profane, vandalize, violate; *opp* revere

**desert** n sand, waste, waste land, wilderness, wilds

**desert** v abandon, forsake, give up, jilt, leave, leave high and dry, leave in the lurch, maroon, strand, turn your back on, walk out on

**deserted** adj abandoned, derelict, desolate, empty, forlorn, godforsaken, isolated, lonely, neglected, solitary, uninhabited, unoccupied, vacant; *opp* bustling

**deserter** n defector, escapee, fugitive, outlaw, renegade, runaway, traitor, truant

**deserve** v be entitled to, be worthy of, earn, gain, have a claim to, have a right to, justify, merit, rate, warrant, win

**design** n 1 (a design of a building) blueprint, draft, drawing, model, outline, plan, sketch. 2 (pattern) arrangement, motif, pattern, shape

**design** v 1 conceive, create, devise, draft, draw, draw up, hatch, invent, originate, outline, plan, sketch, think up.
2 **designed for** aimed at, intended for, tailor-made for

**designer** n architect, creator, inventor, originator, stylist

**desirable** adj 1 advantageous, advisable, beneficial, in sb's interest, profitable, worthwhile; *opp* undesirable. 2 (of a person) alluring, attractive, beguiling, erotic, fetching, seductive, sexually attractive; *opp* undesirable

**desire** n ambition, appetite, ardour, aspiration, craving, hunger, inclination, longing, lust, need, passion, preference, urge, wish, yearning

**desire** v aspire to, covet, crave, dream of, fancy, hanker after, have a yen for, hope for, hunger for, itch for inf, long for, lust after, set your heart on, set your sights on, strive for, thirst for, want, wish for, yearn for

**desolate** adj 1 (of a place) bare, barren, bleak, cheerless, deserted, dreary, godforsaken, inhospitable, isolated, remote, solitary, uninhabited, waste, wild. 2 (of a person) abandoned, alone, dejected, depressed, despairing, despondent, downcast, forlorn, gloomy, grieving, inconsolable, lonely, melancholy, miserable, neglected, sad, unhappy, wretched; **opp** cheerful

**despair** n defeatism, dejection, depression, desperation, despondency, distress, gloom, hopelessness, misery, pessimism, wretchedness; **opp** enthusiasm, happiness, optimism

**despair** v give in, give up, lose heart, lose hope, quit, resign yourself, surrender, throw in the towel; **opp** hope

**desperate** adj 1 at your wits end, despairing, frantic, inconsolable, wretched. 2 (a desperate situation) acute, critical, dangerous, drastic, grave, hopeless, irretrievable, pressing, risky, serious, severe, urgent

**despicable** adj abominable, base, cheap, contemptible, detestable, disgraceful, disgusting, disreputable, hateful, ignominious, loathsome, low, mean, odious, reprehensible, shameful, sordid, vile, worthless, wretched

**despise** v abhor, be contemptuous of,

can't bear, can't stand, detest, disdain, hate, loathe, revile

**despondent** adj blue, dejected, discouraged, disheartened, dismayed, dispirited, down, down in the dumps, downcast, fed up, gloomy, glum, low, melancholy, miserable, unhappy, upset; **opp** cheerful

**despot** n authoritarian, autocrat, dictator, tyrant; **opp** democrat

**destination** n end of the line, journey's end, landing-place, port of call, resting-place, stop, terminus; **opp** starting point

**destined** adj 1 bound for, en route to, heading for. 2 bound to, certain, doomed, fated, intended, meant, pre-ordained, unavoidable

**destiny** n chance, doom, fate, fortune, lot, providence

**destitute** adj badly off inf, bankrupt, bereft, broke inf, disadvantaged, hard up inf, impoverished, in need, lacking, needy, on the breadline, penniless, poor, poverty-stricken, skint inf, without two pennies to rub together; **opp** rich

**destroy** v annihilate, break, break down, crush, decimate, demolish, devastate, dismantle, knock down, level, obliterate, ravage, raze, ruin, shatter, smash, spoil, trash sl, wipe out, wreck

**destruction** n annihilation, decimation, demolition, devastation, dismantling, downfall, end, extermination, havoc, obliteration, ruin, ruination, wrecking

**destructive** adj damaging, deadly, detrimental, devastating, fatal, harmful, hurtful, injurious, lethal, malignant, pernicious; **opp** beneficial

**detach** v cut loose, cut off, disconnect,

disengage, disentangle, free, isolate, loosen, part, pull off, release, remove, sever, take off, tear off, uncouple, undo, unfasten; *opp* attach

**detached** adj 1 disconnected, disengaged, disentangled, free, isolated, loose, released, removed, separate, severed, uncoupled, undone, unfastened; *opp* connected. 2 aloof, cool, disinterested, dispassionate, distant, formal, remote, removed, reserved, standoffish, unapproachable; *opp* friendly. 3 fair, impartial, neutral, objective, unbiased, uncommitted, uninvolved, unprejudiced; *opp* biased

**detail** n aspect, component, element, fact, factor, feature, intricacy, item, part, particular, point, respect, technicality

**detail** v 1 (detail sb to a place/job) allocate, appoint, assign, charge, commission, delegate, detach, send. 2 (detail in a list) catalogue, cite, enumerate, indicate, itemize, list, point out, set out, specify, spell out, relate

**detailed** adj all-inclusive, blow-by-blow, complete, comprehensive, elaborate, exact, exhaustive, full, intricate, in (minute) detail, specific, thorough; *opp* vague

**detain** v 1 (make sb late) delay, hinder, hold up, keep, slow down. 2 (in custody) arrest, confine, hold, impound, imprison, incarcerate, intern, lock up, restrain; *opp* release

**detect** v ascertain, catch, discern, discover, distinguish, find, find out, identify, note, notice, observe, recognize, scent, spot, uncover

**detective** n investigator, police officer,

private eye, sleuth *inf*

**detention** n arrest, confinement, custody, imprisonment, incarceration, internment, quarantine, restraint

**deter** v daunt, discourage, dissuade, frighten, inhibit, intimidate, prevent, put off, scare, stop, talk sb out of, warn off; *opp* encourage

**deteriorate** v crumble, decay, decline, decompose, degenerate, depreciate, disintegrate, fade, fall apart, get worse, go downhill *inf*, go to pot *inf*, go to the dogs *inf*, spoil, weaken, worsen; *opp* improve

**determination** n backbone, commitment, conviction, dedication, doggedness, drive, fortitude, grit *inf*, guts *inf*, perseverance, persistence, resolution, resolve, single-mindedness, staying power, tenacity, will-power

**determine** v 1 (determine what will happen) agree on, arbitrate, decide, decree, judge, ordain, regulate, settle. 2 (learn) ascertain, calculate, detect, discover, establish, find out, learn, work out. 3 (determine to do sth) choose, decide, elect, make up your mind, resolve

**determined** adj 1 (determined to do sth) bent on, fixed on, intent on, resolved, set on. 2 (a determined person) dedicated, dogged, firm, focused, insistent, persistent, purposeful, resolute, resolved, single-minded, steadfast, strong-willed, tenacious, tough, unwavering; *opp* irresolute

**deterrent** n check, curb, discouragement, disincentive, restraint, turn-off *inf*; *opp* encouragement

**detest** v abhor, abominate, despise, disdain, dislike, hate, loathe, scorn; *opp* love

**detract from** v devalue, diminish, lessen, lower, reduce, take away from; *opp* enhance

**detrimental** adj adverse, damaging, destructive, harmful, inimical, injurious, pernicious, prejudicial, unfavourable; *opp* advantageous, helpful

**devastate** v 1 demolish, destroy, flatten, lay waste, level, obliterate, ravage, raze, ruin, spoil, trash *sl*, wreck. 2 disappoint, horrify, overwhelm, shock, take aback, traumatize

**devastating** adj 1 deadly, destructive, ruinous, savage. 2 (devastating news) disappointing, horrifying, overwhelming, shocking, traumatic, upsetting

**develop** v 1 advance, enlarge, evolve, expand, flourish, grow, mature, progress, ripen, spread. 2 (develop an idea) amplify, augment, broaden, dilate on, elaborate, enlarge on, expand. 3 (develop a habit, illness) acquire, catch, contract, get, pick up

**development** n 1 advance, advancement, enlargement, evolution, expansion, flourishing, growth, increase, maturing, maturity, progress, progression, ripening, spreading. 2 change, circumstance, event, happening, incident, occurrence, outcome, result, situation, turn of events, upshot

**deviate** v branch off, deflect, depart, differ, digress, diverge, drift, err, part, stray, swerve, turn aside, vary, veer, wander

**device** n 1 apparatus, appliance, contraption, gadget, gizmo *inf*, implement, instrument, machine, tool, utensil, widget *inf*. 2 (a trick) artifice, con, expedient, fraud, gambit, machination, manoeuvre, plan, ploy, ruse, scheme, sleight, stratagem, stunt, subterfuge, tactic, trick, wile

**devil** n 1 Beelzebub, demon, Evil One, evil spirit, fiend, Lucifer, Old Nick *inf*, Prince of Darkness, Satan. 2 beast, brute, fiend, monster, ogre, savage, terror, thug, villain

**devious** adj artful, calculating, crafty, crooked, cunning, deceitful, dishonest, evasive, guileful, indirect, insidious, insincere, misleading, scheming, sly, sneaky, surreptitious, treacherous, tricky, underhand, wily; *opp* direct, ingenuous

**devise** v arrange, come up with, conceive, concoct, construct, contrive, cook up *inf*, create, design, dream up, engineer, form, formulate, frame, imagine, invent, plan, plot, prepare, scheme, think up, work out

**devoid** adj barren, bereft, deficient, denuded, destitute, empty, free from, lacking, missing, vacant, void, wanting, without

**devote** v allocate, allot, apply, assign, commit, consign, dedicate, give, pledge, reserve, set aside

**devoted** adj adoring, ardent, attentive, besotted, caring, committed, concerned, conscientious, constant, dedicated, devout, dutiful, enthusiastic, faithful, fond, loving, loyal, passionate, staunch, steadfast, true, unswerving, zealous

**devotion** n adherence, adoration,

allegiance, ardour, attentiveness, caring, commitment, concern, constancy, dedication, devotedness, enthusiasm, faithfulness, fervour, fidelity, fondness, love, loyalty, passion, staunchness, steadfastness, zeal

**devout** adj dutiful, God-fearing, godly, holy, orthodox, pious, prayerful, religious, reverent, righteous, zealous

**dexterous** adj adept, adroit, agile, clever, deft, expert, handy, neat, nimble, proficient, sharp, skilful, skilled; *opp* clumsy

**diagnose** v detect, determine, distinguish, identify, interpret, isolate, pinpoint, recognize

**diagnosis** n analysis, conclusion, explanation, interpretation, judgement, opinion, pronouncement, recommendation, verdict

**diagram** n chart, drawing, figure, illustration, outline, picture, representation, sketch, symbol, table

**dialect** n accent, argot, idiom, jargon, language, patois, regionalism, slang, speech, tongue, variety, vernacular

**dialogue** n 1 chat, communication, conference, conversation, discourse, discussion, exchange, interchange, talk. 2 (of a film) conversation, lines, script

**diary** n annals, appointment book, calendar, chronicle, engagement book, journal, log, memoir, personal organizer, record

**dictate** n 1 command, declare, decree, direct, enjoin, give orders, impose, lay down, ordain, order, prescribe. 2 read out, say, speak, recite, transmit, utter

**dictator** n absolute ruler, autocrat,

despot, oppressor, tyrant

**die** v 1 be no more, bite the dust *inf*, cease to exist, croak *sl*, decease, depart, expire, kick the bucket *inf*, lose your life, meet your end, pass away, pass on, perish, snuff it *inf*. 2 come to an end, decay, decline, decrease, disappear, dwindle, ebb, end, fade, lapse, pass, sink, vanish, wane, wilt, wither. 3 (of a machine) break down, come to a halt, fail, fizzle out, halt, lose power, peter out, run down, stop

**diet** n alimentation, consumption, fare, food, intake, nourishment, nutrition, provisions, rations, regime, regimen, subsistence, viands, victuals

**diet** v abstain, cut down, fast, go on a diet, lose weight, reduce, slim

**differ** v 1 be different, be dissimilar, be distinct, be unlike, contrast, deviate, diverge, vary. 2 argue, be at odds; clash, conflict, contradict, debate, disagree, dispute, dissent, diverge, object, oppose, quarrel, quibble, take issue; *opp* agree

**difference** n 1 contrast, discrepancy, disparity, dissimilarity, distinction, divergence, incongruity, nonconformity, peculiarity, singularity, variation, variety; *opp* similarity. 2 altercation, argument, clash, conflict, controversy, debate, difference of opinion, disagreement, dispute, objection, quarrel, quibble, tiff, wrangle; *opp* agreement

**different** adj 1 assorted, clashing, contradictory, contrasting, contrastive, disparate, dissimilar, distinct, diverging, diverse, incongruous, inconsistent, miscellaneous, mixed, other, peculiar, separate, singular, various, varying, unlike; **opp** similar. **2** abnormal, bizarre, distinctive, eccentric, interesting, novel, odd, original, peculiar, singular, special, strange, striking, uncommon, unconventional, unique, unorthodox, unusual, weird; **opp** ordinary

**differentiate** v contrast, discern, discriminate, distinguish, identify, make a distinction, mark off, separate, sort, tell apart, tell the difference

**difficult** adj **1** arduous, burdensome, challenging, complex, complicated, demanding, daunting, exacting, formidable, gruelling, hard, laborious, onerous, painful, problematic, strenuous, taxing, thorny, tough, tricky, wearisome; **opp** easy. **2** (of a person) argumentative, awkward, contrary, demanding, fastidious, fractious, fussy, intractable, obstreperous, perverse, quarrelsome, stroppy *inf*, tiresome, troublesome, trying, unco-operative, unmanageable; **opp** co-operative

**difficulty** n **1** adversity, arduousness, awkwardness, challenge, hardship, laboriousness, labour, ordeal, pain, problem, strain, struggle, toughness, tribulation. **2** dilemma, distress, fix *inf*, jam *inf*, mess, pickle *inf*, plight, predicament, quandary, scrape *inf*, spot *inf*, straits

**diffident** adj apprehensive, backward, bashful, constrained, coy, doubtful, fearful, hesitant, humble, inhibited, insecure, introverted, meek, modest, nervous, shy, reluctant, reserved, retiring, self-conscious, self-effacing, sheepish, shrinking, tentative, timid,

timorous, unassertive, unassuming, unconfident, unsure, withdrawn; **opp** brash

**dig** v **1** burrow, delve, excavate, fork, gouge, grub, harrow, hoe, hollow, mine, penetrate, pierce, plough, quarry, scoop, till, tunnel, turn over. **2** (dig for information) delve, go into, investigate, probe, research, search. **3** (dig sb in the ribs) jab, nudge, poke, prod, punch, push, shove

**digest** v **1** absorb, assimilate, break down, consume, dissolve, eat, incorporate, take in. **2** (digest information) absorb, assimilate, comprehend, consider, contemplate, grasp, master, mull over, ruminate, ponder, study, take in, understand

**dignified** adj ceremonious, decorous, distinguished, elegant, formal, graceful, gracious, grave, honourable, imposing, impressive, lofty, noble, proper, proud, regal, solemn, stately, tasteful; **opp** undignified

**dignitary** n celebrity, luminary, notability, notable, official, personage, public figure, VIP, worthy

**dignity** n ceremony, class, decorum, distinction, elegance, formality, grace, grandeur, gravitas, gravity, hauteur, honour, loftiness, majesty, nobility, pride, propriety, solemnity, stateliness, taste

**digress** v depart, deviate, diverge, drift, get off the subject, get side-tracked, go off at a tangent, lose your thread, meander, ramble, stray, veer, wander

**digression** n aside, departure, detour, deviation, divergence, diversion, drifting, footnote, meander, rambling, straying, wandering

**dilapidated** adj battered, broken-down, crumbling, decaying, decrepit, derelict, falling apart, falling down, in disrepair, in ruins, neglected, peeling, ramshackle, rickety, ruined, run-down, shabby, tumbledown, uncared-for, worn out

**dilemma** n catch-22, difficulty, fix inf, impasse, jam inf, perplexity, pickle inf, plight, predicament, problem, puzzle, quandary, scrape inf, spot inf, straits, vicious circle

**diligent** adj assiduous, attentive, busy, careful, conscientious, dutiful, earnest, hard-working, indefatigable, industrious, meticulous, painstaking, patient, persevering, persistent, punctilious, scrupulous, sedulous, studious, thorough, tireless; *opp* careless, slapdash

**dilute** v adulterate, cut inf, mix, thin, water down, weaken; *opp* concentrate

**dim** adj 1 bleary, blurred, blurry, cloudy, dark, dingy, dull, dusky, faint, foggy, fuzzy, gloomy, hazy, indistinct, misty, murky, muted, obscure, obscured, shadowy, unclear, vague; *opp* bright. 2 dense, dozy inf, dull, dull-witted, dumb inf, obtuse, slow, stupid, thick inf; *opp* bright

**dim** v blur, cloud, darken, dull, fade, fog, lower, mask, obscure, shade, shadow, shroud, turn down

**dimensions** n amplitude, area, bulk, capacity, extent, greatness, largeness, magnitude, measurements, proportions, range, scale, scope, size, volume

**diminish** v abate, contract, curtail, cut, decline, decrease, dwindle, ebb, lessen,

lower, peter out, recede, reduce, shrink, subside, wane, weaken

**dine** v banquet, eat, feast, feed, have dinner, sup

**dingy** adj cheerless, dark, depressing, dim, dirty, dismal, drab, dreary, dull, faded, gloomy, grimy, murky, run-down, seedy, shabby, soiled, sombre, threadbare, worn; *opp* bright

**dinner** n banquet, feast, meal, repast, spread inf, supper

**dip** n 1 bathe, ducking, dunking, immersion, plunge, rinse, soak, soaking, sousing, submersion, swim. 2 concavity, declivity, dent, depression, hole, hollow, incline, slope, valley. 3 (a dip in amount) decline, dive, drop, fall, lowering, plunge, slip, slump

**dip** v 1 bathe, douse, drench, duck, dunk, immerse, lower, plunge, rinse, soak, souse, steep, submerge. 2 decline, descend, dive, drop, fall, go down, lower, plunge, sag, slip, slump

**diplomacy** n adroitness, delicacy, discretion, finesse, sensitivity, skill, subtlety, tact

**diplomat** n ambassador, conciliator, emissary, envoy, go-between, intermediary, mediator, moderator, negotiator, peace-maker, politician, representative, statesman

**diplomatic** adj adept, adroit, careful, considerate, delicate, discreet, judicious, politic, prudent, sensitive, subtle, tactful

**dire** adj alarming, appalling, atrocious, awful, calamitous, catastrophic, chronic, disastrous, dreadful, frightful, ghastly, grievous, horrendous, horrible, horrifying, shocking, terrible, unspeakable, woeful

**direct** *adj* **1** immediate, non-stop, shortest, straight, through, unbroken, uninterrupted; *opp* indirect. **2** blunt, candid, categorical, clear, explicit, forthright, frank, honest, open, outspoken, plain, plain-spoken, straight, straightforward, to the point, unambiguous, unequivocal, upfront; *opp* indirect. **3** (direct opposite) absolute, complete, diametrical, downright, exact, thorough, total, utter

**direct** *v* **1** administer, be in charge of, conduct, control, govern, guide, handle, head, manage, orchestrate, oversee, preside, regulate, run, superintend, supervise. **2** bid, command, dictate, enjoin, instruct, order, require, tell. **3** (direct sb to a place) conduct, escort, give directions, guide, indicate, lead, navigate, pilot, point, show the way, steer, usher

**direction** *n* **1** bearing, course, line, orientation, path, road, route, tack, track, way. **2** administration, command, control, government, guidance, handling, leadership, management, orchestration, order, overseeing, regulation, running, supervision. **3** bidding, command, decree, edict, injunction, instruction, order, ruling

**directions** *n* briefing, guidance, guide, guidelines, indications, instructions, map, plan, recommendations

**director** *n* administrator, boss, chair, chairman, chairwoman, chief, conductor, controller, executive, governor, head, manager, managing director, organizer, overseer, president,

principal, regulator, supervisor

**dirt** *n* dust, earth, filth, gunge, gunk, impurity, mire, muck, mud, ordure, pollution, slime, smudge, spot, stain, soil, tarnish

**dirty** *adj* **1** contaminated, dusty, filthy, foul, grimy, grotty *inf*, grubby, gungy *inf*, gunky *inf*, impure, marked, messy, mucky *inf*, muddy, nasty, polluted, smudged, soiled, spotted, stained, sticky, sullied, tainted, tarnished, unclean; *opp* clean. **2** corrupt, crooked, deceitful, dishonest, dishonourable, fraudulent, illegal, treacherous, unfair, unscrupulous, unsporting; *opp* honest. **3** bawdy, blue, coarse, improper, indecent, lascivious, lewd, obscene, offensive, pornographic, ribald, risqué, rude, salacious, sleazy *inf*, smutty, suggestive, vulgar; *opp* clean

**disability** *n* affliction, ailment, defect, disadvantage, disorder, handicap, impairment, incapacity, infirmity, malady

**disabled** *adj* afflicted, crippled, debilitated, disadvantaged, handicapped, immobilized, impaired, incapacitated, infirm, lame, maimed, mutilated, paralysed, weak, weakened; *opp* able-bodied

**disadvantage** *n* defect, disability, downside, drawback, fault, flaw, handicap, hindrance, hitch, impediment, inconvenience, minus, obstacle, problem, snag, weakness; *opp* advantage

**disagree** *v* argue, bicker, clash, conflict, contend, contest, contradict, counter, debate, differ, discuss, dispute, dissent, diverge, fall out, fight, object, oppose, quarrel, question, quibble, squabble, take issue, wrangle; *opp* agree

**disagreeable** *adj* bad-tempered, churlish, cross, crotchety, difficult, horrible, ill-natured, irritable, nasty, objectionable, obnoxious, peevish, rude, surly, unfriendly, ungracious, unpleasant; *opp* agreeable

**disagreement** *n* altercation, argument, clash, conflict, contention, contradiction, controversy, debate, difference, discord, discussion, dispute, dissent, divergence, division, falling out, fight, objection, opposition, quarrel, row, squabble, strife, tiff, wrangle; *opp* agreement

**disallow** *v* ban, bar, boycott, cancel, deny, dismiss, embargo, forbid, prohibit, proscribe, refuse, reject, repudiate, veto; *opp* allow

**disappear** *v* 1 become invisible, be lost to view, dematerialize, dissolve, evaporate, fade, flee, melt away, recede, vanish, vaporize, wane; *opp* appear. 2 become extinct, cease, come to an end, die, die out, end, evaporate, expire, go, pass away, perish, stop, vanish; *opp* appear

**disappearance** *n* dissolving, ebbing, ending, evaporation, fading, fleeing, going, invisibility, melting, passing, receding, vanishing; *opp* appearance

**disappoint** *v* depress, disenchant, dishearten, disillusion, dismay, dispirit, dissatisfy, fail, frustrate, let down, sadden, thwart, upset; *opp* satisfy

**disappointed** *adj* cast down, depressed, despondent, discouraged, disenchanted, disheartened, disillusioned, dismayed, dispirited, dissatisfied, downcast,

frustrated, let down, sad, saddened, thwarted; *opp* satisfied

**disappointing** *adj* depressing, discouraging, disenchanting, disheartening, disillusioning, dismaying, dispiriting, dissatisfying, frustrating, inadequate, insufficient, paltry, pathetic, unsatisfactory, upsetting; *opp* encouraging, satisfying

**disappointment** *n* 1 depression, discouragement, disenchantment, disillusionment, dismay, dissatisfaction, frustration, regret, sadness; *opp* satisfaction. 2 blow, disaster, failure, fiasco, let-down, setback; *opp* success

**disapprove** *v* be against, censure, condemn, criticize, deplore, deprecate, dislike, frown on, look askance at, not take kindly to, object to, reject, take a dim view, take exception; *opp* approve

**disaster** *n* accident, act of God, adversity, blow, calamity, cataclysm, catastrophe, misadventure, mischance, misfortune, mishap, reverse, ruin, tragedy, trouble

**disastrous** *adj* adverse, appalling, awful, calamitous, cataclysmic, catastrophic, destructive, devastating, dire, dreadful, fatal, fateful, ill-fated, ill-starred, ruinous, terrible, tragic, unfortunate, unlucky

**discard** *v* abandon, cast aside, chuck out *inf*, dispense with, dispose of, ditch *inf*, drop, dump *inf*, get rid of, jettison, junk *inf*, reject, repudiate, scrap, shed, sling out *inf*, throw away, throw out

**discharge** *n* 1 emission, excretion, matter, pus, secretion. 2 dismissal, expulsion, firing, redundancy, removal, sacking. 3 acquittal, clearance, exoneration, freeing, liberation, pardon, release

**discharge** v 1 belch, eject, emit, excrete, exude, give off, produce, release, secrete, send out, spew. 2 dismiss, expel, fire, let go, make redundant, relieve, remove, sack. 3 absolve, acquit, clear, exonerate, free, let go, liberate, pardon, release, set free. 4 detonate, fire, let off, shoot

**disciple** n acolyte, adherent, apostle, believer, convert, devotee, follower, partisan, proselyte, pupil, supporter

**discipline** n 1 chastisement, control, correction, drilling, exercise, punishment, regime, regulation, rules, strictness, training. 2 control, organization, restraint, self-control, self-discipline, self-restraint, strength, will-power

**discipline** v chastise, control, correct, penalize, punish, rebuke, regulate, reprimand, train

**disclose** v admit, bring to light, confess, divulge, expose, impart, let slip, make known, make public, reveal, tell, unveil

**discomfort** n ache, disquiet, distress, hardship, hurt, inconvenience, irritation, nuisance, pain, pang, soreness, trouble, twinge, uneasiness, vexation; *opp* comfort

**disconcerting** adj alarming, baffling, bewildering, dismaying, distracting, disturbing, off-putting, perplexing, perturbing, puzzling, troubling, unnerving, unsettling, upsetting, worrying; *opp* reassuring

**disconnect** v break off, cut off, detach, disengage, divide, part, separate, sever, uncouple, undo, unplug

**discontented** adj annoyed, disaffected, disgruntled, displeased, dissatisfied, fed up, fretful, impatient, restless, troubled, unfulfilled, unhappy, unsatisfied, unsettled; *opp* contented

**discontinue** v abandon, axe inf, break off, cancel, cease, cut, drop, end, give up, halt, interrupt, put an end to, quit, stop, suspend, terminate; *opp* continue

**discord** n 1 arguing, argument, clashing, conflict, contention, controversy, difference, disagreement, disharmony, dispute, dissent, disunity, division, falling-out, friction, hostility, opposition, quarrelling, rowing, rupture, strife, variance, wrangling; *opp* agreement. 2 cacophony, din, dissonance, harshness, jangle, jarring, racket; *opp* harmony

**discount** v 1 disbelieve, disregard, gloss over, ignore, overlook, pass over, pay no attention to, reject, take no notice of. 2 cut, lower, mark down, reduce, take off, slash

**discourage** v 1 abash, cast down, dampen, daunt, demoralize, depress, deter, dishearten, dismay, dissuade, intimidate, put off, unnerve; *opp* encourage. 2 advise against, caution against, disapprove, dissuade, deter, frown on, oppose, put off, repress, take a dim view, urge against; *opp* encourage

**discouraged** adj abashed, cast down, cowed, crestfallen, dashed, daunted, dejected, demoralized, depressed, despondent, deterred, disheartened, dismayed, dispirited, downhearted, intimidated, put off, unnerved; *opp* encouraged

**discouragement** n 1 dejection, demoralization, depression, despondency, dismay, downheartedness; *opp* encouragement. 2 barrier, check, constraint, curb, damper, deterrent, disincentive, hindrance, impediment, obstacle, restriction; *opp* encouragement

**discouraging** adj daunting, demoralizing, depressing, disheartening, dismaying, dispiriting, inauspicious, intimidating, off-putting, unnerving, worrying; *opp* encouraging

**discourse** n 1 chat, communication, conversation, dialogue, discussion, exchange, interchange, speech, talk. 2 address, dissertation, essay, lecture, oration, paper, speech, study, treatise

**discourse** v 1 chat, communicate, confer, converse, debate, discuss, have a conversation, speak, talk. 2 declaim, deliver a paper, expatiate, give a talk, hold forth, lecture, make a speech, orate, speak

**discover** v 1 come across, come upon, dig up, find, light on, locate, track down, turn up, uncover, unearth. 2 ascertain, come to know, detect, determine, disclose, expose, find out, identify, learn, perceive, realize, recognize, see, spot, suss out *inf*, uncover

**discovery** n 1 detection, digging up, disclosure, exposing, finding, identification, locating, location, recognition, spotting, tracking down, uncovering, unearthing. 2 breakthrough, coup, find, innovation, invention

**discredit** v blacken sb's name, cast doubt on, decry, denigrate, disparage, rubbish, show up

**discreet** adj careful, circumspect, diplomatic, judicious, polite, politic, prudent, tactful, tasteful; *opp* indiscreet

**discrepancy** n anomaly, contradiction, difference, disparity, error, inconsistency, inequality, miscalculation, mismatch, mistake, shortfall

**discretion** n care, circumspection, diplomacy, politeness, prudence, tact, tactfulness

**discriminate** v 1 **discriminate against** be biased against, be intolerant of, be prejudiced against, pick on, segregate, single out, treat unfairly, victimize. 2 choose, differentiate, distinguish, draw a distinction, judge, make a distinction, select

**discriminating** adj choosy, cultivated, discerning, fastidious, refined, selective, tasteful

**discrimination** n 1 ageism, apartheid, bias, bigotry, heterosexism, intolerance, male chauvinism, prejudice, racism, segregation, sexism, victimization. 2 culture, discernment, fastidiousness, judgement, refinement, sensitivity, taste

**discuss** v argue, confer, consider, converse, debate, deliberate, put your heads together, talk, talk about, talk over, weigh up

**discussion** n argument, conference, conversation, debate, deliberation, dialogue, pow-wow *inf*, talk

**disdainful** adj aloof, contemptuous, disparaging, disrespectful, proud, scornful, sneering, superior

**disease** n ailment, bug *inf*, complaint, disorder, illness, infection, malady, sickness, syndrome, virus

**diseased** adj 1 ailing, festering, infected, ill, septic, sick, swollen, unhealthy; *opp* healthy. 2 (with a particular disease) arthritic, asthmatic, cancerous, gangrenous, leprous, rabid

**disembark** v alight, arrive, get off, get out, go ashore, land; *opp* embark

**disentangle** v 1 disengage, extricate, loose, undo, unravel, untangle, untie, unwind; *opp* entangle. 2 ascertain, decipher, disembroil, resolve, solve, sort out, straighten out, understand

**disgrace** n abasement, abjection, discredit, dishonour, disrepute, embarrassment, humiliation, rejection, shame, stigma

**disgrace** v 1 discredit, drag through the mud, dishonour, embarrass, humiliate, shame, stigmatize. 2 **disgrace yourself** abase yourself, blot your copy-book, degrade yourself, demean yourself, prostitute yourself, stoop to

**disgraceful** v 1 (morally) abject, contemptible, corrupt, degrading, disgusting, dishonourable, ignominious, outrageous, shameful. 2 (very bad) appalling, awful, dreadful, pathetic, shocking, terrible

**disguise** n 1 camouflage, concealment, costume, cover, false identity, fancy dress, mask. 2 **in disguise** disguised, incognito, under cover

**disguise** v 1 camouflage, cloak, cover, cover up, conceal, dissemble, fake, falsify, hide, mask. 2 **disguise yourself as** dress up as, impersonate, masquerade as

**disgust** n contempt, dislike, distaste, loathing, nausea, offence, outrage, repugnance, repulsion, revulsion

**disgust** v appal, make sick, nauseate, offend, outrage, put off, repel, revolt, sicken

**disgusting** adj appalling, awful, disgraceful, distasteful, gross, horrible, nauseating, obscene, offensive, offputting, outrageous, repugnant, repellent, repulsive, revolting, sickening, ugly, unpleasant, unsavoury

**dish** n 1 (container) bowl, plate, platter, serving dish, vessel. 2 (food) course, creation, delicacy, meal, recipe, speciality

**dishearten** v dampen sb's spirits, deflate, deject, depress, demoralize, deter, discourage, dismay, put off, sadden; *opp* hearten

**dishevelled** adj bedraggled, messy, ruffled, slovenly, tousled, unkempt, untidy

**dishonest** adj cheating, criminal, crooked, deceitful, dishonourable, duplicitous, economical with the truth *inf*, lying, unscrupulous, untrustworthy; *opp* honest

**dishonesty** n cheating, criminality, deceit, deception, duplicity, lies, unscrupulousness

**disillusioned** adj alienated, browned off *inf*, cynical, disabused, disaffected, disappointed, disenchanted, fed up

**disinfect** v bathe, clean, clean out, cleanse, sterilize

**disintegrate** v break down, collapse, decay, fall apart, fall to pieces, implode

**disinterested** adj above the fray, aloof, detached, dispassionate, impartial, objective, unbiased, unselfish, with no axe to grind

**dislike** n antipathy, aversion, detestation, distaste, hate, hatred, hostility; **opp** liking

**dislike** v be disgusted by, be hostile to, be put off by, detest, hate, have an aversion to; **opp** like

**disloyal** adj disobedient, false, mutinous, perfidious, traitorous, treacherous, seditious, unfaithful; **opp** faithful, loyal

**dismal** adj **1** bleak, cheerless, demoralizing, depressing, disheartening, dispiriting, gloomy, miserable, sad. **2** (of weather) appalling, awful, dark, dreadful, gloomy, murky, rainy, miserable, shocking, terrible, unpleasant, wet, wretched; **opp** lovely, wonderful

**dismantle** v disassemble, strip down, take apart, take down, take to pieces

**dismay** n annoyance, disappointment, consternation, displeasure, frustration, shock

**dismay** v annoy, disconcert, dishearten, disappoint, displease, frustrate, shatter, sadden, shock, upset

**dismiss** v **1** (from sb's presence) banish, cast out, chuck out inf, exclude, excuse, send away, send out, throw out. **2** (from a job) down-size, fire, get rid of, kick out inf, remove, sack. **3** (dismiss an idea) brush aside, brush off, discount, disregard, forget about, ignore, reject, ridicule

**disobedient** adj cheeky, defiant, disrespectful, dissenting, dissident, disloyal, insubordinate, mutinous, naughty, unruly; **opp** obedient

**disobey** v **1** (disobey a rule) break, contravene, defy, disregard, flout,

infringe, transgress; **opp** obey. **2** (act disobediently) answer back, mutiny, rebel, refuse, resist, revolt, stand firm, stand up to; **opp** obey

**disorder** n **1** chaos, clutter, disarray, jumble, muddle, untidiness; **opp** order. **2** (violent) anarchy, chaos, civil disobedience, discontent, insurrection, rioting, trouble, turbulence, turmoil, unrest, unruliness, violence; **opp** order. **3** (medical) ailment, complaint, disease, dysfunction tech, illness, malady, sickness, syndrome

**disorganized** adj **1** anarchic, chaotic, disorderly, in disarray, jumbled, random, uncontrolled, unplanned, unstructured, unsystematic, untidy; **opp** organized. **2** (of a person) aimless, in disarray, illogical, muddled, undisciplined, unsystematic; **opp** organized

**disown** v deny, disclaim, dissociate yourself from, distance yourself from, reject, repudiate

**disparaging** adj belittling, contemptuous, critical, disapproving, disdainful, insulting, scornful

**dispassionate** adj calm, cool, detached, disinterested, distant, unbiased, unsentimental

**dispatch** n consignment, message, missive, package, parcel, report

**dispatch** v **1** distribute, forward, mail Am, post, send, send off, send out. **2** (dispatch a task) conclude, deal with, dispose of, expedite, finish off, make short work of, polish off inf

**dispel** v clear up, deny, put an end to, put a stop to, scotch

**dispense** v **1** distribute, disseminate, give,

give out, hand out, impart, prescribe, provide, vend. **2 dispense with** cancel, do without, eliminate, forget, forget about, get rid of, go without, not bother with, remove, scrap

**disperse** v 1 (of a crowd) break up, separate, scatter, leave, melt away, spread out. 2 banish, drive away, scatter

**displace** v 1 (move out of position) disturb, misplace, move, remove, shift, transpose. 2 (cause sb to lose their position) dislodge, drive out, force out, oust, replace, supplant, take the place of

**display** n array, demonstration, exhibition, exposure, presentation, show

**display** v 1 (display goods) arrange, exhibit, present, put on view, show, show off. 2 (display an emotion) betray, reveal, show

**displease** v anger, annoy, disappoint, frustrate, irk, irritate, offend, upset; *opp* please

**displeasure** n anger, annoyance, disappointment, dissatisfaction, frustration, indignation, irritation, offence; *opp* pleasure

**disposable** adj 1 biodegradable, expendable, non-returnable, paper, plastic, temporary, throwaway. 2 (disposable income) after tax, available, net, take-home, to spend

**disposal** n 1 clearance, destruction, dumping, elimination, removal, scrapping. **2 at your disposal** accessible, at your discretion, available, free, handy, obtainable, to hand

**dispose of** v chuck away *inf*, dispense with, dump, eliminate, finish off, get rid of, polish off *inf*, remove,

scrap, throw away

**disprove** v demolish, explode, invalidate, prove wrong, refute; *opp* prove

**dispute** n 1 altercation, argument, battle, conflict, controversy, difference of opinion, differences, disagreement, feud, fight, friction, quarrel, row. 2 (between workers and management) go-slow, grievance, industrial action, lock-out, strike, work-to-rule. **3 beyond dispute** crystal clear, definite, incontrovertible, unarguable, undisputed

**dispute** v 1 contest, deny, reject, oppose, question, wrangle over. 2 (dispute the leadership) battle for, challenge for, compete for, contend for, contest, fight over, vie for

**disqualify** v ban, bar, debar, disallow, exclude, make ineligible, rule out

**disregard** v brush aside, discount, dismiss, ignore, reject, take no notice of

**disreputable** adj crooked, dishonest, dishonourable, dubious, louche, of ill repute, shady, unscrupulous

**disrespect** n cheek, contempt, disdain, disobedience, impertinence, impudence, insolence, insults, irreverence, insubordination, scorn; *opp* respect

**disrespectful** adj cheeky, contemptuous, disdainful, disobedient, impertinent, impolite, impudent, insolent, insubordinate, insulting, irreverent, scornful; *opp* respectful

**disrupt** v disturb, impede, interfere with, interrupt, sabotage, throw into disarray, upset

**disruptive** adj badly behaved, distracting, ill-behaved, interfering, naughty, troublesome, unruly

**dissatisfied** *adj* angry, annoyed, displeased, frustrated, irked, irritated, unfulfilled, unsatisfied; *opp* satisfied

**dissent** *n* argument, defiance, disagreement, discontent, disobedience, dissension, dissidence, non-conformism, opposition; *opp* agreement

**dissent** *v* break ranks, contest, defy, disagree with, disobey, dissociate yourself from, distance yourself from, oppose, reject, speak out against

**dissident** *n* critic, dissenter, non-conformist, opponent, political prisoner, prisoner of conscience

**dissipate** *v* **1** blow away, break up, disappear, disperse, evaporate, melt away, scatter, vanish. **2** (use wastefully) consume, expend, fritter, misspend, spend, squander, use up, waste

**dissociate** *v* **dissociate yourself from** break away from, break ranks with, deny, disclaim, dissent from, disown, distance yourself from, repudiate, reject, say no to, sever your connections with

**dissolve** *v* **1** (add to liquid) dilute, melt, mix, mix in, stir in. **2** (of feelings) crumble, disappear, dissipate, evaporate, fade, fade away, melt away, vanish. **3** (dissolve a partnership, an organization) annul, break up, disband, end, terminate, wind up

**dissuade** *v* deter, discourage, persuade against, prevent, put off, stop, talk sb out of

**distance** *n* **1** interval, length, long way, remoteness, space, way. **2 in the distance** a long way away, distantly, far away, far off, just in sight, just in view, on the horizon, yonder

**distant** *adj* **1** faint, far, faraway, far-off, remote, yonder. **2** (of a person) aloof, cold, day-dreaming, detached, haughty, other-worldly, preoccupied, private, superior, unfriendly

**distaste** *n* antipathy, aversion, disgust, disapproval, dislike, displeasure, repugnance

**distasteful** *adj* disgusting, gross, in bad taste, in poor taste, obscene, repugnant, repellent, unpleasant, unsavoury

**distinct** *adj* **1** (that can be noticed) audible, clear, clear as a bell, definite, discernible, noticeable, perceptible, tangible, unmistakable, visible; *opp* indistinct. **2** (distinct from each other) contrasting, different, discrete, independent, individual, separate, unconnected

**distinction** *n* **1** contrast, difference, differentiation, dissimilarity, dividing line, division, separation. **2** (personal quality) eminence, excellence, prestige, refinement, standing. **3** award, commendation, credit, decoration, honour

**distinctive** *adj* characteristic, distinguishing, own, peculiar, specific, tell-tale

**distinguish** *v* **1** discern, hear, make out, notice, perceive, see. **2** (distinguish between two things) differentiate, discriminate, draw a distinction, make a distinction, tell apart, tell the difference

**distinguished** *adj* award-winning, celebrated, eminent, experienced, favoured, honoured, respected

**distort** *v* bend out of shape, change, deform, falsify, misrepresent, pervert, twist, warp

**distract** v beguile, confuse, disturb, disturb sb's concentration, divert sb's attention, put off, sidetrack

**distracted** adj confused, day-dreaming, inattentive, other-worldly, preoccupied, wandering

**distraction** n 1 confusion, day-dreaming, inattention, lack of concentration, other-worldliness. 2 (sth which distracts) amusement, digression, disturbance, diversion, interruption, irruption, sideshow. 3 to distraction bonkers inf, crazy, frantic, insane, mad, nuts inf, round the bend inf, round the twist inf, up the wall inf

**distress** n agony, anguish, anxiety, grief, misery, pain, sadness, suffering, torment, trauma, trouble, worry

**distress** v afflict, aggrieve, grieve, perturb, traumatize, trouble, upset, worry

**distressed** adj anguished, anxious, distraught, grieving, in distress, in pain, jumpy, nervous, panicky, suffering, traumatized, troubled, upset, worried

**distressing** adj difficult, disturbing, painful, sad, stressful, traumatic, troubling, trying, upsetting, worrisome, worrying

**distribute** v allocate, allot, deal, deal out, deliver, dispense, dispatch, disseminate, divide up, give out, hand out, issue, send out, share out

**distribution** n allocation, delivery, dispatch, dissemination, division, transport

**district** n area, borough, constituency, division, locality, neighbourhood, part of town, postal district, quarter, ward

**distrust** v be sceptical of, be suspicious of, be wary of, disbelieve, doubt, have doubts about, have no confidence in, have no faith in, mistrust, suspect; opp trust

**disturb** v 1 bother, butt in, distract, hassle inf, harass, hinder, interrupt, intrude, pester; opp leave alone. 2 (upset) agitate, alarm, concern, distress, fluster, perturb, shake, trouble, unnerve, unsettle, upset, worry; opp reassure. 3 (disturb sth) interfere with, jumble up, mess about inf, mix up, move, muddle, rearrange, throw into confusion, touch; opp leave alone

**disturbance** n agitation, confusion, disorder, fracas, interruption, intrusion, riot, upheaval, uproar

**disturbed** adj 1 (a disturbed child) neurotic, psychotic, troubled, unbalanced, upset. 2 (feeling disturbed) alarmed, concerned, distracted, distraught, troubled, uneasy, worried

**disturbing** adj alarming, distressing, frightening, harrowing, troubling, unsettling, upsetting, worrying; opp reassuring

**disused** adj abandoned, dead, discarded, idle, neglected, unused

**ditch** n channel, drain, dike, gully, gutter, moat, trench

**ditch** v abandon, chuck inf, discard, dispose of, drop, dump inf, get rid of, junk inf, scrap, throw out

**dive** v 1 (dive into water) go under, jump, leap, plunge. 2 (dive behind a hedge) dart, disappear, dodge, drop, duck. 3 (dive through the air) fall, nosedive, plummet, swoop

**diverse** *adj* assorted, different, differing, dissimilar, distinct, miscellaneous, mixed, separate, several, sundry, varied, various

**diversify** *v* branch out, broaden, change, develop, expand, mix, spread out, vary

**diversion** *n* **1** amusement, entertainment, fun, game, hobby, interest, play, recreation, relaxation, sport. **2** alternative route, detour

**diversity** *n* difference, diverseness, mixture, range, variety

**divert** *v* **1** alter, change the course of, deflect, redirect, reroute, switch, turn aside. **2** deflect, distract, side-track. **3** amuse, delight, enchant, entertain, keep happy, occupy

**diverting** *adj* amusing, enjoyable, entertaining, fun, interesting

**divide** *v* **1** cut, detach, disconnect, halve, part, partition, quarter, segregate, separate, sever, shear, split, subdivide. **2** (share out) allocate, deal out, dole out, measure out, parcel out, share out. **3** (of a road) branch, diverge, fork, split. **4** (divide into categories) arrange, classify, group, organize, separate, sort

**divine** *adj* **1** angelic, celestial, godlike, heavenly, holy, saintly. **2** (to do with God) holy, religious, sacred. **3** beautiful *inf*, glorious, lovely, marvellous, perfect, splendid, super *inf*, wonderful

**divinity** *n* **1** deity, god, goddess, spirit. **2** divine nature, holiness, sanctity

**division** *n* **1** category, class, compartment, department, group, part, piece, portion, section, sector, segment, share, slice. **2** border, boundary, frontier, line, partition, wall. **3** arm, branch, department, unit

**divorce** *n* annulment, break-up *inf*, separation, split *inf*

**divorce** *v* (get divorced) annul the marriage, dissolve the marriage, part, separate, split up

**divulge** *v* betray, disclose, impart, leak, let slip, make known, reveal, tell

**dizzy** *adj* dazed, faint, giddy, light-headed, muddled, reeling, shaky, staggering, swimming, unsteady, weak at the knees, wobbly, woozy *inf*

**do** *v* **1** accomplish, achieve, carry out, cause, complete, finish, perform, undertake. **2** (make sth) arrange, create, design, get ready, look after, make, manufacture, organize, prepare, produce, provide, see to. **3** (do a crossword) complete, figure out, solve, understand, work out. **4** (do a play) act, perform, present, put on. **5** (this will do) be adequate, be enough, be sufficient, satisfy, serve, suffice. **6** (doing well) fare, get on, keep, make out, manage, proceed, progress, survive. **7** (cheat sb) cheat, con *inf*, deceive, defraud, diddle *inf*, take sb for a ride, trick

**docile** *adj* compliant, co-operative, obedient, passive, submissive

**dock** *n* boatyard, harbour, jetty, landing stage, marina, pier, quay, waterfront, wharf

**doctor** *n* consultant, general practitioner, GP, medic *inf*, physician, quack *inf*, surgeon

**doctrine** *n* belief, canon, conviction, creed, dogma, principle, teaching, theory

**document** *n* certificate, diploma,

documentation, manuscript, paper, record, report

**document** v authenticate, back up, certify, chart, corroborate, prove, record, report, support, validate, verify

**dodge** v 1 (dodge sb) elude, escape, evade, give sb the slip. 2 (move) dart, dive, sidestep, swerve, veer, weave. 3 (dodge doing sth) avoid, get out of, shirk, skive *inf*, steer clear of, wriggle out of

**dog** n bitch, canine, cur, hound, mongrel, mutt *inf*, pooch *inf*, puppy

**dogma** n article, belief, creed, doctrine, orthodoxy, principle, tenet, truth

**dogmatic** adj arrogant, assertive, authoritarian, dictatorial, hard-line *inf*, imperious, insistent, overbearing

**dole** n benefit, income support, social security, unemployment benefit, welfare

**dole out** v administer, allocate, deal out, dispense, distribute, divide, give out, hand out, share

**domestic** adj 1 (domestic problems) family, home, personal, private. 2 (domestic animal) domesticated, house-trained, pet, tame; *opp* wild. 3 (domestic affairs) home, internal, national; *opp* foreign

**domesticated** adj 1 (of an animal) broken-in, house-trained, tame, tamed, trained; *opp* wild. 2 (of a person) domestic, home-loving, house-trained *inf*

**dominant** adj 1 assertive, controlling, domineering, leading, most influential, ruling, superior; *opp* self-effacing, passive. 2 (of a feature) biggest, conspicuous, eye-catching, highest, imposing, largest, main, major, tallest

**dominate** v 1 (of a person) be in the driver's seat, boss *inf*, command, control, direct, govern, have the upper hand, influence, lead, monopolize, outnumber, prevail, rule, take control, tyrannize, wear the trousers. 2 (of a feature) dwarf, loom over, overlook, overshadow, stand over, tower above

**domineering** adj bossy *inf*, bullying, forceful, high-handed, menacing, overbearing, strict, threatening, tyrannical; *opp* passive

**donate** v chip in *inf*, contribute, give, kick in *Am inf*, make a gift of, present, supply

**donation** n contribution, gift, grant, offering, present

**donor** n backer, benefactor, contributor, giver, sponsor, supporter

**doom** n 1 destiny, end, fate, kismet. 2 annihilation, catastrophe, death, destruction, downfall, extinction, ruin. 3 doomsday, end of the world, Judgement Day, Last Judgement

**doomed** adj condemned, fated, hopeless, ill-fated, ill-omened, ruined, star-crossed, unlucky

**door** n barrier, doorway, entrance, entry, exit, gate, opening

**dormant** adj asleep, hibernating, inactive, motionless, quiet, resting, sleeping, sluggish, slumbering; *opp* active

**dose** n amount, measure, portion, prescribed amount, quantity

**dot** n 1 circle, dab, fleck, jot, mark, point, speck, speckle, spot. 2 decimal point, full stop

**dote on** v admire, adore, idolize, love, prize, treasure, worship

**doting** adj adoring, devoted, fond, indulgent, loving

**double** adj coupled, doubled, dual, duplicate, in pairs, paired, twice, twin, twofold, two-ply

**double** v enlarge, grow, increase, magnify, multiply by two, rise; *opp* halve

**doubt** n apprehension, cynicism, disbelief, fear, hesitation, incredulity, lack of confidence, lack of conviction, lack of faith, misgivings, mistrust, qualms, reservations, scepticism, suspicion, uncertainty, uneasiness, worries

**doubt** v be dubious, be undecided, be sceptical, be suspicious, distrust, fear, have doubts, have misgivings, have reservations, have scruples, hesitate, question, suspect

**doubtful** adj 1 (not likely to happen) iffy inf, improbable, in doubt, uncertain, unconfirmed, unlikely, unsettled, vague; *opp* certain. 2 (feeling doubt) distrustful, hesitating, incredulous, mistrustful, sceptical, suspicious, tentative, unconvinced, unsure, wavering; *opp* certain. 3 (open to doubt) ambiguous, debatable, dodgy inf, dubious, equivocal, inconclusive, obscure, open to question, problematic, questionable

**downfall** n collapse, defeat, disgrace, fall, overthrow, ruin, undoing

**downpour** n cloudburst, deluge, flood, rainstorm, torrents of rain

**downward** adj descending, downhill, earthbound, earthward, going down

**drab** adj colourless, dingy, dismal, dowdy, dreary, dull, flat, grey, lacklustre, mousy, sombre; *opp* bright

**draft** n first version, outline, plan, rough version, sketch

**draft** v compose, design, draw, draw up, formulate, outline, plan, put together, sketch, work out

**drag** v 1 haul, lug, pull, tow, trail, tug, yank. 2 (the afternoon dragged) be tedious, crawl, creep, go on too long, go slowly, move slowly, stretch out

**drain** n channel, conduit, culvert, ditch, drainpipe, gutter, outlet, pipe, sewer, sink, trench, watercourse

**drain** v 1 (get liquid out) bleed, draw off, dry, empty, filter, milk, pump, remove, tap, withdraw. 2 (of liquid) drip, ebb, flow, leak, ooze, seep, trickle. 3 (use up resources) consume, deplete, expend, exhaust, spend, strain, use up. 4 (make sb tired) enervate, exhaust, sap, tax, weary

**drama** n 1 (a play) comedy, dramatization, melodrama, play, production, show, tragedy. 2 (studying drama) acting, dramatic art, improvisation, stagecraft, theatre. 3 crisis, excitement, histrionics, scene, spectacle

**dramatic** adj 1 breath-taking, electrifying, exciting, impressive, melodramatic, powerful, sensational, startling, tense, thrilling, unexpected, vivid. 2 (a dramatic gesture) artificial, exaggerated, flamboyant, large, overdone, showy, stagy. 3 stage, theatrical

**drastic** adj desperate, dire, extreme, radical, severe, strong

**draught** n breeze, current, flow, movement, wind

**draw** n 1 allure, attraction, enticement, lure, pull inf. 2 (in a game) dead heat, stalemate, tie. 3 lottery, raffle, sweepstake

**draw** v 1 colour, depict, design, make a drawing, make a picture, paint, pencil, sketch, trace. 2 (draw the crowds) attract, coax, entice, lure, persuade, pull. 3 (draw a caravan) haul, pull, tow. 4 (draw a weapon) bring out, produce, pull out, remove, take out, unsheathe. 5 (draw in a game) be equal, be neck and neck, tie. 6 **draw up** compose, draft, frame, put in writing, put together, write out

**drawback** n catch, disadvantage, downside, flaw, fly in the ointment inf, hitch, hurdle, obstacle, problem, snag, stumbling-block; **opp** advantage

**drawing** n cartoon, depiction, diagram, illustration, outline, picture, portrait, portrayal, representation, sketch, study

**dread** n alarm, apprehension, cold feet inf, dismay, fear, foreboding, fright, horror, terror, trepidation, uneasiness, worry

**dread** v be afraid of, be terrified of, fear, shrink from, worry about

**dreadful** adj appalling, awful, dire, disgusting, distressing, fearful, frightful, ghastly, grim, gruesome, harrowing, hideous, horrible, horrifying, monstrous, nasty, repugnant, revolting, shocking, terrible, very bad

**dream** n 1 daydream, delusion, fantasy, hallucination, illusion, imagination, mirage, nightmare, reverie, stupor, trance, vision. 2 aim, ambition, aspiration, desire, fantasy, goal, hope, pipedream, wish

**dream** v daydream, fantasize, hallucinate, have dreams, have nightmares, have visions, imagine, muse, think

**dreary** adj 1 boring, colourless, comfortless, depressing, drab, dull, flat, funereal, gloomy, joyless, melancholy, miserable, monotonous, mournful, sad, sombre, sorrowful, uninteresting, wretched. 2 (dreary weather) bleak, dark, dismal, downcast, gloomy, overcast; **opp** bright

**dregs** n deposit, dross, grounds, remains, residue, scum, sediment

**drench** v douse, drown, flood, saturate, soak, wet

**dress** n 1 frock, gown, robe, shift. 2 (in strange dress) attire, clothes, clothing, costume, garb, gear inf, get-up inf

**dress** v 1 (put clothes on) don, get changed, get dressed, put on, slip on. 2 (decorate) adorn, decorate, trim. 3 (dress a wound) attend to, bandage, bind, cover, put a plaster on, tend, treat. 4 **dress up** dress smartly, get dolled up inf, put your glad rags on inf. 5 **dress up** (dress up as sb) disguise yourself, put fancy dress on, wear a disguise. 6 **dress up** (make sth look better) beautify, decorate, embellish, improve, ornament, trim

**dribble** v 1 drip, drop, leak, ooze, run, seep, trickle. 2 drool, slaver, slobber

**drift** v be carried, coast, float, ramble, roam, stray, waft, wander

**drill** n discipline, exercise, instruction, practice, training

**drill** v 1 bore, make a hole, pierce,

puncture. **2** coach, discipline, exercise, instruct, practise, put sb through their paces, rehearse, teach, train

**drink** *n* **1** alcohol, beverage, booze *inf*, grog, hard stuff *inf*, hooch *inf*, liquid refreshment, liquor, spirits. **2** cup, dram *inf*, glass, gulp, nip *inf*, pint, sip, slug *inf*, swig *inf*, tot

**drink** *v* **1** gulp, guzzle, knock back *inf*, lap, sip, suck, swallow, swig *inf*. **2** (drink alcohol) booze *inf*, carouse, get drunk, have a few, hit the bottle *inf*, indulge, take a drop *inf*

**drip** *n* **1** bead, dribble, drop, leak, plop, splash, spot, tear, trickle. **2** coward, weakling, weak person, weed *inf*, wimp *inf*

**drip** *v* dribble, drizzle, drop, filter, plop, splash, sprinkle, trickle

**drive** *n* **1** excursion, jaunt, journey, outing, ride, run, spin *inf*, trip. **2** (determination) ambition, determination, energy, enterprise, get-up-and-go *inf*, initiative, motivation, vigour. **3** (sales drive) campaign, effort, push

**drive** *v* **1** (make sth or sb go) direct, guide, herd, move, propel, push, send, steer, urge. **2** (go in a car) chauffeur, give sb a lift, go by car, motor, ride, run. **3** (drive a machine) operate, push, work. **4** (make sb do sth) coerce, compel, force, goad, impel, oblige, prod, put pressure on, spur. **5** (push sth in) bang, hammer, hit, knock, ram, thrust

**droop** *v* bend, dangle, drop, fall, flop, hang, sag, sink, slump, stoop, wilt

**drop** *n* **1** (drop of liquid) bead, blob, drip, droplet, globule, pearl, tear. **2** (amount)

dab, dash, mouthful, sip, smidgen *inf*, splash, spot, taste, trace, trickle. **3** (a drop in unemployment) cut, decline, decrease, dip, downturn, fall-off, reduction; *opp* rise. **4** (a steep drop) cliff, descent, precipice, slope

**drop** *v* **1** (go downwards) descend, dip, dive, fall, fall away, go downhill, plummet, plunge, sink, subside, tumble; *opp* rise. **2** (of liquid) dribble, drip, fall, plop. **3** (of prices) collapse, decrease, dip, fall, lessen, plummet; *opp* rise. **4** (drop sth) let fall, let go; *opp* hold. **5** (lose interest in) abandon, chuck *inf*, chuck in *inf*, desert, discontinue, ditch *inf*, finish with, give up, kick *inf*, stop; *opp* take up. **6 drop off** decline, decrease, diminish, drop, dwindle, fall off, lessen; *opp* increase. **7 drop off** doze off, fall asleep, nod off *inf*. **8 drop out** abandon, back out, cop out *sl*, give up, leave, quit, resign, stop

**drought** *n* dry spell, lack of rain

**drown** *v* **1** deluge, drench, engulf, flood, immerse, inundate, submerge, swamp. **2** (of people) go under, sink. **3** (of noise) deaden, drown out, muffle, overpower, swallow up

**drudge** *n* dogsbody *inf*, hack, menial, servant, skivvy *inf*, slave, worker

**drudgery** *n* chores, donkey-work, grind *inf*, hard work, labour, slavery, slog, toil

**drug** *n* **1** medication, medicine, remedy, treatment. **2** barbiturate, illegal substance, narcotic, opiate

**drug** *v* anaesthetize, knock out, sedate, tranquillize. **2** dope *inf*, dose, give drugs to, medicate, poison, treat

**drum** *v* beat, pulsate, rap, reverberate,

tap, throb, thrum

**drunk** *adj* blind drunk, inebriated, intoxicated, legless *inf*, loaded *sl*, merry *inf*, out of it *inf*, paralytic *inf*, plastered *inf*, sloshed *inf*, smashed *inf*, tiddly *inf*, tight *inf*, tipsy, under the influence; **opp** sober

**drunk** *n* alcoholic, boozer *inf*, drunkard, heavy drinker, soak *inf*, wino *inf*

**dry** *adj* 1 arid, baked, barren, dead, dehydrated, dried up, moistureless, parched, shrivelled, waterless, wilted, withered, wizened. 2 (of food) desiccated, dried, hard, stale; **opp** fresh. 3 (of humour) deadpan, droll, ironic, laconic, sarcastic. 4 (of a text) boring, dreary, dull, monotonous, tedious, uninteresting; **opp** exciting

**dry** *v* dehydrate, desiccate, drain, dry off, dry out, dry up, make dry, parch, sear, shrivel, wither, wilt

**dual** *adj* binary, double, duplicate, linked, matched, paired, twin, twofold

**dubious** *adj* 1 (dubious about sth) doubtful, hesitant, sceptical, suspicious, uncertain, unconvinced, undecided, unsure, wavering; **opp** sure. 2 ambiguous, debatable, dodgy *inf*, doubtful, equivocal, fishy *inf*, iffy *inf*, indefinite, obscure, problematical, unclear, unresolved, unsettled, up in the air, vague

**duck** *v* 1 bend, bob, bow, crouch, drop, lower yourself, squat, stoop. 2 (duck sb) dunk, immerse, plunge, push under, submerge

**due** *adj* 1 (the money due) in arrears, outstanding, owed, owing, payable, unpaid. 2 (with the respect that was due) appropriate, decent, deserved, fit, fitting, merited, proper, right. 3 (train is due) awaited, expected, scheduled

**duel** *n* battle, clash, competition, contest, engagement, fight

**dull** *adj* 1 (of a person) dense, dim, dim-witted, dozy *inf*, obtuse, slow, stupid, thick *inf*, unintelligent; **opp** bright. 2 boring, dreary, mind-numbing, tame, tedious, unexciting, unimaginative, uninteresting; **opp** exciting. 3 (of colours) dark, dingy, drab, dreary, faded, flat, lacklustre, matt, muted, sombre, toned down, washed-out; **opp** bright. 4 (of weather) cloudy, dark, dismal, gloomy, grey, murky, overcast; **opp** bright, sunny. 5 (a dull expression) apathetic, blank, dead, empty, expressionless, lifeless, unresponsive. 6 (feeling dull) depressed, drowsy, idle, inactive, lethargic, listless, sleepy, slow, sluggish, stagnant. 7 (a dull blade) blunt, blunted, dulled, unsharpened; **opp** sharp. 8 (a dull thud) deadened, indistinct, muffled, muted

**dumb** *adj* 1 at a loss for words, inarticulate, mute, silent, soundless, speechless, tongue-tied, unable to speak, wordless. 2 (stupid) dense, dim, slow, stupid, thick *inf*, unintelligent; **opp** clever

**dump** *n* junkyard, refuse heap, rubbish heap, tip

**dump** *v* 1 (put) deposit, drop, fling down, park *inf*, put, throw. 2 (dump rubbish) dispose of, ditch *inf*, empty out, get rid of, jettison, scrap, throw away, throw out, tip out, unload. 3 (dump sb) (*inf*) chuck *inf*, ditch *inf*, finish with, leave, stop going out with

**dungeon** *n* cage, gaol, keep, pit, prison

**duplicate** *adj* alternative, copied, corresponding, identical, matched, matching, second, twin

**duplicate** *n* carbon copy, clone, copy, double, exact match, facsimile, imitation, photocopy, replica, spitting image *inf*, twin

**duplicate** *v* clone, copy, do again, double, echo, photocopy, print, repeat, replicate, reproduce

**dusk** *n* dark, evening, gloaming, nightfall, sundown, sunset, twilight

**dust** *n* dirt, earth, grime, grit, powder, smut, soil, soot

**dusty** *adj* **1** dirty, dust-covered, filthy, grimy, sooty, undusted, unswept. **2** chalky, crumbly, dry, fine, gritty, powdery, sandy

**dutiful** *adj* attentive, conscientious, devoted, faithful, hard-working, obedient, obliging, reliable, respectful, submissive, willing

**duty** *n* **1** (sth you have to do) assignment, chore, job, mission, obligation, responsibility, task. **2** (a sense of duty) allegiance, deference, loyalty, obligation, respect, responsibility. **3** (pay duty on sth) charge, customs, dues, levy, tariff, tax, toll

**dwarf** *adj* baby, miniature, pocket, small, tiny, undersized

**dwarf** *n* midget, pygmy

**dwarf** *v* dominate, overshadow, tower above, tower over

**dwell** *v* hang out *inf*, inhabit, live, lodge, remain, reside, rest, settle, stay, stop

**dwelling** *n* abode, home, house, residence

**dye** *n* colour, colouring, pigment, stain, tint

**dye** *v* colour, stain, tint

**dynamic** *adj* active, energetic, enterprising, enthusiastic, forceful, go-ahead *inf*, go-getting, high-powered, lively, motivated, powerful, spirited, vigorous

**eager** *adj* agog, anxious, ardent, bursting, committed, enthusiastic, excited, greedy, hungry, impatient, intent, itching *inf*, keen, longing, passionate, raring, thirsty; *opp* unenthusiastic

**early** *adj* 1 advanced, ahead of time, before time, forward, precocious, premature, untimely. 2 (early people) ancient, first, prehistoric, primitive

**earn** *v* 1 (earn money) bring in *inf*, clear *inf*, gain, get, gross, make, net, pocket, pull in, realize, receive, take home *inf*. 2 (earn points) accumulate, collect, gain, qualify for, receive, win. 3 (earn respect) be entitled to, be worthy of, deserve, gain, have a right to, merit, rate, secure, win

**earnest** *adj* 1 (of people) committed, conscientious, dedicated, determined, grave, hard-working, intense, purposeful, resolved, serious, solemn, studious, zealous. 2 (an earnest plea) heartfelt, impassioned, passionate,

sincere, wholehearted

**earnings** *n* fee, income, pay, remuneration, return, reward, salary, wages

**earth** *n* 1 globe, planet, sphere, world. 2 clay, dirt, ground, land, loam, soil, turf

**earthly** *adj* human, material, mortal, terrestrial, worldly

**ease** *n* 1 calmness, comfort, composure, contentment, enjoyment, happiness, leisure, peace, relaxation, serenity, tranquillity. 2 (do sth with ease) casualness, dexterity, easiness, effortlessness, nonchalance

**easy** *adj* 1 (easy work) cushy *inf*, light, simple, soft, straightforward, undemanding; *opp* demanding, difficult. 2 (easy to do) child's play, clear, foolproof, idiot-proof *inf*, not difficult, simple, uncomplicated, user-friendly; *opp* complicated. 3 (an easy climb) gentle, leisurely, smooth, undemanding, unhurried; *opp* hard. 4 (an easy life) carefree, comfortable, cosy, peaceful, pleasant, quiet, trouble-free, uncomplicated; *opp* hard

**easy-going** *adj* calm, carefree, casual, even-tempered, flexible, informal, laid-back *inf*, lenient, liberal, mellow, permissive, patient, placid, relaxed, tolerant, understanding

**eat** *v* 1 (eat food) bolt, chew, consume, devour, digest, gobble, graze *inf*, munch, nibble, put away *inf*, scoff *inf*, stuff yourself *inf*, swallow, tuck in, wolf. 2 (time to eat) dine, feast, have a meal, lunch, snack *inf*

**eavesdrop** *v* bug *inf*, listen, listen in, monitor, overhear, snoop, spy, tap

**ebb** v 1 (of the tide) fall away, flow back, go out, recede, retreat, subside, withdraw. 2 (of sb's confidence) decline, decrease, die, diminish, drop, dwindle, fade, flag, lessen, peter out, sink, wane, weaken

**eccentric** adj abnormal, bizarre, cranky, dotty inf, erratic, freakish, idiosyncratic, irregular, nutty inf, odd, outlandish, peculiar, queer, strange, uncommon, unconventional, unusual, wacky sl, way-out inf, weird, zany

**echo** n 1 answer, repetition, resounding, reverberation, ringing. 2 (echoes of another occasion) hint, memory, overtones, reminder, suggestion, trace

**echo** v 1 (of a sound) repeat, resound, reverberate, ring, sound again. 2 (echo sb) copy, imitate, mimic, mirror, parrot, reflect

**eclipse** n 1 blocking, blotting out, dimming, shading, veiling. 2 decline, deterioration, failure, fall, weakening; *opp* rise

**eclipse** v 1 block, blot out, cloud, darken, dim, obscure, overshadow, shroud, veil. 2 dwarf, exceed, excel, outdo, outshine, outstrip, put in the shade, surpass, transcend

**economic** adj 1 (for economic reasons) business, commercial, financial, industrial, trade. 2 (not economic) cost-effective, money-making, productive, profitable, profit-making, solvent, viable. 3 (economic policy) budgetary, financial, fiscal, monetary

**economical** adj 1 cheap, cost-effective, efficient, inexpensive, money-saving, time-saving; *opp* uneconomical. 2 (of a

person) careful, economizing, frugal, mean, miserly, parsimonious, prudent, scrimping, sparing, thrifty; *opp* wasteful

**economics** n budgeting, finance, money

**economize** v be economical, be frugal, be sparing, cut back, cut corners, save, scrimp, tighten your belt; *opp* splash out

**economy** n 1 carefulness, meanness, miserliness, prudence, restraint, saving, stinginess, thrift. 2 (a country's economy) budget, economic affairs, financial management, wealth

**edge** n 1 border, boundary, brim, brink, circumference, fringe, limit, line, lip, margin, outline, perimeter, periphery, rim, side, threshold, verge. 2 (have the edge) advantage, dominance, head start, lead, superiority, upper hand

**edible** adj digestible, eatable, fit to eat, good to eat, palatable, safe to eat, wholesome; *opp* inedible

**edit** v adapt, annotate, arrange, assemble, censor, check, compile, correct, emend, polish, prepare, put together, rephrase, revise, rewrite

**edition** n copy, impression, issue, number, printing, publication, version, volume

**educate** v 1 (educate sb at school) coach, discipline, drill, indoctrinate, inform, instruct, lecture, nurture, prepare, school, teach, train, tutor. 2 (travel educates you) civilize, cultivate, develop, edify, enlighten, inform

**educated** adj civilized, cultivated, cultured, enlightened, experienced, informed, knowledgeable, learned, literate, well-informed, well-read; *opp* ignorant

**education** n instruction, knowledge,

scholarship, schooling, teaching, training, tuition

**educational** *adj* edifying, enlightening, improving, informative, instructive

**eerie** *adj* awesome, creepy *inf*, fearful, frightening, ghostly, mysterious, scary *inf*, spine-chilling, spooky *inf*, strange, uncanny, unearthly, unnatural, weird

**effect** *n* 1 (the effect of sth) aftermath, conclusion, consequence, outcome, repercussion, result, upshot. 2 (create an effect) feeling, illusion, impression, sensation, sense

**effect** *v* (effect a change) accomplish, achieve, bring about, carry out, cause, complete, create, execute, fulfil, give rise to, implement, initiate, make, perform, produce, put into effect

**effective** *adj* 1 (effective argument, lighting) compelling, convincing, impressive, moving, noticeable, persuasive, powerful, striking, strong. 2 (working well) capable, competent, efficacious, efficient, powerful, productive, serviceable, strong, successful, useful. 3 (in force) active, current, in force, in operation, valid

**effeminate** *adj* camp *inf*, feminine, girlish, unmanly, weak, wimpish *inf*, womanly; *opp* manly

**effervescent** *adj* 1 (of liquid) bubbling, bubbly, carbonated, fizzing, fizzy, foaming, foamy, frothing, gassy, sparkling. 2 (of personality) animated, bubbly, exuberant, irrepressible, lively, vivacious

**efficiency** *n* ability, capability, competence, economy, effectiveness, organization, power, skill

**efficient** *adj* 1 (an efficient worker) able, businesslike, capable, competent, effective, organized, productive, proficient. 2 (an efficient use of time) cost-effective, economic, effective, productive, profitable, sensible; *opp* inefficient

**effort** *n* 1 application, challenge, diligence, elbow grease *inf*, endeavour, energy, exertion, force, labour, muscle, power, strain, stress, struggle, trouble, work. 2 (a good effort) attempt, crack *inf*, shot *inf*, stab *inf*, try. 3 accomplishment, achievement, attainment, exploit, feat, outcome, result

**effortless** *adj* easy, painless, simple, uncomplicated, undemanding; *opp* difficult

**egotism** *n* egocentricity, egoism, narcissism, pride, self-absorption, self-centredness, self-importance, selfishness, vanity

**egotist** *n* bighead *inf*, egomaniac

**egotistic(al)** *adj* boastful, conceited, egocentric, egoistic, full of yourself, narcissistic, proud, self-centred, self-important, selfish, vain

**eject** *v* 1 (get rid of sb) banish, boot out *inf*, cast out, chuck out *inf*, deport, discharge, dismiss, evict, exile, expel, get rid of, kick out *inf*, oust, remove, sack, throw out, turn out. 2 (get rid of sth) disgorge, emit, excrete, expel, exude, release, send out, shoot out, spew, spout, throw out, vomit. 3 (remove) dislodge, extract, remove, take out; *opp* insert

**elaborate** *adj* 1 (worked out carefully) careful, detailed, exact, exhaustive,

painstaking, precise, thorough;
*opp* vague. 2 (complicated) complex,
complicated, fancy, fussy, intricate,
involved, ornate, showy; *opp* simple

**elaborate** *v* add detail, add to, amplify,
develop, embellish, embroider, enlarge,
expand, fill out, flesh out, improve,
polish, refine

**elapse** *v* go by, lapse, pass, roll, slip away,
slip by

**elastic** *adj* bendy, bouncy, flexible, plastic,
pliable, resilient, rubbery, springy,
stretchy, supple, yielding

**elect** *v* adopt, appoint, cast your vote,
choose, decide upon, nominate, opt for,
pick, plump for, prefer, select, settle on,
vote

**election** *n* ballot, hustings, poll,
referendum, vote, voting

**elector** *n* constituent, voter

**electric** *adj* 1 (of a speech) charged,
dynamic, electrifying, galvanizing,
rousing, stimulating, stirring, tense,
thrilling. 2 (of an appliance) battery-
operated, electrical, mains-operated

**elegant** *adj* 1 (elegant clothes) beautiful,
chic, fashionable, stylish, tasteful.
2 (of sb's body) delicate, fine, handsome.
3 (elegant manners) charming,
debonair, genteel, graceful, nice,
polished, refined, sophisticated, suave.
4 (an elegant apartment) beautiful,
luxurious, posh *inf*, smart, stylish,
sumptuous, tasteful

**element** *n* component, constituent,
factor, feature, ingredient, part, piece,
unit

**elementary** *adj* 1 easy, plain,
rudimentary, simple, straightforward,

understandable. 2 basic, early, first,
fundamental, initial, primary,
introductory

**elements** *n* 1 basics, essentials, first
principles, foundations, principles,
rudiments. 2 atmosphere, climate,
environment, weather

**elevate** *v* 1 hoist, lift, make higher, raise;
*opp* lower. 2 advance, promote, upgrade

**eligible** *adj* acceptable, allowed,
authorized, equipped, fit, qualified,
suitable, suited, worthy

**eliminate** *v* cut out, exclude, get rid of,
leave out, reject, remove, take out

**elite** *n* 1 best, cream *inf*, flower, pick, top.
2 aristocracy, nobility, upper class

**elope** *v* abscond, run away, run off, slip
away, steal away

**eloquent** *adj* articulate, fluent, graceful,
moving, persuasive, plausible, powerful,
well-expressed

**elude** *v* avoid, dodge, escape, evade, get
away, give the slip to, lose, shake off, slip
away from, throw sb off the scent

**elusive** *adj* evasive, hard to find, hard to
pin down, indefinable, intangible,
shifting, shifty, slippery, subtle

**emanate** *v* arise, come forth, derive,
emerge, flow, issue, originate, proceed,
spring, stem

**emancipate** *v* 1 deliver, free, let go,
liberate, release, set free, unchain,
unshackle; *opp* enslave. 2 enfranchise,
give rights to, give the vote to

**embargo** *n* ban, bar, boycott, prohibition,
restriction, seizure, stoppage

**embark** *v* 1 (board a ship) board, go on
board, go aboard. 2 (embark on a
venture) begin, enter into, go into, have

a go at, launch, set about, set out, take on, take the plunge, take up, undertake, venture into

**embarrass** v fluster, humiliate, make sb blush, make sb feel awkward, make sb go red, mortify, shame, show up

**embarrassed** adj ashamed, awkward, blushing, flustered, humiliated, mortified, red, red-faced, self-conscious, shamefaced, sheepish

**embarrassing** adj awkward, humiliating, mortifying, tricky, uncomfortable

**embarrassment** n awkwardness, bashfulness, humiliation, mortification, self-consciousness, shame

**emblem** n badge, crest, insignia, logo, symbol, sign

**embody** v 1 (include) comprise, constitute, embrace, encompass, include, incorporate, take in. 2 (represent) personify, represent, stand for, symbolize, typify

**embrace** v 1 (hug) clasp, cuddle, fold sb in your arms, hold, hug. 2 (include) comprise, embody, encompass, include, incorporate, take in, subsume. 3 (welcome) adopt, espouse, support, take up, take on board, welcome

**emerge** v 1 appear, come into view, come out, emanate, materialize, surface. 2 arise, become apparent, become known, crop up, come out, come to light, develop, get around, transpire, turn out

**emergency** n accident, crisis, critical situation, danger, dire straits, disaster, fix, hole, pickle inf, predicament, red alert

**emigrate** v go to live abroad, migrate,

move, relocate

**eminent** adj celebrated, distinguished, esteemed, important, notable, prominent, renowned, respected

**emission** n discharge, leakage, outflow, output, radiation, release

**emit** v belch, discharge, disgorge, exude, give off, leak, let out, pour out, radiate, release, send out, spew out, spout

**emotion** n excitement, feeling, fervour, passion, sensation, sentiment, sentimentality

**emotional** adj ardent, demonstrative, excitable, fervent, fiery, heated, hot-blooded, impassioned, moved, moving, passionate, poignant, sensitive, sentimental, warm

**emotive** adj 1 controversial, delicate, sensitive. 2 emotional, heart-rending, moving, touching

**emphasis** n accent, attention, force, importance, priority, significance, stress, weight

**emphasize** v accentuate, bring out, feature, focus on, give prominence to, heighten, highlight, point up, press home, spotlight, stress, underline, underscore

**emphatic** adj absolute, categorical, decided, definite, determined, firm, forceful, positive, powerful, pronounced, strong, unequivocal, unmistakable; opp hesitant, tentative

**empire** n colonies, commonwealth, domain, dominion, jurisdiction, kingdom, protectorate, realm, territory

**employ** v 1 (hire) commission, engage, hire, put on the payroll, recruit, sign up, take on. 2 (use) exercise, make use of, use

**employed** adj earning, in a job, in employment, in work, working, waged; *opp* unemployed

**employee** n member of staff, worker, workforce

**employer** n boss, gaffer *inf*, management, manager, owner

**employment** n business, job, livelihood, living, occupation, profession, trade, vocation, work

**emptiness** n 1 bareness, barrenness, blank, vacuum, void. 2 futility, hollowness, meaninglessness, senselessness, triviality, worthlessness

**empty** adj 1 bare, barren, blank, clear, deserted, unfilled, vacant, with nothing inside. 2 futile, hollow, meaningless, purposeless, senseless, trivial, worthless

**enable** v allow, authorize, empower, entitle, equip, facilitate, make sth possible, open the way for, prepare, qualify; *opp* prevent

**enamoured** adj besotted, captivated, crazy about *inf*, infatuated, in love, keen on, nuts about *inf*, smitten *inf*, sweet on

**enchant** v allure, bewitch, captivate, cast a spell on, charm, delight, entrance, fascinate

**enchanted** adj 1 bewitched, captivated, charmed, delighted, entranced, fascinated, spellbound. 2 charmed, magic, magical, under a spell

**enchanting** adj alluring, attractive, bewitching, captivating, charming, delightful, fascinating, spellbinding

**enclose** v 1 cocoon, encase, encircle, fence off, ring, shut in, surround, wall in, wrap. 2 (enclose sth with a letter)

include, insert, put in with, send with

**enclosure** n arena, compound, corral, paddock, pen, pound, ring, run, stockade, yard

**encounter** n confrontation, meeting

**encounter** v be faced with, bump into, come across, come up against, confront, meet, run into

**encourage** v be conducive to, bolster, buoy up, cheer on, egg on *inf*, foster, give courage to, give hope to, hearten, inspire, reassure, root for, spur on, stimulate, strengthen, support, urge; *opp* discourage

**encouragement** n boost, incentive, inspiration, pep talk, reassurance, shot in the arm, support; *opp* discouragement

**encouraging** adj heartening, hopeful, inspiring, optimistic, promising, reassuring, supportive, uplifting; *opp* discouraging

**encroach** v barge in *inf*, get in on *inf*, impinge, interfere, intrude, invade, make inroads, muscle in, obtrude, poke your nose in *inf*, tread on sb's toes, trespass

**end** n 1 cessation, climax, close, completion, conclusion, culmination, finale, finish. 2 boundary, edge, extent, limit, margin, terminus, tip. 3 (remnant) butt, leftover, remnant, stub. 4 (death) curtains *inf*, death, demise, destruction, downfall, extermination, extinction, ruin. 5 (objective) aim, goal, intention, motive, object, objective, purpose

**end** v 1 abolish, conclude, finish, halt, phase out, put an end to, put a stop to, stop, terminate, wind up; *opp* begin, start. **2** break off, cease, close, come to an end, conclude, culminate, finish, peter out, stop, terminate; **opp** begin, start. **3** end up become, come to, come to rest, finish up, reach, turn out, wind up

**endanger** v expose, jeopardize, put at risk, risk, threaten

**endearing** adj adorable, captivating, charming, cute, engaging, lovable, sweet; **opp** repulsive

**endless** adj continual, continuous, everlasting, incessant, interminable, limitless, never-ending, non-stop, perpetual, unbroken, unending, uninterrupted, unremitting

**endorse** v **1** advocate, approve, authorize, back, champion, give approval to, give sth the go-ahead, give sth the red light, okay, sanction, second, support, vote for. **2** countersign, initial, sign

**endure** v bear, cope with, face, go through, put up with, stand, stick inf, stomach, tolerate, withstand. **2** carry on, continue, exist, last, live, persist, prevail, survive

**enemy** n adversary, foe, opponent, rival, them inf, the opposition, the other side; **opp** ally, friend, one of us

**energetic** adj active, animated, brisk, dynamic, forceful, hard-working, lively, spirited, tireless, vigorous; **opp** lethargic, sluggish

**energy** n animation, drive, dynamism, enthusiasm, get-up-and-go inf, life, liveliness, potency, stamina, strength, vigour, vitality, vivacity; **opp** lethargy, weakness

**enforce** v administer, carry out, implement, impose, insist on, put into force

**engage** v **1** (engage sb's interest) attract, allure, captivate, capture, catch, draw, engross, gain, grip, hold, occupy. **2** (engage gear) interconnect, interlock, lock on. **3** (employ) appoint, commission, employ, hire, put on the payroll, take on. **4** engage in be/get involved in, join in, participate in, practise, tackle, take part in

**engaged** adj **1** busy, occupied, tied up, unavailable. **2** betrothed, spoken for

**engagement** n **1** appointment, commitment, date, meeting. **2** betrothal

**engine** n generator, locomotive, machine, motor, turbine

**engineer** n architect, designer, mechanic, planner, technician

**engineer** v bring about, create, devise, effect, manage, mastermind, orchestrate, plan

**engrave** v carve, chisel, cut, etch, gouge, inscribe, scratch

**engraving** n block, carving, etching, inscription, plate, print

**engrossed** adj absorbed, fascinated, immersed, intent, involved, preoccupied, rapt, riveted, wrapped up

**enhance** v add to, augment, boost, emphasize, enrich, improve, increase, intensify, reinforce, strengthen, upgrade

**enigma** n conundrum, mystery, paradox, puzzle, riddle

**enigmatic** adj baffling, curious, inexplicable, mysterious, obscure, puzzling, strange, weird

**enjoy** v **1** adore, get a buzz from inf, get a kick out of inf, get pleasure from, go in for *inf*, like, love, luxuriate in, relish, revel in; *opp* dislike, hate. **2 enjoy yourself** celebrate, have a field day, have a good time, have fun, have the time of your life, let your hair down, party, treat yourself

**enjoyable** *adj* brilliant, entertaining, fun, good, good fun, great, lovely, nice, pleasant, super, superb, wonderful; *opp* awful, dreadful

**enjoyment** *n* amusement, delight, entertainment, fun, gratification, joy, pleasure, relish, satisfaction

**enlarge** *v* add to, blow up, broaden, deepen, expand, extend, increase, inflate, lengthen, let out, magnify, make bigger, stretch, widen; *opp* contract, reduce, shrink

**enlighten** *v* advise, edify, educate, fill sb in on, inform, instruct, make aware, make sb understand, put sb in the picture, put sb right, teach, tell sb about

**enlightened** *adj* **1** aware, educated, informed, knowledgeable, learned, well-informed, wise; *opp* ignorant. **2** broad-minded, fair-minded, liberal, open-minded, tolerant; *opp* bigoted, prejudiced

**enlist** *v* employ, engage, enrol, hire, join up, recruit, register, sign up, take on, volunteer for

**enormous** *adj* astronomic, big, colossal, excessive, giant, gigantic, huge, immense, jumbo, mammoth, massive, vast; *opp* minuscule, small, tiny

**enough** *adj* adequate, ample, as much as you need, plenty, sufficient

**enrich** *v* augment, embellish, enhance, improve, make richer, supplement;

*opp* impoverish

**enrol** *v* admit, enlist, join, recruit, register, sign on, sign up, take on

**ensue** *v* come after, derive, flow, follow, happen afterwards, occur as a result, result, stem from, turn out

**ensure** *v* certify, confirm, guarantee, make certain, make sure, secure

**entail** *v* call for, give rise to, involve, lead to, necessitate, require, result in

**enter** *v* **1** (go inside) board, come in, come inside, get into, get onto, go in, go inside, penetrate. **2** (enter information) add, document, log, note, put down, register, take down, write down, write in. **3** (enrol) become a member, enlist, enrol, go in for, join, participate in, put your name down for, sign up for, take part in

**enterprise** *n* **1** business, effort, endeavour, operation, project, scheme, undertaking, venture. **2** ambition, drive, enthusiasm, get-up-and-go *inf*, gumption, imagination, initiative

**enterprising** *adj* adventurous, ambitious, entrepreneurial, go-ahead, imaginative, resourceful; *opp* staid, stick-in-the-mud, unimaginative

**entertain** *v* amuse, divert, keep sb amused, keep sb happy, keep sb's attention, occupy

**entertainer** *n* artist, artiste, performer

**entertaining** *adj* amusing, diverting, funny, hilarious, interesting, witty; *opp* boring, dull

**entertainment** *n* **1** amusement, distraction, diversion, enjoyment, fun, pleasure, treat. **2** performance, presentation, production, show, spectacle

**enthralled** *adj* captivated, engrossed, fascinated, gripped, intrigued, hypnotized, riveted, spellbound, taken up with

**enthusiasm** *n* commitment, eagerness, excitement, exuberance, fervour, gusto, keenness, passion, relish; *opp* apathy

**enthusiast** *n* addict, buff *inf*, devotee, fan, fanatic, fiend *inf*, follower, freak *inf*, lover, supporter

**enthusiastic** *adj* avid, crazy *inf*, dead keen *inf*, eager, keen, excited, fanatical, mad about *inf*, passionate, raring to go, vehement, wholehearted; *opp* apathetic, half-hearted

**entice** *v* allure, encourage, induce, lead on, lure, seduce, tempt

**entire** *adj* complete, full, total, whole

**entitle** *v* authorize, empower, enable, give sb the right, license, make sb eligible, permit, qualify

**entourage** *n* attendants, band, camp followers, escort, followers, groupies *inf*, retinue

**entrails** *n* bowels, guts *inf*, innards, insides, intestines

**entrance** *n* **1** (way in) access point, door, doorway, entry, foyer, gate, gateway, lobby, mouth, opening, portal, threshold, way in. **2** (admission) access, admission, admittance, entry, right of entry

**entrant** *n* applicant, candidate, competitor, contestant, participant, player

**entrenched** *adj* deep-rooted, deep-seated, established, firmly held, fixed, ingrained, well-established

**entry** *n* **1** (way in) access point, door, doorway, entrance, foyer, gate, gateway, lobby, opening, threshold, way in. **2** (admission) access, admission, admittance, entrance, right of entry. **3** (in a diary) account, description, item, note, record

**envelop** *v* blanket, cover, encase, enclose, enfold, engulf, shroud, surround, swathe, veil, wrap

**envelope** *n* bubble bag, case, casing, cover, covering, folder, jiffy bag [TM], mailing bag, sheathe, skin, wrapper

**enviable** *adj* desirable, favoured, fine, fortunate, privileged, plum *inf*, sought-after, worth having

**envious** *adj* green-eyed, green with envy, jealous, resentful

**environment** *n* conditions, context, environs, habitat, locale, locality, milieu, setting, situation, surroundings

**envisage** *v* anticipate, conceive of, contemplate, expect, imagine, picture, see, suppose, visualize

**envoy** *n* agent, ambassador, consul, delegate, emissary, go-between, intermediary, messenger, representative

**envy** *n* enviousness, jealousy, resentfulness, resentment

**ephemeral** *adj* brief, evanescent, fleeting, momentary, passing, short-lived, temporary, throwaway, transient

**epidemic** *n* outbreak, plague, rash, scourge, wave

**epidemic** *adj* global, pandemic, prevalent, rampant, rife, spreading, sweeping, universal, widespread

**episode 1** *n* affair, chapter, escapade, event, experience, incident, interlude, matter, occasion, occurrence. **2** edition, instalment, part, scene, section

**epitome** *n* embodiment, essence, model, personification, prototype

**epoch** *n* age, date, day, era, generation, period, time

**equal** *adj* **1** alike, comparable, identical, equivalent, on a par, similar, the same, uniform. **2** even, evenly matched, fifty-fifty, level, neck-and-neck. **3** egalitarian, even-handed, fair, impartial, just, unbiased

**equal** *n* clone, counterpart, equivalent, match, twin

**equality** *n* egalitarianism, equal opportunity, fairness, impartiality, justice; *opp* discrimination, inequality

**equalize** *v* balance, compensate, equate, even up, level, level the score, make equal, match, standardize

**equate** *v* associate, be equivalent, compare, correspond to, draw a parallel between, group together, liken, link, pair, regard as the same, talk of in the same breath

**equation** *n* calculation, sum

**equilibrium** *n* balance, evenness, stability, symmetry

**equip** *v* arm, fit out, furnish, kit out, prepare, provide, supply

**equipment** *n* apparatus, gear, instruments, kit *inf*, machinery, materials, rig, stuff, supplies, tackle, things, tools, trappings, utensils

**equivalent** *adj* alike, analogous, comparable, corresponding, equal, identical, interchangeable, matching, on a par, similar, the same, twin; *opp* dissimilar

**equivocal** *adj* ambiguous, ambivalent, doubtful, dubious, evasive, hesitant, qualified, questionable, uncertain, vague; *opp* categorical, definite, unequivocal

**era** *n* age, date, day, epoch, generation, period, stage, time

**eradicate** *v* abolish, annihilate, destroy, eliminate, expunge, exterminate, get rid of, obliterate, remove, root out, stamp out, take out, weed out, wipe out

**erase** *v* blot out, cancel, cross out, delete, remove, rub out, scratch out, scrub out, wipe out

**erect** *adj* perpendicular, rigid, standing, stiff, straight, straight as a ramrod, upright, vertical

**erect** *v* assemble, build, construct, pitch, put together, put up, set up; *opp* demolish, dismantle, take down

**erode** *v* abrade, corrode, eat away, rub away, wash away, wear away, weather

**erotic** *adj* amorous, aphrodisiac, pornographic, raunchy, sensual, sexual, sexy, steamy, suggestive

**err** *v* be mistaken, be wrong, blunder, do wrong, get it wrong, get the wrong end of the stick, go wrong, make a mistake, make an error, miscalculate, slip up

**errand** *n* assignment, chore, job, message, task

**erratic** *adj* changeable, chaotic, fickle, inconsistent, irregular, meandering, sporadic, unpredictable, unreliable; *opp* constant, regular

**error** *n* blunder, boo-boo *inf*, bug, fault, gaffe, howler *inf*, miscalculation, misprint, mistake, oversight, slip-up *inf*

**erupt** *v* blow up, burst out, explode, flare

up, go off, gush, spew out, spout

**escalate** v accelerate, climb, get worse, grow, heighten, increase, intensify, mount, rise, spiral, step up

**escapade** n adventure, affair, episode, exploit, incident, prank, stunt

**escape** n 1 breakout, flight, flit, getaway, jail-break. 2 discharge, emission, leak, leakage, seepage

**escape** v 1 abscond, bolt, break loose, break out, do a bunk *inf*, get away, get free, get out, run away, run off, flit *inf*, scarper *inf*. 2 (escape doing sth) avoid, dodge, duck, evade, skive off *inf*. 3 (leak) bleed, discharge, drain, leak, ooze, seep

**escort** n attendant, bodyguard, chaperon, companion, date, entourage, guard, outrider, partner, retinue

**escort** v accompany, conduct, go with, guide, lead, partner, shepherd, take

**essay** n article, assignment, comment, composition, critique, paper, piece, treatise, review, writings

**essence** n 1 core, crux, essential part, fundamental principle, heart, innermost being, marrow, nature, spirit, substance. 2 concentrate, essential oil, extract, flavouring, tincture

**essential** adj critical, crucial, important, indispensable, key, necessary, vital. 2 basic, cardinal, fundamental, inherent, intrinsic, principal

**establish** v 1 create, form, found, install, put in place, set up, start. 2 confirm, demonstrate, prove, show, verify

**established** adj accepted, deep-rooted, entrenched, ingrained, long-standing, orthodox, official, settled,

traditional, tried-and-tested

**establishment** n 1 creation, formation, foundation, inauguration, inception, setting up. 2 business, company, concern, firm, household, office, organization, outfit *inf*, residence, shop, store. 3 the Establishment big brother *inf*, bureaucracy, the authorities, the government, the powers that be, the ruling classes, the system

**estate** n 1 domain, holding, land, park, property. 2 assets, belongings, fortune, inheritance, possessions, property. 3 housing development

**esteem** n acclaim, admiration, approbation, favour, good opinion, honour, kudos, prestige, regard, respect, reverence

**estimate** n approximation, assessment, ballpark figure, calculation, evaluation, guess, guesstimate *inf*, judgement, reckoning, rough figure

**estimate** v 1 (cost) assess, calculate, evaluate, gauge, judge, reckon, value, work out. 2 (believe) appraise, assess, believe, consider, judge, rate, reckon, surmise, think, view

**estimation** n 1 (opinion) appraisal, assessment, belief, consideration, considered opinion, evaluation, judgement, opinion, view, way of thinking. 2 (esteem) admiration, approval, esteem, good opinion, regard, respect

**estranged** adj alienated, antagonized, apart, at odds, divided, going their separate ways, separated

**eternal** adj 1 abiding, everlasting, deathless, immortal, infinite, permanent, perpetual, timeless, unceasing, undying, without end. **2** ceaseless, constant, continual, continuous, endless, everlasting, incessant, interminable, never-ending, non-stop, perpetual, unending

**eternity** n **1** ages, an age, endlessness, forever, infinity, long time, timelessness. **2** afterlife, heaven, paradise, the hereafter, the next world, world without end

**ethical** adj correct, decent, fair, good, honest, honourable, just, moral, principled, proper, right, upright, virtuous

**ethics** n moral code, morality, morals, principles, standards, values

**ethnic** adj **1** cultural, national, native, racial, tribal. **2** folk, traditional

**etiquette** n **1** (politeness) civility, courtesy, decorum, good manners, politeness, propriety. **2** (convention) accepted behaviour, code of behaviour, code of conduct, code of practice, convention, custom, manners, propriety, protocol, the proprieties

**evacuate** v abandon, desert, flee, go away from, leave, move out of, pull out of inf, quit, retreat from, vacate, withdraw from

**evade** v **1** avoid, dodge, duck inf, elude, escape, give sb the slip, keep out of the way of, shake off, sidestep, steer clear of; **opp** confront. **2** (evade a question or issue) avoid, beat about the bush, dodge, equivocate, fudge, hedge, not give a straight answer to, quibble about, prevaricate. **3** (evade work) avoid, dodge, shirk, skive inf

**evaluate** v appraise, assess, estimate,

gauge, judge, put a value on, rate, reckon, size up, value, weigh up

**evaporate** v **1** dry, dry up, vaporize. **2** disappear, disperse, dissipate, dissolve, fade away, melt away, vanish

**evasive** adj **1** (of a person, tactic) artful, cagey inf, cunning, devious, disingenuous, elusive, shifty. **2** (of a reply) ambiguous, disingenuous, equivocal, indirect, misleading, oblique, prevaricating; **opp** direct

**even** adj **1** (level) flat, flush, horizontal, level, plane, smooth, true, uniform. **2** (steady, constant) consistent, constant, regular, stable, steady, unbroken, unchanging, uniform, unvarying. **3** (equal) alike, balanced, equal, identical, level, much the same, on an equal footing, similar, the same, tied. **4** (fair) balanced, disinterested, equitable, even-handed, fair, impartial, just, unbiased. **5** get even be revenged, get your own back, get your revenge, give as good as you get, pay sb back, reciprocate, revenge yourself, settle the score

**event** n **1** episode, experience, happening, occasion, occurrence, phenomenon. **2** (sporting event) competition, contest, fixture, game, match, race, round, tournament

**even-tempered** adj calm, cool, easy-going, equable, laid back inf, imperturbable, peaceable, placid, relaxed, serene, unflappable, unruffled

**eventful** adj action-packed, active, busy, exciting, full, lively, never a dull moment

**eventual** adj concluding, consequent,

ensuing, final, future, later, resulting, ultimate

**eventually** adv after all, at last, at the end of the day, finally, in the end, in the long run, in time, sooner or later, one day, one fine day inf, some day, sooner or later, when all is said and done

**everlasting** adj 1 deathless, enduring, eternal, immortal, imperishable, indestructible, infinite, lasting, never-ending, perpetual, timeless, undying, unending. 2 ceaseless, constant, continual, continuous, eternal, incessant, interminable, never-ending, non-stop, perpetual, tiresome, without let-up

**everyday** adj common, commonplace, customary, familiar, habitual, mundane, nothing special, ordinary, regular, routine, run-of-the-mill, standard, usual, workaday

**evict** v bounce inf, chuck out inf, dislodge, dispossess, drive out, eject, expel, give notice to quit, kick out inf, oust, put out, remove, show sb the door, throw out, throw sb out on their ear, turf out inf, turn out

**evidence** n 1 confirmation, corroboration, data, facts, indication, information, mark, proof, sign, substantiation, support, verification. 2 affidavit, declaration, deposition, statement, testimony. 3 **give evidence** swear on oath, testify, witness. 4 **in evidence** conspicuous, evident, having a high profile, noticeable, obvious, on display, on view

**evident** adj 1 (easy to see or understand) apparent, clear, easy to see, manifest,

noticeable, palpable, perceptible, plain, plain as the nose on your face inf, self-explanatory, tangible, transparent, unmistakable, visible. 2 (true) clear, incontestable, incontrovertible, indisputable, obvious, undeniable, undoubted

**evidently** adv 1 apparently, as far as you can tell, from all appearances, it appears, it seems, ostensibly, outwardly, seemingly. 2 clearly, obviously, surely, undoubtedly, without question

**evil** adj atrocious, bad, base, black-hearted, corrupt, cruel, demonic, diabolic, depraved, fiendish, foul, heinous, immoral, iniquitous, malicious, malevolent, shameful, sinful, vicious, vile, villainous, wicked; *opp* good

**evil** n 1 atrocity, badness, corruption, cruelty, depravity, immorality, vice, villainy, wickedness, wrong, wrong-doing. 2 affliction, calamity, curse, disaster, hardship, harm, misery, misfortune, pain, suffering, wrong

**evocative** adj bringing to mind, redolent, reminiscent, suggestive

**evoke** v 1 (a response or emotion) arouse, awaken, cause, elicit, excite, give rise to, induce, inspire, kindle, provoke, stimulate, stir up. 2 (an image or memory) call to mind, call up, conjure up, invoke, inspire, recall, summon up

**evolution** n 1 advance, development, emergence, growth, maturing, progress, progression, unfolding. 2 natural selection

**evolve** v change, develop, grow, expand, improve, mature, open out, progress, unfold

**exact** *adj* 1 (an exact copy) accurate, careful, correct, explicit, faithful, literal, precise, spot on *inf*, strict, true, word for word. 2 (of a person) accurate, careful, conscientious, meticulous, painstaking, precise, punctilious

**exact** *v* call for, compel, demand, enforce, extort, extract, impose, insist on, require

**exactly** *adv* 1 (quite right) absolutely, bang on *inf*, certainly, definitely, indeed, precisely, quite, quite right, quite so. 2 accurately, carefully, correctly, faithfully, precisely, strictly, to the letter, word for word. 3 **not exactly** by no means, not at all, not really

**exaggerate** *v* amplify, embellish, embroider, magnify, make a drama out of, make a mountain out of a molehill, make too much of, overemphasize, overestimate, overrate, overstate, stretch the truth, talk up *inf*

**exaggeration** *n* embellishment, embroidery, hyperbole, inflation, overestimation, overstatement

**examination** *n* 1 (the examination of sth) appraisal, analysis, consideration, exploration, inspection, investigation, observation, perusal, probe, review, scrutiny. 2 (undergo an examination) check-up, inspection, the once-over *inf*. 3 (of a witness) cross-examination, interrogation, questioning. 4 assessment, exam, test

**examine** *v* 1 analyse, appraise, assess, check out, consider, explore, look into, scrutinize, study, weigh, weigh up. 2 check, give the once-over *inf*, go over, inspect, look at, look over, observe, peruse, scan, take a look at. 3 (examine

a witness) cross-examine, grill *inf*, interrogate, question, test

**example** *n* 1 case, case in point, illustration, instance, sample, specimen. 2 ideal, model, paragon, pattern, standard. 3 **for example** as an illustration, e.g., for instance, such as

**exasperate** *v* anger, annoy, drive crazy *inf*, enrage, get on your nerves, incense, infuriate, irk, irritate, madden, make your blood boil, needle *inf*, provoke, rouse, try the patience of, vex, wind up *inf*

**excavate** *v* burrow, dig, dig out, dig up, hollow out, mine, tunnel, uncover, unearth

**exceed** *v* 1 (be better than) beat, be better than, be greater than, better, do more than, excel, outdo, outshine, outstrip, surpass. 2 (be more than) be greater than, be more than, go beyond, pass, top. 3 (go beyond a limit) do more than, go beyond, go over, go over the top, overstep

**excel** *v* 1 (be better than) beat, beat hollow, be better than, be superior to, do better than, eclipse, outdo, outclass, outshine, outstrip, overshadow, surpass. 2 (be very good) be excellent, be outstanding, be very good, do well, shine, stand out

**excellence** *n* distinction, eminence, greatness, high quality, merit, quality, perfection, superiority, value, worth

**excellent** *adj* 1 (very good) ace *inf*, brilliant *inf*, exceptional, fabulous *inf*, fantastic *inf*, great, marvellous, outstanding, perfect, superb, superior, wonderful; *opp* awful, dreadful.

**2** (of good quality) A1, choice, exquisite, fine, first-class, first rate, good quality, of high quality, prime, select. **3** (admirable) admirable, exemplary, superior, supreme, worthy

**exception** n **1** anomaly, departure, deviation, freak, irregularity, oddity, special case. **2** exclusion, omission. **3 with the exception of** apart from, bar, but for, except, except for, excepting. **4 take exception** be offended, object to, resent, take offence, take umbrage

**exceptional** adj **1** (unusually good) excellent, outstanding, phenomenal, prodigious, rare, special. **2** (unusual) abnormal, atypical, odd, out of the ordinary, peculiar, rare, unusual; **opp** normal, usual

**excerpt** n clip, extract, part, passage, quotation, quote, selection

**excess** n **1** abundance, glut, more than enough, overdose, overkill inf, surfeit, surplus, too much, too many. **2** leftovers, overflow, remainder, residue. **3** debauchery, dissipation, intemperance, over-indulgence

**excessive** adj exaggerated, extravagant, immoderate, inordinate, lavish, needless, OTT inf, overdone, over the top inf, superfluous, uncalled-for, undue, unnecessary, unreasonable, unwarranted

**exchange** n barter, dealing, give and take, interchange, substitution, swap inf, switch, trade, trade-off

**exchange** v **1** barter, do a swap inf, reciprocate, swap inf, trade. **2** change, interchange, replace, substitute, swap inf, switch, trade in

**excitable** adj **1** edgy, emotional, highly strung, jumpy, lively, nervous, restive, volatile. **2** hasty, hot-headed, quick-tempered, temperamental, testy, touchy; **opp** calm

**excite** v **1** (make sb excited) agitate, arouse, disturb, get sb going inf, inflame, provoke, rouse, set off inf, stimulate, stir up, thrill, titillate, turn on inf, upset, wind up inf, work up inf. **2** (arouse feelings) arouse, awaken, cause, evoke, incite, inspire, kindle, stir up

**excited** adj **1** agog, animated, aroused, boisterous, enthusiastic, exhilarated, exuberant, high inf, in high spirits, intoxicated, thrilled, turned on inf. **2** agitated, at fever pitch, frantic, frenzied, hysterical, in a frenzy, overwrought, wound up

**excitement** n **1** agitation, animation, anticipation, elation, exhilaration, enthusiasm, ferment, tumult. **2** adventure, kick inf, thrill

**exciting** adj **1** (of an experience) dramatic, electrifying, exhilarating, heady, stimulating, stirring, thrilling; **opp** dull, boring. **2** (of a story, film) action-packed, dramatic, fast-moving, gripping, riveting, spectacular, spine-tingling; **opp** dull, boring

**exclaim** v blurt out, call, call out, come out with, cry, cry out, shout, utter, yell

**exclude** v **1** (keep out) ban, bar, blacklist, debar, forbid, ignore, keep out, leave out, ostracize, pass over, prohibit, proscribe, refuse, reject, repudiate, send to Coventry, shut out. **2** (be exclusive of) be apart from, be exclusive of, except; **opp** include

**exclusive** adj **1** closed, limited, posh inf,

private, restricted, select, selective, smart, snobbish. **2** only, single, sole, unique. **3 exclusive of** apart from, excluding, not including

**excursion** n day trip, expedition, jaunt, outing, pleasure trip, tour, trip

**excuse** n **1** apology, defence, explanation, justification, mitigation, mitigating circumstances, plea, pretext, reason. **2** cop-out inf, ostensible reason, pretence, pretext, rationalization

**excuse** v **1** (a person) absolve, allow sb to get away with, exonerate, forgive, let off, make allowances for, pardon. **2** (excuse bad behaviour) condone, defend, explain, explain away, forgive, ignore, justify, mitigate, pardon. **3** (excuse sb from doing sth) exempt, free sb from, let sb off, liberate sb from, release sb from, relieve, spare

**execute** v **1** carry out the death sentence, kill, lynch, put to death. **2** (execute a plan) accomplish, achieve, carry out, discharge, do, effect, enact, fulfil, implement, perform, put into practice, realize

**execution** n **1** capital punishment, death sentence, killing, putting to death. **2** (the execution of a plan) accomplishment, achievement, carrying out, discharge, effecting, fulfilment, implementation, performance, realization

**executioner** n hit-man inf, killer

**executive** adj administrative, controlling, decision-making, directing, governing, managerial

**executive** n **1** administrator, boss inf, chief inf, director, manager, officer,

official. **2** administration, government, leadership, management, top brass inf

**exemplify** v **1** (give an example of) demonstrate, give an example, illustrate, show. **2** (be an example) be an example of, be typical of, epitomize, represent, symbolize, typify

**exempt** adj excepted, excused, free from, immune, let off, not liable to, released from, spare

**exempt** v except, exclude, excuse, free sb from, grant immunity from, let sb off, make an exception for, release sb from, spare

**exercise** n **1** (physical exercise) activity, effort, exertion, games, gym, gymnastics, keep fit, movement, physical jerks inf, sport, training, workout. **2** (use) application, employment, practice, use, utilization

**exercise** v **1** (take exercise) do exercises, drill, exert yourself, take exercise, train, work out. **2** (use) apply, employ, exert, make use of, practise, use, utilize

**exert** v **1** apply, bring to bear, employ, make use of, use, utilize, wield. **2** (exert yourself) apply yourself, do your best, do your utmost, drive yourself hard, give your all, go all out, make an effort, push yourself, put your back into it inf, put yourself out, strain, strive, struggle, toil, work hard

**exertion** n activity, action, effort, endeavour, exercise, hard work, strain, toil, work

**exhaust** v **1** (tire) burn out inf, debilitate, do in inf, drain, enervate, fatigue, knock out inf, overtax, sap your strength, take it out of you, tire, tire out, wear out, weary. **2** (use up) consume, deplete, dissipate, drain, empty, finish off, finish up, run out of, run through, spend, squander, use up, waste

**exhausted** *adj* **1** (tired) all in, burnt out, bushed *Am*, dead beat *inf*, dead on your feet *inf*, debilitated, dog-tired *inf*, drained, enervated, faint, fatigued, prostrate, ready to drop, shattered *inf*, spent, tired out, worn out. **2** (used up) all gone, at an end, depleted, finished, spent, used up

**exhausting** *adj* arduous, back-breaking, debilitating, enervating, fatiguing, gruelling, laborious, punishing, tiring, taxing, wearing, wearying; *opp* easy

**exhaustive** *adj* all-embracing, careful, complete, comprehensive, full, in-depth, intensive, thorough

**exhibit** *v* **1** (exhibit things) demonstrate, display, flaunt, parade, present, put on display, put on show, put on view, show, show off, unveil. **2** (exhibit a quality, feeling) betray, disclose, display, express, give away, flaunt, indicate, reveal, show, show off

**exhibition** *n* **1** (of things) demonstration, display, exposition, fair, presentation, show. **2** (of feelings) demonstration, display, expression, indication, revelation

**exhilarating** *adj* breathtaking, exciting, thrilling

**exile** *n* **1** banishment, deportation, expulsion, transportation. **2** (a person) deportee, displaced person, outcast, refugee

**exile** *v* banish, bar, deport, drive out, eject, evict, expel, send into exile, uproot

**exist** *v* **1** be, be extant, be found, be in existence, be real, happen, live, occur. **2** (survive) continue, endure, last, live, persist, remain, stay alive, stay in existence, subsist, survive

**existence** *n* **1** actuality, being, existing, fact, living, reality. **2** (survival) duration, endurance, persistence, subsistence, survival. **3** (way of life) life, lifestyle, way of life

**exit** *n* **1** escape, outlet, passage, vent, way out. **2** departure, escape, exodus, going, leaving, retreat, withdrawal

**exodus** *n* emigration, escape, exit, flight, leaving, migration, retreat; *opp* arrival

**exorbitant** *adj* excessive, extortionate, extreme, high, inordinate, outrageous, preposterous, ridiculous, steep, unreasonable; *opp* modest

**exotic** *adj* **1** (foreign) alien, foreign, imported, introduced, non-native. **2** (different and exciting) bizarre, colourful, curious, extraordinary, fascinating, glamorous, mysterious, novel, odd, outlandish, peculiar, sensational, striking, unusual

**expand** *v* **1** (make sth bigger) amplify, augment, broaden, build up, develop, dilate, distend, diversify, elaborate, enlarge, extend, fill out, increase, inflate, make bigger, make larger, open up, widen. **2** (become bigger) become bigger, become larger, get bigger, grow, increase in size, open out, stretch, swell, widen; *opp* contract

**expanse** *n* **1** (size) area, breadth, extent, range, spread, vastness. **2** (expanse of land, sea) area, plain, stretch, sweep, tract

**expect** v 1 assume, believe, calculate, guess, imagine, presume, reckon, suppose, surmise, suspect, think, think likely, trust. 2 anticipate, await, be prepared for, envisage, foresee, hope for, look forward to, plan for, predict, wait for. 3 call for, consider necessary, demand, insist on, look for, require, want

**expectant** adj 1 anxious, eager, expecting, hopeful, in suspense, keyed up, looking forward to, on tenterhooks, ready, ready and waiting. 2 (expecting a baby) expecting, having a baby, in the family way inf, pregnant

**expectation** n 1 assumption, belief, calculation, conjecture, forecast, likelihood, presumption, probability, reckoning, surmise, supposition, trust. 2 anticipation, expectancy, hope, readiness

**expectations** n hopes, outlook, prospects

**expedition** n enterprise, excursion, exploration, journey, mission, outing, pilgrimage, quest, safari, tour, trek, trip, voyage

**expel** v 1 (send sb away) ban, banish, cast out, chuck out inf, deport, drive out, eject, evict, exile, kick out inf, oust, remove, send away, send packing inf, throw out, turn out, turf out inf. 2 (send sth out) belch, discharge, eject, emit, force out, give off, push out, send out, spew out

**expend** v 1 (time, money) disburse, dish out inf, fork out inf, fritter, fritter away, lavish, lay out, pay out, shell out inf, spend, squander, waste. 2 (use up)

consume, deplete, drain, exhaust, finish off, use, use up

**expendable** adj dispensable, disposable, inessential, non-essential, replaceable, unimportant, unnecessary

**expenditure** n costs, disbursements, expenses, outgoings, overheads, payments, spending; **opp** income, revenue

**expense** n 1 cost, expenditure, investment, money, outlay, price, spending. 2 **at the expense of** in place of, instead of, rather than, to the detriment of, to the disadvantage of

**expensive** adj beyond sb's means, costly, dear, exorbitant, extortionate, overpriced, pricey, prohibitive; **opp** cheap, inexpensive

**experience** n 1 (sth that happens to you) encounter, episode, event, incident, occurrence, perception, sensation. 2 competence, expertise, familiarity, grounding, knowledge, maturity, record, track record, wisdom; **opp** inexperience

**experienced** adj competent, expert, familiar, knowledgeable, mature, versed, well-versed, wise; **opp** inexperienced

**experiment** n 1 attempt, pilot study, test, trial, try-out, venture. 2 (the practice of experimenting) experimentation, innovation, research, testing, trial and error

**experiment** v 1 carry out experiments, conduct experiments, explore, improvise, innovate, play around. 2 **experiment with** explore, investigate, pilot, research, test, try, try out

**experimental** adj avant-garde, exploratory, innovative, new, pilot, probatonary

**expert** *adj* adept, advanced, brainy *inf*, capable, competent, experienced, practised, proficient, qualified, skilful, skilled, specialist, technical

**expert** *n* academic, authority, boffin *inf*, brain, brains, connoisseur, egghead *inf*, maestro, mastermind, professional, pundit, sage, specialist

**expertise** *n* command, competence, dexterity, experience, proficiency, skilfulness, skill, mastery, professionalism, proficiency, specialism

**expire** *v* 1 breathe your last, depart this world, die, kick the bucket *inf*, give up the ghost *inf*, pass away, pass on, perish, snuff it *inf*. 2 (of a document) become invalid, cease, come to an end, end, finish, go out of date, lapse, run out

**explain** *v* account for, answer, clarify, clear up, describe, give a reason for, interpret, make clear/plain, solve, spell out, throw light on

**explanation** *n* account, answer, clarification, defence, description, elucidation, excuse, explication, hypothesis, interpretation, justification, reason, reply

**explanatory** *adj* descriptive, illuminating, illustrative, informative, revealing, theoretical

**explicit** *adj* categorical, clear, crystal clear, definite, detailed, direct, distinct, exact, express, obvious, overt, patent, plain, precise, specific, straightforward, unambiguous, unequivocal; *opp* implicit

**explode** *v* 1 (sth explodes) blow up, burst, erupt, fly apart, go bang, go off, go up, implode. 2 (explode sth) blast, blow up, detonate, drop, let off, set off, trigger

**exploit** *n* accomplishment, achievement, adventure, deed, feat, stunt, triumph

**exploit** *v* 1 (use sth) capitalize on, develop, employ, make use of, press into service, put to good use, take advantage of, use, utilize, work. 2 (use sb unfairly) abuse, impose on, manipulate, overwork, take advantage of, use, walk all over

**exploration** *n* 1 discovery, expedition, journey, travel, visit, voyage. 2 (of an issue, problem) analysis, consideration, discussion, enquiry, examination, investigation, research, study, survey

**explore** *v* 1 discover, journey, look around, travel, visit, voyage. 2 analyse, consider, discuss, enquire into, examine, go into, investigate, look into, probe, research, survey

**explosion** *n* 1 bang, blast, boom, burst, detonation, eruption, gunshot, mushroom cloud, report. 2 (of new developments, ideas) escalation, expansion, flowering, growth, increase, outbreak, mushrooming

**explosive** *adj* 1 combustible, exploding, flammable, incendiary, inflammable, unstable, volatile. 2 (likely to cause trouble) controversial, highly charged, sensational, tense, unstable, volatile

**explosive** *n* charge, dynamite, gelignite, gunpowder, plastic explosive, TNT

**exponent** *n* advocate, apologist, backer, champion, practitioner, propagandist, promoter, proponent, supporter

**expose** *v* 1 bare, denude, display, exhibit, flash, lay bare, reveal, show, uncover, unveil. 2 (expose dishonesty) bring to light, draw attention to, highlight, reveal, uncover, unmask

**exposed** *adj* bare, for all to see, in full view, naked, on display, open, public, unprotected, vulnerable

**exposure** *n* 1 (publicity) advertising, coverage, publicity. 2 (revealing of sth) baring, disclosure, display, revelation, showing, uncovering, unmasking, unveiling

**express** *adj* 1 clear, conscious, deliberate, distinct, explicit, expressed, intentional, manifest, plain, wilful. 2 fast, first-class, non-stop, prompt, quick, rapid, special, speedy, swift

**express** *v* announce, articulate, communicate, convey, declare, describe, display, give vent to, indicate, make known, manifest, put into words, say, show, speak, state, utter, verbalize, voice

**expression** *n* 1 announcement, articulation, communication, declaration, demonstration, description, display, exhibition, indication, manifestation, reflection, statement, voicing. 2 (group of words) figure of speech, idiom, phrase, proverb, saying, utterance. 3 (on sb's face) air, appearance, countenance, face, look, mien

**expressive** *adj* articulate, colourful, demonstrative, descriptive, eloquent, emotional, explicit, lyrical, moving, poetic, poignant, suggestive, vivid

**exquisite** *adj* artistic, beautiful, delicate, excellent, fine, high-quality, lovely, ornate, perfect, refined, superb, sublime, tasteful

**extend** *v* 1 (make bigger) add to, augment, elongate, enlarge, expand, increase, lengthen, prolong, spread, stretch, stretch out. 2 (extend to full size) pay out, pull out, put up, stretch out, uncoil, unfold, unroll. 3 (extend over an area) cover, range, reach, span, spread, stretch. 4 (extend a deadline) postpone, protract, put back, put off, relax, reschedule. 5 (give) advance, give, grant, hold out, impart, offer, make available, proffer

**extension** *n* 1 accessory, addition, adjunct, add-on, appendage, enlargement, expansion. 2 (to a house) annexe, conservatory, lean-to, outbuilding, outhouse, wing

**extensive** *adj* comprehensive, considerable, enormous, great, large, lengthy, long, prolonged, sizeable, vast, wide, wide-ranging, widespread

**extent** *n* area, breadth, dimensions, expanse, length, magnitude, range, scope, size, spread

**extenuating** *adj* exceptional, exonerating, justifying, mitigating, qualifying

**exterior** *adj* external, outer, outermost, outside, outward, surface

**exterior** *n* façade, face, outside, outward appearance, shell, surface

**exterminate** *v* annihilate, destroy, eliminate, eradicate, extirpate, kill, massacre, slaughter, wipe out

**external** *adj* exterior, outer, outermost, outside, outward, surface

**extinct** *adj* dead, defunct, died out, exhausted, extinguished, gone, lost, vanished, wiped out

**extinguish** *v* 1 destroy, end, eradicate, kill, quench, snuff out, stifle, suppress.

**2** (extinguish a fire, light) blow out, put off, put out, smother, snuff out, switch off, turn off, turn out

**extortionate** adj daylight robbery inf, dear, excessive, exorbitant, expensive, outrageous, overpriced

**extra** adj added, additional, bonus, further, more, supplementary, surplus

**extra** n **1** accessory, addition, additive, add-on, bonus, supplement, surplus. **2** (in a film) bit part, chorus girl, non-speaking part, walk-on part

**extract** n **1** concentrate, derivative, essence. **2** (piece of writing) cutting, excerpt, highlight, part, quotation, quote, selection

**extract** v abstract, derive, distil, draw, draw out, obtain, pull out, remove, select, take out

**extraordinary** adj amazing, astonishing, exceptional, incredible, marvellous, out of the ordinary, outstanding, rare, remarkable, singular, striking, unique, unusual, wonderful; **opp** ordinary

**extravagant** adj excessive, immoderate, over-generous, spendthrift, squandering, wasteful

**extreme** adj **1** (great) absolute, acute, drastic, great, high, intense, severe, utmost. **2** furthest, furthest away, most distant, outer, remotest. **3** (extreme views, measures) drastic, exaggerated, excessive, fanatical, harsh, radical, uncompromising, unreasonable, over-the-top, OTT

**extreme** n absolute, boundary, edge, end, extremity, height, limit, maximum, ultimate

**extremist** n diehard, fanatic, militant,

radical, ultra, zealot; **opp** moderate

**extremity** n boundary, edge, end, extreme, limit, tip

**extricate** v disembroil, disentangle, free, loose, rescue, unravel, untangle

**extroverted** adj boisterous, extrovert, friendly, fun-loving, gregarious, lively, loud, outgoing, outward-looking, sociable, talkative; **opp** introverted

**exuberant** adj celebrating, cheerful, effervescent, elated, enthusiastic, irrepressible, joyful, joyous, jubilant, rejoicing, sparkling, vivacious

**eye** v gaze at, glance at, inspect, keep an eye on, look at, peer at, regard, scrutinize, stare at, study, survey, watch

**eyesight** n eyes, perception, powers of observation, range of vision, sight, vision

**eyesore** n blemish, blight, blot on the landscape, disfigurement, monstrosity, scar

**eye-witness** n bystander, observer, onlooker, spectator, witness

**fabric** *n* 1 cloth, material, textile. 2 (the fabric of society) constitution, essence, framework, make-up, nature, structure

**fabricate** *v* 1 (falsely) concoct, fake, forge, invent, make up. 2 assemble, construct, make, make up, manufacture, produce, put together

**fabulous** *adj* 1 (good) ace *inf*, brilliant, fantastic, good, great, super, superb, wonderful. 2 (imaginary) fantastic, imaginary, invented, legendary, make-believe, mythical

**face** *n* 1 complexion, countenance, expression, fizzog *inf*, head, mug *inf*, physiognomy, visage. 2 (outward appearance) appearance, aspect, facet, side, surface

**face** *v* 1 (of a person) gaze at, look sb in the face, look towards, stare at, turn to, turn towards. 2 (of a building) be opposite, front onto, give onto, have a view of, look out on, overlook. 3 (in a contest) be opposed to, confront, meet, play, play against. 4 (face a problem) accept, come to terms with, confront, deal with, face up to; *opp* avoid.
5 (a problem that faces sb) be before sb, be in store, be on sb's plate *inf*, confront, lie ahead, present itself

**facetious** *adj* flippant, frivolous, humorous, ironic, jocular, jokey, joking, sarcastic, silly, teasing, tongue-in-cheek

**facile** *adj* banal, glib, oversimplified, shallow, silly, trite; *opp* profound

**facilitate** *v* aid, allow, assist, enable, encourage, help, make easier, permit, simplify, speed up

**facility** *n* 1 **facilities** amenities, comforts, mod cons *inf*, equipment, resources, service. 2 dexterity, ease, effortlessness, elegance, fluency, simplicity

**fact** *n* 1 actuality, certainty, reality, truth. 2 **in fact** actually, as a matter of fact, as it happens, in actual fact, indeed, in point of fact, in reality, in truth, really

**faction** *n* band, camp, caucus, clique, group, lobby, party, pressure group, ring, section, set, splinter group

**factor** *n* aspect, component, consideration, detail, element, facet, influence, ingredient, part

**factory** *n* foundry, industrial unit, mill, plant, works, workshop

**factual** *adj* accurate, authentic, exact, faithful, informative, objective, real, real-life, true, true to life, truthful, unbiased; *opp* fictional

**faculty** *n* 1 (in a university) department, division, section, school. 2 ability, aptitude, capability, capacity, sense. 3 **faculties** awareness, cognition, consciousness, perception, reason, understanding

**fade** v 1 (of colours) become pale, dim, dull, grow pale. 2 (become less) decline, die away, disappear, dwindle, grow faint, vanish, wane

**fail** v 1 be defeated, break down, collapse, come a cropper *inf*, come to grief, crash, draw a blank, fall down, fall flat, fall short, fall through, founder, go bankrupt, go under, lose, malfunction, miscarry, misfire, miss, stumble; *opp* succeed. 2 fail to do sth avoid, decline, neglect, omit, refuse. 3 (fail a person) abandon, desert, disappoint, forsake, let down. 4 (fail an exam) be unsuccessful, drop out *Am*, flunk *Am*; *opp* pass

**failing** n defect, drawback, failure, fault, imperfection, inadequacy, shortcoming, weakness

**failure** n 1 bankruptcy, breakdown, collapse, defeat, malfunction; *opp* success. 2 (failure to do sth) dereliction of duty, inability, omission, oversight, refusal. 3 (sb who has failed) incompetent, loser, no-hoper. 4 (sth that has failed) damp squib, disaster, dud, flop, wash-out; *opp* success

**faint** adj 1 barely audible, barely perceptible, barely visible, blurred, dim, feeble, indistinct, quiet, soft, unclear, weak; *opp* bright, loud. 2 (feel faint) dizzy, giddy, light-headed, weak, woozy *inf*

**faint** v black out, collapse, lose consciousness, pass out, swoon; *opp* come round, come to

**fair** adj 1 balanced, equitable, even-handed, honest, impartial, just, legitimate, objective, reasonable, right,

sporting, unbiased, unprejudiced. 2 (of hair) blond, blonde, flaxen, yellow. 3 (of skin) light, pale, white

**faith** n 1 commitment, confidence, conviction, expectation, hope, loyalty, sincerity, trust. 2 (religious belief) belief, communion, confession, congregation, creed, denomination, religion

**faithful** adj 1 committed, loyal, reliable, true, trusting, trusty. 2 be faithful to believe in, have confidence in, keep faith with, stand by, stick to, trust in

**fake** adj artificial, counterfeit, fabricated, false, forged, fraudulent, imitation, sham; *opp* genuine

**fake** v copy, counterfeit, fabricate, falsify, forge, pretend, simulate

**fall** n 1 collapse, descent, slip, stumble, trip, tumble. 2 collapse, decline, decrease, dip, drop, falling-off; *opp* rise. 3 (the fall of sb in power) defeat, demise, dismissal, downfall, end, fall from grace, impeachment, removal, resignation; *opp* rise

**fall** v 1 (move downwards) be dropped, collapse, come crashing down, descend, drop, plop, plummet, sink, stumble, tip over, topple over, trip, tumble. 2 (of a person) collapse, fall down, fall over, keel over, lose your balance, slip, stumble, trip, tumble. 3 (of a price, amount) be marked down, collapse, come down, decline, decrease, drop, fall off, go down, plummet, slump, tumble; *opp* rise. 4 (of sb in power) be defeated, be dismissed, be impeached, be kicked out *inf*, be ousted, be voted out, fall from grace, lose office, lose power, resign, stand down. 5 fall out argue, disagree, have a difference of opinion, quarrel, row

**fallacy** n error, misconception, mistake, paradox

**fallible** adj erring, error-prone, flawed, human, imperfect, sinful, unreliable, weak; *opp* infallible

**false** adj 1 erroneous, fallacious, incorrect, invalid, mistaken, spurious, unfounded, untrue, wrong; *opp* true. 2 (of a person) deceitful, dishonest, disloyal, insincere, unfaithful. 3 artificial, counterfeit, fake, forged, imitation, mock, synthetic; *opp* real

**falsify** v alter, counterfeit, doctor, fabricate, fake, forge, lie about, manipulate, misrepresent, retouch, tamper with, touch up

**falter** v bumble, go wrong, hesitate, stammer, stutter

**fame** n celebrity, distinction, eminence, esteem, greatness, importance, infamy, note, notoriety, pre-eminence, renown, reputation, stardom

**familiar** adj 1 common, commonplace, conventional, customary, everyday, frequent, habitual, household, mundane, normal, ordinary, predictable, recognizable, regular, routine, run-of-the mill, stock, usual, well-known; *opp* unusual. 2 (of people) amiable, casual, close, confidential, cordial, easy, free, friendly, informal, intimate, open, relaxed, sociable, unceremonious, unreserved; *opp* formal. 3 **familiar with** acquainted with, at home with, aware of, conscious of, conversant with, expert in, informed about, no stranger to, trained in, versed in, well up in

**familiarize** v accustom, acquaint, get to know, habituate, make familiar with, make conversant with

**family** n brood, flesh and blood, household, issue, kin, nearest and dearest *inf*, relations, relatives, tribe

**famine** n food shortage, hunger, lack of food, starvation

**famished** adj dying of hunger, dying of starvation, hungry, ravenous, starved, starving, undernourished; *opp* full

**famous** adj acclaimed, big, celebrated, eminent, famed, illustrious, legendary, much-publicized, notorious, prominent, renowned, well-known, world-famous; *opp* unknown

**fan** n adherent, admirer, aficionado, buff *inf*, devotee, enthusiast, fanatic, follower, lover, nut *inf*, supporter, zealot

**fanatic** n 1 (football fanatic) enthusiast, fan, follower, lover, nut *inf*, supporter. 2 (religious fanatic) activist, extremist, maniac, militant, radical, zealot

**fanatical** adj enthusiastic, excessive, extreme, fervent, fervid, frenzied, mad, obsessive, over-enthusiastic, passionate, rabid, wild, zealous; *opp* moderate

**fanciful** adj 1 (of a design) extravagant, fabulous, fairy-tale, fancy; *opp* simple. 2 (of an idea) fabulous, fantastic, ideal, imaginary, legendary, mythical, poetic, romantic, unreal, wild; *opp* realistic. 3 (of a person) capricious, imaginative, inventive, whimsical

**fancy** adj decorated, decorative, elaborate, elegant, embellished, embroidered, glitzy *inf*, intricate, jazzy *inf*, lavish, ornamental, ornamented, ornate, posh *inf*, showy, snazzy *inf*,

**opp** plain

**fancy** v 1 (fancy that sth will happen) believe, conceive, conjecture, guess, imagine, infer, reckon, suppose, surmise, think. 2 (fancy a drink) crave, feel like, long for, want, would like, wish for, yearn for. 3 (fancy sb) be attracted to, be infatuated by, be mad on, desire, fall for, have a crush on, lust after, take a shine to, take to

**fantastic** adj 1 ace inf, brilliant, cracking inf, excellent, fabulous, first-class, first-rate, great, magnificent, marvellous, outstanding, phenomenal, sensational, splendid, super, superb, terrific, tremendous, wonderful; **opp** terrible. 2 (fantastic notions) absurd, amazing, eccentric, exaggerated, exotic, fanciful, far-fetched, freakish, grotesque, incredible, odd, peculiar, quaint, queer, strange, weird, whimsical, wild; **opp** ordinary

**fantasy** n day-dream, delusion, fancy, illusion, imagination, invention, make-believe, reverie; **opp** reality

**far** adv 1 afar, a good way, a great distance, a long way, deep. 2 (far better) considerably, decidedly, greatly, incomparably, much; **opp** slightly. 3 so far thus far, to date, until now, up to now, up to the present, up to this point

**farce** n 1 (type of humour) buffoonery, comedy, parody, satire, slapstick. 2 joke, mockery, nonsense, sham, travesty

**farcical** adj 1 (of a type of humour) amusing, comic, custard-pie, droll, funny, satirical, slapstick. 2 (not good) absurd, derisory, foolish, laughable, ludicrous, nonsensical, preposterous,

ridiculous, risible, silly; **opp** reasonable

**far-fetched** adj doubtful, dubious, improbable, ridiculous, unbelievable, unconvincing, unlikely, unnatural, unrealistic; **opp** realistic

**farm** n croft, holding, homestead, land, plantation, ranch, smallholding

**farm** v cultivate, operate, plant, plough, work

**farming** n agriculture, crofting, cultivation, food-production, husbandry

**far-reaching** adj broad, comprehensive, extensive, important, significant, sweeping, widespread

**fascinate** v absorb, beguile, bewitch, captivate, charm, delight, enchant, engross, enrapture, enthral, entrance, hypnotize, intrigue, mesmerize, rivet, transfix; **opp** bore

**fascinated** adj absorbed, captivated, enchanted, engrossed, enraptured, enthralled, entranced, hypnotized, intrigued, mesmerized, riveted, spellbound, transfixed; **opp** uninterested

**fascinating** adj absorbing, captivating, compelling, enchanting, engaging, engrossing, enrapturing, enthralling, entrancing, gripping, hypnotizing, interesting, intriguing, irresistible, mesmerizing, riveting; **opp** dull

**fashion** n 1 (the latest fashion) convention, craze, custom, fad, the latest thing, trend, vogue. 2 (in such a fashion) manner, method, mode, style, system, way

**fashionable** adj à la mode, chic, current, in inf, in fashion, in vogue, latest, modern, trendy inf, up-to-date, up-to-the-minute, with it inf;

*opp* unfashionable

**fast** *adj* breakneck, brisk, hasty, high-speed, hurried, nippy *inf*, quick, rapid, speedy, supersonic, swift; *opp* slow

**fast** *n* abstinence, fasting, hunger strike

**fast** *v* abstain, go hungry, go on hunger strike, go without food

**fasten** *v* affix, anchor, attach, bind, bolt, buckle, chain, clamp, connect, couple, do up, fix, hitch, join, link, seal, secure, tether, tie; *opp* unfasten

**fastener** *n* anchor, binding, bolt, buckle, chain, clamp, connection, coupling, link, seal

**fat** *adj* beefy, chubby, corpulent, flabby, heavy, large, like a house end, obese, overweight, plump, podgy, portly, rotund, solid, squat, stocky, stout, tubby, weighty; *opp* thin

**fat** *n* blubber, bulk, corpulence, extra weight, flab, paunch

**fatal** *adj* 1 (resulting in sb's death) deadly, final, incurable, killing, lethal, malignant, mortal, pernicious, terminal; *opp* harmless. 2 (resulting in sth unpleasant) calamitous, catastrophic, dire, disastrous, lethal, ruinous; *opp* harmless

**fatality** *n* casualty, death, loss, victim; *opp* survivor

**fate** *n* 1 chance, destiny, doom, fortune, lot, predestination, providence. 2 (the fate of sth) end, future, issue, outcome, result, upshot

**fateful** *adj* catastrophic, disastrous, lethal, fated, ruinous

**father** *n* 1 dad, daddy, male parent, old man *inf*, pa *inf*, papa, pop *inf*. 2 (the father of sth) architect, creator, discoverer, founder, initiator, maker, originator

**fatigue** *n* exhaustion, heaviness, languor, lethargy, listlessness, over-tiredness, tiredness, weariness; *opp* liveliness

**fault** *n* 1 blemish, defect, deficiency, drawback, failing, flaw, imperfection, shortcoming, snag, weakness, weak point. 2 blunder, boob *inf*, error, faux pas, gaffe *inf*, howler *inf*, inaccuracy, miscalculation, misspelling, mistake, omission, oversight, slip, slip-up

**faulty** *adj* bad, broken, damaged, defective, deficient, flawed, erroneous, impaired, imperfect, malfunctioning, on the blink *inf*, out of order, unusable, weak, wrong; *opp* faultless

**favour** *n* 1 (win sb's favour) acceptance, approbation, approval, backing, benevolence, esteem, good opinion, good will, liking, partiality, support. 2 (do sb a favour) courtesy, good turn, kindness, service

**favour** *v* 1 (favour doing sth) advocate, approve, back, be in sympathy with, endorse, promote, recommend, sanction, support; *opp* disapprove. 2 (favour sb) indulge, pamper, reward, show favouritism towards, spoil. 3 (favour sth) be partial to, go for *inf*, go in for *inf*, incline towards, like best, prefer; *opp* dislike

**favourable** *adj* 1 advantageous, appropriate, auspicious, beneficial, conducive, convenient, fair, fit, good, helpful, hopeful, in your favour, on your side, opportune, positive, promising, suitable, timely; *opp* unfavourable. 2 (favourable comments) approving, complimentary, congratulatory, encouraging, enthusiastic, good, laudatory, praising, well-disposed; *opp* unfavourable

**favourite** *adj* best, best-loved, choice, chosen, dearest, favoured, ideal, most-liked, preferred, selected

**favourite** *n* choice, first choice, pick, preference. **2** (a child) apple of your eye, blue-eyed boy, darling, idol, pet, teacher's pet

**fear** *n* **1** alarm, anxiety, apprehension, butterflies, cowardice, dread, fearfulness, faintheartedness, foreboding, fright, horror, nervousness, panic, qualms, shivers, terror, timidity, trepidation, uneasiness; *opp* courage. **2** (a fear of sth) aversion, hang-up, horror, neurosis, nightmare, phobia; *opp* love

**fear** *v* be afraid of, be scared of, dare not, dread, live in fear/terror of, shrink from, shudder at, take fright, tremble at, worry about

**fearful** *adj* **1** (fearful of sth) afraid, alarmed, anxious, apprehensive, frightened, intimidated, nervous, panic-stricken, scared, scared stiff, terrified, timid, uneasy. **2** (a fearful noise) appalling, awful, dire, dreadful, frightful, ghastly, horrible, terrible

**fearless** *adj* bold, brave, confident, courageous, daring, gallant, gutsy *inf*, hard *inf*, heroic, intrepid, plucky, unafraid, undaunted, valiant; *opp* cowardly

**fearsome** *adj* alarming, awesome, daunting, formidable, frightening, hair-raising, horrifying, intimidating, menacing, terrifying, unnerving

**feasible** *adj* achievable, attainable, doable, likely, possible, practicable, realizable, reasonable, viable, workable; *opp* impossible

**feast** *n* banquet, blow out *sl*, dinner, spread *inf*, treat

**feat** *n* accomplishment, achievement, act, action, attainment, deed, exploit, performance

**feature** *n* **1** aspect, attribute, characteristic, detail, facet, factor, mark, peculiarity, point, property, quality, side, trait. **2** (in a newspaper) article, column, item, piece, report, story

**feature** *v* **1** accentuate, emphasize, focus on, give prominence to, highlight, play up, present, promote, spotlight, stress. **2** (in a film) act, appear, figure, participate, perform, play a role, star

**features** *n* appearance, countenance, face, look

**fed up** *adj* annoyed, bored, depressed, discontented, dissatisfied, down, gloomy, glum, miserable, sad, weary; *opp* happy

**fee** *n* bill, charge, cost, dues, fare, payment, price, rate, remuneration, subscription, tariff, toll

**feeble** *adj* **1** decrepit, debilitated, delicate, doddering, exhausted, failing, faint, fragile, frail, infirm, languid, listless, poorly, puny, sickly, weak; *opp* strong. **2** (not determined) inadequate, incompetent, indecisive, ineffectual, irresolute, namby-pamby *inf*, spineless, weedy, wimpy, wishy-washy *inf*; *opp* tough. **3** (a feeble excuse) flimsy, futile, inadequate, ineffective, insubstantial, lame, paltry, poor, unconvincing; *opp* good

**feed** v 1 cater for, give food to, nourish, nurture, provide for, provision, suckle, support, supply, sustain. 2 (feed on sth) devour, dine, eat, graze, live on, pasture, subsist

**feel** n 1 (a leathery feel) finish, surface, texture. 2 (the feel of a place) ambience, atmosphere, aura, impression, mood

**feel** v 1 (with your fingers) caress, finger, fondle, handle, manipulate, maul, paw, stroke, thumb, touch. 2 (in your mind) be aware of, be conscious of, detect, discern, endure, enjoy, experience, go through, have, know, notice, observe, perceive, suffer, undergo. 3 (feel your way) explore, fumble, grope, test, try. 4 (have an opinion) be convinced, believe, be of the opinion that, consider, have a (funny) feeling, intuit, judge, sense, think. 5 **feel like** desire, fancy, want, wish for, would like, yearn for

**feeling** n 1 sensation, sense of touch, sensitivity. 2 (have a feeling) funny feeling, hunch, idea, impression, inkling, notion, suspicion. 3 (sb's feeling about sth) attitude, belief, inclination, instinct, opinion, thought, view

**feelings** n ego, emotions, self-esteem, sensitivities, sentiments, susceptibilities

**fell** v chop down, cut down, demolish, flatten, floor, hew, knock down, level

**feminine** adj delicate, elegant, gentle, girlish, girly inf, graceful, ladylike, soft, tender, womanly; **opp** masculine

**fen** n bog, lowland, marsh, quagmire, swamp

**fence** n barricade, barrier, defence, fencing, hedge, hurdle, paling, palisade, railings, rampart, stockade, wall, wire

**fence** v bound, circumscribe, confine, coop, encircle, enclose, hedge, pen, surround

**ferment** v 1 boil, brew, bubble, fizz, foam, froth, heat, leaven, rise. 2 agitate, excite, incite, inflame, instigate, provoke, rouse, stir up; **opp** calm

**ferocious** adj barbaric, bloodthirsty, brutal, fierce, predatory, ruthless, savage, vicious, violent, wild; **opp** harmless

**ferry** v bring, carry, chauffeur, convey, fetch, shift, ship, shuttle, take, taxi, transport

**fertile** adj fecund, fruitful, lush, productive, prolific, rich, yielding; **opp** infertile

**fertilize** v 1 impregnate, inseminate, make pregnant, pollinate. 2 (fertilize soil) compost, dress, enrich, feed, make fertile, manure, mulch, nourish

**fervent** adj ardent, avid, devout, eager, earnest, emotional, enthusiastic, excited, fanatical, fiery, heartfelt, heated, impassioned, intense, keen, passionate, vehement, wholehearted, zealous; **opp** lukewarm

**fester** v 1 become infected, become inflamed, become poisoned, discharge, go septic, ooze, putrefy, ulcerate. 2 decay, decompose, disintegrate, go bad, go off, rot

**festival** n 1 (a public festival) anniversary, bank holiday, commemoration, day of observance, feast, holiday, holy day, saint's day. 2 carnival, celebration, festivities, gala, jubilee

**festive** adj celebratory, cheerful, convivial, gay, happy, holiday, jolly, jovial, joyful, joyous, merry

**festivity** n amusement, celebration, conviviality, entertainment, fun, fun and games, gaiety, joviality, joyfulness, merriment, merrymaking, mirth, pleasure, revelry

**fetch** v 1 bring, carry, conduct, convey, deliver, escort, get, go and get, import, obtain, retrieve, transport. 2 (fetch a price) bring in, earn, go for, make, raise, realize, sell for, yield

**fête** n bazaar, fair, festival, gala, garden party, jumble sale, sale of work, show

**feud** n 1 argument, conflict, disagreement, dispute, falling-out, quarrel, running battle. 2 (a state of feud) animosity, antagonism, argument, bad blood, conflict, disagreement, discord, dispute, dissension, estrangement, grudge, hostility, rivalry, strife, unfriendliness; *opp* harmony

**fever** n delirium, feverishness, high temperature, temperature

**feverish** adj 1 (of a person) burning up inf, delirious, flushed, hot. 2 (of activity) agitated, desperate, excited, distracted, excited, frantic, frenetic, frenzied, hectic, passionate; *opp* calm

**fiasco** n catastrophe, debacle, disaster, failure, farce, flop inf, mess, rout, washout; *opp* success

**fibre** n filament, hair, strand, thread

**fickle** adj capricious, changeable, changing, disloyal, erratic, fitful, flighty, inconstant, unpredictable, up and down inf, vacillating, volatile; *opp* constant

**fiction** n 1 fable, fantasy, legend, make-believe, myth, romance, story, tale; *opp* real life. 2 (sth not true) cock and

bull story inf, deception, fabrication, falsehood, fancy, fantasy, fib, imagination, invention, lie, tall story, untruth, whopper inf; *opp* truth

**fictional** adj fictitious, imaginary, invented, made-up, make-believe, pretend, non-existent, unreal; *opp* real

**fictitious** adj assumed, bogus, counterfeit, fabricated, fake, false, feigned, imaginary, imagined, invented, made-up, mythical, sham, spurious, unreal, untrue; *opp* genuine

**fiddle** v 1 fidget, finger, fuss, interfere, meddle, mess about, mess around, play, tamper, tinker, toy, trifle. 2 cheat, cook the books, falsify, fix, manoeuvre, racketeer, swindle, wangle

**fidelity** n 1 allegiance, commitment, constancy, dependability, devotion, faithfulness, integrity, loyalty, reliability, staunchness, trustworthiness; *opp* disloyalty. 2 accuracy, adherence, authenticity, closeness, correspondence, exactness, faithfulness, precision; *opp* inaccuracy

**fidget** v fiddle, fuss, have ants in your pants, mess about, mess around, play about, shuffle, squirm, twitch, wriggle

**fidgety** adj agitated, frisky, impatient, jerky, jittery, jumpy, nervous, on edge, restless, twitchy, uneasy; *opp* still

**field** n 1 clearing, enclosure, grassland, green, meadow, paddock, pasture. 2 (a sports field) arena, court, ground, pitch, playing field, recreation ground, stadium, turf. 3 (a field of activity) area, discipline, domain, line, province, speciality, sphere, subject, territory

**fiend** n 1 demon, devil, evil spirit, goblin,

imp, Satan, spirit. **2** addict, devotee, enthusiast, fan, fanatic, follower, freak *inf*, lover, maniac, nut *inf*, supporter, zealot

**fiendish** *adj* accursed, atrocious, barbaric, bloodthirsty, brutal, cruel, demonic, devilish, diabolical, hellish, implacable, infernal, inhuman, malevolent, malicious, malignant, merciless, monstrous, pitiless, ruthless, satanic, savage, ungodly, unspeakable, vicious, wicked; *opp* godly, good

**fierce** *adj* barbaric, brutal, cold-blooded, cruel, dangerous, fearsome, ferocious, menacing, murderous, passionate, ruthless, savage, threatening, uncontrollable, untamed, vicious, violent, wild; *opp* gentle

**fight** *n* **1** action, affray, attack, battle, bout, brawl, clash, conflict, contest, dust-up *inf*, engagement, fracas, fray, joust, punch-up *inf*, scrap *inf*, set-to *inf*, skirmish, struggle, tussle, war, wrestle. **2** altercation, argument, brush, disagreement, dispute, falling out, feud, quarrel, squabble, wrangle

**fight** *v* **1** attack, battle, box, brawl, clash, come to blows, contend, engage, grapple, have a fight, joust, scrap *inf*, skirmish, spar, struggle, tussle, war, wrestle. **2** challenge, contest, defy, dispute, oppose, resist, struggle against, take a stand against, withstand. **3** argue, be at odds, bicker, clash, dispute, fall out, feud, quarrel, squabble, wrangle. **4 fight back** counter-attack, defend yourself, hit back, put up a fight, reply, resist, retaliate, stand up for yourself. **5 fight off** beat off, fend off, hold at bay,

repel, repulse, stave off, ward off

**fighter** *n* boxer, combatant, contender, pugilist, soldier, warrior, wrestler

**figure** *n* **1** amount, cipher, digit, integer, number, numeral, sum, value. **2** body, build, form, frame, outline, physique, shape, silhouette. **3** chart, diagram, graph, illustration, symbol, table

**figure** *v* **1** comprehend, decipher, fathom, make out, see, realize, understand, work out. **2 figure out** assess, calculate, compute, reckon, solve, work out

**file** *n* **1** data, document, dossier, folder, portfolio, record. **2** column, line, procession, queue, row, stream, string, train

**file** *v* **1** categorize, classify, document, enter, organize, put on record, record, register. **2** march, parade, troop. **3** abrade, rasp, rub, scrape, shape, smooth

**fill** *v* block, bung up *inf*, cram, crowd, gorge, jam, load, pack, refill, replenish, satisfy, stock, stuff

**filling** *n* contents, insides, middle, padding, stuffing, wadding

**film** *n* **1** flick *inf*, motion picture, movie, picture, video. **2** coat, coating, covering, haze, layer, membrane, scum, skin, tissue, veil, veneer

**filter** *v* clarify, filtrate, purify, refine, screen, sieve, sift, strain

**filth** *n* **1** contamination, dirt, dung, effluent, excrement, faeces, filthiness, foulness, grime, grot *inf*, muck, ordure, pollution, refuse, sewage, sludge, squalor. **2** impurity, indecency, obscenity, pornography, smut, vulgarity

**filthy** *adj* **1** contamination, begrimed,

defiled, dirty, foul, grimy, grotty *inf*,
grubby, mucky, polluted, squalid;
*opp* clean. 2 bawdy, blue *inf*, coarse,
impure, indecent, lewd, licentious,
obscene, pornographic, raunchy, rude,
smutty, sordid, vulgar

**final** *adj* closing, concluding, conclusive,
dying, end, eventual, finishing, last,
parting, terminating, ultimate; *opp* first

**finale** *n* climax, close, conclusion,
culmination, denouement, end,
epilogue, finish, last act

**finalize** *v* agree, arrange, clinch,
complete, conclude, confirm, decide,
settle, tie up, wrap up

**finance** *n* 1 (dealing with money)
accounting, banking, business,
commerce, economics, investment,
stock market. 2 (money) accounts,
assets, capital, cash, funds, money,
resources, revenue, wealth, wherewithal

**finance** *v* back, fund, guarantee, invest
in, pay for, subsidize, support, underwrite

**financial** *adj* budgetary, commercial,
economic, fiscal, monetary, money,
pecuniary

**find** *n* acquisition, asset, bargain,
discovery, good buy, innovation,
invention

**find** *v* 1 (find sth new) chance upon,
come across, discover, encounter, espy,
happen on, hit on, light on, spot, turn
up, uncover, unearth. 2 (find sth lost)
get back, locate, recoup, recover,
rediscover, regain, retrieve, trace, track
down; *opp* lose. 3 become aware,
conclude, discover, note, notice,
observe, perceive, realize. 4 **find out**
become aware, bring sth to light, detect,

discover, expose, learn, observe, realize,
reveal, see

**fine** *adj* 1 admirable, beautiful, choice,
classic, consummate, elegant, excellent,
exceptional, exquisite, first-class, first-
rate, good, great, high-class, high-
quality, magnificent, outstanding,
quality, rare, refined, select, splendid,
superb, superior, supreme, top-notch *inf*,
world-class. 2 acceptable, agreeable, all
right, OK *inf*, satisfactory, suitable.
3 (a fine day) balmy, bright, clear,
cloudless, dry, fair, pleasant, sunny;
*opp* wet. 4 (fine porcelain) dainty,
delicate, flimsy, fragile, light, minute,
narrow, slender, slim, small, thin,
translucent; *opp* coarse. 5 (a fine
distinction) abstruse, discriminating,
exact, fastidious, fine-drawn, hair-
splitting, minute, nice, precise, subtle;
*opp* clear, obvious

**fine** *n* charge, forfeit, penalty, punishment

**finesse** *n* adroitness, artfulness,
cleverness, craft, delicacy, expertise,
grace, polish, refinement, savoir-faire,
skill, subtlety

**finish** *n* 1 cessation, close, closing,
completion, conclusion, culmination,
denouement, end, ending, finale,
termination; *opp* start. 2 coating, gloss,
lacquer, lustre, patina, polish, sheen,
shine, smoothness, surface, veneer

**finish** *v* 1 accomplish, achieve, bring to
an end, clinch, close, complete,
conclude, culminate, discharge, end,
execute, finalize, fulfil, get done, perfect,
settle, wrap up. 2 break off, cease, desist,
discontinue, halt, interrupt, pack up,
phase out, stop, suspend, terminate,

wind up. **3** annihilate, beat, be too much for, bring down, conquer, destroy, dispose of, exterminate, get rid of, get the better of, kill, overcome, overpower, ruin. **4** consume, devour, dispatch, dispose of, drink up, eat up, get through, polish off *inf*

**finished** *adj* **1** clinched, closed, complete, completed, done, ended, final, finalized, over, perfect, settled, through, tied up, wrapped up. **2** beaten, defeated, done for *inf*, doomed, overcome, past it *inf*, ruined, through, undone, washed up *inf*, wrecked

**finite** *adj* calculable, certain, countable, definable, defined, determinable, fixed, limited, measurable, numbered, restricted; *opp* infinite

**fire** *n* **1** blaze, burning, combustion, conflagration, flame, inferno, pyre. **2** barrage, bombardment, gunfire, salvo, shelling, shooting, shot, sniping. **3** ardour, energy, fervour, intensity, life, passion, spark, spirit, vehemence, vigour, vivacity, zeal

**fire** *v* **1** (set fire to sth) burn, ignite, kindle, put a match to, set sth alight, set fire to, set sth on fire, torch. **2** (fire a gun) detonate, discharge, launch, let off, pull the trigger, set off, shoot. **3** (fire sb) discharge, dismiss, down-size, get rid of, give sb the boot *inf*, let sb go, make sb redundant, sack, throw sb out

**firm** *adj* **1** compact, compressed, condensed, dense, hard, inflexible, resilient, resistant, rigid, set, solid, solidified, strong, taut, tight, stiff, unyielding; *opp* soft. **2** anchored, braced, embedded, fast, fixed, immovable,

motionless, rooted, secured, solid, stable, steady, strong, sturdy, tight, unmoving; *opp* loose. **3** adamant, certain, constant, definite, determined, fixed, immovable, inflexible, intransigent, obdurate, resolute, resolved, set, settled, staunch, stalwart, steadfast, strict, stubborn, sure, unalterable, unbending, unmoving, unshakable, unswerving, unwavering, unyielding

**firm** *n* association, business, company, concern, corporation, enterprise, establishment, house, group, organization, partnership

**first** *adj* **1** earliest, initial, maiden, opening, original, preliminary, primeval, primitive, primordial. **2** chief, dominant, foremost, head, highest, leading, pre-eminent, premier, prime, principal, ruling, superior, supreme, uppermost. **3** axiomatic, basic, cardinal, elementary, essential, fundamental, key, primary, rudimentary

**first-rate** *adj* admirable, choice, classic, consummate, excellent, exceptional, first class, high-class, high-quality, magnificent, outstanding, quality, rare, refined, select, splendid, superb, superior, superlative, top-notch *inf*, world class

**fit** *adj* **1** energetic, healthy, in shape, in trim, robust, strapping, strong, toned, trim, vigorous, well; *opp* unfit. **2** able, adequate, appropriate, capable, competent, correct, decent, eligible, equipped, fitting, good enough, qualified, proper, right, suitable, up to the job *inf*, worthy; *opp* unfit

**fit** *n* attack, bout, convulsion, eruption,

explosion, outbreak, outburst, paroxysm,
seizure, spasm, spell, turn

**fit** v **1** accord, agree, be right, belong,
concur, dovetail, interlock, match, meet,
suit, tally. **2** arrange, assemble, build,
construct, install, interlock, join, match,
put in, put together. **3** adapt, adjust,
alter, cut, modify, shape, tailor

**fitting** adj adequate, appropriate,
becoming, correct, decent, decorous,
good enough, proper, right, seemly,
suitable, worthy

**fix** n bind inf, corner, difficulty, dilemma,
jam inf, mess, pickle inf, plight,
predicament, problem, quandary,
scrape inf, spot inf

**fix** v **1** anchor, attach, connect, embed,
fasten, fit, install, join, secure, stick, tie.
**2** agree, appoint, arrange, arrive at,
conclude, decide, define, determine,
establish, finalize, limit, name, resolve,
set, settle, specify. **3** mend, patch up, put
right, remedy, repair, restore, sort out

**fixed** adj **1** attached, immobile,
permanent, rigid, secured; **opp** movable.
**2** agreed, arranged, definite, established,
planned, pre-arranged, predetermined,
set, settled

**fixture** n arrangement, date, engagement,
event, game, match, meeting

**fizzy** adj bubbling, bubbly, carbonated,
effervescent, gassy, sparkling; **opp** still

**flag** n banner, bunting, colours, ensign,
pennant, standard, streamer

**flag** v **1** fade, fail, decline, decrease,
diminish, ebb, taper off, tire, wane,
weaken, weary. **2** indicate, label, mark,
pick out, signal

**flagrant** adj bare-faced, blatant, bold,

brazen, glaring, gross, obvious, open,
ostentatious, outrageous, overt,
scandalous, shameless, shocking,
unashamed, unconcealed, undisguised

**flair** n **1** ability, aptitude, facility, feel,
genius, gift, knack, skill, talent. **2** chic,
dash, elegance, panache, style, taste

**flamboyant** adj bold, colourful, dashing,
dazzling, extravagant, fancy, flashy,
gaudy, glamorous, ostentatious,
outrageous, shocking, showy, splendid,
swashbuckling, theatrical

**flame** n **1** blaze, conflagration, fire,
tongue. **2** ardour, fervour, fire, intensity,
passion, warmth

**flame** v be ablaze, blaze, burn, flare, flash,
glare, glow, shine

**flap** v **1** agitate, beat, flail, flutter,
oscillate, shake, swing, swish, thrash,
wag, waggle, wave. **2** be agitated, be
in a state, fuss, get flustered, panic

**flare** v blaze, burn, dazzle, flash, flicker,
glare, gleam, glint, shine

**flash** n **1** beam, blaze, bolt, burst, flare,
flicker, glare, gleam, glimmer, glint, ray,
shaft, shimmer, shine, spark, sparkle,
twinkle. **2** instant, jiffy inf, minute,
moment, second, split second, trice,
twinkling of an eye

**flash** v beam, blaze, dazzle, flare, flicker,
glare, gleam, glimmer, glint, glisten,
glitter, light up, reflect, shimmer, shine,
sparkle, twinkle

**flashy** adj bold, brash, bright,
extravagant, fancy, flamboyant, garish,
gaudy, glitzy, loud, ostentatious, showy,
tacky inf, tasteless, tawdry, vulgar; **opp**
understated

**flat** adj **1** even, horizontal, level, levelled,

plane, smooth, unbroken. **2** lying down, outstretched, prone, prostrate, reclining, recumbent, sprawling, spread-eagled, stretched out, supine. **3** bland, boring, dead, dry, dull, insipid, lacklustre, lifeless, monotonous, prosaic, stale, tedious, uninteresting, unvarying, vapid; **opp** interesting

**flat** *n* apartment, bedsit, bedsitter, maisonette, pad *inf*, penthouse, rooms, suite

**flatten** *v* **1** compact, compress, even out, iron out, level out, plane, press down, smooth out. **2** crush, demolish, destroy, knock down, level, raze, squash, trample

**flatter** *v* blandish, butter up, cajole, compliment, court, crawl *inf*, eulogize, fawn, get round *inf*, gush, humour, lay it on thick *inf*, lick sb's boots *inf*, pander to, pay court to, play up to *inf*, praise, soft-soap *inf*, suck up to *sl*, sweet-talk *inf*, wheedle

**flattery** *n* adulation, blandishments, blarney, boot-licking *inf*, buttering-up, cajoling, compliments, eulogy, fawning, gushing, obsequiousness, pandering, praise, soft soap *inf*, sucking-up *sl*, sweet talk *inf*, wheedling

**flavour** *n* **1** aroma, essence, extract, odour, piquancy, relish, savour, seasoning, smack, tang, taste, tastiness, zest. **2** ambience, atmosphere, aura, character, essence, feel, feeling, nature, quality, soul, spirit, tone

**flavour** *v* add flavour to, add piquancy to, imbue, infuse, lace, season, spice

**flaw** *n* blemish, defect, failing, fault, foible, imperfection, shortcoming, weakness

**flawed** *adj* blemished, broken, chipped, cracked, damaged, defective, faulty, imperfect, marred, spoilt, unsound; **opp** perfect

**flee** *v* abscond, beat a retreat, beat it *inf*, bolt, decamp, disappear, do a runner *sl*, escape, fly, leg it *inf*, make off, run away, run off, scarper *inf*, take flight, take off, take to your heels *inf*, vanish

**fleet** *n* armada, convoy, flotilla, naval force, navy, task force, warships

**fleeting** *adj* brief, ephemeral, momentary, passing, quick, rapid, short, short-lived, swift, transient, transitory

**flesh** *n* **1** brawn, carrion, fat, meat, muscle, tissue. **2** body, carnality, physicality, sensuality

**flexible** *adj* **1** bendable, bendy, ductile, giving, elastic, malleable, plastic, pliable, springy, stretchy, supple, yielding; **opp** rigid. **2** adaptable, amenable, biddable, compliant, fluid, malleable, open, responsive, tractable, yielding; **opp** inflexible

**flicker** *v* blink, flash, flutter, glimmer, glint, glitter, oscillate, quiver, tremble, twinkle, vibrate, waver, wink, wobble

**flicker** *n* blink, flash, flutter, glimmer, glint, glitter, twinkle, spark, wink

**flight** *n* **1** journey, trajectory, trip. **2** aviation, flying, soaring, winging. **3** absconding, decamping, departure, disappearance, escape, exit, exodus, fleeing, getaway, retreat, vanishing

**flimsy** *adj* **1** breakable, brittle, delicate, fine, fragile, frail, insubstantial, lightweight, makeshift, ramshackle, rickety, shaky, slight, thin, weak; **opp** strong. **2** (a flimsy excuse) feeble, implausible, inadequate, pathetic, poor, thin, transparent, trifling, trivial, unconvincing, unsatisfactory, weak; *opp* sound

**flinch** v baulk, blench, cower, cringe, dodge, duck, flee, jib at, jump, quail, recoil, retreat, shirk, shrink, shy away, start, swerve, wince, withdraw

**fling** v cast, chuck *inf*, heave, hurl, launch, lob *inf*, pitch, propel, send, shy, sling, throw, toss

**flippant** adj casual, cheeky, disrespectful, facetious, flip, frivolous, glib, light-hearted, impertinent, impudent, irreverent, jokey, offhand, pert, shallow, superficial, thoughtless

**flirt** n coquette, heart-breaker, philanderer, tease

**flirt** v chat sb up *inf*, lead sb on, make advances, ogle, philander, tease, toy with, trifle with

**flirtatious** adj coquettish, coy, flirty, philandering, playful, provocative, teasing

**float** v be buoyant, bob, drift, glide, hang, hover, poise, sail, slide, slip, stay afloat; *opp* sink

**floating** adj 1 afloat, bobbing, buoyant, drifting, gliding, hanging, hovering, poised, sailing, suspended. 2 changeable, fluctuating, unattached, uncommitted, undecided, variable, wandering

**flock** n 1 (of animals) drove, flight, gaggle, herd. 2 (of people) assembly, company, congregation, crowd, gathering, group, horde, host, mass, multitude, throng

**flock** v amass, assemble, congregate, converge, crowd, gather, group, herd, huddle, mass, swarm, throng, troop

**flog** v beat, birch, cane, chastise, flagellate, flay, lash, scourge, thrash, whip

**flood** n 1 deluge, downpour, flash flood, inundation, overflow, spate, tidal wave, tide, torrent. 2 abundance, excess, flow, glut, plethora, profusion, rush, stream, surfeit, surge

**flood** v 1 (to flood an area) cover, deluge, drown, engulf, fill, immerse, inundate, submerge, sweep. 2 (of a river) break its banks, brim over, overflow, pour, stream, surge, swell

**floor** n deck, level, stage, storey, tier

**flop** n débâcle, disaster, dud *inf*, failure, fiasco, loser, no-hoper *inf*, non-starter, washout *inf*; *opp* success

**flop** v 1 collapse, dangle, droop, drop, fall, flag, hang, sag, slump, topple, tumble, wilt. 2 bomb *inf*, close, fail, fall flat, founder

**flounder** v blunder, flail, fumble, grope, muddle, struggle, stumble, thrash, wallow

**flourish** n brandishing, display, gesture, shaking, show, swing, swish, twirl, wave

**flourish** v 1 be fruitful, be successful, bloom, blossom, burgeon, grow, prosper, succeed, thrive; *opp* fail. 2 brandish, hold up, shake, swing, swish, twirl, wave, wield

**flourishing** adj blooming, blossoming, booming, burgeoning, fruitful, growing, prosperous, successful, thriving; *opp* ailing, failing

**flout** v defy, disobey, disregard, ignore, insult, jeer at, laugh at, make a mockery of, mock, ridicule, scorn, show contempt for, sneer at, spurn, treat sth with disdain

**flow** v cascade, circulate, course, dribble, drip, ebb, glide, gush, leak, move, ooze, pour, roll, run, rush, seep, slide, slip, spill, spout, squirt, stream, surge, sweep, swirl, trickle, well, whirl

**flower** n 1 bloom, blossom, bud, floret. 2 best, choice, cream, elite, height, pick

**flower** v bloom, blossom, bud, burgeon, flourish, open, unfold

**fluctuate** v alternate, be unsteady, change, hesitate, oscillate, move, seesaw, shift, swing, vacillate, vary, veer, waver, yo-yo

**fluent** adj articulate, easy, effortless, eloquent, flowing, fluid, mellifluous, natural, ready, smooth, voluble

**fluid** adj 1 flowing, liquefied, liquid, melted, molten, running, runny, sloppy, watery; **opp** solid. 2 adaptable, adjustable, changeable, flexible, floating, indefinite, mobile, mutable, open, shifting, variable; **opp** fixed

**flurry** n bustle, commotion, excitement, flap, fluster, flutter, hubbub, stir, tumult, whirl

**flush** n bloom, blush, colour, glow, radiance, redness, rosiness

**flush** v 1 (of a face) blush, burn, colour, flame, glow, go red, redden. 2 clean out, cleanse, flood, hose down, rinse, wash down, wash out

**fly** v 1 flit, flutter, glide, hover, sail, soar, swoop, take flight, take to the air, take wing. 2 (of a pilot) control, manoeuvre, operate, pilot, take off. 3 (of a flag) display, flap, flutter, hoist, raise, show, wave. 4 (of time) elapse, pass, race, roll on, slip away, slip past. 5 dart, dash, hare

inf, hurry, race, rush, shoot, sprint, tear, zoom

**foam** n bubbles, froth, head, lather, scum, spray, spume, suds

**foam** v boil, bubble, effervesce, fizz, froth, lather

**focus** n centre, core, focal point, heart, hub, pivot, target

**focus** v 1 aim, concentrate, direct attention, fix, home in, pinpoint, spotlight. 2 (of a lens) bring into focus, turn, zoom in

**fog** n cloud, gloom, haze, mist, mistiness, murk, murkiness, smog

**foggy** adj blurred, blurry, clouded, cloudy, dim, grey, hazy, indistinct, misty, murky, obscure, smoggy; **opp** clear

**foil** v baffle, defeat, frustrate, outwit, prevent, stop, thwart

**fold** n bend, corrugation, crease, crinkle, furrow, gather, layer, line, overlap, pleat, pucker, turn, wrinkle

**fold** v 1 bend, crease, crimp, crinkle, crumple, double, gather, jack-knife, overlap, pleat, pucker, tuck, turn. 2 (fold sth in your arms) embrace, enclose, enfold, entwine, envelop, hold, wrap. 3 (of a business) close, collapse, crash, fail, go bankrupt, go bust inf, go under inf, go to the wall

**follow** v 1 (go behind sb or sth) chase, dog, hound, hunt, pursue, shadow, stalk, tag along inf, tail inf, track, trail. 2 (follow a rule) abide by, comply with, conform, honour, obey, observe, stick to. 3 (come after sb or sth) replace, step into sb's shoes, succeed, supersede, supplant, take sb's place

**follower** n admirer, apostle, believer,

convert, devotee, disciple, enthusiast, fan, groupie *inf*, pupil, supporter, worshipper

**folly** *n* foolishness, idiocy, insanity, lunacy, madness, nonsense, silliness, stupidity

**fond** *adj* **1** adoring, affectionate, amorous, caring, devoted, loving, warm. **2 fond of** addicted to, attached to, enamoured of, hooked on, in love with, keen on, mad about, partial to

**fondle** *v* caress, cuddle, pat, pet, stroke, touch

**food** *n* **1** cooking, cuisine, diet, eats *inf*, fare, foodstuffs, grub *inf*, meals, nosh *sl*, nourishment, provisions, refreshments, sustenance. **2** fodder, feed

**fool** *n* **1** blockhead, clot *inf*, dope *inf*, fat-head *inf*, half-wit, idiot, jerk *sl*, moron, nerd *sl*, nincompoop, nit, nitwit, twerp *inf*, twit *inf*, wally *sl*. **2** buffoon, clown, comedian, comic, jester

**fool** *v* **1** bamboozle, beguile, bluff, cheat, con *inf*, deceive, delude, dupe, have sb on *inf*, hoax, hoodwink, kid *inf*, make a fool of, mislead, play a trick on, string sb along *inf*, take sb in, trick. **2 fool around** act the fool, clown around, joke, mess about *inf*, play tricks, tease

**foolish** *adj* barmy *inf*, brainless, crazy, daft, dumb *inf*, hare-brained, idiotic, ill-advised, inane, ludicrous, mad, ridiculous, senseless, silly, simple, stupid, thoughtless, unintelligent, unwise; *opp* sensible

**foolproof** *adj* certain, guaranteed, infallible, safe, sure

**foot** *n* **1** base, bottom, end, foundation. **2** claw, hoof, paw, trotter

**forbid** *v* ban, bar, deny, exclude, inhibit, make illegal, prevent, prohibit, refuse, rule out, say no to, stop, veto; *opp* allow

**forbidden** *adj* against the law, banned, outlawed, out of bounds, prohibited, restricted, secret, taboo, wrong

**force** *n* **1** effort, energy, exertion, impact, might, muscle, power, pressure, stamina, strength, stress. **2** (making sb do sth) aggression, arm-twisting *inf*, coercion, compulsion, duress, pressure, violence. **3** (force of an argument) effect, effectiveness, influence, persuasiveness, power, strength, validity, weight. **4** (spoke with force) drive, emphasis, feeling, fierceness, intensity, passion, persistence, vehemence, vividness. **5** army, battalion, body, corps, division, group, squad, squadron, troops, unit

**force** *v* **1** (make sb do sth) bulldoze *inf*, coerce, compel, constrain, dragoon, impose, make, oblige, press-gang, pressurize, railroad *inf* , twist sb's arm. **2** (force sth open) blast, break open, prise, thrust, use force, wrench. **3** (force sth out) drag, exact, extort, wring. **4** (force sth along) drive, press, propel, push, urge

**forced** *adj* (a forced smile) affected, artificial, false, insincere, self-conscious, stiff, strained, unnatural, wooden; *opp* natural

**forceful** *adj* assertive, compelling, convincing, dynamic, effective, powerful, strong; *opp* weak

**foreboding** *n* anxiety, apprehension, chill, dread, fear, feeling, forewarning, intuition, misgiving, omen, premonition, presentiment, suspicion, warning, worry

**forecast** n guess, outlook, prediction, prognosis, projection, prophecy, speculation

**forecast** v divine, estimate, foresee, foretell, forewarn, predict, prophesy

**foreign** adj 1 (foreign lands) alien, distant, exotic, faraway, outlandish, remote, strange, unfamiliar, unknown. 2 (foreign affairs) external, international, outside, overseas; *opp* domestic

**foreigner** n alien, immigrant, newcomer, outsider, stranger, visitor

**forerunner** n 1 ancestor, forebear, forefather, predecessor. 2 harbinger, herald, precursor

**foresee** v anticipate, divine, envisage, expect, forebode, forecast, foretell, predict, prophesy

**foresight** n anticipation, care, farsightedness, forethought, looking ahead, precaution, prescience, vision

**forest** n coppice, copse, jungle, plantation, trees, wood, woodland

**foretell** v forecast, foresee, foreshadow, forewarn, herald, predict, prophesy

**forfeit** n damages, fee, fine, loss, penalty

**forfeit** v be deprived of, give up, hand over, lose, relinquish, renounce, surrender

**forge** v 1 (forge metal) beat, cast, form, hammer, make, mould, shape, work. 2 (forge an object) coin, copy, counterfeit, fake, falsify, imitate, make illegally, reproduce

**forgery** n copy, counterfeit, fake, imitation, replica, reproduction

**forget** v disregard, fail to remember,

ignore, lose sight of, neglect, omit, overlook, put out of your mind; *opp* remember

**forgetful** adj absent-minded, careless, distracted, dreamy, inattentive, neglectful, oblivious, preoccupied, vague

**forgive** v absolve, acquit, condone, excuse, exonerate, ignore, let off, overlook, pardon, spare

**forgiveness** n absolution, amnesty, clemency, compassion, exoneration, leniency, mercy, pardon, reprieve

**forgiving** adj compassionate, lenient, magnanimous, merciful, mild, soft-hearted, tolerant, understanding

**forgo** v do without, give up, go without, relinquish, renounce, sacrifice, surrender

**forgotten** adj blotted out, buried, dead, gone, left behind, lost, obliterated, out of mind, past

**forlorn** adj 1 alone, desolate, lonely, miserable, pathetic, pitiable, pitiful, unhappy, wretched. 2 abandoned, deserted, forgotten, forsaken, neglected. 3 (a forlorn hope) desperate, hopeless

**form** n 1 (the shape of sth) arrangement, configuration, design, formation, pattern, shape, structure. 2 (type) kind, sort, type, variety. 3 (form to fill in) application, document, paper, sheet. 4 (form at school) class, grade, group, set, stream. 5 (a slim form) anatomy, body, build, figure, frame, outline, physique, shape, silhouette

**form** v 1 build, cast, concoct, construct, create, fashion, forge, make, model, mould, produce, shape, stamp. 2 appear, arise, become visible, come into existence, develop, grow, materialize,

take shape. **3** devise, draw up, dream up *inf*, formulate, plan, think up.
**4** assemble, bring about, establish, found, organize, set up. **5** comprise, constitute, make up

**formal** *adj* **1** (of an occasion) ceremonial, dignified, elaborate, official, posh *inf*, ritualistic, sophisticated; *opp* informal.
**2** (of people) aloof, conventional, correct, prim, reserved, rigid, stuffy, unbending, unfriendly; *opp* relaxed.
**3** (of an agreement) binding, contractual, legal, official, proper; *opp* informal

**formality** *n* **1** (a formality) ceremony, convention, custom, form, gesture, rite, ritual, rule. **2** ceremoniousness, correctness, decorum, etiquette, procedure, protocol, red tape

**formative** *adj* developing, forming, growing, impressionable, shaping, susceptible

**former** *adj* **1** (his former wife) ex-, last, late, one-time, previous. **2** (former times) ancient, bygone, earlier, long gone, old, past

**formidable** *adj* **1** (of a person) alarming, daunting, frightening, intimidating, scary *inf*. **2** (of a sight) awe-inspiring, awesome, daunting, fearful, frightful, horrible, menacing, petrifying, terrifying.
**3** (of a task) arduous, challenging, daunting, difficult, onerous, overwhelming; *opp* simple. **4** (of an enemy) mighty, invincible, powerful, strong

**formula** *n* blueprint, method, prescription, procedure, recipe, technique

**formulate** *v* **1** articulate, define, express, frame, give form to, set out, specify.
**2** create, devise, draw up, evolve, map out, plan, work out

**fort** *n* camp, castle, citadel, fortification, fortress, garrison, stronghold, tower

**forthcoming** *adj* **1** (the forthcoming exam) approaching, coming, imminent, impending, prospective, upcoming.
**2** (of a person) chatty, communicative, talkative, voluble

**fortification** *n* barricade, battlement, bulwark, castle, defence, fort, fortress, parapet, rampart, stronghold

**fortify** *v* **1** (make sth stronger) brace, buttress, defend, guard, protect, reinforce, secure, shore up, stiffen, strengthen. **2** (encourage yourself) boost, buoy up, cheer, embolden, encourage, hearten, invigorate, reassure, revive, sustain; *opp* discourage

**fortress** *n* castle, citadel, fort, stronghold

**fortunate** *adj* **1** blessed, favoured, happy, jammy *inf*, lucky, prosperous, successful; *opp* unfortunate. **2** auspicious, favourable, felicitous, opportune, propitious, timely

**fortune** *n* **1** affluence, assets, inheritance, millions *inf*, money, prosperity, riches, treasure, wealth. **2** accident, chance, destiny, fate, kismet, luck, providence

**fortune-teller** *n* astrologer, clairvoyant, crystal-gazer, oracle, palmist, prophet, seer, soothsayer, stargazer *inf*

**forward** *adj* **1** advanced, early, precocious, premature, well-developed; *opp* backward. **2** bold, brash, brazen, impudent, insolent, over-familiar, presumptuous, shameless; *opp* shy

**forward** v **1** dispatch, post on, re-address, send, send on, transmit. **2** advance, encourage, further, hasten, help, promote, speed up

**foster** v **1** adopt, bring up, care for, look after, raise, rear, take care of. **2** (foster links) cultivate, encourage, promote, support. **3** (foster hopes) cherish, entertain, harbour, sustain

**foul** adj **1** bad, contaminated, dirty, disgusting, fetid, filthy, impure, infected, polluted, putrid, rank, repugnant, repulsive, revolting, rotten, smelly, squalid, stinking, unclean; *opp* clean. **2** atrocious, contemptible, cruel, disgraceful, evil, horrible, scandalous, sordid, vicious, wicked. **3** (foul language) blasphemous, coarse, filthy, obscene, offensive, rude, vulgar. **4** (a foul day) blustery, foggy, rainy, rough, stormy, wet, wild, windy; *opp* beautiful, lovely

**foul** v blacken, contaminate, defile, dirty, pollute, smear, stain, taint

**found** v begin, bring about, create, endow, establish, organize, set up, start

**foundation** n **1** base, basis, bottom, cornerstone, footing, substructure. **2** basis, fundamentals, origin, principles, rudiments

**founder** n beginner, benefactor, builder, designer, inventor, maker, organizer, originator

**founder** v **1** be lost, be wrecked, capsize, go down, run aground, sink. **2** come to grief, fail, fall through, go wrong

**fountain** n fount, jet, spout, spray, spring, well

**fraction** n division, part, portion, small part, subdivision

**fracture** n break, crack, fissure, opening, rift, rupture, split

**fracture** v break, crack, rupture, split, suffer a fracture

**fragile** adj breakable, brittle, delicate, feeble, flimsy, frail, insubstantial, thin, weak; *opp* robust

**fragment** n bit, chip, crumb, fraction, morsel, part, particle, piece, portion, remnant, scrap, shard, shred, sliver

**fragment** v break, chip, crack, disintegrate, fall apart, fracture, shatter, shiver, smash, splinter

**fragrance** n **1** aroma, bouquet, perfume, scent, smell. **2** cologne, perfume, scent

**fragrant** adj aromatic, perfumed, sweet-scented, sweet-smelling

**frail** adj **1** (of a person) decrepit, delicate, feeble, fragile, ill, infirm, puny, sickly, slight, unwell, unsteady, vulnerable, weak; *opp* strong. **2** (of an object) breakable, dainty, easily damaged, flimsy, fragile, insubstantial, rickety, thin; *opp* strong

**frame** n **1** body, casing, chassis, framework, scaffolding, shell, skeleton, structure, substructure. **2** border, edge, mount, mounting, setting

**frame** v **1** compose, devise, draft, draw up, formulate, sketch. **2** box in, encase, enclose, mount, put in a frame, set off, surround. **3** (frame sb) accuse, implicate, incriminate, point the finger at, set up

**framework** n bare bones, core, fabric, foundation, groundwork, outline, plan, shell, skeleton, structure, support

**frank** adj blunt, candid, direct, forthright, free, honest, no-nonsense *inf*, open, outspoken, plain, sincere, straight, straightforward, truthful, unconcealed, undisguised, upfront *inf*

**frantic** *adj* agitated, berserk, beside yourself, crazy, desperate, distracted, distraught, excitable, frenetic, frenzied, furious, hectic, hysterical, mad, overwrought, panic-stricken, raving, wild

**fraternize** *v* associate, consort, go around with, hang around with *inf*, keep company with, mingle, mix, socialize

**fraud** *n* 1 (accused of fraud) cheating, deceit, deception, dishonesty, double-dealing, fraudulence, sharp practice, skulduggery, treachery, trickery. 2 (a trick) con *inf*, deception, hoax, put-up job *inf*, ruse, scam *sl*, trick. 3 (a person) cheat, confidence trickster, con man *inf*, fake, hoaxer, imposter, phoney *inf*, pretender, quack, scoundrel, swindler. 4 (sth not genuine) counterfeit, fake, forgery, phoney *inf*

**fraudulent** *adj* bent *inf*, bogus, corrupt, criminal, crooked *inf*, deceitful, deceptive, dishonest, false, forged, illegal, phoney *inf*, spurious, unscrupulous; *opp* honest

**freak** *adj* abnormal, atypical, bizarre, exceptional, extraordinary, freakish, odd, peculiar, queer, rare, unexpected, unpredictable, unusual, weird; *opp* normal, usual

**freak** *n* 1 aberration, abnormality, anomaly, curiosity, monster, monstrosity, mutant, quirk, rarity. 2 addict, buff *inf*, enthusiast, fan, fanatic

**free** *adj* 1 (free tickets) at no cost, complimentary, for nothing, free of charge, on the house *inf*. 2 (free to move) able, allowed, at large, at liberty, clear, liberated, loose, unchained, unhindered, unblocked, unobstructed, unrestrained. 3 easygoing, footloose, independent, liberated, relaxed, unconstrained, uninhibited; *opp* tied down. 4 (a free country) autonomous, democratic, independent, self-governing. 5 (available for use) available, empty, extra, spare, unoccupied, unused, vacant. 6 **free with** generous, hospitable, lavish, open-handed, unsparing

**free** *v* cut loose, discharge, emancipate, extricate, let go, let out, liberate, loose, release, rescue, save, turn loose, unchain, undo, unleash, untie

**freedom** *n* 1 (freedom to do what you want) carte blanche, flexibility, free hand, free rein, latitude, leeway, licence, opportunity, range, scope. 2 (fighting for freedom) autonomy, deliverance, emancipation, home rule, independence, liberty, sovereignty

**freely** *adv* 1 (go freely) of your own accord, of your own free will, voluntarily, willingly. 2 (speak freely) bluntly, candidly, frankly, honestly, openly

**freeze** *v* 1 become frozen, chill, harden, ice over, ice up, solidify; *opp* thaw. 2 be cold, chill, cool, go numb, make cold, numb. 3 be immobilized, go rigid, stand still, stop dead, stop in your tracks; *opp* move

**freezing** *adj* arctic, biting, bitter, cutting, frosty, ice-cold, icy, raw, snowy, wintry; *opp* boiling

**freight** n cargo, consignment, goods, load, merchandise, shipment

**frenzied** adj agitated, excited, frantic, frenetic, furious, hysterical, maniacal, rabid, uncontrolled, wild; **opp** calm

**frenzy** n 1 agitation, delirium, excitement, fury, hysteria, insanity, lunacy, madness, mania, paroxysm, passion, rage, seizure. 2 bout, fit, outburst

**frequent** adj common, constant, continual, customary, everyday, familiar, habitual, incessant, innumerable, many, numerous, persistent, recurrent, repeated; **opp** rare

**frequent** v go to, hang out at inf, haunt, spend time at, visit

**fresh** adj 1 (fresh colours) bright, clean, crisp, unfaded, vivid. 2 (fresh food) crisp, healthy, natural, raw, unprocessed, untreated; **opp** processed. 3 (fresh water) clean, clear, drinkable, pure, refreshing, sweet, uncontaminated; **opp** stale. 4 (fresh ideas) different, innovative, modern, new, novel, original, up-to-date; **opp** old. 5 (fresh-faced) bright, clear, fair, healthy, pink, rosy, wholesome. 6 (feel fresh after a shower) alive, awake, bright, energetic, full of beans inf, invigorated, lively, perky inf, refreshed, restored, revived, tingling; **opp** tired. 7 (a fresh wind) bracing, brisk, chilly, cool, invigorating, strong; **opp** gentle. 8 (fresh supplies) additional, extra, further, more, other. 9 (fresh bedding) clean, crisp, laundered, starched, unused, washed; **opp** dirty

**freshen** v 1 liven up, refresh, restore, revitalize, revive, rouse. 2 air,

purify, ventilate

**fret** v agonize, be distressed, brood, complain, feel unhappy, grumble, lose sleep, whine, worry

**friction** n 1 abrasion, chafing, erosion, grating, irritation, resistance, rubbing, scraping. 2 (friction between people) antagonism, arguing, bad feeling, conflict, disagreement, dissension, hostility, resentment

**friend** n boyfriend, buddy Am inf, chum, companion, comrade, girlfriend, mate inf, pal inf, partner, pen-friend, playfellow, playmate

**friendliness** n amiability, helpfulness, hospitality, kindliness, kindness, neighbourliness, sociability, warmth

**friendly** adj affectionate, agreeable, amicable, approachable, civil, companionable, helpful, hospitable, intimate, kind, kind-hearted, kindly, neighbourly, sociable, sympathetic, warm, welcoming; **opp** unfriendly

**friendship** n affection, closeness, companionship, harmony, intimacy, rapport, relationship

**fright** n 1 (fear) alarm, apprehension, dismay, dread, fear, horror, panic, terror, trepidation. 2 (have a fright) scare, shock, surprise

**frighten** v 1 alarm, intimidate, make you afraid, make your blood run cold, make your hair stand on end, petrify, put the wind up you inf, scare, spook inf, startle, terrify, unnerve, upset. 2 browbeat, bully, menace, persecute, terrorize, threaten, tyrannize

**frightened** adj afraid, alarmed, anxious, apprehensive, cowardly, fearful, horrified, horror-struck, panicky, panic-stricken, petrified, scared, shocked, startled, terrified, trembling, unnerved, upset

**frightening** adj alarming, blood-curdling, creepy inf, daunting, dreadful, eerie, fearful, fearsome, ghostly, hair-raising, horrifying, intimidating, menacing, scary, shocking, sinister, spine-chilling, terrifying, weird

**frigid** adj 1 aloof, forbidding, formal, icy, remote, rigid, stiff, unfeeling, unfriendly, unresponsive; *opp* warm. 2 arctic, bitter, cold, cool, frosty, frozen, glacial, icy, wintry

**fringe** n 1 border, boundary, edge, limits, margin, outskirts, perimeter, periphery. 2 edging, flounce, frill, ruffle, tassel, trimming

**frisk** v 1 caper, cavort, dance, frolic, gambol, jump, play, romp, skip. 2 inspect, search

**frisky** adj active, bouncy, full of beans inf, high inf, high-spirited, lively, playful, sprightly

**frivolous** adj empty-headed, facetious, flighty, flip inf, flippant, foolish, giddy, idle, inconsequential, juvenile, pointless, puerile, shallow, silly, superficial, trivial, unimportant; *opp* serious

**frolic** v caper, cavort, dance, frisk, gambol, have fun, play, prance, romp, skip

**front** adj first, foremost, head, lead, leading

**front** n 1 exterior, façade, face, foreground, forepart, frontage. 2 beginning, front line, head, top, vanguard. 3 (just a front) blind, cover, disguise, façade, pretext, show

**frontier** n border, boundary, confines, edge, limit

**froth** n bubbles, foam, head, lather, scum, suds

**froth** v bubble over, bubble up, effervesce, fizz, foam, lather

**frothy** adj 1 bubbly, foaming, foamy, lathery. 2 frivolous, insignificant, insubstantial, light, slight, trivial, worthless

**frown** v glare, glower, knit your brows, look daggers, look sullen, scowl

**frozen** adj 1 (frozen wastes) arctic, chilled, frosted, glacial, hard, icebound, icy, polar, Siberian. 2 (without feeling) anaesthetized, asleep inf, deadened, frigid, numb. 3 (not able to move) petrified, rooted to the spot, stock-still, suspended

**fruit** n 1 crop, harvest, produce, yield. 2 effect, outcome, profit, result, return, reward

**fruitful** adj 1 beneficial, productive, profitable, rewarding, successful, useful, well-spent, worthwhile; *opp* fruitless. 2 abundant, copious, fertile, flourishing, lush, luxurious, plentiful, potent, prolific, rich

**frustrate** v annoy, defeat, disappoint, discourage, dishearten, embitter, foil, hinder, prevent, spoil, stymie, thwart, vex

**frustrated** adj annoyed, disappointed, discontented, discouraged, disheartened, embittered, resentful, unfulfilled, unsatisfied

**frustration** n anger, annoyance, dissatisfaction, disappointment, exasperation, irritation, resentment, vexation

**fudge** v 1 avoid, dodge, equivocate, hedge, waffle. 2 bodge, botch, fake

**fuel** n 1 coal, diesel, electricity, gas, kerosene, oil, paraffin, petrol. 2 ammunition, encouragement, fodder, incentive, provocation, stimulus

**fugitive** n deserter, escapee, refugee, runaway

**fulfil** v 1 (do sth) accomplish, achieve, bring about, carry out, complete, do, execute, finish, implement, make sth come true, realize. 2 (satisfy sth) answer, comply with, conform to, fill, meet, obey, satisfy

**full** adj 1 (full of sth) brimful, brimming, bursting, filled, gorged, loaded, overflowing, replete, sated, satisfied, saturated, stuffed, well-stocked; *opp* empty. 2 (detailed) complete, comprehensive, copious, detailed, entire, exhaustive, thorough, unabridged, whole. 3 (full lips) ample, broad, curvaceous, fat, generous, large, plump, rounded; *opp* thin. 4 (a full bus) chock-a-block inf, chock-full inf, crammed, crowded, jammed, jam-packed inf, packed; *opp* empty

**full-grown** adj adult, developed, fully grown, grown-up, mature, ripe

**full-scale** adj all-out, comprehensive, extensive, in-depth, major, proper, thorough, wide-ranging

**fumble** v 1 botch, bungle, drop, flounder, fluff inf, make a hash of inf, mess up, mishandle, miss, muff, spoil, stumble. 2 (fumble in your pocket) feel around, grope, scrabble

**fume** v 1 emit fumes, smoke, smoulder. 2 be angry, be enraged, be incensed, be livid, blow your top inf, boil, flip your lid inf, fly off the handle inf, rage, rant, rave, see red inf, seethe, storm

**fumes** n exhaust, gases, pollution, smog, smoke, vapour

**fun** n amusement, distraction, diversion, enjoyment, entertainment, games, jokes, joking, joy, laughter, merriment, pleasure, recreation, relaxation, sport

**function** n 1 aim, purpose, raison d'être, use. 2 capacity, duty, job, responsibility, role. 3 affair, do inf, event, occasion, party, reception, social occasion

**function** v act, behave, go, operate, perform, run, serve, work

**functional** adj hard-wearing, practical, serviceable, useful, utilitarian, working

**fund** n hoard, kitty, mine, pool, repository, reserve, reservoir, stock, store, storehouse, supply, treasury

**fund** v finance, pay for, subsidize, support, underwrite

**fundamental** adj basic, central, crucial, elementary, essential, first, important, inherent, intrinsic, key, necessary, principal, quintessential, underlying, vital

**funds** n assets, capital, cash, dosh sl, endowments, finance, investments, means, money, resources, riches, savings, wealth

**funeral** n burial, cremation, entombment, interment

**funny** adj 1 amusing, comic, comical, daft inf, droll, entertaining, hilarious, humorous, ironic, ludicrous, mad, nonsensical, preposterous, ridiculous, riotous, satirical, side-splitting, uproarious, witty. 2 (strange) curious, mysterious, odd, peculiar, puzzling, strange, suspicious, unusual; *opp* normal. 3 (feel funny) (*inf*) dizzy, ill, off-colour *inf*, queasy, sick

**fur** *n* bristles, coat, down, fleece, hair, wool

**furious** *adj* 1 angry, beside yourself, enraged, foaming at the mouth *inf*, fuming, hot under the collar *inf*, incensed, infuriated, irate, livid *inf*, mad. 2 fierce, frantic, frenetic, intense, stormy, turbulent, violent, wild

**furnish** *v* 1 decorate, equip, fit out, kit out *inf*. 2 give, offer, present, provide, supply

**furniture** *n* equipment, fittings, furnishings, household goods, possessions

**furtive** *adj* clandestine, conspiratorial, covert, disguised, hidden, secret, secretive, shifty, skulking, slinking, sly, sneaking, sneaky, stealthy, surreptitious, underhand

**fury** *n* 1 anger, frenzy, madness, passion, rage, wrath. 2 ferocity, force, intensity, power, savagery, tempestuousness, violence

**fuss** *n* 1 bother, bustle, confusion, excitement, flurry, tumult, uproar. 2 (make a fuss) argument, dispute, furore, objection, protest, row, squabble, trouble, upset

**fuss** *v* bustle about, complain, create *inf*, fidget, flap, fret, get in a stew *inf*, get worked up *inf*, gripe *inf*, grumble, kick up a fuss, make a fuss, take on *inf*, worry

**fussy** *adj* choosy, difficult, faddy, finicky, hard to please, nit-picking *inf*, particular, picky *inf*

**futile** *adj* fruitless, ineffectual, in vain, pointless, to no avail, unproductive, unsuccessful, useless, wasted, worthless; *opp* useful

**future** *n* 1 (in the future) hereafter, time ahead, time to come, tomorrow. 2 (no future) expectations, outlook, prospects

**future** *adj* 1 (a future time) approaching, awaited, coming, forthcoming, impending, prospective, subsequent, to come. 2 (his future wife) destined, eventual, expected, intended, planned, prospective

**gadget** n appliance, contraption, contrivance, device, instrument, invention, novelty, tool, utensil

**gag** n crack inf, funny remark, jest, joke, one-liner inf, quip, wisecrack inf, witticism

**gag** v 1 keep sb quiet, muffle, muzzle, quiet, silence, smother, stifle, suppress. 2 choke, gasp, heave, retch

**gain** n acquisition, advantage, attainment, benefit, earnings, improvement, income, increase, profit, return, rise, winnings, yield; opp loss

**gain** v achieve, acquire, attain, build up, capture, collect, earn, get, make, net, obtain, profit, pick up, reach, secure, win, yield

**gale** n blast, cyclone, hurricane, squall, storm, tempest, tornado, typhoon, wind

**gallant** adj attentive, bold, brave, chivalrous, courageous, courteous, courtly, daring, dashing, fearless, heroic, honourable, intrepid, manly, noble, polite, valiant, valorous

**gallop** v canter, go at full speed, hurry, hurtle, race, run, rush, sprint, tear

**galvanize** v arouse, awaken, electrify, excite, inspire, jolt, shock, spur, stimulate, stir, urge

**gamble** v 1 (bet money) bet, have a flutter inf, lay bets, punt, stake money, wager. 2 (take a chance) speculate, stick your neck out inf, take a chance, take a risk, trust, venture

**game** adj 1 brave, courageous, daring, plucky, unafraid. 2 agreeable, eager, happy, interested, ready, willing

**game** n 1 amusement, entertainment, pastime, recreation, sport, toy. 2 (just a game) fun, joke, laugh, prank, trick. 3 (a game you play) competition, contest, match, round, tournament

**gang** n band, clique, club, crew inf, crowd, group, herd, horde, lot, mob, pack, posse, team

**gangster** n bandit, brigand, desperado, gunman, robber, thug, tough

**gap** n 1 (gap between two things) aperture, blank, breach, break, cavity, chink, crack, crevice, divide, gulf, hole, opening, rift, space, void. 2 (gap in time) break, breathing-space, interlude, interruption, interval, lull, pause, respite, rest, suspension, wait. 3 (gap between people) difference, distance, division, divergence, gulf, incompatibility

**gape** v 1 gawk, gawp inf, gaze, goggle, ogle, stare. 2 crack, open, part, split, yawn

**garbled** adj confused, distorted, jumbled, misquoted, mixed up, twisted; opp clear

**garish** adj brassy, bright, crude, flash inf,

flashy, gaudy, loud, lurid, showy, tacky *inf*, tasteless, vulgar

**garland** *n* crown, loop, wreath

**garment** *n* article of clothing, attire, clothing, costume, dress, garb, item of clothing, outfit

**garnish** *v* adorn, beautify, decorate, embellish, enhance, grace, ornament, set off, trim

**gash** *n* cut, incision, laceration, slash, slit, tear, wound

**gash** *v* cut, gouge, lacerate, nick, score, slash, slit, split, tear, wound

**gate** *n* barrier, door, doorway, entrance, exit, gateway, portal, portcullis, turnstile

**gather** *v* 1 (collect) accumulate, amass, collect, heap, hoard, pile up, stockpile. 2 (of people) assemble, congregate, convene, crowd, get together, flock, group, herd, marshal, mass, mobilize, round up, summon, swarm, throng. 3 (understand) assume, believe, deduce, draw the conclusion, guess, hear, infer, learn, understand. 4 (gather flowers) harvest, pick, pluck, reap

**gathering** *n* assembly, congregation, convention, crowd, get-together *inf*, group, horde, meeting, mob, party, rally

**gaudy** *adj* bright, brilliant, flash *inf*, flashy, garish, glaring, harsh, loud, ostentatious, showy, tasteless, tawdry, vivid, vulgar

**gauge** *n* 1 (size) bore, calibre, capacity, depth, dimensions, height, measure, size, thickness, width. 2 (instrument) dial, indicator, instrument, meter. 3 (yardstick) benchmark, guide, guideline, indication, indicator, model, standard, yardstick

**gauge** *v* 1 (gauge an amount) ascertain, calculate, check, count, determine, measure, value, weigh, work out. 2 (gauge sb's response) assess, discern, estimate, evaluate, guess, judge, reckon

**gaunt** *adj* angular, bony, drawn, emaciated, haggard, hollow-cheeked, lanky, pinched, scrawny, skinny, starving, thin, wasted; *opp* fat, plump, well-rounded

**gay** *adj* 1 (of colours) bright, colourful, jolly, rich, showy, vivid; *opp* dull. 2 (happy) cheerful, happy, jolly, merry, vivacious; *opp* sad. 3 homosexual, lesbian; *opp* straight

**gaze** *n* look, stare

**gaze** *v* eye, gape, gawp *inf*, look, stare, watch

**gear** *n* 1 belongings, bits and pieces, equipment, kit, paraphernalia, possessions, stuff, things, tools, trappings. 2 cog, cogwheel, gearwheel, machinery, mechanism. 3 clothes, clothing, dress, get-up *inf*, kit *inf*, outfit, rig, togs *inf*

**gem** *n* 1 gemstone, jewel, precious stone, stone. 2 pearl, prize, star, treasure

**general** *adj* 1 across-the-board, all-encompassing, blanket, broad, comprehensive, global, inclusive, overall, universal; *opp* specific. 2 accepted, common, customary, normal, regular, typical, usual. 3 approximate, ballpark, broad, loose, outline, rough, vague; *opp* precise

**generally** *adv* 1 (on the whole) as a rule, broadly speaking, by and large, commonly, mostly, normally, on the whole, typically, usually. 2 (widely) commonly, popularly, universally, widely

**generate** v arouse, bring about, cause, engender, give rise to, lead to, produce, stir up

**generation** n 1 age group, contemporaries, day, era, period, time. 2 arousal, creation, production, stirring up

**generic** adj across-the-board, broad, typical, universal

**generosity** n benevolence, kindness, lavishness, magnanimity, munificence, philanthropy; opp meanness

**generous** adj 1 benevolent, big-hearted, charitable, kind, magnanimous, philanthropic; opp mean. 2 abundant, huge, large, lavish, plentiful

**genius** n 1 clever-clogs inf, expert, know-all inf, mastermind, prodigy, boy wonder, girl wonder, master, virtuoso, whiz-kid inf, whiz inf. 2 ability, aptitude, brains, brilliance, flair, gift, talent

**genteel** adj cultured, elegant, ladylike, polished, polite, posh inf, refined, well-mannered

**gentle** adj 1 (of a person) amiable, easy-going, kind, kindly, mild, placid, soft-hearted, soft, tender. 2 delicate, easy, light, mild, muted, peaceful, quiet, soft, soothing. 3 (of a slope) easy, gradual, moderate, slight, smooth, steady; opp steep

**genuine** adj 1 authentic, bona fide, guaranteed, kosher, legitimate, original, pukka inf, real, solid, true. 2 candid, honest, open, sincere, straight, unaffected

**germ** n bacteria, bug inf, infection, micro-organism, virus

**germinate** v develop, grow, shoot, sprout, start growing, start, take root

**gesticulate** v gesture, indicate, motion, sign, signal, wave

**gesture** n gesticulation, hand movement, indication, motion, sign, signal, wave

**gesture** v gesticulate, indicate, motion, sign, signal, wave

**get** v 1 (obtain) achieve, acquire, attain, come by, come into possession of, earn, gain, inherit, land inf, lay your hands on, make, obtain, procure, receive, secure, win. 2 (get old) become, go, grow, turn. 3 collect, fetch, pick up. 4 arrest, capture, collar, grab, nail, seize, trap. 5 (get sb to do sth) encourage, make, persuade, prevail on. 6 (get flu) be infected by, catch, come down with, contract, develop, fall ill with, go down with, pick up. 7 (get to a place) arrive, come, reach. 8 **get along** (be friendly) be friendly, be on good terms, get on, hit it off. 9 **get at** (criticize) attack, blame, carp, criticize, make fun of, nag, pick on, take the mickey, taunt, tease. 10 **get at** (imply) hint, imply, insinuate, mean, suggest. 11 **get away** (escape) abscond, break free, break out, depart, disappear, do a bunk inf, escape, get out, leave, run away. 12 **get on** (get on a bus, ferry, bike) board, catch, climb on, embark, get, go on board, mount. 13 **get on** (manage) cope, do, get along, make out, manage, progress. 14 **get on** (carry on working) carry on, continue, crack on inf, get cracking inf, press on. 15 **get on** (be friendly) be friendly, be on good terms, get along, hit it off. 16 **get round** avoid, bypass, circumvent, evade, skirt

**ghastly** adj appalling, awful, bad, dreadful, foul, grim, gruesome, hideous, horrendous, horrible, horrid, nasty, terrible

**ghost** n apparition, ghoul, phantom, poltergeist, shade, spectre, spirit, spook inf, wraith

**ghostly** adj creepy, eerie, ghostlike, phantom, spectral, spooky inf, supernatural, unearthly

**giant** n behemoth, colossus, Goliath, leviathan, monster, titan, whopper inf

**giddy** adj dizzy, faint, light-headed, reeling, spinning, unsteady

**gift** n 1 bequest, contribution, donation, endowment, freebie inf, gratuity, hand-out, honorarium, legacy, offering, present, tip. 2 ability, flair, genius, knack, power, talent

**gifted** adj accomplished, brainy inf, bright, brilliant, clever, expert, skilful, talented

**gigantic** adj colossal, enormous, giant, huge, immense, jumbo inf, king-size, mammoth, massive, monstrous, towering, vast

**giggle** v chortle, chuckle, laugh, snigger, titter

**gimmick** n dodge, gizmo, publicity stunt, stunt, trick

**girdle** n 1 band, cummerbund, sash, waistband. 2 corset, pantie-girdle

**girl** n daughter, female, kid, lass, schoolgirl, woman, young woman, youngster

**girlfriend** n date, lover, sweetheart, young lady, woman

**girth** n circumference, perimeter

**gist** n drift, essence, idea, meaning, nub, point, sense, significance, substance

**give** v 1 allocate, award, contribute, deliver, dish out, dole out, donate, grant, hand over, let sb have, present, provide, share out, supply. 2 (give a speech, information) announce, communicate, deliver, make, reveal, tell, utter. 3 (give sb medicine, a punishment) administer, dish out, dispense, impose, inflict, prescribe. 4 (give a party) arrange, have, organize, put on. 5 (yield) buckle, fall, give way, sink, yield. 6 give in capitulate, comply, concede defeat, give up, quit, submit, succumb, surrender, throw in the towel. 7 give out (share out) deal, distribute, dole out inf, hand out, share out. 8 give out (emit) discharge, emit, exude, give off, produce, release. 9 give out (announce) advertise, announce, broadcast, make known, make public, notify, publish. 10 give up (give up an attempt) abandon the attempt, capitulate, comply, concede defeat, give in, lose heart, quit, submit, succumb, surrender, throw in the towel. 11 give up (give up smoking) abandon, cut out, leave off, quit, stop

**glad** adj 1 (happy) cheerful, chuffed inf, delighted, elated, happy, joyful, over the moon, pleased, satisfied, thrilled, well-pleased; opp disappointed. 2 (willing) delighted, eager, happy, keen, more than willing, pleased, ready, willing; opp unwilling

**glamorous** adj appealing, attractive, beautiful, beguiling, dazzling, exciting, flash inf, glittering, glitzy inf, glossy, prestigious, smart

**glamour** n appeal, attraction, beauty, glitter, magic, prestige

**glance** n glimpse, look, peek, peep,

quick look

**glance** v cast an eye over, dip into, flick through, have a quick look at, leaf through, look, peek, peep, scan

**glare** n 1 black look, frown, look, scowl, stare. 2 blaze, brightness, brilliance, dazzle

**glare** v frown, give sb a black look, glower, look daggers at, scowl, stare

**glaring** adj 1 blatant, conspicuous, obvious. 2 blazing, bright, dazzling

**glass** n beaker, crystal, flute, glassware, goblet, tumbler, wine-glass

**glaze** v coat, enamel, lacquer, varnish

**gleam** v flash, glimmer, glint, glisten, glow, shine, sparkle, twinkle

**glee** n delight, excitement, happiness, joy, pleasure, triumph; *opp* misery

**glide** v coast, drift, free-wheel, sail, skate, skim, slide, slip, soar

**glimmer** n flash, flicker, gleam, glow, shimmer, sparkle, twinkle

**glimmer** v blink, flicker, gleam, glint, glow, shimmer, shine, sparkle, twinkle

**glimpse** v catch sight of, notice, see, spot

**glint** v flash, gleam, glisten, glitter, shimmer, shine, sparkle, twinkle

**glisten** v gleam, glint, glitter, shimmer, shine, sparkle

**glitter** v flash, glint, glisten, shine, sparkle, twinkle

**gloat** v boast, brag, crow about, revel in, rub it in, show off, wallow in

**global** adj 1 international, universal, worldwide; *opp* local, parochial. 2 across-the-board, all-encompassing, all-inclusive, general, universal, wide-ranging

**globe** n 1 ball, orb, sphere. 2 earth,

planet, planet earth, world

**gloom** n 1 dejection, depression, despair, despondency, low spirits, misery, pessimism, sadness, unhappiness; *opp* happiness. 2 dark, darkness, dimness, dusk, murkiness, shadow; *opp* brightness

**gloomy** adj 1 dejected, depressed, dismal, down in the dumps *inf*, down, low, miserable, pessimistic, sad; *opp* cheerful. 2 dark, dim, dull, murky, overcast; *opp* bright

**glorious** adj beautiful, brilliant, fine, gorgeous, lovely, magnificent, splendid, superb, terrific, wonderful; *opp* awful, dreadful, terrible

**glory** n 1 credit, distinction, fame, honour, kudos, prestige, triumph. 2 brilliance, grandeur, magnificence, radiance, splendour, wonder

**glory** v exult in, revel in, take pride in

**gloss** n 1 gleam, lustre, polish, sheen, shine, varnish. 2 (outward appearance) appearance, outward appearance, semblance, veneer. 3 (explanation) comment, definition, explanation, note, paraphrase, translation

**glossy** adj gleaming, lustrous, polished, shining, shiny, sleek; *opp* dull, matt

**glow** n brightness, flush, gleam, light, lustre, radiance, redness, rosiness, shine

**glow** v burn, gleam, light up, redden, shine, smoulder

**glower** v give sb a black look, glare, look daggers at sb, scowl

**glowing** adj 1 bright, flushed, radiant, red, rich, rosy, vivid. 2 complimentary, enthusiastic, favourable, full of praise, warm

**glue** n adhesive, cement, fixative, paste

**glue** v bond, cement, fasten, fix, paste, stick

**glut** n excess, overabundance, oversupply, surplus; *opp* scarcity

**glutton** n gannet *inf*, greedy guts *inf*, pig *inf*

**gnarled** adj arthritic, contorted, knotted, twisted

**gnaw** v bite, chew, chomp, eat, eat away, munch, nibble, wear away

**go** v 1 (leave) beat it *inf*, buzz off *inf*, depart, disappear, get away, get going, get moving, leave, retreat, set off, set out, shove off *inf*, vanish. 2 (move) make for, move, pass, proceed, progress, travel. 3 (work) be working, function, operate, run, work. 4 (this road goes to Paris, our land goes as far as the river) continue, extend, lead to, reach, spread, stretch. 5 (time goes quickly) elapse, fly, pass, slip by. 6 (go grey) become, get, grow, turn. 7 (the interview went well, how is the project going?) develop, end up, fare, happen, pan out, proceed, turn out, work out. 8 go by (time goes by) elapse, fly, pass. 9 go by (use as a guide) be guided by, follow, obey, observe, use as a guide. 10 go for (fetch) collect, fetch, go and get, go to pick up. 11 go for (attack) assault, attack, launch yourself at, lunge at. 12 go for (like) choose, like, prefer. 13 go off (go bad) deteriorate, go bad, go mouldy, rot, turn sour. 14 go off (explode) detonate, explode, go bang. 15 go over check, examine, inspect, look through, rehearse, review, run through, scan, study. 16 go through (look through)

check, examine, hunt through, inspect, look through, run through, scan, study. 17 go through (endure) brave, endure, experience, have to put up with, suffer, undergo. 18 go without abstain from, deny yourself, do without, forego, go short, manage without

**goad** v chivvy, egg on *inf*, prod, prompt, provoke, push, spur, stimulate, urge

**goal** n aim, ambition, aspiration, end, objective, target

**godforsaken** adj desolate, dismal, dreary, gloomy, in the back of beyond, miserable, wretched

**godsend** n bit of luck, blessing, boon, miracle, unexpected bonus

**golden** adj 1 (gold) fair, gilded, gilt, gold, yellow. 2 (golden opportunity) excellent, fortuitous, ideal, opportune, wonderful

**good** adj 1 brilliant, delicious, enjoyable, excellent, first-class, great, hunky-dory *inf*, interesting, lovely, nice, pleasant, satisfactory, suitable; super; *opp* awful, bad, terrible. 2 (good at a job) accomplished, capable, clever, competent, conscientious, efficient, professional, proficient, skilful, skilled, talented. 3 (a good person) caring, considerate, decent, generous, honest, honourable, kind, kind-hearted, trustworthy, virtuous; *opp* bad, evil, wicked. 4 (well-behaved) obedient, well-behaved; *opp* naughty

**goodbye** interj adieu, au revoir, bye, bye-bye, cheerio, ciao *inf*, farewell, see you, so long, ta-ta

**good-looking** adj attractive, beautiful, bonny, gorgeous, handsome, pretty; **opp** ugly

**goods** n 1 freight, merchandise, products, stock. 2 belongings, effects, possessions, property, stuff, things

**gorge** n canyon, chasm, gully, ravine

**gorge** v be greedy, cram, devour, eat as much as you can, eat ravenously, fill yourself up, gobble, gulp down, make a pig of yourself inf, overeat, shovel, stuff, wolf

**gorgeous** adj beautiful, brilliant, glorious, good-looking, handsome, impressive, lovely, magnificent, stunning, superb, terrific, wonderful

**gory** adj blood-and-guts inf, blood-stained, bloody, brutal, grisly, gruesome, savage, violent

**gospel** n creed, doctrine, message, teaching, word

**gossip** n 1 hearsay, report, rumour, scandal, tittle-tattle. 2 (have a gossip) chat, chinwag, natter inf. 3 (a person) busybody, nosy parker inf, scandalmonger, tell-tale

**gossip** v blab, chat, chatter, natter inf, spread rumours, talk

**gourmet** n connoisseur, epicure

**govern** v 1 administer, be in power, control, look after, manage, oversee, reign, rule, run. 2 affect, control, decide, determine, influence

**government** n 1 administration, authorities, executive, parliament, regime, ruling party, state, the powers that be. 2 control, leadership, management, regulation, rule

**governor** n administrator, commissioner, director, executive, head, leader, manager, ruler

**grab** v catch hold of, collar inf, get hold of, grasp, seize, snap up, snatch, take hold of

**grace** n charm, elegance, finesse, gracefulness, poise, polish

**grace** v adorn, decorate, dignify, enhance, favour, honour

**graceful** adj attractive, charming, deft, elegant, natural, polished, tasteful

**grade** n category, class, level, position, rank, rung, stage

**grade** v categorize, classify, group, order, rank, size, sort

**gradient** n hill, incline, rise, slope

**gradual** adj 1 continuous, even, progressive, regular, steady, step-by-step; **opp** abrupt, sudden. 2 easy, gentle, moderate; **opp** steep

**gradually** adv bit by bit, evenly, gently, little by little, progressively, slowly, steadily, step by step; **opp** abruptly, suddenly

**graduate** v 1 become a graduate, get your degree, pass, qualify. 2 calibrate, classify, grade, group, mark off, order, rank, sort

**grain** n 1 cereal, corn, seed. 2 atom, bit, crumb, granule, iota, jot, piece, scrap, speck

**grand** adj elegant, imposing, impressive, luxurious, magnificent, majestic, palatial, regal, stately

**grandeur** n elegance, luxury, magnificence, opulence, pomp, splendour

**grandiose** adj ambitious, extravagant, grand, imposing, majestic, ostentatious, OTT inf, over-the-top inf, pretentious, splendid

**grant** n allowance, award, bursary,

donation, endowment, scholarship

**grant** v **1** allocate, allot, assign, award, bestow, confer, donate, give. **2** (allow) accept, acknowledge, admit, allow, concede, go along with, permit

**graph** n bar chart, chart, diagram, pie chart

**graphic** adj blow-by-blow, clear, descriptive, detailed, explicit, realistic, striking, vivid

**grapple** v clash, fight, struggle, tackle, tussle, wrestle

**grasp** n **1** clutches, grip, hold. **2** (understanding) awareness, comprehension, knowledge, mastery, understanding. **3** (ability to achieve sth) capabilities, capacity, limitations, limits, reach. **4** (power) clutches, control, domination, dominion, possession, power

**grasp** v **1** grab, catch, clutch, grip, hold, seize, take hold of. **2** comprehend, cotton on to inf, follow, get your mind round, get, realize, see, understand

**grasping** adj avaricious, grabbing, greedy, mean, mercenary, miserly, selfish, stingy, tight-fisted

**grateful** adj appreciative, full of gratitude, indebted, pleased, thankful; opp ungrateful

**gratitude** n appreciation, gratefulness, thankfulness, thanks; opp ingratitude

**gratuitous** adj needless, uncalled-for, undeserved, unjustifiable, unjustified, unnecessary, unprovoked, unwarranted, without reason

**grave** adj **1** grim, serious, sober, solemn, sombre, stony-faced. **2** (a grave situation) critical, crucial, serious, severe, worrying

**grave** n burial chamber, crypt, mausoleum, sepulchre, tomb, vault

**graveyard** n burial ground, cemetery, churchyard

**gravity** n consequence, importance, magnitude, seriousness, solemnity, urgency, weightiness

**graze** n abrasion, cut, scrape, scratch

**graze** v cut, scrape, scratch

**grease** n fat, lubrication, oil, tallow

**greasy** adj fatty, oily, slimy, slippery, smeary, waxy

**great** adj **1** (excellent) brilliant, classic, excellent, marvellous, outstanding, superb, terrific, wonderful; opp awful, dreadful, terrible. **2** (large) big, enormous, huge, immense, large, massive, vast. **3** (considerable) acute, considerable, extreme, intense, severe. **4** (important) celebrated, chief, distinguished, eminent, famous, important, leading, main, prominent, renowned. **5** (very skilful) ace inf, expert, gifted, good, skilful, talented

**greed** n **1** gluttony, greediness, piggishness inf, voraciousness. **2** avarice, miserliness, selfishness, tight-fistedness

**greedy** adj **1** gluttonous, gutsy inf, piggish inf, voracious. **2** avaricious, grasping, miserly, money-grabbing, selfish, tight-fisted

**green** adj **1** grassy, leafy, lush, verdant. **2** callow, gullible, inexperienced, naïve, new, raw, wet behind the ears. **3** eco-friendly, ecological, environmental, environmentally friendly, environmentally sound

**greet** v meet, receive, say hello

to, welcome

**greeting** n good wishes, hello, message, nod, reception, regards, tidings, wave, welcome

**grey** adj 1 (of sb's face) ashen, pale, white. 2 (of weather) cloudy, dull, foggy, gloomy, leaden, misty, murky, overcast

**grief** n anguish, bereavement, despair, heartache, misery, mourning, sadness, unhappiness

**grievance** n allegation, charge, complaint, dispute, gripe inf, grouse inf, injustice

**grieve** v be distressed, be in mourning, be sad, despair, fret, lament, mourn, suffer; **opp** rejoice

**grim** adj 1 (gruesome) appalling, dreadful, ghastly, grisly, gruesome, harrowing, shocking, terrible. 2 (unpleasant) awful, dire, dreadful, horrendous, horrid, unattractive, unpleasant. 3 (stern) gloomy, morose, serious, sombre, sour, stern, sullen. 4 (stubbornly determined) determined, obdurate, obstinate, resolute, unrelenting

**grimace** n expression, face, frown, scowl, wry expression

**grind** v 1 crush, granulate, mill, powder, pulverize. 2 file, polish, sharpen, smooth

**grip** n 1 grasp, hold. 2 clutches, control, influence, power

**grip** v 1 clasp, grab, grasp, hold, seize, take hold of. 2 capture, enthral, fascinate, hold spellbound, mesmerize

**gripping** adj absorbing, compulsive, exciting, fascinating, heady, interesting, riveting, sensational, thrilling; **opp** boring

**grisly** adj appalling, dreadful, ghastly,

gory, grim, gruesome, horrifying, macabre, shocking, sickening

**groan** v cry out, moan, object, protest, sigh, wail

**groom** v 1 arrange, brush, clean, comb, fix, make tidy, smarten up, spruce up, tidy, titivate. 2 coach, drill, get ready, instruct, prepare, prime, school, teach, train

**groove** n channel, cutting, furrow, gouge, gutter, hollow, indentation, rut, slot, track

**grope** v 1 feel, finger, touch. 2 (seek by touch) feel about for, feel for, fish for, fumble for, search blindly, seek

**gross** adj 1 (fat) bloated, bulky, fat, heavy, huge, massive, obese, overweight; **opp** skinny, thin. 2 coarse, crude, disgusting, offensive, rude, vulgar. 3 (a gross error) blatant, flagrant, glaring, outrageous, serious, shameful, shocking

**grotesque** adj 1 absurd, bizarre, curious, fantastic, outlandish, peculiar, strange, surreal, unnatural, weird. 2 deformed, distorted, gnarled, misshapen, twisted, ugly

**ground** n 1 (soil) dirt, earth, mud, soil. 2 (under your feet) deck inf, earth, floor, terra firma. 3 (for sports) arena, field, pitch, playing field, stadium

**ground** v 1 base, establish, found, set. 2 (teach) coach, drill, familiarize sb with, give sb training in, initiate, instruct, teach, train

**groundless** adj baseless, false, irrational, unfounded, unjustified, unreasonable, unwarranted, without cause, without foundation; **opp** true

**grounds** n pl 1 (around a building) area,

estate, gardens, land, park, parkland, surroundings. 2 (reason) basis, cause, excuse, foundation, justification, motive, pretext, rationale, reason, reasons

**groundwork** n elements, essentials, fundamentals, preparation, preparations, spadework

**group** n 1 (small group of people) band, bunch inf, cluster, company, congregation, crew, gaggle inf, gang, party, team. 2 (large group of people) assembly, crowd, flock, gathering, horde, host, mob, multitude, rabble, swarm, throng. 3 (exclusive group of people) association, cadre, circle, clique, club, faction, ring, school, sect, set. 4 (of animals) flock, herd, swarm. 5 (of things) assortment, batch, bunch, bundle, category, class, cluster, collection, lot, set

**group** v 1 (make a group) arrange, assemble, bring together, categorize, classify, collect, gather, marshal, organize, put together, set out. 2 (become a group) associate, cluster, come together, congregate, flock, gather, get together, swarm, team up, throng

**grovel** v abase yourself, bow and scrape, crawl, creep, fawn, humble yourself, ingratiate yourself with, kowtow, lick sb's boots inf, prostrate yourself, suck up to

**grow** v 1 (get bigger) develop, enlarge, expand, extend, fill out, get bigger, get taller, heighten, increase, lengthen, multiply, spread, swell, thicken, widen. 2 (come from) arise, issue, originate, spring, stem. 3 (grow old) become, come to be, get, turn. 4 (of a business) develop, expand, flourish, make

headway, make progress, progress, prosper, thrive. 5 (of plants) come up, flourish, shot up, spring up, sprout. 6 cultivate, farm, plant, produce, propagate, raise

**growth** n 1 development, enlargement, evolution, expansion, extension, increase, multiplication. 2 advance, expansion, improvement, progress, proliferation, rise, success. 3 (of plants) crop, harvest, produce, yield. 4 (on the body) cancer, cyst, lump, swelling, tumour

**grub** n 1 caterpillar, larva, maggot. 2 (food) a bite inf, a bite to eat inf, fast food inf, junk food inf, meal, nosh inf, refreshments, snacks, something to eat

**grudge** n bitterness, grievance, hard feelings, pique, rancour, resentment

**grudge** v 1 begrudge, give unwillingly. 2 begrudge, be jealous of, envy, mind, resent

**grudging** adj envious, guarded, half-hearted, hesitant, jealous, reluctant, resentful, unenthusiastic, ungracious; **opp** enthusiastic

**gruelling** adj arduous, back-breaking, demanding, exhausting, laborious, punishing, strenuous, taxing, tiring, tough, wearying; **opp** easy

**gruesome** adj awful, disgusting, dreadful, ghastly, grim, grisly, horrendous, horrible, horrific, horrifying, macabre, repulsive, shocking, sickening

**gruff** adj 1 (of a voice) hoarse, husky, rasping, rough, throaty. 2 (of a person) abrupt, bad-tempered, brusque, crabby inf, crotchety, crusty, curt, grouchy inf, grumpy, impolite, rough, rude, surly, uncivil

**grumble** v bellyache inf, bitch inf, carp, complain, find fault with, go on about inf, groan, gripe inf, grouch inf, grouse inf, moan, object, protest, whine, whinge inf

**guarantee** n 1 (of good quality) warranty. 2 assurance, bond, oath, pledge, promise, word, word of honour. 3 (financial) bond, collateral, security, surety

**guarantee** v 1 assure, certify, give a guarantee, give an assurance, give your word, pledge, promise, vouch for, swear, vow, warrant. 2 (guarantee a loan) back, be a guarantor for, provide collateral for, provide security for, underwrite

**guard** n 1 (of a person) bodyguard, escort, guardian, heavy inf, minder inf, protector. 2 (of a place) bouncer inf, custodian, defender, lookout, night watchman, patrol, picket, security guard, sentry, watch, watchman. 3 (prison guard) jailer, prison officer, screw inf, warder. 4 off (your) guard unprepared, unready, with your defences down. 5 on your guard alert, careful, cautious, on the lookout, prepared, ready, vigilant, wary

**guard** v 1 (people or animals) escort, keep, keep under guard, keep watch over, mind, protect, save, secure, shelter, shield, tend, watch, watch over. 2 (a place) cover, defend, patrol, police, secure, watch over. 3 guard against be alert, be on the lookout for, beware of, be wary of, keep an eye out for, keep your eyes open, take care

**guardian** n 1 caretaker, curator, custodian, keeper, steward, warden. 2 champion, defender, protector, preserver, trustee

**guerrilla** n freedom fighter, irregular soldier, member of the resistance, partisan, terrorist

**guess** n assumption, conjecture, estimate, feeling, guesstimate, hypothesis, prediction, speculation, suspicion, surmise

**guess** v conjecture, estimate, have a feeling, have a hunch, have an idea, hazard a guess, make a guess, postulate, predict, speculate, surmise, suppose, think likely

**guest** n 1 caller, house guest, visitor. 2 (in a hotel) boarder, patron, resident

**guidance** n advice, brief, counsel, counselling, direction, guidelines, hint, instruction, leadership, management, supervision, teaching, tip

**guide** n 1 attendant, courier, director, escort, leader, usher. 2 advisor, counsellor, guru, mentor, teacher, tutor. 3 beacon, clue, guiding light, key, landmark, sign. 4 directory, guidebook, guidelines, handbook, instructions, manual, tourist guide

**guide** v 1 (to a place) accompany, conduct, direct, escort, lead, lead the way, pilot, shepherd, show, show the way, steer, usher. 2 advise, brief, counsel, give counselling to, give advice, give a hint, give a pointer, give a tip, give guidance, influence, inform, instruct, make suggestions, take sb by the hand inf. 3 command, control, govern, handle, manage, preside over, regulate, steer, superintend, supervise

**guilt** n 1 blame, culpability, fault, liability, responsibility; *opp* innocence. 2 bad conscience, contrition, disgrace, dishonour, penitence, regret, remorse, repentance, self-reproach, shame

**guilty** adj 1 at fault, blameworthy, convicted, criminal, culpable, responsible, to blame; *opp* innocent. 2 (feel guilty) ashamed, conscience-stricken, contrite, penitent, remorseful, repentant, shamefaced, sheepish

**gulf** n 1 bay, bight, inlet. 2 abyss, breach, canyon, chasm, cleft, gap, gorge, ravine, rent, rift, split. 3 (between people) difference, division, rift, split

**gullible** adj credulous, easily taken in, foolish, green, innocent, naive, silly, simple, trusting, unsuspecting; *opp* shrewd

**gulp** v bolt, devour, gobble, guzzle, knock back *inf*, swallow, swig *inf*, toss off, wolf, wolf down

**gumption** n ability, acumen, common sense, enterprise, get-up-and-go, horse sense *inf*, initiative, judgement, nous *inf*, resourcefulness, savvy *inf*, sense, shrewdness

**gun** n firearm, machine-gun, musket, pistol, revolver, rifle, shooter *inf*, shot-gun

**gunman** n armed robber, bandit, gangster, gunfighter, gunslinger *inf*, hired gun, hit man *inf*, hold-up man, terrorist

**gurgle** v 1 (of water) babble, bubble, murmur, splash, tinkle. 2 (of a baby) babble, burble, chuckle, crow

**gush** n burst, cascade, flood, jet, spate, spurt, stream, surge, torrent

**gush** v 1 burst out, cascade, flood, flow, pour, rush, spout, spurt, stream, surge; *opp* trickle. 2 (of a person) babble, be effusive, be over-enthusiastic, bubble over, get carried away *inf*, make too much of sth, prattle, speak effusively, wax lyrical

**gust** n blast, flurry, puff, rush, squall

**gusto** n appetite, delight, enjoyment, enthusiasm, excitement, pleasure, relish, verve, zest

**guts** n 1 alimentary canal, entrails, innards *inf*, intestines, viscera. 2 boldness, bottle *inf*, bravery, courage, daring, grit, mettle, nerve, pluck, spirit

**gutter** n channel, conduit, culvert, ditch, drain, open sewer, sluice, trench, trough

**guzzle** v bolt, cram yourself, devour, gobble, gulp down, knock back *inf*, swallow, swig *inf*, swill, toss off *inf*, stuff yourself *inf*, wolf down

**habit** n **1** convention, custom, practice, procedure, routine, rule, second nature, tradition, way, wont. **2** bent, inclination, leaning, predisposition, propensity, tendency. **3** addiction, compulsion, craving, dependence

**habitation** n abode, accommodation, domicile, dwelling, home, housing, lodging, pad *inf*, place *inf*, quarters, residence

**habitual** adj **1** accustomed, common, customary, established, familiar, fixed, natural, normal, ordinary, regular, routine, standard, traditional, usual. **2** (having a habit) addicted, chronic, confirmed, hardened, inveterate

**hack** v carve, chop, cut, cut down, gash, hew, lacerate, mutilate, slash

**hackneyed** adj banal, clichéd, commonplace, conventional, corny *inf*, overworked, platitudinous, predictable, stale, stereotyped, stock, trite, unoriginal, worn-out; *opp* new, original

**haggard** adj drawn, emaciated, gaunt, pinched, scraggy, thin, tired, wan, wasted, worn out

**haggle** v **1** bargain, beat sb down, drive a hard bargain. **2** argue, bicker, dispute, quarrel, squabble, wrangle

**hail** v **1** acknowledge, greet, salute, say hello to, welcome. **2** accost, call out to, flag down, signal to, shout to, wave to. **3** acclaim, applaud, extol, glorify, honour, praise, sing the praises of

**hair** n **1** head of hair, locks, mop, shock, tresses. **2** coiffure, cut, haircut, hair-do, hairstyle, style. **3** (of an animal) bristles, coat, fleece, fur, mane, pelt, wool

**hairy** adj bearded, bristly, fleecy, furry, hirsute, long-haired, shaggy, unshaven, woolly

**half** n division, equal part, equal share, fifty per cent, percentage

**half-hearted** adj apathetic, cool, cursory, indifferent, lacklustre, lukewarm, perfunctory, superficial, unenthusiastic; *opp* enthusiastic

**hall** n **1** assembly room, auditorium, meeting room. **2** entrance hall, entry, foyer, lobby, vestibule

**hallmark** n **1** authentication, endorsement, mark, seal, sign, stamp, symbol. **2** badge, indicator, mark, sign, stamp, sure sign, trademark

**hallucination** n apparition, delusion, dream, fantasy, figment of the imagination, illusion, mirage, vision

**halt** n **1** (temporary) break, breather *inf*, breathing space, hiatus, interruption, interval, pause, stoppage, time out *inf*. **2** (permanent) cessation, end, standstill, stop, termination; *opp* start

**halt** v 1 break off, cease, come to a standstill, come to a stop, draw up, pull up, stand still, stop, wait. 2 (stop sth happening) arrest, block, check, crush, end, nip in the bud, put an end to, put a stop to, stop, terminate

**halve** v bisect, cut in half, cut in two, divide equally, reduce by fifty per cent, share equally, split in half, split in two

**hamper** v block, delay, encumber, foil, frustrate, hinder, hold back, hold up, impede, inhibit, interfere with, obstruct, restrain, slow down, stymie, throw a spanner in the works *inf*, thwart; *opp* help

**hand** n 1 fist, mitt *inf*, palm, paw *inf*. 2 (of a dial) indicator, needle, pointer. 3 (helping hand) aid, assistance, help, helping hand, support. 4 (worker) artisan, employee, labourer, worker. 5 calligraphy, handwriting, penmanship, script. 6 **a big hand** applause, ovation, round of applause. 7 **at hand** about to happen, approaching, imminent, impending. 8 **to hand** accessible, available, handy, ready, within reach. 9 **try your hand** attempt, have a go, have a shot *inf*, make an attempt, try your skill

**hand** v 1 convey, deliver, give, offer, pass, present. 2 **hand down** bequeath, hand on, leave, pass down, pass on, will. 3 **hand out** deal out, disburse, dish out *inf*, dispense, distribute, dole out *inf*, give out, share out. 4 **hand over** deliver, donate, give, present, surrender, turn over

**handicap** n 1 disability, impairment. 2 disadvantage, hindrance, impediment, limitation, obstacle, problem, stumbling block

**handiwork** n 1 artefacts, craft, craftsmanship, handicraft. 2 achievement, creation, design, doing, product, production, work

**handle** n grip, haft, hand-grip, hilt, knob, shaft, stock

**handle** v 1 feel, finger, grasp, hold, maul, paw *inf*, stroke, turn over in your hands. 2 administer, be in charge of, control, cope with, deal with, direct, manage, take care of. 3 (handle goods) deal in, market, sell, stock, trade in, traffic in

**handsome** adj 1 (of a man) attractive, dishy *inf*, good-looking, gorgeous, hunky *inf*. 2 (of a woman) elegant, fine, fine-looking, good-looking, striking. 3 (of a gift) big, bountiful, generous, large, lavish, liberal, magnanimous, sizeable, valuable

**handy** adj 1 accessible, at your fingertips, available, close at hand, convenient, get-at-able *inf*, nearby, on tap *inf*, ready, to hand, within reach. 2 convenient, easy to use, functional, helpful, practical, serviceable, useful. 3 (handy with sth) adept, capable, clever, competent, deft, dexterous, good with your hands, nimble-fingered, proficient, skilful

**hang** v 1 be suspended, dangle, droop, flap, swing. 2 attach, drape, fix, pin up, put up, suspend. 3 (in the air) be poised, drift, float, hover. 4 (hang sb) execute, lynch, put the noose around sb's neck, send sb to the gallows. 5 **hang on** (hold on to sth) cling, cling on to, clutch, grasp, grip, hold, hold on to. 6 **hang on**

(wait) hold on, hold the line, stop, wait, wait a minute. **7 hang on sb's words** be all ears, be rapt, be very attentive, concentrate on, give sb your undivided attention, listen closely

**haphazard** *adj* **1** accidental, chance, random, unplanned. **2** aimless, careless, casual, disorganized, hit-or-miss, indiscriminate, slapdash, slipshod, unmethodical, unplanned, unsystematic

**happen** *v* **1** arise, come about, come to pass, crop up, occur, take place, transpire. **2** (happen to sb) become of, befall. **3** (happen by chance) chance, fall out, pan out *inf*, turn out *inf*

**happening** *n* accident, adventure, affair, event, incident, occurrence

**happiness** *n* **1** bliss, good fortune, heaven *inf*, prosperity, well-being; *opp* misery. **2** (happy feeling) cheerfulness, cheeriness, contentment, delight, ecstasy, elation, enjoyment, euphoria, gaiety, gladness, high spirits, joy, merriment, pleasure; *opp* misery

**happy** *adj* **1** carefree, cheerful, cheery, contented, glad, in a good mood, in good spirits, jolly, jovial, light-hearted, merry, pleased, satisfied, smiling, untroubled; *opp* miserable, sad, unhappy. **2** (very happy) blithe, delighted, ecstatic, euphoric, in high spirits, in seventh heaven *inf*, joyful, joyous, on cloud nine *inf*, on top of the world *inf*, overjoyed, over the moon *inf*, radiant, rapt, starry-eyed *inf*, thrilled, thrilled to bits *inf*. **3** (fortunate) advantageous, auspicious, beneficial, convenient, fortunate, lucky, opportune, welcome

**harass** *v* annoy, badger, be on sb's back

*inf*, bother, exasperate, give sb a hard time *inf*, harry, hassle *inf*, hound, persecute, pester, plague, tease, torment, trouble, vex

**harassed** *adj* agitated, careworn, distraught, hassled *inf*, strained, stressed, under pressure, vexed

**harbour** *n* **1** anchorage, dock, haven, marina, port. **2** asylum, haven, place of safety, refuge, safe house, sanctuary, shelter

**harbour** *v* **1** (a person) conceal, give shelter to, grant asylum to, hide, protect, shelter, shield. **2** (a feeling) brood over, cherish, cling on to, hold on to, nurse, maintain, retain

**hard** *adj* **1** (of a substance) close-packed, compact, dense, firm, inflexible, rigid, rock-like, solid, solidified, stiff, stony, tough, unyielding; *opp* soft. **2** (of work) arduous, back-breaking, daunting, difficult, exhausting, gruelling, heavy, Herculean, laborious, no easy task, onerous, strenuous, taxing, tiring; *opp* easy. **3** (of a problem) baffling, complex, complicated, daunting, difficult, perplexing, puzzling, thorny *inf*, tough; *opp* easy. **4** (of a person) callous, cold, cruel, hard-hearted, harsh, heartless, implacable, inflexible, merciless, pitiless, ruthless, severe, stern, strict, unbending, unfeeling, unkind. **5** (of conditions) austere, bad, difficult, distressing, grim, harsh, intolerable, unbearable, unpleasant; *opp* good. **6** (of a worker) assiduous, conscientious, diligent, dogged, enthusiastic, indefatigable, industrious, keen, steady, untiring, zealous. **7** (of a blow) forceful,

heavy, powerful, strong, violent;
*opp* light, soft

**hard and fast** *adj* binding, immutable,
inflexible, invariable, rigorous, strict,
stringent, unalterable

**harden** *v* 1 bake, cake, clot, coagulate,
congeal, freeze, jell, ossify, petrify, set,
solidify, stiffen; *opp* soften. 2 (a person)
brutalize, deaden, make callous, make
tough, numb, toughen

**hardened** *adj* 1 (a hardened criminal)
experienced, habitual, incorrigible,
inveterate, irredeemable, reprobate,
shameless. 2 (hardened to sth)
accustomed, habituated, inured,
seasoned, toughened, used to

**hardheaded** *adj* astute, practical,
pragmatic, rational, realistic, sensible,
shrewd, tough, unsentimental

**hardhearted** *adj* callous, cold, cruel,
hard, heartless, insensitive, merciless,
pitiless, stony-hearted, uncaring,
unfeeling, unkind, unmoved,
unsympathetic

**hardly** *adv* barely, faintly, just, only just,
scarcely, with difficulty

**hardship** *n* adversity, affliction, austerity,
deprivation, destitution, difficulty,
misery, misfortune, need, poverty,
privation, tribulation, trouble, want

**hard-working** *adj* assiduous, busy,
conscientious, diligent, energetic,
indefatigable, industrious, zealous;
*opp* lazy

**hardy** *adj* fit, hale, healthy, hearty, robust,
rugged, sound, stalwart, stout, strong,
sturdy, tough, vigorous; *opp* delicate,
weak

**harm** *n* abuse, damage, detriment,
disservice, hurt, impairment, injury, loss,
misfortune, ruin

**harm** *v* abuse, be harmful to, damage,
hurt, ill-treat, impair, injure, maltreat,
spoil, wound

**harmful** *adj* damaging, destructive,
detrimental, evil, hurtful, injurious,
noxious, pernicious, poisonous,
prejudicial, toxic, unhealthy,
unwholesome

**harmless** *adj* benign, innocent,
innocuous, inoffensive, non-violent,
safe, tame; *opp* dangerous

**harmony** *n* accord, agreement, concord,
conformity, co-operation, peace,
peacefulness, unison, unity; *opp* discord

**harness** *n* bridle, gear, lead, reins, straps,
tack, tackle, yoke

**harness** *v* 1 attach, bind, couple, fasten,
hitch, hitch up, join, tether, tie, yoke.
2 appropriate, channel, control, employ,
exploit, put to use, use, utilize

**harrowing** *adj* distressing, excruciating,
frightening, heartbreaking,
heartrending, horrifying, painful,
terrifying, traumatic

**harsh** *adj* 1 (of a voice) croaking, grating,
gravelly, guttural, rasping, raucous,
rough. 2 (harsh conditions) austere,
bleak, difficult, grim, hard, Spartan.
3 (of a person, a punishment) brutal,
cruel, despotic, domineering, draconian,
excessive, hard, heavy-handed, severe,
stern, strict, unfair, unjust, unkind;
*opp* lenient

**harvest** *n* 1 crops, flowers, fruit, grain,
produce, vintage, yield. 2 (things won
or gained) fruits, gains, haul, prize,
return, reward, spoils, winnings

**harvest** v 1 (harvest crops) bring in, dig
up, gather in, pick, pluck, pull up, reap,
uproot. 2 be rewarded with, collect,
cream off, gain, obtain, reap, secure, win

**hassle** n annoyance, aggravation, aggro
inf, argument, bother, difficulty, grief inf,
harassment, irritation, pain inf, problem,
trouble, upset

**hassle** v annoy, argue with, bother, get on
sb's back inf, get up sb's nose inf, harass,
harry, irritate, pester, plague, trouble

**haste** n hurry, impetuosity, recklessness,
rush, speed, urgency

**hasten** v bring forward, bring on,
encourage, speed, speed up, urge on

**hasty** adj hurried, impetuous, premature,
rash, rushed, urgent

**hatch** v 1 be born, break open, breed,
emerge, incubate. 2 (hatch a plot)
conceive, concoct, cook up inf, design,
devise, formulate, instigate, think up

**hate** n abhorrence, antipathy, aversion,
contempt, detestation, dislike, enmity,
hatred, hostility, ill-will, loathing,
odium, spite; opp love

**hate** v 1 abhor, be contemptuous of, be
unable to bear, be unable to stand,
despise, detest, dislike, loathe; opp love.
2 (hate doing sth) be averse to, be
reluctant to, be unwilling to, shy away
from, shrink from

**hateful** adj 1 abominable, abhorrent,
atrocious, contemptible, despicable,
detestable, foul, hated, heinous,
obnoxious, odious, ugly, unpleasant.
2 (feeling hate) angry, bitter,
contemptuous, hostile, jealous,
resentful, spiteful

**hatred** n abhorrence, antipathy, aversion,

contempt, detestation, dislike, enmity,
hate, hostility, ill-will, loathing, odium,
spite

**haughty** adj aloof, arrogant,
condescending, disdainful, proud, snooty
inf, superior

**haul** n bag, booty, catch, gains, harvest,
loot, spoils, swag slang, winnings

**haul** v drag, draw, heave, lug, pull, tow,
tug

**haunt** v 1 (go to a place frequently)
frequent, hang around inf, inhabit,
patronize, visit. 2 (haunt a person)
beset, hang over, nag at, obsess,
preoccupy, worry

**haunted** adj 1 cursed, possessed, scary,
spooky inf. 2 (haunted look) haggard,
hag-ridden, troubled, tormented,
tortured, worried

**haunting** adj eerie, evocative,
fascinating, nagging, poignant, spine-
tingling, unforgettable

**have** v 1 be blessed with, enjoy, hold,
keep, own, possess, retain. 2 (have a
walk, bath, meal) enjoy, go for, indulge
in, manage, partake of, take. 3 (have an
illness, accident, operation) be affected
by, experience, get, meet with, suffer,
sustain, undergo. 4 (have a baby) bear,
beget, bring into the world, give birth
to, produce. 5 (have sb do sth) ask,
command, commission, compel, direct,
force, instruct, make, order, request, tell.
6 **have to** be bound to, be compelled to,
be forced to, be made to, be obliged to,
be ordered to, be required to, be to, be
told to, must, need to

**haven** n hideaway, hideout, love nest,
oasis, refuge, retreat, safe haven,

sanctuary, shelter

**havoc** n anarchy, chaos, destruction, mayhem, trouble, violence

**hazard** n danger, difficulty, obstacle, pitfall, problem, risk

**hazardous** adj dangerous, difficult, poisonous, risky, toxic, tricky

**haze** n fog, heat haze, mist, pollution, smog, smoke, steam, vapour

**hazy** adj 1 foggy, misty, polluted, smoky, steamy, vaporous. 2 (a hazy memory) blurred, confused, distant, faint, indistinct, obscure, unclear, vague

**head** adj chief, commanding, first, foremost, highest, leading, principal, senior, supreme, top

**head** n 1 block inf, bonce inf, brain, cranium, face, mind, skull. 2 boss, chairman, chief, chief executive, director, headmaster, headmistress, head teacher, leader, manager, principal, supremo. 3 (highest part) apex, beginning, start, summit, tip, top, vertex; opp foot

**head** v 1 be in charge of, control, direct, head up, lead, manage, run. 2 (head a list) be at the head of, be at the top of, begin, lead, lead off, start, start off, top. 3 (go in a particular direction) aim, go, make a beeline inf, move, set off, set out, travel. 4 **head off** block, counter, deflect, forestall, obstruct, pre-empt, prevent, stop

**heading** n 1 caption, headline, name, rubric, subheading, title. 2 category, class, classification, division, head, section

**headlong** adj direct, fast, non-stop, onrushing, straight, wild

**headstrong** adj determined, driven, overconfident, rash, reckless, self-willed, uncontrollable, wilful

**heal** v cure, make better, mend, remedy, restore to health, soothe, treat

**health** n 1 (good health) fitness, healthiness, strength, vigour, vitality, well-being; opp illness, sickness. 2 (state of your body) condition, constitution, medical history, shape, state of health. 3 (public health) health care, health service, hygiene, medical science, medicine, NHS, public health, sanitation

**healthy** adj 1 fit, fit as a fiddle inf, hale and hearty, in fine fettle, in good health, in good shape, in tiptop condition inf, sound, strong, vigorous, well; opp ill, sick, unhealthy. 2 good for you, health-giving, hygienic, invigorating, nourishing, nutritious, restorative, wholesome; opp unhealthy

**heap** n 1 accumulation, collection, hoard, lot, mass, mound, mountain, pile, quantity, stack. 2 **heaps** a lot, a great deal, loads, lots, masses, plenty, stacks, tons

**heap** v amass, heap up, pile, pile up, stack, stack up

**hear** v catch, detect, hark, heed, listen, notice, overhear, perceive

**hearing** n 1 ears, earshot, hailing distance, sound. 2 audience, case, court martial, inquest, proceedings, session, trial

**heart** n 1 centre, core, hub, kernel, middle, nerve centre, nucleus. 2 affection, courage, emotions, feelings, love, mercy, pity, soul, sympathy, tenderness, warmth. **3 by heart** by rote, from memory, off pat *inf*, parrot-fashion, without looking, without notes, word for word

**heartbreaking** *adj* agonizing, crushing, devastating, distressing, heart-rending, painful, shattering, upsetting

**heartbroken** *adj* anguished, crushed, devastated, grief-stricken, sad, shattered

**heartfelt** *adj* deep, earnest, emotional, from the heart, genuine, honest, sincere, warm

**heartless** *adj* cold, cruel, harsh, merciless, pitiless, ruthless, uncaring, unfeeling, unsympathetic

**heart-to-heart** *adj* confessional, frank, intimate, man-to-man, personal, sincere, woman-to-woman

**hearty** *adj* **1** cordial, expansive, extrovert, hail-fellow-well-met, jolly, jovial, loud, welcoming. **2** (a hearty meal) big, filling, large, nourishing, square, substantial, sumptuous

**heat** *n* **1** energy, fire, heating, sun, temperature, warmth. **2** (emotional) anger, emotion, energy, excitement, pressure, urgency, vehemence

**heat** *v* boil, heat up, microwave, raise the temperature of, reheat, warm, warm up

**heated** *adj* angry, emotional, energetic, excited, fierce, frenzied, furious, het up *inf*, passionate, vehement, vigorous, violent, worked up

**heathen** *n* barbarian, idolater, infidel, pagan, savage

**heave** *v* cart *inf*, drag, lift, lug, pull, push, raise, shove, struggle with, tow, tug

**heaven** *n* **1** Elysian Fields, Elysium, heavens, Olympus, paradise, sky,

Valhalla; *opp* hell. **2** (happiness) bliss, dream come true, heaven on earth, Nirvana, paradise, perfection; *opp* hell

**heavy** *adj* **1** big, cumbersome, dense, fat, heavyweight, large, overweight, weighty; *opp* light. **2** (heavy pressure, rainfall) abundant, considerable, great, hard, high, intense, severe, strong; *opp* light. **3** (of a discussion) deep, dense, difficult, profound, serious, solemn, weighty; *opp* light

**heckle** *v* answer back, argue, catcall, interrupt, jeer, mock, shout, take issue with

**hectic** *adj* busy, chaotic, exciting, fevered, feverish, frantic, frenetic, frenzied, rushed

**hedge** *n* border, boundary, bushes, fence, hedgerow, hurdle, privet, shrubs, topiary

**hedge** *v* dither, dodge, duck, equivocate, evade, flannel *inf*, hesitate, prevaricate, play for time, sidestep

**heed** *v* acknowledge, bear in mind, consider, follow, hearken, listen to, notice, obey, pay attention to, pay heed to, pay regard to, respect, take account of, take heed of, take notice of; *opp* ignore

**hefty** *adj* big, cumbersome, enormous, great, heavy, huge, large, strong, weighty, whopping *inf*, whopping *inf*

**height** *n* **1** altitude, depth, elevation, size, stature. **2** (high place) apex, cliff, crest, hill, mountain, peak, pinnacle, summit. **3** (the height of bad manners) acme, apogee, culmination, embodiment, essence, pinnacle, ultimate

**heighten** *v* add to, augment, boost, enhance, improve, increase, intensify, pile on, sharpen, stimulate, wind up

**heir** *n* beneficiary, daughter, heiress, inheritor, next in line, son, successor

**hell** *n* **1** Hades, inferno, nether world, other place, purgatory, underworld; *opp* heaven. **2** (unhappiness) agony, hell on earth, misery, murder *inf*, nightmare, suffering, torture; *opp* heaven

**help** *n* aid, assistance, contribution, donation, hand, helping hand, hint, service, succour

**help** *v* **1** advise, aid, assist, come to the rescue, contribute, give sb a hand, help out, lend sb a hand, rescue, serve, succour, volunteer. **2** (can't help doing sth) avoid, prevent, resist, stop

**helper** *n* aide, adviser, assistant, collaborator, contributor, helpmate, minder *inf*, partner, volunteer

**helpful** *adj* **1** (of a person) accommodating, amenable, benevolent, co-operative, friendly, kind, generous, obliging, supportive. **2** beneficial, constructive, convenient, handy, positive, practical, productive, profitable, serviceable, useful, valuable

**helping** *n* dollop *inf*, plate, plateful, portion, ration, serving, share

**helpless** *adj* **1** (not knowing what to do) all at sea, at a loss, bewildered, floundering, forlorn, hapless, incapable, incompetent, struggling, uncomprehending, useless. **2** (unable to defend yourself) defenceless, exposed, impotent, powerless, unprotected, vulnerable, weak

**herd** *n* crowd, flock, group, mob, rabble, troop

**herd** *v* assemble, bring together, collect, drive, flock, gather, rally, muster, rally, shepherd

**hereditary** *adj* **1** (in biology) congenital, family, genetic, inborn, inherited, innate. **2** (hereditary wealth) ancestral, by divine right, family, genealogical, handed down, inherited

**heresy** *n* blasphemy, dissent, idolatry, non-conformism, sacrilege

**heretic** *n* agnostic, atheist, blasphemer, dissenter, free thinker, idolater, infidel, nonconformist, pagan, renegade, sceptic, unbeliever

**heretical** *adj* agnostic, atheistic, blasphemous, dissenting, idolatrous, nonconformist, pagan, renegade, sacrilegious, sceptical

**heritage** *n* birthright, culture, endowment, inheritance, legacy, patrimony, tradition

**hermit** *n* anchorite, loner, recluse, solitary

**hero** *n* **1** (brave person) celebrity, champion, conqueror, dare-devil, star, superhero, superman, superstar, victor. **2** (of a story) lead, leading man, main character, protagonist, star. **3** (person who is looked up to) example, exemplar, ideal, idol, inspiration, role model

**heroic** *adj* **1** bold, brave, courageous, daring, gallant, fearless, intrepid, valiant. **2** (a heroic achievement) enormous, epic, huge, monumental, painstaking, tremendous

**heroine** *n* **1** celebrity, champion, dare-devil, star, superstar, superwoman *inf*, victor. **2** (of a story) lead, leading lady, main character, protagonist, star. **3** (woman who is looked up to) example, exemplar, ideal, idol, inspiration, role model

**heroism** n bravery, courage, daring, fearlessness, gallantry, valour; *opp* cowardice

**hesitant** adj dithering, doubting, equivocal, evasive, hesitating, indecisive, reluctant, reticent, uncertain, undecided, unsure

**hesitate** v delay, dither, equivocate, falter, hang back, have doubts, have second thoughts, hedge, pause, stall, think carefully, think twice, wait

**hesitation** n delay, dithering, doubt, equivocation, evasion, hedging, indecision, pause, reluctance, reticence, thought, uncertainty, wait

**hidden** adj concealed, in disguise, in hiding, invisible, lurking, secret, undetectable, under cover

**hide** v 1 conceal, cover, cover up, disguise, hide away, keep secret, mask, obscure, put away, secrete; *opp* reveal. 2 go into hiding, go to ground, hole up, lie low, lurk, take cover, take refuge

**hideous** adj disfigured, disgusting, ghastly, gruesome, horrible, horrific, nightmarish, repulsive, ugly, unsightly

**hiding** n 1 in hiding hidden, incommunicado, on the run, under cover. 2 (a good hiding) beating, corporal punishment, drubbing, flogging, smack, spanking, thrashing

**high** adj 1 elevated, lofty, high up, raised, tall, top, upper; *opp* low. 2 (high in an organization) chief, commanding, elevated, high-ranking, high up, influential, leading, powerful, senior, superior, supreme, top; *opp* lowly.

3 (high in amount) abundant, buoyant, considerable, elevated, excessive, expensive, extreme, great, heavy, hot, intense, loud, severe; *opp* low. 4 (a high voice) alto, falsetto, fluting, high-pitched, soprano, squeaky, treble; *opp* deep

**high-class** adj aristocratic, choice, classy *inf*, de luxe, élite, first-class, five-star, high-quality, luxurious, pedigree, posh *inf*, quality, select, superior, top, up-market, upper-class

**highlight** n best bit *inf*, climax, excerpt, extract, good point, strong point

**highly** adv abundantly, considerably, extremely, greatly, intensely, really, seriously, severely, very

**highly strung** adj delicate, edgy *inf*, emotional, irritable, nervous, nervy, neurotic, temperamental, tense, unstable

**hijack** v appropriate, car-jack, commandeer, expropriate, seize, skyjack, take control of, take over, steal

**hike** n march, ramble, tramp, trek, trudge, walk, wander

**hike** v back-pack, march, ramble, tramp, trek, trudge, walk, wander

**hilarious** adj a great laugh, amusing, comic, comical, funny, humorous, hysterical *inf*, side-splitting, uproarious, witty, zany

**hill** n elevation, fell, foothill, height, high land, hillock, hillside, hilltop, knoll, mound, mount, mountain, peak, pike, prominence, ridge, summit

**hinder** v arrest, bar, block, check, curb, delay, deter, encumber, frustrate, get in the way, hamper, handicap, hold back, hold up, impede, inhibit, interrupt, keep back, limit, obstruct, oppose, prevent, restrain, restrict, retard, sabotage, slow down, slow up, stand in the way, stop, thwart; *opp* aid, help

**hindrance** *n* bar, barrier, block, check, curb, deterrent, difficulty, disadvantage, drawback, encumbrance, handicap, hitch, hold-up, impediment, inconvenience, limitation, obstacle, obstruction, restraint, restriction, snag, stumbling-block; *opp* aid, help

**hinge** *v* centre, depend, hang, pivot, rest, revolve, turn

**hint** *n* 1 allusion, clue, idea, implication, indication, inkling, innuendo, insinuation, intimation, mention, reminder, sign, suggestion, tip-off. 2 (give sb a hint) advice, help, pointer, suggestion, tip. 3 (a hint of sth) breath, dash, scent, soupçon, speck, sprinkling, suggestion, suspicion, taste, tinge, touch, trace, undertone, whiff, whisper

**hint** *v* allude, imply, indicate, insinuate, intimate, mention, signal, suggest, tip off

**hire** *n* charge, cost, fee, lease, price, rent, rental

**hire** *v* 1 (hire a vehicle) charter, engage, lease, let, rent. 2 (hire a person) appoint, book, contract, employ, engage, enlist, sign on, sign up, take on

**hiss** *n* 1 buzz, fizz, purr, rasp, rustle, shrill, sizzle, wheeze, whir, whistle, whizz. 2 boo, catcall, condemnation, damnation, derision, hoot, jeer, mocking, ridiculing, scoff, taunt; *opp* applause

**hiss** *v* 1 buzz, fizz, purr, rasp, rustle, shrill, sizzle, wheeze, whir, whistle, whizz.

2 boo, catcall, condemn, damn, decry, deride, hoot, jeer, mock, ridicule, scoff, scorn, taunt; *opp* applaud

**historic** *adj* celebrated, extraordinary, famous, important, memorable, momentous, notable, outstanding, remarkable, significant; *opp* ordinary

**historical** *adj* 1 (historical reasons) ancient, bygone, former, old, past, prior; *opp* current. 2 (a historical figure) actual, attested, authentic, chronicled, confirmed, documented, factual, real, real-life, recorded, true, verifiable; *opp* fictional

**history** *n* 1 antiquity, before, bygone days, former times, the good old days, the old days, the past, time gone by, yesterday, yesteryear; *opp* today. 2 (a history) account, biography, chronicle, diary, memoirs, narration, narrative, recital, record, relation, report, saga, story, study, tale

**hit** *n* 1 bang, bash, blow, bump, clash, clout *sl*, clip, collision, crash, cuff, impact, knock, punch, slap, smack, smash, spank, strike, swat, thump, wallop, whack. 2 sellout, sensation, success, triumph, winner *inf*; *opp* flop

**hit** *v* 1 (deliberately) bang, bash, batter, beat, belt *sl*, clout *sl*, clobber *sl*, cuff, deck *sl*, knock, lay one on *sl*, punch, slap, smack, sock *sl*, spank, strike, swat, thump, wallop, whack. 2 (accidentally) bang into, bump, cannon, clip, collide, crash, run into, smash into

**hitch** *n* catch, check, delay, difficulty, drawback, encumbrance, hindrance, hold-up, impediment, inconvenience, mishap, obstacle, obstruction, problem,

**restraint**, snag, stumbling-block, trouble

**hitch** v attach, bind, connect, couple, fasten, harness, join, tether, tie, yoke; *opp* unhitch

**hoard** n accumulation, cache, collection, fund, heap, mass, pile, reserve, reservoir, stash *inf*, stock, stockpile, store, supply

**hoard** v accumulate, amass, assemble, buy up, collect, deposit, gather, put by, save, stash *inf*, stockpile, stock up, store

**hoarse** adj croaky, grating, gravelly, growling, gruff, guttural, harsh, husky, rasping, rough, throaty; *opp* smooth

**hoax** n cheat, con *inf*, deception, fake, fast one *inf*, fraud, jest, joke, leg-pull *inf*, practical joke, prank, ruse, scam, spoof, swindle, trick

**hobby** n diversion, interest, leisure activity, pastime, pursuit, recreation, relaxation, sideline

**hoist** n crane, elevator, jack, lift, pulley, tackle, winch

**hoist** v elevate, erect, heave, jack up, lift, pull up, raise, rear, winch

**hold** n 1 clasp, clutch, grasp, grip. 2 anchorage, foothold, footing, leverage, prop, purchase, stay, support, vantage

**hold** v 1 (hold sth in your hand) bear, carry, clasp, clinch, cling to, clutch, grasp, grip, hang on to, hug. 2 (hold sb in your arms) cradle, cuddle, embrace, enfold, hug . 3 (hold a passport) have, keep, maintain, own, possess, retain. 4 (hold sb in custody) arrest, bind, check, confine, detain, impound, imprison, incarcerate, keep in custody, lock up, put behind bars, restrain; *opp* release. 5 (hold a view) assume, believe, consider, deem, esteem, judge,

maintain, presume, reckon, regard, think. 6 (hold a meeting) assemble, call, conduct, convene, have, organize, run. 7 (a theatre holding 500 people) accommodate, comprise, contain, have a capacity of, seat, take. 8 (hold the weight of sth) bear, brace, buttress, carry, keep up, prop, shoulder, support, sustain, take. 9 (my offer still holds) be unaltered, carry on, continue, endure, go on, persist, remain, stay. 10 **hold out** carry on, continue, endure, hang on *inf*, keep going, last, persevere, persist, remain, resist, stand fast, stand firm, stick at it, withstand; *opp* give in. 11 **hold up** delay, detain, hinder, impede, obstruct, retard, set back, slow, slow down, stop; *opp* speed up

**holder** n bearer, custodian, incumbent, keeper, owner, possessor, proprietor, purchaser

**hold-up** n bottleneck, delay, difficulty, hindrance, hitch, impediment, inconvenience, obstacle, obstruction, restraint, setback, snag, stoppage, trouble, wait

**hole** n 1 aperture, breach, break, chink, crack, fissure, gap, opening, orifice, perforation, puncture, rift, rip, slit, slot, space, split, tear, vent. 2 (in the ground) abyss, cavity, chasm, crater, dent, depression, dip, excavation, hollow, indentation, pit, pocket, pothole, shaft. 3 (in sb's argument) crack, defect, discrepancy, error, fault, flaw, inconsistency

**holiday** n 1 break, day/week off, half-term, leave, recess, respite, rest, sabbatical, time off, vacation. 2 (public holiday) bank holiday, celebration, day of observance, feast, festival, gala, holy day, saint's day

**hollow** adj 1 cavernous, concave, deep-set, depressed, dimpled, indented, sunken; *opp* convex. 2 empty, hollowed-out, unfilled, vacant, void; *opp* solid. 3 (a hollow sound) deep, dull, flat, low, muffled, muted, rumbling, toneless; *opp* clear. 4 (a hollow promise) artificial, empty, false, hypocritical, insincere, two-faced; *opp* sincere. 5 (a hollow victory) fruitless, futile, insignificant, meaningless, pointless, useless, vain, worthless; *opp* meaningful

**hollow** n cavity, crater, dent, depression, dimple, dint, dip, excavation, hole, indentation, pit, trough

**holocaust** n annihilation, bloodbath, butchery, carnage, destruction, devastation, ethnic cleansing, extermination, genocide, massacre, mass murder, ravaging, slaughter

**holy** adj 1 (of an object) blessed, consecrated, divine, hallowed, revered, sacred, sacrosanct. 2 (of a person) devout, faithful, God-fearing, godly, pious, pure, religious, reverent, righteous, saintly, spiritual, virtuous; *opp* atheistic

**home** n 1 abode, base, domicile, dwelling, dwelling-place, habitation, house, lodging, pad *inf*, quarters, residence. 2 birthplace, country of origin, fatherland, homeland, home town, motherland, native land. 3 (the home of the cheetah) environment, habitat, haunt, home ground, range, territory. 4 **at home** at ease, comfortable, familiar,

relaxed; *opp* uncomfortable

**homeless** adj abandoned, destitute, displaced, dispossessed, down-and-out, evicted, exiled, itinerant, nomadic, of no fixed abode, rootless, vagrant, wandering, without a roof over your head

**homicidal** adj dangerous, deadly, lethal, maniacal, mortal, murderous, violent

**homicide** n assassination, bloodshed, killing, manslaughter, murder, slaughter, slaying

**honest** adj 1 (of a person) above-board, decent, ethical, genuine, high-minded, honorable, law-abiding, reliable, reputable, scrupulous, straight *inf*, trustworthy, trusty, truthful, upright, upstanding, virtuous; *opp* dishonest. 2 (an honest answer) blunt, candid, direct, forthright, frank, open, outright, plain, sincere, upfront

**honesty** n ethics, honour, incorruptibility, integrity, morality, morals, reliability, reputability, scrupulousness, straightness, trustworthiness, truthfulness, uprightness, veracity, virtue; *opp* dishonesty

**honorary** adj complimentary, ex-officio, formal, nominal, titular, unofficial, unpaid

**honour** n 1 (a sense of honour) decency, fairness, goodness, honesty, integrity, loyalty, morality, principle, rectitude, righteousness, uprightness, virtue. 2 (it would be an honour) compliment, credit, pleasure, privilege. 3 (the honour of representing your country) credit, dignity, distinction, eminence, esteem,

fame, glory, good name, prestige, rank,
renown, reputation, repute. **4** (treat sb
with honour) acclaim, accolade,
commendation, deference, homage,
kudos, prestige, recognition, regard,
respect, reverence, tribute;
*opp* disrespect

**honour** *v* acclaim, admire, applaud,
appreciate, celebrate, commemorate,
commend, dignify, esteem, exalt, glorify,
hallow, praise, prize, respect, revere,
value, venerate, worship

**honourable** *adj* admirable, chivalrous,
creditable, decent, dependable, ethical,
fair, faithful, good, honest,
irreproachable, just, law-abiding, moral,
principled, proper, reliable, righteous,
straight *inf*, true, truthful, trustworthy,
trusty, upright, upstanding, virtuous,
worthy; *opp* dishonourable

**honours** *n* awards, decorations, dignities,
distinctions, prizes, rewards, titles

**hook** *n* **1** (on clothing) catch, clasp, clip,
fastener, hasp, link, lock. **2** (coat hook)
holder, nail, peg

**hook** *v* catch, clasp, fasten, fix, secure

**hooligan** *n* bully, delinquent, hoodlum,
lout, ruffian, tearaway, thug *inf*, troublemaker, vandal, yob *inf*, yobbo *inf*

**hoop** *n* band, circle, girdle, loop, ring,
wheel

**hoot** *n* **1** (of an owl) call, cry, screech,
toot, whoop. **2** (of people) boo, catcall,
hiss, jeer, scoff, taunt. **3** (it was a hoot)
laugh, scream

**hoot** *v* **1** (of an owl) call, cry, screech,
toot, whoop. **2** (of people) boo, catcall,
condemn, damn, decry, deride, hiss,
jeer, mock, ridicule, scoff, scorn,

taunt; *opp* applaud

**hop** *v* bounce, bound, caper, dance, jump,
leap, prance, skip, spring, vault, trip

**hope** *n* **1** ambition, aspiration, craving,
desire, dream, longing, wish, yearning.
**2** anticipation, assumption, assurance,
belief, conviction, expectation

**hope** *v* **1** aspire, crave, desire, dream,
long, wish, yearn. **2** anticipate, assume,
await, be hopeful, believe, contemplate,
expect, foresee, look forward to, trust

**hopeful** *adj* **1** (of a person) buoyant,
confident, expectant, optimistic,
positive, sanguine; *opp* pessimistic.
**2** (of news) auspicious, cheerful,
cheering, encouraging, favourable,
heartening, promising, propitious,
reassuring, rosy; *opp* gloomy

**hopefully** *adv* **1** (full of hope)
confidently, expectantly, full of hope,
optimistically, positively, with
anticipation, with assurance, with hope;
*opp* pessimistically. **2** all being well, if
everything goes according to plan, most
likely, probably, with any luck

**hopeless** *adj* **1** (feel hopeless) defeated,
dejected, demoralized, despairing,
desperate, despondent, disconsolate,
downhearted, forlorn, in despair,
negative, pessimistic, resigned, without
hope; *opp* hopeful. **2** (a hopeless case)
beyond (all) hope, helpless, incurable,
irremediable, irreparable, irretrievable,
irreversible, lost. **3** (a hopeless task)
forlorn, futile, impossible, impracticable,
no-win, pointless, unattainable, useless,
vain

**horde** *n* army, band, crew, crowd, drove,
flock, gang, group, host, mass, mob,

multitude, pack, press, swarm, throng, tribe, troop

**horizontal** *adj* even, face-down, flat, level, lying down, prone, prostrate, supine; *opp* vertical

**horrible** *adj* abominable, appalling, awful, cruel, disagreeable, disgusting, dreadful, fearful, frightful, ghastly, grim, grisly, gruesome, hateful, heinous, hideous, horrendous, horrid, loathsome, macabre, mean, nasty, objectionable, obnoxious, repulsive, revolting, shameful, shocking, terrible, unkind, unpleasant, vile; *opp* pleasant

**horrid** *adj* abominable, appalling, awful, cruel, disagreeable, disgusting, dreadful, fearful, frightful, ghastly, hateful, heinous, hideous, horrendous, horrible, loathsome, mean, nasty, objectionable, obnoxious, repulsive, revolting, shameful, shocking, terrible, unkind, unpleasant, vile; *opp* pleasant

**horrific** *adj* appalling, atrocious, blood-curdling, disgusting, dreadful, frightening, grisly, gruesome, hair-raising, harrowing, horrendous, horrifying, nauseating, shocking, sickening, unthinkable

**horrified** *adj* 1 alarmed, frightened, petrified, scared, scared out of your wits, scared stiff, scared to death, terrified. 2 appalled, disgusted, dismayed, outraged, revolted, scandalized, shocked, sickened

**horrify** *v* 1 alarm, frighten, petrify, scare, scare sb out of their wits, scare sb stiff, scare sb to death, terrify. 2 appal, disgust, dismay, outrage, revolt, scandalize, shock, sicken

**horrifying** *adj* 1 alarming, frightening, petrifying, scary, terrifying. 2 appalling, disgusting, dismaying, outrageous, revolting, shocking, sickening

**horror** *n* 1 alarm, apprehension, consternation, dismay, dread, fear, fearfulness, fright, panic, terror, trepidation, uneasiness; *opp* delight. 2 (have a horror of sth) abhorrence, antipathy, aversion, disgust, dislike, distaste, hatred, loathing, repugnance, revulsion; *opp* love

**horse** *n* carthorse, colt, filly, foal, gelding, hack, mare, mount, mule, mustang, nag *inf*, packhorse, pony, racehorse, stallion, steed

**hospitable** *adj* amicable, convivial, cordial, courteous, friendly, generous, genial, gracious, kind, neighbourly, sociable, warm, warm-hearted, welcoming; *opp* unwelcoming

**hospital** *n* clinic, health centre, hospice, infirmary, medical centre, nursing home, sanatorium, sick bay

**hospitality** *n* cheer, conviviality, cordiality, courtesy, friendliness, generosity, geniality, graciousness, kindness, neighbourliness, sociability, warm-heartedness, warmth, welcome; *opp* unfriendliness

**host** *n* 1 anchor man, announcer, compère, entertainer, interviewer, master of ceremonies, MC, presenter. 2 hostess, landlord, owner, proprietor. 3 army, band, crew, crowd, drove, flock, gang, group, hoard, mass, mob, multitude, pack, press, swarm, throng, tribe, troop

**host** *v* compère, introduce, officiate, present, preside

**hostage** n captive, pawn, prisoner, security, surety

**hostile** adj 1 aggressive, antagonistic, anti inf, belligerent, combative, confrontational, contrary, inimical, malevolent, opposed, unfriendly, unkind, unsympathetic, unwelcoming; **opp** friendly. 2 (hostile conditions) adverse, inauspicious, unfavourable, unhelpful; **opp** favourable

**hostilities** n conflict, confrontation, fighting, military action, strife, war, warfare

**hostility** n aggression, anger, animosity, antagonism, antipathy, aversion, bad feeling, belligerence, enmity, friction, hatred, ill will, malevolence, malice, opposition, rancour, resentment, spite, unfriendliness, unkindness, wrath; **opp** friendliness

**hot** adj 1 baking, blistering, boiling, burning, fiery, flaming, heated, piping, red-hot, roasting, scalding, scorching, searing, steaming, sultry, sweltering, thermal, torrid, tropical, warm; **opp** cold. 2 (spicy) peppery, piquant, pungent, sharp, spicy, strong; **opp** mild

**hound** v 1 annoy, badger, browbeat, bully, harass, harry, nag, persecute, pester. 2 chase, drive, follow, hunt, pursue, shadow, stalk, trail

**house** n 1 abode, building, domicile, dwelling, edifice, habitation, home, pad inf, place inf, residence. 2 (a publishing house) business, company, concern, corporation, enterprise, establishment, firm, organization, outfit inf

**house** v accommodate, board, harbour, keep, lodge, place, put up, shelter, sleep,

take in

**hovel** n cabin, den, dump inf, hole inf, hut, shack, shanty, shed

**hover** v 1 be suspended, drift, float, flutter, fly, hang, poise. 2 hang about, hang around, linger, loiter, wait about

**howl** v 1 bay, bellow, cry, holler Am, roar, scream, shout, shriek, yell, yelp. 2 bawl, cry, sob, wail, weep

**huddle** n band, bevy, bunch, cluster, crowd, gang, gathering, group, knot, mass, pack, posse, throng, troupe

**huddle** v 1 bunch, cluster, converge, cram, crowd, flock, gather, group, herd, jam, pile, squeeze, swarm, throng; **opp** spread out. 2 crouch, cuddle, curl up, hug, hunch, nestle, snuggle; **opp** stretch

**hug** n bearhug, clinch inf, cuddle, embrace, squeeze

**hug** v 1 (hug a person) cuddle, embrace, enfold, hold, squeeze. 2 (hug sth) clasp, cling, crush, nurse, squeeze

**huge** adj colossal, elephantine, enormous, extra-large, gargantuan, giant, gigantic, great, hulking, immense, jumbo inf, large, mammoth, massive, mighty, monster inf, mountainous, outsize, vast, whopping inf; **opp** tiny

**hulk** n body, carcass, frame, hull, shell, skeleton, wreck

**hull** n body, casing, covering, frame, framework, skeleton, structure

**hum** v 1 buzz, drone, murmur, purr, sing, throb, thrum, vibrate, whir. 2 (be humming with activity) be active, be busy, bustle, buzz, pulsate, pulse, stir, vibrate

**human** adj 1 anthropoid, hominid, mortal. 2 compassionate, considerate, humane, kind, rational, reasonable, sensible, sensitive, sympathetic, thoughtful, understanding; *opp* inhuman. **3** (only human) fallible, frail, mortal, natural, normal, vulnerable, weak

**humane** *adj* altruistic, benevolent, benign, charitable, compassionate, feeling, forgiving, gentle, good, humanitarian, kind, kindhearted, lenient, magnanimous, merciful, mild, sympathetic, tender, understanding, unselfish, warmhearted; *opp* inhumane

**humanitarian** *adj* altruistic, beneficent, benevolent, charitable, compassionate, gentle, good, humane, kind, lenient, merciful, philanthropic, public-spirited, sympathetic

**humanity** *n* humankind, man, mankind, men, mortals, people, the human race

**humanize** *v* civilize, cultivate, educate, polish, refine, soften, tame

**humble** *adj* **1** deferential, docile, meek, modest, submissive, unostentatious, unpretentious; *opp* brash. **2** (a humble cottage) common, commonplace, ignoble, insignificant, low, lowly, modest, ordinary, poor, simple, undistinguished, unimportant; *opp* great

**humdrum** *adj* banal, boring, dreary, dull, everyday, mind-numbing, monotonous, mundane, ordinary, repetitious, routine, run-of-the-mill, tedious, tiresome, uninteresting; *opp* exciting

**humid** *adj* clammy, close, damp, dank, moist, muggy, steamy, sticky, sultry, wet

**humiliate** *v* abase, chasten, crush, deflate, debase, degrade, demean, disgrace, embarrass, humble, make sb feel small, mortify, put down, put sb in their place, shame, show sb up *inf*, take sb down a peg *inf*

**humiliating** *adj* chastening, crushing, deflating, degrading, demeaning, embarrassing, humbling, ignominious, mortifying, shameful, shaming

**humiliation** *n* abasement, crushing, debasement, degradation, disgrace, dishonour, embarrassment, humbling, ignominy, indignity, loss of face, mortification, shame

**humility** *n* deference, diffidence, humbleness, lack of pride, lowliness, meekness, modesty, self-effacement, servility, submissiveness, unpretentiousness; *opp* arrogance

**humorist** *n* caricaturist, comedian, comic, jester, joker, satirist, sketch-writer, wag, wit

**humorous** *adj* amusing, comic, comical, droll, entertaining, facetious, farcical, funny, hilarious, laughable, ludicrous, ridiculous, satirical, witty

**humour** *n* **1** banter, comedy, drollness, farce, fun, hilarity, jesting, jocularity, jokes, joking, laughter, ludicrousness, merriment, quips, repartee, ridiculousness, satire, wisecracks, wit, witticisms. **2** (mood) disposition, frame of mind, mood, state of mind, spirits, temper, temperament

**hump** *n* bulge, bump, growth, hunch, lump, mound, projection, protrusion, protuberance, swelling

**hunch** *n* **1** feeling, guess, idea, impression, inkling, intuition, premonition, presentiment, sixth sense, suspicion. **2** bulge, bump, growth, hump, lump, swelling

**hunger** n 1 appetite, emptiness, famine, hungriness, ravenousness, starvation. 2 (have a hunger for sth) appetite, craving, desire, eagerness, greed, hankering, itch, keenness, longing, lust, pining, yearning

**hunger** v crave, desire, hanker, have a hankering, have an appetite for, itch, long, lust, pine, yearn

**hungry** adj 1 empty, famished, hollow, malnourished, peckish inf, ravenous, starved, starving, underfed, undernourished, voracious. 2 (hungry for sth) aching, craving, desperate, eager, greedy, hankering, itching, keen, longing, lusting, pining, yearning

**hunk** n block, chunk, lump, mass, piece, slab, wedge

**hunt** n chase, course, pursuit, quest, search, trail

**hunt** v 1 chase, course, hound, pursue, stalk, track, trail. 2 ferret out, forage, look for, search, seek, scour, trace, track down

**hurdle** n barrier, block, handicap, hindrance, impediment, obstacle, obstruction, stumbling-block

**hurl** v cast, chuck inf, fire, fling, heave, launch, lob inf, pitch, propel, send, shy, sling, throw, toss

**hurricane** n cyclone, gale, storm, tempest, tornado, typhoon, whirlwind, windstorm

**hurry** n acceleration, bustle, dispatch, expeditiousness, flurry, haste, rush, rushing, speed, urgency

**hurry** v 1 belt, dash, fly, hasten, get a move on inf, make haste, run, rush,

scurry, speed, step on it inf. 2 (hurry sth) accelerate, expedite, hasten, press, push through, quicken, speed up, urge; *opp* slow down

**hurt** n 1 (emotional) affliction, distress, grief, offence, pain, sadness, upset. 2 (physical) burning, discomfort, pain, smarting, soreness, stinging, throbbing

**hurt** v 1 bruise, cut, damage, disable, harm, impair, injure, mar, spoil, wound. 2 (sth hurts) ache, be painful, be sore, burn, smart, sting, throb. 3 affect, afflict, aggrieve, be hurtful, cut, distress, grieve, insult, offend, pain, sadden, sting, upset, wound

**husky** adj croaking, croaky, deep, gravelly, gruff, harsh, hoarse, low, rasping, rough, throaty

**hut** n cabin, den, hovel, lean-to, refuge, shack, shanty, shed, shelter

**hybrid** adj amalgam, blend, composite, compound, cross, crossbreed, half-blood, half-breed, mix, mixture, mongrel

**hygiene** n cleanliness, health, purity, sanitation

**hygienic** adj aseptic, clean, disinfected, healthy, germ-free, pure, salubrious, sanitary, sterile, sterilized, uncontaminated, unpolluted; *opp* unhygienic

**hype** n advertising, build-up, exaggeration, plugging inf, PR, promotion, propaganda, publicity

**hypnotic** adj fascinating, magnetic, mesmeric, mesmerizing, narcotic, soporific, spell-binding, stupefying

**hypnotize** v entrance, fascinate, magnetize, mesmerize, put a spell on, put sb in a trance, spellbind, stupefy

**hypocrisy** *n* cant, deceit, deception, dissembling, double standards, duplicity, falsity, humbug, insincerity, pretence, sham, two-facedness *inf*

**hypocrite** *n* charlatan, deceiver, dissembler, fake, fraud, imposter, liar, phoney *inf*, pretender

**hypocritical** *adj* deceitful, dishonest, dissembling, duplicitous, fake, false, fraudulent, hollow, inconsistent, insincere, phoney *inf*, pretended, sanctimonious, sham, spurious, two-faced *inf*

**hypothesis** *n* assumption, axiom, conjecture, guess, idea, postulate, premise, proposition, speculation, theorem, theory, thesis

**hypothetical** *adj* academic, assumed, conjectured, imaginary, notional, possible, presumed, proposed, putative, speculative, suggested, theoretical

**hysteria** *n* delirium, frenzy, hysterics, madness, mania, panic

**hysterical** *adj* berserk, beside yourself, crazed, delirious, distracted, distraught, frantic, frenzied, in hysterics, irrational, manic, out of control, raving, uncontrollable

**icy** *adj* **1** arctic, biting, bitter, chill, chilly, freezing, frosty, frozen, glacial, ice-cold, polar, raw, Siberian; *opp* hot. **2** aloof, cold, cool, chilly, distant, frigid, frosty, glacial, steely, stony, unfriendly; *opp* warm

**idea** *n* **1** abstraction, belief, concept, conception, construct, hypothesis, image, impression, notion, opinion, perception, principle, tenet, thought, theory, understanding, view. **2** (a new idea) brainwave, creation, design, inspiration, plan, proposal, scheme, suggestion. **3** (give an idea of sth) approximation, clue, estimate, estimation, guess, guidelines, impression, inkling, intimation

**ideal** *adj* archetypal, classic, complete, consummate, exemplary, faultless, flawless, model, optimum, perfect, quintessential, supreme

**idealist** *n* dreamer, optimist, romantic, Utopian, visionary

**idealistic** *adj* impracticable, impractical, optimistic, quixotic, romantic, starry-eyed, unrealistic, Utopian, visionary; *opp* realistic

**identical** *adj* alike, duplicate, equal, indistinguishable, interchangeable, like, matching, the same, twin; *opp* different

**identify** *v* **1** discern, distinguish, label, name, pick out, pinpoint, recognize, single out, specify, spot. **2** (identify a problem) ascertain, detect, diagnose, discover, establish, find, find out, uncover

**identity** *n* **1** ID *inf*, name. **2** character, distinctiveness, ego, existence, individuality, nature, personality, self, selfhood, uniqueness

**ideology** *n* belief, convictions, credo, creed, doctrine, dogma, philosophy, politics, principles, teaching, tenets, theory, thesis

**idiom** *n* **1** colloquialism, expression, manner of speaking, phrase, turn of phrase. **2** argot, dialect, jargon, language, parlance, patois, speech, usage, vernacular

**idiosyncrasy** *n* characteristic, eccentricity, feature, habit, mannerism, oddity, peculiarity, quirk, trait, trick, way

**idiosyncratic** *adj* characteristic, distinctive, eccentric, individual, odd, particular, peculiar, personal, quirky, singular, unique, unusual

**idiot** *n* blockhead, bonehead *inf*, dimwit, dummy *inf*, dunce, fool, halfwit, ignoramus, imbecile, moron, nitwit, numbskull, simpleton, twit *inf*, wally *sl*

**idiotic** *adj* asinine, crazy, daft *inf*, dense, dimwitted, dumb *inf*, fatuous, foolish, half-witted, inane, moronic, senseless, stupid

**idle** adj 1 apathetic, indolent, lazy, loafing, shiftless, slothful, sluggish, torpid, work-shy; **opp** hard-working, industrious.
2 (not working) inactive, inoperative, jobless, not working, out of action, out of use, redundant, unemployed, unoccupied, unproductive, unused.
3 (idle gossip) fatuous, frivolous, fruitless, futile, inane, insignificant, irrelevant, pointless, superficial, trivial, useless, worthless; **opp** serious

**idle** v coast, drift, hang around *inf*, laze around, lie around, loaf, loll, lounge, mess around *inf*, shirk, sit around, slack, take it easy *inf*, vegetate, waste time

**idol** n deity, god, guru, hero, heroine

**idolize** v adore, adulate, deify, glorify, hero-worship, look up to, love, revere, venerate, worship

**idyllic** adj Arcadian, blissful, ideal, heavenly, lovely, perfect, picturesque, wonderful; **opp** awful, terrible

**ignite** v burn, catch fire, fire, inflame, kindle, light, set alight, set fire to, set on fire, spark off

**ignorant** adj benighted, blind, ill-informed, inexperienced, innocent, naïve, oblivious, stupid, unaware, unconscious, uneducated, unenlightened, unknowing, unwitting; **opp** knowledgeable

**ignore** v brush aside, discount, disregard, neglect, omit, overlook, pass over, pay no attention, reject, shut your eyes, take no notice, turn a blind eye

**ill** adj 1 ailing, groggy *inf*, indisposed, infected, infirm, invalid, not well, off-colour, out of sorts, poorly, sick, sickly, under the weather, unhealthy, unwell; **opp** well. 2 bad, damaging, detrimental, evil, foul, harmful, injurious, ruinous, unfavourable, unfortunate, unlucky, vile, wicked; **opp** good

**ill-bred** adj badly brought up, bad-mannered, boorish, coarse, crass, discourteous, ill-mannered, impolite, indelicate, loutish, rude, uncivil, uncouth, ungentlemanly, unladylike, unmannerly, vulgar, yobbish *inf*

**illegal** adj against the law, banned, barred, black-market, criminal, felonious, forbidden, illegitimate, illicit, lawless, outlawed, prohibited, proscribed, unauthorized, unlawful, unlicensed, unofficial, wrongful; **opp** legal

**illegible** adj incomprehensible, indecipherable, indistinct, obscure, scrawled, scribbled, unintelligible, unreadable; **opp** legible

**illegitimate** adj 1 illegal, illicit, improper, incorrect, invalid, irregular, unauthorized, unlawful, unwarranted, wrongful; **opp** legitimate. 2 (of a person) bastard, born out of wedlock, fatherless; **opp** legitimate

**illicit** adj banned, forbidden, furtive, illegal, illegitimate, immoral, improper, irregular, prohibited, proscribed, unauthorized, unlawful, unlicensed, wrong, wrongful

**illiterate** adj unable to read, uncultured, uneducated, unlettered, unschooled, untaught; **opp** educated, literate

**illness** n affliction, ailment, attack, bug *inf*, complaint, condition, disease, disorder, ill-health, indisposition, infection, infirmity, invalidity, malady, malaise, sickness

**illogical** *adj* absurd, fallacious, faulty, inconsistent, incorrect, invalid, irrational, meaningless, senseless, specious, spurious, unreasonable, unscientific, unsound, untenable; *opp* logical

**ill-treat** *v* abuse, be cruel, damage, harm, hurt, injure, maltreat, mistreat, misuse, oppress, treat sb badly, wrong

**illusion** *n* 1 apparition, daydream, fantasy, figment, hallucination, mirage, phantasm, phantom. 2 delusion, error, fallacy, false impression, misapprehension, misconception, mistake

**illustrate** *v* 1 bring home, clarify, demonstrate, elucidate, emphasize, exemplify, exhibit, explain, interpret, prove, show. 2 adorn, decorate, embellish, illuminate

**illustrated** *adj* decorated, embellished, graphic, illuminated, pictorial, with pictures

**illustration** *n* 1 decoration, diagram, drawing, embellishment, figure, graphic, picture, plate, sketch. 2 analogy, case, clarification, demonstration, elucidation, example, explanation, instance, sample, specimen

**image** *n* 1 depiction, figure, likeness, photograph, picture, portrayal, projection, reflection, representation, semblance. 2 conception, idea, mental picture, notion, perception. 3 (improve your image) impression, name, perception, reputation, repute, standing, status

**imaginable** *adj* conceivable, credible, feasible, likely, plausible, possible, thinkable; *opp* unimaginable

**imaginary** *adj* dreamed-up, fabulous, fanciful, fantastic, fictional, ideal, illusory, imagined, invented, legendary, made-up, mythical, mythological, non-existent, shadowy, supposed, unreal, visionary; *opp* real

**imagination** *n* creativity, fancy, ingenuity, insight, inspiration, inventiveness, originality, vision

**imaginative** *adj* clever, creative, fanciful, ingenious, innovative, inspired, inventive, novel, original, unique, visionary; *opp* unimaginative

**imagine** *v* 1 conceive, conjure up, create, devise, dream up, envisage, fantasize, invent, make believe, picture, pretend, project, think of, think up, visualize. 2 assume, believe, conjecture, deduce, gather, guess, infer, judge, presume, reckon, suppose, surmise, suspect, think

**imitate** *v* 1 ape, caricature, counterfeit, do an impression of, duplicate, echo, impersonate, mimic, mirror, mock, parody, repeat, simulate. 2 copy, emulate, follow, follow sb's example, model yourself on, take a leaf out of sb's book

**imitation** *n* 1 aping, copying, impersonation, impression, mimicry, parody. 2 clone, copy, counterfeit, dummy, duplication, fake, forgery, look-alike, mock-up, model, replica, reproduction, sham, simulation

**imitative** *adj* copied, derivative, mock, parrot-like, plagiarized, unoriginal; *opp* original

**immaculate** adj 1 clean, impeccable, neat, spick and span, spotless, spruce, squeaky-clean. 2 faultless, flawless, guiltless, impeccable, innocent, irreproachable, perfect, pure, sinless, spotless, squeaky-clean, unpolluted, unstained, unsullied, untainted, untarnished, virtuous

**immature** adj 1 (not fully developed) crude, green, half-formed, raw, undeveloped, unformed, unripe, young; *opp* mature. 2 (of a person) adolescent, babyish, backward, callow, childish, infantile, juvenile, puerile; *opp* mature

**immediate** adj 1 instant, instantaneous, on the spot, prompt, quick, rapid, speedy, sudden, swift, unhesitating. 2 adjacent, close, direct, near, next

**immense** adj colossal, elephantine, enormous, extensive, gargantuan, giant, gigantic, great, huge, infinite, mammoth, massive, mighty, monumental, prodigious, stupendous, titanic, tremendous, vast; *opp* tiny

**immerse** v 1 bathe, cover, dip, douse, drench, duck, dunk, lower, plunge, sink, soak, submerge. 2 absorb, engage, engross, lose yourself, occupy, preoccupy

**immigrant** n alien, expatriate, incomer, migrant, newcomer, settler

**imminent** adj approaching, at hand, close, coming, forthcoming, gathering, impending, looming, near, on the horizon, on the way

**immobilize** v bring to a standstill, cripple, disable, freeze, halt, paralyze, put out of action, stop, transfix

**immoral** adj bad, base, corrupt, debauched, degenerate, depraved, dishonest, dissolute, evil, impure, indecent, lewd, licentious, obscene, sinful, unethical, unprincipled, unscrupulous, vicious, vile, villainous, wicked, wrong; *opp* moral

**immortal** adj abiding, ageless, constant, deathless, endless, enduring, eternal, evergreen, everlasting, imperishable, indestructible, infinite, lasting, never-ending, perennial, perpetual, timeless, undying, unfading

**immortalize** v celebrate, commemorate, enshrine, exalt, glorify, keep alive, memorialize, perpetuate, preserve

**immovable** adj 1 anchored, fast, firm, fixed, immobile, jammed, riveted, rooted, secure, set, stable, stationary, stuck. 2 adamant, constant, determined, dogged, immutable, inflexible, obdurate, resolute, staunch, steadfast, stubborn, unbending, unchanging, unshakable, unswerving, unwavering

**immune** adj exempt, free, immunized, invulnerable, proof against, protected, resistant, safe, unaffected

**immunize** v inoculate, protect, safeguard, vaccinate

**impact** n 1 bang, blow, bump, collision, contact, crash, force, impetus, jolt, knock, shock, smash, stroke, thump. 2 bearing, consequence, effect, force, impression, influence, repercussions, result

**impair** v blunt, damage, debilitate, deteriorate, diminish, disable, enfeeble, harm, hinder, hurt, impede, injure, lessen, mar, reduce, spoil, undermine, weaken, worsen

**impart** v 1 communicate, convey,

disclose, make known, pass on, relate, reveal, tell, transmit. 2 accord, bestow, confer, contribute, give, grant, lend

**impartial** *adj* balanced, detached, disinterested, dispassionate, equal, equitable, even-handed, fair, fair-minded, just, neutral, objective, open-minded, unbiased, unprejudiced; *opp* biased

**impassable** *adj* blocked, closed, impenetrable, insurmountable, obstructed, unconquerable

**impasse** *n* dead end, deadlock, full stop, stalemate, stand-off, standstill, stop

**impatience** *n* abruptness, agitation, eagerness, edginess, impetuosity, intolerance, irritability, restiveness, restlessness, shortness; *opp* patience

**impatient** *adj* 1 (waiting for sth) agitated, edgy, fidgety, intolerant, irritable, restive, testy; *opp* patient. 2 (eager to do sth) anxious, eager, keen, longing, raring *inf*. 3 (impatient with sb) abrupt, brusque, hasty, irritable, peevish, quick-tempered, short-tempered, snappish, terse; *opp* patient

**impeccable** *adj* 1 exact, exquisite, faultless, flawless, perfect, precise. 2 innocent, irreproachable, pure, virtuous

**impediment** *n* bar, block, defect, deterrent, difficulty, disadvantage, handicap, obstacle, problem, snag, stumbling-block

**impending** *adj* approaching, at hand, brewing, close, coming, gathering, imminent, looming, menacing, near, on the horizon, threatening

**imperative** *adj* critical, crucial, essential, important, necessary, vital

**imperceptible** *adj* faint, fine, inaudible, indistinct, insignificant, invisible, microscopic, negligible, shadowy, slight, subtle, tiny, undetectable, unnoticeable, unobtrusive, vague; *opp* obvious

**imperfect** *adj* blemished, broken, chipped, cracked, damaged, defective, faulty, flawed, incomplete, limited, partial, spoilt, unfinished; *opp* perfect

**imperfection** *n* blemish, defect, deficiency, failing, fault, flaw, inadequacy, shortcoming, spot, stain, weakness, weak point

**imperial** *adj* 1 kingly, majestic, princely, queenly, regal, royal, sovereign. 2 grand, great, high, imposing, magnificent, majestic, noble, stately, superior

**impersonal** *adj* businesslike, cold, cool, detached, disinterested, dispassionate, distant, formal, mechanical, remote, stiff, unfriendly, without emotion; *opp* friendly, warm

**impersonate** *v* do *inf*, do an impression of, imitate, masquerade as, mimic, parody, pose as, pretend to be, take off *inf*

**impertinent** *adj* brazen, cheeky, cocky *inf*, disrespectful, forward, fresh *inf*, impolite, impudent, insolent, irreverent, rude, saucy; *opp* respectful

**impervious** *adj* 1 (not letting sth in) impenetrable, impermeable, non-porous, resistant, sealed, waterproof, watertight. 2 (impervious to her charms) immune, resistant, unaffected, unmoved, unreceptive, untouched

**impetuous** *adj* ardent, careless, eager, hasty, hot-headed, impromptu, impulsive, quick, rash, reckless, spontaneous, spur-of-the-moment, thoughtless, unplanned, unthinking

**impetus** n 1 encouragement, impulse, incentive, inducement, motivation, push, spur, stimulus. 2 force, momentum, power, propulsion, thrust

**implement** v achieve, bring about, carry out, enforce, execute, fulfil, perform, put into effect, put into practice

**implicate** v 1 connect, concern, embroil, entangle, imply, include, involve. 2 (implicate sb in the crime) accuse, blame, compromise, incriminate, involve

**implication** n assumption, hint, inference, innuendo, meaning, overtone, significance, suggestion

**implicit** adj 1 (implicit in sth) contained, hinted at, implied, indirect, inherent, tacit, understood, unspoken; **opp** explicit. 2 (implicit obedience) absolute, complete, total, unconditional, unquestioning, utter

**implied** adj implicit, indirect, inherent, insinuated, suggested, tacit, unspoken

**imply** v hint, indicate, insinuate, intimate, mean, point to, signify, suggest

**impolite** adj bad-mannered, discourteous, disrespectful, ill-mannered, impertinent, insolent, rough, rude, uncivil, uncouth, vulgar; **opp** polite

**import** v bring in, introduce, ship in; **opp** export

**importance** n 1 gravity, momentousness, newsworthiness, prestige, rarity, seriousness, significance, status. 2 (of no importance) consequence, interest, relevance, usefulness, value, worth

**important** adj 1 (of things, issues) basic,

big, cardinal, central, chief, far-reaching, grave, historic, key, main, major, momentous, principal, salient, serious, significant, urgent, weighty; **opp** unimportant. 2 (of a person) celebrated, distinguished, eminent, famous, high-ranking, influential, leading, powerful, prominent, well-known; **opp** ordinary. 3 (it's important that you do this) critical, crucial, essential, necessary, pivotal, pressing, vital

**impose** v 1 (impose sth on sb) apply, dictate, enforce, exact, foist, force, inflict, introduce, levy, prescribe, put, saddle inf, set. 2 (don't want to impose) abuse, be a burden, butt in inf, exploit, force yourself, gatecrash inf, intrude, take advantage

**imposing** adj commanding, effective, grand, impressive, lofty, majestic, striking

**impossible** adj 1 (not possible) difficult, hopeless, impracticable, impractical, inconceivable, insoluble, insuperable, out of the question, unattainable, unimaginable, unthinkable, unworkable; **opp** possible. 2 (not true) absurd, incredible, outrageous, preposterous, unbelievable. 3 (of people) (inf) insufferable, unbearable, unmanageable

**impostor** n charlatan, cheat, con man inf, fake, fraud, hypocrite, phoney inf, swindler, trickster

**impotent** adj feeble, helpless, inadequate, incapable, incapacitated, ineffective, ineffectual, paralysed, powerless, unable, weak

**impoverished** adj 1 bankrupt, needy, penniless, poor, poverty-stricken, ruined;

*opp* rich, wealthy. **2** barren, bare, depleted, desolate, empty, exhausted, spent, weakened

**impracticable** *adj* awkward, impossible, inconvenient, not feasible, unattainable, unsuitable, useless

**impractical** *adj* abstract, academic, idealistic, impossible, ineffective, romantic, theoretical, unbusinesslike, unrealistic, visionary; *opp* practical

**imprecise** *adj* ambiguous, approximate, estimated, hazy, inaccurate, indefinite, inexact, loose, rough, sloppy *inf*, unscientific, vague, woolly *inf*; *opp* precise

**impregnable** *adj* impenetrable, invincible, invulnerable, safe, secure, strong, unassaiiable

**impress** *v* **1** (impress sb) affect, be memorable, excite, influence, inspire, leave your mark, make an impression, make an impact, persuade, stick in sb's mind *inf*, stir, sway, touch. **2** (impress sth on sb) emphasize, instil, stress. **3** emboss, engrave, print, stamp

**impression** *n* **1** (do an impression of sb) imitation, impersonation, parody, send-up *inf*, take-off *inf*. **2** (I had the impression that she was lying) feeling, hunch, idea, inkling, sensation, sense, suspicion. **3** (made a good impression) effect, impact, mark, response. **4** (your impression of sth) idea, memory, opinion, recollection, view. **5** (an impression on the grass) dent, hollow, imprint, indentation, mark

**impressionable** *adj* easily influenced, gullible, inexperienced, open, receptive, sensitive, susceptible, vulnerable

**impressive** *adj* awe-inspiring, awesome, exciting, formidable, grand, inspiring, magnificent, memorable, moving, powerful, stirring, striking, touching; *opp* unimpressive

**imprison** *v* confine, detain, incarcerate, jail, lock up, put away, put in prison, remand, send down *inf*, send to prison, shut up; *opp* free

**improbable** *adj* doubtful, dubious, fanciful, far-fetched, hard to believe, highly unlikely, implausible, incredible, questionable, unbelievable, unconvincing, unlikely; *opp* likely

**impromptu** *adj* ad-lib, improvised, off the cuff *inf*, off the top of your head *inf*, spontaneous, unplanned, unpremeditated, unrehearsed, unscripted

**improve** *v* **1** (make sth better) correct, enhance, enrich, help, mend, modernize, put right, rectify, refine, reform, repair, revise, touch up, update, upgrade. **2** (get better) advance, develop, gain strength, get better, get well, increase, look up *inf*, make headway, pick up *inf*, progress, rally, recover; *opp* worsen

**improvement** *n* advance, amendment, correction, development, enhancement, gain, growth, increase, progress, recovery, rise, upswing, upturn

**improvise** *v* **1** ad-lib, make it up as you go along, play it by ear. **2** concoct, devise, invent, make do, throw together

**imprudent** *adj* careless, foolish, ill-advised, ill-judged, indiscreet, irresponsible, rash, reckless, thoughtless, unwise; *opp* prudent, wise

**impudent** adj bad-mannered, bold, brazen, cheeky inf, disrespectful, forward, fresh inf, immodest, impertinent, insolent, presumptuous, rude, saucy

**impulse** n 1 force, impetus, momentum, movement, pressure, push, stimulus. 2 desire, drive, instinct, urge, whim

**impulsive** adj 1 (of an action) automatic, hasty, impetuous, instinctive, quick, rash, spontaneous, sudden, unplanned; **opp** planned. 2 (of a person) demonstrative, emotional, hot-headed, intuitive, passionate, spontaneous; **opp** cautious

**impurity** n contamination, dirt, dirtiness, filth, foreign body, infection, pollution

**inability** n impotence, incapability, incompetence, powerlessness, uselessness

**inaccessible** adj cut off, god-forsaken, impassable, inconvenient, isolated, off the beaten track inf, out of reach, remote, unattainable, unobtainable

**inaccuracy** n error, falsehood, fault, imprecision, inconsistency, miscalculation, misprint, mistake, slip, slip-up inf, unreliability

**inaccurate** adj 1 careless, erroneous, false, faulty, flawed, imprecise, incorrect, inexact, misleading, mistaken, out, unfaithful, untrue, wrong; **opp** accurate. 2 (an inaccurate shot) off-target, out, wide, wild; **opp** accurate

**inactive** adj asleep, dormant, hibernating, idle, immobile, inert, lazy, lethargic, out of action, passive, quiet, sedentary, sleepy, slothful, sluggish, unoccupied, unused, vegetating; **opp** active

**inadequate** adj 1 deficient,

disappointing, incapable, incompetent, incomplete, unacceptable, unqualified, unsatisfactory, unsuitable; **opp** adequate. 2 (inadequate rainfall) insubstantial, insufficient, limited, meagre, not enough, scanty, scarce

**inadvisable** adj foolish, ill-advised, ill-judged, imprudent, misguided, unwise; **opp** advisable, wise

**inane** adj fatuous, foolish, frivolous, idiotic, mindless, senseless, silly, stupid

**inanimate** adj cold, dead, defunct, extinct, inert, lifeless, unconscious; **opp** living

**inarticulate** adj dumb, faltering, halting, hesitant, incoherent, incomprehensible, indistinct, muffled, mute, shy, silent, speechless, stammering, stuttering, tongue-tied, unclear, unintelligible, wordless; **opp** articulate

**inaudible** adj faint, hard to hear, indistinct, low, muted, quiet, soft, unheard, whispered; **opp** audible

**inaugural** adj first, initial, introductory, maiden, opening

**inaugurate** v begin, commence, get off the ground, initiate, institute, introduce, launch, originate, set up, start

**inauspicious** adj bad, black, discouraging, ill-fated, ill-starred, ominous, unfortunate, unlucky, unpromising, untimely; **opp** auspicious

**incapable** adj feeble, helpless, inadequate, incompetent, ineffective, inept, powerless, unfit, unqualified, useless, weak; **opp** capable

**incapacitated** adj disabled, disqualified, immobilized, indisposed, laid up inf, out of action inf, unfit

**incarnation** n bodily form, embodiment, life, manifestation

**incentive** n bait, carrot inf, encouragement, impetus, impulse, inducement, lure, motivation, motive, reward, spur, stimulus, sweetener inf

**incessant** adj ceaseless, constant, continual, endless, interminable, never-ending, non-stop, persistent, relentless, unbroken, unrelenting

**incident** n 1 adventure, affair, episode, event, experience, happening, matter, occasion, occurrence. 2 brush, clash, confrontation, disturbance, fight, row, scene, skirmish

**incidental** adj accidental, chance, fortuitous, odd, random, unplanned

**incisive** adj acute, biting, clear, clever, cutting, decisive, direct, keen, penetrating, piercing, precise, sarcastic, sharp, shrewd, telling

**incite** v drive, egg on, encourage, excite, goad, inflame, provoke, rouse, whip up, work up

**inclement** adj bitter, blustery, foul, rough, severe, squally, stormy

**inclination** n 1 aptitude, bent, bias, habit, leaning, tendency. 2 desire, fancy, fondness, liking, partiality, penchant, preference, wish. 3 ascent, descent, gradient, slant, slope

**incline** n ascent, descent, drop, gradient, hill, ramp, rise, slope

**incline** v bank, bend, bow, drop, lean, rise, slope, tilt, tip, veer

**inclined** adj apt, disposed, given to, having a tendency to, in the habit of, liable to, likely to, prone to, willing

**include** v comprise, contain, cover, embrace, encompass, hold, incorporate, involve, take in; opp exclude

**inclusion** n incorporation, insertion, introduction; opp exclusion

**inclusive** adj 1 all-embracing, all in, comprehensive, full, general, overall. 2 including, taking into account

**incoherent** adj confused, disjointed, garbled, illogical, inarticulate, incomprehensible, muddled, rambling, unintelligible; opp coherent

**income** n earnings, interest, pay, profit, revenue, salary, takings, wages

**incoming** adj approaching, arriving, coming in, entering, landing, new, next

**incompatible** adj clashing, conflicting, contradictory, contrasting, different, incongruous, inconsistent, jarring, mismatched, unsuitable; opp compatible

**incompetent** adj clumsy, hopeless inf, incapable, ineffectual, inept, inexpert, unable, unqualified, unskilful, untrained, useless; opp competent

**incomplete** adj bitty inf, fragmentary, imperfect, insufficient, lacking, partial, short, undeveloped, undone, unfinished

**incomprehensible** adj baffling, beyond comprehension, complicated, deep, illegible, impenetrable, inexplicable, inscrutable, meaningless, mysterious, obscure, opaque, puzzling, strange, unfathomable, unintelligible, unreadable

**inconceivable** adj impossible, incredible, mind-boggling inf, out of the question, unbelievable, unheard-of, unimaginable, unthinkable; opp conceivable

**inconclusive** adj ambiguous, indecisive, open, open-ended, uncertain,

undecided, unresolved, unsettled, up in
the air *inf*, vague; *opp* conclusive

**incongruous** *adj* conflicting,
contradictory, inappropriate,
incompatible, inconsistent, odd, out of
keeping, out of place, surprising

**inconsiderate** *adj* careless, insensitive,
intolerant, rude, self-centred, selfish,
tactless, thoughtless, uncaring,
unhelpful, unkind, unsympathetic;
*opp* considerate

**inconsolable** *adj* broken-hearted,
desolate, despairing, grief-stricken,
heart-broken, miserable, sick at heart,
unhappy

**inconspicuous** *adj* camouflaged,
discreet, hidden, insignificant, in the
background, invisible, low-key *inf*,
modest, muted, ordinary, plain, quiet,
small, unassuming, unobtrusive,
unremarkable; *opp* conspicuous

**inconvenient** *adj* annoying, awkward,
difficult, disrupting, embarrassing,
inappropriate, irritating, tiresome,
troublesome, unmanageable, unsuitable;
*opp* convenient

**incorporate** *v* absorb, amalgamate,
assimilate, blend, combine, comprise,
consist of, contain, fuse, include,
integrate, meld, merge, mix, take in,
unify, unite

**incorrect** *adj* erroneous, false, faulty,
flawed, inaccurate, misleading,
mistaken, out, untrue, wide of the mark,
wrong; *opp* correct

**incorrigible** *adj* beyond redemption,
confirmed, dyed-in-the-wool *inf*,
habitual, hardened, hopeless *inf*,
incurable, inveterate,

shameless, unrepentant

**incorruptible** *adj* honest, honourable,
moral, straight, trustworthy, upright,
virtuous

**increase** *n* addition, boost, development,
enlargement, escalation, expansion,
extension, gain, growth, rise, upturn;
*opp* decrease

**increase** *v* 1 (of size) add to, augment,
broaden, build up, dilate, enlarge,
expand, extend, gain, get bigger, grow,
inflate, lengthen, magnify, make bigger,
maximize, multiply, mushroom,
proliferate, prolong, snowball, spread,
strengthen, stretch, swell, widen;
*opp* decrease. 2 (of sound) amplify,
boost, intensify, swell, turn up;
*opp* decrease. 3 (of quality) advance,
broaden, develop, enhance, improve,
step up *inf*. 4 (of seriousness, tension)
build, escalate, grow, heighten, intensify,
mount, raise

**increasing** *adj* developing, escalating,
greater than ever, growing, on the
increase, spreading; *opp* decreasing

**incredible** *adj* 1 absurd, beyond belief,
far-fetched, highly unlikely, implausible,
impossible, improbable, inconceivable,
miraculous, preposterous, surprising,
unbelievable, unconvincing,
unimaginable. 2 (good) amazing,
extraordinary, fantastic *inf*, great,
wonderful; *opp* dreadful, terrible

**incriminate** *v* accuse, blame, charge,
implicate, involve, point your finger at
*inf*, put the blame on

**incur** *v* 1 (incur sb's anger) arouse, bring
upon yourself, draw, provoke. 2 (incur a
fine) be liable to, earn, get, lay yourself

open to, run up, suffer

**incurable** adj fatal, hopeless, inoperable, terminal, untreatable; **opp** curable

**indebted** adj grateful, in sb's debt, obliged, thankful, under an obligation

**indecent** adj 1 blue, crude, dirty, filthy, impure, lewd, naughty, obscene, pornographic, risqué, sexy inf, smutty, suggestive, vulgar. 2 improper, in bad taste, offensive, outrageous, unbecoming, unseemly, unsuitable

**indecipherable** adj illegible, unclear, unintelligible, unreadable

**indecisive** adj dithering, faltering, hesitating, in two minds inf, shilly-shallying, sitting on the fence, tentative, uncertain, undecided, unsettled, up in the air inf, wavering; **opp** decisive

**indefensible** adj inexcusable, unforgivable, unjustifiable, unpardonable, wrong

**indefinite** adj 1 (not decided) ambiguous, doubtful, inconclusive, open, uncertain, undecided, undetermined. 2 (not clear) blurred, confused, dim, fuzzy, hazy, indistinct, unclear, vague

**indelible** adj enduring, fast, fixed, indestructible, ingrained, lasting, permanent, unfading

**independence** n 1 (of countries) freedom, home rule, liberty, self-determination, self-government, self-rule, sovereignty. 2 (of people) freedom, individualism, liberty, self-confidence, self-sufficiency

**independent** adj 1 (of countries) free, liberated, neutral, self-governing. 2 (of things) distinct, free-standing, individual, private, self-contained, separate, unconnected, unrelated. 3 (of people) carefree, footloose, free, free-thinking, individualistic, liberated, open-minded, self-reliant, self-sufficient, self-supporting, unbiased

**indescribable** adj beyond words, indefinable, unspeakable, unutterable

**indestructible** adj durable, enduring, eternal, everlasting, immortal, indelible, lasting, permanent, solid, strong, tough, unbreakable; **opp** breakable, delicate

**index** n catalogue, directory, guide, key, table of contents

**indicate** v be a sign of, communicate, convey, denote, imply, manifest, mean, point to, reveal, say, show, signal, signify, stand for, suggest, symbolize

**indication** n clue, evidence, explanation, hint, sign, signal, symptom, token, warning

**indicator** n display, gauge, guide, index, marker, meter, needle, pointer, sign, signal, signpost, symbol

**indictment** n accusation, allegation, charge, prosecution, summons

**indifferent** adj 1 (indifferent to sth) aloof, apathetic, blasé, callous, cold, cool, detached, distant, uncaring, unconcerned, unfeeling, uninterested, unmoved, unresponsive. 2 (not very good) average, fair, mediocre, ordinary, undistinguished, uninspired

**indigestion** n acidity, dyspepsia, heartburn

**indignant** adj angry, annoyed, disgruntled, exasperated, furious, in a huff, incensed, infuriated, irate, miffed inf, peeved inf, put out inf, resentful, vexed; **opp** pleased

**indirect** *adj* 1 (not straight) circuitous, crooked, meandering, rambling, roundabout, tortuous, wandering, winding, zigzag; *opp* direct. 2 (not intended) accidental, incidental, secondary, unintended. 3 (not open) devious, disguised, euphemistic, implicit, implied, oblique, sneaky *inf*, surreptitious; *opp* open

**indiscreet** *adj* careless, foolish, ill-considered, imprudent, insensitive, tactless, undiplomatic; *opp* discreet

**indiscretion** *n* 1 blunder, error, faux pas, gaffe, mistake, slip, slip of the tongue. 2 carelessness, foolishness, lack of diplomacy, tactlessness, thoughtlessness

**indiscriminate** *adj* 1 (indiscriminate bombing) careless, general, haphazard, random, sweeping, unsystematic, wholesale. 2 (not choosing carefully) aimless, casual, desultory, promiscuous, uncritical, undiscerning, unsystematic; *opp* selective

**indispensable** *adj* basic, crucial, essential, imperative, important, necessary, needed, required, vital; *opp* dispensable

**indistinct** *adj* 1 bleary, blurred, dim, faint, fuzzy, hazy, misty, out of focus, shadowy, vague; *opp* clear, distinct. 2 ambiguous, confused, doubtful, indefinite, muffled, slurred, unclear, weak; *opp* clear, distinct

**indistinguishable** *adj* alike, identical, interchangeable, the same

**individual** *adj* 1 characteristic, distinct, distinctive, exclusive, idiosyncratic, original, own, particular, personal, specific, unique. 2 (for one person) for one, private, separate, single

**individual** *n* character, human being, person, type

**individualist** *n* free spirit, individual, loner, maverick, nonconformist, original

**indoctrinate** *v* brainwash, drill, instil, re-educate, school, teach, train

**induce** *v* coax, convince, encourage, get, impel, incite, motivate, persuade, prompt, talk into, tempt, urge

**inducement** *n* attraction, bait, encouragement, incentive, lure, motive, provocation, reward, stimulus, sweetener *inf*

**indulge** *v* 1 (indulge sb's wishes) cater to, fulfil, give in to, give way to, gratify, pander to, satisfy, yield to. 2 (indulge in sth) bask, give yourself up to, luxuriate, revel, wallow. 3 (indulge sb) baby, be indulgent to, cosset, mollycoddle, pamper, spoil, treat

**indulgence** *n* 1 fulfilment, gratification, satisfaction. 2 excess, extravagance, luxury, self-gratification. 3 compassion, fondness, forgiveness, kindness, tolerance, understanding

**indulgent** *adj* compassionate, doting, easy-going, fond, humane, kind, lenient, liberal, permissive, sympathetic, tolerant, understanding

**industrious** *adj* active, busy, conscientious, diligent, energetic, hard-working, keen, productive, tireless, unflagging; *opp* lazy

**industry** *n* 1 business, commerce, manufacturing, production, trade. 2 activity, application, busyness, diligence, effort, energy, industriousness, labour, perseverance, steadiness, tirelessness, toil, zeal

**inedible** adj bad, harmful, indigestible, not fit to eat, off inf, poisonous, rotten, uneatable, unpalatable; **opp** edible

**ineffective** adj 1 (not having any effect) fruitless, futile, ineffectual, unavailing, unsuccessful, vain; **opp** effective.
2 (an ineffective leader) hopeless inf, inadequate, incapable, incompetent, inefficient, inept, powerless, unproductive, useless, weak, worthless; **opp** effective

**inefficient** adj 1 extravagant, uneconomical, wasteful; **opp** efficient.
2 (of a person) disorganized, incapable, ineffectual, inept; **opp** efficient

**ineligible** adj disqualified, inappropriate, out of the running inf, ruled out, unacceptable, undesirable, unfit, unqualified, unsuitable, unworthy; **opp** eligible

**inept** adj 1 (inept handling of the crisis) awkward, bungling, cack-handed inf, clumsy, gauche, heavy-handed, incompetent, ineffectual, unskilful.
2 (an inept remark) ill-timed, inappropriate, out of place, tactless, tasteless, unsuitable

**inequality** n bias, discrepancy, discrimination, lack of balance, imbalance, prejudice, unevenness, variation; **opp** equality

**inert** adj comatose, dead, dormant, immobile, inactive, inanimate, lifeless, motionless, passive, stationary, still, torpid, unresponsive; **opp** active

**inertia** n apathy, drowsiness, idleness, inactivity, laziness, lethargy, listlessness, passivity, sloth, stillness, torpor

**inevitable** adj assured, bound to happen, certain, destined, fixed, inescapable, inexorable, ordained, sure, unavoidable

**inexcusable** adj indefensible, outrageous, reprehensible, unforgivable, unjustifiable, unpardonable

**inexpensive** adj bargain, budget, cheap, dirt-cheap inf, economical, low-cost, low-priced, modest, reasonable; **opp** expensive

**inexperienced** adj amateur, immature, innocent, naïve, new, raw, unpractised, unqualified, unskilled, unsophisticated, untrained, wet behind the ears inf, young; **opp** experienced

**inexplicable** adj baffling, bewildering, incomprehensible, mysterious, mystifying, puzzling, strange, unaccountable, unfathomable, weird

**infallible** adj 1 (of a method) certain, dependable, foolproof, reliable, sound, sure, sure-fire inf, trustworthy, unfailing.
2 (of a person) faultless, flawless, perfect, without fault

**infamous** adj 1 (well-known) ill-famed, notorious, renowned, well-known.
2 (bad) disgraceful, dishonourable, disreputable, monstrous, outrageous, scandalous, shameful, shocking, villainous, wicked

**infant** n babe, baby, child, little child, toddler, tot

**infatuated** adj besotted, bewitched, captivated, enamoured, enchanted, fascinated, in love, obsessed, smitten inf, spellbound, swept off your feet, under sb's spell

**infatuation** n crush inf, fixation, mania, obsession, passion, thing inf

**infect** v 1 blight, contaminate, corrupt, poison, pollute, spoil, taint, touch. 2 pass on, spread, transmit

**infection** n 1 bacteria, bug *inf*, disease, epidemic, germs, septicaemia, virus. 2 contamination, poison, pollution

**infectious** adj catching, contagious, spreading, transmissible, transmittable

**infer** v conclude, deduce, draw a conclusion, gather, presume, read between the lines, understand

**inference** n assumption, conclusion, conjecture, deduction, presumption

**inferior** adj 1 (in rank) humble, junior, lesser, lower, lowly, minor, secondary, second-class, subordinate, unimportant; *opp* superior. 2 (in quality) cheap, defective, faulty, imperfect, poor, second-rate, shoddy, substandard; *opp* good, superior

**infertile** adj arid, barren, childless, sterile, unfruitful, unproductive; *opp* fertile

**infest** v crawl over, flood, invade, overrun, plague, ravage, swarm

**infested** adj alive, crawling, overrun, plagued, ridden, swarming, teeming

**infiltrate** v creep in, enter secretly, filter through, insinuate into, intrude, penetrate, pervade, seep in, soak into, spy on, worm into

**infinite** adj bottomless, boundless, enormous, eternal, huge, immense, incalculable, inexhaustible, limitless, measureless, never-ending, numberless, unbounded, uncounted, unending, untold, vast, wide, without end, without number

**infinity** n endlessness, eternity, space, vastness

**infirm** adj decrepit, doddering, doddery, feeble, frail, weak; *opp* healthy, strong

**infirmity** n ailment, disability, disease, disorder, illness, impairment, sickness, weakness

**inflame** v anger, arouse, enrage, exasperate, excite, ignite, incense, infuriate, kindle, madden, provoke, rile, stir up, whip up

**inflamed** adj angry-looking, festering, fevered, hot, infected, red, septic, sore, swollen

**inflammable** adj combustible, flammable, incendiary, likely to burn, volatile

**inflammation** n abscess, boil, burning, heat, infection, irritation, painfulness, rash, redness, sore, soreness, swelling, tenderness

**inflate** v balloon, blow up, boost, dilate, enlarge, expand, increase, puff out, puff up, pump up, swell

**inflexible** adj 1 (of a person) adamant, firm, obstinate, pig-headed *inf*, strict, stubborn, unbending, uncompromising, unhelpful; *opp* flexible. 2 (of a material) firm, fixed, hard, inelastic, rigid, stiff, unyielding; *opp* flexible

**inflict** v apply, deal out, deliver, exact, impose, levy, wreak

**influence** n ascendancy, authority, clout *inf*, control, dominance, hold, importance, power, prestige, standing

**influence** v affect, bias, change, determine, have an effect, manipulate, persuade, prejudice, pull strings *inf*, put pressure on, sway

**influential** adj authoritative, important, instrumental, momentous, persuasive, potent, powerful, prestigious, significant, strong

**influx** n arrival, flood, flow, inflow, inrush, invasion, rush, stream

**inform** v 1 advise, announce, enlighten, fill sb in inf, give information, give sb the low-down inf, leak, let sb know, notify, put sb in the picture inf, teach, tell. 2 (inform on sb) blab, blow the whistle inf, grass sl, rat sl, sneak inf, split inf, squeal inf, tell inf, tell tales inf, tip off inf

**informal** adj 1 (of an event) casual, cosy, friendly, relaxed, simple, unceremonious, unofficial; opp formal. 2 (of a person) approachable, easy-going, free and easy, friendly, unpretentious. 3 (of language) chatty, colloquial, everyday, slangy inf; opp formal

**information** n advice, data, evidence, facts, info inf, intelligence, knowledge, news, statistics

**informative** adj chatty, educational, enlightening, factual, gossipy, helpful, illuminating, instructive, newsy, revealing; opp uninformative

**informed** adj 1 (keep sb informed) posted, primed, up-to-date, well-briefed. 2 (knowing a lot) clued-up, enlightened, intelligent, knowledgeable, well-informed, well-read

**informer** n betrayer, grass sl, informant, sneak, spy, stool-pigeon inf, tell-tale inf, traitor

**infrequent** adj few and far between, irregular, occasional, once in a blue moon inf, rare, sporadic, uncommon, unusual; opp frequent

**infringe** v break, defy, disobey, disregard,

flout, ignore, overstep

**infuriate** v aggravate inf, anger, bug inf, drive sb mad inf, enrage, exasperate, incense, irritate, madden, make sb's blood boil, make sb see red, outrage, provoke, rile

**infuriating** adj aggravating inf, annoying, exasperating, galling, irritating, maddening, provoking

**ingenious** adj brilliant, clever, crafty, cunning, imaginative, inventive, neat, original, smart

**ingenuous** adj guileless, honest, inexperienced, innocent, naïve, simple, sincere, trusting, unsophisticated; opp crafty

**ingredient** n component, constituent, contents, element, factor, part

**inhabit** v colonize, dwell, live, make your home, occupy, populate, rent, reside, set up home, settle, stay, take up residence in

**inhabitable** adj habitable, in reasonable condition, livable in, livable, weatherproof; opp uninhabitable

**inhabitant** n dweller, tenant, occupant, householder, citizen, resident, inmate, lodger, native, townspeople

**inhale** v breathe in, draw in, suck in, take down into your lungs; opp exhale

**inherent** adj basic, built-in, congenital, essential, fundamental, hereditary, inbred, inbuilt, ingrained, inherited, innate, intrinsic, natural

**inherit** v accede to, be heir to, be left, be willed, come into, succeed to, take over

**inheritance** n bequest, birthright, endowment, estate, heritage, legacy

**inhibit** v check, constrain, curb, hold

back, interfere with, prevent, repress, restrict, stem, straitjacket, suppress

**inhibited** *adj* constrained, embarrassed, guarded, reserved, self-conscious, shy, uptight *inf*; *opp* uninhibited

**inhibition** *n* angst, constraint, embarrassment, reserve, reticence, self-consciousness, shyness

**inhospitable** *adj* 1 (of a person) aloof, antisocial, cold, cool, hostile, unfriendly, unsociable, unwelcoming. 2 (of a landscape) barren, bleak, desolate, forbidding, godforsaken, hostile, uninviting

**inhuman** *adj* barbaric, barbarous, cruel, heartless, inhumane, merciless, pitiless, savage, unfeeling, unnatural

**inhumane** *adj* brutal, callous, cold-blooded, cruel, hard-hearted, heartless, inhuman, pitiless, unfeeling; *opp* humane

**iniquitous** *adj* corrupt, criminal, evil, immoral, infamous, outrageous, scandalous, unfair, unjust, wicked, wrong; *opp* fair, right

**initial** *adj* early, first, inaugural, introductory, opening; *opp* final

**initiate** *v* begin, commence, get under way, instigate, launch, originate, pioneer, prompt, set up, start, stimulate, trigger; *opp* terminate

**initiation** *n* admission, baptism, debut, enrolment, induction, initiation rite, introduction, investment, ordination, rite of passage

**initiative** *n* 1 ambition, creativity, drive, dynamism, enterprise, resourcefulness, self-motivation. 2 plan, programme, project, proposal, scheme, suggestion.

3 advantage, first move, first step, lead, opening gambit

**inject** *v* 1 inoculate, mainline *inf*, shoot *inf*, shoot up *inf*, squirt in, vaccinate. 2 (inject cash into sth) add, bring in, infuse, insert, instil, introduce, put

**injection** *n* 1 booster, fix *inf*, immunization, inoculation, jab *inf*, shot *inf*, vaccination. 2 (an injection of cash) addition, introduction

**injure** *v* 1 (wound) cut, damage, disable, disfigure, fracture, harm, hurt, mutilate, wound. 2 (spoil) damage, harm, ruin, spoil, undermine, weaken

**injured** *adj* 1 (wounded) disabled, fractured, hurt, sore, wounded. 2 (spoilt) damaged, harmed, spoilt, undermined, weakened. 3 (an injured look) aggrieved, hurt, put out, reproachful, wounded

**injury** *n* bruising, cut, fracture, gash, laceration, sore, wound

**injustice** *n* bias, discrimination, favouritism, inequity, offence, one-sidedness, prejudice, unfairness, wrong; *opp* justice

**inn** *n* ale house, hostelry, hotel, local, pub, public house, tavern, watering hole *inf*

**innate** *adj* built-in, inborn, inbuilt, inherent, inherited, instinctive, intrinsic, natural

**inner** *adj* 1 central, innermost, inside, interior, internal, middle; *opp* external, outer. 2 intimate, personal, private, secret; *opp* external, outer, public

**innocence** *n* 1 honesty, probity, purity, virtue; *opp* guilt. 2 gullibility, inexperience, naivety, simplicity

**innocent** *adj* 1 blameless, in the clear,

not guilty; **opp** guilty. **2** childlike, credulous, gullible, inexperienced, naïve; **opp** experienced

**innovation** *n* change, creativity, introduction, invention, new method, novelty, reform

**innuendo** *n* allusion, hint, implication, insinuation, rumour, suggestion, whisper

**inquest** *n* hearing, inquiry, investigation, probe, study

**inquire** *v* ask, explore, investigate, look into, make inquiries, query

**inquiry** *n* **1** examination, exploration, investigation, review, study, survey. **2** query, question, request

**inquisitive** *adj* curious, interested, interfering, meddlesome, nosy, prying

**insane** *adj* **1** crazy, deranged, disturbed, dotty *inf*, mad, mental, mentally disordered, mentally ill, not all there, off your rocker *inf*, out of you mind, round the bend *inf*, senile, unbalanced, unhinged; **opp** sane. **2** (an insane idea) crackpot *inf*, crazy, daft *inf*, foolish, harebrained, mad, ridiculous, stupid; **opp** sensible

**insanity** *n* **1** dementia, madness, mental disability, mental disorder, mental illness, senility. **2** (stupidity) folly, foolhardiness, lunacy, madness, stupidity

**insatiable** *adj* avid, greedy, inordinate, irrepressible, never satisfied, voracious

**inscribe** *v* carve, cut, engrave, etch, mark, sign, write

**inscription** *n* dedication, engraving, legend, lettering, message, signature, words

**inscrutable** *adj* blank, cryptic, deadpan, enigmatic, impenetrable, mysterious, poker-faced

**insect** *n* beetle, bug *inf*, creepy-crawly *inf*, fly

**insecure** *adj* anxious, exposed, lacking confidence, nervous, uncertain, unsafe, vulnerable; **opp** secure

**insecurity** *n* anxiety, lack of confidence, nervousness, uncertainty, vulnerability; **opp** security

**insensitive** *adj* crass, heartless, impervious, indifferent, oblivious, tactless, thoughtless, unaffected, uncaring, unfeeling, unmoved, unsympathetic, unthinking; **opp** sensitive

**inseparable** *adj* close, devoted, indivisible, inextricable, integral, intimate

**insert** *v* add, enclose, enter, implant, interject, introduce, pop in, put in, set in, slide in, stick in

**inside** *adj* **1** indoor, inner, innermost, interior, internal; **opp** outside. **2** (inside information) classified, confidential, secret

**insidious** *adj* furtive, pervasive, sneaking, sneaky, stealthy, subtle, surreptitious

**insight** *n* acumen, awareness, grasp, intuition, perception, perceptiveness, understanding, vision

**insignificant** *adj* inconsequential, irrelevant, minor, negligible, paltry, petty, trivial, unimportant; **opp** significant

**insincere** *adj* deceitful, dishonest, disloyal, evasive, false, feigned, hypocritical, lying, phoney *inf*, put on *inf*, shifty, two-faced, underhand, untruthful; **opp** honest, open, sincere

**insinuate** v give the impression, hint, imply, intimate, suggest

**insinuation** n hint, implication, innuendo, intimation, slur, suggestion

**insipid** adj 1 anaemic, bland, colourless, pale, washed-out, watery, weak, wishy-washy inf. 2 boring, dead, dull, flat, humdrum, lifeless, stale, unimaginative, uninteresting

**insist** v assert, be firm, demand, emphasize, persist, put your foot down inf, stand firm, stick to your guns inf, stress

**insistent** adj demanding, determined, dogged, forceful, incessant, urgent, persistent, unrelenting

**insolence** n cheek, disrespect, impertinence, impudence, insubordination, nerve, rudeness

**insolent** adj bad-mannered, cheeky, disrespectful, impertinent, impudent, offensive, rude

**insoluble** adj impenetrable, incomprehensible, inexplicable, mystifying, obscure, perplexing, puzzling, unanswerable, unsolvable; opp simple, straightforward

**insolvent** adj bankrupt, broke, failed, finished, gone bust inf, in debt, in the hands of the receivers, in the red, penniless, ruined

**insomnia** n sleeplessness

**inspect** v audit, check out, examine, give sth the once-over inf, go over, go through, look at, look over, scrutinize, study

**inspection** n audit, check, examination, once-over inf, scrutiny

**inspector** n auditor, checker, examiner, investigator, superintendent, supervisor

**inspiration** n 1 brainstorm, brainwave, bright idea, brilliant idea, idea, insight, revelation, thought. 2 creativity, encouragement, imagination, motivation, muse, stimulus

**inspire** v encourage, enthuse, fire sb's imagination, galvanize, motivate, prompt, spark off, spur, stimulate, trigger

**inspired** adj brilliant, dazzling, excellent, exciting, impressive, stunning, supreme, thrilling, wonderful

**instability** n 1 precariousness, shakiness, unsteadiness, wobbliness. 2 insecurity, precariousness, uncertainty, unpredictability, variability, volatility

**install** v ensconce, fit, fit in, inaugurate, instate, load, locate, position, put in place, put in, set up

**instalment** n chapter, edition, episode, part, section

**instance** n case, example, occasion, occurrence, time

**instant** adj direct, fast, immediate, instantaneous, on-the-spot, quick, rapid, snap

**instigate** v bring about, encourage, incite, prompt, put into action, set in motion, set up, start, stir up, whip up

**instil** v din into inf, implant, inculcate, infuse, ingrain, inject, teach

**instinct** n aptitude, feel, feeling, gut feeling, hunch, impulse, intuition, natural ability, predisposition, sixth sense

**instinctive** adj automatic, inborn, inbred, innate, intuitive, involuntary, natural, reflex

**institute** n academy, association,

establishment, foundation, institution, organization, society

**institute** v bring about, develop, establish, found, initiate, introduce, launch, organize, originate, set in motion, set up, start

**institution** n 1 (organization) academy, association, establishment, foundation, home, hospital, institute, organization, society. 2 (custom) convention, custom, practice, tradition. 3 (the process of instituting) creation, establishment, formation, foundation, initiation, introduction

**institutional** adj bureaucratic, clinical, conventional, drab, formal, impersonal, orderly, regimented, unimaginative, unvarying

**instruct** v 1 (teach) coach, drill, educate, inform, teach, train. 2 (order) brief, direct, order, tell

**instruction** n 1 (order) brief, command, direction, injunction, order, requirement. 2 (education) classes, coaching, drilling, education, grounding, guidance, lessons, preparation, training, tuition

**instructions** n 1 brief, directions, orders. 2 directions, instruction leaflet, manual, rule book

**instructive** adj edifying, educational, enlightening, helpful, illuminating, informative, revealing, useful

**instructor** n coach, guru, lecturer, mentor, teacher, trainer, tutor

**instrument** n 1 apparatus, appliance, contraption, device, gadget, implement, machine, musical instrument, tool, utensil. 2 dial, meter, gauge

**instrumental** adj a prime mover in, contributory, helpful, influential, involved, significant

**insubordinate** adj defiant, disobedient, disorderly, mutinous, rebellious, recalcitrant, undisciplined, unruly; *opp* obedient

**insufficient** adj inadequate, meagre, not enough, pathetic *inf*, scant, scanty, skimpy; *opp* ample, plentiful

**insular** adj closed, cut off, independent, isolated, limited, narrow, parochial, remote, self-contained, self-sufficient, solitary

**insulate** v 1 cover, encase, lag, protect, put insulation in, soundproof. 2 cushion, cut off, protect, shelter, shield

**insult** n abuse, affront, insolence, libel, rudeness, slander, slight, slur; *opp* compliment

**insult** v abuse, affront, be rude to, call names, hurt sb's feelings, libel, offend, slag off *inf*, slander, snub; *opp* compliment, praise

**insulting** adj abusive, disparaging, insolent, offensive, rude, scurrilous

**insurance** n assurance, cover, indemnity, protection, provision, safeguard, surety

**insure** v cover, indemnify, protect, take out insurance, underwrite

**insurgent** n freedom fighter, guerrilla, rebel, revolutionary, terrorist

**insurrection** n coup, insurgency, mutiny, rebellion, revolt, uprising

**intact** adj in one piece, perfect, sound, unbroken, undamaged, unharmed, unscathed, whole

**integral** adj basic, constituent, essential, fundamental, indispensable, inherent, intrinsic, necessary, requisite

**integrate** v amalgamate, assimilate, combine, fuse, incorporate, interweave, knit, merge, mesh, unite

**integrity** n decency, honesty, honour, morality, principle, probity, rectitude, virtue

**intellect** n brain, intelligence, mind, reason, understanding

**intellectual** adj academic, bookish, cerebral, mental, scholarly, studious

**intellectual** n academic, don, egghead inf, member of the intelligentsia, scholar, thinker

**intelligence** n aptitude, brains, brilliance, cleverness, gumption inf, intellect, IQ, mental capacity, nous inf, wit

**intelligent** adj brainy inf, bright, brilliant, clever, educated, gifted, knowledgeable, learned, quick, sensible, sharp, smart, well-informed; *opp* slow, unintelligent

**intelligible** adj clear, comprehensible, lucid, meaningful, straightforward, unambiguous, understandable; *opp* incomprehensible, unintelligible

**intend** v aim, be determined, expect, have in mind, mean, plan

**intense** adj acute, deep, extreme, fierce, forceful, heavy, keen, passionate, powerful, severe, strong, vehement

**intensify** v add to, boost, deepen, emphasize, escalate, exacerbate, fuel, increase, inflame, magnify, reinforce, step up, strengthen

**intensity** n degree, depth, fierceness, force, power, severity, strength

**intensive** adj all-out, concentrated, detailed, exhaustive, in-depth, total

**intent** adj absorbed, attentive, concentrated, concentrating, engrossed, fixed, focused, rapt

**intention** n aim, ambition, goal, idea, objective, plan, purpose, wish

**intentional** adj calculated, conscious, deliberate, done on purpose, intended, meant, planned, premeditated, wilful; *opp* accidental, unintentional

**intercept** v block, catch, cut off, head off, stop

**interchangeable** adj equivalent, exchangeable, identical, standard

**intercourse** n 1 (sexual) copulation, love-making, sex, sexual intercourse, sexual relations. 2 (social) association, connection, conversation, dealings, interaction

**interest** n 1 (attention) absorption, attention, curiosity, notice. 2 (be of interest) concern, consequence, note, relevance, significance. 3 (a leisure activity) hobby, leisure activity, pastime, pursuit. 4 (an appealing quality) appeal, attraction, charm, fascination. 5 (in sb's interest) advantage, benefit. 6 (on a loan or investment) APR, charge, dividend, profit, rate, return

**interest** v amuse, appeal to, arouse sb's curiosity, attract, captivate, divert, fascinate, hold sb's attention, intrigue; *opp* bore

**interested** adj 1 absorbed, attracted, captivated, curious, engrossed, enthusiastic, fascinated, intent, into inf, keen; *opp* bored. 2 (an interested party) concerned, involved, partial

**interesting** adj absorbing, appealing, compelling, curious, entertaining, fascinating, intriguing, thought-provoking; *opp* dull, boring

**interfere** *v* 1 butt in, fiddle with, intrude, meddle, poke your nose in *inf*, pry, stick your oar in *inf*. 2 **interfere with** frustrate, get in the way of, hamper, hinder, hold up, impede, inhibit, prevent

**interference** *n* intervention, intrusion, meddling, nosiness *inf*, prying

**interim** *adj* acting, makeshift, pro tem, provisional, stopgap, temporary

**interior** *adj* central, core, inland, inner, inside, internal; *opp* exterior, outside

**interlude** *n* break, breather *inf*, breathing-space, delay, intermission, interval, pause, recess, respite

**intermediary** *n* arbitrator, broker, go-between, mediator, negotiator

**intermediate** *adj* halfway, in-between, mid, midway, transitional

**interminable** *adj* constant, continual, endless, incessant, innumerable, long-winded, never-ending, perpetual, rambling, tedious, unending

**intermission** *n* break, interlude, interval, let-up, lull, pause, respite

**intermittent** *adj* erratic, fitful, irregular, occasional, on-and-off, periodic, spasmodic, sporadic; *opp* regular

**internal** *adj* 1 central, core, inland, inner, inside, interior; *opp* external. 2 civil, domestic, home, in-house, national

**international** *adj* cosmopolitan, global, intercontinental, worldwide

**interpret** *v* clarify, crack, decipher, decode, elucidate, explain, expound, gloss, make sense of, read, translate, understand

**interpretation** *n* analysis, explanation,

meaning, reading, sense, translation, understanding, version

**interpreter** *n* commentator, exponent, translator

**interrogate** *v* cross-examine, cross-question, debrief, give sb the third degree, grill, put sb through the mill, question, quiz

**interrogation** *n* cross-examination, cross-questioning, debriefing, grilling, inquisition, investigation, probing, questioning, third degree

**interrupt** *v* 1 barge in *inf*, break in, butt in *inf*, chime in *inf*, chip in *inf*, disturb, heckle, interject, intervene, muscle in *inf*, put your oar in *inf*. 2 block, break off, break, bring to a standstill, cut off, obstruct, postpone, punctuate, suspend

**interruption** *n* break, delay, disruption, disturbance, gap, hitch, interval, intrusion, pause, postponement, stoppage, suspension

**interval** *n* 1 break, delay, gap, intermission, interlude, lull, pause, pause, recess. 2 interim, intervening, time, meantime, period, space, spell, time

**intervene** *v* 1 (intervene in sth) butt in *inf*, get in the way, get involved, intercede, put your oar in *inf*, step in. 2 (sth intervenes) come between, happen, occur

**interview** *n* 1 (for a job or award) assessment, evaluation procedure, oral examination, viva. 2 (discussion with sb) audience, consultation, dialogue, discussion, exchange, face-to-face, one-to-one, press conference, question and answer session

**interview** v cross-examine, grill, interrogate, put questions to, question, see, talk to, vet

**interviewer** n 1 assessor, examiner, interrogator, questioner. 2 (in the media) chat-show host, reporter, talk-show host

**intimate** adj 1 affectionate, close, familiar, informal, loving, sexual, warm. 2 confidential, personal, private, secret

**intimate** v communicate, hint, impart, imply, indicate, insinuate, let it be known, signal, suggest

**intimidate** v browbeat, bulldoze, bully, coerce, cow, frighten, lean on inf, menace, overawe, pressurize, push around, put pressure on, scare, subdue, terrify, terrorize, threaten, twist sb's arm inf, tyrannize

**intimidation** n arm-twisting inf, browbeating, bullying, coercion, pressure, terror, threatening behaviour

**intolerable** adj 1 impossible to bear, more than you can stand, unbearable, unendurable. 2 (of behaviour) insupportable, offensive, unacceptable

**intolerant** adj bigoted, chauvinistic, dogmatic, illiberal, narrow-minded, one-sided, prejudiced, racist, sexist, small-minded, uncharitable, xenophobic; opp tolerant

**intransigent** adj die-hard, hard-line, immovable, implacable, inflexible, intractable, obdurate, obstinate, stubborn, tough, uncompromising

**intrepid** adj adventurous, bold, brave, courageous, daring, fearless, game, plucky, resolute, stalwart

**intricate** adj complex, complicated, convoluted, detailed, elaborate, entangled, fiddly inf, involved, tangled; opp simple

**intrigue** n 1 collusion, conspiracy, double-dealing, plot, scheme. 2 affair, liaison, love affair, romance

**intrigue** v 1 appeal to, arouse sb's curiosity, attract, beguile, captivate, capture sb's interest, charm, fascinate, interest, rivet. 2 connive, conspire, plot, scheme

**intriguing** adj appealing, captivating, exciting, fascinating, interesting, riveting, tantalizing

**intrinsic** adj basic, built-in, central, congenital, essential, fundamental, inborn, in-built, inherent, native, natural, real

**introduce** v 1 acquaint, bring together, familiarize, make acquainted, make known, present. 2 begin, bring in, establish, found, inaugurate, initiate, introduce, institute, launch, organize, originate, pioneer, set in motion, set up, start, usher in. 3 announce, begin, lead into, lead up to, preface

**introduction** n 1 foreword, lead-in, opening, preamble, preface, preliminaries, prelude, prologue. 2 (first experience of sth) baptism, debut, inauguration, induction, initiation, launch, presentation. 3 (the start of sth) beginning, establishment, inauguration, institution, launch, start

**introductory** adj 1 first, inaugural, initial, opening, prefatory, preliminary. 2 basic, fundamental, preparatory, rudimentary

**introspective** adj brooding,

contemplative, introverted, inward-looking, meditative, pensive

**introverted** adj introspective, inward-looking, reserved, self-absorbed, shy, withdrawn; *opp* extroverted

**intrude** v barge in, break in, butt in, encroach, enter uninvited, gatecrash, interfere, interrupt, invade sb's privacy, invade sb's space, poke your nose in, stick your nose in, trespass

**intruder** n 1 burglar, housebreaker, invader, prowler, stalker, trespasser. 2 gatecrasher, infiltrator, interloper, uninvited guest, unwelcome visitor

**intrusion** n encroachment, infringement, interference, interruption, invasion, trespass, violation

**intrusive** adj impertinent, interfering, meddlesome, nosy, officious, pushy *inf*, uncalled-for, unwanted

**intuition** n feeling, hunch, insight, instinct, perception, presentiment, sixth sense

**invade** v 1 (a place) assail, assault, attack, march into, occupy, overrun, penetrate, raid, storm, take over. 2 (sb's privacy) encroach, infringe, interfere, intrude, trespass on, violate

**invader** n aggressor, assailant, attacker, occupying force, raider, trespasser

**invalid** adj 1 ailing, bed-ridden, chronically sick, disabled, feeble, frail, ill, infirm, sick, weak. 2 (of an agreement) null and void, unusable, void, worthless; *opp* valid. 3 (of criticism) baseless, false, spurious, unfounded, unreasonable, wrong; *opp* valid

**invalid** n chronic patient, convalescent,

patient, sick person, sufferer, valetudinarian

**invalidate** v annul, cancel, negate, nullify, overrule, overthrow, quash, repeal, rescind, revoke, terminate

**invaluable** adj beyond price, indispensable, irreplaceable, precious, priceless, worth its weight in gold

**invasion** n 1 (of a place) assault, attack, foray, incursion, inroad, offensive, onslaught, raid. 2 (of sb's privacy) breach, infringement, interference, intrusion, trespass, violation

**invent** v 1 coin, come up with, conceive, contrive, create, design, devise, formulate, frame, improvise, originate, think up. 2 (a story) come up with, concoct, cook up *inf*, dream up, fabricate, make up, think up

**invention** n 1 (the act of inventing) coinage, contrivance, creation, design, devising, innovation, origination. 2 (sb's invention) brainchild, coinage, contraption, contrivance, construction, design, device. 3 (the ability to invent) creativeness, creativity, genius, imagination, ingenuity, inventiveness, resourcefulness. 4 (sth made-up) cock-and-bull story, fabrication, falsehood, fiction, figment of sb's imagination, lie, story, tall story

**inventive** adj creative, imaginative, ingenious, innovative, original, resourceful

**inventor** n architect, author, boffin *inf*, creator, designer, initiator, innovator, maker, originator, prime mover, producer

**inventory** n account, catalogue,

checklist, description, list, record,
register, schedule, statement

**inverse** adj 1 opposite, reverse,
transposed. 2 flip side inf, obverse,
opposite side, other side, reverse

**invert** v capsize, overturn, reverse,
transpose, turn upside down, upset,
upturn

**invest** v 1 (in a business) buy shares,
endow, fund, provide capital for, put
money into, sink money into.
2 (money) expend, lay out, play the
market, put in, put to work, speculate,
spend, use profitably, venture

**investigate** v analyse, conduct an inquiry,
conduct a survey, consider, inquire into,
examine, explore, go into inf, hold an
inquiry, inspect, look into, make
inquiries, probe, research, search, study,
suss out inf, weigh up

**investigation** n analysis, inquiry,
examination, exploration, inquest,
inquiry, inspection, probe, research,
review, scrutiny, search, study, survey

**investigator** n 1 examiner, inquirer,
researcher. 2 detective, private
detective, private eye, sleuth inf

**investment** n 1 risk, speculation,
venture. 2 capital, finance, funding,
stake money

**invigorate** v brace, energize, enliven,
quicken, pep up, perk up, put new
strength into, refresh, rejuvenate,
stimulate, strengthen

**invigorating** adj bracing, enlivening,
exhilarating, refreshing, rejuvenating,
revitalizing, strengthening, tonic

**invincible** adj impregnable,
indestructible, indomitable, insuperable,

invulnerable, unassailable, unbeatable,
unconquerable, unstoppable;
**opp** vulnerable

**invisible** adj camouflaged, concealed,
disguised, hidden, indiscernible,
obscured, out of sight, unseen;
**opp** visible

**invitation** n 1 asking, call, invite inf,
request, summons. 2 encouragement,
enticement, incitement, overture,
provocation, temptation, welcome

**invite** v 1 ask, request sb's company,
summon. 2 appeal for, ask for, request,
seek, solicit. 3 (invite disaster) bring sth
on yourself, make sth liable to happen,
provoke

**inviting** adj alluring, attractive,
captivating, delightful, engaging,
enticing, pleasing, seductive, tempting,
warm, welcoming, winning

**invoice** n account, bill, statement of
charges

**invoke** v 1 appeal to, beg, call for, call
upon, entreat, implore, pray, solicit,
supplicate. 2 (invoke a law) apply,
implement, put into effect, resort to, use

**involuntary** adj 1 automatic, knee-jerk
inf, instinctive, mechanical,
spontaneous, unintentional, unthinking.
2 against sb's will, compulsory,
obligatory, reluctant, unwilling

**involve** v 1 entail, imply, mean,
necessitate, require. 2 comprise, bring
in, draw in, hold, include, incorporate,
take in. 3 affect, concern, interest, touch

**involved** adj 1 complex, complicated,
confused, confusing, convoluted,
intricate, knotty, mixed up, tangled;

*opp* simple. 2 (involved in sth) busy, concerned, interested, participating, taking part. 3 (involved in a crime) associated, implicated, incriminated

**involvement** *n* association, commitment, concern, connection, interest, participation

**ironic** *adj* 1 derisive, double-edged, mocking, sarcastic, sardonic, satirical, wry. 2 paradoxical

**irony** *n* 1 double meaning, mockery, sarcasm, satire. 2 paradox

**irrational** *adj* 1 (of an idea) absurd, crackpot *inf*, groundless, illogical, implausible, ridiculous, senseless, unreasonable, unsound, wild, without foundation; *opp* sensible. 2 (of a person) confused, crazy, demented, illogical, insane, mad, muddled, muddle-headed, unintelligent, unstable, unthinking

**irreconcilable** *adj* 1 (of ideas) at odds, clashing, conflicting, contrary, diametrically opposed, incompatible. 2 (of enemies) hard-line, implacable, inflexible, intransigent, uncompromising

**irrefutable** *adj* beyond doubt, certain, conclusive, incontestable, incontrovertible, indisputable, indubitable, sure, unanswerable, undeniable

**irregular** *adj* 1 abnormal, eccentric, extraordinary, odd, peculiar, quirky, unusual. 2 (in shape) asymmetric, bumpy, crooked, craggy, jagged, lumpy, ragged, rough, uneven; *opp* regular. 3 erratic, fitful, fluctuating, haphazard, intermittent, occasional, patchy, random, shaky, spasmodic, sporadic, uneven, unsteady, varying; *opp* regular.

4 (not honest) against the rules, illegal, improper, out of order, unconventional, unofficial, unorthodox. 5 (of troops) guerrilla, mercenary, partisan, resistance, underground

**irregularity** *n* 1 aberrance, abnormality, deviation, eccentricity, oddity, peculiarity. 2 (an irregularity on a surface) asymmetry, bump, bumpiness, hole, lump, pothole, roughness, unevenness. 3 fluctuation, inconsistency, inconstancy, patchiness, shakiness, unevenness, unsteadiness, variability; *opp* regularity. 4 (dishonest behaviour) breach, malpractice, unconventionality, unorthodoxy

**irrelevant** *adj* beside the point, extraneous, immaterial, inapplicable, inappropriate, neither here not there, nothing to do with it, out of place, unconnected, unrelated; *opp* relevant

**irreparable** *adj* beyond repair, incurable, irremediable, irreversible, irretrievable, past mending, unalterable

**irresistible** *adj* 1 compelling, imperative, inevitable, inexorable, overpowering, overwhelming, powerful, unavoidable. 2 alluring, enticing, fascinating, seductive, tempting

**irresponsible** *adj* careless, feckless, flighty, immature, negligent, reckless, shiftless, thoughtless, unreliable, untrustworthy, wild; *opp* responsible

**irreverent** *adj* 1 blasphemous, heretical, impious, irreligious, profane, sacrilegious, ungodly. 2 cheeky, derisive, disrespectful, flippant, impertinent, impudent, rude; *opp* respectful

**irrigate** *v* flood, spray, sprinkle, water, wet

**irritable** adj bad-tempered, cantankerous, crabby inf, cross, crotchety, fractious, grumpy, impatient, irascible, peevish, petulant, querulous, ratty inf, short-tempered, tetchy, touchy

**irritate** v 1 anger, annoy, bother, drive sb mad, drive sb up the wall inf, exasperate, get on sb's nerves, get sb's back up, get up sb's nose inf, nettle, pester, provoke, ruffle, try sb's patience, vex. 2 (irritate the skin) chafe, cause irritation, itch, rub, tickle

**irritated** adj 1 annoyed, cross, exasperated, nettled, ruffled, vexed. 2 (of skin) inflamed, itchy

**irritating** adj annoying, irksome, maddening, nagging, provoking, troublesome, trying, upsetting

**irritation** n 1 anger, annoyance, exasperation, impatience, irritability, vexation. 2 (on the skin) inflammation, itch, rash

**island** n isle, islet

**isolate** v cloister, cordon off, cut off, detach, disconnect, exclude, insulate, keep apart, quarantine, segregate, separate, sequester, shut out, single out

**isolated** adj 1 (of a person) alone, excluded, forlorn, lonely, segregated, separated, solitary. 2 (of a place) cut off, hidden, lonely, off the beaten track, out of the way, remote, secluded. 3 (of an incident, example) abnormal, anomalous, exceptional, freak, single, solitary, unique

**issue** n 1 affair, argument, bone of contention, controversy, matter, point, problem, question, subject, topic. 2 edition, impression, instalment,

number, printing, version. 3 conclusion, consequence, effect, end, outcome, result, upshot inf. 4 children, descendants, offspring

**issue** v 1 circulate, distribute, emit, give out, publish, put out, release. 2 come out, emanate, emit, exude, flow, gush, ooze, pour out, seep. 3 appear, come out, emerge, leave

**itch** n 1 irritation, itchiness, prickling, tickling, tingle. 2 craving, desire, hankering, hunger, longing, thirst, yearning, yen

**itch** v 1 be itchy, irritate, prickle, tickle, tingle. 2 (be itching to do sthg) ache, burn, crave, hanker, hunger, long, wish, yearn

**item** n 1 account, article, bit, feature, piece, report, story. 2 aspect, component, consideration, detail, element, ingredient, matter,. 3 (on a list) entry, record. 4 (for sale) article, lot, object, thing

**itinerary** n journey, plan, programme, schedule, timetable, travel arrangements, travel plan

**jab** n 1 dig, nudge, poke, prod, punch, stab. 2 injection, inoculation, vaccination

**jab** v dig, elbow, nudge, poke, prod, punch, stab, thrust

**jacket** n 1 (garment) anorak, blazer, cardigan, cardi *inf*, doublet, sports jacket. 2 case, casing, covering, envelope, folder, sheath, wrapper

**jagged** adj angular, barbed, chipped, craggy, indented, irregular, notched, ragged, rough, serrated, sharp, spiky, toothed, uneven, zigzag

**jail** n can *Am*, clink *inf*, cooler *inf*, inside, jailhouse *Am*, lockup, nick, pen *Am inf*, penitentiary *Am*, prison, slammer *inf*

**jail** v confine, detain, immure, imprison, incarcerate, intern, lock up, send down, send to jail, send to prison

**jailer** n guard, keeper, prison officer, screw *inf*, warder

**jam** n 1 conserve, jelly, marmalade, preserve. 2 blockage, bottleneck, congestion, gridlock, hold-up, obstruction, stoppage, traffic jam. 3 crowd, crush, press, squeeze, swarm, throng. 4 (be in a jam) dilemma, fix, hole, hot water, plight, predicament, quandary, spot of bother, straits, tight spot, trouble

**jam** v 1 block, clog, congest, cram, fill, obstruct, overcrowd, pack, stop up, stuff. 2 (people jam into a place) cram, crowd, crush, force, pack, ram, squash, squeeze. 3 (jam sth in) force, press, ram, thrust, wedge. 4 become stuck, stall, stick, stop

**jangle** v 1 clang, clank, clash, clatter, clink, jingle, rattle, vibrate. 2 (on sb's nerves) disturb, grate on, irritate, jar on

**jar** n bottle, container, crock, jam jar, pot, tub, urn

**jar** v 1 jerk, jog, jolt, rattle, shake, shock, vibrate. 2 be at odds with, clash, conflict, oppose. 3 annoy, disturb, grate, grate on, irritate, jangle, offend, upset

**jargon** n 1 argot, cant, dialect, idiom, language, patois, slang, vernacular. 2 (of a profession) buzz words, language, slang, specialized language, technical terms, usage

**jaundiced** adj bitter, cynical, distrustful, envious, pessimistic, resentful, sceptical, suspicious

**jaunt** n airing, excursion, expedition,

outing, ramble, stroll, trip

**jealous** adj **1** bitter, covetous, envious, green with envy, grudging, jaundiced, resentful. **2** distrustful, possessive. **3** careful, on guard, protective, vigilant, watchful, wary

**jeer** v barrack, boo, deride, gibe, heckle, hiss, laugh, make fun of, mock, ridicule, scoff, scorn, sneer, taunt

**jeopardize** v chance, endanger, gamble with, imperil, put at risk, put in jeopardy, risk, take a chance with, threaten

**jeopardy** n **in jeopardy** at risk, compromised, endangered, imperilled, in danger, in peril, jeopardized, threatened, under threat

**jerk** v **1** pull, shake, snatch, tug, wag, waggle, wrench, yank. **2** (move unevenly) jolt, judder, jump, lurch, rattle, shake, twitch

**jerky** adj disjointed, fitful, irregular, juddering, jumpy, lurching, spasmodic, staccato, twitchy

**jest** n gag, jape, joke, lampoon, laugh inf, prank, practical joke

**jest** v banter, clown, crack a joke, have sb on, joke, kid inf, pull sb's leg, quip, tease

**jester** n buffoon, clown, comedian, comedienne, comic, entertainer, fool, funny man, joker

**jet** n cascade, flow, fountain, rush, spurt, stream

**jetty** n breakwater, groyne, landing stage, marina, mole, mooring, pier, quay

**jewel** n **1** gem, gemstone, item of jewellery, ornament, piece of jewellery,

precious stone, semi-precious stone, sparkler inf, stone. **2** (types of jewel) diamond, emerald, lapis lazuli, onyx, pearl, ruby

**jewellery** n **1** adornments, costume jewellery, jewels, regalia, trinkets, valuables. **2** (item of jewellery) anklet, bracelet, brooch, earring, medallion, necklace, pendant, ring, tiara

**jingle** v chime, chink, clink, jangle, ping, ring, sound, tinkle

**jinx** n bad luck, curse, evil eye, gremlin, malediction, spell

**job** n **1** (paid employment) appointment, employment, opening, position, post, situation, vacancy, work. **2** (type of work) career, duties, occupation, business, line, profession, trade, vocation. **3** (thing to be done) chore, commission, errand, matter, mission, odd job, piece of work, project, task, undertaking

**jobless** adj at a loose end, between jobs, idle, on the dole inf, out of a job, out of work, redundant, resting, seeking employment, signing on, unemployed, unoccupied, workless

**jog** v **1** canter, run, run-walk, shuffle, toddle, trot, waddle, warm up. **2** (hit sth lightly) agitate, brush, bump, jar, jolt, jostle, knock, nudge, prod, push, set in motion, shake, tap

**join** n boundary, connection, dividing line, edge, joint, junction, meeting point, seam

**join** v **1** (join two things) attach, bind, bring together, connect, join up, merge, put together, tie, unify, unite; 
*opp* separate. **2** (two things join) come

together, connect, converge, join up,
meet, merge, unite; *opp* separate. 3 (join
a club, the army) become a member of,
enlist, enrol, join up, register, subscribe;
*opp* leave

**joint** *adj* collective, common, communal,
concerted, co-operative, mutual, shared

**joint** *n* 1 angle, articulation, binding,
connection, join, junction. 2 (in the
body) ankle, elbow, hip, knee, knuckle,
shoulder, wrist

**joke** *n* crack *inf*, funny story, gag, jape,
jest, laugh *inf*, one-liner, practical joke,
prank, punch line, quip, riddle, shaggy-
dog story, sketch, spoof, story, wisecrack,
witticism

**joke** *v* banter, clown, crack a joke, have
sb on, jest, josh, kid *inf*, laugh, pull sb's
leg, quip, tease, wisecrack

**joker** *n* clown, comedian, comedienne,
comic, funny man, jester, satirist, wag,
wit

**jolly** *adj* bright, cheerful, cheery, happy,
hearty, jovial, joyful, laughing, merry,
pleasant

**jolt** *v* agitate, bump, jar, jerk, jog, knock,
nudge, push, shake, shock, shove

**jostle** *v* brush, crowd, elbow, manhandle,
push, push out of the way, shove

**journal** *n* bulletin, diary, newsletter,
newspaper, magazine, periodical, record,
review

**journalist** *n* broadcaster, columnist,
critic, correspondent, cub reporter,
editor, feature writer, gentleman
of the press, hack *slang*, news-hound,
press man, reporter, reviewer,
writer

**journey** *n* crossing, drive, excursion,

expedition, flight, hike, holiday, odyssey,
passage, pilgrimage, ride, trek, trip,
voyage, walk

**joy** *n* bliss, delight, ecstasy, elation,
euphoria, happiness, joie de vivre,
jubilation, pleasure, rapture, rejoicing;
*opp* dismay

**joyful** *adj* blissful, cheerful, delighted,
ecstatic, elated, euphoric, glad, happy, in
seventh heaven, jolly, jovial, joyous,
jubilant, merry, on cloud nine *inf*, on top
of the world, over the moon *inf*,
rapturous; *opp* miserable

**jubilee** *n* anniversary, celebration,
centenary, centennial *Am*, festival,
festivities, royal occasion

**judge** *n* 1 circuit judge, jurist, justice,
Law Lord, Lord Chancellor, Lord
Chief Justice, magistrate, Master
of the Rolls, recorder, your Honour.
2 (in a competition) adjudicator,
arbiter, assessor, official, referee,
umpire

**judge** *v* 1 appraise, assess, calculate,
consider, decide, estimate, evaluate,
form an opinion, gauge, guess, weigh,
weigh up. 2 (judge a competition)
adjudge, adjudicate, arbitrate, decide,
referee, umpire. 3 (in law) find, hear,
pass sentence, preside, pronounce, rule,
sentence, sit in judgement, try

**judgement** *n* 1 (official) adjudication,
arbitration, award, decision, finding,
ruling, sentence, verdict. 2 (sb's
judgement of sth) appreciation,
appraisal, assessment, calculation,
consideration, estimate, estimation,
evaluation, guess, opinion, view.
3 (ability to make the right decision)

common sense, discretion, discrimination, good sense, level-headedness, maturity, objectivity, sense of proportion, sensitivity, sobriety, tact. **4** (mental ability) awareness, balance of your mind, clear head, control, co-ordination, faculties, mind, perception, self-control, senses, sobriety

**judicial** adj constitutional, institutional, juridical, legal, official, statutory

**jug** n carafe, ewer, pitcher, pot, urn, vase, vessel

**juggle** v (juggle your responsibilities) combine, keep all your balls in the air, manipulate, play off, prioritize, reorder, shuffle, swap, switch

**juice** n cordial, crush, essence, gravy, liquid, mineral, sap, squash

**juicy** adj dripping, moist, ripe, sappy, squashy, squelchy inf, succulent, watery

**jumble** n chaos, confusion, heap, mixture, muddle, randomness

**jumble** v confuse, entangle, mix, mix up, muddle, shuffle, tangle

**jump** n **1** bounce, bound, dive, hop, leap, skip, spring, take-off, vault. **2** high jump, long jump, pike, pole vault, ski-jump, straddle, triple jump, parachute jump. **3** (thing jumped over) bar, barrier, ditch, fence, hurdle, obstacle, wall, water jump

**jump** v **1** bounce, bound, dive, hop, leap, pogo, prance, rise, skip, soar, spring, take off, vault. **2** (over an obstacle) clear, cross, jump over, leap, leapfrog, straddle, traverse. **3** (with fright) flinch, jump out of your skin inf, recoil, shiver,

start, twitch

**jumpy** adj agitated, edgy inf, fidgety, jittery, like a cat on hot bricks, nervy inf, nervous, on edge, on tenterhooks, restless, twitchy inf

**junction** n crossroads, fork, intersection, roundabout, T-junction

**juncture** n moment, moment in time, occasion, point, position, present time, situation, stage

**jungle** n bush, forest, rain forest, tropical forest, vegetation

**junior** adj inferior, lowly, low-ranking, second, subordinate, young, younger; **opp** senior

**junk** n antiques, bric-a-brac, odds and ends, refuse, rubbish, scrap, trash

**jurisdiction** n ambit, authority, brief, command, competence, control, department, orbit, patch inf, power, remit

**just** adj **1** (of a decision) equitable, fair, justifiable, justified, legitimate, right; **opp** unjust. **2** (of a person) equitable, even-handed, fair, fair-minded, honest, honourable, impartial, objective, respectful, righteous, unbiased, upright; **opp** unjust

**justice** n **1** (legal concept) constitutionality, jurisprudence, law, lawfulness, legality, right. **2** (quality of being just) decency, equity, fairness, fair play, impartiality, plain dealing, rectitude, respect; **opp** injustice. **3** (after being wronged) amends, compensation, expiation, redress, reparation, retribution, revenge

**justifiable** adj defensible, fair, just,

justified, legitimate; *opp* unjustifiable

**justify** *v* account for, defend, excuse, exonerate, explain, legitimize, vindicate

**jut** *v* jut out, overhang, poke out, project, protrude, stick out

**juvenile** *adj* 1 adolescent, immature, underage, young, youthful. 2 (juvenile attitude) adolescent, childish, immature, infantile, puerile, silly

**juvenile** *n* adolescent, child, minor, young person, youngster, youth

**juxtapose** *v* compare, contrast, draw parallels, place side by side

**keen** adj 1 ardent, avid, crazy about inf, desirous, eager, earnest, enthusiastic, fervent, mad inf, passionate. 2 (a keen sense of smell) acute, astute, penetrating, sensitive, sharp, shrewd, strong

**keep** n 1 castle, fort, inner sanctum, stronghold, tower. 2 (pay for your keep) bed and board, living, maintenance, means, survival

**keep** v 1 conserve, detain, guard, have, hold, own, possess, preserve, retain. 2 (keep a person) care for, feed, look after, maintain, pay for, nurture, provide for, subsidize, sustain, take care of. 3 (keep doing sth) carry on, continue, go on, keep on, persevere, persist. 4 (keep a promise) abide by, adhere to, fulfil, honour, observe, realize, respect. 5 **keep up** conserve, hold, maintain, look after, persevere with, preserve

**keeper** n caretaker, curator, guard, guardian, jailer, minder inf, warden, warder

**key** adj crucial, essential, important, indispensable, major, vital

**key** n acid test, answer, clue, criterion, explanation, solution

**kick** v 1 boot inf, drive, pass, shoot, strike. 2 (kick a habit) beat inf, forswear, give up, quit, renounce. 3 **kick out** banish, chuck out inf, dismiss, eject, exclude, exile, expel, send out, throw out, vote out

**kidnap** v abduct, capture, hold to ransom, seize, snatch, take hostage

**kill** v assassinate, butcher, cut down, destroy, do sb in, electrocute, eliminate, execute, exterminate, gas, gun down, hang, massacre, murder, poison, slaughter, put down, put out of its misery, put to death, put to sleep, shoot, slay, smother, stone, strangle, suffocate

**killer** n assassin, butcher, executioner, gunman, hangman, murderer, murderess, poisoner, strangler

**killing** n 1 assassination, atrocity, butchery, capital punishment, death, death penalty, electrocution, elimination, euthanasia, execution, extermination, hanging, homicide Am, manslaughter, massacre, mercy killing, murder, shooting, slaying, strangulation, suffocation. 2 (make a killing) bonanza, fortune, gain, profit, success, windfall

**kin** n blood, family, kindred, kinsfolk, kinsmen, kinswomen, kith, relations, relatives, you and yours

**kind** adj benevolent, compassionate, considerate, fair, friendly, generous, helpful, kind-hearted, kindly, obliging, sympathetic, understanding, warm, welcoming, well-meaning; *opp* cruel, unkind

**kind** *n* category, class, sort, species, type

**kindle** *v* 1 (kindle a fire) get going, ignite, light, set fire to, set light to, start. 2 (kindle emotions) excite, inspire, rouse, stimulate, stir, stir up

**kindness** *n* benevolence, compassion, consideration, fairness, friendliness, generosity, kind-heartedness, sympathy, warmth; *opp* cruelty, unkindness

**king** *n* Crown, head of state, His Majesty, liege, lord, monarch, ruler, sire

**kingdom** *n* country, domain, fiefdom, land, monarchy, realm, territory

**kiosk** *n* booth, box, office, pavilion, stall, window

**kiss** *v* canoodle *inf*, neck *inf*, peck, smooch *inf*, snog *inf*

**kit** *n* 1 (items for making or doing sth) apparatus, implements, outfit, set, tools, utensils. 2 (items carried or worn) belongings, clothes, equipment, gear *inf*, stuff *inf*, tackle, things

**knack** *n* ability, aptitude, gift, habit, instinct, talent, trick

**knead** *v* manipulate, massage, press, pummel, roll, squeeze, work

**kneel** *v* be on your knees, fall to your knees, genuflect, get down on your knees, kneel down

**knickers** *n* bloomers, briefs, drawers, pants, panties, smalls, underpants, undies *inf*

**knife** *n* blade, carving knife, chopper, cutter, dagger, flick-knife, penknife, sheath knife, Stanley knife, stiletto

**knit** *v* bind, intertwine, make, purl, sew, stitch, weave

**knob** *n* 1 button, doorknob, handle, lever, switch. 2 boss, bulge, bump, lump, nub, protuberance, protrusion

**knock** *v* 1 bump, collide, hit, jog, push, strike, tap. 2 knock down cut down, demolish, fell, floor, pull down, push over, raze, run over. 3 knock out (make sb lose consciousness) anaesthetize, chloroform, floor, knock unconscious, KO *inf*, put to sleep. 4 knock out (from a competition) beat, defeat, eliminate, overcome, put out, vanquish

**knot** *n* 1 bow, granny knot, loop, nexus, reef knot, tangle. 2 (knot of people) bunch, circle, cluster, gaggle, gathering, group, huddle, ring

**knot** *v* bind, entangle, tangle, tie, tie up

**know** *v* 1 (know a fact) be aware, be certain, be conscious, be familiar with, be informed, be sure, comprehend, understand. 2 (know a person, place) be a friend of, be acquainted with, be familiar with, be friends with, get to know, have been introduced to, have met

**knowing** *adj* 1 (a knowing grin, remark) conspiratorial, meaningful, sardonic, self-satisfied, sly, superior, worldly-wise, wry. 2 calculated, conscious, deliberate, intended, intentional, purposeful, wilful

**knowledge** *n* 1 awareness, certainty, cognition, comprehension, consciousness, erudition, intelligence, learning, understanding. 2 (things that are known) data, facts, findings, information, learning, lore, observations, scholarship, science

**knowledgeable** *adj* aware, brainy *inf*, clever, informed, learned, intelligent, scholarly, well-informed; *opp* ignorant

**label** n 1 brand, flag, marker, stamp, sticker, tab, tag, ticket. 2 category, classification, designation, epithet, heading, name, pigeonhole, stigma, term

**label** v 1 brand, flag, mark, stamp, tag. 2 brand, categorize, classify, designate, name, pigeonhole, stigmatize, term

**laborious** adj difficult, hard, laboured, painstaking, tedious, wearisome; *opp* easy

**labour** n 1 (work) chores, donkey work *inf*, drudgery, effort, grind *inf*, hard labour, hard work, manual work, strain, toil, work. 2 (workers) hands, labourers, manpower, workers, workforce, workmen. 3 (giving birth) birth pangs, childbirth, contractions, delivery

**labour** v 1 exert yourself, slave, strain, strive, sweat, toil, work, work your fingers to the bone, work your socks off *inf* . 2 (labour a point) behaviour, dwell on, elaborate, emphasize, get bogged down on, get stuck on, overdo, over-elaborate, over-emphasize, repeat, stress

**labourer** n blue-collar worker, hand, manual worker, unskilled worker, worker, workman

**lace** n crochet, embroidery, filigree, net, string

**lace** v 1 (lace a shoe) attach, bind, close, do up, fasten, secure, strap, string, thread, tie. 2 (lace a drink) add to, blend, fortify, mix, spike

**lack** n absence, dearth, deficiency, insufficiency, need, scarceness, scarcity, shortage, want; *opp* abundance

**lack** v be lacking in, be short of, be without, have need of, miss, need, require, want

**lacking** adj 1 (the system is sadly lacking) defective, flawed, impaired, inadequate, unsatisfactory, weak; *opp* satisfactory. 2 (be lacking in social skills) missing, needing, wanting, without

**laden** adj burdened, charged, encumbered, hampered, heavily laden, loaded, piled high, weighed down, weighted

**lady** n 1 female, girl, lass *inf*, wife *inf*, woman; *opp* gentleman. 2 baroness, countess, dame, duchess, marchioness, noblewoman, peeress, viscountess; *opp* lord

**ladylike** adj courtly, cultivated, dainty, decorous, elegant, genteel, gracious, modest, polished, polite, proper, refined, respectable, well-bred, well-mannered; *opp* coarse

**lag** v bring up the rear, dawdle, delay, dilly dally *inf*, drag your feet, drop behind, fall behind, go slow, hang about, hang back, idle, linger, loiter, saunter, straggle, trail; *opp* lead

**laid-back** adj at ease, calm, casual, easy-going, nonchalant, relaxed, unflappable, unhurried; *opp* anxious

**lair** n burrow, covert, den, earth, hide-out, hole, nest, refuge, resting place, retreat, shelter

**lake** n lagoon, lido, loch, pool, pond, reservoir, sea, tarn, water

**lame** adj 1 crippled, disabled, handicapped, hobbling, limping. **2** (a lame excuse) feeble, flimsy, inadequate, pathetic, poor, tame, thin, unconvincing, weak; *opp* convincing

**lament** v 1 (lament sth) bemoan, bewail, complain, deplore, regret; *opp* praise. **2** (lament sb's death) beat your breast, cry, grieve, mourn, shed tears, sorrow, wail, weep; *opp* rejoice

**lamp** n lantern, light, night light, standard lamp, street light, table lamp, torch

**land** n 1 (back on land) coast, dry land, earth, ground, shore, solid ground, terra firma; *opp* sea, space. **2** (fertile land) dirt, earth, ground, loam, soil. **3** (own a lot of land) acres, estate, grounds, property, realty. **4** (a distant land) country, district, nation, province, region, state, territory, tract

**land** v alight, arrive, berth, come ashore, come in to land, debark, disembark, dismount, dock, touch down; *opp* set off

**landlord** n 1 host, hostess, hotelier, innkeeper, landlady, licensee, publican, restaurateur; *opp* customer. **2** landowner, letter, manager, manageress, owner, proprietor; *opp* tenant

**landmark** n 1 feature, guidepost, identification, monument. **2** (landmark in sth's history) critical point, milestone, new era, turning point, watershed

**landscape** n aspect, countryside, outlook, panorama, prospect, rural scene, scene, scenery, view, vista

**landslide** n avalanche, landslip, rockfall

**language** n 1 communication, conversation, discourse, expression, parlance, speaking, speech, talk, talking, verbal expression, vocalization, words. **2** (a particular language) argot, dialect, idiom, jargon, lingo *inf*, patois, tongue, vernacular, vocabulary. **3** (the language of a novel) expression, phraseology, phrasing, style, terminology, vocabulary, wording

**languish** v decline, droop, fade, fail, faint, flag, go downhill *inf*, stagnate, suffer, waste, weaken, wilt, wither; *opp* flourish

**lank** adj 1 (of hair) drooping, dull, lifeless, limp, long, lustreless, straggling, straight; *opp* bouncy. **2** (of a person) bony, emaciated, gangling, gaunt, lanky, lean, scraggy, scrawny, skinny, slender, slim, tall, thin; *opp* chubby

**lanky** adj awkward, gangling, lank, lean, scrawny, skinny, tall, thin, ungraceful, weedy *inf*; *opp* chubby

**lap** n 1 circle, circuit, coarse, loop, orbit, revolution, round, tour. **2** (sit on sb's lap) knee

**lap** v 1 (waves lapping the shore) ripple, slap, slosh, splash, swish, wash. **2** (a cat lapping milk) drink, gulp, guzzle, lick, sip, sup

**lapse** v 1 decline, deteriorate, diminish, drop, fail, fall, go downhill *inf*, go to pot *inf*, sink, slide, slip; *opp* improve. **2** (a passport lapses) become invalid,

become void, end, expire, finish, run
out, stop, terminate

**lapse** *n* blunder, error, failing, fault,
indiscretion, mistake, omission,
oversight, slip, slip-up *inf*

**large** *adj* ample, big, broad, bulky, colossal,
considerable, elephantine, enormous,
extensive, generous, giant, gigantic,
grand, great, huge, immense, jumbo *inf*,
king-size, liberal, lofty, massive, mighty,
monumental, roomy, sizable, spacious,
sweeping, substantial, vast, wide;
*opp* small

**lash** *n* blow, hit, strike, stripe, stroke,
thwack *inf*, wallop *inf*, whack *inf*, whip

**lash** *v* 1 (lash one thing to another) bind,
fasten, hitch, join, leash, rope, secure,
strap, tether, tie. 2 (rain lashing the
windows) batter, beat, buffet, dash,
drum, hammer, hit, knock, pound,
smack, strike. 3 (lash sb) beat, birch,
flog, horsewhip, strike, thrash, wallop
*inf*, whack *inf*, whip

**last** *adj* 1 closing, concluding, final,
terminal, ultimate; *opp* first. 2 latest,
most recent; *opp* first. 3 (last in a line)
back, end, final, hindmost, rearmost;
*opp* front

**last** *v* abide, carry on, continue, endure,
go on, hold, keep, linger, live, persist,
remain, survive; *opp* end

**lasting** *adj* abiding, ceaseless, constant,
continuing, durable, enduring, eternal,
long-lasting, long-term, ongoing,
permanent, perpetual, unceasing,
undying, unending; *opp* temporary

**late** *adj* 1 behind, behind schedule,
behind time, belated, delayed, overdue,
slow, tardy; *opp* early. 2 (the late Mr

Smith) dead, deceased, defunct,
departed

**lately** *adv* latterly, of late, recently;
*opp* previously

**latitude** *n* carte blanche, elbow-room *inf*,
freedom, free play, indulgence, leeway,
liberty, licence; *opp* restriction

**latter** *adj* 1 last-mentioned, later, second;
*opp* former. 2 (the latter part) closing,
concluding, end, final, last; *opp* opening

**laugh** *n* 1 belly laugh *inf*, chortle,
chuckle, giggle, guffaw, roar of laughter,
snigger, titter. 2 (sb is a laugh) card *inf*,
case *inf*, hoot, scream, wag.
3 (sth is a laugh) fun, lark, scream

**laugh** *v* 1 be in stitches, burst out
laughing, chortle, chuckle, crack up *inf*,
fall about, giggle, guffaw, roll about,
snigger, split your sides, titter. 2 **laugh at**
deride, jeer, lampoon, make fun of,
mock, ridicule, scoff, send up, take the
mickey, taunt, tease

**laughable** *adj* absurd, derisory, derisive,
ludicrous, outrageous, preposterous,
ridiculous, risible; *opp* reasonable

**laughing stock** *n* butt, dupe, everybody's
fool, fair game, fall guy *inf*, figure of fun,
target, victim

**laughter** *n* 1 chortling, chuckling,
giggling, guffawing, laughing, laughs,
sniggering, tittering. 2 amusement,
entertainment, glee, hilarity, hysterics,
light-heartedness, merriment, mirth

**launch** *v* 1 (launch a new business)
begin, commence, embark, establish, get
going, inaugurate, initiate, instigate,
introduce, open, set up, start. 2 (launch
a rocket) cast, catapult, discharge,
dispatch, fire, hurl, let fly, project,

propel, send off, set off, shoot, throw

**lavatory** n bathroom, cloakroom,
convenience, john Am inf, latrine, little
boy's room inf, little girl's room inf, loo
inf, powder room, the gents, the ladies,
toilet, urinal, washroom, WC

**lavish** adj exuberant, lush, luxuriant,
luxurious, opulent, sumptuous;
**opp** simple. 2 (lavish with sth)
bountiful, extravagant, free, generous,
liberal, munificent, open-handed,
unselfish, unstinting; **opp** mean

**law** n act, bill, bylaw, code,
commandment, covenant, decree,
directive, edict, enactment, injunction,
mandate, order, ordinance, regulation,
rule, statute

**law-abiding** adj compliant, decent,
dutiful, good, honest, lawful, obedient,
peaceable, respectable, upright, well-
behaved; **opp** criminal, trouble-making

**lawful** adj allowable, allowed, authorized,
constitutional, just, legal, legalized,
legitimate, permissible, permitted,
prescribed, proper, rightful, sanctioned,
valid; **opp** unlawful

**lawsuit** n action, case, dispute,
indictment, industrial tribunal,
litigation, proceedings, prosecution,
suit, trial

**lawyer** n advocate, attorney Am,
barrister, brief inf, counsel, legal advisor,
legal practitioner, member of the bar,
solicitor

**lax** adj careless, casual, neglectful,
negligent, remiss, slack, slipshod,
unreliable, vague

**lay** adj 1 (lay preacher) non-clerical,
non-ordained, part-time, secular;

**opp** ordained. 2 (lay person) amateur,
inexpert, non-professional;
**opp** professional

**lay** v 1 (lay sth somewhere) deposit,
leave, place, plant, put, rest, set, settle.
2 (lay sth out) arrange, dispose,
organize, position, set out. 3 (lay eggs)
bear, deposit, produce. 4 (lay blame)
allot, ascribe, assign, attribute, charge,
impose, impute. 5 (lay plans) arrange,
concoct, contrive, create, design, devise,
make, plan, plot, prepare, set up, work
out. **6 lay down** (a law) command,
formulate, ordain, order, prescribe,
proclaim, set down, stipulate.
**7 lay on** furnish, give, provide, supply

**layabout** n dosser inf, good-for-nothing,
idler, laggard, loafer, shirker, skiver inf,
waster inf; **opp** grafter

**layer** n 1 (of rock) bed, row, seam,
stratum, thickness, tier. 2 (of paint)
coat, coating, covering, film, skin

**layman** n amateur, lay person,
non-professional, non-specialist;
**opp** professional

**layout** n 1 (of a place) arrangement,
design, geography, plan. 2 (of a page)
arrangement, design, format, outline

**laze** v do nothing, idle, lie around, loaf,
lounge, relax, sit around, unwind

**laziness** n idleness, inactivity, indolence,
lax, slackness inf, sloth

**lazy** adj idle, inactive, indolent, laxity,
skiving inf, slack inf, slothful, work-shy;
**opp** hard-working

**lead** n 1 (the lead) advantage, edge, first
place, precedence, priority, supremacy,
vanguard. 2 (follow sb's lead) direction,
example, guidance, leadership. 3 (get a

lead) clue, guide, hint, indication, line, suggestion, tip-off . **4** (lead role) hero, heroine, leading role, pointer, principal, protagonist, starring role, title role. **5** (extension lead) cable, flex, wire

**lead** v **1** (lead sb somewhere) conduct, draw, escort, guide, pilot, show the way, steer, usher. **2** (lead sb to think sth) cause, dispose, draw, incline, induce, influence, move, persuade, prevail, prompt. **3** (lead an army) be in charge of, captain, command, direct, govern, head, manage, rule, supervise. **4** (be in the lead) be ahead, be first, be in the lead, exceed, excel, head, leave behind, outdo, outstrip, surpass; *opp* trail. **5** (lead an exciting life) experience, have, live, pass, spend. **6 lead on** deceive, delude, dupe, hoodwink, mislead, string along *inf*, trick

**leader** n boss, captain, chief, commander, conductor, director, foreman, guide, head, number one *inf*, principal, ruler, skipper *inf*, supremo *inf*

**leading** *adj* best, chief, first, foremost, greatest, highest, major, main, number-one *inf*, premier, principal, ruling, senior, top; *opp* minor

**leaf** n **1** blade, foliage, frond, greenery, needle. **2** (in a book) folio, flyleaf, page, sheet

**leaflet** n booklet, circular, flyer, handout, notice, pamphlet

**league** n alliance, association, band, coalition, compact, confederacy, confederation, consortium, corporation, fellowship, fraternity, group, guild, order, partnership, society, syndicate, union

**leak** n **1** discharge, drip, emission, leakage, seepage, trickle. **2** (of information) disclosure, divulgence, revelation

**leak** v **1** discharge, drip, escape, exude, issue, ooze, seep, spill, trickle. **2** (leak information) disclose, divulge, give away, let out, let slip, let the cat out of the bag, make known, reveal, spill the beans

**lean** *adj* bony, emaciated, gaunt, lanky, scrawny, skinny, slender, slim, thin, wiry; *opp* fat

**lean** v **1** be propped, be supported, recline, repose, rest. **2** be at an angle, bend, incline, slant, slope, tilt, tip

**leaning** n aptitude, bend, bias, fondness, inclination, instinct, liking, partiality, penchant, predilection, preference, propensity, taste, tendency

**leap** v bounce, bound, caper, cavort, frisk, gambol, hop, jump, skip, spring

**learn** v **1** acquire, assimilate, attain, grasp, imbibe, master, pick up. **2** (learn your lines) commit sth to memory, get off pat, learn by heart, memorize. **3** (learn that sth is true) ascertain, discover, find out, gather, hear, understand

**learned** *adj* academic, cultured, erudite, expert, intellectual, knowledgeable, scholarly, skilled, versed, well-educated, well-read; *opp* uneducated

**learner** n apprentice, beginner, cadet, novice, pupil, student, trainee

**learning** n education, knowledge, letters, scholarship, schooling, study, tuition, wisdom

**lease** v charter, hire, let, loan, rent

**leave** n **1** (leave to do sth) authorization, consent, dispensation, freedom, liberty, permission, sanction. 2 (on leave) break, holiday, sabbatical, time off, vacation

**leave** v 1 (leave a place) be off inf, check out, depart, disappear, exit, go, hop it inf, move, quit, retire, scarper, slope off, split inf, withdraw; **opp** arrive. 2 (leave your wife) abandon, break up with, desert, dump inf, finish with, split with. 3 (leave your job) cease, chuck in, desist, drop out, give up, pull out, relinquish, resign, stop, walk out.

4 (leave sth to sb) bequeath, endow, hand down, transmit, will. 5 **leave out** disregard, exclude, ignore, miss out, neglect, omit, overlook, reject, skip; **opp** include

**lecture** n 1 (a history lecture) address, class, lesson, paper, seminar, speech, talk. 2 (telling off) chiding, rebuke, remonstration, reprimand, reproof, scolding, sermon, talking to, telling-off

**lecture** v 1 (lecture in history) address, expound, hold forth, instruct, speak, talk, teach. 2 (lecture a child) admonish, castigate, censure, chide, read the riot act, reprimand, reprove, scold, tear into, tear sb off a strip, tell off

**ledge** n mantle, overhang, projection, protrusion, ridge, shelf, sill, step

**left** adj communist, Labour, leftist, left-wing, liberal, progressive, radical, red, socialist

**leftover** adj excess, extra, remaining, surplus, uneaten, unused, unwanted

**leftovers** n excess, extra, remainder, remains, remnants, scraps, surplus

**leg** n 1 (of a person) limb, member, peg inf, pin inf. 2 (of a piece of furniture)

column, pillar, prop, support, upright. 3 (leg of a journey) bit, lap, part, portion, section, segment, stage, stretch

**legacy** n bequest, endowment, estate, gift, heirloom, inheritance

**legal** adj above-board, allowed, approved, authorized, decriminalized, lawful, legalized, legitimate, licensed, permissible, proper, sanctioned, valid; **opp** illegal

**legalize** v allow, approve, authorize, decriminalize, legitimize, license, make legal, permit, sanction, validate; **opp** ban

**legend** n epic, fable, fairy tale, fiction, folk tale, myth, narrative, saga, story, tale

**legendary** adj acclaimed, celebrated, famed, famous, glorious, great, immortal, proverbial, world-famous; **opp** unknown

**legible** adj clear, decipherable, distinct, easy to read, intelligible, neat, plain, readable; **opp** illegible

**legislate** v authorize, decree, enact, establish, ordain, order, prescribe

**legislation** n 1 authorization, codification, enactment, law-making, prescription. 2 (a piece of legislation) act, bill, charter, code, constitution, law, measure, regulation, rule, statute

**legitimate** adj above-board, allowed, approved, authorized, decriminalized, lawful, legal, legalized, licensed, permissible, sanctioned, valid; **opp** illegal

**legitimize** v allow, approve, authorize, legalize, license, make legal, permit, sanction, validate; **opp** ban

**leisure** n holiday, recreation, relaxation, relief, rest, spare time, time off, vacation; **opp** work

**leisurely** adj comfortable, easy, gentle, laid-back, lazy, relaxed, relaxing, restful, slow, unhurried; **opp** frantic

**lend** v 1 advance, give sb the loan of, loan; **opp** borrow. 2 add, afford, bestow, contribute, endow, furnish, give, grant, impart, provide, supply

**length** n 1 distance, extent, footage, measure, mileage, reach, span. 2 duration, period, span, stretch, time

**lengthen** v continue, drag out, draw out, elongate, expand, extend, increase, prolong, protract, stretch; **opp** shorten

**lengthy** adj extended, interminable, long, long-drawn-out, long-winded, protracted

**lenient** adj charitable, clement, forbearing, forgiving, gentle, humane, indulgent, kind, lax, magnanimous, merciful, mild, soft, sparing, tolerant

**lessen** v 1 assuage, curtail, decrease, diminish, ease, lighten, lower, mitigate, reduce, relieve, tone down; **opp** intensify. 2 abate, decline, decrease, die down, diminish, ease off, ebb, let up, moderate, slacken, subside, tail off, weaken; **opp** intensify

**lesson** n 1 class, coaching, drill, instruction, period, schooling, seminar, session, teaching, tutoring. 2 admonition, deterrent, example, exemplar, message, model, moral, warning

**let** v 1 agree to, allow, authorize, consent, give leave, give permission, give the go-ahead, grant, permit, sanction, tolerate. 2 contract out, hire, lease, rent, sublet. 3 **let down** disappoint, disillusion, fail, fall short. 4 **let off** detonate, discharge,

explode, fire, launch, set off, trigger. 5 **let off** (forgive) absolve, acquit, discharge, excuse, exempt, forgive, let sb go, pardon, release, reprieve, spare. 6 **let out** (information) betray, disclose, leak, let slip, make known, reveal, tell. 7 **let out** (a person) free, discharge, let sb go, liberate, release, set sb free

**letdown** n anticlimax, damp squib inf, disappointment, disillusionment, failure, flop inf, wash-out inf

**lethal** adj deadly, devastating, fatal, mortal, murderous, virulent

**lethargic** adj apathetic, drowsy, dull, enervated, fatigued, heavy, inactive, indolent, inert, languid, languorous, lazy, listless, passive, sleepy, slothful, slow, sluggish, somnolent, torpid, weary; **opp** energetic

**lethargy** n apathy, drowsiness, dullness, fatigue, heaviness, indolence, inertia, lack of energy, languor, lassitude, laziness, listlessness, passivity, sleepiness, sloth, slowness, sluggishness, somnolence, torpor, weariness; **opp** energy

**letter** n 1 card, communication, dispatch, epistle, line, missive, note. 2 character, consonant, initial, sign, symbol, vowel

**level** adj 1 even, flat, flush, horizontal, smooth, straight, true, uniform; **opp** uneven. 2 aligned, balanced, comparable, equal, equivalent, identical, in line, matching, on a par, proportionate, the same

**level** n 1 degree, echelon, grade, plane, position, rank, rung, stage, standing, status. 2 altitude, depth, elevation, height. 3 floor, layer, storey, stratum

**level** v 1 even out, flatten, plane, smooth. 2 bulldoze, demolish, destroy, flatten, knock down, lay low, pull down, raze, tear down

**lever** n crowbar, jemmy, handle, grip

**lever** v crowbar, force, jemmy, prise, raise, wrench

**levy** n charge, dues, duty, excise, imposition, tariff, tax, toll

**levy** v charge, collect, demand, exact, gather, impose, tax

**liability** n 1 accountability, blame, culpability, duty, obligation, onus, responsibility. 2 (sth is a liability) burden, disadvantage, drag, drawback, encumbrance, handicap, hindrance, impediment, millstone, nuisance

**liable** adj 1 (liable for sth) accountable, answerable, bound, culpable, obligated, responsible. 2 (liable to do sth) apt, disposed, inclined, in the habit of, likely, predisposed, prone, susceptible, tending, vulnerable

**liaison** n 1 communication, connection, co-operation, contact, interchange, linkage, link-up, tie. 2 affair, amour, entanglement, intrigue, relationship, romance

**liar** n deceiver, false witness, fibber inf, perjurer

**libel** n aspersion, calumny, defamation, denigration, lie, obloquy, slander, slur, smear, vilification

**libel** v blacken sb's name, calumniate, cast aspersions, defame, denigrate, malign, misrepresent, slander, smear, traduce, vilify

**libellous** adj calumnious, damaging, defamatory, false, injurious, malicious, scurrilous, slanderous, untrue

**liberal** adj 1 broad-minded, easy-going, enlightened, lenient, libertarian, moderate, open-minded, permissive, progressive, reformist, tolerant, unprejudiced. 2 (a liberal amount) abundant, ample, bountiful, copious, generous, lavish, magnanimous, munificent, plentiful, profuse, unstinting

**liberalize** v broaden, ease, expand, extend, free up, loosen, moderate, open up, relax, slacken, soften, stretch; *opp* tighten

**liberate** v deliver, discharge, emancipate, free, let go, let out, redeem, release, rescue, set free, unchain, untie

**liberation** n deliverance, discharge, emancipation, freedom, liberty, release, unchaining

**liberty** n autonomy, emancipation, freedom, independence, release, self-determination, sovereignty

**licence** n 1 (permission) authorization, authority, dispensation, entitlement, leave, liberty, permission, privilege, right. 2 (document giving permission) certificate, charter, credentials, permit, warrant. 3 (in behaviour) abandon, anarchy, decadence, disorder, dissipation, dissoluteness, excess, immorality, indulgence, laxity, liberality, licentiousness, unruliness

**license** v accredit, allow, authorize, certify, empower, entitle, grant a license to, permit, sanction, warrant

**lick** v brush, flick, lap, taste, tongue

**lid** n cap, cover, covering, stopper, top

**lie** n bluff, deceit, deception, equivocation, fabrication, falsehood, fib *inf*, fiction, invention, mendacity, misrepresentation, perjury, porky *sl*, pretence, story, untruth, whopper *inf*; **opp** truth

**lie** *v* **1** bear false witness, bluff, deceive, dissemble, equivocate, fabricate, falsify, fib *inf*, invent, make up, misrepresent, perjure, pretend, tell a falsehood, tell a lie. **2** be horizontal, be lying, be prone, be prostrate, be recumbent, be supine, lean back, lounge, recline, repose, rest, sprawl, stretch out

**life** *n* **1** animation, being, breath, entity, existence, living; **opp** death. **2** activity, animation, dynamism, energy, enthusiasm, exuberance, liveliness, oomph *inf*, spark, sparkle, spirit, sprightliness, verve, vigour, vitality, vivacity, zest; **opp** dullness. **3** (sb's life) career, days, lifespan, lifetime, time on earth. **4** autobiography, biography, history, life story, memoir

**lifeless** *adj* **1** cold, dead, deceased, defunct, extinct, inanimate, inert, insensate; **opp** living. **2** colourless, dull, flat, heavy, lacklustre, unexciting, uninspired, wooden; **opp** lively

**lifelike** *adj* authentic, convincing, exact, faithful, graphic, natural, real, realistic, true-to-life, vivid

**lifelong** *adj* abiding, constant, enduring, lasting, long-standing, long-term, perennial, permanent, persistent

**lift** *n* **1** amelioration, boost, enhancement, fillip, improvement, promotion, shot in the arm *inf*. **2** (give sb a lift) drive, ride, run, transport, transportation

**lift** *v* **1** carry, elevate, hoist, pick up, raise,

**2** ameliorate, boost, buoy up, cheer, enhance, improve, promote

**light** *adj* **1** airy, delicate, flimsy, gossamer, lightweight, portable, slight; **opp** heavy. **2** bright, full of light, glowing, illuminated, lit-up, sunny, well-lit; **opp** dark. **3** (of a knock, touch) delicate, faint, gentle, indistinct, mild, soft, weak; **opp** heavy. **4** amusing, easy, entertaining, diverting, fun, frivolous, light-hearted, simple, superficial, trivial, undemanding; **opp** serious

**light** *n* **1** beam, blaze, brightness, brilliance, flare, flash, glare, gleam, glint, glitter, glow, illumination, incandescence, luminescence, luminosity, lustre, phosphorescence, radiance, ray, scintillation, shaft, shine, sparkle, twinkle. **2** beacon, bulb, candle, lamp, lantern, taper, torch

**light** *v* fire, flame, ignite, kindle, put a match to, set alight

**lighten** *v* **1** brighten, cast light on, illuminate, irradiate, light up, make sth bright, shed light on, shine on. **2** allay, alleviate, assuage, ease, lessen, mitigate, reduce, relieve

**like** *adj/prep* akin, alike, allied, analogous, corresponding, equal, equivalent, identical, matching, parallel, relating, resembling, same, similar

**like** *v* admire, appreciate, approve of, be fond of, be keen on, be partial to, cherish, delight in, enjoy, esteem, have a soft spot for *inf*, love, prize, relish, revel in, take pleasure in; **opp** dislike, hate

**likeable** *adj* agreeable, amiable, appealing, charming, congenial, endearing, engaging, friendly, genial, lovable, nice, personable, pleasant, pleasing, sympathetic, winning

**likelihood** n chance, hope, liability, possibility, probability, prospect

**likely** adj **1** anticipated, expected, feasible, on the cards, plausible, probable. **2** (likely to do sth) apt, disposed, inclined, liable, prone, tending

**liken** v compare, draw an analogy between, equate, link, match, relate

**likeness** n **1** affinity, congruity, correspondence, link, match, resemblance, similarity. **2** depiction, drawing, effigy, image, model, painting, picture, portrait, representation, sketch, statue, study

**liking** n admiration, affinity, appreciation, approval, bent, esteem, fondness, keenness, love, partiality, penchant, predilection, preference, soft spot inf, taste, weakness

**limb** n appendage, arm, extension, extremity, leg, member, offshoot, projection, wing

**limelight** n attention, celebrity, fame, prominence, public eye, publicity, recognition, spotlight, stardom

**limit** n **1** border, bound, boundary, brim, brink, confines, edge, end, extent, frontier, perimeter, periphery. **2** cap, ceiling, check, curb, cut-off, deadline, limitation, maximum, restraint, restriction

**limit** v cap, check, circumscribe, confine, control, curb, delineate, demarcate, fix, put a limit on, ration, restrain, restrict

**limitation** n **1** cap, ceiling, check, curb, cut-off, deadline, limit, maximum, restraint, restriction. **2** defect, deficiency, fault, inadequacy, shortcoming, weakness

**limited** adj **1** capped, checked, circumscribed, confined, controlled, curbed, delineated, demarcated, fixed, rationed, restrained, restricted. **2** basic, inadequate, insufficient, minimal, restricted, scanty, sparse; opp unlimited

**limitless** adj boundless, countless, endless, everlasting, immeasurable, incalculable, inexhaustible, infinite, innumerable, never-ending, numberless, unbounded, unconfined, unending, unlimited

**limp** adj drooping, flabby, flaccid, floppy, loose, relaxed, sagging, slack, soft, wilting; opp firm, stiff

**limp** v be lame, falter, hobble, shamble, shuffle, totter

**line** n **1** band, bar, border, boundary, contour, dash, hyphen, mark, rule, streak, striation, strip, stripe, stroke, trail, underscore. **2** channel, corrugation, crease, fold, furrow, groove, wrinkle. **3** cable, cord, filament, lead, rope, strand, string, thread, wire. **4** (of people) chain, column, cordon, crocodile, file, parade, procession, queue, rank, row, series. **5** approach, avenue, course, direction, drift, method, tack, track, way

**line** v **1** crease, furrow, inscribe, mark, rule, score, wrinkle. **2** border, edge, fringe, hem, rim. **3 line up** (form a line) get in line, form a line, form a queue, queue up. **4 line up** (put into a line) align, arrange in a line, marshal, place in line, straighten up

**lines** n **1** configuration, contour,

delineation, figure, form, outline, shape.
2 part, script, speech, words

**linger** v 1 dally, dawdle, hang around,
hover, lag, loiter, pause, remain, stay,
stop, take your time, tarry, wait;
*opp* hurry. 2 abide, continue, endure,
persist, remain

**lingering** adj abiding, continuing,
enduring, long, long-drawn-out,
persistent, protracted, remaining

**link** n 1 affiliation, association,
attachment, bond, connection,
relationship, tie. 2 (joining two things
together) connection, connector,
coupling, join, joint, loop, ring

**link** v 1 attach, bind, connect, couple,
fasten, join, tie, yoke. 2 associate,
attach, bracket, connect, join, put
together, relate, tie up

**lip** n brim, brink, edge, margin, rim, verge

**liquid** adj flowing, fluid, liquefied, melted,
molten, running, runny, sloppy

**liquid** n fluid, juice, liquor, solution

**liquidate** v annihilate, bump off *inf*,
destroy, dispatch, do away with *inf*,
eliminate, exterminate, get rid of *inf*,
kill, murder, obliterate, remove, silence,
wipe out

**list** n catalogue, directory, file, index,
inventory, listing, record, register, roll,
schedule, table, tally

**list** v catalogue, enter, enumerate, file,
index, itemize, make a list, make an
inventory, note, record, register,
tabulate, write down

**listen** v attend, concentrate, hark, hear,
heed, mind, note, observe, pay
attention, take notice

**listless** adj apathetic, enervated, feeble,

heavy, inactive, indolent, inert, languid,
lethargic, limp, passive, sluggish, supine,
torpid, weary; *opp* energetic

**literal** adj 1 actual, authentic, genuine,
real, true, unexaggerated. 2 (a literal
translation) accurate, close, exact,
faithful, strict, verbatim, word-for-word

**literary** adj bookish, cultivated, cultured,
educated, erudite, highbrow, learned,
literate, scholarly, well-read, widely read

**literate** adj able to read, cultivated,
educated, informed, lettered, schooled,
well-read; *opp* illiterate

**literature** n 1 books, fiction, letters,
writing. 2 booklet, brochure, circular,
handout, information, leaflet, pamphlet

**litigation** n action, case, dispute, lawsuit,
legal proceedings, suit

**litter** n clutter, debris, detritus, garbage,
jetsam, junk, mess, refuse, rubbish, trash
*Am*, waste

**litter** v clutter, make untidy, mess up,
scatter, strew

**little** adj 1 baby, compact, diminutive,
dinky *inf*, dwarf, infinitesimal,
Lilliputian, microscopic, midget, mini
*inf*, miniature, minuscule, minute,
petite, short, small, teeny *inf*, tiny, titchy
*inf*, wee *inf*; *opp* big. 2 (a little child)
infant, junior, small, young; *opp* big.
3 (not much) inadequate, insufficient,
meagre, mean, measly *inf*, miserly,
negligible, paltry, piddling *inf*, scant,
skimpy, sparse

**live** adj 1 active, actual, alive, animate,
breathing, existing, living, sentient,
vital; *opp* dead. 2 (a live issue) burning,
current, hot, important, pertinent,
pressing, relevant, topical, vital.

**3** (a live broadcast) as it happens, in real time, unedited; *opp* pre-recorded

**live** *v* **1** be, be alive, breathe, draw breath, exist, have life. **2** abide, dwell, have your home, inhabit, lodge, occupy, reside, settle. **3** (of a custom) abide, continue, endure, last, persist, prevail, remain, stay alive, survive. **4** exist, get by *inf*, make a living, make ends meet, subsist, support oneself, survive

**livelihood** *n* daily bread, job, keep, living, means of support, occupation, subsistence, sustenance, trade, work

**lively** *adj* active, alert, animated, bouncy, bubbly *inf*, buoyant, bustling, cheerful, chirpy *inf*, energetic, enthusiastic, exuberant, frisky, high-spirited, irrepressible, jolly, nimble, perky *inf*, quick, spirited, sprightly, spry, vigorous, vital, vivacious; *opp* dull, lethargic

**livid** *adj* **1** angry, boiling *inf*, enraged, fuming, furious, hopping mad *inf*, incensed, infuriated, mad *inf*, outraged, seething. **2** (of a bruise) black-and-blue, bluish, bruised, discoloured, purplish. **3** (of sb's face) ashen, deathly, ghastly, ghostly, grey, pale, pallid, white

**living** *adj* active, actual, alive, animate, breathing, existing, live, sentient, vital; *opp* dead

**living** *n* crust, daily bread, employment, income, job, keep, livelihood, means of support, occupation, subsistence, sustenance, wage, work

**load** *n* **1** bale, cargo, charge, consignment, freight, shipment. **2** burden, cross, duty, encumbrance, millstone, pressure, responsibility, strain, trouble, weight, worry

**load** *v* **1** cram, fill, freight, heap, pack, pile, stack, stuff. **2** burden, charge, oppress, pressure, saddle, trouble, weigh down, worry

**loan** *n* advance, credit, mortgage

**loath, loth** *adj* against, averse to, disinclined, opposed, reluctant, resistant, shy, unenthusiastic, unwilling; *opp* eager

**loathe** *v* abhor, abominate, despise, detest, execrate, hate, have an aversion to, recoil from, revile, shrink from, shudder at; *opp* love

**lobby** *n* **1** anteroom, entrance hall, foyer, hall, hallway, reception, waiting room. **2** (pressure group) campaign, campaigners, interest group, lobbyists, pressure group

**lobby** *v* campaign for, petition, pressurize, promote, push for, try to influence

**local** *adj* **1** community, neighbourhood, parish-pump *inf*, parish, provincial, regional, district; *opp* central, national. **2** adjoining, nearby, neighbouring

**local** *n* **1** native, neighbour, resident, villager. **2** ale house, boozer *inf*, inn, pub, public house, watering hole *inf*

**locality** *n* area, community, district, locale, neighbourhood, vicinity

**localize** *v* confine, contain, limit, restrain, restrict

**locate** *v* **1** discover, find, pin down, pinpoint, put your hands on, run to earth, track down, unearth. **2** establish, place, put, set up, site, situate

**location** *n* place, position, setting, site, situation, spot, venue, whereabouts

**lock** *n* bolt, catch, clasp, fastening, latch, mortise-lock, padlock, rim-lock,

Yale lock TM

**lock** v **1** bolt, fasten, padlock, secure, shut. **2** entangle, entwine, fix, jam, join, mesh. **3 lock up** detain, imprison, incarcerate, put behind bars, remand, take away sb's freedom, throw sb in jail

**lodge** n cabin, chalet, cottage, gate-house, house, hut

**lodge** v **1** (lodge an appeal) enter, file, make, put in, register, submit. **2** (get stuck) become embedded, embed, get caught, get stuck, jam, stick. **3** (live) have digs, have lodgings, have rooms, kip down inf, live, stay, stop with inf

**lodger** n boarder, paying guest, resident, tenant

**lodgings** n accommodation, apartment, a roof over your head, boarding house, digs inf, flat, pad inf, rooms, somewhere to live

**log** n **1** block of wood, branch, chunk of wood, fuel, timber, trunk, twig, wood. **2** account, diary, journal, logbook, record, register

**logic** n argument, deduction, rationale, reasoning, sense

**logical** adj cogent, coherent, consistent, plausible, rational, reasonable, sensible, sound, structured, valid, well-organized; opp illogical

**loiter** v hang about, hang around, linger, loaf about, skulk, stand about, wait around

**loll** v flop, languish, lean, lie, lounge, slouch, slump, sprawl

**lone** adj isolated, single, solitary, unaccompanied

**lonely** adj abandoned, alone, deserted, desolate, forlorn, forsaken, isolated, lonesome, solitary

**long** adj **1** drawn out, elongated, endless, extended, interminable, lengthy, long-winded, never-ending, prolonged, protracted. **2** (four metres long) in length, lengthways

**long** v covet, crave, dream of, hanker after, have a craving for, want, yearn for

**longing** n ambition, craving, desire, hunger, urge, wish

**look** n **1** butcher's inf, examination, gander inf, gaze, glance, glare, glimpse, glower, inspection, peek, scan, stare. **2** appearance, expression, face, impression

**look** v **1** browse through, cast your eye over, examine, eye, eyeball inf, gawp inf, gaze, glance, have a look, peep, peer, scan, see, stare, study, watch. **2** (seem) appear, give the appearance of being, seem, strike you as being. **3** (look everywhere for sth) hunt, search, scour. **4 look after** care for, keep an eye on, mind, nurse, nurture, take care of, tend, watch. **5 look forward to** anticipate, count the days until, long for. **6 look into** check out, inquire about, examine, explore, go into, investigate, make some inquiries, research, study, suss out inf. **7 look out** be careful, be on the watch for, beware, keep an eye out, mind yourself, watch out. **8 look up** (look up sth in a reference book) consult, locate, refer to, search for, track down. **9 look up** (visit sb) call on, drop in on, go and see, visit. **10 look up** (improve) get better, improve, look rosy, pick up, shape up

**lookout** n **1** guard, sentry, watch. **2** (that's your lookout) affair, business, concern, pigeon inf, problem

**loom** *v* appear, dominate, hang over, materialize, overshadow, take shape, threaten, tower over

**loop** *n* circle, coil, curl, curve, hoop, noose, ring, spiral, turn, twist, whorl

**loop** *v* bend, coil, curl, spiral, twist, wind

**loophole** *n* excuse, flaw, pretext, way of avoiding sth, way out

**loose** *adj* **1** baggy, floppy, free, hanging, slack, straggling, trailing, unattached, wobbly. **2** at large, escaped, free, out, untethered. **3** approximate, ballpark *inf*, general, rough, vague

**loose** *v* free, let out, liberate, release, set free, let go, set loose, slacken, turn loose, undo, untether, untie

**loosen** *v* ease off, relax, slacken, undo, unfasten, untie; *opp* tighten

**loot** *n* bounty, goodies *inf*, haul, plunder, spoils

**lopsided** *adj* awry, crooked, skew-whiff *inf*, tilting, uneven, wonky *inf*; *opp* straight

**lord** *n* **1** aristocrat, baron, count, duke, earl, noble. **2** chief, leader, master, ruler

**lordly** *adj* **1** arrogant, condescending, disdainful, haughty, imperious, patronizing. **2** aristocratic, noble

**lose** *v* **1** be unable to find, mislay, misplace; *opp* find. **2** be defeated, get beaten, get hammered *inf*, get thrashed *inf*; *opp* win

**loser** *n* also-ran, failure, no-hoper, runner-up

**loss** *n* bereavement, cost, damage, defeat, deficit, deprivation, disappearance, failure, harm, hurt, impairment, privation

**lost** *adj* **1** (sth is lost) disappeared, misplaced, missing, vanished. **2** (sb is lost) adrift, disorientated, off course. **3** (feel lost) baffled, bewildered, confused, mystified, puzzled. **4** (from the past) dead, extinct, forgotten, past, vanished, wiped out

**lot** *n* **1 a lot** a good deal, loads *inf*, lots, many, masses, piles *inf*, plenty, scores, stacks *inf*, tons *inf*. **2 a lot** a good deal, frequently, often, regularly. **3** batch, bunch, bundle, crowd, group

**lotion** *n* cream, liquid, milk, ointment

**lottery** *n* **1** draw, raffle, sweepstake. **2** gamble, game, the luck of the draw

**loud** *adj* **1** blaring, booming, deafening, ear-splitting, noisy, raucous, rowdy, shrill, thudding, thundering, tumultuous; *opp* quiet. **2** (of a colour) flashy *inf*, garish, gaudy, lurid, ostentatious, showy; *opp* subdued, subtle

**lounge** *n* drawing room, front room, living room, parlour, sitting room

**lounge** *v* flop, laze, lie about, lie back, loll, relax, sprawl

**lout** *n* hoodlum, hooligan, oaf, slob, thug, tough, yahoo, yob

**lovable** *adj* adorable, appealing, attractive, cuddly, cute, endearing, gorgeous, lovely, sweet

**love** *n* **1** adoration, affection, devotion, fondness, infatuation, liking, partiality, passion, soft spot, tenderness, weakness. **2** darling, dear, poppet, sweetheart, sweetie

**love** *v* **1** (be in love with) adore, be devoted to, be fond of, be in love with, be infatuated with, be keen on, be soft on *inf*, dote on, fancy *inf*, have a crush on, have a thing about *inf*, idolize, think

the world of, worship. 2 (love
strawberries, a song, dancing) adore,
be keen on, be partial to, enjoy, get a
kick out of, go for, have a weakness for,
really like

**lovely** adj 1 (a lovely holiday) brilliant,
fabulous, gorgeous, great, marvellous,
superb, terrific, wonderful. 2 (good-
looking) attractive, beautiful, cute,
good-looking, handsome, pretty, sweet

**lover** n another man, another woman, bit
on the side inf, boyfriend, fiancé,
fiancée, girlfriend, mistress, old flame,
partner, toy boy

**loving** adj adoring, affectionate, amorous,
ardent, caring, close, devoted,
passionate, tender, warm; opp cold

**low** adj 1 (short) dwarf, low-growing, low-
lying, shallow, short, small, squat,
stunted, sunken; opp tall. 2 (stocks are
low) cut, deficient, depleted,
inadequate, insufficient, meagre,
modest, poor, reduced, scant, scarce,
under-strength; opp high. 3 (low
volume, light) gentle, hushed, muffled,
muted, pianissimo, quiet, soft, subdued;
opp bright, loud, strong. 4 (bass) bass,
deep; opp high-pitched, soprano.
5 (unhappy) brassed off inf, depressed,
despondent, dispirited, down, down in
the dumps inf, downhearted, fed up inf,
gloomy, miserable, sad, unhappy;
opp happy, on a high inf

**lower** adj 1 inferior, junior, lesser,
secondary, subordinate; opp higher.
2 (lower prices) cut, decreased, reduced,
slashed; opp higher, increased

**lower** v 1 drop, haul down, let down, take
down. 2 (lower prices) bring down, cut,

decrease, discount, mark down, reduce,
slash; opp put up. 3 (lower the volume)
reduce, turn down; opp turn up

**low-key** adj casual, downbeat, laid-back,
muted, played down, restrained,
understated

**loyal** adj committed, dependable,
devoted, dutiful, faithful, reliable,
staunch, true, trusted, trustworthy;
opp disloyal

**loyalty** n allegiance, dedication,
dependability, devotion, faithfulness,
fidelity, reliability, trustworthiness;
opp disloyalty

**lubricate** v grease, moisturize, oil

**lucid** adj 1 (a lucid explanation) clear,
comprehensible, distinct, explicit,
logical, plain, simple, straightforward,
understandable. 2 (clear-headed) all
there inf, clear-headed, compos mentis,
in your right mind, rational, sane,
thinking straight

**luck** n 1 chance, destiny, fate, fluke,
fortune, serendipity, the stars. 2 (good
luck) best of luck, break inf, good luck,
prosperity, stroke of luck, success,
windfall

**lucky** adj auspicious, charmed, fortuitous,
fortunate, handy, jammy inf, opportune,
timely; opp unlucky

**lucrative** adj beneficial, fruitful, high-
income, juicy inf, profitable, well-paid,
worthwhile

**ludicrous** adj absurd, comic, crazy, daft
inf, farcical, incongruous, preposterous,
ridiculous, silly, stupid; opp sensible

**luggage** n baggage, bags, belongings,
cases, gear inf, possessions, things

**lukewarm** adj 1 at room temperature,

hand-hot, tepid. **2** half-hearted, indifferent, unenthusiastic, uninterested; *opp* enthusiastic

**lull** *n* calm, hush, let-up, pause, quiet, quiet period, stillness, tranquillity

**lull** *v* calm down, die down, dwindle, let up, pacify, quieten down, soothe

**luminous** *adj* bright, fluorescent, glowing, lustrous, phosphorescent, radiant, shining, vivid; *opp* dull

**lump** *n* **1** (swelling) bulge, bump, growth, swelling, tumour. **2** (piece) blob, chunk, clump, hunk, piece, wad, wedge

**lump** *v* bunch, clump, combine, consolidate, fuse, group, merge, mix, pool, put

**lunatic** *adj* absurd, crackpot *inf*, crazy, daft *inf*, foolish, idiotic, insane, mad, stupid; *opp* sensible

**lunatic** *n* headbanger *inf*, insane person, madman, maniac, nutcase *inf*, nutter *inf*, psychopath

**lunge** *v* dive, fall on, jump, leap, lurch, plunge, pounce, thrust

**lurch** *v* list, lunge, pitch, reel, roll, stagger, stumble, sway, weave

**lure** *n* attraction, carrot, decoy, inducement, invitation, magnet, temptation

**lure** *v* attract, beckon, draw, ensnare, entice, invite, lead on, seduce, tempt

**lurid** *adj* **1** bright, garish, gaudy, glaring, loud, vivid. **2** disgusting, gory, grisly, gruesome, nasty, repulsive, revolting, shocking, unpleasant

**lurk** *v* hide, lie in wait, linger, skulk, sneak, snoop

**luscious** *adj* appetizing, delicious, juicy, mouth-watering, succulent, yummy *inf*

**lush** *adj* dense, flourishing, green, luxuriant, prolific, rich, thick

**lust** *n* craving, desire, lechery, longing, passion

**lust after** *v* crave, desire, fancy *inf*, need, want

**luxurious** *adj* affluent, comfortable, deluxe, expensive, extravagant, grand, lavish, opulent, plush, rich, ritzy *inf*, sumptuous, swanky *inf*; *opp* poor, Spartan

**luxury** *n* **1** comfort, extravagance, grandeur, indulgence, opulence, richness, splendour, sumptuousness. **2** (a luxury) extra, extravagance, optional extra, treat, trimmings

**lyrical** *adj* emotional, expressive, impassioned, poetic, romantic

**lyrics** *n* libretto, text, words

**macabre** *adj* eerie, frightening, grisly, gruesome, horrible, morbid, sick *inf*

**machine** *n* apparatus, appliance, contraption, device, gadget, mechanism, robot, tool

**machinery** *n* **1** apparatus, equipment, gear, plant, tools. **2** channels, organization, procedure, set-up *inf*, structure, system, workings

**mad** *adj* **1** crazy *inf*, demented, dotty *inf*, insane, mentally handicapped, mentally ill, mentally unstable, nuts *inf*, out of your mind, round the bend *inf*, senile, unbalanced, unhinged; *opp* sane. **2** (idiotic) crackers *inf*, crackpot *inf*, crazy, daft *inf*, foolish, idiotic, insane, lunatic, ridiculous, silly, stupid; *opp* sensible

**madden** *v* anger, annoy, enrage, exasperate, gall, get sb's back up *inf*, get up sb's nose *inf*, infuriate, irritate, make angry, make sb's blood boil, upset; *opp* please

**made-up** *adj* **1** fabricated, false, fictional, imaginary, invented, spurious; *opp* true. **2** off-the-peg, pre-built, ready-made

**madman** *n* head case *inf*, loony *inf*, madwoman, mentally handicapped person, nutcase *inf*, nutter *inf*, psychopath

**madness** *n* **1** dementia, insanity, mania, mental illness, psychosis. **2** absurdity, craziness, folly, foolishness, stupidity

**magazine** *n* colour supplement, journal, monthly, periodical, weekly

**magic** *adj* **1** brilliant, excellent, marvellous, terrific, wonderful. **2** charmed, enchanted, magical

**magic** *n* **1** black magic, conjuring, enchantment, illusion, sleight of hand, sorcery, the occult, the supernatural, voodoo, witchcraft. **2** charm, fascination, magnetism, spell

**magician** *n* conjuror, illusionist, sorcerer, warlock, witch, wizard

**magnanimous** *adj* benevolent, big-hearted, big, charitable, generous, kind

**magnetic** *adj* appealing, attractive, captivating, charismatic, enchanting, fascinating, gripping, inviting, irresistible, mesmerizing, seductive, tantalizing, tempting

**magnetism** *n* appeal, attraction, charm, draw, fascination, lure, magic, pull, spell, temptation

**magnificent** *adj* brilliant, excellent, fine, glorious, gorgeous, grand, magic, marvellous, out of this world, splendid, sumptuous, superb, tremendous, wonderful

**magnify** *v* amplify, blow up, boost, build up, enhance, enlarge, exaggerate, expand, heighten, increase, inflate, make bigger; **opp** reduce

**magnitude** n degree, enormity, extent, greatness, immensity, importance, significance, size, vastness

**maid** n 1 domestic servant, domestic, girl, housemaid, lady-in-waiting, lady's maid, servant. 2 girl, lass, young woman

**mail** n collection, delivery, letters, parcels, post, postal service

**mail** v email, post, send, send off, transfer

**maim** v disable, handicap, damage permanently, injure, mutilate, wound

**main** adj basic, central, chief, critical, crucial, essential, first, foremost, key, major, most important, number one, paramount, predominant, primary, prime, principal, top, vital

**main** n cable, channel, conduit, line, pipe, water main

**maintain** v 1 (keep up) continue, keep up, keep, retain, sustain. 2 (maintain a building) carry out repairs, keep in good order, look after, preserve, repair, take care of. 3 (say that sth is true) allege, argue, assert, believe, claim, contend, profess, state

**majestic** adj grand, imperial, imposing, impressive, magnificent, noble, regal, splendid, stately

**majesty** n grandeur, magnificence, nobility, pomp, royalty, splendour, stateliness

**major** adj chief, considerable, crucial, extensive, great, important, key, leading, main, outstanding, principal, significant; **opp** minor

**majority** n best part, bulk, greater part, largest part, lion's share, main body,

more than half, most; **opp** minority

**make** n brand, marque, sort, type, variety

**make** v 1 (produce) assemble, bake, build, cook, create, draw up, fashion, fix inf, form, manufacture, prepare, produce, put together, synthesize. 2 (cause) bring about, cause, generate, give rise to. 3 (compel) coerce, compel, force, oblige, push sb into, require. 4 (earn) bring home, bring in, clear, earn, gain, net. 5 (one and one makes two) add up to, come to, constitute, equal, total. 6 (make a statement, speech) deliver, give, say, utter. 7 **make off** bolt, clear off inf, cut and run inf, decamp, do a runner inf, escape, get away, run off, sacrper. 8 **make out** (be able to see or hear) detect, discern, distinguish, hear, pick out, recognize, see. 9 **make out** (understand) decipher, figure out, follow, get inf, grasp, see, understand, work out. 10 **make out** (make out a receipt) complete, fill in, fill out, write out. 11 **make up** compose, concoct, create, dream up, fabricate, hatch, invent. 12 **make up** comprise, constitute, form

**make-believe** n dream, fantasy, fiction, imagination, invention, play-acting, pretence, role-play; **opp** reality

**make do** v cope, get by, improvise, manage, put up with, survive

**maker** n architect, author, builder, composer, creator, manufacturer, originator, producer, writer

**makeshift** adj emergency, improvised, make-do, provisional, rough-and-ready, stop-gap, temporary; **opp** permanent

**make-up** n cosmetics, face-paint, greasepaint, war-paint

**makings** n beginnings, capability, ingredients, potential, promise, qualities, talent

**maladjusted** adj disturbed, neurotic, unbalanced, unstable, with behavioural problems; **opp** well-adjusted

**male** adj boyish, manlike, manly, masculine; **opp** female

**malevolent** adj cruel, evil, fierce, hostile, malicious, malign, spiteful, unfriendly, venomous, vindictive; **opp** good

**malice** n animosity, bitchiness inf, bitterness, enmity, hatred, hostility, ill-will, rancour, spite, venom, vindictiveness

**malicious** adj bitchy inf, bitter, hostile, hurtful, malignant, pernicious, spiteful, venomous, vicious, vindictive

**malignant** adj 1 hostile, malicious, pernicious, spiteful, venomous, vicious. 2 dangerous, destructive, life-threatening; **opp** benign

**man** n 1 bloke inf, chap inf, gentleman, guy inf, human being, individual, lad, male, young man. 2 Homo sapiens, human race, humankind, humans, men and women, people

**man** v crew, operate, staff, work

**manacle** n chain, fetter, handcuffs, irons, shackle

**manage** v 1 accomplish, bring off, cope, crack it inf, deal with, get by, handle, succeed, survive. 2 administer, be in charge of, control, direct, head, lead, organize, oversee, pilot, run, supervise

**manageable** adj 1 attainable, doable, feasible, possible, viable. 2 accommodating, amenable, compliant, controllable, docile, submissive

**management** n 1 administration, board, bosses, directors, employers, executive, managers, owners, top brass inf. 2 administration, command, control, direction, handling, organization, overseeing, running, supervision

**manager** n administrator, boss, controller, director, employer, executive, foreman, gaffer inf, governor, head of department, head, line manager, owner, person in charge, proprietor, superintendent, supervisor

**mandate** n approval, authority, authorization, command, decree, direction, edict, order, power, ruling, sanction, support

**mangle** v crush, destroy, distort, hack, maul, twist, wreck

**mangy** adj moth-eaten, scabby, scruffy, shabby, tatty inf, threadbare, wretched

**manhandle** v haul, heave, hump, push, shove

**mania** n 1 derangement, insanity, madness, mental illness. 2 addiction, craving, craze, obsession, passion

**maniac** n deranged person, idiot, loony inf, lunatic, madman, madwoman, nutcase inf, nutter inf, psychopath

**manifest** adj clear, conspicuous, glaring, obvious, patent, plain, unmistakable

**manifestation** n demonstration, display, embodiment, evidence, expression, indication, sign, symbol, testimony

**manipulate** v 1 handle, manoeuvre, operate, use, work. 2 (people) exploit, influence, misuse, take advantage of, use

**mankind** n Homo sapiens, human race, humanity, humans, men and women, people

**manly** *adj* **1** macho, male, masculine, virile; *opp* effeminate. **2** brave, chivalrous, gallant, strong, vigorous

**man-made** *adj* artificial, imitation, manufactured, simulated, synthetic, synthesized; *opp* natural

**manner** *adj* **1** approach, means, method, procedure, process, style, technique, way. **2** air, appearance, attitude, bearing, behaviour, demeanour, look, mien, way. **3** all manner of all kinds of, a mixture of, an assortment of, assorted, different, various, varying

**mannerism** *n* characteristic, gesture, foible, habit, idiosyncrasy, peculiarity, quirk

**manners** *n* **1** bearing, behaviour, conduct, deportment. **2** civility, correct behaviour, courtesy, decorum, etiquette, good form, politeness, protocol, propriety, social graces, the done thing *inf*

**manoeuvre** *n* action, dodge, intrigue, machination, plan, plot, ploy, ruse, scheme, subterfuge, tactic, trick

**manoeuvre** *v* **1** contrive, engineer, intrigue, manage, manipulate, plan, plot, pull strings, scheme. **2** direct, drive, guide, move, steer

**manoeuvres** *n* deployment, exercise, military exercise, movement, training

**manual** *adj* **1** by hand, hand-operated. **2** (manual work) labouring, physical, with your hands

**manufacture** *v* **1** build, construct, create, fabricate, forge, form, make, mass-produce, process, produce, shape, turn out. **2** (a story) concoct, cook up *inf*,

dream up, invent, think up

**manure** *n* compost, droppings, dung, fertilizer, guano, muck

**many** *adj* abundant, a lot of, copious, countless, frequent, heaps of *inf*, innumerable, loads of *inf*, lots of, myriad, numerous, oodles of *inf*, plenty of, profuse, tons of *inf*, umpteen *inf*

**map** *n* chart, guide, plan, street guide, road-map, town plan

**march** *n* **1** march-past, parade, route march, tramp, trek, walk. **2** demo *inf*, demonstration, parade, procession, protest

**march** *v* file, footslog, parade, stride, tramp

**margin** **1** border, boundary, brink, edge, perimeter, periphery, rim, side, verge. **2** allowance, latitude, leeway, room, room for manoeuvre, scope, space

**marginal** *adj* **1** borderline, peripheral. **2** doubtful, insignificant, low, minimal, negligible, slight, small, unimportant

**marginalize** *v* decrease the influence of, exclude, make marginal, make unimportant, push out, push to the margins

**marital** *adj* conjugal, married, matrimonial, nuptial, wedded

**mark** *n* **1** blemish, blot, blotch, dent, dot, impression, pockmark, scar, scratch, smear, smudge, smut, speck, spot, stain, streak. **2** badge, brand, device, emblem, hallmark, seal, signature, symbol, trademark. **3** evidence, indication, proof, sign, symbol, token. **4** aim, goal, intention, objective, purpose, target. **5** below the mark below par, below the norm, below the standard, inadequate,

inferior, not up to scratch, substandard.
**6 leave its mark** affect, have an effect,
have an impact, impress, influence,
make an impression. **7 wide of the mark**
erroneous, fallacious, inaccurate,
incorrect, wrong

**mark** v 1 blemish, blot, damage, deface,
disfigure, dent, dirty, draw on, make a
mark on, scar, scrawl on, scribble on,
smudge, spot, stain, streak, write on.
2 brand, label, put a mark on, tag.
3 (mark sb's work) appraise, assess,
correct, evaluate, grade, tick. 4 (mark
sb's words) attend to, heed, listen to,
mind, note, notice, observe, pay
attention to, see, take notice of, take
seriously, take to heart, watch. 5 (mark
an occasion) celebrate, commemorate,
honour, observe

**marked** adj apparent, blatant, clear,
conspicuous, decided, distinct, evident,
notable, obvious, patent, pronounced,
remarkable, striking

**market** n 1 bazaar, fair, market-place,
mart. 2 call, demand, desire. 3 business,
buying and selling, commerce, dealing

**market** v advertise, peddle, promote,
push inf, put on the market, retail, sell,
trade in, vend

**marketable** adj desirable, in demand,
salable, sought after, wanted

**marksman** n crack shot inf, good shot,
markswoman, sharpshooter

**maroon** v abandon, desert, forsake, leave,
leave behind, leave stranded, put ashore,
strand

**marriage** n 1 matrimony, union, wedlock.
2 marriage ceremony, nuptials, wedding.
3 alliance, association, combination,

link, merger, union

**married** 1 (of people) hitched inf, joined,
spliced inf, united, wed, wedded.
2 conjugal, connubial, marital,
matrimonial, wedded

**marry** v 1 become man and wife, be
married, get hitched inf, get married, get
spliced inf, join in matrimony, tie the
knot inf, unite, walk down the aisle inf,
wed. 2 ally, combine, join, link, merge,
unite

**marsh** n bog, fen, marshland, mire,
morass, quagmire, quicksand, swamp,
wetland

**marshy** adj boggy, miry, muddy, quaggy,
soft, squelchy, swampy

**marvel** v admire, applaud, be amazed by,
be astonished by, be surprised by, praise,
wonder at

**marvellous** adj amazing, astounding,
breathtaking, brilliant, extraordinary,
fantastic, out of this world inf,
remarkable, sensational, stupendous,
superb, terrific, wonderful

**masculine** adj 1 macho, male, manly,
virile; opp feminine. 2 (of a woman)
butch inf, manly, unfeminine,
unwomanly; opp feminine

**mash** v crush, mangle, pound, pulp,
pulverize, purée, smash, squash

**mask** n camouflage, cover, disguise,
façade, false colours, front, guise,
pretence, screen, shield, smokescreen,
veil

**mask** v cloak, conceal, cover up, disguise,
hide, obscure, screen, veil

**mass** adj extensive, general,
indiscriminate, large-scale, popular,
universal, wholesale, widespread

**mass** n 1 accumulation, collection, concentration. 2 body, crowd, horde, host, lot, mob, multitude, throng. 3 body, bulk, greater part, lion's share, main body, majority, preponderance. 4 bulk, magnitude, size

**mass** v 1 accumulate, amass, assemble, bring together, collect, gather. 2 assemble, collect, flock together, gather, gather together, meet, marshal, rally, swarm, throng

**massacre** n annihilation, blood bath, butchery, carnage, genocide, mass execution, mass murder, slaughter

**massacre** v annihilate, butcher, kill, kill off, mow down, slaughter, slay, wipe out

**massage** v knead, manipulate, rub, rub down

**masses** n 1 an abundance, bags inf, heaps inf, hundreds, loads, lots, millions, oodles inf, thousands. 2 **the masses** the common people, the mob, the hoi polloi, the proletariat, the rabble

**massive** adj colossal, enormous, gigantic, ginormous inf, huge, immense, large, mammoth, vast, whopping inf; opp tiny

**master** adj chief, main, most important, predominant, principal

**master** n 1 boss, chief, controller, director, employer, governor, head, lord, lord and master, ruler, top dog inf. 2 (of a ship) captain, commander, skipper. 3 head, headmaster, head teacher, instructor, schoolmaster, schoolteacher, teacher, tutor. 4 (a master at sth) ace inf, authority, dab hand inf, expert, genius, maestro, past-master, virtuoso, wizard

**master** v 1 become expert in, become

proficient in, get the hang of inf, grasp, know, learn, learn thoroughly. 2 control, dominate, govern, overcome, overpower, quell, subdue, subjugate, tame

**masterly** adj accomplished, ace inf, adept, consummate, deft, dexterous, excellent, expert, first-rate, masterful, proficient, skilful, skilled

**mastermind** n 1 brains, brainbox, expert, genius, intellect, intellectual. 2 architect, author, brains behind sth, creator, director, initiator, organizer, originator, planner

**mastermind** v be the brains behind inf, conceive, devise, direct, initiate, manage, organize, plan, think up

**masterpiece** n best work, chef d'oeuvre, magnum opus, masterwork, pièce de résistance, tour de force

**match** n 1 bout, competition, contest, game, tournament. 2 counterpart, equal, equivalent, peer, rival. 3 copy, double, duplicate, look-alike, spitting image inf, twin. 4 complement, counterpart, mate, pair, twin. 5 affiliation, alliance, marriage, pairing, partnership, union

**match** v 1 agree with, be a pair, be compatible with, be similar to, be the same as, blend with, complement, coordinate with, correspond to, fit, go with, harmonize, make a set, suit, tone with; opp contrast. 2 be a match for, be equal to, be in the same category as, be on a level with, compare with, compete with, keep pace with, keep up with, measure up to, rival. 3 bring together, combine, link, marry, pair off, pair up, put together, team up

**matching** adj 1 alike, identical, just

like, the same, twin. 2 blending, complementing, coordinating, equivalent, harmonizing, identical, like, parallel, similar, twin

**mate** n 1 better half inf, husband, other half inf, partner, spouse, wife. 2 colleague, co-worker, fellow-worker, workmate. 3 (a plumber's mate) apprentice, assistant, helper, subordinate. 4 buddy inf, chum inf, companion, comrade, friend, pal inf

**mate** v 1 breed, couple, copulate. 2 bring together, marry, match, join, pair, wed

**material** adj 1 concrete, palpable, physical, solid, substantial, tangible. 2 essential, grave, important, key, meaningful, pertinent, relevant, serious, significant, weighty

**material** n 1 element, matter, medium, stuff, substance. 2 cloth, fabric, stuff, textiles. 3 data, details, evidence, facts, gen inf, info inf, information, notes

**materialize** v 1 come about, come into being, happen, occur, take place. 2 appear, become visible, come to light, emerge, present itself, show itself, turn up inf

**maternal** adj 1 motherly. 2 (maternal relations) on the distaff side, on your mother's side

**matter** n 1 material, medium, stuff, substance. 2 affair, business, episode, event, incident, issue, occurrence, question, situation, subject, topic. 3 consequence, import, importance, note, significance, weight

**matter** v be important, be relevant, be significant, carry weight, count, make a difference, make any difference, signify

**matter-of-fact** adj deadpan, down-to-earth, dull, factual, flat, literal, mundane, plain, prosaic, straightforward, unvarnished

**mature** adj 1 adult, full-grown, fully-developed, fully-grown, grown-up, of age, well-developed. 2 experienced, responsible, sensible, wise. 3 mellow, ready, ripe, ripened, seasoned

**mature** v 1 become adult, come of age, develop, grow up, reach adulthood. 2 become responsible, become sensible, become wise. 3 become ripe, grow ripe, mellow, ripen

**maturity** n 1 adulthood, coming-of-age, majority, manhood, womanhood. 2 sense, sense of responsibility, wisdom. 3 mellowness, ripeness

**maul** v 1 claw, lacerate, mangle, mutilate, savage, tear to pieces. 2 abuse, handle roughly, manhandle, molest, paw

**maxim** n adage, aphorism, axiom, motto, proverb, rule, saying

**maximum** adj biggest, extreme, full, fullest, greatest, highest, largest, most, supreme, top, topmost, utmost; opp minimum

**maximum** n acme, apex, ceiling, crest, height, highest point, peak, summit, top, upper limit, utmost, zenith; opp minimum

**maybe** adv conceivably, could be inf, perhaps, possibly, who knows? inf, you never know inf; opp certainly, definitely

**maze** n confusion, jungle, labyrinth, mesh, network, puzzle, tangle, web

**meadow** n field, grassland, paddock, pasture

**meagre** adj deficient, inadequate, measly,

paltry, poor, scanty, short, skimpy, sparse, stingy; *opp* generous

**mean** *adj* 1 cheese-paring *inf*, close, close-fisted, illiberal, mingy *inf*, miserly, niggardly, parsimonious, stingy, tight, tight-fisted, ungenerous; *opp* generous. 2 bad-tempered, callous, disagreeable, hard-hearted, obnoxious, spiteful, surly, uncharitable, unfriendly, unkind, unpleasant. 3 (of an action) base, contemptible, despicable, ignoble, nasty, odious, shameful, vile. 4 (of a place) humble, miserable, poor, seedy, shabby, squalid, wretched

**mean** *n* average, balance, median, middle, mid-point, norm

**mean** *v* 1 convey, denote, drive at *inf*, express, imply, indicate, insinuate, represent, say, signify, spell, stand for, suggest, symbolize. 2 aim, have in mind, intend, plan, propose, set out. 3 bring about, cause, engender, entail, give rise to, involve, lead to, necessitate, produce

**meander** *v* 1 bend, curve, loop, snake, twist and turn, wind, zigzag. 2 ramble, stray, stroll aimlessly, wander, wander about

**meaning** *n* 1 drift, essence, explanation, gist, implication, import, message, sense, significance, substance, thrust, upshot. 2 consequence, effect, point, purpose, significance, value, worth. 3 aim, design, end, goal, intention, object, plan

**meaningful** *adj* 1 important, material, relevant, serious, significant, valid, worthwhile; *opp* meaningless. 2 eloquent, expressive, pointed, significant

**meaningless** *adj* 1 aimless, empty, futile,

hollow, insignificant, pointless, trifling, trivial, useless, vain, worthless; *opp* important. 2 inane, incoherent, incomprehensible, nonsensical, senseless, unintelligible

**means** *n* 1 avenue, course, expedient, method, process, way. 2 affluence, capital, finance, fortune, funds, money, property, resources, riches, wealth

**measure** *n* 1 amount, capacity, degree, expanse, extent, proportion, quantity, range, reach, scope, size. 2 allotment, allowance, division, part, percentage, portion, quota, ration, share. 3 scale, standard, unit. 4 gauge, measuring-spoon, measuring-cup, meter, ruler, scale, tape-measure. 5 benchmark, criterion, litmus test, test, yardstick. 6 action, course, course of action, expedient, procedure, proceeding, step. 7 act, bill, law, resolution, statute

**measure** *v* 1 assess, calculate, calibrate, compute, count, determine, evaluate, judge, mark out, meter, quantify, rate, reckon, size, survey, take measurements, value, weigh. 2 **measure out** allocate, allot, deal out, distribute, divide, dole out, share out. 3 **measure up** be adequate, be as good as, be equal to, be good enough, be on a level with, be suitable, come up to, come up to scratch *inf*, fit the bill, fulfil expectations, make the grade, match, meet, pass muster

**measurement** *n* 1 amount, capacity, depth, dimensions, extent, height, length, proportions, quantity, range, size, weight, width. 2 assessment, calculation, evaluation, judgement, quantification, quantifying, sizing, weighing

**meat** *n* **1** animal flesh, flesh, offal.
**2** (meat and drink) food, grub *inf*, nosh
*inf*, nourishment, provisions, rations,
scoff *inf*, sustenance, victuals

**mechanical** *adj* **1** automated, automatic,
machine-driven, motor-driven,
technological. **2** automatic, cursory,
habitual, instinctive, involuntary, knee-
jerk *inf*, machine-like, perfunctory,
reflex, routine, soulless, unconscious,
unthinking

**mechanism** *n* **1** apparatus, appliance,
contraption, contrivance, device,
gadget, machine, system, tool.
**2** components, innards *inf*, machinery,
workings, works. **3** agency, channel,
means, method, operation, procedure,
proceeding, system

**mechanize** *v* automate, bring up to date,
equip with machines, make automatic,
modernize

**medal** *n* award, decoration, honour,
medallion, prize, reward, trophy

**meddle** *v* be a busybody, butt in, interfere,
intervene, intrude, poke your nose in *inf*,
pry, stick your nose in *inf*, stick your oar
in *inf*, tamper

**mediate** *v* act as go-between, act as
mediator, act as middleman, act as
peacemaker, arbitrate, conciliate,
intercede, intervene, liaise, make peace,
negotiate, reconcile, referee, umpire

**medicinal** *adj* curative, healing, remedial,
restorative, therapeutic

**medicine** *n* **1** cure, drug, medication,
medicament, remedy, panacea.
**2** healing, medical science,
therapy, treatment

**mediocre** *adj* average, fair, indifferent,
middling, no great shakes *inf*, nothing to
write home about *inf*, ordinary, passable,
pedestrian, run-of-the-mill, second-rate,
so-so, undistinguished, uninspired

**meditate** *n* **1** be lost in thought, cogitate,
deliberate, muse, ponder, reflect, study,
think. **2** brood over, chew over *inf*,
contemplate, consider, mull over,
ponder, reflect on, think over

**medium** *adj* **1** average, fair, intermediate,
mean, median, mediocre, middle,
middling, moderate,

**medium** *n* **1** average, centre,
compromise, mean, median, middle,
middle way. **2** agency, approach,
channel, form, means, means of
communication, means of expression,
method, vehicle, way. **3** conditions,
element, environment, habitat, milieu,
setting. **4** clairvoyant, seer, spiritualist

**medley** *n* assortment, hotchpotch,
jumble, miscellany, mishmash, mixed
bag, mixture

**meek** *adj* **1** docile, forbearing, gentle,
humble, long-suffering, mild, modest,
patient, peaceable, resigned, self-
effacing, unassuming, unpretentious.
**2** acquiescent, compliant, deferential,
docile, soft, spineless, submissive, timid,
tractable, weak, weak-kneed *inf*,
wimpish *inf*; *opp* aggressive

**meet** *v* **1** (meet sb) bump into, chance
upon, come across, come face to face
with, come upon, encounter, happen
upon, join, make contact with, meet
with, rendezvous with, run into.
**2** (people meet) assemble, come
together, congregate, gather, mingle,

rendezvous. **3** (lines, roads meet) come together, connect, converge, intersect, join, link up, touch. **4** (one line, road meets another) abut, adjoin, reach. **5** (meet certain conditions) answer, comply with, correspond to, fulfil, measure up to, observe, satisfy

**meeting** *n* **1** (to discuss business) assembly, conclave, conference, convention, discussion, gathering, get-together *inf*, session. **2** (between two people) appointment, assignation, confrontation, contact, encounter, rendezvous. **3** (of roads, lines, rivers) confluence, convergence, crossroads, intersection, junction

**melancholy** *adj* dejected, depressed, disconsolate, doleful, down *inf*, down in the dumps *inf*, down in the mouth, gloomy, glum, inconsolable, melancholic, miserable, nostalgic, sad, sombre, sorry for yourself, tearful, unhappy, wistful

**mellow** *adj* **1** (of food, taste) fruity, full-bodied, juicy, matured, rich, ripe, smooth, soft, tender. **2** (of a voice, sound) baritone, contralto, deep, mellifluous, resonant, rich, smooth, sweet. **3** (of colours) autumnal, golden, rich, soft, warm. **4** (of a person) calm, gentle, mature, indulgent, relaxed, serene, warm

**mellow** *v* **1** age, improve with age, mature, ripen, soften. **2** (of a person) chill out *inf*, lighten up *inf*, relax, relent, warm to sth

**melodramatic** *adj* dramatic, exaggerated, histrionic, sensational, sentimental, theatrical

**melody** *n* air, descant, music, song, strain, theme, tune

**melt** *v* **1** defrost, dissolve, liquefy, soften, thaw, unfreeze; *opp* freeze, solidify. **2** (of fears, anger) abate, die down, disappear, disperse, evaporate, fade, fade away, vanish

**member** *n* **1** adherent, associate, fellow, initiate, subscriber. **2** (of a set) component, constituent, element, part

**memoirs** *n* autobiography, diary, journal, life story, memories, recollections, reminiscences

**memorable** *adj* extraordinary, distinctive, historic, impressive, momentous, not to be forgotten, notable, noteworthy, remarkable, striking, unforgettable; *opp* unmemorable

**memorial** *adj* celebratory, commemorative, in celebration of sb/sth, in commemoration of sb/sth, in honour of sb/sth, in memory of sb/sth, in remembrance of sb/sth, monumental

**memorial** *n* cairn, cenotaph, homage, monument, plaque, shrine, statue, time capsule, tribute

**memorize** *v* absorb, commit to memory, learn, learn by heart, learn by rote, make a mental note of, remember, take in

**memory** *n* **1** (ability to remember) attention span, mind, powers of recall, recall, remembrance, retention. **2** (sth remembered) impression, recollection, reminiscence. **3** (in computing) bits, bytes, cache, capacity, data bank, data storage, gigabytes, hard disk, kilobytes, megabytes, RAM, random access memory, read-only memory, ROM

**menace** *n* **1** (dangerous thing, person)

bane, danger, evil, hazard, nuisance, peril, risk, sword of Damocles, thorn in sb's side, threat. **2** (an atmosphere of menace) danger, evil, fear, foreboding, intimidation, peril, threat. **3** (naughty child) devil, hooligan, imp, mischief-maker, pest, rapscallion, rascal, scamp *inf*, terror *inf*, troublemaker

**menace** *v* **1** alarm, browbeat, bully, cow, frighten, intimidate, scare, terrify, terrorize, threaten. **2** (the dangers that menace our society) beset, endanger, hang over, imperil, threaten

**menacing** *adj* **1** frightening, glowering, intimidating, lowering, ominous, terrifying, threatening. **2** (of future threats) dangerous, forbidding, impending, looming, ominous, threatening

**mend** *v* darn, fix, patch up *inf*, rebuild, reconstruct, renew, repair, restore, sew up

**menial** *adj* demeaning, dirty, domestic, humble, labouring, low-grade, lowly, low-status, routine, unglamorous, unskilled

**mental** *adj* cerebral, cognitive, emotional, in the mind, intellectual, psychological; *opp* physical

**mentality** *n* attitude, cast of mind, character, make-up, mind, mode of thought, personality, psyche, psychology

**mentally** *adv* cognitively, emotionally, in your mind, in your mind's eye, intellectually, psychologically, silently; *opp* physically

**mention** *n* acknowledgement, allusion, citation, comment, disclosure, indication, notice, quotation, reference, remark, report, statement

**mention** *v* acknowledge, allude to, cite, comment on, declare, disclose, divulge, indicate, quote, refer to, remark on, report, say, speak of, state, talk about, talk of

**mercenary** *adj* acquisitive, avaricious, covetous, grasping, greedy, in it for the money *inf*, materialistic, money-grubbing *inf*, selfish, venal

**merchandise** *n* articles, commodities, goods, items, products, wares

**merchant** *n* businessman, capitalist, entrepreneur, exporter, importer, seller, supplier, trader, tradesman, tradesperson, vendor

**merciful** *adj* compassionate, forgiving, indulgent, kind, lenient, pitying, soft-hearted, tender-hearted; *opp* merciless

**merciless** *adj* cruel, hard, pitiless, remorseless, ruthless, severe, without pity; *opp* merciful

**mercy** *n* **1** charity, clemency, compassion, forgiveness, indulgence, kindness, lenience, pity. **2 at the mercy of** exposed to, in the clutches of, in the power of, threatened by, under the control of, vulnerable to

**merge** *v* **1** (of companies, organizations) ally, amalgamate, be absorbed, be incorporated, be taken over, combine, form a coalition, form an alliance, join forces, join together, team up, unite. **2** (of substances, colours, feelings) be absorbed, be assimilated, be submerged, be swallowed up, blend, converge, fade into, fuse, intermingle, mingle, mix, seep into

**merger** *n* absorption, alliance,

amalgamation, coalition, combination, conglomeration, incorporation, takeover

**merit** n 1 advantage, bonus, credit, good point, pro, quality; *opp* demerit. 2 ability, excellence, praiseworthiness, skill, talent, value, worth

**merry** adj 1 celebrating, cheerful, festive, happy, jolly, joyful, joyous, laughing, lively, rejoicing, revelling. 2 drunk, inebriated, intoxicated, tipsy

**mesh** n lattice, net, netting, network, tangle, web

**mesh** v agree, be in harmony, be on the same wavelength, coincide, combine, connect, dovetail, fit, fit in, fit together, go together, harmonize, interlock, match, tally

**mess** n 1 chaos, confusion, debris, dirt, disorder, filth, jumble, muddle, pigsty *inf*, rubbish, untidiness. 2 (unsatisfactory situation) calamity, crisis, débâcle, disarray, disaster, foul-up *inf*, hole, pickle *inf*, trouble. 3 (place where soldiers eat) bar, cafeteria, canteen, club, dining hall, mess hall

**mess** v 1 mess about act up, have a laugh *inf*, joke, fool about, fool around, misbehave, play up, tease. 2 mess with sth fiddle with, fuss, meddle, play with, tinker with, trifle with. 3 mess up botch, bungle, get sth wrong, make a mess of, make a pig's ear of *inf*

**message** n 1 cable, communication, E-mail, fax, letter, memo, memorandum, missive, note, telegram, telephone call, signal, transmission, wire *Am*. 2 (of a literary work) idea, import, interpretation, meaning, moral, purport, significance, theme

**messenger** n bearer, carrier, courier, emissary, envoy, errand-boy, go-between, harbinger, herald, runner

**messy** adj chaotic, complicated, confused, dirty, filthy, jumbled, untidy

**metaphorical** adj allegorical, emblematic, figurative, non-literal, proverbial, symbolic

**meteoric** adj brilliant, dazzling, fast, irresistible, overnight, quick, rapid, spectacular, speedy, sudden, swift

**method** n approach, arrangement, manner, means, methodology, mode, modus operandi, plan, practice, procedure, process, rule, style, system, technique, way

**methodical** adj careful, deliberate, logical, meticulous, orderly, precise, step-by-step, systematic

**meticulous** adj accurate, careful, conscientious, correct, detailed, exact, methodical, painstaking, punctilious; *opp* sloppy

**microbe** n amoeba, bacillus, bacterium, bug *inf*, germ, micro-organism, virus

**middle** adj 1 central, halfway, intermediate, mean, medial, median, mid-. 2 (between two extreme qualities) average, medium, middling

**middle** n centre, core, halfway mark, heart, kernel, midpoint, midst, nucleus

**might** n energy, force, forcefulness, power, strength, sturdiness, vigour

**mighty** adj 1 (of person) all-powerful, almighty, forceful, great, powerful, strong, sturdy. 2 (of sound, force) extreme, great, heavy, intense, powerful, severe, strong, vigorous, violent

**migrant** adj globe-trotting, itinerant,

migrating, migratory, travelling, wandering

**migrant** n asylum seeker, emigrant, exile, globe-trotter, guest worker, gypsy, immigrant, itinerant, nomad, refugee, Romany, traveller, voyager, wanderer

**migrate** v emigrate, flee, fly away, go away, journey, move, relocate, travel, trek, voyage, wander

**migration** n emigration, flight, immigration, journey, relocation, travel, trek, voyage, wandering

**mild** adj 1 (of taste, smell) bland, gentle, insipid, inoffensive, soft, subtle, sweet, unobtrusive, weak; **opp** harsh, strong. 2 (of a person) docile, gentle, inoffensive, kind, meek, mild-mannered, placid, unassertive; **opp** aggressive. 3 (of weather) balmy, clement, moderate, temperate, warm, warmish

**milieu** n background, environment, location, setting, social circle, surroundings

**militant** adj aggressive, campaigning, combative, committed, extreme, extremist, hardline, radical, strident, uncompromising; **opp** moderate

**military** adj armed, martial, naval, service, soldierly, warlike

**military** n armed forces, army, forces, militia, services

**milk** v (milk sb) bleed, drain, exploit, extort, extract, siphon, soak, squeeze, suck dry

**mill about** v circulate, hang about, hang around, loiter, mill around, move about, move around, saunter, stroll, walk, wander

**mimic** n chameleon, copycat inf,

impersonator, impressionist, mime, mime artist

**mimic** v ape, caricature, copy, do an impression of, imitate, impersonate, mime, parody, resemble

**mind** n brain, head, imagination, intellect, intelligence, memory, mental capacity, mental health, mentality, opinion, psyche, psychology, sanity, soul, thinking, thought, will

**mind** v 1 guard, keep, keep an eye on, look after, protect, take care of, watch, watch over. 2 (mind the step) avoid, be aware, be careful, be mindful, beware, look out, pay attention, take care, watch, watch out. 3 (not mind sth) be bothered, be offended, be upset, care, disapprove, give a damn inf, give a tinker's cuss inf, object, take offence

**mindful** adj 1 attentive, aware, careful, conscious, thoughtful, wary, watchful. 2 be mindful of be alert to, be alive to, beware of, make allowances for, heed, pay attention to, take account of, take into account, take into consideration, think about

**mindless** adj brainless inf, cretinous, daft, hare-brained, idiotic, moronic, stupid, thoughtless, vacuous

**mine** n 1 colliery, deep mine, excavation, open-cast mine, pit, quarry, shaft, supply, tunnel, working. 2 bomb, booby trap, detonator, explosive charge, landmine

**mine** v 1 bore, dig, drill, excavate, extract, hew, quarry, tunnel, work. 2 booby-trap, lay mines, plant mines

**mingle** v 1 blend, combine, confuse, fold, intermingle, melt, merge, mix. 2 (talk to people) associate, chat, circulate, fraternize, hobnob *inf*, join in, move around, socialize

**minimal** *adj* **1** basic, essential, indispensable, minimum. **2** little, nominal, low, meagre, slight, small, tiny, token

**minimize** *v* **1** curtail, cut back, cut down, decrease, keep down, keep to a minimum, prune, reduce, shrink; *opp* maximize. **2** (think sth is unimportant) dismiss, downgrade, laugh off, play down, shrug off, underestimate, underplay, understate

**minimum** *adj* barest, least, lowest, minimal, smallest, slightest

**minimum** *n* least, low point, lowest level, nadir, smallest amount, trough; *opp* maximum

**minion** *n* aide, assistant, attendant, bodyguard, dogsbody *inf*, flunkey, helper, henchman, hireling, lackey, menial, minder *inf*, servant, sidekick, subordinate, underling

**minister** *n* **1** cabinet member, chancellor, Chancellor of the Exchequer, First Lord of the Treasury, Foreign Secretary, Home Secretary, junior minister, Minister of the Interior, Minister of State, premier, President of the Board of Trade, Prime Minister, secretary, Secretary of State. **2** clergyman, man of the cloth, moderator, parson, pastor, preacher, priest, rector, vicar

**minor** *adj* inconsequential, inferior, insignificant, lesser, negligible, slight, small, trivial, unimportant; *opp* major

**mint** *adj* new, perfect, pristine, unblemished, unsullied, untarnished, unused, virgin

**mint** *v* cast, coin, issue, press, print, produce, stamp, strike

**minute** *adj* diminutive, microscopic, mini-, miniature, miniaturized, minuscule, small, tiny; *opp* enormous, huge

**minute** *n* instant, jiffy *inf*, moment, second, short time, tick *inf*

**minutes** *n* notes, proceedings, record, transactions, transcript

**miracle** *n* marvel, mystery, phenomenon, prodigy, wonder

**miraculous** *adj* **1** inexplicable, magical, mysterious, paranormal, supernatural. **2** (extremely impressive) fantastic, incredible, marvellous, phenomenal, prodigious, stunning, superb, unbelievable, wonderful, wondrous

**mirage** *n* chimera, delusion, hallucination, illusion, image, optical illusion, trick of the light, vision

**mirror** *n* glass, looking-glass, reflector

**mirth** *n* comedy, fun, hilarity, joking, laughing, laughter, merriment

**misapprehension** *n* aberration, error, false impression, misreading, mistake, mistaken impression, misconception, misinterpretation, misjudgement, misunderstanding

**misbehave** *v* act up, be cheeky, be impolite, be naughty, be rude, be unruly, behave badly, break the rules, bully, fool about, fool around, make a scene, make mischief, mess about, mess around, play up, show off; *opp* behave

**misbehaviour** *n* bad behaviour, bullying, cheek, delinquency, disobedience, fooling about, fooling around, hooliganism, impoliteness, messing

about, messing around, mischief,
misconduct, naughtiness, rudeness,
showing off, tantrum, tomfoolery,
trouble, unruliness

**miscalculate** v err, get sth wrong, go
wrong, make a mistake, misjudge, slip up

**miscarriage** n 1 abortion, stillbirth.
2 (miscarriage of justice) failure,
injustice, mistake, travesty, unsafe
conviction, wrongful conviction

**miscarry** v 1 abort, have a miscarriage,
lose a baby. 2 (of a plan) come to
nothing, fail, fall through, fall flat, flop,
founder, go amiss, go awry, go up in
smoke, go wrong, misfire

**miscellaneous** adj assorted, different,
disparate, diverse, jumbled, mixed,
motley, odd, sundry, various

**mischief** n 1 delinquency, misbehaviour,
misconduct, monkey business inf,
naughtiness, pranks, shenanigans,
trickery, unruliness. 2 damage,
deception, dishonesty, evil, harm, hurt,
lies, malice, scheming, trouble,
vindictiveness, wickedness

**mischievous** adj 1 bad, badly behaved,
cheeky, disobedient, impish,
misbehaving, naughty, playful, unruly.
2 deceitful, dishonest, evil, injurious,
libellous, malicious, slanderous, spiteful,
untrue, vindictive, vicious, wicked

**misconception** n error, fallacy, false
impression, misapprehension,
misinterpretation, mistaken impression,
misunderstanding

**miser** n cheapskate inf, hoarder, money-
grubber inf, penny-pincher, scrooge,
skinflint inf

**miserable** adj 1 blue inf, broken-hearted,

crestfallen, cut-up inf, dejected,
depressed, despondent, down inf,
down in the dumps inf, downcast,
downhearted, forlorn, gloomy, glum,
low, melancholy, mournful, sad,
sorrowful, unhappy, wretched;
opp cheerful. 2 churlish, contemptible,
cross, despicable, disagreeable, grumpy,
ill-natured, low, mean, sour, sulky,
sullen, surly, taciturn, unfriendly,
unhelpful, unsociable; opp pleasant.
3 (of a place) awful, dilapidated, filthy,
foul, seedy, shabby, sordid, sorry, squalid,
uncomfortable, wretched; opp luxurious

**misery** n 1 anguish, depression,
desolation, despair, despondency,
distress, gloom, grief, hardship,
heartache, hell inf, hopelessness,
melancholy, pain, sadness, sorrow,
suffering, torment, torture, unhappiness,
woe; opp happiness. 2 (an unfortunate
event) adversity, blow, hardship, load,
misfortune, ordeal, trial, tribulation,
trouble, woe; opp fortune

**misfire** v fail, fall through, flop, founder,
go amiss, go awry, go up in smoke, go
wrong

**misfit** n eccentric, fish out of water,
maverick, nonconformist, oddball inf,
square peg in a round hole, weirdo inf

**misfortune** n accident, adversity, bad
luck, blow, calamity, catastrophe,
disaster, hardship, harm, loss,
misadventure, mishap, setback, tragedy,
trial, tribulation, trouble, woe

**misguided** adj deluded, erroneous,
foolish, ill-advised, imprudent,
inappropriate, misled, misplaced,
mistaken, unreasonable, unsound,

unwise, wrong; **opp** well-advised

**misjudge** v be wrong about, get the wrong end of the stick, get the wrong idea, jump to the wrong conclusion, make a mistake, miscalculate, misconstrue, misinterpret, misread, overestimate, overrate, underestimate, underrate, undervalue

**mislay** v be unable to find, lose, lose track of, misplace, miss; **opp** find

**mislead** v beguile, bluff, confuse, deceive, delude, fool, give sb the wrong idea, give sb the wrong impression, hoodwink, lead sb up the garden path, misdirect, misguide, misinform, take sb for a ride, take sb in, throw sb off the scent, trick

**misleading** adj ambiguous, confusing, deceitful, deceptive, false, spurious, unreliable; **opp** clear

**miss** n blunder, botch, bungle, error, failure, fault, loss, mistake, omission, oversight, slip, slip-up

**miss** v **1** (miss a lesson) be too late for, forego, omit, play truant, skip inf, skive off inf. **2** (not include) fail to include, fail to mention, omit, overlook. **3** (narrowly miss being hit) avoid, dodge, escape, evade, side-step, steer clear of. **4** (miss a target) blunder, botch, bungle, err, fail, fall short, lose, slip up. **5** (miss a person) grieve for, lament, long for, need, pine for, want, yearn for

**misshapen** adj bent, contorted, crooked, crumpled, deformed, disfigured, distorted, gnarled, grotesque, knotted, malformed, out of shape, screwed up, tangled, twisted, warped

**missile** n bomb, grenade, projectile, rocket, shell, torpedo, weapon

**missing** adj absent, astray, gone, lost, mislaid, misplaced, nowhere to be found, unaccounted for; **opp** present

**mission** n **1** aim, assignment, charge, duty, function, goal, job, objective, purpose, task, undertaking, work. **2** delegation, deputation, task force

**missionary** n crusader, evangelist, minister, preacher, priest

**misspent** adj dissipated, misapplied, squandered, thrown away, wasted

**mist** n cloud, condensation, fog, haze, smog, spray, steam, vapour

**mistake** n blunder, boob inf, botch, clanger inf, error, fault, faux pas, gaffe, howler inf, inaccuracy, miscalculation, misjudgement, misprint, misspelling, misunderstanding, omission, oversight, slip, slip-up

**mistake** v **1** (mistake one thing for another) confuse, mix up, take sth for sth else. **2** (understand sth wrongly) get the wrong end of the stick, get wrong, misapprehend, misconstrue, misinterpret, misjudge, misread, misunderstand; **opp** understand

**mistaken** adj erroneous, false, inaccurate, incorrect, inexact, misguided, misinformed, wide of the mark, wrong; **opp** correct

**mistress** n concubine, fancy woman inf, girlfriend, kept woman, lover, paramour

**mistrust** v be sceptical, be suspicious, be unsure, be wary, disbelieve, doubt, fear, have doubts, have misgivings, have suspicions, question, suspect; **opp** trust

**misty** adj **1** (of weather) cloudy, foggy, hazy, murky; **opp** clear. **2** (of an image) bleary, blurred, dim, faint, fuzzy, indistinct, obscure, smoky, steamy, vague; *opp* distinct

**misunderstand** *v* be barking up the wrong tree *inf*, get the wrong end of the stick, get the wrong idea, get wrong, misapprehend, misconceive, misconstrue, mishear, misinterpret, misjudge, miss the point, mistake; *opp* understand

**misunderstanding** *n* error, misapprehension, misconception, misjudgement, misreading, mistake, mix-up

**misuse** *n* abuse, corruption, misapplication, squandering, waste

**mitigate** *v* allay, alleviate, appease, assuage, calm, check, decrease, diminish, dull, ease, extenuate, lessen, lighten, moderate, mollify, pacify, placate, quiet, reduce, relieve, soothe, subdue, take the edge off *inf*, temper, weaken; *opp* worsen

**mitigating** *adj* exonerating, extenuating, justifying, qualifying, vindicating

**mix** *n* amalgam, assortment, blend, combination, compound, mixture, range, union, variety

**mix** *v* 1 amalgamate, blend, coalesce, combine, cross, fuse, incorporate, intermingle, interweave, join, jumble up, merge, mingle, muddle, unite; *opp* separate. 2 (mix with people) associate, fraternize, go out with, hobnob, keep company, mingle, socialize. 3 mix up confuse, mistake, muddle up

**mixed** *adj* 1 (a mixed bunch) assorted, diverse, heterogeneous, miscellaneous, motley, varied; *opp* similar. 2 (mixed feelings) ambiguous, ambivalent,

confused, muddled, uncertain, unsure; *opp* clear-cut

**mixed-up** *adj* 1 at sea, bewildered, confused, muddled, perplexed, puzzled. 2 (a crazy mixed-up kid) disturbed, ill-adjusted, maladjusted, screwed-up *inf*; *opp* together

**mixture** *n* amalgam, amalgamation, association, blend, brew, collection, compound, cross, fusion, hotchpotch *inf*, medley, mélange, mishmash *inf*, mix, union, variety

**mix-up** *n* confusion, disorder, mistake, misunderstanding, muddle

**moan** *n* 1 (complaint) beef *inf*, complaint, grouch *inf*, grouse, grumble, whine, whinge *inf*; *opp* praise. 2 (a moan of pain) cry, groan, sigh, wail, whimper, whine

**moan** *v* 1 (complain) beef *inf*, carp, complain, grouch *inf*, grouse, grumble, whine, whinge *inf*. 2 (moan in pain) cry, groan, sigh, wail, whimper, whine

**mob** *n* body, bunch, collection, crowd, drove, flock, gang, gathering, herd, hoard, host, mass, pack, press, rabble, swarm, throng

**mob** *v* besiege, crowd, hem in, jostle, overrun, surround, swarm

**mobile** *adj* 1 (of an object) movable, portable, transportable; *opp* fixed. 2 (of people) itinerant, migrant, nomadic, peripatetic, travelling, wandering. 3 (of a face) animated, changeable, ever-changing, expressive, flexible; *opp* inexpressive

**mobilize** *v* activate, assemble, call up, gather, get together, marshal, muster, organize, prepare, rally, ready

**mock** adj artificial, bogus, counterfeit, dummy, fake, false, feigned, forged, imitation, pretend inf, sham, simulated, spurious; opp real

**mock** v deride, insult, jeer, laugh at, make fun of, parody, poke fun at, rib inf, ridicule, satirize, scoff, scorn, send up inf, sneer, take the mickey inf, taunt, tease, wind up inf

**mockery** n contempt, derision, disdain, jeering, laughter, mickey-taking inf, parody, ribbing inf, ridicule, satire, scoffing, scorn, sending up inf, sneering, taunting, teasing, wind-up inf

**model** adj 1 imitation, miniature, mock-up, replica. 2 (a model student) exemplary, ideal, perfect; opp terrible

**model** n 1 copy, facsimile, image, imitation, miniature, mock-up, replica, representation. 2 (a model of excellence) archetype, byword, epitome, example, ideal, paradigm, paragon, standard

**model** v v 1 carve, cast, design, fashion, form, mould, sculpt, shape. 2 (model clothes) display, show off, wear

**moderate** adj 1 average, light, limited, medium, middle, mild, steady, temperate. 2 (of a person) balanced, calm, cautious, cool, fair, gentle, middle-of-the-road, peaceable, reasonable, sober; opp extreme

**moderate** v 1 (become less) abate, calm, decrease, diminish, ease, lessen, lighten, reduce, weaken. 2 (make sth less) alleviate, appease, assuage, calm, check, pacify, placate, quiet, soothe, subdue, take the edge off inf

**moderation** n calmness, composure, control, coolness, fairness, justice, mildness, reasonableness, restraint, temperance

**modern** adj 1 avant-garde, contemporary, current, fresh, new, newfangled, novel, present, recent. 2 fashionable, in inf, in vogue, latest, modish, progressive, stylish, trendy inf, up to date, up to the minute, with it inf; opp old-fashioned

**modernize** v bring up to date, do up inf, refurbish, regenerate, rejuvenate, remake, renew, renovate, revamp, update

**modest** adj 1 bashful, coy, demure, diffident, discreet, humble, meek, quiet, reserved, restrained, reticent, retiring, self-effacing, shy, unassuming, unpretentious; opp brash. 2 (a modest amount) limited, medium, moderate, normal, ordinary, small; opp huge

**modesty** n bashfulness, coyness, demureness, diffidence, discretion, humility, meekness, quietness, reticence, self-effacement, shyness, unpretentiousness; opp brashness

**modification** n adaptation, adjustment, alteration, change, conversion, refinement, reorganization, revision, transformation, variation

**modify** v adapt, adjust, alter, change, convert, recast, refine, reorganize, revise, transform, vary

**moist** adj clammy, damp, dank, dewy, humid, runny, steamy, watery, wet; opp dry

**moisten** v damp, dampen, soak, sponge, spray, water, wet; opp dry

**moisture** n damp, dew, humidity, liquid, spray, water, wet, wetness; opp dryness

**molest** v 1 abuse, accost, assault, attack, ill-treat, interfere with, mistreat, rape. 2 annoy, badger, bother, bug *inf*, disturb, harass, harry, hassle, hector, interfere with, irk, irritate, persecute, pester, torment, upset, vex, worry

**moment** n 1 (in a moment) flash, instant, jiffy *inf*, minute, second, tick *inf*, twinkling of an eye *inf*. 2 (at that moment) instant, juncture, point, stage, time

**momentary** adj brief, ephemeral, fleeting, hasty, passing, quick, short, short-lived, transient, transitory; *opp* drawn-out

**momentum** n drive, energy, force, impulse, power, propulsion, push, thrust

**monarch** n emperor, empress, king, potentate, prince, princess, queen, ruler, sovereign

**monetary** adj budgetary, capital, cash, financial, fiscal

**money** n brass *inf*, bread *inf*, capital, cash, coin, currency, dosh *inf*, dough *inf*, finance, funds, income, lolly *inf*, means, resources, revenue, savings

**mongrel** n cross, cross-breed, hybrid, mixed breed; *opp* pure-bred

**monitor** n 1 (person) examiner, observer, overseer, prefect, supervisor, watchdog. 2 (device) detector, recorder, scanner, security camera

**monitor** v check, examine, follow, keep an eye on, keep track of, observe, oversee, record, supervise, survey, trace, track, watch

**monk** n abbot, brother, friar, hermit

**monkey** n 1 ape, primate, simian. 2 (you little monkey) devil, imp, rascal,

rogue, scamp, terror

**monopolize** v control, corner, dominate, hog *inf*, take over

**monotonous** adj boring, colourless, dreary, droning, dull, flat, humdrum, mindnumbing, plodding, repetitive, soporific, tedious, tiresome, toneless, unchanging, unexciting, uninteresting; *opp* exciting

**monster** n barbarian, beast, bogey-man, brute, demon, devil, fiend, ghoul, ogre, savage, troll, villain

**monstrosity** n carbuncle, eyesore, horror

**monstrous** adj 1 (a monstrous act) abhorrent, abominable, atrocious, awful, brutal, cruel, diabolical, disgraceful, evil, foul, heinous, horrific, horrifying, inhuman, intolerable, loathsome, odious, outrageous, repulsive, scandalous, shocking, vicious, vile, villainous. 2 (a monstrous building) colossal, enormous, giant, gigantic, great, huge, hulking, immense, mammoth, massive, mighty, prodigious, tremendous, vast; *opp* tiny

**monument** n cenotaph, gravestone, mausoleum, memorial, obelisk, relic, shrine, statue, tombstone

**monumental** adj 1 awe-inspiring, awesome, classic, enduring, exceptional, extraordinary, great, historic, immortal, important, impressive, lasting, memorable, outstanding, significant, unforgettable

**mood** n disposition, frame of mind, humour, inclination, spirit, temper

**moody** adj abrupt, bad-tempered, cantankerous, crabby, cross, crotchety, curt, doleful, dour, frowning, grumpy, huffy *inf*, ill-tempered, irritable, miserable, morose, petulant, sulky, sullen, temperamental, testy, touchy, unpredictable; *opp* cheerful

**moor** *v* anchor, berth, dock, fasten, fix, lash, secure, tie up

**moot** *adj* arguable, contestable, controversial, debatable, disputable, questionable; *opp* uncontroversial

**mope** *v* brood, despair, fret, grieve, languish, pine, sulk

**moral** *adj* decent, ethical, fair, good, honest, irreproachable, just, law-abiding, noble, principled, proper, pure, respectable, responsible, righteous, upright, upstanding, virtuous; *opp* immoral

**morale** *n* cheerfulness, confidence, determination, heart, hope, hopefulness, mettle, self-confidence, self-esteem, spirit, zeal

**morality** *n* decency, fairness, goodness, honesty, integrity, justice, principle, righteousness, uprightness, virtue; *opp* immorality

**moralize** *v* lecture, pontificate, preach

**morals** *n* ethics, ideals, manners, mores, principles, scruples, standards

**morbid** *adj* brooding, ghastly, ghoulish, gloomy, grim, grisly, gruesome, hideous, horrid, macabre, sick *inf*, sombre, unhealthy, unwholesome

**more** *adj* added, additional, extra, fresh, further, increased, new, other, renewed, spare, supplementary; *opp* less

**morose** *adj* bad-tempered, churlish, depressed, dour, gloomy, glum, grim, humourless, melancholy, moody, mournful, pessimistic, sombre, sour,

sulky, sullen, taciturn; *opp* cheerful

**morsel** *n* bit, bite, crumb, fragment, grain, mouthful, nibble, piece, scrap, segment, slice, titbit

**mortal** *adj* 1 earthly, ephemeral, fleshly, human, temporal, transient, worldly; *opp* immortal. 2 (a mortal injury) deadly, fatal, killing, lethal, terminal; *opp* minor

**mortality** *n* 1 earthliness, humanity, impermanence, transience, worldliness; *opp* immortality. 2 (infant mortality) deaths, dying, fatalities, loss of life

**mortified** *adj* ashamed, crushed, deflated, embarrassed, filled with shame, humiliated, shamed; *opp* proud

**mortify** *v* crush, deflate, embarrass, fill with shame, humiliate, put down, shame

**mostly** *adv* as a (general) rule, chiefly, commonly, customarily, for the most part, generally, in general, in the main, largely, mainly, normally, on the whole, ordinarily, particularly, predominantly, primarily, principally, typically, usually

**mother** *n* female parent, ma *inf*, mama, mom *Am inf*, mum *inf*, mummy *inf*, old lady *inf*

**mother** *v* care for, cherish, fuss over, indulge, look after, nourish, nurse, nurture, pamper, protect, raise, rear, spoil, take care of

**motherly** *adj* affectionate, caring, fond, kind, loving, maternal, nurturing, protective, tender, warm

**motion** *n* 1 action, activity, agitation, flow, move, movement, progress, shift, stirring, travel. 2 gesticulation, gesture, movement, signal, wave

**motion** *v* beckon, direct, gesticulate,

gesture, nod, signal, sign, wave

**motionless** *adj* at rest, frozen, halted, immobile, inert, lifeless, paralysed, static, stationary, still, stopped, unmoving; *opp* moving

**motivate** *v* activate, arouse, cause, drive, egg on, encourage, galvanize, goad, impel, incite, induce, influence, inspire, instigate, lead, move, persuade, prod, prompt, provoke, push, set, spur, stimulate, stir, urge

**motivated** *adj* ambitious, ardent, committed, dedicated, driven, eager, enthusiastic, fervent, galvanized, industrious, inspired, intent, keen

**motivation** *n* 1 (desire to do sth) ambition, desire, drive, eagerness, enthusiasm, fervour, hunger, inspiration, keenness. 2 (the thing that motivates sth) cause, encouragement, goading, incitement, inducement, inspiration, persuasion, prodding, prompting, pushing, spur

**motive** *n* basis, cause, grounds, incentive, inducement, influence, inspiration, intention, lure, motivation, occasion, prompting, provocation, purpose, push, rationale, reason, spur, stimulus

**motley** *adj* assorted, diverse, heterogeneous, ill-matched, mingled, miscellaneous, mixed, rag-bag, varied, various

**mottled** *adj* blotched, blotchy, dappled, flecked, freckled, marbled, marked, patchy, piebald, speckled, splotchy, spotted, stippled, streaked, variegated

**motto** *n* adage, catch-phrase, dictum, epigram, maxim, precept, proverb, rule, saying, slogan, watchword

**mould** *n* 1 (for making sth) cast, die, form, model, pattern, shape, stamp, template. 2 blight, fungus, growth, mildew, rot

**mould** *v* carve, cast, construct, fashion, forge, form, model, sculpt, shape, stamp, work

**mouldy** *adj* blighted, decayed, decaying, fusty, mildewed, mouldering, musty, rotten, rotting

**mound** *n* bank, dune, heap, hill, hillock, hummock, knoll, pile, rise, stack

**mount** *n* 1 backing, base, fixture, frame, setting, stand, support. 2 elevation, hill, mound, mountain, peak, summit

**mount** *v* 1 ascend, climb, go up, rise, scale. 2 climb on, get astride, get on, jump on. 3 (tension mounts) accumulate, build, escalate, expand, grow, increase, intensify, multiply, pile up, swell. 4 (mount an exhibition) display, exhibit, prepare, produce, put on, stage

**mountain** *n* alp, crest, elevation, height, mount, peak, pinnacle, range, sierra, summit

**mountainous** *adj* alpine, craggy, high, highland, rocky, rugged, soaring, steep, towering, upland

**mourn** *v* bemoan, bewail, cry for, feel the loss of, grieve, lament, miss, pine for, regret, sorrow, wail, weep

**mournful** *adj* depressing, dismal, distressing, doleful, gloomy, heart-breaking, heart-rending, melancholy, miserable, painful, piteous, pitiful, plaintive, sad, sorrowful, tragic, unhappy, woeful

**mouth** *n* 1 gob *sl*, jaws, lips, muzzle.

**2** aperture, door, entrance, gateway, inlet, opening, orifice, portal, way in

**mouthful** *n* bit, bite, drop, forkful, gulp, morsel, sample, sip, spoonful, swallow, taste

**movable** *adj* bendable, detachable, flexible, mobile, moving, plastic, portable, transportable; *opp* immovable

**move** *n* **1** action, agitation, change, motion, movement, shift, stirring. **2** act, action, deed, gambit, manoeuvre, measure, play, step, stratagem, stroke, tactic, turn. **3** change, relocation, shift, transfer

**move** *v* **1** (sth or sb moves) budge, change places, change position, go, shift, stir. **2** (move sth) carry, transport, shift, take. **3** (move forward) advance, go, head, journey, make headway, make progress, pass, proceed, travel. **4** (move house) go away, leave, migrate, move away, move house, relocate. **5** (make sb feel moved) affect, arouse, fire, impassion, incite, induce, inspire, lead, motivate, persuade, prompt, provoke, push, rouse, spur, stimulate, stir, touch

**movement** *n* **1** action, activity, advance, agitation, change, gesture, motion, move, progress, shift, stirring. **2** carrying, moving, shifting, transfer, transferral, transport, transportation. **3** campaign, coalition, crusade, drive, faction, front, group, lobby, organization, party, pressure group

**moving** *adj* **1** affecting, emotional, emotive, heart-rending, heart-warming, inspiring, pathetic, poignant, powerful, rousing, stirring, touching. **2** active, dynamic, in motion, mobile, movable

**mow** *v* **1** clip, crop, cut, scythe, shear, trim. **2** mow down butcher, cut down, massacre, slaughter, slay

**mud** *n* clay, dirt, mire, ooze, silt, slime, sludge, soil

**muddle** *n* chaos, clutter, confusion, disarray, disorder, jumble, mess, mix-up, shambles *inf*, tangle

**muddle** *v* **1** clutter, disarrange, disorder, disorganize, get sth mixed up, jumble, mess up, mix up, scramble, tangle. **2** bemuse, bewilder, confound, confuse, daze, disorient, disorientate, perplex, puzzle

**muddy** *adj* **1** caked, dirty, filthy, messy, mucky. **2** boggy, marshy, slimy, sludgy, soft, spongy, waterlogged

**muffle** *v* **1** cloak, cover, enfold, hood, shroud, swathe, wrap up. **2** (muffle a sound) dampen, deaden, disguise, dull, hush, mask, mute, quieten, silence, smother, soften, stifle, suppress

**muffled** *adj* dampened, deadened, dull, faint, hushed, indistinct, muted, smothered, stifled, suppressed, unclear

**mug** *n* beaker, cup, flagon, jug, pot, tankard

**mugger** *n* assailant, attacker, bag-snatcher, robber, thief, thug

**muggy** *adj* clammy, close, damp, humid, oppressive, steamy, sticky, stuffy, sultry

**multiple** *adj* collective, many, numerous, several, sundry, various

**multiply** *v* accumulate, breed, expand, extend, increase, proliferate, propagate, reproduce, spread

**multitude** *n* army, assembly, congregation, crowd, horde, host, legion, mass, mob, sea, swarm, throng

**mumble** v grumble, murmur, mutter, speak indistinctly

**munch** v champ, chew, chomp, crunch, eat, gnaw, masticate

**mundane** adj banal, commonplace, dull, everyday, humdrum, ordinary, pedestrian, prosaic, quotidian, routine, unexciting, uninteresting, workaday; *opp* extraordinary

**municipal** adj borough, city, civic, civil, community, district, local, metropolitan, public, town, urban

**murder** n assassination, bloodshed, butchery, carnage, homicide, killing, manslaughter, massacre, slaughter, slaying

**murder** v assassinate, bump off *inf*, butcher, destroy, dispatch, do away with *inf*, do in *inf*, kill, massacre, put to death, slaughter, slay

**murderer** n assassin, butcher, cut-throat, gunman, killer, slaughterer, slayer

**murderous** adj barbaric, barbarous, bloodthirsty, bloody, butchering, death-dealing, homicidal, massacring, psychopathic, savage, slaughtering

**murmur** n 1 (sound) buzz, drone, hum, rumble, rumbling. 2 (way of speaking) grumble, mumble, mumbling, mutter, muttering, undertone, whisper

**murmur** v breathe, grumble, mumble, mutter, purr, rumble, speak in an undertone, whisper

**muscle** n 1 biceps, ligament, sinew, tendon. 2 brawn, clout *inf*, force, might, potency, power, strength

**muscular** adj athletic, beefy *inf*, brawny, burly, hefty, hunky *inf*, lusty, mighty, powerful, robust, sinewy, stalwart, strapping, strong, sturdy, tough, vigorous, well-built

**muse** v brood, cogitate, consider, contemplate, daydream, deliberate, dream, meditate, mull over, ponder, reflect, ruminate, speculate, think, weigh, wonder

**musical** adj dulcet, harmonious, lilting, melodic, melodious, sweet-sounding, tuneful

**muster** v assemble, call up, collect, congregate, convene, gather, group, marshal, mobilize, rally, round up, summon

**musty** adj airless, damp, dank, decaying, fusty, mildewed, mouldy, smelly, stale, stuffy, unused

**mutation** n alteration, change, evolution, metamorphosis, modification, transformation, transmutation, variation

**mute** adj dumb, silent, speechless, unspoken, voiceless, wordless

**mutilate** v butcher, cripple, damage, deface, disable, disfigure, dismember, hack, lame, maim, mangle

**mutinous** adj defiant, disobedient, insubordinate, rebellious, restive, revolutionary, riotous, seditious, subversive, uncontrollable, ungovernable, unmanageable, unruly

**mutiny** n defiance, disobedience, insubordination, insurgence, insurrection, rebellion, resistance, revolt, revolution, riot, rising, sedition, subversion, uprising

**mutiny** v defy, disobey, rebel, resist, revolt, riot, rise up

**mutter** v complain, grumble, mumble, murmur, rumble, talk under your breath

**mutual** *adj* common, joint, reciprocal, reciprocated, requited, returned, shared

**muzzle** *v* censor, curb, gag, restrain, silence, stifle, suppress

**mysterious** *adj* abstruse, arcane, baffling, bizarre, cryptic, curious, dark, enigmatic, furtive, hidden, impenetrable, inexplicable, inscrutable, mystifying, obscure, perplexing, puzzling, secret, strange, uncanny, unexplained, unfathomable, unknown, weird

**mystery** *n* conundrum, enigma, paradox, problem, puzzle, riddle, secret

**mystical** *adj* arcane, hidden, metaphysical, mysterious, occult, otherworldly, paranormal, preternatural, spiritual, supernatural, transcendental

**mystify** *v* baffle, bemuse, bewilder, confound, confuse, elude, escape, flummox, nonplus, perplex, puzzle, stump *inf*

**myth** *n* 1 allegory, fable, fairy-tale, legend, parable, saga, story, tale. 2 delusion, fabrication, falsehood, fiction, figment of sb's imagination, invention, misconception, untruth

**mythical** *adj* 1 allegorical, fabled, fabulous, fairy-tale, fantastical, legendary, mythic, mythological. 2 fabricated, false, fantasy, imaginary, invented, made-up, non-existent, pretended, unreal, untrue

**nadir** *n* bottom, depths, low point, rock bottom

**nag** *n* harpy, pest, scold, shrew, virago

**nag** *v* annoy, badger, be on sb's back *inf*, carp, chivvy, goad, go on at *inf*, harass, harp on at, hassle *inf*, hector, henpeck, pester, plague, worry

**nagging** *adj* continuous, ever-present, irritating, painful, persistent, worrying

**nail** *v* attach, fasten, fix, hammer, join, pin, secure, tack

**naïve** *adj* artless, childlike, credulous, green *inf*, guileless, gullible, inexperienced, ingenuous, innocent, open, simple, trusting, unsophisticated, unsuspicious, unwary, unworldly; *opp* knowing

**naked** *adj* bare, exposed, in your birthday suit *inf*, in the altogether *inf*, in the buff *inf*, in the nude, in the raw *inf*, nude, starkers *inf*, stark-naked, stripped, unclothed, uncovered, undressed; *opp* clothed, dressed

**name** *n* 1 appellation, epithet, label, nickname, tag, term, title. 2 (make your name in sth) distinction, eminence, esteem, fame, honour, note, prestige, prominence, reputation, repute, renown

**name** *v* 1 baptize, call, christen, designate, dub, entitle, label, nickname, style, tag, term. 2 (name a new chairman) appoint, choose, commission, delegate, designate, elect, identify, nominate, pick, select, specify

**nameless** *adj* 1 anonymous, incognito, obscure, unidentified, unknown, unsung. 2 abominable, appalling, dreadful, horrible, indescribable, unmentionable, unspeakable, unutterable

**nap** *n* doze, forty winks *inf*, kip *inf*, rest, siesta, sleep, snooze *inf*

**nap** *v* doze, drowse, have a nap, kip *inf*, nod off *inf*, rest, sleep, snooze *inf*

**narrate** *v* chronicle, describe, detail, recite, recount, rehearse, relate, repeat, report, tell, unfold

**narration** *n* commentary, description, explanation, reading, recital, relation, reporting, story-telling, telling

**narrative** *n* account, chronicle, description, history, report, statement, story, tale

**narrator** *n* author, chronicler, commentator, reporter, story-teller, writer

**narrow** *adj* close, confined, cramped, fine, limited, meagre, pinched, restricted, scanty, slender, slim, squeezed, straitened, thin, tight; *opp* wide

**narrow** *v* diminish, limit, reduce, shrink, straiten, tighten; *opp* widen

**narrow-minded** *adj* biased, bigoted, conservative, hidebound, inflexible, insular, intolerant, mean-spirited, old-fashioned, parochial, petty, prejudiced, reactionary, rigid, small-minded, strait-laced; *opp* broad-minded

**nasty** *adj* **1** awful, disgusting, filthy, foul, horrible, horrid, nauseating, odious, repellent, repugnant, repulsive, revolting, sickening, unpleasant, vile, yucky *inf*; *opp* nice. **2** (be nasty to sb) bitchy *sl*, catty, cruel, disagreeable, horrible, horrid, malicious, mean, spiteful, unkind, unpleasant, vicious; *opp* nice

**nation** *n* country, domain, kingdom, land, people, population, power, realm, republic, society, state

**national** *adj* **1** (not local) countrywide, federal, general, nationwide. **2** (not international) domestic, internal, patriotic, popular

**nationalism** *n* chauvinism, jingoism, loyalty, patriotism, xenophobia

**native** *adj* **1** (native to a place) aboriginal, domestic, indigenous, local, original. **2** (native intelligence) congenital, hereditary, inborn, inbred, inherited, innate, instinctive, intuitive, natural

**native** *n* citizen, countryman, dweller, inhabitant, local, resident

**natter** *v* chat, chatter, chin-wag *inf*, chit-chat *inf*, gab *inf*, gossip, jaw *inf*, prattle, rabbit on *inf*, talk

**natural** *adj* **1** authentic, genuine, real, sincere, spontaneous, unaffected, unfeigned; *opp* artificial. **2** (normal) common, logical, ordinary, normal, predictable, regular, routine, standard, typical, understandable, unsurprising, usual; *opp* unnatural. **3** (a natural ability) characteristic, congenital, god-given, hereditary, inborn, inbred, inherited, innate, instinctive, intuitive, native; *opp* learned

**naturally** *adv* **1** (behave naturally) candidly, ingenuously, unpretentiously. **2** as you would expect, certainly, of course

**nature** *n* **1** ecology, landscape, Mother Nature, natural history, scenery, the countryside, the earth, the environment, the universe, the world, wildlife. **2** (sth of that nature) description, kind, sort, species, style, type, variety. **3** (sb's nature) character, disposition, make-up, mood, outlook, personality, temperament, traits. **4** (the nature of a thing) character, essence, features, properties, quality

**naughty** *adj* bad, badly-behaved, defiant, delinquent, disobedient, disruptive, impolite, mischievous, rascally, rude, stubborn, undisciplined, unmanageable, unruly, wicked, wilful

**nausea** *n* **1** biliousness, faintness, queasiness, seasickness, sickness, vomiting. **2** disgust, loathing, repugnance, revulsion

**nauseate** *v* disgust, horrify, make sb sick, make sb want to throw up *inf*, offend, repel, repulse, revolt, sicken, turn sb's stomach

**nautical** *adj* boating, marine, maritime, naval, sailing, seafaring, seagoing, yachting

**navigate** *v* **1** cross, cruise, journey, sail, sail across, voyage. **2** (navigate a ship) captain, drive, handle, manoeuvre, pilot, skipper, steer. **3** (find the way) direct, find the way, guide, map-read, plan the route

**navigation** n **1** directing, manoeuvring, steering. **2** (the skills of navigation) map-reading, sailing, seamanship

**navigator** n helmsman, mariner, pilot, seaman

**navy** n armada, convoy, fleet, flotilla

**near** adj **1** (near in space) accessible, adjacent, adjoining, at close quarters, beside, bordering, close, close by, connected, handy, nearby, neighbouring, next-door, touching, within reach. **2** (near in time) approaching, coming, forthcoming, imminent, impending, in the offing, looming, next, round the corner inf

**nearly** adv about, all but, almost, approaching, approximately, around, as good as, just about, not quite, practically, roughly, virtually

**neat** adj **1** accurate, clean, dapper, fastidious, methodical, meticulous, orderly, organized, precise, shipshape, smart, spick and span, spruce, straight, systematic, tidy, trim, uncluttered, well-groomed, well-kept, well-turned-out; **opp** untidy. **2** (neat movements) agile, dainty, deft, dexterous, elegant, graceful, nimble, practised, precise, skilful, stylish; **opp** clumsy. **3** (neat whisky) pure, straight, undiluted

**necessary** adj compulsory, essential, imperative, important, indispensable, mandatory, needed, obligatory, required, vital

**necessitate** v call for, demand, entail, involve, make necessary, require

**necessity** n (sth is a necessity) essential, must inf, need, prerequisite, requirement

**need** n **1** (need for affection) desire, lack, longing, shortage, wish, yearning. **2** (children in need) deprivation, destitution, distress, poverty. **3** (the need to do sth) call, necessity, obligation. **4** (a basic human need) demand, essential, requirement, want

**need** v **1** (need sth) be short of, be without, call for, demand, lack, require, want. **2** (need sb) depend on, desire, miss, rely on, want. **3** (need to do sth) be compelled, be obliged, have to

**needless** adj excessive, gratuitous, groundless, pointless, redundant, superfluous, uncalled for, unnecessary, unwanted

**needy** adj badly off, deprived, destitute, disadvantaged, hard up inf, penniless, poor, poverty-stricken, underprivileged

**negate** v cancel, contradict, deny, disprove, invalidate, neutralize, oppose, repeal, reverse, revoke, wipe out

**negative** adj **1** (negative outlook) complaining, cynical, gloomy, jaundiced, pessimistic, unenthusiastic, unhelpful; **opp** positive. **2** (saying no) anti inf, contradicting, contradictory, contrary, denying, disagreeing, opposing, refusing, resisting

**neglect** n carelessness, forgetfulness, inattention, indifference, lack of concern, negligence

**neglect** v **1** (leave sb or sth) abandon, forget, forsake, ignore, leave alone, pay no attention to. **2** (neglect to do sth) fail, forget, not remember, omit, overlook, shirk, skimp, skip

**neglected** adj 1 (of a place) abandoned, derelict, forgotten, overgrown, run-down. 2 (of a child) abandoned, ignored, left alone, mistreated, uncared for

**negligent** adj careless, forgetful, irresponsible, neglectful, reckless, remiss, slack, slapdash, sloppy, thoughtless, unthinking; **opp** careful

**negligible** adj inconsequential, insignificant, minor, petty, slight, small, tiny, trifling, trivial, unimportant

**negotiate** v agree, bargain, deal, discuss, haggle, hold talks, settle, work out

**negotiation** n arbitration, bargaining, diplomacy, discussion, mediation, talks

**neighbourhood** n area, community, district, locality, part, place, region, vicinity, zone

**neighbouring** adj adjacent, adjoining, bordering, close, closest, near, nearby, nearest, next, next-door, surrounding

**neighbourly** adj amiable, friendly, helpful, hospitable, kind, obliging, sociable

**nerve** n 1 (bravery) bottle inf, bravery, coolness, courage, daring, determination, fearlessness, guts inf, resolve, spirit, will-power. 2 (cheek) audacity, brazenness, cheek, impertinence, impudence, insolence, presumptuousness, rudeness

**nerve-racking** adj anxious, difficult, distressing, frightening, harrowing, nail-biting inf, stressful, tense, worrying

**nerves** n anxiety, butterflies in your stomach inf, jitters inf, nervousness, strain, stress, tension

**nervous** adj afraid, agitated, anxious, apprehensive, edgy, fearful, highly strung, impatient, insecure, jumpy, on edge, on tenterhooks inf, restless, shaky, strained, tense, timid, trembling, uneasy, unnerved, uptight inf, worried; **opp** calm

**nestle** v cuddle, curl up, huddle, nuzzle, snuggle

**net** n lattice, mesh, netting, web

**net** v capture, catch, enmesh, entangle, snare, trap

**network** n 1 criss-cross inf, grid, labyrinth, lattice, maze, mesh, net, tangle, web. 2 arrangement, interconnection, organization, structure, system

**neurosis** n anxiety, depression, fixation, obsession, phobia

**neurotic** adj anxious, compulsive, disturbed, mentally ill, nervous, obsessive, overwrought, unstable

**neuter** v castrate, geld, spay, sterilize

**neutral** adj 1 (neutral in an argument) disinterested, fair, impartial, objective, open-minded, unbiased, uncommitted, undecided, uninvolved, unprejudiced. 2 (neutral colours) colourless, dull, indeterminate, pale, vague

**neutralize** v cancel, cancel out, compensate for, counteract, make ineffective, negate, undo, wipe out

**never-ending** adj boundless, constant, continual, endless, eternal, everlasting, incessant, infinite, limitless, non-stop, perpetual, relentless, unbroken, uninterrupted, without end

**new** adj advanced, brand-new, contemporary, current, different, fashionable, fresh, futuristic, latest, modern, newfangled, novel, original, recent, revolutionary, state-of-the-art, topical, trendy *inf*, unfamiliar, unknown, unused, unusual, up-to-date; *opp* old

**newcomer** *n* immigrant, new arrival, outsider, settler, stranger

**newfangled** *adj* gimmicky, modern, new, novel, state-of-the-art, ultra-modern

**news** *n* 1 (a news report) announcement, bulletin, dispatch, exposé, facts, headlines, leak, release, report, statement, story. 2 (catching up on the news) gossip, information, rumour, scandal, talk, the latest *inf*, tittle-tattle, word

**newspaper** *n* broadsheet, daily *inf*, gazette, journal, paper, rag *inf*, tabloid, weekly

**next** *adv* after, afterwards, later, subsequently, then

**nibble** *v* bite, eat, gnaw, munch, nip, peck at, pick at, snack on *inf*

**nibble** *n* bite, crumb, morsel, piece, snack, taste

**nice** *adj* 1 (of a person) agreeable, amiable, charming, courteous, friendly, kind, likeable, pleasant, polite, understanding; *opp* horrible, nasty. 2 (of the weather) dry, fine, pleasant, sunny, warm; *opp* awful, dreadful. 3 (a nice time) enjoyable, exciting, good, interesting, marvellous, pleasant, pleasurable; *opp* awful, horrible. 4 (of behaviour) appropriate, cultivated, polite, proper, refined, respectable, seemly; *opp* bad

**niche** *n* alcove, corner, cranny, hollow, nook, opening, recess

**nick** *n* chip, cut, dent, mark, notch, scratch

**nick** *v* 1 (nick the edge of sth) chip, cut, mark, notch, scratch. 2 (steal) filch, lift, pilfer, pinch, pocket, shoplift, steal, swipe, take, walk off with

**nickname** *n* alias, family name, pet name

**niggle** *n* complaint, concern, misgiving, objection, worry

**niggle** *v* 1 criticize, find fault, fuss, nag, nit-pick *inf*. 2 (sth niggles you) annoy, irritate, rankle, trouble, worry

**niggling** *adj* 1 finicky, fussy, nit-picking *inf*, picky *inf*. 2 insignificant, minor, petty, trifling, unimportant. 3 (niggling doubts) gnawing, irritating, persistent, troubling, worrying

**night** *n* dark, darkness, night-time

**nightfall** *n* dusk, evening, sundown, sunset, twilight

**nimble** *adj* acrobatic, active, agile, deft, graceful, lithe, lively, quick, skilful, sprightly, spry

**nip** *n* 1 bite, nibble, pinch, tweak. 2 (nip of whisky) dram, draught, drop, sip, taste

**nip** *v* 1 catch, clip, grip, hurt, pinch, snag, squeeze, tweak, twitch. 2 bite, sink your teeth into, snap at

**nobility** *n* aristocracy, elite, gentry, high society, lords, nobles, peerage, peers, upper class

**noble** *adj* 1 (of noble birth) aristocratic, blue-blooded, born with a silver spoon in your mouth, distinguished, highborn, princely, titled, upper-class. 2 (a noble gesture) brave, gallant, generous, heroic, honourable, magnanimous, self-sacrificing, virtuous, worthy. 3 (a noble oak tree) awesome, great, imposing, impressive, splendid

**noble** n aristocrat, lady, lord, nobleman, noblewoman, peer

**nocturnal** adj night, nightly, night-time

**nod** v 1 bob your head, bow your head, incline your head. 2 (as a signal) gesture, indicate, motion, sign, signal. **3 nod off** doze, drop off, drowse, fall asleep, nap, nod off, slumber

**noise** n babble, blare, cacophony, clamour, clatter, commotion, din, hubbub, hullabaloo inf, racket, row, screaming, shouting, sound, talk, uproar

**noiseless** adj hushed, inaudible, mute, muted, quiet, silent, soft, soundless, still; *opp* noisy

**noisy** adj blaring, blasting, boisterous, deafening, ear-splitting, loud, piercing, raucous, riotous, rowdy; *opp* quiet, silent

**nomad** n migrant, rambler, roamer, rover, traveller, wanderer

**nomadic** adj migrant, roaming, roving, travelling, wandering

**nominal** adj 1 (the nominal leader of the country) formal, in name only, ostensible, puppet, self-styled, so-called, supposed. 2 (a nominal fee) minimal, minor, small, symbolic, token; *opp* large

**nominate** v appoint, assign, choose, designate, elect, name, propose, put forward, put up inf, recommend, select, submit

**nonchalant** adj blasé, calm, casual, composed, cool, indifferent, laid-back inf, offhand, self-possessed, unconcerned, unemotional; *opp* tense, uptight

**noncommittal** adj careful, cautious, discreet, evasive, giving nothing away, guarded, neutral, tactful, unrevealing, vague, wary

**non compos mentis** adj crazy, insane, mad, mentally ill, mentally unbalanced, of unsound mind

**nondescript** adj characterless, dull, featureless, indeterminate, ordinary, undistinguished, uninteresting, unmemorable, unremarkable; *opp* special

**nonentity** n lightweight inf, nobody, nothing inf, person of no account

**non-existent** adj fancied, fanciful, fantasy, fictional, fictitious, hypothetical, illusory, imaginary, imagined, legendary, made-up, mythical, unreal; *opp* real

**nonplussed** adj astonished, astounded, amazed, baffled, disconcerted, dumbfounded, flummoxed, mystified, speechless, stunned, taken aback

**nonsense** n 1 balderdash, baloney inf, claptrap inf, codswallop inf, double Dutch inf, drivel, gibberish, gobbledegook inf, hogwash inf, piffle sl, poppycock inf, rubbish, stuff and nonsense, twaddle. 2 clowning, foolishness, idiocy, joking, madness, silliness, stupidity

**non-stop** adj ceaseless, constant, continuous, endless, incessant, never-ending, steady, unbroken, unending, uninterrupted

**norm** n average, benchmark, mean, measure, par, pattern, rule, scale, standard, type, yardstick

**normal** adj accepted, average, common, customary, established, everyday, familiar, general, natural, ordinary, predictable, regular, routine, run-of-the mill inf, standard, typical, usual; *opp* abnormal

**normality** *n* naturalness, ordinariness, regularity, routine, usualness

**normally** *adv* as a rule, as usual, commonly, in general, mostly, naturally, ordinarily, regularly, routinely, typically, usually

**nose** *v* 1 detect, scent, smell out, sniff out. 2 interfere, look around, meddle, poke your nose in *inf*, pry, search, snoop *inf*

**nostalgia** *n* homesickness, longing, memory, pining, regret, reminiscence, sentiment, sentimentality, wistfulness, yearning

**nostalgic** *adj* emotional, homesick, longing, pining, regretful, remembering, romantic, sentimental, wistful, yearning

**nosy** *adj* curious, eavesdropping, inquisitive, interfering, intrusive, meddlesome, prying, snooping *inf*

**notable** *adj* 1 extraordinary, famous, impressive, memorable, noteworthy, noticeable, obvious, outstanding, rare, remarkable, singular, uncommon, unforgettable, unusual. 2 celebrated, distinguished, eminent, famous, great, noted, prominent, renowned, well-known

**notation** *n* characters, code, script, signs, symbols, system

**note** *n* 1 comment, correspondence, explanation, footnote, inscription, jotting, letter, memo *inf*, memorandum, message, minute, record, reference, reminder. 2 (a note of sarcasm in his voice) element, feeling, hint, intonation, quality, tone

**note** *v* detect, enter, indicate, jot down, make a note, mark, mention, notice, observe, record, register, remark, see, take note, take notice, write down

**noted** *adj* acclaimed, celebrated, distinguished, eminent, famous, great, illustrious, notable, of note, prominent, recognized, renowned, well-known

**noteworthy** *adj* exceptional, extraordinary, important, rare, remarkable, significant, striking, unique, unusual; *opp* ordinary

**nothing** *n* 1 nil, nought, zero. 2 vacuum, void, blankness, naught, not anything, not a thing, nothingness, zilch *inf*

**notice** *n* 1 (a notice on the notice-board) advertisement, announcement, bulletin, handout, leaflet, message, note, poster, sign, warning. 2 (come to sb's notice) attention, awareness, consciousness, observation, regard. 3 (receive notice of sth) advice, information, news, notification, warning. 4 (be given your notice) dismissal, marching orders *inf*, redundancy, the boot *inf*, the push *inf*, the sack *inf*, your cards *inf*

**notice** *v* be aware, detect, discern, discover, distinguish, feel, find, make out, note, observe, pay attention, perceive, register, see, spot, take note

**noticeable** *adj* apparent, clear, conspicuous, discernible, distinct, evident, marked, obvious, plain, prominent, pronounced, salient, striking, unmistakable, visible

**notify** *v* advise, declare, inform, let sb know, make known, proclaim, publish, report, tell, warn

**notion** *n* assumption, belief, concept, idea, impression, opinion, theory, thought, understanding, view

**notional** *adj* abstract, conceptual, hypothetical, illusory, imaginary, theoretical, unreal

**notoriety** *n* bad reputation, dishonour, disrepute, ill repute, infamy, scandal

**notorious** *adj* disgraceful, dishonourable, disreputable, ill-famed, infamous, of ill repute, outrageous, scandalous, well-known

**nought** *n* naught, nil, nothing, zero

**nourish** *v* care for, feed, maintain, nurture, provide for, strengthen, support, sustain

**nourishing** *adj* good for you, healthy, nutritious, sustaining, wholesome

**nourishment** *n* diet, food, goodness, nutrition, sustenance

**novel** *adj* different, fresh, ground-breaking, imaginative, innovative, new, original, trail-blazing, uncommon, unconventional, unfamiliar, unique, unusual; *opp* old

**novel** *n* best-seller, book, fiction, narrative, romance, story, work of fiction

**novelty** *n* **1** (the novelty of his plan) difference, freshness, newness, originality, strangeness, unusualness. **2** (cheap novelties) curiosity, gadget, gimmick, knick-knack, memento, souvenir, trinket

**novice** *n* amateur, apprentice, beginner, learner, newcomer, new recruit, probationer, pupil, rookie *inf*, student, trainee

**now** *adv* at once, at present, at the moment, for the time being, immediately, instantly, just now, nowadays, promptly, right away, right now, straightaway; *opp* later

**nowadays** *adv* any more, at present, at the moment, in this day and age, now, these days, today

**noxious** *adj* corrosive, foul, harmful, nasty, poisonous, polluting, toxic, unhealthy, unwholesome; *opp* harmless

**nucleus** *n* centre, core, heart, kernel, middle, nub

**nude** *adj* bare, exposed, in your birthday suit *inf*, in the altogether *inf*, in the buff *inf*, naked, in the raw *inf*, starkers *inf*, stark naked, stripped, unclothed, uncovered, undressed; *opp* clothed, dressed

**nudge** *v* bump, dig, dig sb in the ribs, elbow, jog, poke, prod, push, shove, touch

**nuisance** *n* annoyance, bore, bother, drag *inf*, hassle *inf*, inconvenience, irritation, pain *inf*, problem, trouble, worry

**nullify** *v* abolish, annul, cancel, declare null and void, do away with, invalidate, negate, neutralize, quash, repeal, revoke, set aside

**numb** *adj* anaesthetized, asleep *inf*, cold, dead, deadened, frozen, paralysed, stunned, stupefied, without feeling

**numb** *v* anaesthetize, deaden, desensitize, dull, freeze, immobilize, make numb, paralyse

**number** *n* **1** digit, figure, integer, numeral, unit. **2** (of a magazine) copy, edition, imprint, issue, printing

**number** *v* add up, calculate, compute, count, reckon, total, work out

**numberless** *adj* countless, endless, infinite, innumerable, many, more than you can count, myriad, numerous, untold

**numeral** *n* Arabic numeral, character, digit, figure, integer, number, Roman numeral, symbol

**numerous** *adj* abundant, copious, countless, lots *inf*, many, multitudinous, myriad, plentiful, several, untold, various; *opp* few

**nurse** *v* care for, look after, minister to, take care of, tend, treat

**nurture** *v* bring up, cultivate, educate, feed, nourish, nurse, provide for, rear, sustain, tend, train

**nut** *n* 1 kernel, pip, seed, stone.
2 crackpot *inf*, crank *inf*, eccentric, loony *inf*, lunatic, madman, maniac, nutcase *inf*, nutter *inf*, psycho *sl*, psychopath, weirdo *inf*

**nutritious** *adj* good for you, health-giving, healthy, nourishing, wholesome

**oasis** *n* 1 spring, watering-hole, well.
2 haven, hiding-place, island, refuge,
retreat, sanctuary

**oath** *n* 1 (oath of allegiance) affirmation,
avowal, bond, pledge, promise, sworn
statement, undertaking, vow, word of
honour. 2 blasphemy, curse, expletive,
obscenity, profanity, swearword

**obedient** *adj* acquiescent, amenable,
compliant, docile, dutiful, law-abiding,
manageable, respectful, submissive, well-
behaved, well-trained; *opp* disobedient

**obese** *adj* corpulent, fat, fleshy, heavy,
overweight, podgy, portly, stout, tubby;
*opp* thin

**obey** *v* 1 (obey a rule) abide by, accept,
adhere to, agree to, comply with, follow,
keep, observe, respect, stick to *inf.*
2 (obey sb) be obedient to, be ruled by,
bow to, defer to, heed, honour, submit
to, take orders from, yield to. 3 (you
must obey) be dutiful, be obedient, do
what you are told, follow orders. 4 (obey
the instructions) act upon, carry out,
fulfil, perform

**object** *n* 1 (a useful object) article, item,
thing. 2 (the object of the game) aim,
goal, idea, intention, motive, objective,
point, purpose, reason. 3 (the object of
abuse/frustration) butt, focus, recipient,
target, victim

**object** *v* argue, beg to differ, be opposed,
complain, grumble, mind *inf*, oppose,
protest, raise objections, take a stand
against, take exception to

**objection** *n* argument, challenge,
complaint, disapproval, dissatisfaction,
doubt, grievance, opposition, protest,
query, quibble

**objectionable** *adj* abhorrent, deplorable,
disgusting, distasteful, foul, horrible,
insufferable, intolerable, nasty,
obnoxious, offensive, repugnant,
revolting, unacceptable, undesirable,
unpleasant, vile

**objective** *n* aim, ambition, aspiration,
design, desire, end, goal, hope, intent,
intention, object, plan, point, purpose,
target

**objective** *adj* detached, disinterested,
dispassionate, even-handed, fair,
impartial, just, neutral, open-minded,
rational, unbiased, unemotional,
uninvolved, unprejudiced; *opp* biased

**obligation** *n* commitment, compulsion,
constraint, demand, duty, liability,
necessity, need, requirement,
responsibility

**obligatory** *adj* binding, compulsory,
essential, imperative, mandatory,
necessary, required, unavoidable;
*opp* optional, voluntary

**oblige** v 1 (make sb do sth) bind, coerce, compel, constrain, force, leave sb no choice, make, put sb under an obligation, require. 2 (do sb a favour) accommodate, help, indulge, please, serve

**obliged** adj 1 (feel obliged to sb) appreciative, grateful, indebted, thankful. 2 (obliged to do sth) bound, compelled, constrained, duty-bound, forced, made, required

**obliging** adj agreeable, amiable, considerate, co-operative, courteous, eager to please, friendly, generous, good-natured, helpful, kind, polite, willing; *opp* difficult, unhelpful

**oblique** adj 1 (oblique line) angled, aslant, at an angle, diagonal, inclined, slanted, slanting, sloped, sloping. 2 (oblique mention) back-handed, implicit, implied, indirect, roundabout; *opp* direct

**obliterate** v blot out, cancel, delete, demolish, destroy, efface, eradicate, erase, leave no trace, remove, rub out, wipe out

**oblivion** n 1 absent-mindedness, abstraction, amnesia, forgetfulness, unawareness, unconsciousness. 2 (consigned to oblivion) anonymity, disuse, extinction, neglect, obscurity. 3 blackness, darkness, senselessness, stupor, unconsciousness

**oblivious** adj absent-minded, absorbed, blind, careless, deaf, forgetful, heedless, ignorant, neglectful, regardless, unaware, unconcerned, unheeding; *opp* aware

**obnoxious** adj disgusting, foul, horrid, insufferable, loathsome, nasty,

nauseating, objectionable, odious, offensive, repellent, repugnant, repulsive, revolting, unpleasant; *opp* nice, pleasant

**obscene** adj blue, coarse, crude, depraved, dirty, disgusting, filthy, foul, foul-mouthed, immoral, indecent, lewd, offensive, perverted, pornographic, rude, shocking, sick *inf*, suggestive, vulgar

**obscenity** n 1 (shout an obscenity) curse, dirty word, expletive, four-letter word, naughty word, swearword. 2 (prosecuted for obscenity) blasphemy, evil, filth, immorality, indecency, lewdness, offensiveness, perversion, pornography, vulgarity

**obscure** adj 1 (not obvious) ambiguous, concealed, confusing, cryptic, deep, enigmatic, hidden, mysterious, puzzling, secret, unclear; *opp* obvious. 2 (not clear) blurred, cloudy, dark, dim, faint, fuzzy, gloomy, hazy, indistinct, masked, misty, murky, shadowy, shady, shrouded, unlit, vague; *opp* clear, distinct. 3 (not known about) forgotten, hidden, insignificant, remote, undistinguished, unheard-of, unknown

**obscure** v block, blur, cloak, cloud, conceal, cover, darken, dim, disguise, eclipse, hide, mask, overshadow, screen, shade, shroud, veil

**observant** adj alert, attentive, aware, eagle-eyed, having your eyes peeled, on the ball *inf*, on the lookout, perceptive, sharp, sharp-eyed, vigilant, watchful; *opp* unobservant

**observation** n 1 (watching sth or sb) attention, examination, inspection, monitoring, review, scrutiny, study,

surveillance, watch, watching. **2** (sth
that you notice) conclusion, finding,
information, result. **3** (sth that you say
or write) comment, opinion, reflection,
remark, statement, thought

**observe** *v* **1** (notice) detect, discern,
discover, note, notice, perceive, see,
spot, witness. **2** (observe sth or sb)
check out *inf*, keep an eye on *inf*, keep
tabs on *inf*, keep under observation, keep
under surveillance, monitor, scrutinize,
spy on, stare at, study, view, watch.
**3** (observe a religious custom) celebrate,
follow, honour, keep, mark, obey,
remember. **4** (make an observation)
announce, comment, mention,
remark, say

**observer** *n* bystander, commentator, eyewitness, looker-on, onlooker, spectator,
viewer, watcher, witness

**obsess** *v* become an obsession, be on your
mind, consume, control, dominate, grip,
haunt, plague, possess, preoccupy, prey
on, take hold of, torment

**obsessed** *adj* gripped, haunted, hung up
on *inf*, in the grip of, preoccupied

**obsession** *n* addiction, bee in your
bonnet *inf*, complex, compulsion, fetish,
fixation, hang-up *inf*, infatuation, mania,
phobia, preoccupation, thing *inf*

**obsessive** *adj* addictive, compulsive,
consuming, gripping, passionate

**obsolete** *adj* antiquated, antique, archaic,
bygone, dated, discarded, extinct, old,
old-fashioned, outmoded, out of date,
passé, unfashionable

**obstacle** *n* bar, barrier, block, blockage,
check, difficulty, hindrance, hitch,
hurdle, interruption, obstruction,

problem, snag, stumbling-block

**obstinate** *adj* defiant, determined,
dogged, firm, headstrong, inflexible,
persistent, pigheaded, self-willed, single-
minded, stubborn, tenacious,
unbending, unreasonable, wilful

**obstreperous** *adj* boisterous, disorderly,
loud, naughty, noisy, out of control, out
of hand, rampaging, rough, rowdy,
stroppy *inf*, uncontrolled, undisciplined,
unruly, wild

**obstruct** *v* block, bring to a standstill,
bung, check, choke, clog, curb, cut off,
delay, frustrate, halt, hamper, hinder,
hold up, impede, interrupt, prevent,
restrict, shut off, slow, stop, thwart

**obstruction** *n* bar, barrier, block,
blockage, deterrent, hurdle, obstacle,
restriction, snag, stumbling-block

**obstructive** *adj* awkward, difficult,
unco-operative, unhelpful, unwilling;
*opp* co-operative, helpful

**obtain** *v* achieve, acquire, buy, come by,
earn, find, gain, get, get hold of, get your
hands on, pick up *inf*, secure, win

**obtrusive** *adj* blatant, conspicuous,
intrusive, noticeable, obvious, out of
place, prominent; *opp* unobtrusive

**obvious** *adj* apparent, blatant, clear,
conspicuous, evident, glaring, manifest,
noticeable, open, overt, patent, plain,
pronounced, self-evident, straightforward, transparent, unmistakable,
visible

**occasion** *n* **1** (special occasion) affair,
celebration, do *inf*, event, function,
party. **2** (happy occasion) episode,
event, experience, happening, incident,
occurrence. **3** (a different occasion)

circumstance, instance, situation, time

**occasional** *adj* casual, incidental, infrequent, intermittent, irregular, odd, rare, sporadic; *opp* regular

**occupant** *n* householder, inhabitant, inmate, occupier, renter, resident, tenant

**occupation** *n* **1** business, employment, job, profession, trade, work. **2** activity, craft, diversion, hobby, interest, pursuit, recreation. **3** (occupation of a country) capture, colonization, conquest, invasion, overthrow, possession, seizure, take-over

**occupied** *adj* **1** (doing sth) active, at work, busy, employed, hard at it *inf*, tied up *inf*, working; *opp* idle. **2** (being used) engaged, full, in use, taken, unavailable; *opp* free

**occupy** *v* **1** (occupy sb) amuse, divert, engage, engross, entertain, interest, keep busy. **2** (occupy a country) capture, colonize, conquer, invade, overrun, seize, take over. **3** (occupy a house) inhabit, live in, move into, reside in, take up residence in. **4** (occupy your time) fill, fill up, preoccupy, take up, use up

**occur** *v* **1** appear, arise, come about, crop up, develop, happen, materialize, result, take place, turn up. **2 occur to sb** come to mind, cross your mind, dawn on you, enter your head, strike you

**occurrence** *n* affair, circumstance, development, episode, event, happening, incident, matter, occasion, phenomenon

**odd** *adj* **1** abnormal, bizarre, curious, different, eccentric, extraordinary, freak, funny, idiosyncratic, incongruous, irregular, outlandish, peculiar, puzzling,

rare, remarkable, strange, uncommon, unconventional, unexpected, unusual, weird; *opp* normal. **2** extra, left-over, lone, remaining, single, solitary, spare, surplus, uneven, unmatched, unpaired, unused

**oddity** *n* aberration, abnormality, anomaly, curiosity, freak, irregularity, peculiarity, phenomenon, quirk, rarity, strangeness, uniqueness

**odds** *n* (the odds of sth happening) chance, likelihood, probability, prospect

**odious** *adj* disgusting, foul, hateful, horrible, loathsome, offensive, repellent, repugnant, repulsive, revolting, unpleasant; *opp* lovely, nice, pleasant

**odour** *n* aroma, bouquet, fragrance, perfume, pong *inf*, scent, smell, stench, stink

**offence** *n* **1** (commit an offence) breach, crime, felony, illegal act, misdemeanour, sin, transgression, wrong. **2** (cause offence) anger, annoyance, disapproval, disgust, displeasure, hurt, irritation, outrage, resentment, upset *inf*

**offend** *v* **1** (offend sb) anger, annoy, displease, embarrass, give offence, humiliate, hurt sb's feelings, insult, irritate, outrage, pain, provoke, repel, revolt, sicken, slight, snub, upset, wound. **2** (commit a crime) break the law, commit a crime, do wrong, sin

**offended** *adj* affronted, annoyed, disgusted, embarrassed, hurt, insulted, miffed *inf*, outraged, put out, resentful, revolted, sickened, stung, upset, wounded

**offender** *n* criminal, culprit, delinquent, felon, lawbreaker, outlaw, villain, wrongdoer

**offensive** *adj* 1 (of behaviour) abusive, annoying, antisocial, disgusting, embarrassing, hurtful, indecent, insolent, insulting, irritating, provocative, objectionable, outrageous, rude, tasteless, uncivil, unpleasant, vulgar, wounding; *opp* inoffensive.
2 (of a smell) disgusting, distasteful, nasty, nauseating, obnoxious, odious, repellent, revolting, sickening, unsavoury, vile, yucky *sl*; *opp* pleasant.
3 (invading a country) aggressive, attacking, belligerent, hostile, invading, on the warpath *inf*, threatening, warlike; *opp* defensive

**offensive** *n* assault, attack, drive, incursion, onslaught, push, raid, strike

**offer** *n* approach, bid, chance, incentive, invitation, opportunity, proposal, proposition, suggestion, tender

**offer** *v* bid, give, make an offer, make available, propose, provide, put forward, submit, suggest, tender, volunteer

**offering** *n* contribution, donation, gift, hand-out

**offhand** *adj* abrupt, brusque, casual, cavalier, cool, curt

**office** *n* 1 base, place of work, study, workplace. 2 (have the office of chairman) appointment, business, duty, job, place, position, post, responsibility, role, situation, work

**officer** *n* 1 administrator, agent, bureaucrat, committee-member, dignitary, office-holder, official.
2 (police officer) bobby *inf*, constable, copper *inf*, PC, police officer, WPC

**official** *adj* accredited, approved,

authorized, bona fide, certified, formal, kosher *inf*, legitimate, licensed, recognized, sanctioned, valid, validated; *opp* unofficial

**official** *n* administrator, agent, authorized person, bureaucrat, civil servant, committee-member, dignitary, jobsworth *inf*, mandarin, office-holder, officer, public servant

**officiate** *v* be in charge, be responsible, conduct, lead, preside, referee, run, take charge, take the chair, umpire

**officious** *adj* bossy, bumptious, dictatorial, domineering, interfering, obtrusive, opinionated, overbearing, pushy *inf*, self-important

**off-putting** *adj* daunting, demoralizing, disconcerting, discouraging, formidable, intimidating, unnerving, unsettling, upsetting; *opp* encouraging

**offset** *v* balance out, cancel out, compensate for, counteract, counterbalance, make up for, neutralize, set off

**offshoot** *n* arm, branch, by-product, derivative, limb, spin-off, splinter group

**offspring** *n* brood, children, descendants, family, heirs, issue, kids *inf*, litter, progeny, successors, young

**often** *adv* again and again, all the time, constantly, frequently, generally, many times, much, regularly, repeatedly, time after time, time and again; *opp* seldom

**oil** *v* anoint, grease, lubricate, wax

**ointment** *n* cream, liniment, lotion

**okay** *adj* acceptable, adequate, all right, convenient, fine, good, not bad, O.K., passable, reasonable

**okay** *v* agree, approve, authorize, consent

to, endorse, give sth the go-ahead, give sth the green light, give sth the thumbs up, O.K., pass, rubber-stamp, sanction; **opp** block, prevent

**old** *adj* **1** (of a person) aged, ageing, ancient, doddery, elderly, geriatric, getting on, grey, in your dotage, mature. **2** (of objects) aged, ancient, antiquated, antique, early, prehistoric, veteran, vintage. **3** (dilapidated) crumbling, decrepit, dilapidated, past it, threadbare, worn-out, worn. **4** (old-fashioned) antiquated, dated, obsolete, old-fashioned, out of the ark, outdated, passé, stale, time-worn. **5** (traditional) age-old, original, time-honoured, traditional. **6** erstwhile, former, previous

**old-fashioned** *adj* antiquated, dated, obsolescent, obsolete, old-hat *inf*, outdated, outmoded, out of fashion, out of the ark, passé, stale, time-worn, unfashionable

**omen** *n* bad sign, foreboding, harbinger, portent, sign, warning, writing on the wall

**ominous** *adj* bad, black, dark, dire, gloomy, inauspicious, menacing, sinister, unfavourable, unpromising; **opp** auspicious

**omission** *n* error, exclusion, gap, neglect, oversight

**omit** *v* drop, exclude, forget, leave out, miss, miss out, neglect, overlook

**omnipotent** *adj* all-powerful, almighty, supreme

**onerous** *adj* burdensome, difficult, exacting, hard, heavy, taxing, troublesome, unpleasant; **opp** easy, simple

**one-sided** *adj* biased, partial, partisan, unbalanced, unequal, uneven, unfair; **opp** balanced, fair, impartial, unbiased

**onlooker** *n* bystander, observer, passer-by, spectator, viewer, witness

**onslaught** *n* assault, attack, bombardment, offensive, raid, thrust

**onus** *n* burden, duty, obligation, responsibility

**ooze** *v* bleed, drain, dribble, emit, escape, flow, leak, percolate, secrete, seep, trickle, weep

**opaque** *adj* **1** cloudy, dirty, filmy, hazy, muddy, murky; **opp** clear, transparent. **2** difficult, impenetrable, incomprehensible, obscure; **opp** clear, obvious, straightforward, understandable

**open** *adj* **1** ajar, uncovered, undone, unfastened, unlocked. **2** spread out, unfolded. **3** (of countryside) broad, clear, exposed, free, rolling, spacious, sweeping, treeless, unenclosed, unrestricted. **4** (of information) available, free, public, unrestricted; **opp** classified, secret. **5** (open aggression) blatant, clear, evident, flagrant, manifest, obvious, overt, plain, undisguised. **6** (the matter is still open) undecided, unresolved, unsettled, up for grabs *inf*

**open** *v* **1** unbolt, uncork, uncover, undo, unfasten, unlock, untie, unwrap; **opp** close, do up, fasten, shut, wrap up. **2** spread out, unfold, unfurl, unroll; **opp** close, fold up. **3** (open a meeting) begin, commence, get going, initiate, kick off *inf*, launch, set in motion, set up, start; **opp** close

**opening** adj first, inaugural, initial, introductory, preliminary; opp closing

**opening** n 1 aperture, chink, crack, doorway, gap, hatch, hole, orifice, slot, split, way in. 2 beginning, birth, dawn, launch, outset, start. 3 break inf, chance, opportunity

**open-minded** adj detached, dispassionate, enlightened, impartial, liberal, objective, open to suggestions, receptive, unbiased; opp narrow-minded

**operate** v 1 function, go, run, work. 2 (operate a machine) control, drive, handle, use, work. 3 (operate on sb) cut sb open inf, do an operation, perform surgery, put sb under the knife inf

**operation** n 1 control, management, performance, use, working. 2 (undertaking) business, campaign, effort, enterprise, process, project, task, undertaking, venture. 3 (surgery) biopsy, laparoscopy, surgery, transplant

**operational** adj functioning, going, in operation, in use, in working order, ready, up and running, viable, working

**opinion** n assessment, belief, estimation, feeling, idea, impression, judgement, stance, view, viewpoint, way of thinking

**opinionated** adj arrogant, dictatorial, doctrinaire, dogmatic, inflexible, pigheaded inf, pompous, single-minded, uncompromising

**opponent** n adversary, antagonist, competitor, contender, contestant, enemy, player, rival

**opportune** adj advantageous, appropriate, apt, favourable, good, right, suitable, timely, well-timed

**opportunity** n break inf, chance, moment, opening, possibility, time

**oppose** v attack, be hostile to, campaign against, combat, counter, defy, fight, obstruct, stand up to, take a stand against, take issue with, take on; opp support

**opposed** adj 1 against, antagonistic, anti, hostile, in opposition, on the other side. 2 conflicting, incompatible, opposing, opposite

**opposite** adj 1 facing, on the other side, overlooking. 2 conflicting, contradictory, converse, different, hostile, irreconcilable, opposed, rival, unlike; opp similar

**opposite** n antithesis, converse, inverse, reverse, the other side of the coin

**opposition** n 1 enemy, opponent, other side, rival. 2 antagonism, competition, defiance, disapproval, hostility, objection, resistance; opp support

**oppress** v 1 crush, intimidate, persecute, put down, subjugate, suppress, terrorize, tyrannize. 2 (make sb unhappy) afflict, depress, torment, weigh down

**oppressed** adj 1 browbeaten, crushed, downtrodden, enslaved, persecuted, subjugated, tyrannized. 2 (unhappy) depressed, desolate, despondent, downhearted, weighed down

**oppressive** adj 1 harsh, repressive, tyrannical, unjust. 2 burdensome, onerous. 3 airless, close, humid, muggy, stifling, stuffy, suffocating

**oppressor** n autocrat, bully, despot, dictator, tormentor, tyrant

**opt for** v choose, decide on, go for inf, pick, prefer, settle on

**optimistic** adj buoyant, cheerful,

confident, hopeful, looking on the bright side, looking through rose-tinted spectacles, positive, sanguine; *opp* pessimistic

**optimum** *adj* best, ideal, maximum, optimal, peak, prime, top; *opp* worst

**option** *n* alternative, choice, possibility, route

**optional** *adj* discretionary, extra, up to you, voluntary; *opp* compulsory

**oral** *adj* by mouth, spoken, verbal, vocal

**orator** *n* lecturer, public speaker, speaker, speechifier, speech-maker

**orbit** *n* circuit, course, path, revolution, track

**orbit** *v* circle, go round

**orchestrate** *v* arrange, organize, plan, put together, set up, stage-manage

**ordeal** *n* distress, hardship, misery, nightmare, suffering, tribulation, trouble

**order** *n* 1 command, court order, directive, injunction, instruction, regulation, requirement. 2 (sth you have ordered) booking, choice, commission, request, requirement, requisition, selection. 3 (way things are arranged) arrangement, categorization, grouping, method, pattern, plan, sequence, structure. 4 (restore order) calm, control, discipline, harmony, law and order, peace, symmetry; *opp* chaos, disorder, disruption

**order** *v* 1 (tell sb to do sth) decree, direct, give orders to, instruct, require, tell. 2 (put things in order) arrange, categorize, classify, organize, put in order, sort out. 3 (order goods) ask for, book, choose, commission, put in an order for, request, reserve, send off for

**orderly** *adj* 1 businesslike, efficient, methodical, neat, organized, systematic, tidy; *opp* chaotic, disorganized. 2 controlled, disciplined, quiet, well-behaved; *opp* rebellious, undisciplined

**ordinary** *adj* common, common-or-garden, customary, everyday, familiar, humdrum, normal, plain, regular, run-of-the-mill, standard, unexceptional, unremarkable

**organic** *adj* 1 chemical-free, natural, organically grown. 2 animate, biological, living

**organism** *n* animal, being, creature, living thing, plant, structure

**organization** *n* 1 (group) association, body, business, club, combine, company, confederation, consortium, corporation, federation, firm, group, institution, league, society. 2 (structure) arrangement, composition, configuration, construction, design, make-up, order, pattern, structure. 3 (the organizing of sth) logistics, management, operation, planning, regulation, running, setting up

**organize** *v* 1 (put in order) arrange, categorize, classify, configure, order, put in order, structure. 2 (organize a campaign) arrange, co-ordinate, design, establish, form, look after, manage, orchestrate, plan, run, see to, set up, sort out, take care of

**orgy** *n* 1 (wild party) binge *inf*, revel, wild party. 2 (an orgy of sth) binge, bout, fling, splurge, spree

**orient** *v* 1 design for, direct at, intend for, orientate, make sth suitable for. 2 align, get your bearings, locate, orientate, position, turn

**origin** n 1 basis, derivation, provenance, root, source, starting point. 2 ancestry, background, extraction, family, heritage, lineage, parentage, pedigree, stock

**original** adj 1 fresh, ground-breaking, imaginative, innovative, new, novel, unusual, untried. 2 earliest, first, initial, primary

**originality** n creativity, freshness, imagination, individuality, innovation, invention, new ideas, novelty

**originate** v 1 (create) bring about, coin, create, develop, establish, give birth to, institute, introduce, invent, launch, pioneer, set up, start. 2 (come from) arise, begin, come from, derive from, flow from, spring from, start, stem from

**ornament** n bauble, decoration, knick-knack, trimming, trinket

**ornamental** adj attractive, decorative, elaborate, fancy, intricate, non-essential, showy

**ornate** adj busy, elaborate, fancy, flashy inf, flowery, fussy, grandiose, ornamental, pretentious, rococo, showy; **opp** plain

**orthodox** adj accepted, authorized, conformist, conservative, conventional, established, mainstream, official, standard, traditional;
**opp** nonconformist, revolutionary, unconventional, unorthodox

**orthodoxy** n conformity, conservatism, conventionality, propriety, traditionalism

**ostensible** adj outward, pretended, professed, purported, seeming, so-called, stated, superficial, supposed

**ostentatious** adj affected, flamboyant, flashy inf, garish, gaudy, loud, overdone, pretentious, showy; **opp** quiet, restrained

**ostracize** v cold-shoulder inf, exclude, isolate, reject, send sb to Coventry, shun, shut out, snub

**oust** v depose, dislodge, displace, drive out, expel, force out, kick out inf, overthrow, push out, replace, throw out, topple, unseat

**outbreak** n epidemic, eruption, explosion, flare-up, occurrence, rash, upsurge

**outburst** n burst, eruption, explosion, fit, flare-up, flood, outbreak, outpouring, storm, surge

**outcast** n exile, outsider, pariah, persona non grata, refugee, reject

**outcome** n consequence, effect, result, upshot

**outcry** n clamour, complaints, cries of indignation, fuss, howls of protest, hue and cry, hullabaloo, objections, opposition, row, uproar

**outdated** adj antiquated, dated, dead, fuddy-duddy inf, obsolete, old-fashioned, out, out of date, out of the ark inf, outmoded, out of fashion, passé, unfashionable

**outdo** v beat, eclipse, excel, get the better of, go one better than, outclass, outshine, outsmart, overshadow, run rings around inf, show up, surpass

**outdoor** adj alfresco, exterior, external, open-air, out of doors, outside;
**opp** indoor

**outer** adj 1 exposed, exterior, external, outermost, outside, outward, surface, top; **opp** inner. 2 distant, far, fringe, outlying, peripheral, remote; **opp** inner

**outfit** *n* **1** clothes, costume, gear *inf*, get-up *inf*, kit *inf*, rig *inf*, togs *inf*. **2** (organization) crew, enterprise, group, organization, set-up, team, unit

**outgoing** *adj* **1** (the outgoing president) departing, ex, former, leaving, old, previous, retiring; **opp** incoming. **2** (friendly) approachable, bubbly, extrovert, friendly, genial, gregarious, lively, sociable

**outing** *n* day-trip, excursion, expedition, jaunt, tour, trip, visit

**outlaw** *n* bandit, criminal, fugitive, highwayman, robber

**outlaw** *v* ban, bar, criminalize, forbid, make illegal, prohibit, proscribe

**outlay** *n* charge, cost, disbursement, expenditure, expense, investment, outgoings, spending

**outlet** *n* **1** market, retail outlet, retailer, shop, store. **2** channel, discharge, duct, escape valve, mouth, opening, release, vent; **opp** inlet

**outline** *n* **1** abstract, bare bones, draft, résumé, rough idea, sketch, summary, synopsis. **2** contour, framework, perimeter, profile, shape, sketch, skeleton, tracing

**outline** *v* **1** draft, give a rough idea of, rough out, sketch out, sketch, summarize. **2** sketch, trace

**outlook** *n* **1** (outlook on life) attitude, opinion, perspective, position, standpoint, view. **2** (forecast) expectations, forecast, future, prognosis, prospect. **3** (a building with a pleasant outlook) aspect, panorama, view, vista

**out of date** *adj* antiquated, dated, dead, fuddy-duddy *inf*, obsolete, old-fashioned, outdated, out, out of the ark *inf*, outmoded, out of fashion, passé, unfashionable; **opp** modern, new

**output** *n* crop, efficiency, manufacture, performance, product, production figures, production, productivity, result, yield

**outrage** *n* **1** anger, disgust, fury, horror, indignation, rage, revulsion, shock. **2** affront, atrocity, crime, disgrace, evil, insult, offence, scandal

**outrage** *v* anger, disgust, horrify, incense, infuriate, offend, shock, upset

**outrageous** *adj* **1** disgraceful, disgusting, heinous, horrifying, infuriating, offensive, scandalous, shocking, terrible, upsetting. **2** crazy, excessive, mad, preposterous, unreasonable, wild

**outright** *adj* absolute, categorical, complete, definite, downright, out-and-out, thorough, total, unmitigated, unqualified, utter

**outright** *adv* **1** (frankly) candidly, explicitly, frankly, openly, plainly, straight. **2** (in one go) at once, directly, immediately, in one fell swoop, in one go, instantaneously, there and then. **3** (completely) categorically, completely, entirely, lock, stock and barrel, totally

**outset** *n* beginning, birth, dawn, inception, kick-off *inf*, launch, start

**outside** *adj* **1** exterior, external, open-air, out of doors, outdoor, outer, outermost, outward, surface, top; **opp** inside. **2** (an outside possibility) faint, improbable, marginal, remote, slight, slim, unlikely

**outsider** *n* alien, exile, foreigner, incomer, misfit, odd one out, oddball, stranger

**outskirts** n edge, fringe, margin, outlying areas, periphery, suburbs

**outspoken** adj blunt, direct, explicit, forthright, frank, mouthy inf, tactless, undiplomatic; opp quiet, reserved

**outstanding** adj 1 excellent, exceptional, great, impressive, magnificent, memorable, notable, remarkable, special, stunning, superb, supreme, world-class. 2 (unresolved) ongoing, pending, remaining, to be dealt with, unpaid, unresolved, unsettled

**outward** adj 1 exterior, external, outer, outside, surface. 2 (visible) apparent, discernible, external, noticeable, visible; opp inward. 3 (ostensible) apparent, ostensible, professed, superficial, supposed

**outweigh** v be more important than, cancel out, have the edge on, override, prevail, take precedence over

**outwit** v beat, deceive, dupe, get the better of, outmanoeuvre, outsmart, pull the wool over sb's eyes, put one over on inf

**ovation** n acclaim, accolade, applause, clapping, standing ovation, tribute

**overall** adj all-embracing, blanket, broad, complete, comprehensive, general, global, inclusive, total, umbrella

**overcast** adj cloudy, dark, dull, grey, leaden, murky; opp clear

**overcome** v conquer, defeat, get the better of, master, quash, rise above, subdue, surmount, triumph over

**overcritical** adj carping, fussy, hard to please, hypercritical, pernickety, quibbling

**overcrowded** adj chock-a-block inf, congested, crammed full, full, heaving, jam-packed, overloaded, overrun, packed, swarming, teeming

**overdue** adj behind schedule, delayed, in arrears, late, outstanding, unpaid, unsettled

**overeat** v be greedy, binge, eat like a horse, eat too much, gorge, make a pig of yourself inf, overindulge, pig out inf, stuff your face inf, stuff yourself inf; opp diet, starve yourself

**overflow** v brim over, flood, pour over, run over, spill over

**overgrown** adj overrun, tangled, thick with weeds, unkempt, untidy, weedy, wild

**overhang** v droop over, jut out, loom over, project, protrude, stick out

**overhaul** v check over, fix, inspect, maintain, mend, recondition, refurbish, renovate, repair, restore, service

**overheads** n everyday expenditure, expenditure, expenses, operating costs, running costs

**overjoyed** adj cock-a-hoop inf, delighted, ecstatic, euphoric, in raptures, jubilant, on cloud nine inf, on top of the world inf, over the moon inf, thrilled; opp depressed, miserable

**overlook** v 1 forget, leave out, miss, not notice, omit. 2 excuse, ignore, let sth pass, let sth ride, turn a blind eye to inf, write off. 3 be opposite, face, front onto, have a view of, look out onto

**overpower** v crush, defeat, get the upper hand, get under control, immobilize, overwhelm, pin down, restrain, trounce

**overpowering** adj intolerable, oppressive, overwhelming, powerful, strong, suffocating, unbearable

**overrule** v cancel, countermand, disallow, invalidate, override, overturn, reject, reverse, revoke, set aside, veto

**oversee** v administer, control, keep an eye on, look after, preside over, supervise

**overshadow** v cloud, dwarf, eclipse, obscure, outshine, put in the shade, spoil

**oversight** n blunder, error, gaffe, mistake, omission, slip-up

**overt** adj blatant, evident, explicit, obvious, open, patent, plain, unconcealed, undisguised, visible; *opp* covert, secret

**overtake** v 1 go past, leave behind, outdistance, outstrip, pass, pull ahead of. 2 (events overtake you) befall, catch up with, engulf, hit, overwhelm

**overthrow** v beat, defeat, depose, displace, oust, remove from office, throw out, topple, unseat

**overtone** n connotation, feeling, hint, intimation, sense, suggestion, undercurrent

**overturn** v 1 capsize, keel over, knock over, tip over, topple over, upset, upturn. 2 (overturn a decision) annul, countermand, overrule, quash, reject, repeal, reverse, revoke, set aside, veto

**overweight** adj chubby, corpulent, fat, gross, heavy, massive, obese, outsize, plump, podgy, portly, pudgy, roly-poly, stout, tubby, well-padded inf; *opp* thin

**overwhelm** v 1 engulf, flood, inundate, snow under, swamp. 2 conquer, crush, defeat, overcome, overpower, quell, subjugate, vanquish. 3 bowl over inf, daze, devastate, knock for six inf, leave speechless, move deeply, shake,

prostrate, stagger, stun

**overwhelming** adj 1 (of an emotion) crushing, devastating, overpowering, shattering, staggering, stunning, uncontrollable. 2 (too many or too much) enormous, huge, immense, inordinate, mind-boggling inf, staggering, stupendous

**overwrought** adj agitated, beside yourself, distracted, frantic, frenzied, hysterical, in a state inf, tense, uptight inf

**owe** v 1 (owe money) be in arrears, be in debt, be in the red, be overdrawn. 2 (owe a favour) be indebted to, be obliged to, be under an obligation to

**owing** adj 1 due, in arrears, outstanding, overdue, owed, payable, unpaid. 2 **owing to** as a result of, because of, due to, thanks to

**own** v 1 be the owner of, have, have in your possession, hold, keep, retain, possess. 2 **own up** admit, come clean, confess, make a clean breast of it, put your hand up to inf

**owner** n 1 holder, keeper, possessor. 2 (of land or a business) homeowner, landlady, landlord, proprietor. 3 (of an animal) keeper, master, mistress

**pace** n 1 step, stride. 2 (way of walking) gait, tread, walk. 3 (speed) lick inf, rate, speed, tempo, velocity

**pace** v 1 pad, patrol, pound, stride, tread, walk. 2 give a lead to, set the pace for

**pacifist** n conscientious objector, dove, passive resistor, peace-lover, peacemaker; **opp** warmonger

**pacify** v calm, calm down, conciliate, placate, quieten, soothe, tranquillize

**pack** n 1 bale, bundle, package, parcel, truss. 2 backpack, haversack, kitbag, knapsack, rucksack. 3 box, carton, container, package, packet, parcel. 4 (of animals) drove, flock, herd, troop. 5 (of people) band, gang, group, horde, mob, set, troop

**pack** v 1 (pack things) bale, box, bundle up, package, parcel up, place, put, store, stow, wrap, wrap up. 2 (pack a suitcase) cram, fill, fill up, load, stuff. 3 (pack people in) cram, crowd, fill, jam, press into, squeeze into. 4 pack down

compact, compress, press down, press together, tamp. 5 **pack off** dismiss, dispatch, send away, send off, send packing inf. 6 **pack up** (put things away) clear up, put away, tidy away, tidy up. 7 **pack up** (give up) call it a day inf, cease, finish, give up, leave off, pack it in inf stop. 8 **pack up** (stop working) break down, come to a halt, conk out inf, fail, stop working

**package** n 1 box, carton, container, packet, parcel. 2 combination, lot, package deal, package holiday, whole, whole shebang inf

**package** v box, pack, pack up, parcel up, wrap, wrap up

**packed** adj chock-a-block, congested, crowded, filled, filled to capacity, full, full up, jammed, jam-packed, overflowing; **opp** empty

**packet** n box, carton, container, pack, package

**pact** n agreement, alliance, arrangement, bargain, contract, deal, settlement, treaty, understanding

**pad** n 1 cushion, padding, wadding, wad. 2 jotter, notebook, notepad, writing pad. 3 foot, paw, sole

**pad** v 1 cushion, line, pack, protect, stuff, upholster. 2 amplify, augment, eke, elaborate, fill out, flesh out, pad out, protract, spin out, stretch

**padding** n 1 filling, packing, protection, stuffing, wadding. 2 verbiage, verbosity, waffle inf, wordiness

**paddle** n oar, scull

**paddle** v 1 propel, pull, row, scull. 2 dabble, splash, splash about, wade

**pagan** adj atheistic, godless, heathen,

idolatrous, infidel, polytheistic

**page** n 1 folio, leaf, sheet, side. 2 attendant, bellboy *Am*, pageboy, servant

**pageant** n parade, procession, show, spectacle, tableau

**pageantry** n ceremony, grandeur, magnificence, pomp, ritual, show, spectacle, splendour

**pain** n 1 ache, cramp, discomfort, hurt, irritation, pang, smart, soreness, spasm, sting, tenderness, twinge. 2 agony, anguish, suffering, torment, torture. 3 (mental) anguish, distress, grief, heartache, misery, suffering, torment, torture, unhappiness, woe

**pain** v 1 (hurt) ache, be painful, be sore, cause pain, chafe, hurt, smart, sting, throb. 2 (make sb unhappy) afflict, aggrieve, distress, grieve, hurt, make miserable, sadden, torment, torture

**painful** adj 1 aching, excruciating, hurting, inflamed, smarting, sore, stinging, tender, throbbing. 2 disagreeable, distressing, harrowing, hurtful, nasty, traumatic, trying, unpleasant, upsetting. 3 arduous, difficult, hard, laborious, strenuous, tough; **opp** painless

**painkiller** n anaesthetic, analgesic, anodyne, palliative

**painless** adj 1 pain-free, without pain; **opp** painful. 2 easy, effortless, simple, trouble-free; **opp** difficult

**painstaking** adj assiduous, careful, conscientious, diligent, meticulous, punctilious, thorough

**paint** n colour, colouring, dye, pigment, stain, tint

**paint** v 1 apply paint to, colour, cover, daub, decorate, dye, spray, stain, tint, touch up, varnish, whitewash. 2 (show sth) delineate, depict, describe, picture, portray, represent

**painter** n artist, decorator, illustrator

**pair** n brace, couple, duo, match, twins, twosome

**pair** v 1 pair up (put things together) arrange in pairs, couple, join up, link up, match, match up, put together, twin, yoke. 2 pair off, pair up (of people) double up, find a partner, get together, join up, make a twosome, marry, team up, wed

**palatable** adj appetizing, delicious, moreish *inf*, mouthwatering, savoury, scrumptious, tasty, yummy *inf*; **opp** disgusting

**palatial** adj grand, imposing, luxurious, magnificent, majestic, opulent, posh *inf*, plush *inf*, spacious, splendid, stately, sumptuous; **opp** miserable, tiny

**pale** adj 1 anaemic, ashen, as white as a sheet, colourless, deathly pale, drained, like death, like death warmed up *inf*, pallid, pasty, peaky *inf*, wan, washed-out *inf*, white, white-faced. 2 (of colours) bleached, faded, light, pastel, washed-out, wishy-washy *inf*. 3 (of light) dim, faint, inadequate, weak

**pall** v become boring, become tedious, become tiresome, cloy, lose its attraction, lose its interest, get boring, get/grow tedious, get/grow tiresome

**palpable** adj 1 apparent, blatant, clear, conspicuous, evident, glaring, manifest, obvious, patent, plain, unmistakable. 2 concrete, solid, tangible

**palpitate** v beat rapidly, flutter, pound,

pulsate, throb, thud, thump

**paltry** *adj* 1 (too small) derisory, insignificant, meagre, miserly, piddling *inf*, small, trifling, unimportant, worthless; *opp* generous. 2 contemptible, despicable, low, mean, miserable, sorry

**pamper** *v* cosset, humour, indulge, make a fuss of, mollycoddle, overindulge, pet, spoil, wait on hand and foot

**pamphlet** *n* booklet, brochure, circular, leaflet, tract

**pan** *n* 1 casserole, pot, saucepan. 2 container, receptacle, vessel

**panacea** *n* cure-all, cure for all ills, elixir, nostrum, universal remedy

**panache** *n* dash, élan, flair, flamboyance, pizzazz *inf*, style, verve

**pandemonium** *n* Babel, bedlam, chaos, commotion, hullabaloo, tumult, turmoil, uproar

**panel** *n* 1 insert, pane. 2 board, committee, jury

**pang** *n* 1 ache, pain, sharp pain, sting, twinge. 2 (pang of conscience) misgiving, qualm, remorse, scruple

**panic** *n* alarm, dismay, fear, horror, hysteria, terror

**panic-stricken** *adj* aghast, frightened, frightened to death *inf*, hysterical, panicky, petrified, scared out of your wits *inf*, scared stiff, scared to death *inf*, terrified; *opp* calm

**panorama** *n* aerial view, bird's-eye view, landscape, scene, view, vista

**panoramic** *adj* commanding, extensive, scenic, sweeping, wide

**pant** *v* blow, breathe heavily, gasp, gasp for breath, huff and puff, puff, wheeze

**pants** *n* 1 boxer shorts, briefs, knickers, panties, underpants, Y-fronts. 2 jeans, slacks, trousers

**paper** *n* 1 (newspaper) broadsheet, daily, newspaper, rag *inf*, tabloid. 2 (give a paper) dissertation, monograph, record, study, treatise

**papers** *n* 1 contract, deed, deeds, document, documents, form, forms, legal papers. 2 ID, identification documents, identification papers, identity card, passport. 3 correspondence, diaries, files, letters, personal papers, records

**parable** *n* allegory, fable, moral tale, story with a moral

**parade** *n* 1 cavalcade, cortège, demonstration, march, march-past, motorcade, pageant, procession. 2 display, exhibition, show, spectacle

**parade** *v* 1 file past, march, march past. 2 (show sth off) air, display, exhibit, flaunt, make a show of, show, show off, vaunt. 3 show off, strut, swagger, swank *inf*

**paradise** *n* 1 Eden, Elysian Fields, Elysium, fairyland, Garden of Eden, heaven, heavenly kingdom, kingdom of heaven, Shangri-La, utopia, Valhalla. 2 bliss, delight, ecstasy, joy, seventh heaven

**paradox** *n* anomaly, contradiction, inconsistency, oxymoron, self-contradiction

**paradoxical** *adj* anomalous, contradictory, inconsistent

**paragon** *n* archetype, exemplar, example, ideal, model, model of excellence, pattern, perfect example, standard

**parallel** *adj* 1 equidistant, side by side.

2 analogous, comparable, corresponding, equivalent, like, matching, resembling, similar

**parallel** n 1 corollary, counterpart, duplicate, equal, equivalent, match, twin. 2 analogy, comparison, correspondence, likeness, resemblance, similarity

**paralyse** v 1 cripple, disable, immobilize, incapacitate, make powerless. 2 bring to a halt, bring to a standstill, bring to a stop, freeze, halt, immobilize, put out of action, put out of commission, stop. 3 deaden, desensitize, freeze, numb. 4 (with fear) freeze, petrify, stagger, stop, stun, transfix

**paralysed** adj 1 crippled, disabled, immobilized, paraplegic, unable to move. 2 at a standstill, frozen, halted, immobile, immobilized, rigid, unable to move, unusable. 3 dead, deadened, frozen, numb. 4 (with fear) petrified, stunned, stupefied, transfixed

**paramount** adj cardinal, chief, foremost, main, most important, pre-eminent, primary, principle, supreme, uppermost

**paraphernalia** n 1 baggage, belongings, bits and pieces, clobber inf, effects, impedimenta, luggage, odds and ends, personal belongings, possessions, stuff, things. 2 (things needed for sth) accessories, apparatus, equipment, gear, kit, material, tackle, tools

**paraphrase** v explain, gloss, interpret, put into other words, rephrase, reword

**parasite** n bloodsucker, cadger, drone, freeloader inf, hanger-on, leech, scrounger, sponger

**parcel** n 1 bale, box, bundle, carton, pack, package. 2 (of land) lot, patch, piece, plot

**parcel** v 1 box, bundle up, do up, pack, package, pack up, parcel up, tie up, wrap, wrap up. 2 **parcel out** allocate, allot, carve up, deal out, distribute, divide, share out

**parch** v bake, burn, dehydrate, dessicate, dry, dry up, scorch, shrivel, wither

**parched** adj 1 arid, baked, burned, dessicated, dehydrated, dried out, dried up, dry, scorched, shriveled, waterless, withered. 2 dry inf, dehydrated, thirsty

**pardon** n 1 forgiveness, indulgence, mercy. 2 (an official pardon) amnesty, exoneration, free pardon, release, reprieve

**pardon** v 1 condone, excuse, forgive, forgive and forget, let off, overlook. 2 (pardon sb officially) absolve, exonerate, grant a pardon to, release, reprieve

**pardonable** adj allowable, excusable, forgivable, minor, slight, understandable; opp unpardonable

**parent** n dad inf, father, mother, mum inf, old dear inf, old man inf old lady inf, old woman inf, procreator, progenitor, sire

**parentage** n ancestry, birth, descent, extraction, family, lineage, origin, pedigree, race, stock

**park** n 1 green, playground, public garden, public park, recreation ground. 2 estate, gardens, grounds, parkland

**parliament** n assembly, congress, convocation, council, legislative assembly, legislature, senate

**parody** n burlesque, caricature, imitation, lampoon, satire, send-up inf, spoof inf, take off inf

**parody** v caricature, imitate, lampoon, mimic, satirize, send up *inf*, take off *inf*

**parry** v 1 (parry blows) avert, block, deflect, fend off, rebuff, repel, stave off, turn aside, ward off. 2 (parry awkward questions) avoid, dodge, duck *inf*, evade, elude, sidestep *inf*

**part** n 1 bit, fraction, fragment, percentage, piece, portion, scrap, section, segment, share, slice. 2 component, constituent, element, ingredient. 3 (part of an organization) branch, department, division, section, unit. 4 (theatrical) character, lines, role, words. 5 (your part in an undertaking) capacity, duty, function, job, responsibility, role, task. 6 (part of a town) area, district, neighbourhood, quarter, region, sector, zone. 7 **for the most part** all in all, by and large, generally, mostly, to all intents and purposes, usually. 8 **take part** be involved, contribute, do your share, engage in, have a hand in, have something to do with, join in, participate, play a part

**part** v 1 (part things that are joined) break, break up, cleave, divide, separate, sever, split, tear. 2 (people part) break up, divorce, get a divorce, get a separation, get divorced, go their separate ways, part company, separate, split up. 3 **part from** go away from, leave, say farewell to, say goodbye to, say your goodbyes, separate, split *inf*, take your leave. 4 **part with** cede, give away, give up, let go, let go of, relinquish, sacrifice, sell, yield

**partake** v 1 contribute to, engage in,

have a hand in, have sth to do with, participate in, play a part in, share in, take part in. 2 (partake of food, drink) consume, drink, eat, share in

**partial** adj 1 imperfect, incomplete, in part, limited, part, unfinished. 2 biased, discriminatory, having an interest, inequitable, one-sided, partisan, prejudiced, unfair, unjust; *opp* impartial, unbiased. 3 **be partial to** be fond of, be keen on, care for, have a liking for, have a taste for, have a weakness for, like

**partially** adv fractionally, half, in part, moderately, not completely, not fully, not wholly, partly, slightly, to a certain extent, to a limited extent, to some degree, to some extent

**participant** n competitor, contributor, member, party, shareholder

**participate** v be involved in, contribute to, engage in, join in, have a hand in, have sth to do with, play a part in, take part in

**particle** n 1 bit, crumb, fragment, grain, morsel, scrap, smidgen *inf*, speck, spot, tiny bit, tiny piece. 2 atom, molecule

**particular** adj 1 distinct, individual, precise, individual, specific, unique; *opp* general. 2 exceptional, outstanding, remarkable, singular, special, unusual. 3 choosy *inf*, discriminating, exacting, fastidious, finicky, fussy, pernickety *inf*, selective. 4 **in particular** especially, particularly, specially, specifically

**parting** n 1 adieu, departure, farewell, goodbye, leave-taking, leaving. 2 breaking up, divorce, separation, splitting up. 3 breaking up, detachment, dividing, division, partition, separating, separation, severance, splitting up

**partisan** adj biased, bigoted, doctrinaire, factional, one-sided, partial, prejudiced, sectarian, unbalanced, unfair; *opp* impartial

**partisan** n 1 adherent, backer, devotee, disciple, follower, supporter, sympathizer, upholder. 2 freedom fighter, guerrilla, insurgent, member of the resistance, terrorist

**partition** n 1 barrier, room divider, screen, wall. 2 (act of separating) division, partitioning, segregation, separation, split; *opp* unification

**partition** v divide, section off, segregate, separate, split, split up, wall off

**partner** n 1 (in business, sport) accomplice, ally, associate, collaborator, colleague, comrade, companion, co-worker, fellow worker, sleeping partner, team-mate. 2 (in a couple) boyfriend, common-law husband, common-law wife, companion, girlfriend, husband, live-in lover inf, mate, significant other inf, spouse, wife

**partnership** n 1 alliance, association, brotherhood, collaboration, fellowship, fraternity, joint effort, union. 2 (in business) cartel, company, confederation, conglomerate, co-op inf, co-operative, joint venture, syndicate

**party** n 1 bash inf, do inf, get-together inf, orgy, reception, social, social gathering, soirée. 2 (political) bloc, faction, fraction, grouping. 3 (the parties involved) individual, person. 4 (to a dispute, conspiracy) accomplice, litigant, participant, third party. 5 **be a party to** approve of, condone, get

involved in, participate in, support, take part in

**pass** n 1 (make a pass at sb) advance, approach, assault, fumble, lunge, proposition, harassment. 2 (between mountains) canyon, channel, cutting, gap, gorge, gully, opening, passage, path, ravine, valley. 3 (an official pass) authorization, identification, identity card, licence, passbook, passport, permit, proof of identity, safe conduct, swipe card, ticket, warrant, visa

**pass** v 1 drive by, drive past, go by, go past, move past, overtake, pass by, run by, run past, walk by, walk past. 2 (pass a level, amount) break, exceed, go above, go beyond, outstrip, surpass, transcend. 3 (pass an exam) be successful, get through, graduate, qualify; *opp* fail. 4 (pass a law) accept, agree, approve, confirm, enact, establish, promulgate, ratify, validate, vote through; *opp* reject. 5 (pass sth to sb) circulate, deal, deliver, give, hand, hand over, pass on, present, proffer, transfer. 6 (in a quiz) fail to answer, give in, make no bid, miss a turn, opt out, say nothing. 7 (pass the time) fill, occupy, spend, while away. 8 (time passes) advance, continue, elapse, flow, fly, go on, tick by. 9 **pass away** breathe your last, depart this world, die, expire, go to meet your Maker, kick the bucket inf, pass on, perish. 10 **pass out** black out, collapse, faint, lose consciousness, swoon

**passable** adj adequate, average, fair, satisfactory, tolerable

**passage** n 1 (from a book) excerpt, extract, paragraph, part, quotation, reading, section, text, verse. 2 (narrow lane) alley, arcade, catwalk, channel, corridor, covered way, hall, hallway, lane, tunnel, passageway, walkway. 3 (on a ship) crossing, journey, transit, voyage

**passenger** n commuter, customer, tourist, traveller

**passer-by** n bystander, passing motorist, pedestrian

**passing** adj brief, fleeting, incidental, momentary, short, short-lived, temporary, transient, transitory

**passion** n 1 (strong feeling) animation, ardour, devotion, emotion, enthusiasm, excitement, fervour, fire, heat, keenness, vehemence, zeal. 2 (strong sexual feeling) arousal, desire, craving, fondness, infatuation, love, lust

**passionate** adj 1 animated, ardent, burning, devoted, eager, emotional, enthusiastic, excitable, excited, fervent, fiery, heartfelt, hot, hot-headed, impassioned, intense, tempestuous, vehement, wild, zealous. 2 (sexually) amorous, aroused, hot, loving, lustful, randy inf, sensual, sexy, turned-on inf

**passive** adj inactive, inert, patient, quiescent, unassertive, unresisting, submissive; **opp** active

**past** adj 1 ancient, bygone, earlier, erstwhile, ex-, former, historical, old, onetime, preceding, previous, prior, yesterday's; **opp** future. 2 done, finished, forgotten, gone, in the past, over, over and done with; **opp** continuing, present, ongoing

**past** n 1 antiquity, bygone days, bygones, days gone by, former times, old times,

olden days, history, mists of time, yesterday, yesteryear, yore; **opp** future. 2 (sb's past) background, experiences, former life, life history, origins, record; **opp** future

**paste** n adhesive, cement, glue, gum, putty

**paste** v affix, cement, fasten, fix, glue, gum, stick

**pastiche** n burlesque, copy, imitation, parody, satire, take-off inf

**pastime** n amusement, distraction, diversion, entertainment, hobby, interest, leisure activity, pursuit, recreation, sport

**pastoral** adj 1 agrarian, agricultural, Arcadian, bucolic, country, farming, rural, rustic. 2 (pastoral care) fatherly, in loco parentis, nurturing, parental, paternal

**pasture** n field, grass, grassland, grazing land, meadow, pasturage tech, pastureland

**pat** v dab, hit, slap, tap, touch

**patch** n 1 area, blotch, mark, marking, shape, spot, stain. 2 (patch of land) area, lot, parcel, piece, plot, strip, tract

**patch** v 1 darn, mend, repair. 2 **patch up** (patch up a quarrel) reconcile, repair, resolve, restore, settle

**patchy** adj erratic, good in parts, inconsistent, intermittent, irregular, sketchy, uneven, variable, varying

**patent** adj apparent, blatant, clear, conspicuous, definite, evident, flagrant, glaring, manifest, obvious, palpable, plain, unmistakable

**path** n 1 alley, avenue, bridle path, bridleway, footpath, lane, pathway, pavement, road, route, track, trail, walkway, way. **2** (of a moving object) arc, course, curve, direction, orbit, trajectory

**pathetic** adj **1** abject, abysmal, bad, dismal, feeble, hapless, hopeless, ineffectual, miserable, pitiable, pitiful, poor, sad, sorry, weak, wretched. **2** (upsetting) affecting, heartbreaking, moving, piteous, pitiful, plaintive, poignant, sad, sentimental, sorry, tearjerking, touching, upsetting

**pathos** n emotion, poignancy, sadness, sentimentality

**patience** n calm, calmness, endurance, forbearance, fortitude, passivity, resignation, stoicism, tolerance; *opp* impatience

**patient** adj **1** calm, long-suffering, passive, resigned, stoical, tolerant, waiting; *opp* impatient. **2** (of a piece of work) assiduous, diligent, indefatigable, meticulous, painstaking, persevering, persistent, thorough, unhurried, untiring; *opp* hurried

**patient** n case, client, inmate, invalid, resident, subject, sufferer, victim

**patriot** n chauvinist, loyalist, nationalist

**patriotic** adj chauvinistic, flag-waving, gung-ho *inf*, jingoistic, loyal, loyalist, my-country-right-or-wrong, nationalistic

**patrol** n garrison, guard, guards, posse, rangers, scouts, squad, vigilantes, watch

**patrol** v be on the beat, cruise, do the rounds, guard, inspect, keep vigil, monitor, police, watch

**patron** n **1** backer, benefactor, contributor, donor, friend, protector, sponsor, supporter. **2** client, customer,

habitué, regular, visitor

**patronage** n **1** assistance, backing, endorsement, protection, sponsorship, support. **2** (of an unfair, illegal kind) back-scratching, jobs for the boys, nepotism, old school tie

**patronize** v **1** be condescending, look down on, look down your nose at, sneer at, talk down to. **2** (patronize a shop, restaurant) buy from, do business with, drink at, eat at, frequent, shop at, visit

**patronizing** adj condescending, disdainful, haughty, high-handed, overbearing, scornful, sneering, snobbish, snooty *inf*; *opp* respectful

**pattern** n **1** arrangement, decoration, design, device, figure, marking, motif, ornamentation, shape. **2** (for making sth) blueprint, guide, instructions, model, plan, sample, specimen, stencil, template. **3** (events following a pattern) order, plan, shape, structure, system

**paunch** n abdomen, beer belly *inf*, beer gut *inf*, belly, gut, middle-aged spread, pot *inf*, potbelly *inf*, stomach, spare tyre *inf*, tummy *inf*

**pause** n abeyance, break, cessation, delay, gap, halt, hesitation, interlude, interruption, interval, rest, silence

**pause** v break off, cease, delay, hesitate, interrupt, rest, stop, wait

**pave** v pave the way for allow, enable, foreshadow, make possible, permit, precede, prepare

**pay** n allowance, commission, earnings, emoluments, honorarium, income, payment, take-home pay, remittance, remuneration, reward, salary, stipend, wage, wages

**pay** v 1 buy, cough up inf, fork out inf, foot the bill, hand over, lay out, part with, shell out inf, pay out, pay up, remit, settle up, spend. 2 (produce a profit, benefit) be advantageous, be profitable, be rewarding, be worthwhile, make a profit, make money, pay off. 3 (pay sb to do sth) employ, engage, hire, remunerate, reward, take on. 4 (pay sb for damage, expenses) compensate, defray, indemnify, pay back, recompense, refund, reimburse. 5 **pay for** (suffer as a result of) atone for, be penalized for, be punished for, compensate for, do penance for, expiate, make amends for, make good, make reparations for, make up for, suffer for. 6 **pay off** cancel, clear, close, discharge, liquidate, meet, repay, settle, square

**payable** adj due, outstanding, owed, owing, to be paid, unpaid

**payment** n amount, award, compensation, deposit, instalment, premium, refund, reimbursement, repayment, sum

**peace** n 1 armistice, concord, harmony, pacification, peacetime, reconciliation, truce; opp war. 2 calm, calmness, peacefulness, quiet, repose, rest, serenity, tranquillity

**peaceable** adj amicable, conciliatory, peaceful, peace-loving

**peaceful** adj 1 (wanting, seeking peace) amicable, conciliatory, peaceable, peace-loving; opp warlike. 2 (free of conflict) at peace, calm, harmonious, untroubled. 3 (without noise, movement) at peace, at rest, calm, placid, quiet, restful, serene, still, tranquil

**peak** n 1 brow, crest, hilltop, mountain top, pinnacle, point, summit, tip, top. 2 acme, apex, climax, height, high, high point, high-water mark, maximum, pinnacle, top, zenith; opp trough

**peak** v 1 climax, culminate, reach a crescendo, reach a peak. 2 **have peaked** be in decline, be on the downward slide, be on the way down, be past your best, decline, fall off

**peal** n carillon, chime, clang, ring, ringing, toll, tolling

**peal** v chime, clang, resound, ring, ring out, toll

**peasant** n country dweller, countryman, country cousin inf, farm labourer, farm worker, farmer, farmhand, rustic, serf, smallholder, yokel inf

**peck** v bite, nibble, nip

**peculiar** adj 1 bizarre, eccentric, extraordinary, funny, odd, out of the ordinary, queer, singular, strange, unusual, weird; opp normal. 2 (peculiar to sth) characteristic, distinctive, distinguishing, exclusive, individual, own, particular, proper, special, specific, unique

**peculiarity** n 1 eccentricity, foible, idiosyncrasy, oddity. 2 attribute, characteristic, feature, hallmark, property

**pedantic** adj academic, bookish, didactic, doctrinaire, dogmatic, donnish, nit-picking, over-literal, scholarly, scholastic

**pedestrian** adj boring, commonplace, dull, mediocre, plodding, prosaic, run-of-the-mill, unimaginative, uninspired, unoriginal

**pedestrian** n foot passenger, hiker,

passer-by, rambler, walker

**pedigree** n ancestry, background, descent, family, family tree, genealogy, heritage, lineage

**peel** v pare, skin, strip, uncover

**peep** v glance, glimpse, look, peek, sneak a look, snoop, take a butcher's inf

**peer** n 1 aristocrat, baron, baroness, count, duke, earl, hereditary peer, lady, life peer, lord, marquis, noble, nobleman, peer of the realm, viscount. 2 associate, colleague, companion, equal

**peer** v gaze, look, look closely, squint inf, stare

**peevish** adj bad-tempered, cantankerous, churlish, complaining, crabby inf, cross, crotchety inf, crusty inf, disagreeable, discontented, fractious, fretful, grouchy inf, grumbling, grumpy, ill-natured, irritable, petulant, querulous, ratty inf, rude, sulky, sullen, surly, testy

**peg** v fix, keep, maintain, pin, secure, stabilize

**pelt** v batter, beat, bombard, riddle, shower, sprinkle, stone

**pen** n 1 ballpoint, ballpoint pen, biro, cartridge pen, felt-tip, felt-tip pen, fountain pen, quill. 2 cage, coop, corral, enclosure, fold, pound, sheep fold, pigsty, stall, stockade, sty

**pen** v 1 author, compose, draft, draw up, write. 2 **pen in** box in, corral, enclose, enfold, fence in, hem in, imprison, pin down, restrict

**penal** adj corrective, criminal, disciplinary, prison, punitive

**penalize** v 1 book, caution, discipline, fine, punish. 2 (a situation which penalizes sb) disadvantage, place at a disadvantage, handicap

**penalty** n caution, endorsement, fine, forfeit, punishment, sentence

**penance** n amends, atonement, expiation, penitence, punishment, repentance

**pending** adj 1 on the table, outstanding, undecided, unfinished. 2 approaching, coming, imminent, impending, in store, in the offing, on the cards, on the way

**penetrate** v bore, enter, go in, go into, go through, perforate, permeate, pervade, pierce, stab

**penitent** adj apologetic, contrite, guilty, remorseful, repentant, sheepish, sorry

**pen name** n alias, assumed name, nom de guerre, nom de plume, pseudonym, stage name

**penniless** adj bankrupt, broke inf, cleaned out inf, destitute, impecunious, impoverished, indigent, poor, poverty-stricken, without a penny, without a penny to your name

**pension** n allowance, annuity, benefit, income support, private income

**pensioner** n OAP, old age pensioner, oldie inf, retired person, senior citizen, veteran

**pensive** adj contemplative, day-dreaming, deep in thought, meditative, reflective, ruminating, thinking, thoughtful, withdrawn, wistful

**pent-up** adj accumulated, built-up, frustrated, repressed

**people** n 1 folk, folks inf, human beings, human race, humanity, humankind, man, mankind, men, mortals, individuals. 2 (the people) citizenry, citizens, common people, commoners, electorate, hoi polloi, lower orders, masses, ordinary people, plebs *inf*, populace, population, proletariat, public, society, subjects, voters. 3 clan, community, ethnic group, nation, race, tribe

**people** *v* colonize, inhabit, live in, occupy, populate, settle, stock

**perceive** *v* apprehend, appreciate, be aware of, be conscious of, detect, discern, distinguish, espy, experience, hear, note, notice, observe, recognize, register, see, sense

**perceptible** *adj* apparent, appreciable, audible, detectable, discernible, observable, noticeable, palpable, perceivable, recognizable, visible; *opp* imperceptible

**perception** *n* awareness, consciousness, discernment, experience, knowledge, grasp, insight, perceptiveness, recognition, understanding

**perceptive** *adj* acute, alert, astute, attentive, aware, bright, clever, discerning, intelligent, keen-eyed, observant, on the ball *inf*, penetrating, perspicacious, quick, sensitive, sharp, sharp-eyed, smart

**perch** *n* position, roost, seat, station, vantage point

**perch** *v* alight, balance, land, poise, position yourself, rest, roost, settle, sit, station yourself

**percussion** *n* bass drum, bongos, drum, kettledrum, glockenspiel, maracas, tambourine, snare drum, timpani, tom-tom, triangle, xylophone

**perennial** *adj* 1 constant, continuing, durable, enduring, eternal, everlasting,

lasting, permanent, unceasing. 2 continual, cyclical, recurrent, recurring, regular, seasonal

**perfect** *adj* 1 consummate, faultless, flawless, ideal, immaculate, impeccable, incomparable, irreproachable, matchless, pure, spotless, sublime, unbeatable, unblemished, unmarred, untarnished; *opp* imperfect. 2 (a perfect circle) entire, finished, full, whole; *opp* imperfect. 3 (perfect nonsense) absolute, complete, downright, out-and-out, sheer, total, unadulterated, unmitigated, utter

**perfect** *v* accomplish, achieve, bring to fruition, carry out, complete, consummate, effect, execute, finish, fulfil, perform, realize, see through

**perfection** *n* 1 completeness, faultlessness, flawlessness, incomparability, integrity, precision, purity, spotlessness, wholeness; *opp* imperfection. 2 (the perfection of a technique) accomplishment, achievement, completion, consummation, end, execution, finishing, fruition, fulfilment, realization

**perforate** *v* bore, drill, penetrate, pierce, prick, punch, puncture, stab

**perform** *v* 1 (perform a task) accomplish, achieve, carry out, complete, discharge, do, effect, execute, finish, fulfil, pull off *inf*, satisfy, transact, work. 2 (perform a play) act, depict, enact, play, present, produce, put on, render, represent, stage

**performance** *n* 1 (a gala performance) act, appearance, entertainment, exhibition, gig *inf*, play, portrayal, presentation, production, show. 2 (the performance of a task) accomplishment, achievement, completion, conduct, discharge, effect, execution, finishing, fulfilment, satisfaction, transaction

**performer** n actor, actress, artist, artiste, dancer, entertainer, musician, player, singer, thespian

**perfume** n 1 after-shave, cologne, eau de Cologne, fragrance, scent, toilet water. 2 (the perfume of flowers) aroma, bouquet, fragrance, odour, scent, smell

**perhaps** adv conceivably, feasibly, it could be, maybe, possibly; *opp* definitely

**peril** n danger, hazard, insecurity, jeopardy, menace, risk, susceptibility, uncertainty, vulnerability; *opp* safety

**perilous** adj dangerous, hazardous, insecure, precarious, risky, threatening, uncertain, unsafe; *opp* safe

**perimeter** n border, boundary, bounds, circumference, confines, edge, fringe, frontier, limit, margin, periphery, verge

**period** n interval, phase, season, session, space, span, spell, stage, stint, stretch, term, time, while

**periodical** adj cyclical, every once in a while, every so often, intermittent, occasional, periodic, recurrent, recurring, regular, repeated, spasmodic, sporadic

**perish** v 1 be killed, bite the dust *inf*, die, expire, fall, kick the bucket *inf*, lose, your life, pass away, snuff it *sl*; *opp* live. 2 collapse, crumble, decline, disappear, fall, vanish; *opp* survive. 3 decay, decompose, disintegrate, go bad, go off, go sour, rot, waste, wither

**perishable** adj biodegradable, decaying, destructible, unstable

**perjure** v bear false witness, commit perjury, give false testimony, lie under oath

**perjury** n false testimony, false witness, lying under oath, oath breaking, violation of oath

**permanent** adj abiding, constant, continual, continuous, durable, endless, enduring, eternal, everlasting, fixed, immutable, indestructible, invariable, irreparable, lasting, life-long, never-ending, non-stop, perpetual, persistent, steadfast, unchanging; *opp* temporary

**permeate** v diffuse, filter through, imbue, infiltrate, impregnate, penetrate, percolate, pervade, saturate, soak

**permissible** adj acceptable, allowable, authorized, lawful, legal, legitimate, permitted, sanctioned, within the law, within the rules; *opp* forbidden

**permission** n agreement, allowance, approval, assent, authorization, consent, dispensation, franchise, freedom, go-ahead *inf*, green light, leave, liberty, licence, sanction, thumbs-up *inf*

**permissive** adj broad-minded, easy-going, indulgent, lenient, liberal, tolerant; *opp* strict

**permit** n authority, authorization, licence, pass, passport, permission, sanction, ticket, visa, warrant

**permit** v agree, allow, approve, assent, authorize, consent, countenance, enable, endorse, entitle, grant, legalize, let, license, sanction, tolerate; *opp* forbid

**perpendicular** adj at 90 degrees, at right angles, erect, plumb, straight, upright, vertical

**perpetrate** v bring about, carry out, commit, do, effect, execute, inflict, perform, pull off *inf*

**perpetual** adj abiding, constant, continual, continuous, durable, endless, enduring, eternal, everlasting, fixed, immutable, indestructible, invariable, irreparable, lasting, life-long, never-ending, non-stop, permanent, persistent, steadfast, unchanging; *opp* temporary

**perpetuate** v continue, eternalize, immortalize, keep going, maintain, preserve, sustain; *opp* end

**perplex** v baffle, bamboozle *inf*, bewilder, dumbfound, confound, confuse, flummox, mystify, nonplus, puzzle, stump, throw *inf*

**perplexing** adj 1 baffling, bewildering, confounding, confusing, enigmatic, inexplicable, mysterious, mystifying, puzzling, strange, weird; *opp* normal. 2 complex, complicated, difficult, hard, intricate, involved, knotty; *opp* simple

**perquisite** n advantage, benefit, bonus, dividend, extra, freebie *inf*, gratuity, perk, plus

**persecute** v abuse, afflict, distress, harass, hound, hunt, ill-treat, maltreat, mistreat, oppress, pursue, torment, torture, victimize

**persevere** v carry on, continue, endure, go on, hammer away *inf*, hang on, hold on, hold out, keep at it *inf*, keep going, keep it up *inf*, maintain, persist, pursue, remain, soldier on *inf*; *opp* give up

**persist** v carry on, continue, endure, go on, hammer away *inf*, hang on, hold on, hold out, keep at it *inf*, keep going, keep it up *inf*, maintain, persevere, pursue, remain, soldier on *inf*; *opp* give up

**persistent** adj 1 (of a person) assiduous, determined, dogged, hard-working, immovable, insistent, obstinate, patient, persevering, relentless, resolute, steadfast, stubborn, tenacious, tireless, unflagging, untiring, unwavering. 2 (of a noise) ceaseless, constant, continual, continuous, endless, eternal, everlasting, incessant, interminable, lasting, long-lasting, never-ending, permanent, perpetual, relentless, unending, unrelenting, unrelieved; *opp* intermittent

**person** n being, body, character, figure, human, human being, individual, mortal, soul

**personal** adj 1 characteristic, distinctive, exclusive, idiosyncratic, individual, own, particular, peculiar, personalized, unique. 2 (a personal phone call) confidential, intimate, private

**personality** n 1 (sb's personality) character, disposition, individuality, make-up, nature, persona, temperament. 2 (a TV personality) big name, celebrity, famous name, household name, idol, star, superstar, VIP

**personnel** n employees, helpers, human resources, labour, labour force, manpower, members, people, staff, workers, workforce

**perspective** n 1 (sb's perspective on sth) angle, approach, attitude, opinion, outlook, point of view, position, slant, stance, stand, standpoint, vantage point, view, viewpoint. 2 (in perspective) context, proportion, relation, relativity

**perspiration** n beads of sweat,

moisture, sweat, wetness

**perspire** *v* drip with sweat, glow, pour with sweat, secrete, sweat, swelter

**persuade** *v* allure, cajole, coax, coerce, convince, entice, impel, induce, influence, press, prevail upon, prompt, sway, talk into, tempt, urge, wheedle *inf*, win over; *opp* dissuade

**persuasion** *n* 1 cajoling, coaxing, coercing, convincing, enticement, inducement, influencing, persuading, pressing, prompting, urging, wheedling. 2 (your political persuasion) attitude, belief, conviction, opinion, position, slant, stance, stand, standpoint, view, viewpoint

**persuasive** *adj* 1 (of evidence) compelling, conclusive, convincing, credible, impressive, plausible, sound, strong, telling, unarguable, watertight; *opp* unconvincing. 2 (of a person) effective, eloquent, forceful, impressive, influential, strong

**pertinent** *adj* admissible, applicable, apposite, appropriate, apt, fit, fitting, material, relevant, suitable, to the point; *opp* irrelevant

**perturb** *v* agitate, alarm, bother, disconcert, disquiet, distress, disturb, fluster, frighten, ruffle, scare, trouble, unnerve, unsettle, upset, worry

**perturbed** *adj* agitated, alarmed, anxious, bothered, disconcerted, disquieted, distressed, disturbed, flustered, ill at ease, nervous, restless, ruffled, scared, shaken, troubled, uncomfortable, uneasy, unnerved, unsettled, upset, worried; *opp* unconcerned

**peruse** *v* browse, check, examine, have a

look at, inspect, look over, read, run your eye over, scan, scrutinize, study

**pervade** *v* diffuse, extend, fill, filter through, imbue, infuse, penetrate, percolate, permeate, saturate, spread through

**pervasive** *adj* common, extensive, inescapable, omnipresent, pervading, prevalent, rife, ubiquitous, universal, widespread; *opp* rare

**perverse** *adj* awkward, contrary, difficult, headstrong, inflexible, intractable, obstinate, pig-headed, rebellious, stubborn, uncooperative, unruly, wayward; *opp* reasonable

**perversion** *n* 1 aberration, abnormality, debauchery, depravity, deviance, deviation, immorality, unnaturalness, vice, wickedness. 2 (the perversion of sth) corruption, distortion, falsification, misrepresentation, twisting

**pervert** *n* degenerate, deviant, perv *sl*, weirdo *sl*

**pervert** *v* abuse, bend, distort, falsify, misapply, misconstrue, misrepresent, misuse, twist, warp

**perverted** *adj* abnormal, amoral, corrupt, debased, debauched, depraved, deviant, immoral, sick, twisted, unhealthy, unnatural, warped; *opp* natural

**pessimistic** *adj* bleak, cynical, defeatist, fatalistic, gloomy, negative, resigned; *opp* optimistic

**pest** *n* 1 annoyance, bother, inconvenience, irritation, nuisance, pain, pain in the neck, trial. 2 (on plants) bug, creepy-crawly *inf*, insect, parasite

**pester** *v* annoy, badger, bother, disturb,

harass, harry, hassle, hound, irk, nag, plague, torment, trouble, worry

**pestilence** *n* affliction, blight, cancer, curse, disease, epidemic, plague, scourge

**pet** *n* apple of your eye, blue-eyed boy, blue-eyed girl, darling, favourite, idol, jewel

**pet** *v* caress, fondle, pat, stroke

**petition** *n* 1 (sign a petition) list of signatures, protest document. 2 (file a petition) appeal, application, entreaty, plea, request, suit, supplication

**petition** *v* appeal, apply, ask, beg, beseech, entreat, plead, press, solicit, urge

**petrify** *v* 1 fill sb with fear, frighten, horrify, panic, paralyse, scare, scare sb out of their wits/skin, scare sb to death, stun, stupefy, terrify. 2 calcify, fossilize, turn to stone

**petty** *adj* 1 (petty squabbling) inconsequential, insignificant, little, minor, negligible, paltry, slight, small, trifling, trivial, unimportant; *opp* important, major. 2 (don't be so petty) grudging, mean, nit-picking, small-minded, spiteful, stingy, ungenerous; *opp* generous

**phantom** *n* apparition, ghost, phantasm, spectre, spirit, spook

**phase** *n* chapter, period, part, point, season, spell, stage, step, time

**phenomenal** *adj* amazing, astonishing, astounding, exceptional, extraordinary, fabulous, fantastic, incredible, marvellous, mind-blowing *inf*, mind-boggling *inf*, miraculous, outstanding, remarkable, sensational, singular, staggering, stunning, unbelievable,

unique, wondrous; *opp* unremarkable

**phenomenon** *n* 1 (a natural phenomenon) circumstance, event, happening, incident, occurrence, sight. 2 (a musical phenomenon) marvel, miracle, prodigy, rarity, sensation, wonder

**philanthropist** *n* altruist, humanitarian, giver, good Samaritan, provider

**philistine** *n* barbarian, ignoramus, lout; *opp* intellectual

**philosopher** *n* logician, metaphysician, sage, scholar, theorist, thinker

**philosophical** *adj* 1 (a philosophical discussion) abstract, erudite, learned, theoretical, thoughtful. 2 (be philosophical about sth) accepting, calm, collected, composed, cool, patient, rational, realistic, reasonable, resigned, stoical

**philosophy** *n* 1 (study philosophy) ideology, logic, metaphysics, rationalism, reason, thinking, thought. 2 (your philosophy on sth) attitude, belief, conviction, ideology, opinion, outlook, point of view, principle, thinking, view, viewpoint

**phlegmatic** *adj* 1 calm, cool, composed, imperturbable, philosophical, placid, serene, stoical, undemonstrative, unemotional; *opp* excitable. 2 apathetic, impassive, indifferent, unenthusiastic, unresponsive; *opp* enthusiastic

**phobia** *n* antipathy, aversion, dislike, distaste, dread, fear, hang-up *inf*, hatred, horror, loathing, neurosis, obsession, repulsion, terror, thing *inf*

**phone** *n* blower *inf*, car phone,

mobile phone, telephone

**phone** v call, call up, dial, give sb a bell, give sb a buzz, give sb a call, give sb a ring, give sb a tinkle, make a phone call, ring, ring up, telephone

**phoney** adj artificial, assumed, bogus, counterfeit, fake, false, fictitious, forged, fraudulent, imitation, mock, pretend, pseudo, put-on inf, sham, spurious, trick; **opp** real

**photocopy** n copy, duplicate, photostat, print-off, xerox TM

**photocopy** v copy, duplicate, photostat, print off, reproduce, run off, xerox TM

**photograph** n enlargement, exposure, image, likeness, photo, picture, print, shot, snap inf, snapshot

**photograph** v capture on film, film, record, shoot, snap inf, take a picture

**photographic** adj (a photographic memory) accurate, exact, pictorial, precise, retentive, visual

**phrase** n 1 catchphrase, expression, idiom, proverb, remark, saying, statement, utterance. 2 clause, group of words, sentence

**phrase** v express, formulate, frame, present, put, say, term, utter, voice, word

**physical** adj 1 (physical things) concrete, material, palpable, real, substantial, tangible, visible; **opp** intangible. 2 (physical activity) bodily, corporal, corporeal, physiological; **opp** mental

**physician** n consultant, doc inf, doctor, general practitioner, GP, medic inf, medical practitioner, quack inf, specialist

**physique** n body, build, figure, form, frame, shape

**pick** n best, cream, elite, favourite,

flower, pride; **opp** worst

**pick** v 1 choose, decide, elect, favour, make a choice, opt for, plump for, prefer, select, settle on, single out, vote for; **opp** discard. 2 (pick flowers) collect, cut, gather, harvest, pluck, pull. 3 **pick on** browbeat, bully, give sb a hard time, harass, hector, persecute, push sb around inf; **opp** favour

**picture** n 1 drawing, illustration, image, likeness, painting, photograph, portrait, print, representation, sketch. 2 (a picture of what sth is like) account, depiction, description, image, impression, report. 3 (take a picture) photo, shot, snap inf, snapshot. 4 (a motion picture) blockbuster, film, flick inf, movie, video

**picture** v call to mind, conceive, conjure up, envisage, evoke, imagine, see, think up, visualize

**picturesque** adj attractive, beautiful, charming, idyllic, lovely, pretty, quaint, scenic, striking; **opp** ugly

**piece** n 1 bit, bite, chunk, dollop inf, fraction, fragment, hunk, length, lump, morsel, part, portion, quantity, scrap, section, segment, share, shred, slab, slice, sliver, unit. 2 (a piece in the newspaper) article, column, composition, item, report, review. 3 (a piece by a famous sculptor) creation, specimen, study, work, work of art

**pier** n breakwater, dock, jetty, landing stage, quay, wharf

**pierce** v bore, drill, impale, jab, penetrate, perforate, prick, puncture, spike, stab

**piercing** adj 1 (a piercing sound) ear-splitting, high-pitched, loud, sharp,

shrieking, shrill; *opp* gentle, soft.
2 (a piercing wind) arctic, biting, bitter,
cold, freezing, keen, numbing, wintry;
*opp* warm

**pigment** *n* colour, colourant, dye, stain,
tincture, tint

**pile** *n* 1 accumulation, agglomeration,
bundle, collection, heap, mass, mound,
mountain, stack, stock, store, tower.
2 abundance, heaps *inf*, load, loads *inf*,
mass, masses *inf*, lots *inf*, stacks *inf*

**pile** *v* accumulate, amass, assemble,
collect, gather, heap, hoard, load, pile
up, stack up, stockpile, stock up, store up

**pile-up** *n* accident, collision, crash,
smash, smash-up

**pilgrim** *n* crusader, devotee, seeker,
traveller, wanderer, wayfarer, worshipper

**pilgrimage** *n* crusade, expedition,
journey, mission, quest, search

**pill** *n* capsule, drug, lozenge, medicine,
pastille, pellet, tablet

**pillage** *n* looting, marauding, plunder,
plundering, raiding, ransacking, rifling,
robbery, robbing, sack

**pillage** *v* despoil, loot, plunder, raid,
ransack, ravage, raze, rifle, rob, sack,
strip

**pillar** *n* 1 column, pier, pilaster, pole,
post, prop, shaft, stanchion, support,
upright. 2 (pillar of society) backbone,
mainstay, rock, supporter, upholder,
worthy

**pilot** *n* 1 airman, aviator, captain,
commander, director, driver, flier,
helmsman, navigator. 2 experiment,
model, prototype, test, trial

**pilot** *v* 1 conduct, convey, direct, drive,
fly, guide, lead, navigate, point,

shepherd, steer. 2 model, test, try out

**pimple** *n* acne, blackhead, boil, pustule,
spot, swelling, zit *sl*

**pin** *n* bolt, brooch, clip, fastener, nail, peg,
rivet, spike, staple, tack

**pin** *v* affix, attach, clip, fasten, fix, join,
nail, peg, rivet, secure, staple, stick,
tack. 2 **pin down** constrain, hold down,
immobilize, pinion, restrain

**pinch** *v* 1 compress, grasp, nip, press,
squeeze, tweak. 2 chafe, confine, cramp,
crush, hurt, rub, squeeze. 3 filch *inf*, lift
*inf*, make off with *inf*, nick *inf*, plunder,
poach, rob, shoplift, steal, swipe *inf*,
walk off with

**pine** *v* ache, crave, hanker, hunger, long,
miss, mourn, mope, sicken, yearn

**pinnacle** *n* acme, apex, apogee, cap, crest,
crown, height, high point, peak,
summit, top, zenith

**pinpoint** *v* define, discover, distinguish,
find, home in on, identify, locate,
specify, spot

**pioneer** *n* 1 colonist, discoverer, explorer,
frontiersman, frontierswoman, settler.
2 architect, developer, discoverer,
founder, front-runner, ground-breaker,
innovator, inventor, leader, originator,
trail-blazer, trend-setter

**pioneer** *v* begin, create, develop,
discover, experiment with, found,
initiate, instigate, institute, introduce,
invent, lead the way, launch, originate,
set up, start

**pious** *adj* 1 dedicated, devoted, devout,
God-fearing, godly, holy, religious,
reverent, righteous, saintly, spiritual,
virtuous; *opp* impious. 2 goody-goody
*inf*, holier-than-thou, hypocritical,

**pipe** *n* channel, conduit, cylinder, duct, hose, line, main, passage, pipeline, tube

**pipe** *v* 1 channel, conduct, siphon, transmit. 2 cheep, chirp, flute, peep, shrill, squeak, trill, twitter, warble, whistle

**piquant** *adj* hot, peppery, pungent, salty, savoury, sharp, spicy, tart, tasty; *opp* bland

**pirate** *n* 1 buccaneer, corsair, freebooter, hijacker, marauder, raider, rover. 2 copier, plagiarist

**pirate** *v* appropriate, copy, infringe copyright, plagiarize, poach, reproduce

**pit** *n* 1 abyss, cavity, chasm, crater, dent, depression, ditch, excavation, gulf, hole, hollow, indentation, pot-hole, trench. 2 coal-mine, colliery, mine, quarry, shaft, working

**pitch** *n* 1 arena, field, ground, park, playing-field, stadium. 2 degree, extent, height, intensity, level, point. 3 angle, dip, gradient, incline, slant, slope, steepness, tilt

**pitch** *v* 1 bowl, cast, chuck *inf*, fling, heave, hurl, lob *inf*, sling, throw, toss. 2 (pitch a tent) erect, put up, raise, set up. 3 pitch in assist, chip in *inf*, contribute, do your bit, help, join in, lend a hand, participate, play a part

**pitch-black** *adj* coal-black, ebony, jet-black, pitch-dark, raven

**piteous** *adj* affecting, distressing, grievous, heartbreaking, heart-rending, lamentable, miserable, moving, pathetic, pitiable, pitiful, plaintive, poignant, sad, touching, upsetting, woeful, wretched

**pitfall** *n* catch, danger, difficulty, drawback, hazard, peril, snag, stumbling-block, trap

**pitiful** *adj* 1 affecting, distressing, grievous, heartbreaking, heart-rending, lamentable, miserable, moving, pathetic, piteous, pitiable, plaintive, poignant, sad, touching, upsetting, woeful, wretched. 2 contemptible, hopeless, inadequate, laughable, mean, measly, miserable, paltry, pathetic *inf*, poor, ridiculous, risible, shabby, sorry, useless, worthless; *opp* good

**pitiless** *adj* brutal, callous, cold-blooded, cold-hearted, cruel, hard, hard-hearted, harsh, heartless, implacable, inexorable, inhuman, merciless, relentless, ruthless, sadistic, uncaring, unfeeling, unmerciful, unsympathetic; *opp* merciful

**pittance** *n* chicken-feed *inf*, drop, mite, peanuts *inf*, scrap, trifle

**pity** *n* 1 charity, clemency, commiseration, compassion, compunction, condolence, fellow-feeling, forbearance, kindness, mercy, quarter, sympathy, tenderness, understanding. 2 (a pity) bad luck, crime *inf*, crying shame *inf*, misfortune, shame

**pity** *v* commiserate, feel for, feel sorry for, show compassion, show mercy, sympathize, weep for; *opp* envy

**pivot** *n* 1 axis, axle, fulcrum, hinge, pin, spindle, swivel. 2 centre, focus, heart, hub

**pivot** *v* revolve, rotate, swing, swivel, turn

**placard** *n* advert, advertisement, bill, notice, poster, sign

**placate** *v* appease, assuage, calm,

conciliate, humour, mollify, pacify, propitiate, satisfy, soothe

**place** n 1 area, location, point, position, scene, setting, site, situation, spot, station, venue, whereabouts. 2 city, country, county, district, locale, locality, neighbourhood, quarter, region, state, town, vicinity, village. 3 (sb's home) abode, apartment, domicile, dwelling, house, flat, property, residence, rooms. 4 (second place in a race) grade, position, rank, role, standing, station, status. 5 (a job) employment, job, office, position, post, situation

**place** v 1 deposit, dump inf, lay, leave, locate, plant, pop inf, position, put, rest, settle, situate, stand, station, stick inf. 2 arrange, categorize, class, classify, grade, group, order, put in order, rank, sort

**placid** adj calm, collected, composed, cool, easy-going, equable, even-tempered, gentle, imperturbable, mild, peaceful, phlegmatic, quiet, serene, steady, still, tranquil, unexcitable, unruffled; opp excitable

**plagiarize** v copy, crib inf, lift inf, pirate, reproduce, steal

**plague** n 1 disease, epidemic, infection, outbreak, pestilence. 2 affliction, bane, blight, blot, calamity, cancer, curse, evil, scourge, torment, trial

**plague** v afflict, annoy, badger, bedevil, bother, bug inf, disturb, harass, hassle inf, hound, molest, nag, persecute, pester, tease, torment, torture, trouble, vex

**plain** adj 1 apparent, audible, clear, comprehensible, distinct, evident, legible, lucid, manifest, obvious, patent, transparent, unambiguous, unmistakable, visible. 2 average, common, commonplace, everyday, homely, lowly, modest, ordinary, simple, typical, unaffected, unpretentious; opp sophisticated. 3 austere, bare, basic, discreet, modest, muted, pure, restrained, severe, simple, stark, unadorned, Spartan; opp decorated, fancy. 4 (of sb's appearance) ordinary-looking, ugly, unattractive, unprepossessing; opp pretty. 5 artless, bluff, blunt, candid, frank, guileless, honest, open, outspoken, straightforward, unvarnished, upfront inf

**plain** n flatland, grassland, lowland, pampas, plateau, prairie, savannah, steppe, veld

**plain-spoken** adj artless, bluff, blunt, candid, direct, explicit, forthright, frank, guileless, honest, open, outspoken, straightforward, unvarnished, upfront inf; opp indirect

**plaintive** adj doleful, melancholy, mournful, pathetic, piteous, pitiful, plangent, rueful, sad, sorrowful, unhappy, wistful, woebegone, woeful; opp cheerful

**plan** n 1 aim, course, design, device, formula, idea, intention, method, plot, policy, procedure, programme, project, proposal, proposition, scenario, scheme, strategy, suggestion, system. 2 bird's-eye view, blueprint, chart, diagram, drawing, layout, map, representation, sketch

**plan** v 1 arrange, concoct, contrive, design, devise, draft, draw up, formulate, map out, mastermind, organize, outline, plot, prepare, project, scheme, think up, work out. 2 aim, contemplate, envisage, foresee, intend, mean, propose, purpose, think of

**plane** *adj* even, flat, flush, horizontal, level, regular, smooth, uniform

**plane** *n* 1 flat surface, level, surface. 2 degree, footing, level, position, rank, stratum. 3 aeroplane, aircraft, airplane *Am*, jet, jumbo

**planet** *n* globe, orb, satellite, sphere, world

**plant** *n* 1 bush, flower, greenery, herb, shrub, vegetable, weed. 2 factory, foundry, mill, shop, works, workshop, yard. 3 apparatus, equipment, gear, machinery, machines, tools

**plant** *v* 1 implant, scatter, seed, sow, transplant. 2 locate, place, put, set, situate, station

**plaster** *n* 1 gypsum, mortar, plasterwork, stucco. 2 bandage, dressing, sticking-plaster

**plaster** *v* bedaub, coat, cover, daub, overlay, smear, spread

**plastic** *adj* ductile, flexible, malleable, pliable, pliant, soft, supple, workable; **opp** rigid

**plate** *n* 1 dish, platter, salver. 2 illustration, lithograph, photo, photograph, picture, print

**platform** *n* 1 dais, podium, rostrum, stage, stand. 2 manifesto, objectives, plan, policy, programme, proposals

**platitude** *n* banality, cliché, commonplace, stock phrase, truism

**plausible** *adj* believable, conceivable, credible, imaginable, likely, logical, persuasive, possible, probable, rational, reasonable, sensible, tenable; **opp** implausible

**play** *n* 1 comedy, drama, performance, piece, show, tragedy. 2 amusement, diversion, entertainment, frivolity, frolics, fun, games, horse-play, leisure, merry-making, playing, recreation, revelry, sport

**play** *v* 1 amuse yourself, caper, cavort, enjoy yourself, frisk, frolic, have a good time, have fun, gambol, romp, sport, trifle. 2 (in a game, match) compete, join in, participate, take part. 3 (play a character) act, impersonate, perform, play the part of, portray, represent, take the part of. 4 **play down** belittle, downplay, gloss over, make light of, make little of, minimize, underplay, underrate, understate. 5 **play on** abuse, capitalize on, exploit, impose on, make the most of, profit by, take advantage of, trade on. 6 **play up** accentuate, emphasize, exaggerate, highlight, overstate, spotlight, stress, talk up, underline

**playboy** *n* hedonist, ladies' man, man-about-town, philanderer, pleasure-seeker, rake, roué, socialite, sybarite, womanizer

**player** *n* 1 competitor, contestant, participant, sportsman, sportswoman, team member. 2 (theatre) actor, actress, artiste, entertainer, performer, thespian, trouper. 3 (music) artist, artiste, instrumentalist, musician, performer, soloist, virtuoso

**playful** *adj* cheerful, frisky, frolicsome, fun-loving, high-spirited, humorous, impish, jokey, kittenish, light-hearted, lively, merry, mischievous, puckish, roguish, spirited, sportive, sprightly, teasing, vivacious; **opp** serious

**plea** n 1 appeal, entreaty, petition, prayer, request, suit, supplication. 2 argument, claim, excuse, explanation, justification

**plead** v 1 appeal, beg, beseech, entreat, implore, petition, pray, solicit, supplicate. 2 allege, argue, assert, claim, declare, maintain, put forward, reason

**pleasant** adj 1 agreeable, amusing, delightful, enjoyable, fine, good, gratifying, lovely, nice, pleasing, pleasurable, satisfying, welcome; **opp** unpleasant. 2 (of a person) affable, agreeable, amiable, charming, cheerful, congenial, engaging, friendly, genial, good-humoured, likable, nice, sympathetic, winning; **opp** unpleasant

**pleasantry** n badinage, banter, greeting, jest, joke, quip, remark

**please** v 1 amuse, appeal, charm, cheer, content, delight, divert, entertain, give pleasure, gladden, gratify, indulge, make happy, satisfy, suit, tickle *inf*; **opp** displease. 2 (do as you please) choose, desire, like, prefer, see fit, want, will, wish

**pleased** adj charmed, chuffed *inf*, content, contented, delighted, elated, euphoric, glad, gratified, happy, over the moon *inf*, satisfied, thrilled, tickled *inf*; **opp** annoyed, unhappy

**pleasing** adj agreeable, amusing, attractive, beautiful, charming, delightful, enjoyable, fine, good, gratifying, lovely, nice, pleasant, pleasurable, satisfying

**pleasure** n amusement, bliss, comfort, contentment, delectation, delight, diversion, enjoyment, entertainment, ecstasy, euphoria, fulfilment, gratification, happiness, joy, recreation, satisfaction

**pledge** n 1 assurance, covenant, oath, promise, undertaking, vow, warrant, word. 2 bail, bond, collateral, deposit, gage, guarantee, security, surety

**pledge** v commit yourself, contract, covenant, give your word, guarantee, promise, swear, undertake, vouchsafe, vow, warrant

**plentiful** adj abounding, abundant, bounteous, bountiful, copious, generous, inexhaustible, lavish, liberal, overflowing, plenteous, profuse; **opp** rare

**plenty** n 1 abundance, loads *inf*, lots *inf*, masses *inf*, mountains, plethora, profusion, quantity, stacks *inf*, sufficiency, tons *inf*, wealth. 2 abundance, affluence, bounty, fruitfulness, luxury, opulence, plenitude, prosperity, wealth; **opp** scarcity

**pliable** adj 1 bendy, ductile, elastic, flexible, malleable, plastic, pliant, soft, stretchable, supple, workable; **opp** rigid. 2 (of a person) amenable, compliant, docile, flexible, impressionable, manageable, pliant, receptive, tractable, yielding; **opp** stubborn

**plight** n case, condition, difficulty, dilemma, hot water *inf*, jam *inf*, pickle *inf*, problem, predicament, scrape *inf*, situation, spot *inf*, state, straits, trouble

**plod** v clump, drag, lumber, plough, slog, stomp, tramp, tread, trudge

**plot** n 1 cabal, conspiracy, intrigue, machination, plan, scheme, stratagem. 2 (of a story) action, narrative, outline, scenario, story, story-line, thread.

**3** (plot of land) acreage, allotment, garden, lot, parcel, patch, smallholding, tract

**plot** v **1** collude, conspire, cook up *inf*, devise, hatch, intrigue, manoeuvre, plan, scheme. **2** calculate, chart, compute, draft, draw, locate, map, mark, outline, record, sketch

**plough** v cultivate, dig, furrow, ridge, till, turn over, work

**pluck** v clutch, grab, grasp, jerk, pull, seize, snatch, tug, tweak, yank

**plug** n **1** bung, cork, seal, spigot, stopper. **2** advert *inf*, advertisement, hype *inf*, mention, promotion, publicity, push

**plug** v **1** block, bung, close, cork, seal, stop, stopper, stuff. **2** advertise, hype *inf*, mention, promote, publicize, push

**plume** n feather, plumage, quill

**plump** adj ample, buxom, chubby, corpulent, dumpy, fat, fleshy, full, obese, podgy, portly, pudgy, roly-poly, rotund, round, stout, tubby; *opp* thin

**plunder** n **1** booty, contraband, ill-gotten gains, loot, pickings, prize, spoils, stolen goods, swag *inf*. **2** looting, marauding, pillage, plundering, raiding, ransacking, rifling, robbery, robbing, sack

**plunder** v despoil, lay waste, loot, pillage, raid, ransack, ravage, rifle, rob, sack, spoil, steal, strip

**plunge** v **1** descend, dip, dive, drop, fall, hurtle, nosedive, plummet, pitch, sink, swoop, tumble. **2** dip, douse, immerse, sink, submerge, thrust

**ply** v carry on, engage in, exercise, follow, practise, pursue, work at

**poach** v filch *inf*, lift *inf*, make off with *inf*, nick *inf*, pinch *inf*, plagiarize, plunder,

rob, steal, swipe *inf*, thieve

**pocket** n bag, compartment, hollow, pouch, receptacle, sack

**pocket** v appropriate, filch *inf*, nick *inf*, pinch *inf*, steal, take, walk off with

**pod** n case, hull, husk, shell

**poem** n ditty *inf*, haiku, limerick, lyric, ode, rhyme, song, sonnet, verse

**poet** n bard, lyricist, rhymer, sonneteer, versifier

**poetic** adj flowery, imaginative, lyric, lyrical, musical, rhythmical

**poetry** n poems, rhymes, rhyming, verse

**poignant** adj affecting, bitter, distressing, emotional, evocative, heartbreaking, intense, moving, painful, pathetic, pitiful, sad, sentimental, tender, touching, tragic, upsetting

**point** n **1** (meet at a certain point) location, place, position, site, spot. **2** (a sharp point) apex, end, nib, prong, sharp end, spike, spur, tine, tip, top. **3** (point in time) instant, juncture, moment, second, stage, time. **4** (the point of doing sth) aim, goal, intention, motive, purpose, reason, use. **5** (the point of what sb is saying) crux, drift, essence, gist, meaning, relevance, significance, theme, thrust. **6** (sb's good points) attribute, characteristic, facet, feature, quality, trait

**point** v **1** (point sth at sb) aim, direct, level, train. **2** (point at sth) call attention to, draw attention to, indicate, point out, show, signal. **3** (point sb in the right direction) guide, lead, steer

**pointed** adj barbed, edged, sharp, spiky

**pointer** n **1** arrow, hand, indicator, needle. **2** advice, hint, recommendation, suggestion, tip, warning

**pointless** adj aimless, fruitless, futile, ineffective, in vain, irrelevant, meaningless, senseless, silly, stupid, unproductive, useless, worthless; **opp** useful

**poise** n aplomb, assurance, calmness, composure, cool, coolness, dignity, equanimity, sang-froid, self-assurance, self-possession

**poised** adj 1 calm, collected, composed, dignified, self-confident, self-possessed, unflappable inf. 2 balanced, hovering, in equilibrium, steady, teetering, wavering. 3 (poised for sth) all set, keyed up, prepared, ready, standing by, waiting

**poison** n toxin, venom

**poison** v 1 (poison sth) adulterate, blight, contaminate, infect, pollute, spoil. 2 (poison sb) give poison to, kill, murder. 3 (poison sb's mind) corrupt, deprave, pervert, subvert, warp

**poisonous** adj deadly, fatal, lethal, noxious, toxic, venomous, virulent

**poke** v dig, elbow, hit, jab, nudge, prod, punch, push, stab, stick, thrust

**poky** adj confined, cramped, narrow, small, tiny; **opp** spacious

**pole** n bar, column, mast, post, prop, rod, shaft, spar, stake, stick, upright

**polarize** v diverge, divide, separate, split

**police** n constabulary, police force, the Bill inf, the fuzz inf, the law inf

**police** v control, guard, keep in order, oversee, patrol, protect, regulate, supervise, watch over

**policeman** n bobby inf, constable, cop inf, copper inf, detective, inspector, officer, PC, WPC, policewoman

**policy** n approach, code, course, guidelines, line inf, manifesto, plan, practice, procedure, programme, protocol, rules, scheme, strategy, theory

**polish** n 1 brightness, brilliance, finish, glaze, gleam, gloss, lustre, sheen, shine, sparkle, veneer. 2 beeswax, oil, shellac, varnish, wax. 3 (sb has polish) class inf, elegance, grace, refinement, sophistication, style

**polish** v brighten, buff, burnish, clean, rub, shine, smooth, wax

**polished** adj 1 (a polished surface) bright, gleaming, glossy, lustrous, shining, shiny, slippery, smooth.
2 (polished manners) civilized, classy inf, cultivated, elegant, polite, posh, refined, sophisticated, well-bred; **opp** rough. 3 (a polished performance) accomplished, expert, flawless, impeccable, masterly, perfect, proficient, skilful; **opp** bad, poor

**polite** adj 1 (of a person) attentive, chivalrous, civil, considerate, courteous, gracious, respectful, thoughtful, well-behaved, well-mannered, well-spoken; **opp** rude. 2 diplomatic, discreet, euphemistic, formal, proper, tactful

**political** adj administrative, civic, diplomatic, governmental, legislative, parliamentary, public, state

**politician** n congressman, legislator, member of parliament, MP, senator, statesman

**politics** n affairs of state, civics, diplomacy, government, political science, public affairs, statesmanship

**poll** n 1 ballot, count, election,

referendum, vote, voting. 2 canvass, census, market research, sampling, show of hands, survey

**poll** v ballot, canvass, interview, question, sample, survey

**pollute** v adulterate, contaminate, dirty, foul, infect, make dirty, poison, soil, spoil, stain, taint

**pollution** n adulteration, contamination, dirt, dirtiness, filth, filthiness

**pomp** n ceremony, display, glitter, glory, grandeur, magnificence, majesty, ostentation, pageantry, ritual, spectacle, splendour, show

**pompous** adj affected, arrogant, boastful, bombastic, conceited, grandiose, imperious, inflated, ostentatious, overbearing, pretentious, self-important, showy, smug, snooty inf, stuck-up inf, vain; **opp** modest

**pond** n duck pond, lake, millpond, pool, puddle, tarn

**ponder** v brood, consider, contemplate, deliberate, meditate, mull over, muse, reflect, ruminate, study, think

**ponderous** adj 1 awkward, bulky, cumbersome, heavy, huge, massive, slow, unwieldy; **opp** light. 2 (a ponderous speech) boring, dreary, dull, humourless, laboured, long-winded, plodding, slow, tedious, tiresome

**pool** n lagoon, lake, oasis, paddling pool, pond, puddle, swimming pool, tarn

**pool** v amalgamate, combine, merge, put together, share

**poor** adj 1 (of a person) badly off, broke inf, deprived, destitute, hard up inf, impoverished, needy, penniless, poverty-stricken, skint inf; **opp** rich. 2 (a poor

amount) deficient, inadequate, insufficient, meagre, miserable, reduced, scanty, sparse. 3 (poor quality) bad, cheap, defective, faulty, imperfect, inferior, rubbishy, shoddy, substandard; **opp** good. 4 (unlucky) ill-fated, luckless, miserable, pathetic, pitiable, unfortunate, unhappy, unlucky, wretched; **opp** lucky. 5 (a poor home) humble, lowly, mean, modest, simple. 6 (poor soil) arid, bare, barren, depleted, infertile, unproductive; **opp** rich

**pop** v bang, burst, crack, detonate, explode, go off, snap

**populace** n crowd, general public, masses, mob, multitude, people, public, rabble

**popular** adj 1 (liked by many people) accepted, approved, celebrated, famous, fashionable, favourite, in, in demand, liked, sought-after, well-known, well-liked; **opp** unpopular. 2 (believed by many people) common, conventional, current, general, predominant, prevailing, standard, universal, widespread

**popularity** n acceptance, acclaim, approval, currency, demand, fame, favour, renown, vogue

**popularize** v give credence to, give currency to, make accessible, make available, make popular, promote, spread

**populate** v colonize, dwell in, fill, inhabit, live in, occupy, overrun, people, settle

**population** n citizens, community, folk, inhabitants, people, populace, public, residents, society

**populous** adj crowded, densely

populated, heavily populated, overpopulated, packed

**porch** n doorway, entrance, lobby, vestibule

**pore over** v 1 (pore over a book) examine, peruse, read, scrutinize, study. 2 (pore over a question) brood on, contemplate, dwell on, go over, meditate on, mull over, muse on, ponder, reflect on, think about

**pornographic** adj blue, dirty, erotic, explicit, filthy, indecent, obscene, porn inf, sexual, titillating

**porous** adj absorbent, cellular, penetrable, permeable, sponge-like, spongy

**port** n dock, harbour, haven, sea-port

**portable** adj compact, convenient, easy to carry, handy, light, lightweight, manageable, mobile, movable, pocket, pocket-sized, small, transportable

**porter** n caretaker, concierge, door-keeper, doorman, gatekeeper, janitor, security-guard, watchman

**portion** n 1 bit, chunk, helping, piece, section, segment, serving, slice, sliver, wedge. 2 (sb's portion) allocation, allowance, cut inf, measure, percentage, quantity, quota, ration, share, whack inf

**portrait** n drawing, image, likeness, painting, photograph, picture, portrayal, representation, self-portrait, study

**portray** v 1 delineate, depict, draw, illustrate, paint, render, represent, sketch. 2 characterize, depict, describe, represent, show

**pose** n 1 attitude, bearing, position, posture, stance. 2 act, affectation, façade, front, masquerade, posture, pretence, role

**pose** v 1 (pose for your picture) model, sit, strike a pose. 2 act, be a poser inf, put on airs, put on an act, show off. 3 (pose a question) ask, put, submit, suggest. 4 (pose a problem) cause, create, present

**poseur** n fraud, poser inf, posturer, show-off

**posh** adj 1 (of a person) aristocratic, genteel, rich, snobbish, stuck-up inf, toffee-nosed inf, upper-class; *opp* common. 2 (of a restaurant, shop) classy inf, elegant, expensive, fancy, fashionable, swanky inf, swish inf, up-market inf, upscale inf; *opp* cheap

**position** n 1 (position on a map) bearings, location, reference, whereabouts. 2 (a house in a good position) area, locale, location, place, setting, site, situation, spot. 3 (a comfortable position for driving) angle, pose, posture, stance, way of sitting. 4 (put sb in an awkward position) plight, predicament, situation, state. 5 (opinion) attitude, belief, opinion, point of view, stance, view. 6 (position in society) caste, class, importance, place, rank, station, status. 7 (applying for a position in the company) job, post, situation. 8 (position in the league tables) grade, level, place, rank

**position** v arrange, array, lay out, locate, place, put, set, site, situate, stand, station

**positive** adj 1 absolute, actual, affirmative, categorical, certain, clear, clear-cut, decided, definite, emphatic, firm, incontrovertible, indisputable, real, undeniable, unmistakable. 2 certain,

confident, convinced, sure;
*opp* doubtful. **3** (some positive advice)
constructive, helpful, practical,
productive, useful, worthwhile;
*opp* unhelpful. **4** (a positive approach)
confident, hopeful, idealistic, optimistic;
*opp* negative

**possess** v **1** be the owner of, enjoy, have,
hold, own. **2** (possess a sense of humour)
be blessed with, be endowed with, have.
**3** (take by force) acquire, invade,
occupy, seize, take over, take possession
of. **4** (possess sb's mind) bewitch,
captivate, cast a spell over, charm,
control, dominate, enchant, enthral,
haunt, hypnotize, influence, obsess

**possessions** n assets, belongings, effects,
property, things, worldly goods

**possessive** adj **1** clinging, controlling,
dominating, domineering, jealous,
overprotective, proprietorial, protective.
**2** acquisitive, covetous, grasping, greedy,
selfish; *opp* generous

**possibility** n chance, danger, likelihood,
odds, potential, probability, prospect,
risk

**possible** adj able to be done, attainable,
conceivable, credible, feasible,
imaginable, likely, plausible, potential,
practicable, probable, realizable,
reasonable, viable, within reach;
*opp* impossible

**possibly** adv God willing, hopefully *inf*,
if possible, maybe, perhaps

**post** n **1** (wooden post) column, pillar,
pole, shaft, stake, support, upright.
**2** (job) appointment, job, position,
situation, vacancy. **3** (catch the post)
collection, delivery, mail, postal service.

**4** (deal with your post) correspondence,
letters, mail

**post** v dispatch, mail, send, transmit

**poster** n advertisement, flyer, notice,
placard, sign

**posterity** n **1** future, future generations.
**2** children, descendants, offspring, heirs,
successors

**postpone** v adjourn, defer, delay, hold
over, put back, put off, put on ice *inf*, put
on the back burner *inf*, shelve, suspend

**postscript** n addition, afterthought,
appendix, codicil, PS

**postulate** v advance, assume,
hypothesize, posit, propose, suppose

**posture** n attitude, bearing, carriage,
deportment, pose, stance

**pot** n bowl, cauldron, container, dish, jar,
pan, urn, vessel

**potent** adj effective, forceful, influential,
mighty, overwhelming, powerful, strong,
vigorous; *opp* weak

**potential** adj budding, developing,
embryonic, future, likely, possible,
promising, would-be *inf*

**potion** n brew, concoction, dose, draught,
drink, drug, elixir, liquid, mixture

**potter** v **1** (potter in the garden) dabble,
do odd jobs, fiddle, mess about, tinker.
**2** (potter along) dawdle, dilly-dally,
move slowly

**pottery** n ceramics, china, crockery,
earthenware, porcelain, stoneware,
terracotta

**pouch** n bag, pocket, purse, sack, wallet

**pounce** v ambush, attack, drop, jump,
lunge, snatch, spring, strike, swoop, take
sb by surprise

**pound** n compound, corral,

enclosure, pen, yard

**pound** v **1** batter, beat, knead, press, pummel, thump. **2** crush, grind, mash, powder, pulverize, smash. **3** (pounding along) clump, stamp, stomp, tramp. **4** (heart began to pound) bang, beat heavily, bump, palpitate, pulse, throb, thump

**pour** v **1** (liquid pouring) cascade, course, flood, flow, gush, jet, run, rush, spew, spill, splash, spout, spurt, stream. **2** (rain) bucket down *inf*, pelt down, rain hard, teem, throw it down *inf*. **3** (pour the wine) decant, serve

**poverty** n destitution, distress, hardship, insolvency, need, penury, want; *opp* wealth

**powder** n dust, fine particles, talc

**powder** v crush, granulate, grind, pound, pulverize

**power** n **1** drive, energy, force, might, muscle, potency, powerfulness, strength, vigour. **2** (the power to do sth) ability, capability, competence, potential. **3** (power over sb) ascendancy, authority, clout *inf*, command, control, dominance, domination, influence, mastery, rule, sovereignty, supremacy, sway. **4** (power to grant sth) authority, authorization, licence, prerogative, right

**powerful** adj **1** mighty, robust, strapping, strong, sturdy, tough; *opp* weak. **2** (a powerful ruler) authoritative, commanding, dominant, invincible, mighty, omnipotent, sovereign, strong, supreme; *opp* weak. **3** (a powerful argument) compelling, convincing, effective, eloquent, forceful, persuasive, telling; *opp* weak

**powerless** adj debilitated, defenceless, dependent, disabled, feeble, frail, helpless, impotent, incapable, incapacitated, ineffectual, paralysed, unable, unarmed, vulnerable, weak; *opp* strong

**practicable** adj achievable, attainable, doable *inf*, feasible, possible, realistic, sensible, viable, workable; *opp* impracticable

**practical** adj **1** (a practical person) capable, competent, efficient, expert, hands-on, no-nonsense *inf*, practised, proficient, skilled, trained. **2** (be practical about sth) businesslike, down-to-earth, hard-headed, hard-nosed *inf*, matter-of-fact, pragmatic, realistic, sensible. **3** (practical shoes) functional, sensible, utilitarian

**practice** n **1** drill, exercise, preparation, rehearsal, repetition, study, training. **2** (it's only a practice) dummy-run *inf*, rehearsal, run-through *inf*. **3** (a common practice) custom, habit, tradition, way. **4** (standard practice) method, procedure, tradition. **5** (put sth into practice) action, effect, operation

**practise** v **1** drill, exercise, go over, go through, polish, prepare, refine, rehearse, repeat, run through, study, train, warm up, work out. **2** (practise a religion) follow, observe

**pragmatic** adj businesslike, efficient, matter-of-fact, practical, realistic, sensible

**praise** n **1** acclaim, accolades, applause, approval, commendation, compliments, congratulations, ovation, thanks, tributes. **2** (praise of God) adoration,

**praise** v 1 (praise sb) acclaim, admire, applaud, cheer, clap, commend, compliment, congratulate, pay tribute to, rave about *inf*; *opp* criticize. 2 (praise God) adore, exalt, glorify, honour, offer praise to, worship

**praiseworthy** *adj* admirable, commendable, creditable, deserving, excellent, good, laudable

**prance** v bound, caper, cavort, dance, frisk, gambol, jump, leap, play, romp, skip

**prank** n jape, practical joke, stunt, trick

**prattle** v chatter, gabble, jabber, rabbit *inf*, twitter, waffle *inf*, witter on *inf*

**pray** v 1 ask, beg, beseech, entreat, implore, petition, plead, request, urge. 2 (pray to God) commune with God, offer a prayer, say your prayers

**prayer** n communion, devotion, litany

**preach** v 1 evangelize, give a sermon, spread the gospel, teach. 2 advise, exhort, give advice, harangue, lay down the law, lecture, pontificate, urge

**preacher** n clergyman, cleric, evangelist, minister, missionary, parson, pastor, televangelist

**preamble** n foreword, introduction, opening remarks, overture, preface, prelude

**precarious** *adj* dangerous, dicey, dodgy *inf*, doubtful, dubious, hairy *inf*, hazardous, insecure, perilous, risky, treacherous, uncertain, unreliable, unsafe, unstable, unsure, vulnerable, wobbly; *opp* safe

**precaution** n 1 anticipation, care, caution, foresight, forethought, prudence, wariness. 2 preventive measure, protection, provision, safeguard, safety measure

**precede** v be in front, come before, come first, go ahead, go before, go in front, head, herald, introduce, lead, lead into, lead up to, preface, start, usher in

**precedent** n criterion, example, instance, model, patter, prototype, standard, yardstick

**precious** *adj* 1 (his precious baby) adored, beloved, cherished, darling, dear, favourite, irreplaceable, loved, treasured. 2 (precious stones) invaluable, priceless, prized, rare, valuable

**precipice** n bluff, brink, cliff, cliff face, crag, drop, escarpment, height, rock face

**precipitate** *adj* 1 abrupt, breakneck, brief, headlong, hurried, plunging, rapid, speedy, sudden, swift, unexpected, violent. 2 hasty, heedless, hurried, impetuous, impulsive, rash, reckless

**precipitate** v accelerate, advance, bring on, encourage, expedite, further, hasten, hurry, quicken, spark off, speed up, trigger

**precise** *adj* 1 accurate, clear, exact, explicit, specific, unambiguous. 2 (the precise meaning) actual, correct, faithful, literal, right, strict. 3 (at a precise time) definite, exact, fixed, particular, specific. 4 (precise movements) accurate, careful, exact, meticulous, scrupulous

**preclude** v debar, exclude, forestall, make impossible, prevent, prohibit, rule out, stop, thwart

**precocious** *adj* advanced, ahead, bright,

developed, forward, gifted, intelligent, mature, quick

**preconception** n assumption, bias, expectation, notion, preconceived idea, prejudice, presumption

**precursor** n forerunner, harbinger, herald, predecessor

**predatory** adj hunting, marauding, pillaging, plundering, preying, rapacious, voracious

**predecessor** n ancestor, antecedent, forebear, forefather, forerunner, precursor

**predetermined** adj agreed, fixed, prearranged, set, settled

**predicament** n corner, crisis, difficult situation, dilemma, emergency, fix inf, hole inf, mess, pickle inf, plight, quandary, scrape inf, tight spot inf

**predict** v augur, divine, forebode, forecast, foresee, foreshadow, foretell, portend, presage, prophesy

**predictable** adj anticipated, certain, expected, foreseeable, foreseen, likely, on the cards inf, reliable, sure, unsurprising; **opp** unpredictable

**prediction** n forecast, prognosis, prophecy

**predominant** adj 1 ascendant, controlling, dominant, in control, leading, most powerful, principal, ruling, superior. 2 chief, main, most obvious, most noticeable, prevailing

**predominate** v be dominant, be in the majority, be most noticeable, be predominant, carry weight, have the upper hand, hold sway, outnumber, outweigh, overrule, prevail, rule

**pre-eminent** adj distinguished, excellent, famous, foremost, important, incomparable, outstanding, prominent, renowned, superior, unrivalled, unsurpassed

**pre-empt** v 1 acquire, appropriate, assume, commandeer, seize, take over, usurp. 2 anticipate, forestall, prevent

**preen** v 1 (of animals) arrange, clean, plume, smooth. 2 (of people) array, beautify, deck out, doll up inf, dress up, groom, prettify, primp, spruce up, titivate

**preface** n foreword, introduction, preamble, prelude, prologue

**preface** v begin, introduce, launch, lead into, open, precede, prefix, start

**prefer** v be partial to, choose, desire, elect, fancy, favour, go for inf, incline towards, like, like better, opt for, pick, plump for, select, vote for, want, wish

**preferable** adj advantageous, best, better, chosen, favoured, more desirable, more suitable, nicer, preferred, superior, wanted

**preference** n 1 choice, desire, favourite, first choice, option, pick, selection, wish. 2 advantage, favouritism, partiality, precedence, preferential treatment, priority

**preferential** adj advantageous, better, biased, favourable, favoured, partial, privileged, special, superior

**pregnant** adj carrying a child, expecting inf, having a baby, with child

**prejudge** v anticipate, presume, presuppose

**prejudice** n 1 ageism, bigotry, chauvinism, discrimination, favouritism, intolerance, jingoism, narrow-mindedness, racism, sexism, unfairness, xenophobia. **2** bias, leaning, partiality, preconceived idea

**prejudice** v **1** (make sb prejudiced) bias, colour, distort, influence, interfere with, jaundice, poison, predispose, slant, sway, warp. **2** (prejudice your case) be disadvantageous, be prejudicial, damage, harm, hurt, spoil, undermine

**prejudiced** adj biased, bigoted, discriminatory, intolerant, narrow-minded, unfair, unjust; **opp** impartial

**prejudicial** adj damaging, deleterious, detrimental, harmful, unfavourable

**preliminary** adj **1** first, initial, introductory, opening, prefatory, preparatory, prior. **2** early, experimental, exploratory, pilot, qualifying, tentative, test, trial

**prelude** n **1** introduction, introductory movement, overture, preface, prologue. **2** beginning, curtain-raiser inf, herald, precursor, start, warm-up inf

**premature** adj **1** early, immature, incomplete, raw, too early, too soon, undeveloped, unripe, untimely. **2** hasty, ill-considered, impulsive, rash

**premeditated** adj calculated, considered, deliberate, intended, intentional, planned, wilful; **opp** spontaneous

**premise** n argument, assertion, assumption, basis, grounds, hypothesis, supposition

**premises** n building, establishment, place, property, site

**premium** n bonus, fee, payment, prize, remuneration, reward, surcharge

**premonition** n **1** apprehension, fear, feeling, foreboding, funny feeling, hunch

inf, idea, intuition, misgiving, presentiment, suspicion. **2** indication, omen, portent, sign, warning

**preoccupied** adj absent-minded, absorbed, distracted, engrossed, far-away, immersed, intent, lost in thought, oblivious, pensive, rapt, taken up, thoughtful, unaware

**preparation** n **1** arrangements, briefing, development, gearing up inf, getting ready, groundwork, making ready, making provision, organization, plans, practice, preparing, setting up, spadework, training. **2** (preparation for an exam) coaching, reading, revising, revision, study, studying, working

**preparatory** adj introductory, opening, prefatory, preliminary

**prepare** v **1** (prepare sth) arrange, assemble, draw up, get ready, make ready, put together. **2** (prepare to do sth) brace yourself, exercise, gear up inf, make preparations, plan, practise, psych yourself up inf, steel yourself, take steps, train, warm up. **3** (prepare for an exam) cram inf, practise, revise, study, swot inf. **4** (prepare sb for sth) brief, coach, drill, educate, equip, groom, rehearse, teach, train, tutor. **5** (prepare a meal) cook, fix Am inf, get ready, make, put together

**prepared** adj **1** (prepared to do sth) able, disposed, inclined, minded, of a mind, predisposed, ready, willing. **2** (everything was prepared) arranged, in order, in readiness, ready, set

**preposterous** adj absurd, bizarre, crazy, excessive, impossible, incredible, ludicrous, monstrous, out of the question, outrageous, ridiculous, shocking, unbelievable, unthinkable

**prerequisite** n condition, must inf, necessity, precondition, qualification, requirement

**prescribe** v advise, commend, decree, direct, impose, instruct, lay down, order, recommend, specify, stipulate, suggest

**presence** n 1 (your presence is required) attendance, company. 2 (aware of sb's presence) closeness, nearness, proximity. 3 (sb has presence) charisma, magnetism, personality, poise, self-assurance, self-confidence, self-possession

**present** adj 1 contemporary, current, existing, immediate, instant, present-day, up-to-date. 2 accounted for, at hand, available, here, in attendance, nearby, ready, there, to hand

**present** n 1 (the present) here and now, now, the time being, today. 2 (a present) contribution, donation, gift, offering

**present** v 1 (present sb to people) announce, introduce, make known. 2 (present a gift) award, bestow, confer, donate, give, hand over, offer. 3 (present a proposal) advance, put forward, set forth, submit, suggest, tender. 4 (present a different side of your character) demonstrate, display, exhibit, reveal, show. 5 (present a TV show) compère, host, introduce. 6 (present a show) act, give, mount, perform, put on, stage

**presentable** adj acceptable, all right, becoming, decent, fit to be seen, good enough, okay inf, passable, respectable, suitable, tidy, up to scratch inf, well-groomed

**presentation** n demonstration, display,

exhibition, launch, performance, production, show

**preserve** v 1 care for, conserve, defend, guard, keep, look after, maintain, perpetuate, protect, safeguard, save, secure, uphold. 2 (preserve food) bottle, can, cure, dry, freeze, pickle, salt, smoke

**preside** v administer, be in charge, chair, conduct, control, direct, govern, head, lead, manage, officiate, run, take charge, take the chair

**press** n Fleet Street, journalism, newspapers, magazines, papers, reporters, the media

**press** v 1 compress, condense, crush, jam, mash, push, reduce, squeeze, stuff. 2 (press sb close) clasp, crush, embrace, enfold, hold, hug, squeeze. 3 (press sb to do sth) ask, beg, compel, constrain, enjoin, entreat, exhort, implore, insist, persuade, put pressure on, urge. 4 (people press into a place) cluster, crowd, flock, gather, push, surge, swarm, throng. 5 (press clothes) flatten, iron, make flat, smooth

**pressing** adj critical, crucial, high-priority, imperative, important, serious, urgent, vital; opp non-urgent, unimportant

**pressure** n 1 compression, crushing, force, heaviness, load, squeezing, stress, weight. 2 (pressure in your job) constraints, demands, difficulties, hassle inf, problems, strain, stress, tension. 3 (using pressure to make sb do sth) coercion, compulsion, duress, force, power

**prestige** n cachet, credit, distinction, eminence, esteem, fame, good name, honour, importance, influence, kudos *slang*, reputation, standing, status

**prestigious** *adj* acclaimed, celebrated, distinguished, eminent, famed, famous, glamorous, highly regarded, high-ranking, illustrious, important, influential, respected, well-known

**presume** *v* 1 assume, believe, conjecture, guess, imagine, infer, suppose, surmise, take for granted, take it, think. 2 be presumptuous, dare, go so far as, have the effrontery, have the temerity, make bold, take the liberty, venture

**presumptuous** *adj* arrogant, audacious, bold, cheeky, cocksure, forward, insolent, overconfident, pushy *inf*, too big for your boots *inf*; *opp* modest

**presuppose** *v* assume, imply, presume, suppose, take as read, take for granted

**pretence** *n* 1 act, affectation, appearance, artifice, charade, deceit, deception, dissembling, excuse, façade, falsehood, front, hypocrisy, insincerity, lying, mask, masquerade, pose, posing, posturing, pretext, ruse, sham, show, simulation, trickery, veneer. 2 fantasy, imagination, invention, make-believe, unreality

**pretend** *v* 1 affect, allege, bluff, deceive, dissemble, fake it, falsify, feign, impersonate, make out, pose, put on an act, simulate, trick. 2 (children like to pretend) act, fantasize, imagine, make believe, play, play-act, pretend

**pretentious** *adj* affected, conceited, exaggerated, flamboyant, grandiose, high-flown, ostentatious, pompous, showy, snobbish, superficial; *opp* unpretentious

**pretext** *n* cover, excuse, lie, ploy, pretence, reason, red herring, ruse, wile

**pretty** *adj* 1 (of a person) appealing, attractive, beautiful, bonny, cute, fair, good-looking, lovely, nice-looking; *opp* ugly. 2 (of a place) attractive, charming, delightful, pleasant; *opp* ugly, unattractive

**prevail** *v* be victorious, conquer, overcome, overrule, prove superior, succeed, triumph, win, win out, win through

**prevailing** *adj* common, current, customary, established, fashionable, general, ordinary, popular, prevalent, usual, widespread

**prevalent** *adj* accepted, common, commonplace, current, established, extensive, frequent, rampant, rife, ubiquitous, universal, usual, widespread; *opp* rare

**prevaricate** *v* beat about the bush, be evasive, cavil, dodge, equivocate, evade, fence, fib, flannel *inf*, hedge, lie, quibble, shilly-shally, sidestep

**prevent** *v* avert, avoid, block, check, curb, deter, fend off, foil, forestall, frustrate, hamper, hinder, impede, nip in the bud, obstruct, put a stop to, restrain, stave off, stop, thwart, ward off; *opp* encourage

**preventative** *adj* deterrent, obstructive, precautionary, pre-emptive, preventive, protective

**previous** *adj* earlier, erstwhile, ex-, former, one-time, past, preceding, prior

**prey** *n* game, kill, quarry, victim

**price** *n* amount, bill, charge, cost, damage *inf*, estimate, expenditure, expense, fee, figure, offer, outlay, payment, quotation, rate, sum, terms, valuation, value, worth

**priceless** *adj* 1 costly, dear, expensive, invaluable, irreplaceable, precious, valuable, worth its weight in gold; *opp* worthless. 2 (hilarious) a scream *inf*, comic, funny, hilarious, killing *inf*

**prick** *v* 1 jab, nick, perforate, pierce, puncture, spike, stab. 2 (prickle) hurt, itch, prickle, smart, sting, tickle, tingle

**prickle** *n* barb, spike, spine, thorn

**prickle** *v* hurt, itch, prick, smart, sting, tickle, tingle

**prickly** *adj* 1 (with prickles) brambly, scratchy, sharp, spiky, spiny, thorny, vicious. 2 (of a person or situation) awkward, difficult, irritable, ratty *inf*, shirty *inf*, tetchy, thorny, touchy, tricky, waspish

**pride** *n* 1 dignity, ego, feelings, honour, self-esteem, self-respect. 2 arrogance, big-headedness *inf*, conceit, snobbery, vanity

**priest** *n* chaplain, clergyman, clergywoman, curate, deacon, ecclesiastic, father, member of the clergy, minister, padre, parson, pastor, priestess, rector, shaman, vicar

**priggish** *adj* goody-goody *inf*, moralistic, prim, sanctimonious, smug, strait-laced, stuffy *inf*

**prim** *adj* demure, fastidious, formal, prissy, proper, starchy, strait-laced

**primarily** *adv* basically, chiefly, essentially, first and foremost, in the main, largely, mainly, mostly, particularly, predominantly, principally

**primary** *adj* 1 earliest, elementary, first, initial, primitive. 2 chief, essential, foremost, main, most important,

paramount, prime, principal

**prime** *adj* 1 best, choice, class-one, first-class, grade A, leading, superior, top-quality, top. 2 chief, essential, main, most important, paramount, primary, principal

**prime** *n* best part, height, heyday, peak, zenith

**prime** *v* brief, coach, get ready, groom, inform, prepare, train

**primitive** *adj* basic, crude, early, elementary, naïve, rough, rudimentary, simple, uncivilized, unsophisticated

**prince** *n* monarch, ruler, sovereign

**principal** *adj* chief, first, foremost, fundamental, key, leading, main, major, most important, paramount, prime, top; *opp* minor

**principal** *n* boss *inf*, dean, director, head teacher, head, lead, leader, manager, star, top dog *inf*, vice-chancellor

**principle** *n* 1 axiom, canon, creed, doctrine, law, maxim, rule, theory. 2 decency, honour, integrity, morality, morals, probity, scruples, standards

**print** *n* 1 copy, engraving, etching, painting, photo, photograph, picture, reproduction, woodcut. 2 fingerprint, footprint, impression, indentation, mark. 3 characters, font, lettering, letters, text, type, typeface

**print** *v* 1 issue, publish, reproduce, run off, send to press, write. 2 engrave, etch, imprint, mark, stamp

**priority** *n* first place, first thing, main concern, main thing, most important thing, precedence, preference, prerogative

**prison** *n* 1 cell, clink *inf*, cooler *inf*,

detention centre, dungeon, goal, jail, lock-up, nick *inf*, penitentiary *Am*, place of detention, remand home, youth custody centre. **2** confinement, custodial sentence, custody, detention, incarceration

**prisoner** *n* captive, convict, detainee, hostage, inmate, jail-bird *inf*, POW

**privacy** *n* confidentiality, freedom from interference, isolation, peace and quiet, right to be left alone, seclusion, secrecy, solitude

**private** *adj* **1** (confidential) closed, confidential, off the record, restricted, secret, top secret, unofficial. **2** (secluded) concealed, hidden, isolated, secluded, solitary, withdrawn. **3** (personal) exclusive, intimate, own, personal, privately owned, secret

**privilege** *n* advantage, benefit, concession, entitlement, exemption, honour, licence, perk *inf*, prerogative, right

**privileged** *adj* advantaged, elite, exempt, fortunate, immune, lucky, special

**prize** *adj* best, champion, prize-winning, special, top, winning

**prize** *n* accolade, award, cup, jackpot, medal, purse, reward, trophy, winnings

**prize** *v* cherish, idolize, revere, set great store by, treasure, value, worship

**probability** *n* chance, expectation, likelihood, odds, prospect

**probable** *adj* anticipated, apparent, expected, likely, odds-on *inf*, on the cards *inf*, plausible, very possible

**probably** *adv* doubtless, in all likelihood, in all probability, it is likely that, it is to be expected that, presumably

**probe** *n* examination, exploration, inquiry, investigation, study

**probe** *v* **1** examine, explore, feel, investigate, poke, prod. **2** check out, examine, investigate, look into, research, search

**problem** *adj* difficult, intractable, problematic, troublesome, unruly; *opp* easy

**problem** *n* brain-teaser, can of worms *inf*, conundrum, difficulty, dilemma, headache *inf*, poser *inf*, predicament, puzzle, quandary, snag, trouble

**problematic** *adj* awkward, complicated, delicate, thorny, tricky; *opp* simple

**procedure** *n* approach, drill, formula, means, method, operation, plan of action, policy, process, routine, step, system, technique, way

**proceed** *v* begin, carry on, continue, get going *inf*, go ahead, make progress, move on, press on, start; *opp* stop

**proceedings** *n* **1** affairs, business, events, goings-on *inf*, legal action, matters, measures, moves, steps. **2** account, annals, archives, minutes, report, transactions

**proceeds** *n* earnings, income, profit, receipts, revenue, takings

**process** *n* action, activity, method, operation, procedure, stages, steps, system, technique, way

**process** *v* administer, convert, deal with, handle, manufacture, prepare, produce, refine

**procession** *n* column, convoy, cortège, file, line, march, parade, string, succession

**proclaim** *v* **1** announce, declare, decree,

make known, pronounce, publish.
2 be a sign of, herald, indicate, prove,
reveal, show

**proclamation** n announcement,
declaration, decree, edict, notice,
publication

**procrastinate** v defer, dither, drag your
feet, hesitate, play for time, prevaricate,
put sth off, stall, vacillate

**procure** v acquire, buy, come by, get hold
of, lay your hands on, obtain, pick up,
secure, wangle inf

**prod** v 1 dig, jab, poke. 2 egg on inf,
encourage, goad, motivate, rouse, spur,
stimulate, urge

**prodigal** adj excessive, extravagant,
imprudent, irresponsible, profligate,
reckless, wanton, wasteful; **opp** careful,
thrifty

**prodigious** adj enormous, gigantic, huge,
immense, impressive, magnificent,
massive, phenomenal, staggering,
tremendous, vast

**prodigy** n genius, marvel, phenomenon,
sensation, talent, wonder

**produce** n crops, fruit and vegetables,
goods, groceries, merchandise, products,
stock, stuff

**produce** v 1 (make) compose, construct,
create, develop, form, generate, make,
manufacture, put together, turn out.
2 (cause) bring about, cause, create,
deliver, evoke, generate, give birth to,
give rise to, give, initiate, result in, spark
off, trigger, yield. 3 (produce
information or evidence) disclose,
present, provide, put forward, reveal,
supply. 4 (produce a play) direct, do,
mount, present, put on, stage

**producer** n 1 creator, grower, maker,
manufacturer. 2 administrator, backer,
director, impresario

**product** n 1 commodity, goods, item,
merchandise, produce, wares. 2 by-
product, consequence, effect, legacy,
outcome, result, upshot

**productive** adj beneficial, effective,
efficient, fertile, fruitful, profitable,
prolific, rich, useful, worthwhile;
**opp** fruitless, unproductive

**productivity** n capacity, efficiency,
output, production rate, rate of work

**profess** v announce, assert, claim,
declare, express, maintain, own,
proclaim, state

**profession** n business, career, job, line of
work, occupation, trade, vocation, work

**professional** adj 1 businesslike,
competent, efficient, excellent,
experienced, fine, polished, skilful;
**opp** incompetent, unprofessional.
2 qualified, white-collar; **opp** unskilled.
3 doing sth for a living, paid;
**opp** amateur

**proficient** adj accomplished, capable,
competent, effective, efficient,
experienced, expert, good, skilful,
skilled, talented

**profile** n 1 outline, shape, side view,
silhouette. 2 account, biography, CV,
description, outline, portrait, review,
sketch, study, summary, vignette

**profit** n 1 bottom line, dividend,
earnings, gain, proceeds, receipts, return,
revenue, takings, yield. 2 advantage,
benefit, gain, good, return, value

**profit** v 1 (sth profits you) be an
advantage to, be of use to, benefit,

do sb good, help. 2 **profit from** benefit from, cash in on, exploit, use

**profitable** adj 1 cost-effective, lucrative, money-making, money-spinning, rewarding, successful; *opp* unprofitable. 2 advantageous, beneficial, constructive, useful, worthwhile; *opp* useless, worthless

**profiteer** n extortionist, racketeer, speculator, wheeler-dealer

**profligate** adj 1 excessive, extravagant, wasteful; *opp* careful. 2 degenerate, dissolute, immoral, shameless, unprincipled, wild

**profound** adj 1 (intense) deep, great, intense, keen, marked, passionate, sincere, strong. 2 (learned) difficult, erudite, impenetrable, intellectual, learned, scholarly, weighty

**profuse** adj abundant, copious, lavish, luxuriant, plentiful, prolific, unstinting

**profusion** n abundance, glut, loads inf, masses, mountain inf, plenty, superfluity, surplus, vast quantities, wealth; *opp* scarcity

**programme** n 1 broadcast, edition, production, series, show, transmission. 2 agenda, bill, curriculum, listing, menu, order of events, order of the day, plan, schedule, scheme, syllabus

**programme** v 1 arrange, line up, organize, plan, put together, schedule. 2 (programme a video) adjust, set

**progress** n advance, advancement, development, evolution, growth, headway, improvement, movement, progression, step forward

**progress** v advance, come on, develop, get better, get on, forge ahead, improve,

make headway, make progress, make strides, move, move forward, proceed

**progression** n 1 (headway) advancement, course, development, headway, progress. 2 (succession) chain, series, stream, string, succession

**progressive** adj advanced, avant-garde, contemporary, enlightened, go-ahead, innovative, liberal, modern, radical, trendy inf, up-to-date; *opp* old-fashioned

**prohibit** v ban, forbid, make illegal, make impossible, outlaw, preclude, prevent, proscribe, rule out, stop, veto; *opp* allow, permit

**prohibition** n ban, banning, embargo, injunction, outlawing, prevention, proscription, restriction

**prohibitive** adj 1 discouraging, preventive, restrictive. 2 (a prohibitive price) excessive, exorbitant, impossible, unreasonable; *opp* reasonable

**project** n enterprise, idea, job, operation, plan, programme, proposal, scheme, task, undertaking, venture

**project** v 1 (stick out) bulge, extend, jut out, overhang, protrude, stick out. 2 (propel) cast, direct, fire, hurl, launch, propel, shoot, throw out, throw. 3 (forecast) calculate, compute, estimate, extrapolate, forecast, plan, predict

**projectile** n bullet, missile, rocket, shell, shot

**projection** n 1 bulge, ledge, overhang, protrusion, protuberance, shelf. 2 calculation, computation, estimate, extrapolation, forecast, prediction

**proliferate** v escalate, expand, flourish, grow, increase, multiply, mushroom, reproduce, rocket, snowball

**prolific** adj abundant, lush, luxuriant, plentiful, productive, profuse, riotous, vigorous

**prolong** v drag out, extend, lengthen, make longer, spin out, stretch, string out; *opp* shorten

**prominent** adj 1 bulging, conspicuous, jutting out, noticeable, obtrusive, protruding, sticking out. 2 distinguished, eminent, foremost, important, leading, main, major, top, well-known

**promiscuous** adj dissolute, fast, free, immoral, loose, sleeping around *inf*, wanton, wild

**promise** n 1 assurance, commitment, guarantee, oath, pledge, undertaking, vow. 2 hint, sign, suggestion. 3 (sb shows promise) ability, flair, potential, talent

**promise** v 1 give your word, guarantee, pledge, swear, undertake, vouch, vow. 2 (show signs of) augur, hint at, indicate, show signs of, suggest

**promising** adj 1 bright, encouraging, favourable, good, hopeful, optimistic, rosy; *opp* discouraging. 2 budding, gifted, rising, talented, up-and-coming

**promote** v 1 (encourage) back, boost, encourage, foster, further, nurture, push *inf*, stimulate, support; *opp* discourage. 2 (advertise) advertise, champion, endorse, market, plug *inf*, publicize, recommend, sell. 3 (give sb promotion) advance, give sb promotion, upgrade; *opp* demote

**promotion** n 1 backing, boost, encouragement, furtherance, nurturing, support. 2 advertising, advertising campaign, hype *inf*, marketing, publicity. 3 advancement, elevation, preferment, upgrading; *opp* demotion

**prompt** adj direct, early, immediate, instant, on time, punctual, quick, rapid, speedy, swift, timely; *opp* late, slow, sluggish

**prompt** n cue, hint, nudge, prod, reminder

**prompt** v 1 cause, encourage, induce, inspire, make, motivate, move, urge. 2 give sb a cue, help out, jog sb's memory, prod, remind

**promulgate** v advertise, announce, circulate, issue, make known, publicize, put about, spread

**prone** adj 1 (prone to sth) apt, disposed, given, inclined, liable, likely, subject, susceptible, tending, vulnerable. 2 (lying prone) face down, full-length, horizontal, prostrate, recumbent, stretched out

**prong** n branch, pin, point, spike, tine

**pronounce** v 1 articulate, enunciate, express, say, vocalize, voice. 2 announce, assert, declare, decree, proclaim, state

**pronounced** adj clear, definite, distinct, distinctive, evident, marked, noticeable, obvious, strong

**pronouncement** n announcement, declaration, decree, edict, judgment, proclamation, statement, verdict

**pronunciation** n accent, articulation, delivery, diction, enunciation, inflection, intonation, speech, stress, way of saying sth

**proof** n authentication, confirmation, corroboration, demonstration, evidence, facts, substantiation, verification

**prop** *n* brace, buttress, post, shaft, stanchion, stay, strut, support, truss

**prop** *v* 1 brace, buttress, hold up, shore up, support, underpin. 2 lean, rest, stand

**propaganda** *n* brainwashing, disinformation, hype *inf*, indoctrination, misinformation, promotion campaign, public relations exercise, publicity

**propagate** *v* 1 breed, generate, grow, increase, produce, reproduce, take cuttings. 2 (information) circulate, disseminate, promote, spread, transmit

**propel** *v* fling, hurl, launch, move, project, push, send, shoot, thrust

**propensity** *n* disposition, leaning, liability, proclivity, susceptibility, tendency

**proper** *adj* 1 acceptable, accepted, appropriate, conventional, correct, decent, decorous, fitting, respectable, right, seemly, suitable. 2 genuine, real, right, true; *opp* false

**property** *n* 1 (possessions) belongings, bits and pieces *inf*, effects, gear *inf*, possessions, things. 2 building, land, real estate. 3 attribute, characteristic, feature, power, quality

**prophecy** *n* forecast, fortune-telling, prediction, prognosis, second sight

**prophesy** *v* forecast, foresee, foretell, predict

**prophet** *n* clairvoyant, oracle, seer, sibyl, soothsayer

**prophetic** *adj* far-seeing, inspired, prescient

**propitious** *adj* advantageous, auspicious, favourable, fortunate, lucky, opportune, promising, timely;

*opp* inauspicious, unfavourable

**proportion** *n* 1 amount, distribution, fraction, part, percentage, portion, ratio, share. 2 balance, harmony, symmetry

**proportional** *adj* commensurate, comparable, corresponding, in proportion to, proportionate, relative

**proposal** *n* bid, offer, plan, project, proposition, recommendation, suggestion, tender

**propose** *v* 1 (suggest) offer, put forward, recommend, suggest, table. 2 (propose to do sth) aim, have in mind, intend, mean, plan. 3 (propose a motion or candidate) nominate, put forward, put up, sponsor

**proposition** *n* 1 (suggestion) offer, plan, proposal, recommendation, suggestion. 2 (undertaking) job, prospect, task, undertaking, venture

**proprietor** *n* landlady, landlord, landowner, owner

**propriety** *n* correctness, courtesy, decency, decorum, delicacy, etiquette, good form, good manners, politeness, protocol, rectitude, respectability, seemliness

**prosaic** *adj* dull, flat, lifeless, mundane, pedestrian, stale, trite, unimaginative, uninteresting; *opp* interesting, novel

**proscribe** *v* ban, bar, forbid, make illegal, outlaw, prevent, prohibit; *opp* allow, permit

**prosecute** *v* accuse, bring an action against, bring before the courts, charge, haul up before the bench *inf*, indict, prefer charges against, put on trial, take to court, try

**prospect** *n* chance, expectation, future,

hope, idea, likelihood, odds, outlook, possibility, probability, promise, thought

**prospect** v examine, explore, search, survey

**prospective** adj aspiring, expected, future, likely, possible, potential, probable, would-be

**prospectus** n advertising material, booklet, brochure, catalogue, particulars, promotional material

**prosper** v blossom, boom, do well, flourish, get on, go from strength to strength, grow, succeed, thrive

**prosperity** n affluence, boom, plenty, prosperousness, success, wealth, well-being; *opp* adversity, bust *inf*, failure, poverty, recession

**prosperous** adj affluent, booming, comfortable, doing well, rich, thriving, wealthy, well-heeled, well-off, well-to-do; *opp* deprived, poor, struggling

**prostitute** n call-girl, courtesan, hooker *inf*, pro *inf*, whore, woman of ill repute

**prostitute** v cheapen, debase, demean, lower, sell

**protagonist** n 1 advocate, champion, chief player, exponent, leader, leading light, prime mover, principal, proponent, standard-bearer. 2 competitor, contender, contestant, player

**protect** v conserve, cover, defend, guard, keep safe, look after, preserve, shelter, shield, take care of, watch over

**protection** n care, conservation, custody, defence, guard, guardianship, preservation, safe-keeping, security, shelter, shield

**protective** adj 1 fireproof, safety,

waterproof. 2 over-protective, possessive, solicitous, vigilant, watchful

**protector** n bodyguard, champion, defender, guard, guardian, shield

**protest** n 1 complaint, dissent, objection, opposition, outcry. 2 demo, demonstration, protest march, rally. 3 avowal, claim, declaration, protestation

**protest** v 1 appeal, argue, complain, kick up a fuss *inf*, make a stand against, object, take exception to. 2 campaign, demonstrate, lobby, march. 3 (protest your innocence) assert, declare, maintain, profess, state

**protester** n activist, campaigner, demonstrator, dissident, objector

**protocol** n 1 code of behaviour, courtesies, custom, etiquette, formalities, good form, procedure, propriety. 2 agreement, concordat, convention, pact, treaty

**prototype** n model, original, precursor

**protracted** adj endless, extended, interminable, lengthy, long-winded, long, never-ending, prolonged; *opp* brief, short

**protrude** v bulge out, come through, extend, jut, jut out, poke out, project, stick out

**protruding** adj bulbous, bulging out, distended, jutting out, projecting, prominent, protuberant

**proud** adj 1 delighted, glad, gratified, happy, honoured, pleased, satisfied, well pleased; *opp* ashamed. 2 arrogant, big-headed *inf*, boastful, cocky *inf*, conceited, disdainful, haughty, high-and-mighty *inf*, imperious, overbearing, self-important, snobbish, snooty *inf*, stuck up *inf*, supercilious, toffee-nosed *inf*, vain; *opp* modest. 3 distinguished, glorious, grand, honourable, illustrious, magnificent, noble, splendid, worthy. 4 dignified, independent, self-respecting. 5 (proud day) glorious, gratifying, happy, marvellous, satisfying

**prove** *v* 1 authenticate, bear out *inf*, confirm, corroborate, determine, establish, find proof, produce proof, show, substantiate, verify; *opp* disprove. 2 check, put to the test, test, try out. 3 (prove to be) emerge, end up, be found, turn out

**proverb** *n* adage, axiom, maxim, old saw, saying

**proverbial** *adj* 1 famous, infamous, legendary, notorious, renowned, well-known. 2 axiomatic, traditional, typical

**provide** *v* 1 endow, equip, fix up with *inf*, provision, stock up, supply. 2 contribute, donate, give, grant, lay on, present. 3 give, offer, produce, yield. 4 **provide for** care for, keep, maintain, make provision for, support. 5 **provide for/against** anticipate, be prepared for, guard against, get ready for, make arrangements, make plans, make preparations, make provisions, plan ahead, plan for, prepare for, take precautions

**providence** *n* 1 destiny, divine intervention, fate, fortune, God's will. 2 care, discretion, economy, foresight, good management, prudence, thrift; *opp* improvidence

**provident** *adj* careful, economical, farsighted, prudent, shrewd, thrifty; *opp* improvident

**providential** *adj* chance, fortuitous, happy, fortunate, lucky, opportune; *opp* unfortunate

**province** *n* 1 district, region, section, state, territory. 2 area of activity, area of responsibility, business, concern, field, part, responsibility, role, sphere

**provincial** *adj* 1 local, regional, state; *opp* national. 2 country, outlying, rural, rustic, small-town *Am*. 3 backward, insular, inward-looking, limited, narrow, narrow-minded, parochial, small-minded, unsophisticated; *opp* cosmopolitan

**provision** *n* 1 (the provision of sth) equipping, providing, supply, supplying. 2 (make provision for sth) arrangement, plan, precaution, precautionary measure, preparation. 3 (the provisions of a contract) condition, limitation, proviso, qualification, requirement, restriction, stipulation, term

**provisional** *adj* conditional, contingent, interim, limited, qualified, stopgap, temporary, tentative, transitional

**provisions** *n* food, food and drink, foodstuffs, food supplies, groceries, ration, stores, supplies

**proviso** *n* condition, exception, limitation, provision, qualification, requirement, restriction, stipulation

**provocation** *n* 1 affront, aggravation, annoyance, harassment, insult, irritation, offence, taunt, taunting, teasing. 2 goading, incitement, justification, motive, prompting, rousing, stimulus, stirring

**provocative** *adj* 1 aggravating, annoying,

exasperating, goading, infuriating, insulting, offensive, provoking, stimulating. 2 alluring, erotic, raunchy *inf*, seductive, sexy, suggestive, titillating

**provoke** v 1 arouse, awaken, bring about, cause, elicit, evoke, excite, give rise to, incite, induce, inspire, kindle, occasion, produce, prompt, rouse, spark off, stimulate, stir up, work up. 2 (provoke sb) aggravate, anger, annoy, exasperate, gall, get on your nerves *inf*, harass, infuriate, insult, irritate, madden, make your blood boil *inf*, offend, outrage, pique, rile, rouse, tease, torment, upset, wind up *inf*

**prowess** n 1 ability, aptitude, competence, expertise, mastery, proficiency, skill, talent. 2 boldness, bravery, courage, gallantry, grit *inf*, guts *inf*, mettle, nerve, pluck, spirit, steadfastness, valour

**prowl** v creep, move stealthily, skulk, slink, sneak, stalk, steal

**proximity** n 1 closeness, nearness. 2 locality, neighbourhood, vicinity

**prudent** adj 1 careful, cautious, circumspect, judicious, sagacious, sensible, shrewd, wary, wise; *opp* imprudent, unwise. 2 (prudent use of sth) canny, careful, economical, farsighted, provident, thrifty; *opp* wasteful

**prudish** adj easily shocked, goody-goody *inf*, old-fashioned, puritanical, priggish, prim, straitlaced, Victorian

**prune** v 1 clip, cut back, lop, shape, thin, thin out, trim. 2 curtail, cut, cut back, make cutbacks, make cuts, make reductions, pare down, reduce,

retrench, shorten, trim

**pry** v be a busybody, be inquisitive, be nosy, interfere, intrude, meddle, nose about *inf*, poke your nose in *inf*, search, snoop, stick your nose in *inf*

**prying** adj curious, inquisitive, interfering, intrusive, meddlesome, meddling, nosy *inf*, snooping, spying

**pseudonym** n alias, assumed name, pen name, professional name, stage name

**psyche** n anima, individuality, inner being, personality, self, soul, spirit

**psychiatrist** n analyst, headshrinker *inf*, psychoanalyst, psychotherapist, shrink *inf*

**psychic** adj clairvoyant, extrasensory, mystic, occult, paranormal, preternatural, supernatural, supernormal, telepathic

**psychological** adj 1 cerebral, mental; *opp* physical. 2 emotional, in the mind, mental, irrational, subconscious, unconscious; *opp* physical

**psychology** n 1 science of the mind, study of the mental processes, study of personality. 2 (sb's phychology) attitude, mental processes, mind, mind-set *inf*, thought processes, way of thinking

**psychopath** n headcase *inf*, lunatic, madman, maniac, psycho *inf*

**pub** n bar, boozer *inf*, inn, local *inf*, public house, saloon, tavern, wine bar

**puberty** n adolescence, pubescence, sexual maturity, teenage years, teens

**public** adj 1 (a public place) accessible, communal, open to all, open to the public, unrestricted. 2 (a public institution) civic, communal, community, national, nationalized, social, state. **3** (public awareness) collective, common, democratic, general, majority, popular, universal, widespread. **4** (make sth public) acknowledged, known, notorious, obvious, open, overt, plain, published, well-known, widely known. **5** (public figure) eminent, important, in the public eye, prominent, well-known

**public** n **1** citizens, community, electorate, everyone, ordinary people, people, people in general, populace, society, the country, the hoi polloi, the masses, the nation, the people. **2** (do sth to please your public) admirers, audience, clientele, fans, followers, patrons, supporters. **3 in public** for all to see, in full view, openly, publicly

**publication** n **1** book, booklet, brochure, leaflet, magazine, newspaper, pamphlet, periodical, title. **2** (the publication of information) announcement, broadcasting, declaration, disclosure, dissemination, notification, publicizing, reporting. **3** (the publication of a book) issuing, printing, production, publishing

**publicity** n **1** advertising, ballyhoo inf, hype inf, marketing, plug inf, promotion. **2** attention, limelight, public interest

**publicize** v **1** advertise, give publicity to, hype inf, market, plug inf, promote, push. **2** announce, broadcast, make known, make public, publish, spotlight

**publish** v **1** bring out, issue, print, produce, put out, release. **2** advertise, announce, break the news about, broadcast, circulate, declare, disclose, divulge, leak inf, make known, make

public, publicize, put about inf, report, reveal

**puerile** adj adolescent, childish, immature, infantile, juvenile

**puff** n blast, breath, draught, flurry, gust, whiff

**puff** v **1** blow, breathe heavily, exhale, gasp, pant, wheeze. **2** (a cigarette) drag inf, draw, inhale, inhale, pull on, smoke. **3 puff up** bloat, blow out, blow up, distend, inflate, swell

**puffy** adj bloated, distended, enlarged, puffed up, swollen

**pugnacious** adj aggressive, bellicose, belligerent, combative, irascible, quarrelsome; opp gentle, passive

**pull** n **1** jerk, tug, twitch, yank. **2** attraction, draw, force, lure, magnetism, power. **3** clout inf, influence, power

**pull** v **1** drag, draw, haul, tow, trail, tug, yank; opp push. **2** (pull flowers, vegetables) collect, cull, extract, pick, pluck, pull out, pull up, uproot. **3** (pull a muscle) sprain, strain, tear, wrench. **4** (pull the crowds) attract, bring in, draw, entice, lure. **5 pull down** demolish, destroy, knock down, level, raze. **6 pull through** come through, pull round, rally, recover, survive

**pulp** n **1** flesh, soft part. **2** mash, mush, paste, purée

**pulse** n beat, beating, drumming, heartbeat, pounding, pulsation, rhythm, throb, throbbing, vibration

**pump** v **1** drive, force, inject, push, send. **2** (pump sb for information) cross-examine, give sb the third degree inf, grill inf, interrogate, question.

3 **pump up** blow up, inflate

**pun** n double entendre, play on words

**punch** n bash, blow, bop inf, clout, hit, hook, jab, knuckle sandwich inf, smack, thump, wallop, whack

**punch** v 1 bash, belt inf, box, clout, hit, pound, pummel, slug, sock inf, strike, thump, wallop. 2 (punch a hole) bore, drill, hole, make a hole in, perforate, pierce, prick, puncture

**punctual** adj early, in good time, on the dot, on time, prompt, when expected; opp late

**punctuate** v 1 break, interrupt, intersperse, pepper, sprinkle. 2 insert punctuation, put in punctuation marks

**puncture** n 1 hole, leak, nick, opening, perforation, pin-prick, rupture. 2 blow out, burst tyre, flat inf, flat tyre

**puncture** v bore, deflate, hole, let down, make a hole in, penetrate, perforate, pierce, punch, rupture

**pungent** adj 1 (of a smell) acid, acrid, bitter, caustic, rank, sharp; opp gentle. 2 (of a taste) aromatic, hot, peppery, piquant, spicy, tangy; opp mild

**punish** v 1 castigate, chasten, chastise, correct, discipline, exact retribution from, inflict punishment on, make sb pay for sth, penalize, rap sb over the knuckles inf, take disciplinary action against, teach sb a lesson inf. 2 beat, birch, cane, flog, scourge, spank, thrash, whip

**punishable** adj criminal, culpable, indictable

**punishing** adj arduous, backbreaking, exhausting, gruelling, hard, strenuous, taxing, tiring, tough, wearing; opp easy, light

**punishment** n 1 chastening, chastisement, correction, disciplinary action, discipline, penalty, punitive measure, retribution, sanction. 2 beating, birching, caning, flogging, good hiding, hiding, pain, scourging, spank, spanking, thrashing, whipping

**punitive** adj 1 castigating, disciplinary, penal, penalizing, punishing. 2 cruel, harsh, savage, severe, stiff

**punter** n 1 backer, better, gambler, player. 2 client, customer, patron

**puny** adj feeble, frail, sickly, small, stunted, underdeveloped, undersized, weak, weakly; opp strong

**pupil** n 1 schoolboy, schoolgirl, scholar, student. 2 beginner, learner, novice, trainee. 3 apprentice, disciple, follower, protégé, protégée, student

**puppet** n 1 doll, dummy, marionette. 2 dupe, mouthpiece, pawn, poodle, stooge, tool

**purchase** n 1 acquisition, buy, investment. 2 foothold, grasp, grip, leverage, toe-hold

**purchase** v acquire, buy, get, invest in, obtain, pay for, pick up, procure, secure

**pure** adj 1 (pure gold) flawless, genuine, perfect, real, unadulterated, unalloyed, undiluted, true. 2 (pure air, water) clean, clear, germ-free, immaculate, spotless, sterile, uncontaminated, unpolluted, untainted, wholesome; opp polluted. 3 (of a person) blameless, chaste, decent, good, immaculate, impeccable, innocent, irreproachable, uncorrupted, unsullied, virginal, virtuous. 4 (pure malice) absolute, downright, complete, out-and-out, perfect, sheer, total, utter. 5 (pure science) abstract, theoretical

**purge** n 1 cleansing, purging, purification. 2 clear out, dismissal, expulsion, ousting, rooting out, weeding out. 3 dose of salts, laxative, purgative

**purge** v 1 clean out, cleanse, purify, wash out. 2 clear out, depose, dismiss, eliminate, liquidate, expel, get rid of, oust, root out, weed out

**purify** v clean, cleanse, decontaminate, disinfect, fumigate, make pure, refine, sanitize, sterilize, wash

**purist** n dogmatist, pedant, stickler

**puritanical** adj ascetic, austere, goody-goody inf, narrow-minded, prim, prudish, self-denying, straitlaced, strict

**purpose** n 1 (have a purpose) aim, ambition, design, end, goal, intention, motivation, motive, object, objective, plan, target. 2 (sth lacks purpose) determination, direction, firmness, persistence, resoluteness, resolution, steadfastness, tenacity. 3 (the purpose of sth) point, reason, use, usefulness, value. 4 on purpose by design, consciously, deliberately, intentionally, knowingly, wilfully, with intent; opp accidentally

**purposeful** adj determined, dogged, firm, resolute, persistent, single-minded, steadfast, tenacious

**purposeless** adj aimless, meaningless, motiveless, pointless, senseless, useless

**purse** n 1 pocketbook Am, pouch, wallet. 2 coffers, exchequer, funds, means, money, resources, treasury, wealth. 3 award, prize, reward

**pursue** v 1 chase, dog, follow, give chase,

go after, harry, hound, hunt, hunt down, run after, shadow, stalk, tail, track. 2 (pursue a goal) aim for, aspire to, been intent on, have as a goal, seek, strive for, work for, work towards. 3 (pursue a career, way of life) apply yourself to, carry on, conduct, continue, continue with, engage in, go for inf, go on with, persist in, proceed with, stick with

**pursuit** n 1 (the pursuit of a person, animal) chase, hue and cry, hunt, inquiry, pursuing, trail. 2 (leisure pursuits) activity, enthusiasm, hobby, interest, line, occupation, pastime, pleasure. 3 (the pursuit of knowledge) hunt, inquiry, quest, search, seeking after, striving for

**push** n 1 (give sb a push) butt, jolt, jostle, nudge, poke, prod, shove, thrust. 2 (military) advance, assault, attack, charge, offensive, sortie, thrust. 3 (have a lot of push) ambition, drive, energy, enterprise, enthusiasm, get-up-and-go, gumption inf, initiative

**push** v 1 (push sth) drive, press, propel, ram, shove, thrust. 2 (push past people) barge, bustle, elbow, hustle, jostle, manhandle, nudge, shoulder, shove, squeeze. 3 (push sth into a place) cram, force, jam, press in, ram, squash, squeeze, stuff. 4 (push sb into doing sth) browbeat, coerce, encourage, force, impel, incite, lean on inf, motivate, persuade, press, prompt, put pressure on, urge. 5 (push a product) advertise, hype inf, plug inf, promote, publicize, recommend. 6 push around boss around, browbeat, bully, intimidate, lean on inf, tyrranize

**pushed** adj 1 busy, hurried, in a hurry, pressed, rushed, under pressure, up against it. 2 **pushed for** feeling the need of, lacking, not having enough of, running short of, short of, without

**pushover** n 1 (a person) easy mark, easy prey, mug inf, soft touch, sucker inf, weakling, wimp. 2 (a task) breeze inf, child's play, cinch, doddle inf, easy task, piece of cake inf, walkover

**pushy** adj ambitious, assertive, brash, forceful, overbearing, presumptuous

**put** v 1 fix, install, locate, place, plonk inf, position, set, settle, situate, stand. 2 allocate to, assign to, consign, deploy, dispose, impose, station.
3 **put down** (put sth down somewhere) deposit, lay, lay down, set down, settle.
4 **put down** (put sb down) belittle, criticize, denigrate, deprecate, disparage, find fault with, knock, pick holes in, run down. 5 **put down** (put down a rebellion) crush, defeat, put a stop to, quash, quell, repress stamp out, stop, suppress. 6 **put down** (write down) enter, inscribe, jot down, log, make a note of, note, record, set down, take down, write down. 7 **put down** (put an animal down) destroy, put out of its misery, put to sleep, kill. 8 **put down to** ascribe, attribute, blame, chalk up to, impute, put the blame on. 9 **put forward** advance, introduce, move, nominate, present, propose, recommend, submit, suggest. 10 **put off** (put sth off) defer, delay, postpone, put back, put on ice, put on the back burner, reschedule, shelve. 11 **put off** (put sb off an idea) discourage, dissuade, dishearten, offend, repel. 12 **put off** (put sb off when they are working) distract, divert, divert the attention of, sidetrack. 13 **put off** (put off the light) switch off, turn off.
14 **put on** (put on clothes) change into, dress in, don, slip into. 15 **put on** lay on, make available, provide, supply.
16 **put on** (put on a play, an exhibition) do, mount, present, produce, stage.
17 **put on** (pretend) affect, fake, feign, pretend, sham, simulate. 18 **put on** (put on the light) switch on, turn on.
19 **put on** (put on weight) gain, increase. 20 **put up** (put up a building) build, construct, erect. 21 **put up** (put sb up) accommodate, allow sb to stay, give sb a bed, give sb a place to stay, provide sb with accommodation, take sb in. 22 **put up** (put up money) advance, donate, give, pledge, provide, supply.
23 **put up** (put up prices) increase, raise.
24 **put up to** (put sb up to sth) egg on, encourage, incite, persuade, talk sb into sthg, urge on. 25 **put up with** accept, bear, endure, stand, swallow, take, tolerate

**putrid** adj bad, decayed, decomposed, fetid, foul, off, putrefied, rancid, rotten, rotting, spoiled, stale, stinking; *opp* fresh

**puzzle** n brain-teaser, conundrum, dilemma, enigma, mystery, poser inf, quandary, question, riddle

**puzzle** v 1 baffle, bewilder, confuse, flummox inf, mystify, perplex, stump inf.
2 **puzzle over sth** brood, consider, muse, ponder, study, think about, think over, wonder about. 3 **puzzle out** crack inf, decipher, figure out, find the answer to, solve, think out, unravel, work out

**puzzled** *adj* at a loss, at sea, baffled, bewildered, confused, flummoxed *inf*, mystified, perplexed, stumped

**puzzling** *adj* abstruse, baffling, bewildering, confusing, cryptic, enigmatic, incomprehensible, involved, mind-boggling *inf*, mysterious, mystifying, perplexing, unclear; *opp* clear

cautious, conditional, guarded, half-hearted, limited, modified, provisional, reserved, restricted; *opp* wholehearted

**qualify** *v* **1** be eligible, be entitled, have/gain the right, get through, go through, make the grade *inf*, meet the requirements, pass, reach the required standard, succeed. **2** (sth qualifies sb for a particular responsibility) authorize, empower, entitle, equip, fit, make eligible, make suitable, prepare, suit. **3** (qualify a statement) add a rider to, limit, mitigate, moderate, modify, modulate, nuance, restrict, soften, temper, tone down, weaken

**quality** *n* **1** (extent to which sth is good) calibre, excellence, merit, rating, standard, standing, status, value, worth. **2** (what sth is like) character, description, essence, kind, nature. **3** (the qualities of sth or sb) advantage, aspect, attribute, characteristic, feature, good point, hallmark, mark, property, trait

**qualms** *n* anxiety, apprehension, conscience, disinclination, disquiet, doubt, guilt, hesitancy, hesitation, misgivings, pangs, reluctance, remorse, reservations, reticence, scruples, second thoughts, uncertainty, uneasiness

**quandary** *n* difficulty, dilemma, fix *inf*, impasse, plight, predicament, problem, puzzle, uncertainty

**quantity** *n* aggregate, amount, lot, number, sum, total

**quarrel** *n* altercation, argument, battle, break, conflict, confrontation, difference of opinion, disagreement, dispute, falling-out, feud, fight,

**quail** *v* back away, cower, cringe, falter, flinch, quake, recoil, shake, shrink, shy away, tremble, waver

**quaint** *adj* charming, curious, droll, eccentric, fanciful, odd, offbeat, olde worlde *inf*, old-fashioned, peculiar, queer, strange, sweet, twee *inf*, unusual, whimsical

**quake** *v* quiver, rock, shake, shiver, shudder, tremble, vibrate

**qualification** *n* **1** ability, aptitude, capability, competence, eligibility, fitness, proficiency, skill, suitability, training. **2** condition, exception, limitation, modification, provision, proviso, restriction, stipulation

**qualified** *adj* **1** able, capable, certificated, competent, experienced, fit, proficient, skilled, trained. **2** (qualified acceptance)

rivalry, row *inf*, squabble, tiff *inf*,
vendetta, war, wrangle *inf*

**quarrel** *v* argue, battle, be at daggers
drawn, be estranged, be in conflict,
bicker, cross, cross swords, dispute, fall
out, feud, fight, row *inf*, spar, squabble,
tangle, wrangle *inf*

**quarrelsome** *adj* aggressive, angry,
argumentative, bad-tempered, bloody-
minded, cantankerous, choleric,
confrontational, contrary, disagreeable,
disputatious, explosive, fractious,
impatient, irascible, irritable,
obstructive, pugnacious, querulous,
quick-tempered, stroppy *inf*, testy,
truculent, unfriendly, vengeful, volatile

**quarry** *n* 1 excavation, hole in the
ground, mine, open-cast mine, pit.
2 goal, objective, prey, prize, target,
victim

**quarter** *n* 1 area, district, locality,
neighbourhood, part of town.
2 (advice from a particular quarter)
direction, person, source

**quarters** *n* abode, accommodation,
apartments, barracks, billet, digs *inf*,
dwelling, home, house, lodgings,
residence, rooms

**quash** *v* annul, cancel, nullify, invalidate,
overrule, overthrow, overturn, rescind,
reverse, revoke, suppress; *opp* uphold

**quaver** *v* falter, fluctuate, quake, shake,
tremble, vibrate, waver

**queasy** *adj* bilious, ill, nauseous, queer
*inf*, seasick, sick, travel-sick, unwell,
woozy *inf*

**queen** *n* 1 Crown, head of state, Her
Majesty, lady, matriarch, monarch, ruler,
sovereign. 2 consort, dowager queen

**queer** *adj* aberrant, abnormal, bizarre,
curious, deviant, eccentric, funny,
inexplicable, odd, outlandish, peculiar,
singular, strange, suspicious, unusual,
weird

**quell** *v* allay, beat down, conquer, defeat,
eliminate, extinguish, overcome, pacify,
quash, stifle, subdue, suppress, vanquish

**quench** *v* end, extinguish, gratify, relieve,
sate, satisfy, slake

**query** *n* 1 inquiry, problem, question.
2 (a query over sb's future) doubt,
hesitation, problem, question, question
mark, suspicion, uncertainty

**query** *v* call into question, challenge,
contest, dispute, doubt, mistrust,
question, suspect

**quest** *n* crusade, expedition, journey,
mission, pursuit, search

**question** *n* 1 brain-teaser *inf*,
conundrum, demand, inquiry, poser *inf*,
query, riddle; *opp* answer. 2 (sth to be
considered or decided) affair,
controversy, debate, issue, mystery,
point, problem, puzzle, situation

**question** *v* 1 ask, cross-examine, debrief,
grill *inf*, inquire, interrogate, interview,
poll, probe, pump *inf*, quiz. 2 (question
whether sth is true) argue over, call into
question, challenge, contest, dispute,
doubt, impugn, object to, oppose,
quarrel with, query

**questionable** *adj* arguable, borderline,
contestable, controversial, debatable,
disputable, doubtful, dubious, open to
challenge, problematic, uncertain

**queue** *n* crocodile *inf*, file, line, string,
tailback, waiting list

**queue** *v* file, form a queue, line up, queue

up, stand in line, wait in line

**quibble** *n* argument, complaint, criticism, dispute, nit-picking, objection, pettifogging, point of contention, query

**quibble** *v* argue, carp, dispute, part company, nit-pick, pettifog, split hairs, take issue

**quick** *adj* 1 brisk, fast, fast-moving, fleet of foot, headlong, high-speed, nippy *inf*, rapid, speedy, swift; *opp* slow. 2 (not lasting long) abrupt, hasty, hurried, lightning, momentary, rapid, swift. 3 (not delayed) immediate, instant, instantaneous, prompt, rapid, spur-of-the-moment, swift. 4 (quick to do sth) hasty, in a hurry, precipitate, prompt. 5 (thinking quickly) alert, astute, bright, clever, intelligent, keen, perceptive, quick-thinking, quick-witted, sharp, shrewd, smart

**quicken** *v* 1 (sth quickens) accelerate, gather pace, gather speed, go faster, speed up; *opp* slow down. 2 (quicken sth) accelerate, expedite, hasten, hurry, speed up; *opp* slow down

**quiet** *adj* 1 calm, noiseless, peaceful, placid, restful, serene, silent, sleepy, soundless, still, tranquil, unexciting; *opp* noisy. 2 (of sb's voice) breathy, inaudible, hushed, low, muffled, murmuring, muted, small, soft, subdued, tiny, whispering; *opp* loud. 3 (of a person) docile, inactive, introverted, meek, passive, phlegmatic, placid, quiescent, reserved, retiring, silent, taciturn, uncommunicative, withdrawn; *opp* noisy. 4 (have a quiet word with sb) confidential, discreet, on the quiet *inf*, private, secret

**quiet** *n* calm, calmness, hush, peace, peacefulness, placidity, quietness, repose, rest, silence, stillness, tranquillity; *opp* noise

**quieten** *v* calm, calm down, hush, lull, muffle, mute, pacify, shut up, silence, stifle, subdue

**quip** *n* bon mot, crack *inf*, epigram, gag *inf*, jest, joke, one-liner, wisecrack, witticism

**quirk** *n* 1 caprice, eccentricity, foible, idiosyncrasy, kink, oddity, peculiarity, whim. 2 (quirk of fate, nature) aberration, anomaly, exception, freak, reversal, turn, twist

**quit** *v* 1 depart, give notice, go away, hand in your notice, leave, resign, vacate, withdraw; *opp* stay on. 2 (stop doing sth) abandon, abstain, cease, cut out, desist, discontinue, drop, give up, refrain, renounce, stop; *opp* continue

**quite** *adv* 1 fairly, moderately, pretty *inf*, rather, relatively, somewhat. 2 absolutely, altogether, completely, entirely, fully, totally, wholly

**quits** *adj* equal, even, level, on equal terms, square

**quiver** *v* oscillate, palpitate, pulsate, shake, shiver, shudder, throb, tremble, vibrate

**quiz** *n* competition, contest, game show, questionnaire

**quiz** *v* cross-examine, fire questions at, grill *inf*, interrogate, interview, poll, pump, question

**quota** *n* allocation, allowance, amount, assignment, consignment, cut *inf*, measure, percentage, portion, proportion, quantity, ratio, ration, share, supply

**quotation** *n* 1 citation, excerpt, extract, line, verse, passage, quote *inf*, reference. 2 (a price) bid, costing, estimate, figure, price, rate, tender

**quote** *v* 1 cite, instance, mention, recite, refer to, repeat, reproduce. 2 bid, cost, estimate, price, tender

**rabble** n 1 band, crowd, gang, horde, mob, rioters, troublemakers. 2 (lowest ranks of society) common people, commoners, hoi polloi, lower classes, masses, plebs *inf*, riff-raff

**race** n 1 chase, competition, contest, event, heat, match, pursuit, run. 2 (in particular sports) Grand Prix, handicap, marathon, rally, sprint, stakes, steeplechase. 3 ethnic group, nation, nationality, people, tribe

**race** v 1 (in sport) be pitted against sb, chase, compete, contest, pursue, sprint. 2 (run, move quickly) bowl, career, dash, gallop, hasten, hurry, run, rush, scamper, speed, sprint, whizz *inf*

**racial** *adj* anthropological, communal, ethnic, ethnological, folk, national, tribal

**rack** n frame, framework, holder, pallet, stand, structure

**rack** v 1 (racked by pain, uncertainty) afflict, assail, besiege, crucify, harass,

harrow, oppress, persecute, plague, torment, torture. 2 **rack your brains** search your memory, think hard, turn sth over in your mind, try to remember

**racket** n 1 cacophony, din, disturbance, fracas, noise, sound, tumult, uproar. 2 corruption, extortion, fraud, graft, scam *inf*, scheme

**radiant** *adj* 1 (giving off light) bright, brilliant, dazzling, glittering, luminous, resplendent, shining, shiny, sparkling. 2 (of a person) beaming, delighted, expansive, happy, serene, smiling, warm

**radiate** v 1 (radiate heat, energy) emanate, emit, exude, generate, give off, produce, send forth, shed, send out, shine, spread. 2 (lines radiating from a central point) branch, diverge, fan out, spread, spread out

**radical** *adj* 1 campaigning, left-of-centre, left-wing, militant, progressive, revolutionary, socialist; *opp* conservative, reactionary. 2 (radical change) complete, extreme, fundamental, great, major, severe, thorough, thoroughgoing; *opp* minor

**radio** n 1 receiver, transistor radio, tuner, wireless. 2 (for sending and receiving messages) CB, transmitter, walkie-talkie

**rage** n anger, bile, frenzy, fulmination, fury, rampage, violence, vituperation

**rage** v 1 be angry, be beside yourself, be enraged, be furious, be hopping mad *inf*, be in a frenzy, be in a fury, be incensed, be infuriated, be mad, blow a fuse *inf*, blow a gasket *inf*, blow your top *inf*, boil over, explode *inf*, flip your lid *inf*, foam at the mouth, fume, go berserk, hit the roof *inf*, lose your temper, rail, rant, rave, roar, seethe, shout, swear, throw a wobbly *inf*, thunder. 2 (of a storm, controversy) be at its height, continue, continue unabated; *opp* abate

**ragged** *adj* 1 frayed, in ribbons, in shreds, in tatters, old, patched, ripped, shabby, tattered, tatty *inf*, threadbare, torn, worn through. 2 (not straight) irregular, jagged, serrated, uneven, untidy, wavy, zigzag

**rags** *n* castoffs, old clothes, remnants, shreds, tatters

**raid** *n* 1 assault, attack, foray, incursion, invasion, sally, sortie. 2 (by police) inspection, search, seizure, spot check

**raid** *v* 1 assault, attack, foray, invade, storm. 2 (involving robbery) loot, pillage, plunder, rob. 3 (police) descend on, inspect, search, spot-check

**raider** *n* 1 assailant, attacker, invader. 2 bandit, brigand, looter, marauder, robber, predator, thief

**rain** *n* cloudburst, deluge, downpour, drizzle, flood, precipitation, raindrops, rainfall, shower, storm, thunderstorm, torrent

**rain** *v* bucket *inf*, chuck it down *inf*, drizzle, pour, pour down, rain cats and dogs *inf*, spit

**raise** *v* 1 elevate, hoist, hold up, jack up, lift, lift up, pick up, pull up, push up, rear; *opp* lower. 2 augment, boost, increase, inflate, jack up *inf*, mark up, push up, put up, up *inf*; *opp* lower. 3 (raise the quality, status of sth) enhance, exalt, heighten, improve, promote, upgrade. 4 (sth raises fears, doubts, questions) activate, arouse, awaken, breed, cause, create, engender,

evoke, excite, foment, foster, generate, incite, instigate, kindle, provoke, rouse, set off, spark, stimulate, trigger. 5 (sb raises a question, problem) ask, bring up, broach, express, introduce, mention, moot, pose, present, propose, put forward, state, suggest. 6 (raise cattle, children) breed, bring up, look after, nurture, rear. 7 (raise funds) amass, collect, generate, make, solicit

**rally** *n* 1 drive, Grand Prix, race. 2 (large meeting) assembly, conference, congress, convention, convocation, gathering, mass meeting, meeting, public meeting, reunion. 3 (of share prices) improvement, increase, recovery, resurgence, revival

**rally** *v* 1 be revitalized, be revived, bounce back, improve, make a comeback, recover, regroup, reorganize, resist, revive. 2 (rally the troops) inspire, mobilize, revitalize, revive, revivify, spur on, steel, stir up. 3 **rally round** be supportive, come to the rescue, help, support

**ram** *v* batter, buffet, bump, butt, collide with, cram, crush, hit, impact, pound, strike

**ramble** *n* hike, stroll, walk

**ramble** *v* 1 (talk) chatter, digress, drone on, wander. 2 (walk) amble, hike, range, roam, rove, stroll, walk, wander

**rampage** *n* on the rampage 1 (in an angry mood) angry, berserk, breathing fire, furious, on the warpath, raging. 2 looting, marauding, out of control, pillaging, rampaging, stampeding, violent

**rampage** *v* charge, go berserk, loot,

pillage, run amok, run riot, stampede,
storm

**rampant** adj out of control, raging,
rampaging, riotous, stampeding,
unbridled, uncontrollable, uncontrolled,
unrestrained, wanton, wild

**ramshackle** adj decrepit, dilapidated,
flimsy, jerry-built, rickety, shaky,
unstable, unsteady, tumbledown

**rancid** adj curdled, festering inf, off, rank,
putrid, rotting, sour, spoiled, stale

**random** adj accidental, arbitrary, casual,
chance, disorganized, fortuitous,
haphazard, hit-or-miss, indiscriminate,
irregular, sporadic, spot, stray,
unplanned, unsystematic

**range** n 1 (of sb's interests,
responsibilities) area, breadth, compass,
diversity, extent, gamut, scale, scope,
span, spectrum, sphere, spread, sweep,
variety. 2 (of vision, weapon) area,
distance, extent, field, limit, reach

**range** v comprise, consist of, encompass,
extend, include, reach, span, spread,
stretch, vary

**rank** adj disgusting, fetid, foul, foul-
smelling, putrid, rancid, revolting,
smelly inf, stinking

**rank** n class, grade, level, place, position,
ranking, rating, seniority, standing,
station, status

**rank** v categorize, class, classify, grade,
order, place, rate

**ransack** v plunder, rifle, rummage, scour,
search, trash inf, turn upside-down

**ransom** n bribe, compensation,
deliverance, liberation, pay-off,
redemption

**ransom** v buy back, deliver, liberate,

recover, redeem, rescue

**rant** v bawl, bellow, bluster, go on and
one, harangue, rage, rail, rave, roar,
shout, spout, swear, thunder,
vociferate, yell

**rape** n abuse, assault, attack, indecent
assault, molestation, sexual abuse, sexual
assault, violation

**rape** v abuse, assault, attack, defile,
deflower, force yourself on, indecently
assault, molest, ravish, sexually abuse,
sexually assault, violate

**rapid** adj 1 breakneck, brisk, fast, fast-
moving, headlong, high-speed,
lightning, nippy inf, quick, speedy, swift.
2 (not lasting long) hasty, hurried,
momentary, quick, swift. 3 (not delayed)
immediate, instant, instantaneous,
lightning, prompt, quick, spur-of-the-
moment, swift

**rare** adj 1 few and far between,
infrequent, occasional, scarce, scattered,
sporadic, thin on the ground;
*opp* common. 2 (having unusual
qualities) atypical, exceptional,
extraordinary, singular, uncommon,
untypical, unique, unusual; *opp* common

**rascal** n 1 devil, imp, jackanapes,
mischief-maker, rapscallion inf,
scallywag inf, scamp inf, terror inf.
2 (wicked, criminal) blackguard,
bounder, cad, rat, reprobate, rogue,
scoundrel, villain

**rash** adj devil-may-care, foolhardy, hare-
brained, hasty, headlong, headstrong,
heedless, hot-headed, hurried, ill-
advised, ill-considered, impetuous,
imprudent, impulsive, incautious,
injudicious, madcap, over-adventurous,

precipitate, premature, reckless, spur-of-the-moment, unguarded, unthinking

**rash** n 1 allergic reaction, dermatitis, eczema, eruption, inflammation, irritation, psoriasis, redness, skin irritation, spots. 2 (a rash of burglaries) flood, outbreak, plague, rush, series, spate, wave

**rate** n 1 (rate of change, increase) degree, intensity, level, pace, ratio, scale, speed, tempo. 2 (money to be paid) amount, band, charge, cost, fare, fee, figure, payment, price, scale, sum, tariff, wage. 3 **at any rate** anyhow, anyway, in any case, in any event, nevertheless, whatever the case may be

**rate** v 1 adjudge, appraise, assess, class, classify, estimate, evaluate, gauge, grade, judge, measure, put a value on, rank, regard, value. 2 be worth, be worthy of, deserve, merit

**ratify** v accredit, approve, certify, confirm, countersign, endorse, pass, sanction, sign, underwrite, validate

**rating** n category, class, classification, designation, grade, level, placing, rank, ranking, position, standard, standing, status, tariff, type, value

**ratio** n comparison, fraction, frequency, proportion, quotient, rate

**ration** n allocation, allowance, amount, assignment, dose, helping, measure, portion, provision, quantity, quota, share, supply

**ration** v allot, apportion, distribute, eke out, mete out, parcel out, share, share out

**rational** adj enlightened, intelligent, logical, lucid, reasonable, sane, sensible, sound; **opp** irrational

**rationale** n argument, case, grounds, justification, logic, motivation, philosophy, reason, reasoning, theory

**rationalize** v 1 (rationalize your feelings) account for, clarify, elucidate, excuse, explain, justify, resolve, think through, vindicate. 2 (rationalize an industry) rearrange, reorganize, reshuffle, restructure, streamline, trim

**rattle** v 1 (rattle sth) bang, clang, clank, clatter, jangle. 2 (rattle sb) alarm, disconcert, disturb, fluster, frighten, perturb, put off, scare, shake, unnerve, upset, worry; **opp** calm

**raucous** adj grating, harsh, hoarse, husky, jarring, loud, noisy, piercing, rasping, rough, shrill, squawking, strident; **opp** quiet

**ravage** v 1 demolish, destroy, devastate, lay waste, level, raze, ruin, spoil, wreak havoc on, wreck. 2 loot, pillage, plunder, raid, ransack

**rave** v 1 fume, go crazy, go mad, rage, rant, roar, splutter, storm, thunder. 2 (rave about sb) enthuse, go into raptures inf, gush inf

**raving** adj crazed, crazy, delirious, demented, deranged, frenzied, hysterical, insane, irrational, mad, rabid, raging, unbalanced, wild; **opp** sane

**raw** adj 1 (raw food) fresh, rare, uncooked, underdone, unprepared; **opp** cooked, prepared. 2 (raw materials) basic, coarse, crude, natural, rough, unfinished, unprocessed, unrefined, untreated. 3 (a raw wound) bloody, chafed, grazed, inflamed, open, scraped, scratched, sensitive, sore, tender, unhealed; *opp* healed

**ray** *n* 1 (a ray of light) bar, beam, flash, gleam, glint, laser, shaft, streak, stream. 2 (a ray of hope) flicker, glimmer, hint, spark, trace

**reach** *n* 1 (beyond your reach) distance, extension, extent, grasp, spread, stretch. 2 (the reach of an organization) area, authority, command, control, influence, jurisdiction, power, range, scope, sphere, sway, territory

**reach** *v* 1 (reach a high standard) accomplish, achieve, arrive at, attain, gain, get, make. 2 (reach a place, an object) contact, extend to, get as far as, stretch to, touch. 3 **reach for** extend, outstretch, put out your hand, stretch, try to get

**react** *v* 1 answer, reciprocate, reply, respond, retaliate, retort. 2 act, behave, function, operate, proceed, work

**reaction** *n* answer, reply, response, retaliation, retort, riposte

**reactionary** *adj* conservative, die-hard, old-fashioned, rightist, right-wing, traditionalist; *opp* progressive, radical

**read** *v* 1 (read a book) dip into, look at, peruse, pore over, scan, skim, study. 2 (read the news) announce, deliver, recite, speak, utter. 3 (read sth into sth) assume, comprehend, construe, infer, interpret, see, take sth to mean, understand

**ready** *adj* 1 (prepared) all set *inf*, arranged, completed, equipped, fit, organized, primed, set, waiting; *opp* unprepared. 2 (available) accessible, at hand, at your disposal, at your fingertips *inf*, available, convenient, handy, near, on call, present; *opp* unavailable. 3 (willing) agreeable, consenting, disposed, eager, game *inf*, glad, happy, pleased, willing; *opp* unwilling

**real** *adj* 1 (real leather) authentic, bona fide, genuine, true; *opp* artificial, fake. 2 (a real person) actual, corporeal, existing, genuine, ordinary, non-fictitious; *opp* fictitious

**realistic** *adj* 1 (of a person) clear-sighted, common-sense, down-to-earth, level-headed, matter-of-fact, objective, practical, pragmatic, rational, sensible; *opp* unrealistic. 2 (a realistic copy) convincing, faithful, lifelike, true to life, truthful; *opp* unrealistic

**reality** *n* actuality, experience, fact, life, practice, real life, the real world, truth; *opp* theory

**realize** *v* 1 appreciate, catch on to *inf*, comprehend, conceive, cotton on to *inf*, grasp, imagine, recognize, take in, understand. 2 (realize a plan) accomplish, achieve, bring off, complete, do, effect, fulfil, implement, make happen. 3 (realize £10,000) bring in, earn, gain, get, make, net, obtain

**realm** *n* country, domain, empire, kingdom, land, monarchy, principality, province, state

**reap** *v* 1 (reap rewards) acquire, collect, derive, gain, gather, get, obtain, realize, receive, win. 2 (reap a harvest) cut, gather in, harvest; *opp* sow

**rear** *adj* back, end, following, hind, hindmost, last, posterior; *opp* front

**rear** *n* back, back end, end, hind, rear end, stern, tail, tail end; *opp* front

**reason** n 1 (your reason for doing sth) aim, basis, cause, end, explanation, goal, grounds, impetus, incentive, intention, justification, motive, object, objective, pretext, purpose, rationale. 2 (a man of reason) brains, common sense, intellect, judgment, logic, reasonableness, sanity, sense, understanding, wisdom, wit

**reason** v calculate, conclude, consider, deduce, figure out, infer, judge, reckon, surmise, think, work out

**reasonable** adj 1 (of a person) calm, fair, intelligent, impartial, just, logical, practical, realistic, sane, sensible, sober, sound, thinking, unbiased, wise; *opp* irrational. 2 (quite good) average, fair, moderate, ordinary, passable, tolerable. 3 (of a price) acceptable, appropriate, cheap, competitive, fair, inexpensive, low, modest; *opp* high

**reasoning** n 1 (learn sth through reasoning) analysis, deduction, logic, rationalization, theorizing, thinking, thought. 2 (sb's reasoning) argument, case, hypothesis, line of thought, rationale

**reassure** v calm, cheer, comfort, encourage, hearten, put sb at ease, restore sb's confidence, set sb's mind at rest, support, uplift; *opp* worry

**rebel** n anarchist, dissenter, heretic, insurgent, nonconformist, revolutionary

**rebel** v defy, disobey, dissent, resist, revolt, rise up, take a stand; *opp* obey

**rebellion** n 1 mutiny, resistance, revolt, revolution, riot, rising, uprising. 2 (a mood of rebellion) defiance, disobedience, dissent, heresy, nonconformity; *opp* obedience

**rebellious** adj bolshie inf, defiant, difficult, disloyal, disobedient, disorderly, insurgent, intractable, mutinous, nonconformist, obstinate, rebel, recalcitrant, revolutionary, turbulent, unruly, wild; *opp* obedient

**rebound** n boomerang, bounce, recoil, return, ricochet, spring-back

**rebound** v boomerang, bounce, recoil, return, ricochet, spring back

**rebuild** v overhaul, reassemble, recondition, reconstruct, recreate, redevelop, refashion, regenerate, remake, renovate, restore

**rebuke** v blame, castigate, censure, chide, give sb a (good) talking to inf, haul sb over the coals, lecture, read sb the riot act, reprehend, reprimand, reproach, reprove, scold, take sb to task, tell off inf, tick off inf

**rebuke** n blame, censure, lecture, reprimand, reproach, reproof, scolding, talking-to inf, telling-off inf, ticking-off inf

**recall** v 1 (recall sb's name) recollect, remember, summon up, think of. 2 (recall a product) call in, summon, take back, withdraw

**recede** v 1 (a tide recedes) ebb, fall back, go back, regress, retreat, shrink back, subside, withdraw; *opp* advance. 2 (a threat recedes) decline, decrease, dwindle, fade, lessen, peter out, subside, wane; *opp* increase

**receipt** n 1 (a train ticket receipt) acknowledgment, bill, proof of payment, sales slip, stub, voucher. 2 (on receipt of sth) acceptance, delivery, getting, obtaining, receiving, taking

**receive** v 1 acquire, be given, be sent, collect, gain, get, obtain, pick up, take; *opp* give, send. 2 (receive some news) apprehend, be informed, be notified, be told, find out, gather, hear, learn of; *opp* tell. 3 (receive bad treatment) be subjected to, encounter, endure, experience, go through, meet with, suffer, sustain, undergo; *opp* give. 4 (receive guests) entertain, greet, let in, meet, show in, welcome

**recent** adj brand new, contemporary, current, fresh, late, latest, modern, new, novel, up-to-date, up-to-the-minute, young; *opp* old

**reception** n 1 (get an enthusiastic reception) acknowledgement, greeting, reaction, response, treatment, welcome. 2 (attend a reception) bash inf, do inf, function, gathering, get-together inf, party, social, soirée

**receptive** adj amenable, flexible, interested, open, open-minded, sympathetic, responsive, well-disposed, willing; *opp* hostile

**recess** n 1 alcove, cavity, hollow, niche, nook. 2 adjournment, break, breather inf, closure, holiday, respite, rest, time off, time out, vacation

**recession** n decline, depression, downturn, drop, hard times, slump; *opp* boom

**recipe** n directions, formula, instructions, method, prescription, procedure, process, system, technique

**reciprocal** adj alternate, common, complementary, correlative, corresponding, equivalent, exchanged, give-and-take, interchangeable, mutual, returned, shared; *opp* one-way

**reciprocate** v do the same, give back, match, reply, requite, respond, return

**recital** n 1 concert, performance, programme, show. 2 (a recital of sth you did) account, description, narration, narrative, recounting, relation, report, statement, telling

**recite** v articulate, deliver, narrate, perform, present, rattle off inf, recount, reel off inf, relate, repeat

**reckless** adj careless, crazy inf, daredevil, foolhardy, hasty, heedless, impetuous, imprudent, impulsive, irresponsible, mad inf, rash, thoughtless, wild; *opp* careful, cautious, prudent

**reckon** v (He is reckoned to be the best) believe, consider, deem, hold, judge, rate, regard. 2 (reckon that sth is true) assume, believe, conjecture, fancy, guess, imagine, suppose, surmise, think

**reclaim** v get back, recapture, recover, regain, reinstate, retrieve, take back

**recline** v lean, lie, loll, lounge, rest, stretch out

**recluse** n hermit, loner, monk, nun

**recognition** n (in recognition of sb's bravery) acceptance, admission, appreciation, avowal, endorsement, notice, respect. 2 (act of recognizing) identification, recollection, remembrance

**recognize** v 1 identify, know, place, recall, recollect, remember, spot. 2 (recognize sb's bravery) accept, admit, appreciate, avow, endorse, notice, respect

**recoil** v 1 fly back, rebound, return, ricochet, spring back. 2 (of a person) draw back, falter, flinch, jump, shrink, shy away, start, wince

**recollect** v recall, remember, summon up, think of

**recollection** n impression, memory, remembrance, reminiscence

**recommend** v 1 (recommend a course of action) advise, advocate, counsel, propose, put forward, suggest, urge. 2 (recommend sb for a job) back *inf*, commend, endorse, favour, push *inf*, put in a good word for, speak favourably/highly/well of, support, vouch for

**recommendation** n 1 advice, counsel, hint, proposal, suggestion, tip. 2 approval, backing, blessing, commendation, endorsement, reference, support

**reconcile** v 1 (reconcile yourself to sth) accept, get used to, make the best of, resign, submit, yield; *opp* resist. 2 (reconcile people) appease, bring together, conciliate, pacify, placate, restore harmony, reunite; *opp* divide

**reconnaissance** n examination, exploration, inspection, investigation, observation, patrol, reconnoitering, scrutiny, spying

**reconnoitre** v examine, explore, inspect, investigate, observe, patrol, scan, scrutinize, survey

**reconsider** v change your mind, have a change of heart, reassess, re-examine, rethink, review, revise, think again, think better of, think twice

**record** n 1 (a record of proceedings) account, chronicle, documentation, dossier, file, journal, log, register, report.

2 (have a good record in sales) background, career, curriculum vitae, history, performance. 3 (play a record) album, disc, LP, recording, release, single, vinyl. **4 off the record** confidential, private, secret, unofficial; *opp* public

**record** v 1 catalogue, chronicle, document, enter, file, log, minute, note, put down, note down, register, report, set down, transcribe, write down. 2 tape, tape-record, video

**recording** n album, cassette, CD, compact disc, disc, record, tape, video, videotape

**recount** v communicate, depict, describe, impart, narrate, portray, recite, relate, repeat, report, tell

**recover** v 1 be on the mend, convalesce, get back on your feet, get back to normal, get better, get well, improve, perk up *inf*, pick up, pull through, rally, recuperate, revive; *opp* deteriorate. 2 (recover property) get back, reclaim, recoup, redeem, regain, repossess, retrieve, salvage, win back

**recovery** n 1 convalescence, improvement, progress, rally, recuperation, revival. 2 (recovery of property) reclaiming, recouping, redeeming, regaining, repossession, retrieval, salvage

**recreation** n amusement, distraction, diversion, enjoyment, exercise, fun, hobby, leisure, pastime, play, pleasure, relaxation, relief, sport; *opp* work

**recrimination** n accusation, comeback *inf*, counter attack, counter charge, reprisal, retaliation, retort, retribution, vengeance

**recruit** *n* apprentice, beginner, convert, initiate, learner, new boy *inf*, newcomer, new girl *inf*, novice, trainee

**recruit** *v* draft, employ, engage, enlist, enrol, sign on, sign up, take on

**rectify** *v* correct, cure, fix, improve, put right, redress, remedy, repair, right, square

**recuperate** *v* be on the mend, convalesce, get back on your feet, get back to normal, get better, get well, improve, perk up *inf*, pick up, pull through, rally, recover, revive; *opp* deteriorate

**recur** *v* come back, happen again, persist, reappear, return

**recurrent** *adj* continued, frequent, habitual, intermittent, periodic, persistent, recurring, repeated, returning; *opp* one-off

**recycle** *v* reclaim, reprocess, retrieve, reuse, salvage, save, use again

**red** *adj* crimson, rosy, ruby, ruddy, scarlet, vermilion

**redden** *v* blush, colour up, flush, glow, go red

**redeem** *v* 1 (redeem a voucher) cash in, exchange for cash, use. 2 (redeem property) get back, reclaim, recoup, recover, regain, repossess, retrieve, salvage, win back. 3 (redeem sb) deliver, emancipate, free, liberate, release, rescue, save, set free

**reduce** *v* contract, cut, decrease, diminish, lessen, limit, lower, minimize, moderate, shorten, shrink, slash, truncate; *opp* increase

**reduction** *n* contraction, cut, cutback,

decline, decrease, drop, lessening, limit, lowering, minimizing, moderation, shortening, shrinking, slashing, truncating; *opp* increase

**redundant** *adj* 1 non-essential, superfluous, supernumerary, surplus, unnecessary, unneeded, unwanted; *opp* essential. 2 (be made redundant) dismissed, jobless, laid-off, sacked, unemployed; *opp* employed

**reel** *v* falter, lurch, pitch, rock, roll, stagger, stumble, sway, totter, wobble

**refer** *v* 1 (refer to sth) allude, cite, hint, make reference to, mention, speak of. 2 (refer sb to sth) direct, guide, pass on, point, recommend, send. 3 (refer to a dictionary) consult, go to, look at, study, turn to

**referee** *n* adjudicator, arbiter, arbitrator, judge, ref *inf*, umpire

**reference** *n* 1 (make reference to) allusion, mention, note, remark. 2 (in reference to) concern, connection, consideration, regard, relation, respect. 3 (write a reference) endorsement, recommendation, testimonial

**refine** *v* 1 decontaminate, distill, filter, process, purify, treat. 2 civilize, cultivate, elevate, improve, perfect, polish, temper

**refined** *adj* civilized, courteous, cultivated, cultured, dignified, discerning, discriminating, elegant, genteel, gracious, ladylike, polished, polite, sophisticated, urbane, well-bred; *opp* common

**refinement** *n* 1 breeding, civility, courtesy, cultivation, culture, dignity, discernment, elegance, finesse, gentility, graciousness, polish, politeness, sophistication, taste. **2** (make a refinement) alteration, change, enhancement, improvement, modification

**reflect** v **1** echo, mirror, reproduce, return, send back, scatter, throw back. **2** (reflect on sth) consider, contemplate, deliberate, meditate, mull over, muse, ponder, ruminate, think, wonder

**reflection** n **1** echo, reproduction, image. **2** consideration, contemplation, deliberation, meditation, musing, pondering, thought, wondering

**reform** n change, conversion, correction, improvement, rebuilding, reconstruction, regeneration, remodelling, renovation, reorganization, repair, restoration, revision

**reform** v change, convert, correct, improve, mend, rebuild, reclaim, reconstruct, refashion, regenerate, remodel, renovate, reorganize, repair, restore, revamp, revise

**refrain** v abstain, avoid, cease, desist, do without, eschew, forbear, give up, leave off, quit inf, renounce, stop

**refresh** v **1** brace, cheer, cool, energize, enliven, fortify, freshen, invigorate, perk up inf, pick up, reanimate, renew, restore, revitalize, revive, revivify, stimulate. **2** (refresh sb's memory) activate, awaken, jog, prod, prompt, renew, rouse, stimulate

**refreshing** adj **1** bracing, cheering, cooling, energizing, fortifying, fresh, invigorating, restorative, revitalizing, reviving, stimulating, tonic. **2** different, fresh, original, new,

novel, stimulating, welcome

**refreshments** n drinks, eatables, food, nibbles inf, snacks, titbits

**refuge** n **1** asylum, bolt-hole, haven, hideaway, hide-out, hiding place, protection, retreat, safety, sanctuary, security, shelter, stronghold. **2** expedient, recourse, resort, stratagem, strategy, tactic

**refugee** n displaced person, émigré, escapee, exile, fugitive, runaway

**refund** n rebate, reimbursement, repayment, return

**refund** v give back, make good, pay back, reimburse, repay, restore, return

**refurbish** v do up inf, fix up inf, make over, overhaul, recondition, redecorate, refit, remodel, renovate, restore, revamp, spruce up

**refuse** n debris, detritus, dregs, dross, garbage Am, junk, litter, rubbish, trash Am, waste

**refuse** v decline, deny, rebuff, reject, repudiate, say no, spurn, turn down, withhold

**refute** v counter, discredit, disprove, negate, overthrow, prove wrong, rebut, silence

**regain** v find, get back, recapture, reclaim, recoup, recover, recuperate, retake, retrieve, win back

**regard** n **1** attention, consideration, heed, interest, mind, notice, thought. **2** admiration, affection, appreciation, deference, esteem, honour, love, respect. **3** gaze, look, observation, scrutiny, stare

**regard** v **1** adjudge, believe, consider, deem, esteem, hold, imagine, judge, look upon, perceive, rate, reckon, see,

suppose, think, treat, value, view.
2 (watch) eye, keep an eye on, look at, observe, scrutinize, stare at, study, watch, view

**regarding** prep about, apropos, as regards, as to, concerning, in regard to, in respect of, in the matter of, on the subject of, pertaining to, re, respecting, with reference to, with regard to

**regime** n dictatorship, government, junta, leadership, order, reign, rule, system

**regiment** v bring into line, control, discipline, order, organize, regulate, systematize

**region** n area, county, department, district, division, locality, part, place, province, quarter, section, sector, state, territory, tract, zone

**regional** adj district, local, parochial, provincial, sectional

**register** n annals, archives, catalogue, chronicle, diary, directory, file, index, inventory, journal, ledger, list, log, record, roll

**register** v 1 archive, catalogue, chronicle, enter, file, index, inscribe, list, log, note, record, take down, write down.
2 (register an emotion) betray, display, exhibit, express, indicate, manifest, reflect, reveal, show

**regress** v backslide, degenerate, deteriorate, go back, lapse, lose ground, recede, relapse, retreat, retrogress, return, revert, slip back; *opp* improve

**regret** n 1 compunction, conscience, contrition, guilt, penitence, remorse, repentance, ruefulness, self-reproach, sorrow. 2 bitterness, disappointment, grief, sadness, sorrow

**regret** v 1 accuse yourself, feel guilty, feel remorse, feel sorry, repent, reproach yourself, rue. 2 bemoan, bewail, deplore, deprecate, grieve, lament, miss, mourn, weep over

**regrettable** adj deplorable, disappointing, disgraceful, reprehensible, sad, shameful, unfortunate; *opp* fortunate

**regular** adj 1 (a regular pattern) consistent, constant, equal, even, fixed, measured, ordered, periodic, predictable, recurring, repeated, rhythmic, set, steady, symmetrical, systematic, uniform, unvarying. 2 (a regular route, procedure) common, conventional, customary, daily, established, everyday, familiar, frequent, habitual, known, normal, ordinary, orthodox, prevailing, routine, standard, typical, usual.
3 (a regular job) dependable, reliable, safe, steady

**regulate** v adjust, administer, arrange, balance, control, direct, govern, guide, handle, manage, monitor, order, oversee, rule, run, settle, steer, superintend, supervise

**regulation** n 1 by-law, commandment, decree, dictate, directive, edict, law, order, ordinance, precept, requirement, restriction, rule, ruling, statute.
2 (the regulation of sth) adjustment, administering, administration, control, controlling, directing, direction, government, handling, management, monitoring, ordering, overseeing, running, steering, supervising, supervision

**rehearsal** n drill, dry run, practice, preparation, reading, run-through, try-out

**rehearse** v drill, go over, go through, practise, prepare, read through, repeat, run through, try out

**reign** n administration, command, control, dominion, empire, government, monarchy, power, rule, sovereignty

**reign** v administer, be in power, be on the throne, command, govern, rule

**reincarnation** n rebirth, transmigration

**reinforce** v back up, bolster, brace, buttress, emphasize, fortify, harden, prop, shore up, stiffen, strengthen, stress, support, toughen, underline

**reinforcements** n auxiliaries, back-up, help, reserves, support

**reinstate** v recall, rehabilitate, replace, restore, return, take back

**reject** n cast-off, discard, failure, second

**reject** v 1 (reject a person, thing) cast out, discard, dismiss, disown, eliminate, exclude, jettison, jilt, rebuff, renounce, repudiate, scrap, send back, send packing inf, shun, spurn, throw away, throw out. 2 (reject a request, offer) decline, deny, refuse, say no, turn down, veto; **opp** accept

**rejection** n 1 brush-off inf, casting out, discarding, dismissal, disowning, elimination, exclusion, jilting, knock-back inf, renunciation, repudiation, scrapping, spurning, throwing away, throwing out. 2 denial, no, refusal, thumbs down inf, veto; **opp** acceptance

**rejoice** v celebrate, delight, exult, glory, revel, triumph

**rejoicing** n celebration, delight, elation, euphoria, exultation, gladness, happiness, jubilation, merry-

making, revelry, triumph

**relapse** n degeneration, deterioration, lapse, regression, retrogression, reversion, set-back, weakening, worsening

**relapse** v backslide, degenerate, deteriorate, fail, have a relapse, lapse, regress, revert, sink, weaken, worsen

**relate** v 1 communicate, describe, detail, impart, make known, narrate, present, recount, report, set forth, tell. 2 (establish a connection) ally, associate, connect, correlate, couple, join, link. 3 relate to (be relevant) apply, be relevant, concern, have to do with, pertain, refer to

**related** adj affiliated, akin, allied, associated, connected, correlated, coupled, interconnected, linked, relevant, similar

**relation** n 1 association, bearing, bond, connection, correlation, interconnection, link, relevance, similarity. 2 family member, kin, kith and kin, relative

**relations** n 1 affairs, communication, connections, contact, dealings, interaction, liaison, links. 2 family, kin, kindred, kinsfolk, relatives

**relationship** n 1 affinity, association, bond, conjunction, connection, correlation, interconnection, kinship, link. 2 affair, alliance, friendship, intrigue, liaison, partnership, romance

**relative** adj comparable, comparative, parallel, respective

**relative** n family member, kin, kith and kin, relation

**relax** v 1 calm down, chill out sl, cool

down, laze around, loosen up, put your
feet up *inf*, slow down, take it easy,
unwind. 2 (relax a control) diminish,
ease, lessen, let up, loosen, reduce,
slacken, soften, weaken; *opp* tighten

**relaxation** *n* 1 amusement, diversion,
enjoyment, fun, leisure, pleasure,
recreation, refreshment, repose, rest.
2 (relaxation of a control) diminishing,
easing, lessening, letting up, loosening,
slackening, softening, weakening;
*opp* tightening

**relaxed** *adj* at ease, at home, calm,
carefree, casual, comfortable, cool, easy,
easy-going, informal, insouciant, laid-
back *inf*, leisurely, light-hearted,
nonchalant, peaceful, serene, tranquil,
unconcerned, untroubled; *opp* up-tight

**relay** *n* 1 relief, shift, turn. 2 broadcast,
dispatch, programme, transmission

**relay** *v* broadcast, carry, communicate,
hand on, pass on, send, spread, televise,
transmit

**release** *n* 1 acquittal, deliverance,
discharge, emancipation, freeing,
liberating, setting free, unchaining,
unfastening, unshackling, untying.
2 (a press release) announcement,
bulletin, communication, proclamation,
publication

**release** *v* 1 acquit, deliver, discharge,
emancipate, extricate, free, let go, let
out, liberate, loose, set free, unchain,
unfasten, unshackle, untie. 2 (release
news) announce, break, circulate,
communicate, disseminate, distribute,
issue, make available, make known,
make public, present, publish, put out,
send out

**relent** *v* be merciful, capitulate, forbear,
give way, melt, show mercy, soften, yield

**relentless** *adj* harsh, implacable,
inexorable, merciless, pitiless,
remorseless, ruthless, unbending,
unrelenting, unyielding

**relevant** *adj* applicable, apposite,
appropriate, apt, connected, germane,
material, pertinent, related, salient,
significant, to the point; *opp* irrelevant

**reliable** *adj* certain, consistent, constant,
dependable, faithful, loyal, predictable,
proven, regular, responsible, safe, secure,
solid, sound, stable, staunch, sure, true,
trusty, trustworthy, unfailing;
*opp* unreliable

**relic** *n* fragment, keepsake, memento,
remains, reminder, remnant, scrap,
token, trace, vestige

**relief** *n* aid, alleviation, assistance, balm,
comfort, cure, deliverance, diversion,
ease, help, let-up *inf*, remedy, remission,
rescue, respite, solace, succour, support

**relieve** *v* 1 aid, allay, alleviate, assist,
assuage, calm, comfort, deliver, ease,
help, lessen, lift, lighten, mitigate,
moderate, palliate, reduce, release,
remedy, rescue, soothe, succour, support.
2 (relieve sb at work) fill in for, stand in
for, substitute for, replace, take over
from, take the place of

**religion** *n* belief, creed, denomination,
divinity, doctrine, dogma, faith, sect,
theology

**religious** *adj* devotional, devout, faithful,
God-fearing, godly, holy, pious, pure,
reverent, righteous, spiritual

**relish** *v* appreciate, delight in, enjoy, like,
love, revel in, savour, take pleasure in

**reluctant** *adj* averse, disinclined, grudging, hesitant, loath, slow, unenthusiastic, unwilling; *opp* keen, willing

**rely** *v* **rely on** bank on, be sure of, bet on, count on, depend on, have confidence in, lean on, put your trust in, reckon on, swear by, trust

**remain** *v* abide, be left, carry on, continue, endure, keep on, last, linger, live on, persist, prevail, stand, stay, survive

**remainder** *n* balance, excess, leavings, leftovers, remains, remnants, residue, rest, surplus

**remaining** *adj* left, lingering, outstanding, persisting, surviving, unfinished

**remains** *n* **1** balance, crumbs, debris, dregs, leavings, leftovers, pieces, relics, remnants, residue, rest, scraps, traces, vestiges. **2** ashes, body, bones, cadaver, carcass, corpse

**remark** *n* assertion, comment, declaration, observation, pronouncement, reflection, statement, utterance

**remark** *v* **1** assert, comment, declare, mention, note, observe, pass comment, reflect, say, state. **2** discern, espy, heed, mark, note, notice, perceive, regard, see

**remarkable** *adj* amazing, astonishing, astounding, considerable, distinctive, distinguished, exceptional, extraordinary, impressive, notable, noteworthy, outstanding, phenomenal, pre-eminent, rare, singular, strange, striking, surprising, uncommon, unforgettable, unusual;

*opp* ordinary, unremarkable

**remedy** *n* antidote, corrective, counter-measure, cure, drug, medication, medicine, palliative, panacea, relief, therapy, treatment

**remedy** *v* alleviate, assuage, control, correct, counter, counteract, cure, ease, heal, help, rectify, relieve, soothe, treat

**remember** *v* be mindful of, call up, keep in mind, recall, recognize, recollect, reminisce, retain

**remind** *v* bring to mind, call up, give a reminder, jog your memory, prompt

**reminder** *n* **1** aide-mémoire, cue, hint, memo *inf*, memorandum, mnemonic, note, nudge, prompt. **2** keepsake, memento, relic, remembrance, souvenir

**reminiscent** *adj* evocative, redolent, similar, suggestive

**remiss** *adj* careless, forgetful, heedless, inattentive, lax, neglectful, negligent, slack, slipshod, sloppy *inf*, thoughtless, unmindful, unthinking

**remission** *n* **1** absolution, amnesty, discharge, exemption, exoneration, forgiveness, parole, pardon, release, repeal, reprieve. **2** abatement, alleviation, lull, moderation, reduction, relaxation, respite, suspension

**remittance** *n* allowance, fee, payment, transfer

**remnant** *n* bit, crumbs, debris, dregs, fragment, leavings, leftovers, relic, remnant, residue, rest, scrap, trace, vestige

**remonstrate** *v* argue, challenge, complain, dispute, dissent, expostulate, object, oppose, protest, take exception, take issue

**remorse** n compunction, conscience, contrition, guilt, mortification, penitence, regret, repentance, self-reproach, shame, sorrow

**remorseful** adj ashamed, conscious-stricken, contrite, guilt-ridden, guilty, mortified, penitent, regretful, repentant, sorry

**remorseless** adj cruel, harsh, implacable, inexorable, inhumane, merciless, pitiless, relentless, ruthless, unrelenting, unremitting

**remote** adj 1 cut off, distant, far, faraway, far-off, inaccessible, in the middle of nowhere, isolated, lonely, off the beaten track, out of the way, secluded. 2 aloof, chilly, cool, detached, distant, haughty, removed, reserved, stand-offish, unapproachable, unfriendly, withdrawn; *opp* friendly

**removal** n 1 carrying away, moving, relocating, removing, taking away, transfer, transportation. 2 abolition, deletion, effacing, elimination, eradication, erasure, extermination, liquidation, obliteration, withdrawal. 3 (of a person) deposition, dislodging, dismissal, ejection, expulsion, eviction, firing, ousting, replacement, sacking

**remove** v 1 carry away, convey, move, relocate, take away, transfer, transport. 2 abolish, banish, delete, do away with, eliminate, efface, eradicate, erase, excise, expunge, exterminate, get rid of, kill, liquidate, obliterate, withdraw. 3 (remove a person) depose, dislodge, dismiss, eject, expel, evict, fire, oust, replace, sack. 4 (remove clothes) doff, peel off, shed, slip off, strip off, take off

**render** v 1 cause to be, get, leave, make. 2 (give) cede, contribute, deliver, furnish, give, hand over, make available, offer, present, provide, submit, supply, surrender, tender, turn over, yield. 3 (give a performance of) act, depict, do, execute, interpret, perform, present, portray, represent

**renege** v back out, break your promise, cop out *inf*, default, go back on your word, pull out

**renew** v 1 modernize, overhaul, recondition, refit, refurbish, regenerate, rejuvenate, remodel, renovate, repair, replace, restore, resurrect, revamp, revitalize, revive, transform. 2 (renew efforts) come back to, continue, pick up, recommence, restart, resume, return to. 3 (renew a pledge) confirm, reaffirm, reiterate, repeat, restate

**renounce** v abandon, abstain, cast off, deny, discard, disown, eschew, forgo, forsake, forswear, give up, quit, reject, relinquish, repudiate, spurn, waive

**renovate** v do up *inf*, fix up *inf*, modernize, overhaul, recondition, refit, refurbish, remake, remodel, repair, restore, revamp

**renowned** adj acclaimed, celebrated, distinguished, eminent, famed, famous, illustrious, known, noted, prominent, well-known

**rent** n fee, hire, instalment, lease, payment, rental, tariff

**rent** v charter, hire, hire out, lease, let

**repair** n darn, fixing, mending, overhaul, patch, restoration

**repair** v darn, fix, heal, mend, patch, patch up, put right, renovate, restore

**repay** v 1 (repay money) compensate, pay back, recompense, refund, reimburse, settle up, square. 2 (repay a wrong) avenge, get back at, get even, get your own back *inf*, hit back, reciprocate, retaliate, revenge, settle the score

**repeal** v (repeal a law) abolish, annul, cancel, invalidate, rescind, revoke, withdraw

**repeat** n recap *inf*, repetition, replay, reproduction, rerun

**repeat** v 1 (say sth again) echo, parrot, quote, recap *inf*, recite, reiterate, retell, say again. 2 (do sth again) copy, do again, duplicate, rehearse, replay, replicate, reproduce, rerun, show again

**repel** v 1 (repel invaders) beat back, confront, drive back, fend off, fight, force back, hold off, keep at bay, resist, ward off. 2 (sth repels you) be repellent, disgust, make your flesh creep, make you sick, nauseate, offend, put off *inf*, revolt, shock, sicken, turn your stomach. 3 (repel water) be impermeable to, keep out, resist; **opp** attract

**repellent** adj abhorrent, disgusting, distasteful, foul, horrid, loathsome, nauseating, obnoxious, obscene, odious, offensive, off-putting, repugnant, repulsive, revolting, sickening, vile

**repent** v atone, be contrite, be penitent, be sorry, feel remorse, regret, reproach yourself, rue

**repentance** n compunction, contrition, grief, guilt, penitence, regret, remorse, self-accusation, self-reproach, shame, sorrow

**repentant** adj apologetic, ashamed, chastened, conscience-stricken, contrite, guilt-ridden, penitent, remorseful, sorry; **opp** unrepentant

**repercussion** n backlash, consequence, effect, result, sequel

**repetition** n 1 (too much repetition) copying, duplication, redundancy, repeating, repetitiousness. 2 (a repetition) duplication, echo, recurrence, repeat, restatement, retelling

**repetitive** adj boring, dull, mechanical, monotonous, recurrent, repeated, tedious, unchanging

**replace** v 1 (replace sth) change, make good, put back, renew, restore, substitute. 2 (replace sb) come after, cover for, fill in for, follow, oust, stand in for, succeed, supersede, take the place of, understudy

**replacement** n double, locum, proxy, stand-in, substitute, successor, surrogate, understudy

**replenish** v fill, refill, renew, replace, restock, stock up, top up

**replica** n carbon copy, clone, copy, duplicate, facsimile, imitation, likeness, model, reproduction

**reply** n acknowledgement, answer, comeback *inf*, reaction, rejoinder, response, retort, riposte

**reply** v 1 (reply to what sb says) answer, counter, rejoin, respond, retort, riposte. 2 (reply to a letter) acknowledge, answer, write back. 3 (reply to what sb does) react, reciprocate, respond, retaliate

**report** n 1 account, announcement, article, description, message, news, note, paper, piece, statement, story, write-up. 2 (a loud report) backfire, bang, blast, boom, crack, crash, discharge, echo, explosion, noise, sound

**report** v 1 (tell people about sth) announce, broadcast, circulate, communicate, describe, disclose, document, publish, recount, reveal, tell, write about, write up. 2 (report sb) accuse, complain about, denounce, grass on *inf*, inform against, inform on, rat on *inf*, squeal on *inf*, tell on *inf*. 3 (report for duty) announce yourself, arrive, be present, check in, come, present yourself, sign in, turn up

**reporter** n correspondent, journalist, newscaster, newsman, newspaperman, newspaperwoman, newswoman, presenter, writer

**repose** n calmness, ease, peace, peacefulness, quietness, relaxation, rest, serenity, sleep, slumber, stillness, tranquillity

**reprehensible** adj bad, blameworthy, culpable, delinquent, deplorable, disgraceful, inexcusable, shameful, unpardonable, wicked, wrong

**represent** v 1 correspond to, embody, exemplify, express, mean, stand for, symbolize, typify. 2 (an MP must represent the people) act for, be the representative of, be the spokesperson for, speak for. 3 (represent sb in a picture) depict, draw, evoke, illustrate, paint, portray, render, show, sketch. 4 (represent sb on stage) act out, assume the guise of, enact, impersonate, personify, pose as, pretend to be, show

**representation** n account, depiction, description, figure, icon, illustration, image, likeness, model, painting, picture, portrait, portrayal, statue

**representative** adj 1 (of a sample) archetypal, average, characteristic, illustrative, indicative, normal, symbolic, typical. 2 (of a government) authorized, chosen, delegated, democratic, elected, elective, official, popular

**representative** n 1 ambassador, consul, councillor, delegate, deputy, emissary, envoy, Member of Parliament, MP, ombudsman, spokesman, spokesperson, spokeswoman, stand-in, substitute. 2 (a representative for a company) agent, rep *inf*, salesman, salesperson, saleswoman, traveller *inf*

**repress** v 1 (repress people) control, crush, dominate, intimidate, keep down, oppress, overpower, quash, quell, restrain, subdue, subjugate. 2 (repress feelings) bottle up *inf*, control, inhibit, hold in, keep in, smother, stifle, suppress; *opp* show

**repressed** adj 1 (of people) frustrated, inhibited, restrained, tense, unbalanced, uptight *inf*, withdrawn. 2 (of feelings) hidden, subconscious, suppressed, unconscious

**repression** n control, domination, oppression, subjugation, totalitarianism, tyranny

**repressive** adj absolute, authoritarian, brutal, despotic, dictatorial, fascist, harsh, oppressive, tyrannical, undemocratic; *opp* liberal

**reprieve** n amnesty, pardon, postponement, stay of execution

**reprieve** v forgive, let off, pardon, rescue, save, set free, spare

**reprimand** n condemnation, criticism, dressing-down *inf*, lecture *inf*, rebuke, reproach, scolding, slap on the wrist *inf*, talking-to *inf*, telling-off *inf*, ticking-off *inf*

**reprimand** v castigate, criticize, lecture *inf*, rebuke, reproach, scold, tell off *inf*, tick off *inf*

**reprisal** n redress, retaliation, retribution, revenge, vengeance

**reproach** n blame, contempt, criticism, disapproval, discredit, disgrace, scorn, shame, stigma

**reproach** v blame, censure, condemn, criticize, find fault, reprimand, scold, show disapproval; *opp* praise

**reproachful** adj censorious, critical, disappointed, disapproving, disparaging, reproving, scolding, scornful

**reproduce** v 1 clone, copy, echo, forge, imitate, match, mirror, parallel, recreate, redo, remake, repeat, replicate. 2 copy, duplicate, make a copy of, photocopy, print, reprint, Xerox TM. 3 bear young, breed, give birth, increase, multiply, procreate, produce offspring, spawn

**reproduction** n copy, duplicate, facsimile, fake, fax, forgery, imitation, photocopy, picture, print, replica

**repudiate** v contradict, deny, disagree with, disclaim, dispute, rebuff, reject

**repugnant** adj abhorrent, disagreeable, disgusting, distasteful, hateful, horrible, nauseating, objectionable, offensive, repellent, revolting, sickening, unpleasant

**repulsive** adj abominable, disgusting, distasteful, foul, gross *slang*, hateful, hideous, loathsome, nasty, nauseating,

odious, off-putting *inf*, repellent, repugnant, revolting, sick *inf*, sickening, ugly, vile

**reputable** adj (a reputable company) above-board, excellent, good, highly regarded, honourable, legitimate, of good repute, prestigious, reliable, respectable, respected, trustworthy, upright, well-thought-of; *opp* disreputable

**reputation** n character, good name, name, position, prestige, recognition, renown, repute, respectability, standing, status

**reputed** adj alleged, believed, considered, deemed, judged, reckoned, regarded, rumoured, said, supposed, thought

**request** n appeal, call, demand, desire, entreaty, petition, plea, prayer, question

**request** v apply for, ask, ask for, beg, beseech, call for, claim, demand, desire, implore, invite, pray, seek

**require** v 1 (need) be missing, be short of, crave, desire, lack, miss, need, want, wish. 2 (require sb to do sth) ask, bid, command, compel, force, insist upon, instruct, oblige, order, put pressure on, request. 3 (require a lot of strength) call for, demand, depend on, necessitate, need, take

**requirement** n condition, demand, essential, necessity, need, precondition, qualification, stipulation

**requisite** adj called for, compulsory, essential, indispensable, mandatory, necessary, needed, obligatory, required, vital

**rescue** n deliverance, freeing, liberation, recovery, release, rescuing, salvage, saving

**rescue** v deliver, free, get back, get out, liberate, recover, redeem, release, retrieve, salvage, save, set free

**research** n analysis, enquiry, examination, experimentation, exploration, fact-finding, inquiry, investigation, study, tests

**research** v analyse, examine, experiment, explore, investigate, look into, review, study, test

**resemblance** n analogy, comparison, conformity, congruity, correspondence, kinship, likeness, similarity

**resemble** v bear a resemblance to, be like, duplicate, echo, look like, mirror, put you in mind of, sound like, remind you of, take after

**resent** v begrudge, be resentful about, dislike, envy, feel aggrieved at, feel bitter about, grudge, grumble at, object to, take exception to, take offence at, take umbrage at

**resentful** adj aggrieved, angry, bitter, disgruntled, in a huff inf, indignant, irate, irked, irritated, jealous, miffed inf, offended, peeved inf, piqued, put out inf, spiteful, vindictive

**resentment** n anger, animosity, bitterness, displeasure, fury, hard feelings, hurt, ill-will, indignation, malice, pique, rancour, spite

**reservation** n 1 (have reservations about sth) doubt, hesitation, misgiving, qualm, reluctance, scepticism, scruple. 2 (live on a reservation) enclave, homeland, preserve, reserve, sanctuary, territory, tract. 3 (a reservation at a restaurant) appointment, arrangement, booking

**reserve** adj auxiliary, extra, fall-back, in reserve, spare, substitute

**reserve** n 1 (kept a reserve for emergencies) fund, hoard, savings, stock, stockpile, store, supply. 2 (known for his reserve) aloofness, coolness, detachment, formality, modesty, remoteness, restraint, reticence, self-effacement, shyness. 3 (animals on a reserve) area, game park, park, preserve, protected area, reservation, sanctuary, tract. 4 (an extra person) back-up inf, reinforcements, replacement, stand-in inf, substitute

**reserve** v 1 (reserve a ticket) book, order, pay in advance for, prearrange. 2 (reserve sth for later) conserve, earmark, hang on to inf, hoard, keep, keep back, lay aside, put away, save, set aside, stockpile, store up, withhold

**reserved** adj 1 (of a person) aloof, cautious, cold, cool, demure, diffident, modest, quiet, remote, restrained, reticent, self-effacing, shy, silent, undemonstrative, unfriendly, unsociable. 2 (of a table, seat) booked, engaged, held, kept, retained, taken

**reside** v abide, dwell, inhabit, live, lodge, occupy, settle, stay

**residence** n address, dwelling, flat, home, house, lodgings, quarters

**resident** n citizen, householder, inhabitant, local, lodger, occupant, occupier, tenant

**residue** n dregs, excess, extra, leftovers, remainder, remains, remnant, rest, surplus

**resign** v abdicate, chuck in sl, give notice, give up, hand in your notice, hand over, leave, quit, retire, step down *inf*

**resigned** *adj* 1 compliant, forbearing, long-suffering, passive, patient, philosophical, stoical, subdued, tolerant, unresisting. 2 (resigned to sth) accepting, acquiescent, reconciled, submitting, yielding

**resilient** *adj* 1 (of materials) bouncy, elastic, firm, flexible, plastic, pliable, pliant, rubbery, springy, supple; *opp* brittle. 2 (of a person) adaptable, buoyant, irrepressible, quick to recover, strong, tough, unstoppable

**resist** *v* 1 (stop sth) block, check, counteract, curb, frustrate, halt, hinder, inhibit, keep at bay, obstruct, prevent, rebuff, stop. 2 (resist an enemy) battle against, combat, confront, defy, fight, oppose, repel, stand up to, thwart. 3 (resist moisture) be resistant to, repel, withstand. 4 (try to resist a cake) abstain from, avoid, desist from, do without, refrain from

**resistant** *adj* 1 immune to, impervious to, proof against, strong, tough, unaffected by; *opp* susceptible to. 2 (resistant to change) antagonistic, defiant, hostile, intransigent, obstinate, opposed, recalcitrant, stubborn, unco-operative, unyielding

**resolute** *adj* adamant, bold, committed, decided, decisive, determined, dogged, immovable, obstinate, persistent, resolved, set, single-minded, staunch, steadfast, stubborn, tenacious, unbending, undaunted, unwavering

**resolution** *n* 1 boldness, commitment, courage, dedication, determination, persistence, purpose, resolve, staying

power, steadfastness, will-power. 2 (a resolution) aim, decision, declaration, intent, intention, judgement, motion, plan, pledge, promise, resolve, undertaking, verdict, vow

**resolve** *v* 1 (resolve to do sth) agree, decide, determine, intend, make up your mind, undertake. 2 (resolve a difficulty) clear up, figure out, settle, sort out, solve, unravel, work out

**resort** *n* haunt, holiday town, refuge, retreat, spot

**resort to** *v* employ, exercise, fall back on, make use of, turn to, use, utilize

**resource** *n* 1 fund, reserve, stock, stockpile, supply. 2 course, device, expedient, means, way

**resourceful** *adj* able, bright, capable, clever, creative, enterprising, imaginative, ingenious, inspired, inventive, quick-witted, skilful, talented

**resources** *n* assets, capital, funds, holdings, money, possessions, reserves, supplies, wealth

**respect** *n* 1 (respect for sb) admiration, approval, awe, consideration, esteem, honour, recognition, regard, reverence. 2 (in this/that respect) aspect, attribute, characteristic, detail, feature, matter, particular, point, quality, sense, trait, way. 3 (show respect) consideration, courtesy, deference, politeness, thoughtfulness. 4 (with respect to your letter) reference, regard

**respect** *v* 1 (respect sb) admire, adore, defer to, esteem, have a high opinion of, honour, look up to, revere, think highly of, venerate. 2 (respect rules) abide by, adhere to, comply with, follow, heed, obey, observe; **opp** break. **3** (respect sb's views) recognize, show consideration for, take into account, value

**respectable** adj **1** (of a person) decent, dignified, genteel, good, honest, honourable, law-abiding, of good repute, proper, reputable, trustworthy, upright, venerable, virtuous, worthy. **2** (of an amount) adequate, ample, appreciable, considerable, decent, fair, goodly, presentable, reasonable, satisfactory, sizeable, substantial, tolerable

**respectful** adj admiring, civil, considerate, courteous, deferential, dutiful, humble, polite, reverential, subservient; **opp** disrespectful

**respective** adj individual, own, particular, personal, relevant, special, specific, various

**respite** n break, breather inf, cessation, halt, hiatus, holiday, interval, let-up inf, lull, pause, relief, rest, time off, time out

**respond** v **1** (respond to a letter) acknowledge, answer, reply, write back. **2** (respond to speech or action) answer, counter, react, reciprocate, reply, retort, return

**response** n answer, comeback inf, feedback, reaction, reply

**responsibility** n **1** (have a responsibility) accountability, answerability, authority, duty, importance, liability, obligation, onus, power, trust. **2** (responsibility for sth going wrong) accountability, blame, burden, fault, guilt, liability

**responsible** adj **1** (having responsibility) accountable, in charge, in control, liable. **2** (responsible for sth going

wrong) accountable, answerable, at fault, culpable, guilty, to blame; **opp** innocent. **3** (behaving in a responsible way) adult, conscientious, dependable, level-headed, mature, reasonable, reliable, sensible, steady, trustworthy; **opp** irresponsible. **4** (a responsible job) decision-making, executive, front-line inf, high, important, managerial, powerful; **opp** menial

**rest** n **1** (stop for a rest) break, breather inf, halt, interlude, intermission, interval, lull, pause, respite, time off, time out. **2** (a well-earned rest) break, holiday, vacation. **3** (a sleep) forty winks inf, kip slang, lie-down, nap, siesta, sleep. **4** (need plenty of rest) calmness, ease, hush, inactivity, peace, quiet, relaxation, repose, sleep, tranquillity. **5** (throw away the rest) balance, excess, leftovers, others, remainder, remnants, residue, surplus

**rest** v **1** be still, catnap, doze, have a kip inf, have a nap, have a rest, have a sleep, lie down, nod off, put your feet up, snooze inf, take it easy inf, unwind. **2** (rest on a surface) lean, lie, place, prop, set, sit, stand, steady, support. **3** (everything rests on your answer) depend, hang, hinge, rely, turn

**restful** adj calm, calming, leisurely, peaceful, placid, quiet, relaxed, relaxing, serene, sleepy, soothing, still, tranquil

**restless** adj **1** (not staying in one place) itinerant, nomadic, roaming, roving, transient, travelling, unsettled, wandering; **opp** settled. **2** (constantly moving) active, busy, changeable, changing, in motion, moving, on the move, turbulent; **opp** still. 3 (not getting much sleep) disturbed, fitful, fretful, sleepless, uncomfortable, uneasy, wakeful; **opp** restful. 4 (not patient or calm) agitated, edgy, excitable, fidgeting, fidgety, ill at ease, impatient, jittery *inf*, jumpy, nervous, restive, uneasy, unruly, unsettled, worked up, worried; **opp** calm, relaxed

**restore** v 1 (restore sth old) clean, do up *inf*, fix, fix up *inf*, mend, recondition, redecorate, refurbish, renew, renovate, repair, revamp. 2 (restore a person) build up, refresh, rejuvenate, revive, revitalize, strengthen. 3 (restore stolen property) bring back, give back, hand back, recover, replace, return, send back

**restrain** v 1 (restrain feelings) control, curb, hold in check, inhibit, rein in, repress, stifle, subdue, suppress; **opp** show. 2 (restrain a prisoner) chain up, confine, detain, handcuff, imprison, lock up, manacle, tie up; **opp** let loose. 3 (restrain sb from doing sth) hinder, hold back, keep, obstruct, prevent, save, stop; **opp** encourage

**restrained** adj 1 (of a person) calm, controlled, mild, moderate, reticent, undemonstrative, unemotional. 2 (of colours) discreet, muted, soft, subtle, tasteful, understated, unobtrusive

**restraint** n 1 (show restraint) inhibition, moderation, prudence, self-control, self-discipline. 2 (a restraint on sth) ban, check, constraint, curb, deterrent, embargo, limit, rein, restriction

**restrict** v circumscribe, confine, contain, control, hamper, handicap, hinder,

impede, imprison, limit, moderate, regulate, restrain

**restriction** n ban, check, condition, control, curb, handicap, limit, limitation, proviso, qualification, regulation, restraint, rule, stipulation

**result** n 1 (the result of sth happening) conclusion, consequence, effect, outcome, repercussion, sequel, upshot. 2 (the wrong result) answer, decision, judgement, solution, verdict

**result** v appear, arise, come about, derive, develop, emerge, ensue, follow, happen, occur, proceed, spring, stem, take place, turn out

**resume** v begin again, carry on, continue, proceed, recommence, re-open, restart, take up

**resurrect** v breathe new life into, bring back, raise from the dead, reawaken, reintroduce, renew, restore to life, revive

**resuscitate** v bring round, give the kiss of life to, revive, save

**retain** v 1 absorb, contain, hang on to *inf*, hold, keep, keep hold of, keep in, maintain, preserve, reserve, save, soak up; **opp** lose. 2 keep in mind, learn, memorize, recall, recollect, remember; **opp** forget

**retaliate** v avenge yourself, get even *inf*, get your own back, give as good as you get, hit back, reciprocate, repay, settle a score, strike back, take revenge

**retard** v arrest, delay, handicap, hinder, hold back, impede, obstruct, set back, slow down

**reticent** adj quiet, reserved, retiring, secretive, shy, silent, tight-lipped, uncommunicative

**retire** v 1 give up work, leave, quit, stop working. 2 depart, exit, go away, go out, leave, withdraw. 3 call it a day, go to bed, go to sleep, turn in *inf*

**retiring** adj bashful, coy, demure, diffident, meek, modest, quiet, reserved, reticent, shrinking, shy, timid, unassertive; *opp* outgoing

**retort** n answer, rejoinder, reply, response, riposte

**retort** v answer, answer back, come back at, counter, reply, riposte, say in reply

**retract** v 1 draw in, pull back, pull in, sheathe. 2 backtrack on, cancel, deny, disclaim, disown, renounce, repudiate, reverse, revoke, take back, withdraw

**retreat** n 1 asylum, den, haunt, haven, hideaway, hideout, hiding place, refuge, sanctuary, shelter. 2 departure, evacuation, exit, flight, withdrawal

**retreat** v 1 back away, back down, back off, depart, draw back, evacuate, fall back, flee, give way, go away, go back, leave, move back, pull back, recoil, retire, run away, take flight, take to your heels *inf*, turn tail, withdraw; *opp* advance. 2 ebb, flow back, recede, shrink back; *opp* advance

**retribution** n compensation, justice, punishment, reckoning, recompense, redress, reparation, repayment, reprisal, retaliation, revenge, reward, vengeance

**retrieve** v bring back, fetch, find, get back, recall, recapture, recover, regain, repossess, rescue, salvage, trace, track down, win back

**retrospective** adj backward-looking, looking back, with hindsight

**return** n 1 arrival, coming home, homecoming, reappearance.
2 (a good return on your investment) earnings, gain, income, interest, profit, revenue, yield

**return** v 1 come again, come back, go back, reappear. 2 (return to look for sth) backtrack, double back, go back, retrace your steps. 3 (return a library book) give back, put back, replace, restore, send back, take back. 4 (return a favour) pay back, reciprocate, repay

**reveal** v 1 (reveal a secret) announce, betray, broadcast, confess, disclose, divulge, give away, leak, let on, let out, let slip, make known, publicize, tell.
2 (show sth) bare, display, expose, show, uncover, unmask, unveil

**revel** v 1 celebrate, have fun, live it up *inf*, make merry, paint the town red *inf*, party. 2 (revel in sth) bask, delight, gloat, luxuriate, relish, savour, take pleasure, wallow

**revelation** n admission, betrayal, confession, disclosure, discovery, leak *inf*, publishing, revealing, telling

**revelry** n celebrations, festivities, fun, gaiety, jollification, jollity, living it up *inf*, merrymaking, party, rave *inf*, rave-up *inf*

**revenge** n 1 (get your revenge) redress, reprisal, retaliation, retribution, vengeance. 2 (feelings of revenge) hate, hatred, hostility, malice, spite, spitefulness, vindictiveness

**revenue** n gain, income, interest, money, proceeds, profits, receipts, returns, takings, rewards, yield

**reverberate** v boom, echo, rebound, resonate, resound, ring, thunder, vibrate

**revere** v adore, exalt, glorify, honour, idolize, pay homage to, praise, respect, venerate, worship

**reverent** adj adoring, awed, deferential, devout, humble, pious, religious, respectful, reverential, solemn, submissive, worshipful

**reverse** adj back-to-front, backward, backwards, contrary, converse, inverted, opposite, transposed

**reverse** n 1 contrary, converse, inverse, opposite. 2 back, other side, rear, wrong side

**reverse** v 1 (in a vehicle) back, go backwards, move backwards. 2 (reverse a judgement) annul, cancel, change, countermand, invalidate, overrule, overturn, quash, repeal, revoke, set aside, undo, upset. 3 (reverse an image) invert, put back to front, transpose, turn over, turn round, turn upside down, up-end

**review** n 1 analysis, assessment, fresh look, reassessment, reconsideration, re-examination, rethink. 2 (write a review) appreciation, commentary, criticism, critique, evaluation, judgement, report, study, write-up

**review** v 1 (review a decision) look again at, reassess, reconsider, re-examine, rethink, think over. 2 (review a performance) analyse, appraise, assess, criticize, evaluate, judge, write a review of. 3 (review the year) look back on, look back over, recall, recollect, reflect on, remember, survey

**reviewer** n commentator, critic, judge

**revise** v 1 (revise your opinion) alter, amend, change, modify, reconsider,

review. 2 (revise your work) correct, edit, improve, redraft, rephrase, rewrite, update. 3 (revise for a test) brush up, cram inf, learn, read, reread, study, swot up inf

**revision** n 1 alteration, amendment, change, correction, modification, rewriting, updating. 2 homework, reading, studying, swotting inf

**revival** n reawakening, rebirth, renaissance, renewal, resurgence, resurrection, return, upsurge

**revive** v 1 (revive a person) bring round, give the kiss of life to inf, resuscitate, rouse. 2 (sb revives) come back to life, come round, come to, rally, recover, regain consciousness. 3 (a drink to revive you) cheer, invigorate, refresh, revitalize, strengthen. 4 (revive memories) awaken, call forth, rekindle, stir up

**revolt** n civil war, coup, insurgency, insurrection, mutiny, rebellion, revolution, rising, uprising

**revolt** v 1 defect, disobey, mutiny, rebel, resist, riot, rise up, take to the streets. 2 (sth revolts you) appal, disgust, make your flesh creep, make you sick, nauseate, offend, repel, sicken, turn your stomach

**revolting** adj abhorrent, disgusting, distasteful, foul, horrible, nasty, nauseating, obnoxious, obscene, offensive, repellent, repugnant, repulsive, shocking, sickening, vile

**revolution** n 1 coup, coup d'état, insurgency, mutiny, putsch, rebellion, revolt, rising, uprising. 2 change, reorganization, shift, transformation, upheaval, U-turn *inf.* **3** circle, circuit, cycle, gyration, orbit, rotation, round, spin, turn

**revolutionary** *adj* **1** (revolutionary methods) avant-garde, different, drastic, experimental, ground-breaking, innovative, new, novel, progressive, radical; *opp* conservative. **2** (revolutionary forces) extremist, insurgent, mutinous, rebel, subversive

**revolve** *v* circle, go round, gyrate, orbit, rotate, spin, swivel, turn, turn round, twist, wheel, whirl

**revulsion** *n* abhorrence, aversion, disgust, distaste, hate, hatred, loathing, repugnance

**reward** *n* award, bonus, cut *inf,* decoration, gift, honour, medal, payment, present, prize, remuneration, tribute

**reward** *v* compensate, decorate, give a reward to, honour, pay, recompense, remunerate, tip

**rewarding** *adj* beneficial, fulfilling, gratifying, productive, profitable, satisfying, useful, valuable, worthwhile; *opp* unrewarding

**rhetoric** *n* eloquence, expressiveness, gift of the gab *inf,* oratory, purple prose, rhetorical language, speechifying, verbosity

**rhetorical** *adj* bombastic, extravagant, flamboyant, florid, flowery, high-flown, insincere, long-winded, ostentatious, pretentious, showy, verbose, wordy

**rhyme** *n* ditty, doggerel, jingle, ode, poem, poetry, song, verse

**rhythm** *n* accent, beat, cadence, flow, lilt, metre, movement, pattern, pulse, stress,

swing, tempo, time

**rhythmic** *adj* flowing, harmonious, lilting, measured, melodious, metrical, musical, pulsating, regular, repeated, rhythmical, steady, throbbing

**rich** *adj* **1** affluent, flush *inf,* loaded *inf,* made of money *inf,* moneyed, prosperous, wealthy, well-heeled *inf,* well-off, well-to-do; *opp* poor. **2** (rich furnishings) costly, elaborate, elegant, expensive, exquisite, fine, gorgeous, grand, lavish, opulent, palatial, precious, splendid, sumptuous, valuable; *opp* simple. **3** (rich ground) abundant, ample, copious, fertile, fruitful, lush, luxurious, plentiful, productive, prolific; *opp* poor. **4** (an area rich in wildlife) abounding, full, overflowing, replete, rife, teeming, well-provided, well-stocked, well-supplied. **5** (rich food) cloying, creamy, delicious, fattening, fatty, full-flavoured, heavy, savoury, spicy, succulent, sweet, tasty; *opp* light. **6** (rich sounds) deep, full, mellow, melodious, resonant; *opp* thin. **7** (a rich red) brilliant, deep, intense, strong, vivid, warm

**riches** *n* affluence, assets, fortune, gold, money, possessions, property, resources, treasure, wealth; *opp* poverty

**rid** *v* cleanse, clear, deliver, free, purge, purify, relieve, rescue, save, unburden. **2 get rid of** destroy, dispose of, do away with, dump, eject, eliminate, expel, jettison, remove, throw away, unload

**riddle** *n* brain-teaser *inf,* conundrum, enigma, mystery, poser, problem, puzzle, question

**ride** *n* drive, journey, joy-ride *inf,*

lift, outing, spin *inf*, trip

**ride** v 1 float, gallop, go, journey, move, progress, travel, trot. 2 (ride a bicycle) be mounted on, control, handle, manage, mount, pedal, sit on, steer

**ridicule** n derision, irony, laughter, mockery, sarcasm, satire, scorn, sneering, teasing, taunting

**ridicule** v be sarcastic about, caricature, deride, humiliate, jeer at, laugh at, make jokes about, mock, parody, poke fun at, satirize, send up *inf*, sneer at, take the mickey out of *inf*, taunt, tease

**ridiculous** adj 1 (a ridiculous story) amusing, crazy, droll, farcical, funny, humorous, illogical, incredible, ludicrous, nonsensical, preposterous, surreal, unbelievable. 2 (you look ridiculous) absurd, comical, foolish, funny, hilarious, silly, weird. 3 (a ridiculous price) crazy, derisory, laughable, ludicrous, outrageous, shocking, stupid, unreasonable; *opp* reasonable

**rife** adj abundant, common, general, predominant, prevalent, rampant, ubiquitous, universal, widespread; *opp* rare

**rift** n 1 (a physical rift) breach, break, chink, cleft, crack, crevice, fault, fissure, opening, split. 2 (a rift in a family) breach, difference, disagreement, division, feud, quarrel, separation

**rig** v 1 equip, fit, fit out, furnish, kit out, provide, rig out, set up, supply. 2 (rig the results) arrange, engineer, fake, falsify, fix *inf*, manipulate, tamper with. 3 **rig up** assemble, botch, build, cobble together, construct, improvise, knock up, put together, throw together

**right** adj 1 (what you did was right) correct, decent, equitable, ethical, fair, good, honest, honourable, just, lawful, moral, proper, virtuous; *opp* wrong. 2 (the right time) accurate, correct, exact, precise, true; *opp* wrong. 3 (at the right moment) appropriate, convenient, ideal, opportune, proper; *opp* wrong. 4 (the right thing to wear) appropriate, decent, fit, proper, seemly, suitable; *opp* inappropriate. 5 (do the right way) best, good, normal, preferable, preferred, recommended, sensible, usual; *opp* wrong

**right** n 1 (fight for your rights) claim, due, entitlement, freedom, interest, privilege. 2 (have the right to do sth) authority, licence, permission, power, prerogative. 3 (have right on your side) decency, good, goodness, honour, justice, lawfulness, morality, reason, truth, virtue; *opp* wrong

**right** v 1 (make sth right) amend, correct, fix, make amends for, put right, put to rights, rectify, redress, remedy, repair, settle, sort out, straighten out. 2 (right a fallen chair) pick up, set upright, stand upright, straighten up

**right** adv 1 directly, in a straight line, straight. 2 directly, immediately, promptly, quickly, straightaway. 3 (it fell right off the table) all the way, altogether, completely, quite, totally, utterly. 4 (right on the nose) exactly, slap-bang *inf*, precisely, squarely. 5 (not doing it right) appropriately, correctly, properly, satisfactorily, suitably. 6 (treating her right) equitably,

fairly, honestly, honourably, justly.
**7** (work out right) advantageously,
favourably, for the best, fortunately,
to your advantage, well

**righteous** adj blameless, ethical, fair,
God-fearing, good, honest, honourable,
just, law-abiding, moral, pure,
sanctimonious, upright, upstanding,
virtuous; **opp** immoral

**rightful** adj authorized, bona fide, correct,
lawful, legal, legitimate, proper, real,
true

**rigid** adj **1** (rigid ideas) firm, fixed, hard
and fast, harsh, inflexible, rigorous, set,
strict, unalterable, unrelenting;
**opp** flexible. **2** (rigid materials) hard,
inelastic, inflexible, solid, stiff, strong,
taut, unbending; **opp** flexible

**rigorous** adj challenging, demanding,
exacting, hard, harsh, meticulous,
painstaking, scrupulous, severe, strict,
stringent, thorough, tough

**rigour** n **1** hardship, harshness, rigidity,
severity, sternness, strictness, toughness.
**2** (do sth with rigour) accuracy,
meticulousness, precision, thoroughness

**rim** n border, brim, brink, circumference,
edge, lip, margin, perimeter, verge

**rind** n crust, husk, outer layer, peel, skin

**ring** n **1** band, circle, circlet, disc, halo,
loop, round. **2** arena, enclosure, rink.
**3** alliance, band, clique, gang, gathering,
group, knot, league, mob, organization,
syndicate. **4** (telephone call) bell inf,
buzz inf, call, phone call inf, telephone
call, tinkle inf. **5** (sound of bells) buzz,
chime, clang, clink, jangle, jingle, peal,
ping, ringing, tinkle, tolling

**ring** v **1** buzz, chime, clang, clink, ding-
dong, jangle, jingle, peal, ping, sound,
tinkle, toll. **2** echo, resonate, resound,
reverberate. **3** (telephone) call, phone
inf, ring up, telephone. **4** (make a ring
round sth) circle, encircle, enclose,
fence in, hem in, put a ring round,
surround

**rinse** v bathe, clean, cleanse, dip, flush,
sluice, swill, wash, wash out, wet

**riot** n **1** anarchy, chaos, confusion,
disorder, lawlessness, pandemonium,
rioting, tumult, turbulence, upheaval,
uproar, violence. **2** brawl,
demonstration, fight, fracas, free-for-all,
mutiny, protest, scuffle, rebellion, revolt,
uprising

**riot** v brawl, fight, go berserk, go wild,
mutiny, rampage, rebel, revolt, rise up,
run amok, run wild, take to the streets

**riotous** adj **1** (a riotous crowd) anarchic,
disorderly, lawless, mutinous, rebellious,
rowdy, uncontrollable, unruly, violent.
**2** (a riotous evening) boisterous,
hilarious, loud, noisy, unrestrained,
uproarious, wild

**rip** n gash, hole, opening, slit, split, tear

**rip** v **1** (rip sth to shreds) cut, gash,
lacerate, pull apart, rupture, shred, slit,
split, tear. **2** (rip sth out of sb's hands)
grab, pull, snatch, wrench, yank

**ripe** adj **1** full-grown, mature, mellow,
ready, ready to eat. **2** auspicious,
favourable, ideal, opportune, right,
suitable, timely

**ripen** v age, become ripe, come to
maturity, develop, grow ripe, mature,
mellow

**rise** n **1** advance, escalation,
improvement, increase, jump, leap,

upsurge, upswing, upturn; *opp* drop, fall. **2** ascent, bank, elevation, hill, incline, ramp, ridge, upward slope. **3** increment, pay increase

**rise** v **1** get to your feet, get up, leap up, stand up, surface *inf*, wake up. **2** (go upwards) ascend, climb, come up, go up, levitate, lift, mount, move up, take off; *opp* descend. **3** (of prices) escalate, go up, increase, rocket, soar, spiral; *opp* fall. **4** (of sounds) become louder, grow, increase, intensify, soar, swell; *opp* fall. **5** (rise in the firm) advance, be promoted, do well, get on, progress, prosper. **6** (of a road) climb, get steeper, go uphill, slope upwards; *opp* descend. **7** (of a tower) loom, soar, stand out, tower. **8** (of water) come up, get deeper, get higher, swell; *opp* fall. **9** (of a river) begin, flow from, issue from, originate, spring

**risk** n **1** chance, danger, likelihood, possibility. **2** danger, hazards, jeopardy, peril, speculation, uncertainty. **3** (it's a risk) gamble, venture

**risk** v **1** (risk losing) chance, dare, hazard, take the risk of, venture. **2** (risk your life) endanger, gamble with, imperil, jeopardize, put at risk

**risky** adj chancy *inf*, dangerous, fraught with danger, hazardous, perilous, precarious, touch-and-go, tricky, uncertain, unsafe; *opp* safe

**rite** n ceremony, custom, observance, practice, ritual, service, tradition

**ritual** adj **1** ceremonial, customary, formal, prescribed, traditional. **2** (habitual) customary, habitual, prescribed, regular, routine, set

**ritual** n **1** ceremony, custom, observance, practice, rite, tradition. **2** (routine) ceremony, habit, procedure, routine

**rival** adj competing, conflicting, enemy, opposing, opposite, warring; *opp* friendly

**rival** n adversary, antagonist, challenger, competitor, contender, contestant, enemy, opponent, opposition; *opp* friend, helper, team-mate

**rival** v be as good as, challenge, compete with, equal, match up to, measure up to, oppose, parallel, vie with

**rivalry** n adversary, competition, competitiveness, conflict, contention, hostility, opposition; *opp* co-operation, friendliness

**road** n avenue, bypass, drive, dual carriageway, expressway *Am*, freeway *Am*, highway, lane, motorway, roadway, route, street, thoroughfare, track, trunk road

**roam** v prowl, ramble, range, tramp, travel, walk, wander

**roar** v **1** bawl, bellow, blare, boom, crash, cry, rumble, shout, thunder, yell. **2** (laugh) fall about *inf*, guffaw, hoot, howl with laughter, kill yourself laughing, laugh, roll in the aisles *inf*, split your sides *inf*

**rob** v **1** break into, burgle, hold up, loot, mug, pick sb's pocket, raid, ransack, rifle, steal from, steal, thieve. **2** cheat, con, do *inf*, rip off *inf*, swindle

**robber** n bandit, burglar, cat burglar, housebreaker, looter, mugger, pickpocket, shoplifter, thief

**robbery** n break-in, burglary, embezzlement, fraud, hold-up, housebreaking, larceny, looting, misappropriation, mugging, pilfering, raid, shoplifting, stealing, theft

**robe** *n* attire, ceremonial dress, costume, gown, vestment

**robot** *n* android, automaton, computer-controlled machine, humanoid, machine

**robust** *adj* 1 hardy, powerful, rugged, strong, sturdy, tough, vigorous, well-made. 2 practical, pragmatic, realistic, sensible, sound, strong

**rock** *n* boulder, crag, outcrop, reef, stone

**rock** *v* 1 lurch, move to and fro, pitch, sway, teeter, totter, wobble. 2 astound, shake, shock, stagger, startle, stun, take by surprise

**rocky** *adj* 1 bumpy, craggy, pebbly, rough, rugged, stony. 2 iffy *inf*, shaky, uncertain, unstable, unsteady, wobbly

**rod** *n* bar, baton, pole, shaft, stick, wand

**rogue** *n* cheat, con-man, crook, fraud, rascal, scoundrel, sharper

**role** *n* 1 capacity, contribution, function, job, position, task. 2 (in a play) character, part

**roll** *n* 1 ball, bobbin, cylinder, furl, round, scroll, spool, tube, tube, twist. 2 (rolling movement) cycle, revolution, rotation, spin, turn, twirl. 3 (register) census, directory, inventory, list, listing, record, register, schedule. 4 (rumble) boom, reverberation, roar, rumble

**roll** *v* 1 coil, curl, furl, go round, revolve, rotate, somersault, spin, tumble, turn, twirl, wheel, wind. 2 (of a ship) lurch, pitch, reel, rock, toss. 3 (flatten) compact, compress, flatten, level out, press down, press, smooth

**romance** *n* 1 intrigue, love affair, love,

passion, relationship. 2 love story, romantic fiction. 3 adventure, fascination, glamour

**romantic** *adj* 1 affectionate, amorous, emotional, lovey-dovey *inf*, loving, passionate, sentimental, sloppy *inf*, soppy *inf*, tender; *opp* unromantic. 2 dreamy, exciting, fabulous, fairy-tale, glamorous, idealistic, impractical, starry-eyed; *opp* down-to-earth, practical

**room** *n* 1 capacity, elbow-room, space, volume. 2 (scope) capacity, freedom, latitude, leeway, margin, opportunity, scope. 3 accommodation, bedroom, bedsit, place to stay

**roomy** *adj* baggy, big, extensive, large, sizeable, spacious, voluminous; *opp* small

**root** *n* 1 rhizome, taproot, tuber. 2 (the root of a problem) basis, bottom, cause, core, crux, germ, origin, seat, source, starting point

**root** *v* 1 germinate, sprout, take root. 2 (search) forage, root around, rummage, scrabble, search. 3 **root out** cut out, destroy, dig out, discover, eliminate, eradicate, get rid of, remove, search out, unearth, uproot, weed out

**rope** *n* cable, cord, guy, halter, hawser, line, tether, towrope

**rot** *n* 1 canker, decay, decomposition, mould, putrefaction. 2 (nonsense) bosh *inf*, claptrap *inf*, drivel *inf*, garbage *inf*, gibberish, nonsense, rubbish, tripe *inf*

**rot** *v* crumble, decay, decompose, disintegrate, fester, go bad, go off, go sour, moulder, perish, putrefy

**rota** *n* duty rota, list, roster *Am*, schedule, timetable

**rotate** *v* 1 go round, pivot, revolve, spin,

swirl, swivel, turn, twirl, wind.
**2** alternate, come round, do in turn,
recur, share, take turns at

**rotten** adj **1** (decaying) addled, bad,
decaying, foul, mouldering, off inf,
perished, putrid, rotting, sour; **opp** fresh.
**2** (terrible) awful, bad, disappointing,
dismal, foul inf, inferior, lousy inf,
miserable, nasty, poor, terrible;
**opp** terrific, wonderful. **3** (ill) bad,
grotty inf, ill, off colour, poorly, rough
inf, sick, under the weather, unwell;
**opp** fine, well

**rough** adj **1** bumpy, coarse, jagged, rocky,
rugged, scratchy, stony, uneven;
**opp** smooth. **2** (a rough estimate)
approximate, crude, estimated, general,
quick, raw, rudimentary, sketchy, vague;
**opp** detailed, exact, precise. **3** (of a
person) badly behaved, brusque, curt, ill-
mannered, loutish, rowdy, rude, surly;
**opp** refined. **4** (of work, conditions)
arduous, hard, heavy-handed, severe,
spartan, tough, unfair, unjust, violent.
**5** (of a voice) grating, gruff, harsh,
hoarse, husky, rasping; **opp** smooth, soft.
**6** (of the sea) choppy, heavy, stormy,
wild; **opp** calm. **7** (ill) bad, grotty inf, ill,
off colour, poorly, rotten inf, sick, under
the weather, unwell; **opp** fine, well

**round** adj ball-shaped, bulbous, circular,
curved, cylindrical, disc-shaped,
globular, rounded, spherical, spheroid

**round** n **1** ball, band, circle, disc, globe,
ring, sphere. **2** (in sport or
competitions) bout, cycle, game, heat,
level, series, session, stage. **3** (of a doctor
or guard) beat, circuit, lap, route,
tour, turn

**round** v (go round) circle,
circumnavigate, come round, go
round, skirt, turn

**roundabout** adj circuitous, devious,
evasive, indirect, long-winded,
meandering, oblique, rambling, tortuous;
**opp** direct

**rouse** v **1** (stir up) arouse, awaken, egg on
inf, galvanize, incite, inflame, kindle,
provoke, rally, stimulate, stir up, whip
up, work up; **opp** calm, discourage.
**2** (rouse sb) awaken, wake up, waken

**rousing** adj electrifying, energetic,
exciting, fervent, lively, moving,
spirited, stimulating, stirring, vigorous;
**opp** dull, flat, lifeless, uninspiring

**rout** n conquest, defeat, drubbing,
overthrow, pasting inf, thrashing;
**opp** victory

**rout** v conquer, crush, defeat, drive off,
hammer inf, overthrow, see off, thrash,
trounce

**route** n course, crossing, itinerary,
journey, path, run, way

**routine** adj **1** common, everyday,
familiar, habitual, ordinary, regular,
standard, usual; **opp** special, unusual.
**2** (dull) boring, dull, monotonous,
predictable, run-of-the-mill, tedious,
unexciting; **opp** exciting

**routine** n **1** custom, drill, formula, habit,
pattern, procedure, programme, system.
**2** act, patter, performance, piece, set

**row** n (line) bank, chain, column, file,
line, procession, queue, rank, series,
string, tier

**row** n **1** (argument) altercation,
argument, controversy, disagreement,
dispute, quarrel, ructions inf, scrap,

slanging match *inf*, spat, squabble, tiff, wrangle. **2** (noise) commotion, din, fracas, hubbub, hullabaloo, noise, racket, rumpus, uproar

**row** *v* argue, bicker, quarrel, squabble, wrangle

**rowdy** *adj* badly behaved, boisterous, loutish, noisy, rough, unruly, wild; *opp* quiet, well-behaved

**royal** *adj* imperial, majestic, princely, regal, sovereign, stately

**rub** *v* **1** buff, clean, polish, scour, scrub, shine, smooth, wipe. **2** (stroke) caress, fondle, massage, stroke. **3** (chafe) abrade, chafe, scrape, wear away. **4** apply, put on, smear, spread. **5 rub out** cancel, delete, efface, erase, remove, rub off, wipe out

**rubbish** *adj* **1** (nonsense) balderdash, claptrap, codswallop *inf*, drivel, gobbledegook, nonsense, rot *inf*, twaddle. **2** (refuse) debris, detritus, dross, garbage *Am*, junk, litter, rubble, scrap, trash *Am*, waste, refuse

**ruddy** *adj* blushing, crimson, florid, flushed, healthy, pink, red, rosy, scarlet

**rude** *adj* **1** abusive, bad-mannered, cheeky, discourteous, disrespectful, impertinent, impolite, insolent, insulting, offensive, offhand, short, uncivil, uncouth; *opp* polite.
**2** (of a joke) blue, coarse, crude, dirty, naughty, obscene, risqué, smutty, vulgar; *opp* clean

**rudeness** *n* bad manners, cheek, cheekiness, coarseness, discourtesy, disrespect, impertinence, impudence, insolence, offensiveness, vulgarity; *opp* courtesy, good manners, politeness

**rudimentary** *adj* basic, crude, early, elementary, primitive, simple; *opp* sophisticated

**rudiments** *n* basic principles, basics, essentials, foundations, fundamentals, nuts and bolts

**ruffian** *n* bully, hooligan, lout, rowdy, scamp, thug, tough, yob

**ruffle** *v* **1** disturb, mess up, ripple, rumple, stir, tousle. **2** agitate, annoy, disconcert, disturb, fluster, irritate, nettle *inf*, put out, rattle *inf*, unsettle, upset

**rugged** *adj* barren, craggy, hard, harsh, rocky, rough, tough, weather-beaten, weathered

**ruin** *n* bankruptcy, collapse, defeat, destitution, destruction, downfall, end, failure, havoc, insolvency, undoing, wreck, wreckage

**ruin** *v* bankrupt, bring down, defeat, demolish, destroy, devastate, mess up, shatter, smash, spoil, wreck

**ruined** *adj* bankrupt, crumbling, derelict, destroyed, dilapidated, in ruins, insolvent, ramshackle, spoiled, uninhabitable, wrecked

**ruinous** *adj* catastrophic, crippling, crushing, devastating, dire, disastrous, fatal, injurious, shattering

**rule** *n* **1** axiom, code, direction, formula, guideline, law, maxim, order, principle, regulation, ruling, standard, statute, tenet. **2** (control) administration, authority, command, control, dominion, government, management, power, regime, reign, sovereignty, supervision

**rule** *v* **1** decide, decree, determine, find, judge, lay down, order, pronounce.
**2** (govern) administer, be in power, be

on the throne, control, govern, hold the reigns, lead, manage, reign, run. **3 rule out** disallow, discount, dismiss, disqualify, eliminate, exclude, preclude, prohibit, reject

**ruler** *n* chief, dictator, emperor, governing body, government, governor, head of state, king, leader, monarch, potentate, president, queen, regent, sovereign

**ruling** *adj* controlling, dominant, in power, leading, reigning, supreme

**ruling** *n* adjudication, decision, decree, finding, judgment, pronouncement, verdict

**rumour** *n* dirt *inf*, gossip, grapevine, hearsay, low-down *inf*, news, scandal, story, talk, the latest

**run** *n* **1** canter, gallop, jog, sprint, trot. **2** (a journey) drive, journey, outing, ride, route, spin *inf*, trip. **3** (a series) period, round, series, spell, stretch, succession. **4** enclosure, pen

**run** *v* **1** bolt, career, charge, dash, gallop, hare, hotfoot it *inf*, hurry, jog, race, scurry, sprint, tear. **2** (run a company) administer, control, direct, govern, head, lead, manage, operate, supervise. **3** (function) behave, function, go, operate, perform, work. **4** (trains run every hour) go, move, operate, pass, travel. **5** (extend) continue, extend, go, last, lie, reach, stretch. **6** (run for office) apply, be a candidate, compete, go in for, put your name forward, stand, take part. **7** (flow) cascade, discharge, dribble, flow, gush, pour, spill, spout, stream, trickle. **8** (drip) dissolve, drip, go soft, melt. **9 run away** abscond, do a bunk *inf*, escape, leave home, bolt, run off,

make off. **10 run over** (look at sth again) go through, look through, recap, recapitulate, repeat, run through. **11 run over** (knock down) hit, knock down, knock over, run down. **12 run over** (of liquid) overflow, spill over

**runner** *n* **1** athlete, fell-runner, harrier, jogger, sprinter. **2** shoot, sprout, sucker, tendril

**running** *adj* **1** consecutive, continual, continuous, in a row, incessant, on the trot, ongoing, perpetual, successive, uninterrupted. **2** (running water) flowing, moving; *opp* still

**rupture** *n* **1** breach, break, cleft, fracture, split, tear. **2** hernia. **3** (disagreement) break-up, break, disagreement, division, feud, quarrel, rift, schism

**rupture** *v* breach, break, burst, divide, fracture, separate, sever, split, tear

**rural** *adj* agrarian, agricultural, countrified, country, countryside, pastoral, rustic; *opp* urban

**rush** *n* bustle, dash, flood, haste, hurry, panic, race, scramble, speed, sprint, stampede, surge, urgency

**rush** *v* bolt, charge, dart, dash, flood, fly, get a move on, hotfoot it *inf*, hurry, move fast, race, run, scramble, shoot, speed, sprint, stampede, surge, tear, zoom

**rust** *n* corrosion, oxidation

**rust** *v* corrode, oxidize

**rustic** *adj* agrarian, agricultural, countrified, country, countryside, pastoral, rural

**rustle** *n* crackle, hiss, swish, whisper

**rustle** *v* crackle, hiss, swish, whisper

**rusty** *adj* **1** corroded, oxidized, rusted.

**2** (out of practice) below par, neglected, not up to scratch *inf*, out of practice, poor, stale, weak. **3** brick-red, chestnut, coppery, reddish-brown, rust-coloured

**rut** *n* **1** furrow, gouge, groove, gutter, hollow, track, trough, wheel mark.
**2 in a rut** at a dead end, bored, in a routine, on the treadmill, stuck in the daily grind

**ruthless** *adj* brutal, callous, cold, cruel, harsh, heartless, inhuman, merciless, pitiless, savage, severe, unfeeling, unrelenting, violent

**sabotage** *n* damage, destruction, subversion, vandalism, wrecking

**sabotage** *v* attack, damage, destroy, disable, put out of action, scupper, thwart, vandalize, wreck

**sack** *n* **1** dismissal, notice, redundancy, the axe, the boot *inf*, the push *inf*, your cards. **2** bag, holdall

**sack** *v* axe, discharge, dismiss, down-size, fire, give sb the boot *inf*, give sb the push *inf*, give sb the sack, give sb their marching orders *inf*, lay off, make redundant, put sb on the scrap heap *inf*, terminate sb's contract

**sacred** *adj* blessed, consecrated, devotional, divine, godly, hallowed, heavenly, holy, inviolate, religious, revered, sacrosanct, sanctified, spiritual

**sacrifice** *n* **1** loss, relinquishment, renunciation, surrender. **2** offering

**sacrifice** *v* forfeit, forego, give up, lose, offer, relinquish, renounce, surrender

**sacrilege** *n* blasphemy, desecration, disrespect, godlessness, heresy, irreverence, profanity, violation

**sacrosanct** *adj* inviolable, non negotiable, protected, sacred, untouchable

**sad** *adj* **1** (unhappy) broken-hearted, crestfallen, dejected, depressed, desolate, despondent, disappointed, distressed, down in the dumps *inf*, down *inf*, grief-stricken, heartbroken, low, miserable, tearful, unhappy, upset; *opp* cheerful, happy. **2** (a sad story) depressing, distressing, heartbreaking, heartrending, moving, poignant, touching, tragic, upsetting; *opp* cheerful, heart-warming. **3** (unsatisfactory) bad, deplorable, disastrous, disgraceful, miserable, pitiful, regrettable, sorry, unfortunate, unsatisfactory, wretched; *opp* excellent

**sadden** *v* break sb's heart, depress, disappoint, dishearten, dismay, distress, make unhappy, upset; *opp* cheer

**sadistic** *adj* barbarous, brutal, cruel, heartless, inhuman, perverted, savage

**sadness** *n* dejection, depression, despondency, disappointment, grief, heartache, misery, regret, sorrow, unhappiness; *opp* happiness

**safe** *adj* **1** (unharmed) all right, in one piece, intact, out of danger, safe and sound, unharmed, unhurt, uninjured. **2** (of a place) impregnable, protected, secure; *opp* dangerous. **3** (harmless) fit for human consumption, good, harmless, healthy, non-toxic, pure, tried and tested, uncontaminated, wholesome; *opp* dangerous, harmful. **4** (reliable) careful, cautious, conservative, dependable, prudent, reliable,

**safe** n night safe, repository, safety-deposit box, strongbox, strongroom, vault

**safeguard** n defence, guarantee, insurance, precaution, protection, security, shield, surety

**safeguard** v foster, guard, keep safe, look after, preserve, protect, secure, watch over

**safety** n dependability, protection, reliability, sanctuary, security, shelter

**sag** v bend, dip, droop, drop, fall, flop, give, hang down, sink, slump, wilt

**sail** v 1 cruise, go sailing, put to sea, set sail, steam, tack. 2 captain, navigate, pilot, skipper. 3 (sail into the room) drift, float, fly, glide, skim, soar, sweep, waltz

**sailor** n marine, mariner, matelot inf, seafarer, seaman, skipper

**saintly** adj angelic, blessed, devout, God-fearing, godly, good, holy, pious, pure, religious, righteous, virtuous

**sake** n account, advantage, benefit, good, interest, purpose, reason

**salary** n earnings, fee, income, pay packet, pay, remuneration, stipend, take-home pay, wage

**sale** n auction, deal, marketing, retailing, selling, trade, traffic, transaction

**salient** adj chief, conspicuous, important, main, noticeable, obvious, principal, prominent, striking; opp irrelevant, minor

**sallow** adj pale, pallid, pasty, sickly, unhealthy-looking, wan, yellowish; opp rosy, ruddy

**salt** adj brackish, saline, salted, salty

**salute** n acknowledgement, greeting,

homage, recognition, salutation, tribute

**salute** v acknowledge, greet, honour, pay tribute to, praise, take your hat off to inf

**salvage** v reclaim, recover, redeem, rescue, restore, resurrect, retrieve, save

**salvation** n reclamation, recovery, redemption, rescue, saving

**same** adj 1 alike, corresponding, duplicate, equal, equivalent, identical, interchangeable, like, matching, parallel, similar, twin; opp different. 2 changeless, consistent, constant, unchanging, uniform, unvarying

**sample** n example, foretaste, specimen, swatch, taster, trailer, trial pack

**sample** v taste, trial, try out, try

**sanctify** v 1 anoint, bless, canonize, consecrate, dedicate, make holy, purify. 2 approve, authorize, legitimize, license, permit, sanction, support; opp forbid

**sanctimonious** adj canting, goody-goody inf, holier-than-thou, pious, self-righteous, smug, superior

**sanction** n 1 agreement, approval, authority, authorization, backing, consent, endorsement, the go-ahead, permission, seal of approval, support, the green light inf, the thumbs up inf. 2 penalty, punishment, sentence. 3 ban, boycott, embargo, penalty, restriction

**sanction** v allow, approve, authorize, back, endorse, give sth the thumbs up inf, give the go-ahead to, give the green light inf, okay inf, permit, support; opp forbid, prevent

**sanctity** n devotion, godliness, holiness, righteousness, sacredness, saintliness, spirituality, virtue

**sanctuary** n 1 asylum, cover, haven,

protection, refuge, safety, shelter.
2 animal sanctuary, conservation
area, nature reserve, protected area,
reservation, reserve. 3 altar, chapel,
church, holy place, sanctum, temple

**sane** adj all there inf, balanced, in
possession of all your faculties, in your
right mind, lucid, of sound mind,
rational, reasonable, right-minded,
stable; opp insane, mad

**sanitary** adj clean, germ-free, healthy,
hygienic, pure, salubrious, sterile,
uncontaminated; opp dirty, unhealthy,
unhygienic

**sanity** n common sense, good sense,
level-headedness, normality, rationality,
reason

**sap** n life force, life-blood, vigour, vitality

**sarcasm** n derision, irony, mockery, satire,
scoffing, scorn

**sarcastic** adj caustic, derisive, ironic,
mocking, sarky inf, sardonic, satirical,
scoffing, scornful

**satire** n burlesque, caricature, irony,
mockery, parody, ridicule, sarcasm, send-
up inf, skit, spoof inf, take-off inf

**satirical** adj caustic, ironical, irreverent,
mocking, sarcastic, sardonic

**satirize** v caricature, make fun of, mock,
parody, poke fun at, send up inf, take off
inf, take the mickey out of

**satisfaction** n 1 comfort, contentment,
enjoyment, fulfilment, gratification,
pleasure, pride; opp dissatisfaction.
2 compensation, justice, redress,
reparation, vindication

**satisfactory** adj acceptable, adequate, all
right, average, fair, good enough, not
bad, okay, passable, quite good,

reasonable, sufficient, suitable, up to
scratch inf; opp poor, unacceptable,
unsatisfactory

**satisfy** v 1 (satisfy a need or requirement)
answer, comply with, fulfil, meet,
resolve, supply. 2 (satisfy sb's hunger or
thirst) assuage, gratify, quench, satiate,
suffice. 3 (convince sb) convince, make
happy, persuade, placate, put sb's mind
at rest, reassure

**saturate** v douse, drench, permeate, soak,
steep, suffuse, wet

**sauce** n 1 dressing, coulis, condiment,
gravy. 2 cheek, gall, impertinence,
impudence, nerve, sauciness

**savage** adj 1 (wild) fierce, primitive,
uncivilized, untamed, wild; opp tame.
2 (vicious) barbaric, brutal, cruel,
ferocious, ruthless, vicious, violent

**save** v 1 (keep) collect, conserve, hoard,
hold on to, invest, keep, put aside, put
away, put back, reserve, stash away,
stockpile, store. 2 (economize) cut costs,
cut expenditure, draw in your horns inf,
economize, find savings, make cuts,
make economies. 3 (rescue) bail out,
conserve, defend, deliver, free, preserve,
protect, rescue, safeguard, salvage,
screen, shield. 4 (save you from having
to do sth) make unnecessary, prevent,
spare, stop

**savings** n capital, funds, investments,
nest egg, piggy bank inf, reserves

**saviour** n champion, fairy godmother,
friend in need, Good Samaritan,
guardian angel, knight in shining
armour, rescuer

**savour** v appreciate, enjoy, luxuriate in,
relish, revel in, wallow in

**savoury** adj 1 piquant, salty, spicy, tangy.
2 appetizing, delicious, mouthwatering,
scrumptious inf, tasty

**say** n 1 (have your say) chance to speak,
opinion, right to speak, two
pennyworth. 2 (have no say) authority,
influence, input, part, sway, voice, vote

**say** v 1 (refuse to say the word) enunciate,
mention, mouth, pronounce, utter,
voice. 2 (say that sth is true) affirm,
allege, announce, assert, claim, come out
with inf, declare, maintain, put about inf,
report, state, suggest. 3 (say how you
feel) articulate, communicate, convey,
enunciate, express, intimate, make
known, put into words, tell. 4 answer,
comment, declare, exclaim, remark,
reply, respond, retort. 5 (say a prayer)
deliver, read, read out, recite, repeat

**saying** n 1 adage, axiom, dictum, maxim,
motto, old saw, precept, proverb.
2 catchphrase, cliché, expression,
formula, slogan

**scale** n 1 calibration, gradation,
graduation, measuring system, steps.
2 hierarchy, ladder, order, pecking order
inf, ranking, spectrum, spread. 3 (on a
large/small/grand scale) degree, extent,
range, scope, way. 4 (in music) octave,
sequence, series. 5 (rough skin)
dandruff, flake, plate, scurf. 6 (in a
kettle) coating, crust, deposit,
encrustation, fur, plaque, tartar

**scale** v ascend, clamber up, climb, climb
up, go up, mount, scramble up

**scamper** v dart, dash, frisk, frolic,
gambol, romp, run, scoot, scuttle

**scan** v 1 check, examine, gaze at,
investigate, look at, pore over, scrutinize,
search, stare at, study, survey, sweep.
2 (look at writing) flick through, flip
through, have a look at, leaf through,
glance over, look over, read, read
through, run your eye over, skim, skim
through

**scandal** n 1 crime, impropriety,
misconduct, offence, sin, transgression.
2 (a political scandal) outrage,
sensation. 3 (cause a scandal) disgrace,
dishonour, disrepute, embarrassment,
ignominy, infamy, notoriety, reproach,
shame. 4 (gossip) backbiting,
defamation, dirt, gossip, muck-raking,
rumour, slander, slur, talk, tittle-tattle

**scandalize** v affront, appal, cause raised
eyebrows, disgust, horrify, offend,
outrage, shock, upset

**scandalous** adj 1 disgraceful, disgusting,
odious, immoral, indecent, outrageous,
shameful, shocking, sordid.
2 defamatory, libellous, scurrilous,
slanderous

**scanty** adj inadequate, insufficient,
limited, meagre, measly, paltry, poor,
restricted, scant, skimpy

**scar** n 1 blemish, brand, discolouration,
disfigurement, mark. 2 (emotional scar)
damage, injury, trauma

**scar** v 1 blemish, brand, discolour, deface,
disfigure, mark. 2 (mentally) affect,
damage, injure, leave its mark, leave
scars, traumatize, upset

**scarce** adj at a premium, few and far
between, hard to come by inf, hard to
find inf, inadequate, infrequent, in short
supply, insufficient, lacking, rare, scanty,
seldom seen, short, sparse, thin on the
ground, uncommon, unusual, wanting

**scarcely** *adv* barely, hardly, only just

**scare** *n* alarm, alert, fright, horror, shock, terror

**scare** *v* alarm, daunt, frighten, give sb a fright, intimidate, make sb afraid, make sb jump *inf*, panic, petrify, put the fear of God into sb *inf*, put the wind up sb, startle, terrify, terrorize, unnerve

**scared** *adj* alarmed, fearful, frightened, nervous, panicky, panic-stricken, petrified, shaken, startled, terrified

**scary** *adj* alarming, frightening, hair-raising, horrifying, petrifying, terrifying

**scathing** *adj* biting, caustic, critical, cutting, harsh, sarcastic, scornful, severe, stinging, trenchant, withering

**scatter** *v* **1** (scatter things) diffuse, disseminate, fling, litter, shower, sow, spread, sprinkle, strew, toss about. **2** (people scatter) break up, disband, disperse, go off in all directions, separate

**scene** *n* **1** area, locality, location, place, position, setting, site, spot. **2** landscape, panorama, prospect, scenery, view, vista. **3** backdrop, background, location, set, setting. **4** (make a scene) carry-on *inf*, commotion, kerfuffle *inf*, disturbance, furore, fuss, row, tantrum, to do, upset. **5** picture, sight, spectacle. **6** (not my scene) area of interest, field, interest, milieu, sphere, world. **7** (of a play or film) act, clip, episode, part, section, sequence

**scenery** *n* **1** landscape, panorama, surroundings, terrain, view, vista. **2** backdrop, set, stage set, setting

**scenic** *adj* beautiful, breathtaking, lovely, picturesque, pretty, spectacular

**scent** *n* **1** aroma, bouquet, fragrance, odour, perfume, smell. **2** (an animal's scent) spoor, track, trail. **3** (perfume) cologne, fragrance, perfume, toilet water

**scent** *v* **1** be on the trail of, follow the scent of, nose out, smell, sniff, sniff out. **2** become aware of, detect, discern, get wind of, recognize, sense, sniff out

**sceptic** *n* agnostic, cynic, doubter, doubting Thomas, unbeliever

**sceptical** *adj* cynical, disbelieving, distrustful, doubting, dubious, hesitant, incredulous, mistrustful, suspicious, uncertain, unconvinced, unsure

**schedule** *n* **1** agenda, calendar, diary, itinerary, plan, programme, timetable. **2** catalogue, inventory, list, register

**schedule** *v* arrange, arrange a time, book, fix a time, organize, plan, programme, slot in, time, timetable

**scheme** *n* **1** course of action, plan, procedure, programme, project, strategy, system, tactics. **2** blueprint, design, draft, layout, outline, plan, project, proposal. **3** arrangement, organization, system. **4** conspiracy, game *inf*, intrigue, machinations, plot, ploy, racket *inf*, ruse, stratagem

**scheme** *v* collude, conspire, intrigue, manoeuvre, plan, plot

**scheming** *adj* artful, calculating, conniving, cunning, Machiavellian, sly, underhand, wily

**scholar** *n* **1** academic, egghead *inf*, intellectual, learned person, man of letters, pundit, woman of letters. **2** pupil, schoolboy, schoolgirl, student

**scholarly** *adj* **1** (of a person) academic, bookish, erudite, intellectual, learned, lettered, studious, well-read. **2** (of a piece of work) academic, rigorous, scientific, well-documented, well-argued, well-researched

**scholarship** n 1 academic achievement, education, erudition, knowledge, learning, letters. 2 bursary, endowment, exhibition, fellowship, grant

**school** n 1 academy, college, educational establishment, educational institution, seminary. 2 adherents, circle, devotees, disciples, followers, group, movement, pupils, set. 3 (school of thought) belief, creed, faith, outlook, persuasion, opinion, point of view, school of thought, way of thinking

**schooling** n 1 education, formal education, instruction, learning, teaching, tuition. 2 coaching, drill, grounding, instruction, preparation, training

**science** n 1 branch of knowledge, discipline, organized knowledge, systematic study. 2 art, skill, technique

**scientific** adj analytical, controlled, methodical, rational, regulated, rigorous, systematic

**scintillating** adj bright, brilliant, dazzling, flashing, flickering, lively, sparkling, stimulating, vivacious

**scoff** v 1 be sarcastic, be scornful, gibe, jeer, sneer. 2 (eat) bolt, devour, finish off, guzzle, polish off inf. 3 scoff at belittle, deride, despise, disparage, flout, laugh at, mock, poke fun at, pooh-pooh inf, ridicule, scorn

**scold** v bawl out inf, berate, blame, castigate, chide, give sb a rocket inf, give sb a talking-to, give sb a ticking-off, haul over the coals, lecture, nag, rap over the knuckles, read the riot act to, rebuke, reprimand, reproach, reprove, tear sb off a strip inf, tell off, tick off

**scoop** v bail, dig, excavate, gouge, hollow, ladle, scrape, shovel, spoon

**scoop** n 1 dipper, ladle, spoon. 2 (in a newspaper) exclusive, exposé, inside story, revelation

**scope** n 1 area, compass, competence, extent, field, limit, range, reach, span, sphere, terms of reference. 2 capacity, chance, elbow-room, freedom, latitude, leeway, liberty, opportunity, room, room to manoeuvre

**scorch** v blacken, blister, burn, char, dry up, parch, sear, singe, shrivel

**scorching** adj baking, boiling, fiery, flaming, red-hot, roasting, searing, sizzling, sweltering, very hot;
*opp* freezing

**score** n 1 count, marks, points, result, sum, tally, total. 2 (on a surface) gash, gouge, groove, mark, scratch. 3 (a score to settle) a bone to pick, grievance, grudge. 4 know the score be aware of the situation, know the facts, know what's what

**score** v 1 achieve, chalk up, gain, gain a point, get a goal, notch up, win. 2 add up, count, keep count, keep a record, keep score, record. 3 (score the surface of sth) gash, gouge, mark, scrape, scratch. 4 score out cancel, cross out, delete, put a line through, scratch out, strike out

**scorn** n contempt, derision, disdain, disparagement, mockery, sarcasm

**scorn** v 1 be above, deride, disdain, disparage, flout, look down on, mock, scoff at, slight, treat with contempt; *opp* admire. 2 (scorn sb) rebuff, refuse, reject, spurn, turn down, turn your nose up at *inf*; *opp* accept

**scornful** *adj* contemptuous, derisive, disdainful, haughty, insolent, mocking, sarcastic, slighting, sneering, snide *inf*, supercilious, superior; *opp* respectful

**scoundrel** *n* good-for-nothing, heel *slang*, miscreant, rascal, reprobate, rogue, ruffian, villain

**scour** *v* 1 abrade, clean, rub, scrub, wash. 2 (search) comb, go over, hunt through, ransack, rummage through, search, turn upside down *inf*

**scourge** *n* affliction, bane, burden, curse, evil, infliction, misery, misfortune, plague, punishment, terror, torment, visitation

**scout** *n* advance guard, escort, lookout, outrider, spy, vanguard

**scowl** *v* frown, glare, glower, grimace, look daggers *inf*, lower

**scramble** *v* 1 clamber, climb, crawl, scurry, struggle. 2 compete, contend, jockey, jostle, push, rush, strive, struggle, vie

**scrap** *n* 1 bit, fragment, grain, offcut, part, particle, piece, remnant, snippet, trace. 2 (of food) bit, bite, crumb, grain, morsel, mouthful, scraping. 3 (scrap merchant) junk, offcuts, rejects, rubbish, waste. 4 (fight) argument, barney *inf*, brawl, clash, dust-up *inf*, fight, quarrel, row, scuffle, set-to, squabble, tiff

**scrap** *v* 1 chuck *inf*, demolish, discard, drop, get rid of, jettison, shed, throw away, throw on the scrap heap, write off. 2 (fight) argue, bicker, fall out *inf*,

fight, quarrel, scuffle, squabble

**scrape** *n* 1 abrasion, graze, laceration, scratch, wound. 2 grating, grinding, rasping, scratch, scratching, squeak. 3 mark, scuff, scratch. 4 (awkward situation) escapade, mischief, prank, trouble. 5 difficulty, fix *inf*, mess, plight, predicament, tight corner, tight spot, trouble

**scrape** *v* 1 abrade, bark, graze, lacerate, rub, scratch, scuff, skin. 2 grate, grind, rasp, scratch, squeak. 3 clean, erase, file, remove, rub, scour, scrub

**scrappy** *adj* bitty, careless, disjointed, fragmentary, hurriedly done, incomplete, sketchy, slipshod, thrown together, unfinished

**scratch** *v* 1 abrade, bark, claw, cut, graze, mark, score, scrape, wound. 2 delete, eliminate, pull out, withdraw

**scratch** *n* 1 abrasion, cut, graze, wound. 2 line, mark, scrape. 3 up to scratch acceptable, adequate, competent, good enough, okay *inf*, satisfactory, up to standard

**scream** *v* bawl, cry, howl, screech, shriek, squall, squeal, wail, yell, yowl

**scream** *n* 1 cry, howl, screech, shriek, squeal, wail, yell, yowl. 2 (a real scream) barrel of laughs *inf*, hoot *inf*, laugh, riot

**screen** *n* 1 awning, blind, canopy, curtain, net curtain, shade. 2 guard, protection, shelter, shield. 3 camouflage, cloak, cover, disguise, façade, front, shield, veil. 4 divider, partition

**screen** *v* 1 guard, protect, shade, shelter, shield. 2 camouflage, conceal, disguise, hide, mask, veil. 3 (of people) check, examine, investigate, test, vet

**screw** v rotate, tighten, turn, twist, work

**scribble** v dash off, doodle, jot down, scrawl

**script** n 1 (of a play or film) book, libretto, lines, screenplay, text, words. 2 hand, handwriting, writing

**scripture** n Bible, good book, gospel, holy writ, sacred writings, word of God

**scrounge** v beg, cadge, sponge

**scrounger** n beggar, cadger, freeloader, parasite, sponger

**scrub** v 1 clean, rub, scour, wash. 2 abandon, call off, cancel, do away with, drop, give up

**scruffy** adj 1 (of a person) dishevelled, ragged, shabby, slovenly, tattered, unkempt, untidy. 2 (of a place) disreputable, run-down, shabby, squalid, untidy

**scruples** n compunction, conscience, doubt, hesitation, misgiving, qualm, second thought, twinge of conscience

**scrupulous** adj 1 ethical, fair, honest, honourable, moral, principled, proper, upright. 2 careful, conscientious, diligent, fastidious, finicky, meticulous, painstaking, precise, punctilious, rigorous, strict, thorough

**scrutinize** v check, examine, explore, inspect, investigate, look at closely, peruse, scan, search, study

**scrutiny** n check, checking, examination, exploration, inspection, investigation, perusal, search, study

**scum** n 1 dross, film, froth, grime. 2 dregs of society, rabble, riffraff

**scurrilous** adj 1 abusive, defamatory, insulting, libellous, slanderous. 2 coarse, foul, gross, indecent, low, obscene, offensive, vile, vulgar

**sea** n 1 main, ocean, the briny, the deep, the waves. 2 (a sea of people) expanse, host, mass, multitude, plethora, profusion, sheet. 3 **at sea** at a loss, baffled, bewildered, confused, lost, mystified, perplexed

**seal** v 1 close up, cork, fasten, make airtight, make watertight, plug, secure, stick down, stop, stopper, stop up. 2 (decide sth) clinch, decide, finalize, secure, settle. 3 **seal off** close off, cordon off, isolate, quarantine, segregate

**seal** n 1 badge, crest, emblem, insignia, mark, sign, symbol. 2 (seal of approval) assurance, authentication, confirmation, guarantee, ratification, warrant, warranty

**seam** n 1 join, stitching. 2 layer, lode, stratum, thickness, vein

**search** n 1 check, examination, inspection, look, probe, scrutiny. 2 enquiry, hunt, investigation, pursuit, quest. 3 **in search of** hunting for, in pursuit of, looking for, on the lookout for, on the track of, seeking

**search** v 1 comb, examine, explore, go over, go over with a fine-tooth comb, go through, hunt through, investigate, poke about, pry, ransack, rummage through, sift through, turn inside out, turn upside down. 2 (search sb) check, examine, frisk, inspect, scrutinize. 3 **search for** ferret about for, hunt for, look for, seek, try to find

**searching** adj 1 (a searching look) discerning, intense, intent, keen, penetrating, piercing, sharp. 2 (searching questions) analytic, close, penetrating, probing, thorough

**season** *n* period, phase, spell, term, time, time of year

**season** *v* 1 add flavouring to, add seasoning to, flavour, salt, spice. 2 add spice to, add zest to, colour, enliven, leaven, liven up, pep up

**seasonable** *adj* appropriate, opportune, suitable, timely, well-timed

**seasoning** *n* condiment, dressing, flavouring, herbs, herbs and spices, pepper, salt, salt and pepper, spice

**seat** *n* 1 bench, chair, pew, settle, stool. 2 (place where sth is based) capital, centre, headquarters, heart, hub, location, place, site, situation. 3 (country seat) ancestral home, mansion, family residence, stately home

**seat** *v* 1 place, put, settle. 2 (the room seats 50) accommodate, have room for, have seating for, hold, take

**seating** *n* accommodation, chairs, places, room, seats

**secluded** *adj* 1 concealed, cut off, hidden, inaccessible, isolated, lonely, off the beaten track, out of the way, remote, solitary, tucked away. 2 cloistered, private, sequestered, sheltered, shut away

**second** *adj* 1 (in time, sequence) added, additional, duplicate, extra, following, further, later, next, other, repeated, subsequent, succeeding. 2 (in importance) assistant, deputy, inferior, junior, lesser, lower, secondary, second-best, second-class, subordinate, supporting, vice-

**second** *n* 1 flash, instant, jiffy *inf*, minute *inf*, moment, split second, tick *inf*, trice,

twinkling of an eye, wink of an eye. 2 assistant, backer, helper, right-hand man, supporter

**second** *v* 1 approve, back, endorse, side with, support, take sb's side. 2 assign, move, post, relocate, send sb on placement, transfer

**secondary** *adj* 1 inferior, less important, lesser, minor, subordinate, subsidiary. 2 (not happening or experienced directly) auxiliary, by-, at one remove, derivative, derived, indirect, second-hand; *opp* primary. 2 (of schools) comprehensive, grammar, high, senior; *opp* primary

**secret** *adj* clandestine, concealed, confidential, covert, esoteric, hidden, mysterious, private, undercover, undisclosed, unknown

**secret** *n* coded message, confidence, mystery, skeleton in the closet, skeleton in the cupboard

**secretary** *n* administrative assistant, clerk, gofer *inf*, office junior, PA, personal assistant, typist

**secrete** *v* 1 discharge, exude, generate, produce. 2 conceal, hide, hoard, palm, put away, salt away *inf*, sequester, spirit away, tuck away

**secretive** *adj* enigmatic, furtive, mysterious, reticent, sly, sneaky *inf*, surreptitious, suspicious, uncommunicative; *opp* open

**sect** *n* 1 cult, denomination, faith, religion. 2 camp, caucus, clique, faction, grouping, party, splinter group, tendency

**sectarian** *n* bigot, extremist, partisan, racist, segregationist, zealot

**section** *n* 1 area, division, part, portion,

region, segment, sector, unit. 2 (of an organization) branch, department, division, group, subdivision, unit. 3 (of text) paragraph, part, passage, stretch, subsection

**sector** n 1 area, district, division, section, territory, ward, zone. 2 (sector of industry) area, branch, division, part, section, subdivision, type

**secular** adj 1 civil, humanist, lay, non-religious, profane, temporal, worldly; **opp** religious

**secure** adj 1 (of objects, goods) fastened, locked, locked up, secured, tight, unbreakable. 2 (in a particular position) fast, firm, fixed, held in place, stable, supported; **opp** insecure. 3 (of a person, place) impregnable, invulnerable, protected, safe, unassailable, untouchable; **opp** insecure

**secure** v 1 (secure an object) anchor, batten down, bind, bolt, fasten, fix, fortify, lock, make safe, padlock, reinforce, tie, tighten. 2 (keep a place secure) defend, guard, protect, safeguard. 3 (get sth) achieve, acquire, ensure, gain, get, get hold of, make certain, obtain, procure

**security** n asylum, defence, protection, refuge, safety, shelter

**sedate** adj calm, composed, decorous, deliberate, dignified, majestic, slow, solemn, staid, stately, unhurried; **opp** frantic

**sedative** adj anodyne, calming, hypnotic, narcotic, relaxing, sleep-inducing, soothing, tranquilizing

**sedentary** adj desk-bound, inactive, seated, sitting, stationary; **opp** active

**sediment** n alluvium, deposit, dregs, grounds, lees, residue, silt

**seduce** v 1 (attract sb) attract, charm, entice, flirt with, flutter her eyelashes at inf, tempt. 2 (sexually) bed, corrupt, debauch, deflower, get sb into bed, have your evil way with inf, lead sb astray

**seductive** adj alluring, appealing, attractive, bedroom, charming, come-hither, enticing, erotic, flirtatious, ravishing, sexy, tempting

**see** v 1 behold, catch sight of, descry, discern, distinguish, espy, glimpse, have before your eyes, look, make out, note, notice, observe, perceive, sight, spot, spy, view, watch, witness. 2 (have an image, idea in your mind) conceive, foresee, imagine, picture, visualize. 3 (understand) appreciate, apprehend, comprehend, fathom, follow, grasp, perceive, realize, understand. 4 (see many things during your life) bear witness to, encounter, experience, go through, meet, meet with. 5 (have a meeting with sb) consult, go out with, go to, have a date with, have an appointment with, interview, meet, rendezvous with, spend time with, visit. 6 (see sb somewhere) accompany, come with, conduct, drive, escort, go with, run inf, take. 7 **see about** consider, inquire, investigate, look into, think about. 8 **see through** (see through sb) be wise to, have no illusions about, not be deceived by, not be taken in by, penetrate, unmask. 9 **see through** (see sth through) complete, endure, finish, go all the way, keep at, persevere with, persist with, see out, stick out inf.

**10 see to** attend to, busy yourself with, concern yourself with, concentrate on, deal with, occupy yourself with, organize, see about, turn your attention to

**seed** n 1 ear, germ, grain, pip, stone. 2 (the seeds of sth) beginning, cause, germ, origin, root, source

**seedy** adj decaying, dilapidated, faded, disreputable, dubious, gone to seed, grubby, run-down, shabby, sleazy inf, squalid

**seek** v be after, be on the look-out for, chase after, go in search of, hunt, look for, pursue, search for, want

**seem** v appear, feel, give the impression, look, sound

**seethe** v be agitated, be angry, be furious, be in a rage, be incensed, be livid, boil, foam at the mouth, fume, rage, simmer

**segment** n chunk inf, part, portion, section, sector, share

**segregate** v divide, keep apart, isolate, quarantine, separate, sort; opp mix

**seize** v 1 grab, lay hands on, pick up, snatch, take hold of. 2 (seize a criminal) apprehend, arrest, capture, catch, nab inf, take, take away. 3 (seize goods) confiscate, sequestrate, take, take away. 4 seize up crash, freeze, get stuck, give out, grind to a halt, stick, stiffen

**seizure** n 1 (of a criminal) arrest, capture. 2 (of goods) confiscation. 3 (medical) apoplexy, attack, convulsion, fit, paroxysm, spasm, stroke, turn inf

**select** v choose, cull, draw, elect, pick, pick out, plump for, prefer, sample

**selection** n assortment, choice, collection, range, sample, set

**selective** adj 1 careful, choosy, discriminating, discerning, fastidious, finicky inf, fussy inf, particular, picky inf. 2 (a selective account of events) biased, discriminatory, edited, incomplete, misleading, unbalanced; opp balanced

**self-centred** adj egoistic, egotistical, selfish, self-absorbed, self-interested, self-obsessed, self-regarding, self-seeking, smug, vain

**self-confident** adj assured, brash, cocky inf, confident, self-assured, sure of yourself, swaggering

**self-conscious** adj discomfited, embarrassed, ill at ease, shy, uncomfortable

**self-esteem** n confidence, dignity, pride, self-confidence, self-image, self-respect

**self-evident** adj axiomatic, clear, natural, obvious, plain, self-explanatory

**selfish** adj egoistic, egotistical, greedy, mean, mercenary, miserly, self-centred, self-interested, self-seeking; opp altruistic, generous

**selfless** adj altruistic, generous, heroic, magnanimous, modest, self-effacing, self-sacrificing; opp selfish

**self-respect** n confidence, dignity, pride, self-confidence, self-esteem, self-image

**self-righteous** adj holier-than-thou, pious, pompous, pontificating, sanctimonious, sententious, vain

**sell** v 1 cash in, dispose of, export, find a buyer for, flog inf, get rid of, offload inf; opp buy. 2 (have sth to sell) advertise, deal in, dispense, have for sale, hawk inf, put on sale, offer, stock, trade in, vend

**seller** n commercial traveller, hawker, merchant, sales rep inf, sales representative, salesman, shopkeeper, vendor; **opp** buyer

**send** v 1 (send a letter, parcel) consign, despatch, export, forward, mail Am, post, put in the post, relay, send off, ship; **opp** receive. 2 (send sth into the air) drive, force, kick, propel, throw. 3 (send sb somewhere) assign, force, order, post, second, throw. 4 (send a signal, electronic message) beam, broadcast, emit, send out, transmit; **opp** receive. 5 send for ask for, call, call in, call up, order, request, summon; **opp** send away

**senile** adj confused, demented, doddering, forgetful, gaga inf, in their dotage, in their second childhood, old, soft in the head inf, rambling, raving, suffering from Alzheimer's disease

**senior** adj elder, first, high, outranking, ranking, superior, top; **opp** junior

**sensation** n 1 experience, feeling, impression, perception, sense. 2 animation, commotion, controversy, excitement, shock, stir, surprise

**sensational** adj 1 amazing, astonishing, extraordinary, gob-smacking inf, incredible, surprising, unexpected. 2 brilliant inf, excellent, exciting, fabulous inf, fantastic inf, great, magnificent, marvellous, stupendous inf, thrilling, wonderful. 3 (sensational journalism) down-market, exaggerated, lurid, melodramatic, over-the-top, sensationalist, shock-horror inf, tabloid, titillating

**sense** n 1 (physical, mental attribute) ability, faculty, feel, feeling, instinct, gift, perception, reflex, sensitivity, talent. 2 (a sense of sth about to happen)

awareness, feeling, gut feeling, hunch, instinct, intuition, perception, sensation, sixth sense. 3 (have the sense to do sth) common sense, foresight, gumption inf, intelligence, judgement, nous inf, understanding, wisdom, wit. 4 (the sense of a word) connotation, denotation, implication, import, meaning, purport

**sense** v be aware of, be conscious of, detect, experience, feel, intuit, perceive

**senseless** adj 1 asleep, comatose, out cold inf, out for the count inf, unconscious. 2 absurd, crazy, daft inf, fatuous, foolish, futile, half-witted, idiotic, illogical, inane, irrational, ludicrous, mad, meaningless, mindless, nonsensical, pointless, ridiculous, silly, stupid, useless; **opp** sensible

**sensibility** n delicacy, emotions, feelings, finer feelings, sensitivity

**sensible** adj common-sense, intelligent, judicious, logical, meaningful, practical, rational, sober, wise; **opp** foolish, stupid

**sensitive** adj 1 (feeling emotions deeply) delicate, easily hurt, emotional, feeling, highly strung, touchy. 2 (sensitive to the problems involved) alert, attuned, aware, conscious, in tune, perceptive, responsive, sympathetic; **opp** insensitive. 3 (of a measuring instrument) accurate, delicate, finely tuned, reactive, responsive

**sensual** adj 1 (of pleasure) bodily, carnal, fleshly, material, physical, sexual, tactile; **opp** intellectual. 2 (arousing pleasure) arousing, attractive, exciting, sensuous, sexy, titillating, voluptuous. 3 (seeking pleasure) debauched, decadent, hedonistic, lascivious, lustful, pleasure-seeking

**sensuous** *adj* curvaceous *inf*, curvy, sensual, sinuous, sleek, slinky, smooth, voluptuous, sexy

**sentence** *n* 1 proposition, question, statement, utterance *tech*. 2 decree, decision, edict, judgement, order, penalty, punishment, term of imprisonment, verdict

**sentence** *v* condemn, decree, imprison, judge, order, penalize, pronounce sentence, punish

**sentiment** *n* 1 attitude, feeling, judgement, opinion, view, way of thinking, wish. 2 compassion, emotion, pathos, pity, sadness, sensibility, sympathy, tenderness

**sentimental** *adj* emotional, exaggerated, gooey *inf*, gushing, pathetic, sad, sickly, sloppy, tear-jerking

**sentry** *n* guard, look-out, sentinel, soldier, watchman

**separable** *adj* detachable, divisible, removable, separate; *opp* inseparable

**separate** *adj* 1 (two separate parts) detached, disconnected, discrete, distinct, divided, independent, individual, separable, separated, unattached. 2 (a separate subject) different, in its own right, other, unconnected, unrelated

**separate** *v* 1 (separate two things) break up, cut off, divide, detach, disconnect, dissociate, divorce, isolate, part, pull apart, segregate, sever, sort, split, sunder, take apart, tear asunder. 2 (sth separates into two) break up, come apart, diverge, divide, fork, split. 3 (of a couple)

become estranged, break up, divorce, go their separate ways, lead separate lives, live apart, part, part company, split, split up

**separated** *adj* divorced, estranged, living apart

**separation** *n* break, break-up, divorce, estrangement, parting, parting of the ways, rift, split

**septic** *adj* festering, gangrenous, infected, poisoned, suppurating

**sequel** *n* aftermath, consequence, continuation, fall-out, follow-up, repercussion

**sequence** *n* continuation, list, order, procedure, progression, series, succession

**serene** *adj* calm, content, happy, peaceful, placid, quiet, untroubled

**series** *n* array, column, group, list, row, sequence, set, succession

**serious** *adj* 1 (a serious matter, decision) critical, crucial, far-reaching, grave, important, life-and-death, major, momentous, of consequence, pressing, significant, of urgent, vital, weighty; *opp* trivial. 2 (a serious illness) acute, bad, chronic, critical, dangerous, grave, grievous, life-threatening, severe; *opp* mild. 3 (not laughing) austere, dour, earnest, grave, humourless, long-faced, pensive, po-faced *inf*, poker-faced *inf*, prim and proper, severe, sober, solemn, sombre, stern, thoughtful, unsmiling. 4 (not joking) earnest, genuine, honest, in earnest, sincere, truthful. 5 (serious about doing sth) determined, earnest, firm, in earnest, resolute, resolved

**sermon** *n* 1 (in church) address, discourse, homily, preaching, speech.

2 admonishment, homily, lecture, lesson, reprimand, scolding, talking-to *inf*

**servant** *n* assistant, butler, companion, dogsbody *inf*, drudge *inf*, employee, factotum, flunkey, footman, housekeeper, lackey, maid, menial, minion, retainer, secretary, slave, valet; *opp* master, mistress

**serve** *v* 1 (serve a customer) assist, attend to, deal with, help, see to, wait on. 2 (serve food) bring, dole out *inf*, give out, ladle, serve up, spoon. 3 (be a servant to) assist, be employed by, be in sb's employ, help, work for. 4 (serve a purpose) aid, answer, help, be useful for, fulfil, satisfy

**service** *n* 1 (official, public) authority, body, brigade, bureau, department, force, institution, network, office, organization, unit, utility. 2 (offered by an organization) aid, amenity, assistance, benefit, facility, help, opportunity, product, support, system. 3 (in a shop, restaurant) assistance, attentiveness, help. 4 (in a particular job or cause) assistance, dedication, devotion, duty, employment, help, labour, record, work. 5 (in a church) ceremony, rite, ritual, sacrament. 6 (for a car) adjustment, check, examination, maintenance, MOT, overhaul, repairs

**service** *v* adjust, check, check over, examine, give sth the once-over *inf*, maintain, overhaul, repair

**serviceable** *adj* adequate, in good repair, practicable, usable, useful

**servile** *adj* cringing, grovelling, humble, ingratiating, obsequious, oily *inf*, slavish, submissive, unctuous

**session** *n* 1 period, sitting, spell, stretch, time. 2 assembly, conference, discussion, hearing, meeting, sitting

**set** *adj* 1 definite, definitive, determinate, firm, fixed, inflexible, permanent, pre-arranged, pre-ordained, prescribed, rigid, unalterable, unchanging; *opp* vague. 2 (set to do sth) about to, on the point of, prepared to, primed to, ready to, soon to. 3 (set on doing sth) bent, determined, earnest, intent, resolute, resolved, stubborn

**set** *n* 1 array, assemblage, assortment, batch, collection, combination, lot, group, series, suite. 2 (type) category, class, genus, group, kind, range, type

**set** *v* 1 apply, arrange, locate, lodge, put, place, plant, position, rest, situate, station. 2 (set a clock, machine) adjust, calibrate, prepare, regulate, start, synchronize. 3 (set a time, date) agree, appoint, arrange, decide, determine, fix, schedule, specify. 4 (set sb a task) allocate, assign, designate, give, prescribe, present. 5 (a substance sets) coagulate, congeal, crystallize, gel, harden, solidify, stiffen, thicken. 6 (of the sun, moon) descend, go down, sink; *opp* rise. 7 **set about** approach, begin, deal with, do, get on with, get to grips with, go about, organize, plan, start, tackle. 8 **set in** become established, begin, establish itself, start, take hold, take root. 9 **set off** (start a journey) depart, leave, set forth, set out, set sail, start, start off. 10 **set off** (an explosion, an argument) cause, explode, ignite, initiate, instigate, provoke, spark, spark off, trigger, trigger off. **11 set out** (set things out) arrange, display, exhibit, lay out, present. **12 set out** (set out to do sth) aim, aspire, attempt, intend, plan, set your sights on, try. **13 set up** arrange, construct, equip, establish, install, organize, prepare, put in place

**setback** *n* complication, delay, difficulty, disappointment, failure, hold-up, knock-back *inf*, obstacle, problem, tribulation, vicissitude

**setting** *n* **1** backcloth, backdrop, background, context, décor, location, milieu, scene, scenery, situation, surroundings. **2** (the settings of a machine) adjustment, attribute, calibration, option, property, timing

**settle** *v* **1** agree, arrange, conclude, decide, resolve, reconcile, sort *inf*, sort out. **2** (settle a bill, debt) clear, defray, discharge, liquidate, pay, pay off, redeem, repay, square. **3** (settle in a place) camp, colonize, ensconce yourself *inf*, establish yourself, go to live, install yourself, occupy, people, populate, put down roots, set up home. **4** (of snow) be precipitated, come to rest, lie, stick. **5 settle down** calm down, make yourself at home, make yourself comfortable, relax. **6 settle for** accept, agree to, be content with, be satisfied with

**settlement** *n* **1** agreement, compact, concordat, pact, reconciliation, resolution. **2** colony, community, encampment, habitation, hamlet, township, village

**sever** *v* break, chop, cut, cut off, disconnect, dissociate, part, pull apart, separate, snip, split

**severe** *adj* **1** bad, bitter, dangerous, drastic, extreme, fierce, great, heavy, intense, serious, violent; *opp* mild, minor. **2** (severe test) arduous, demanding, difficult, exacting, hard, rigorous, stringent, taxing, tough. **3** (of punishment) cruel, hard, harsh, oppressive, pitiless, rigid, rigorous, strict, stringent; *opp* lenient. **4** (of sb's character, appearance) austere, cold-hearted, dour, forbidding, grim, humourless, intimidating, serious, sober, solemn, stern, unsmiling; *opp* friendly

**sew** *v* crochet, embroider, darn, knit, mend, stitch

**sex** *n* **1** femininity, masculinity, gender, sexuality. **2** bonking *sl*, coitus, copulation, fornication, hanky-panky *inf*, intercourse, intimacy, it *inf*, love-making, mating, nookie *inf*, penetration, physical love, roll in the hay *inf*, sexual activity, sexual intercourse, sexuality, slap and tickle *inf*

**sexual** *adj* erotic, genital, marital, physical, reproductive, sensual, sex-related

**sexuality** *n* **1** eroticism, libido, lust, sensuality, sex, sex drive. **2** inclinations, proclivities, sexual orientation, sexual preference, tastes

**sexy** *adj* alluring, arousing, attractive, enticing, erotic, ravishing, seductive, sensual, sensuous

**shabby** *adj* **1** dilapidated, dingy, dirty, dowdy, drab, faded, frayed, gone to seed, grubby, moth-eaten, ragged, run-down, old, scruffy, seedy, tatty *inf*, threadbare, worn; *opp* neat, smart. **2** base, contemptible, deceitful, despicable, discreditable, dishonest, dishonourable, disreputable, grubby, ignoble, lowdown *inf*, mean, nasty, shameful, shoddy, sordid, squalid, treacherous, unfair, ungenerous, unkind, unscrupulous, unworthy; *opp* noble

**shade** n 1 dark, darkness, gloom, penumbra, shadow, shelter; *opp* light. 2 (of colour) degree, intensity, nuance, tinge, tint, variation

**shade** v cloud, conceal, cover, darken, dim, hide, mask, obscure, screen, shadow, shield, shroud, veil; *opp* expose

**shadow** n 1 outline, shape, silhouette. 2 (in the shadows) darkness, dimness, gloom, obscurity, shade; *opp* daylight. 3 (no shadow of a doubt) hint, suggestion, suspicion, touch, trace. 4 (cast a shadow over sb) cloud, gloom, sadness, unhappiness

**shadowy** adj 1 dark, dim, dusky, gloomy, murky, obscure, shaded; *opp* well-lit. 2 (a shadowy figure) dreamlike, faint, ghostly, nebulous, obscure, phantom, unreal, vague; *opp* distinct

**shady** adj 1 cool, leafy, shaded, sheltered; *opp* sunny. 2 (a shady character) crooked, disreputable, dodgy *inf*, dubious, fishy *inf*, shifty, slippery, suspicious, untrustworthy; *opp* trustworthy

**shaft** n 1 (a mine shaft) duct, flue, mine, passage, pit, tunnel, well. 2 (shaft of light) beam, gleam, laser, pencil, ray, streak. 3 (shaft of a golf club) handle, pole, post, rod, shank, stem, upright

**shaggy** adj bushy, dishevelled, hairy, hirsute, long-haired, tousled, unkempt, unshorn, woolly; *opp* clean-shaven

**shake** v 1 agitate, bump, convulse, jar, judder, quiver, rattle, rock, shiver, shudder, sway, totter, tremble, vibrate, waver, wobble. 2 (shake your fist) brandish, flourish, wave. 3 shake up alarm, distress, disturb, frighten, perturb, rattle, ruffle, shock, throw *inf*, unnerve, unsettle, upset; *opp* comfort, reassure

**shaky** adj 1 (take your first shaky steps) doddering, faltering, feeble, insecure, precarious, quivery, shaking, staggering, teetering, tottering, trembling, unstable, unsteady, weak, wobbly; *opp* confident. 2 decrepit, dilapidated, flimsy, precarious, ramshackle, rickety, rocky, unstable, unsteady, weak, wobbly; *opp* robust

**shallow** adj empty-headed, facile, foolish, frivolous, glib, ignorant, insincere, puerile, silly, simple, superficial, unintelligent, unthinking; *opp* thinking

**sham** n counterfeit, fake, forgery, fraud, hoax, imitation, pretence

**shambles** n chaos, confusion, disarray, disorder, disorganization, mess, muddle; *opp* order

**shame** n condemnation, discredit, disgrace, dishonour, disrepute, humiliation, ignominy, infamy, loss of face, reproach, scandal, smear, stigma, vilification; *opp* pride

**shame** v condemn, discredit, disgrace, dishonour, humiliate, lose face, reproach, smear, stigmatize, vilify

**shamefaced** adj ashamed, embarrassed, guilty, humiliated, mortified, penitent, red-faced *inf*, remorseful, repentant, shamed, sorry; *opp* proud

**shameful** adj atrocious, base,

contemptible, deplorable, despicable, disgraceful, indecent, low, mean, outrageous, reprehensible, scandalous, wicked; *opp* noble

**shameless** *adj* audacious, brash, brazen, corrupt, depraved, immodest, improper, indecent, unabashed, unashamed, undisguised, unprincipled, unselfconscious, wanton; *opp* modest

**shape** *n* 1 configuration, contours, cut, figure, form, format, formation, lines, model, mould, outline, pattern. 2 (of a person) body, build, figure, physique, profile, silhouette. 3 (in good shape) condition, fettle, health, kilter, state

**shape** *v* 1 (shape an object) carve, cast, create, cut, fashion, form, make, model, mould, produce. 2 (shape a plan) define, develop, devise, organize, plan, prepare

**shapeless** *adj* amorphous, formless, irregular, nebulous, undeveloped, unshaped, unstructured, vague; *opp* well-defined

**share** *n* allocation, allotment, allowance, assignment, cut, division, helping, part, percentage, portion, proportion, quota, ration, serving

**share** *v* allocate, allot, apportion, assign, deal out, distribute, divide, halve, quarter, split

**sharp** *adj* 1 (of a knife) jagged, pointed, serrated, spiky; *opp* blunt. 2 (a sharp bend) abrupt, acute, angular, hairpin, sudden, tight; *opp* wide. 3 (of a person) alert, astute, bright, clever, incisive, intelligent, observant, perceptive, quick, quick-witted, shrewd, smart; *opp* slow. 4 (a sharp pain) acute, cutting, intense, piercing, severe, shooting, stabbing,

stinging, violent; *opp* nagging, slight. 5 (a sharp image) clear, crisp, distinct, focused, well-defined; *opp* unclear. 6 (a sharp tongue) bitter, critical, curt, cutting, harsh, hurtful, sarcastic, sardonic, scathing, severe, venomous, vitriolic; *opp* kind. 7 (a sharp taste) acid, acrid, caustic, hot, piquant, pungent, tangy, tart; *opp* bland

**sharpen** *v* file, grind, hone; *opp* blunt

**shatter** *v* blast, break, burst, crack, crush, demolish, disintegrate, explode, fracture, smash, splinter, split, wreck

**shed** *v* 1 (shed leaves, skin) cast off, discard, drop, moult, slough; *opp* grow. 2 (shed workers) dismiss, fire *inf*, get rid of, make redundant, sack *inf*; *opp* take on

**sheen** *n* brightness, glaze, gleam, glint, gloss, lustre, polish, reflection, shimmer, shine, sparkle; *opp* dullness

**sheepish** *adj* bashful, coy, embarrassed, guilty, meek, reticent, self-conscious, shy, timid, uncomfortable; *opp* brazen

**sheer** *adj* 1 (a sheer drop) abrupt, perpendicular, precipitous, sharp, steep, vertical; *opp* gradual. 2 (sheer stupidity) complete, downright, out-and-out, plain, pure, total, unqualified, utter. 3 (sheer material) filmy, fine, flimsy, gauzy, see-through, thin, translucent, transparent; *opp* thick

**sheet** *n* 1 (a sheet of snow) blanket, coat, covering, film, layer, veneer. 2 (a sheet of glass) pane, panel, piece, plate, slab. 3 (a sheet of paper) folio, leaf, page, piece

**shell** *n* 1 case, casing, covering, husk, pod. 2 (of a ship) chassis, framework, hull, structure

**shell** v attack, barrage, blitz, bomb, bombard, strike, torpedo

**shelter** n 1 (a shelter for the homeless) haven, refuge, retreat, sanctuary. 2 (look for shelter) defence, protection, refuge, safety, sanctuary, security

**shelter** v conceal, defend, enclose, guard, harbour, hide, keep safe, protect, safeguard, shield

**sheltered** adj 1 (of a place) protected, screened, secluded, shaded, shady, shielded,; opp exposed. 2 (of sb's life) cloistered, protected, quiet, unadventurous, unexciting, withdrawn; opp full

**shelve** v defer, delay, mothball, postpone, put off, put on ice, put on the back burner, suspend; opp continue

**shield** n barrier, cover, defence, guard, protector, safeguard, screen

**shield** v cover, defend, guard, keep safe, protect, safeguard, screen; opp expose

**shift** n 1 (in your opinion) about-turn, adjustment, alteration, change, modification, reversal, sea change, switch, transfer, variation. 2 (the night shift) crew, gang, group, team, workforce

**shift** v 1 budge, displace, move, relocate, reposition; opp remain. 2 (shift your opinion) adjust, alter, change, modify, reverse, switch, transfer, vary; opp maintain

**shifty** adj crooked, disreputable, dodgy inf, dubious, fishy inf, shady, slippery, suspicious, untrustworthy; opp trustworthy

**shimmer** v flicker, gleam, glint, glisten, glow, sparkle, twinkle

**shine** n brightness, glare, gleam, glisten, glitter, glow, shimmer, sparkle, twinkle; opp dullness

**shine** v 1 beam, blaze, dazzle, flash, glare, gleam, glisten, glitter, glow, radiate, shimmer, sparkle, twinkle. 2 (shine at sth) be excellent, be exceptional, be outstanding, do well, excel, stand out

**shiny** adj bright, burnished, gleaming, glistening, glittering, glossy, lustrous, polished, shimmering, shinning, sparkling, twinkling; opp dull

**ship** n boat, craft, cruiser, destroyer, ferry, frigate, liner, steamer, tanker, trawler, vessel, yacht

**ship** v carry, convey, deliver, ferry, send, transport

**shirk** v avoid, dodge, duck, evade, get out of, play truant, shun, sidestep, skive

**shiver** v quake, quiver, shake, shudder, tremble

**shock** n 1 (come as a shock) blow, bombshell, thunderbolt, trauma, upset. 2 (a feeling of shock) astonishment, distress, fright, offence, outrage, revulsion

**shock** v astonish, astound, daze, disquiet, distress, frighten, give sb a turn inf, horrify, jar, jolt, offend, outrage, revolt, shake, sicken, stagger, startle, stun, stupefy, traumatize, unsettle

**shocking** adj appalling, astounding, atrocious, awful, disgraceful, distressing, foul, ghastly, hideous, horrific, obscene, offensive, outrageous, revolting, scandalous, sickening, terrible, upsetting

**shoddy** adj cheap, inferior, poor, rubbishy inf, second-rate, shabby, slipshod, tacky inf, trashy inf; opp quality

**shoot** v 1 (shoot sb) bag, bring down, gun down, hit, injure, kill, shell, snipe at, wound. 2 (shoot a gun) aim, discharge, fire, launch. 3 (shoot out of the room) bolt, charge, dart, dash, fly, hurtle, leap, race, rush, speed, streak, tear; *opp* saunter

**shop** n boutique, cash and carry, chain store, department store, outlet, retailer, seller, store, supermarket, wholesaler

**shore** n bank, beach, coast, sands, seashore, seaside, water's edge, waterside

**short** adj 1 (a short speech) abbreviated, abridged, brief, compact, compressed, concise, pithy, succinct, summarized, terse, truncated; *opp* long. 2 (of a person) diminutive, little, midget, petite, pint-sized *inf*, slight, small, squat; *opp* tall. 3 (a short break) brief, cursory, fleeting, momentary, passing, quick, short-lived, transitory; *opp* long. 4 (in short supply) deficient, inadequate, insufficient, lacking, low, scarce, sparse, tight, wanting; *opp* plentiful

**shortage** n dearth, deficiency, deficit, inadequacy, insufficiency, lack, scarcity, shortfall, want; *opp* excess

**shortcoming** n bad thing, defect, drawback, failing, fault, flaw, frailty, imperfection, limitation, weakness, weak point; *opp* strength

**shorten** v abbreviate, abridge, compress, condense, contract, curtail, cut, decrease, dock, lessen, précis, prune, reduce, shrink, summarize, trim, truncate; *opp* lengthen

**short-sighted** adj 1 myopic, near-sighted; *opp* long-sighted. 2 careless, ill-advised, ill-considered, imprudent, injudicious,

rash, unthinking, unwary, unwise; *opp* sensible

**short-tempered** adj crabby *inf*, fiery, hot-tempered, impatient, irascible, irritable, quick-tempered, ratty *inf*, stroppy *inf*, touchy; *opp* patient

**shot** n 1 (take a shot) fling, hurl, lob, pot shot, throw. 2 (fire a shot) ammunition, bullet, lead, missile, pellet, slug *inf*. 3 (hear a shot) blast, crack, explosion, gun fire. 4 (have a shot at sth) attempt, bash *inf*, crack *inf*, effort, endeavour, go *inf*, guess, stab *inf*, try, turn

**shout** v ball, bellow, call, cheer, clamour, cry, holler Am *inf*, rant, roar, scream, screech, shriek, yell; *opp* whisper

**shove** v barge, drive, elbow, force, nudge, press, prod, push, shoulder, thrust

**shovel** v clear, dig, excavate, ladle, scoop, shift, spoon

**show** n 1 (go to see a show) concert, drama, gig *inf*, pageant, parade, performance, play, production. 2 (a motor show) demonstration, display, exhibition, expo *inf*, exposition, fair, presentation. 3 (for show) affectation, appearance, display, façade, illusion, ostentation, pose, pretence

**show** v 1 (sth shows) appear, be in view, be seen, be visible, catch the eye, make an appearance, materialize, stand out, stick out. 2 (show sth is true) demonstrate, divulge, explain, expose, express, indicate, make known, make plain, prove, reveal, teach, uncover. 3 (show symptoms) display, exhibit, manifest, present. 4 (show sb to their seat) accompany, conduct, direct, escort, guide, lead, steer, usher. 5 **show off** be full of yourself *inf*, boast, blow your own trumpet *inf*, brag, crow, swagger around. **6 show up** embarrass, humiliate, let down, mortify, shame

**showdown** *n* clash, climax, confrontation, crisis, decider *inf*, face-off, moment of truth *inf*

**shower** *n* **1** (of rain) deluge, downpour, fall, flurry, rainstorm, sprinkling, torrent. **2** (of bullets) barrage, stream, volley

**shower** *v* deluge, heap, inundate, lavish, load, overwhelm, pour

**show-off** *n* big-head, braggart, egotist, exhibitionist, poser *inf*

**showy** *adj* conspicuous, elaborate, fancy, flamboyant, flashy, fussy, garish, gaudy, lavish, loud *inf*, lurid, ornate, ostentatious, OTT *inf*, over the top *inf*, pretentious, vulgar; *opp* modest

**shred** *n* **1** bit, fragment, piece, rag, scrap, sliver, tatter. **2** (a shred of evidence) grain, iota, jot, scintilla, scrap, speck, trace

**shred** *v* cut, grate, rip, scrap, tear

**shrewd** *adj* astute, canny, clever, crafty, cunning, intelligent, keen, knowing, observant, perceptive, quick-witted, sharp, sly, smart, wily; *opp* ignorant

**shriek** *v* cry, holler *Am inf*, howl, scream, screech, squawk, squeal, wail, whoop, yell; *opp* whisper

**shrill** *adj* acute, ear-splitting, high, jarring, penetrating, piercing, screeching, sharp, shrieking; *opp* soft

**shrink** *v* **1** contract, decrease, diminish, dwindle, lessen, reduce; *opp* grow. **2** (shrink from sth) back off, cower, draw back, flinch, recoil, retreat, shy away, wince, withdraw

**shrivel** *v* curl, dehydrate, droop, dry out, dry up, wilt, wither, wizen, wrinkle

**shroud** *n* blanket, cloak, cloud, cover, mantle, mask, screen, swathe, veil

**shroud** *v* blanket, cloak, cloud, conceal, cover, envelop, hide, mask, screen, swathe, veil, wrap

**shudder** *n* convulsion, jerk, quake, quiver, rattle, shake, shiver, spasm, tremble, tremor, vibration

**shudder** *v* convulse, jerk, quake, quiver, rattle, shake, shiver, tremble, vibrate

**shuffle** *v* **1** (shuffle somewhere) drag your feet, hobble, limp, scrape your feet, shamble, slide; *opp* stride. **2** (shuffle cards) confuse, disarrange, intermix, jumble, mix, rearrange, reorganize

**shun** *v* avoid, elude, evade, flee, give sb a wide berth *inf*, give sb the cold shoulder *inf*, rebuff, reject, spurn, turn away from; *opp* welcome

**shut** *v* **1** bolt, close, draw, fasten, lock, seal, secure, slam; *opp* open. **2 shut up** gag, hush, keep quiet, make silent, muzzle, silence

**shy** *adj* bashful, coy, diffident, hesitant, inhibited, introverted, nervous, reserved, reticent, retiring, self-conscious, self-effacing, sheepish, shrinking, timid, wary, withdrawn; *opp* self-confident

**sick** *adj* **1** (feel sick) nauseated, nauseous, queasy. **2** (ill) ailing, bed-ridden, diseased, feeble, ill, indisposed, infirm, poorly, sickly, under the weather *inf*, unwell, weak; *opp* well. **3** (sick humour) black, ghoulish, grim, macabre, morbid, perverted, sadistic, unhealthy

**sicken** *v* appal, disgust, gross out *Am inf*,

make you sick, nauseate, offend, repel, revolt, turn your stomach

**sickening** adj abhorrent, disgusting, distasteful, foul, gross, hideous, loathsome, nauseating, objectionable, offensive, repugnant, repulsive, revolting, vile

**sickly** adj ailing, delicate, feeble, frail, ill, infirm, languid, nauseating, puny, unhealthy, weak; *opp* healthy

**side** n 1 (a side of a field) border, boundary, division, edge, fringe, limit, margin, perimeter, periphery, rim, verge. 2 (a side of a cube) aspect, face, facet, flank, part, surface, view. 3 (be on opposing sides) camp, faction, group, party, sect, team, wing

**side with** v ally with, back, be on the side of, form an alliance with, join up with, partner, prefer, support, take the side of, team up with; *opp* oppose

**sidestep** v avoid, bypass, circumvent, dodge, duck *inf*, elude, evade, find a way round, skirt, steer clear of; *opp* confront

**sidetrack** v deflect, distract, divert, send off track

**sieve** v filter, screen, separate, sift, strain

**sift** v 1 filter, screen, separate, sieve, strain. 2 (sift evidence) analyze, examine, investigate, probe, screen, scrutinize, sort out, study, pore over, work over

**sigh** n breath, exhalation, murmur

**sight** n 1 (have good sight) eyes, eyesight, seeing, vision. 2 (a wonderful sight) appearance, display, scene, spectacle, view, vista

**sight** v behold, discern, distinguish, glimpse, make out, notice, observe, perceive, recognize, see, spot

**sign** n 1 clue, evidence, hint, indication, manifestation, mark, proof, suggestion, symptom, token, trace. 2 board, marker, notice, placard, signpost. 3 gesticulation, gesture, indication, motion, movement, signal. 4 cipher, code, device, emblem, hieroglyph, insignia, logo, mark, symbol

**signal** n 1 cue, gesticulation, gesture, indication, motion, movement, sign. 2 evidence, hint, indication, mark, proof, token

**signal** v beckon, gesticulate, gesture, give a signal, indicate, motion, nod, sign, wave

**signature** n autograph, mark, name

**significance** n 1 idea, import, meaning, message, point, purpose, sense, signification. 2 consequence, importance, magnitude, moment, seriousness, value, weight

**significant** adj considerable, important, meaningful, momentous, noteworthy, of consequence, of note, serious, valuable, weighty; *opp* insignificant

**signify** adj be a sign of, betoken, connote, denote, imply, indicate, mean, point to, portend, represent, stand for, suggest, symbolize

**silence** n calm, hush, lull, peace, quiet, quietness, soundlessness, stillness, tranquility; *opp* noise

**silent** adj 1 calm, hushed, noiseless, peaceful, quiet, soundless, still, tranquil; *opp* noisy. 2 dumb, mum, mute, speechless, taciturn, tight-lipped, tongue-tied, voiceless, wordless; *opp* talkative

**silhouette** *n* contour, form, outline, profile, shape

**silly** *adj* absurd, asinine, brainless, childish, crazy, daft *inf*, fatuous, foolish, frivolous, giddy, idiotic, immature, inane, infantile, meaningless, mindless, pointless, puerile, ridiculous, simple-minded, stupid; *opp* sensible

**similar** *adj* akin, alike, analogous, close, comparable, corresponding, equivalent, like, matching, parallel, related, resembling, the same, uniform; *opp* different

**similarity** *n* affinity, agreement, closeness, correspondence, equivalence, kinship, likeness, match, relation, resemblance, similitude, uniformity; *opp* difference

**simmer** *v* 1 boil, bubble, cook, poach, stew. 2 fume, rage, seethe, smart, smoulder

**simple** *adj* 1 clear, comprehensible, easy, intelligible, lucid, obvious, plain, straightforward, uncomplicated, understandable; *opp* complicated. 2 austere, basic, classic, clean, modest, natural, plain, pure, restrained, unadorned, unfussy; *opp* elaborate. 3 artless, candid, childlike, frank, guileless, gullible, ingenuous, innocent, naïve, natural, sincere, unaffected, unsophisticated; *opp* sophisticated

**simplicity** *n* 1 clarity, clearness, comprehensibility, ease, intelligibility, lucidity, obviousness, straightforwardness. 2 austerity, cleanness, modesty, naturalness, plainness, purity, restraint. 3 artlessness, candour, frankness,

gullibility, ingenuousness, innocence, naïveté, naturalness, sincerity

**simplify** *v* abridge, clarify, cut, make simpler, edit, prune, shorten, streamline

**simplistic** *adj* facile, glib, inadequate, naïve, over-simplified, shallow, superficial

**simultaneous** *adj* at the same time, coinciding, concurrent, contemporaneous, parallel, synchronized, synchronous

**sin** *n* corruption, crime, depravity, error, evil, guilt, immorality, iniquity, misdeed, misdemeanour, offence, peccadillo, transgression, trespass, vice, wickedness, wrong, wrongdoing

**sin** *v* do wrong, err, fall, go astray, lapse, offend, stray, transgress, trespass

**sincere** *adj* candid, earnest, frank, genuine, guileless, heartfelt, honest, open, real, serious, truthful, unaffected, unfeigned, wholehearted; *opp* insincere

**sincerity** *n* candour, earnestness, frankness, genuineness, good faith, honesty, openness, seriousness, truth, truthfulness; *opp* insincerity

**sinful** *adj* bad, corrupt, criminal, depraved, erring, evil, fallen, guilty, immoral, iniquitous, wicked, wrong; *opp* virtuous

**sing** *v* carol, chant, chirp, chorus, croon, hum, pipe, serenade, trill, warble, yodel

**singe** *v* blacken, burn, char, scorch, sear

**single** *adj* 1 distinct, individual, isolated, lone, one, only, separate, sole, solitary, singular, unique. 2 bachelor, celibate, free, lone, unattached, unmarried, unwed; *opp* married

**single-handed** *adj* alone, by yourself,

independent, on your own, solitary, solo, unaided, unassisted

**single-minded** adj dedicated, determined, dogged, fixed, focused, persevering, purposeful, resolute, set, steadfast, stubborn, tireless, unswerving, unwavering

**singular** adj 1 distinct, individual, isolated, lone, one, only, separate, sole, solitary, single, unique. 2 abnormal, curious, different, distinctive, exceptional, extraordinary, notable, noteworthy, odd, outstanding, peculiar, rare, remarkable, strange, striking, unique, unusual; *opp* normal, usual

**sinister** adj dark, dire, disquieting, disturbing, evil, forbidding, foreboding, frightening, malevolent, malign, malignant, menacing, nefarious, ominous, threatening, villainous

**sink** v 1 collapse, decline, descend, diminish, dip, droop, drop, ebb, fade, fall, flag, founder, lapse, lessen, lower, plummet, plunge, sag, slip, subside, weaken, worsen. 2 be engulfed, be submerged, founder, go down, go under, plummet

**sip** v drink, lap, sample, sup, taste, try

**sit** v 1 be seated, perch, rest, settle, squat, take a seat. 2 (sit an exam) be a candidate, enter, go in for, take. 3 (a court sits) assemble, be in session, convene, gather, meet

**site** n area, ground, location, place, plot, position, setting, situation, spot

**site** v install, locate, place, position, put, set, situate

**sitting-room** n front room, drawing room, living-room, lounge, parlour

**situate** v install, locate, place, position, put, set, site

**situation** n 1 background, case, circumstances, condition, position, state of affairs. 2 environment, locale, location, place, plot, position, setting, site, spot. 3 employment, job, place, position, post

**size** n 1 amount, area, capacity, dimensions, extent, gauge, measurements, proportions, range, scale, scope, volume. 2 (large size) bulk, expanse, hugeness, immensity, largeness, magnitude, mass, vastness, volume

**sizeable** adj ample, big, considerable, decent, generous, large, significant, substantial, worthwhile; *opp* small

**sketch** n depiction, doodle, draft, drawing, outline, plan, representation

**sketch** v delineate, depict, doodle, draft, draw, indicate, outline, plot, portray, represent, rough out

**sketchy** adj bitty *inf*, cursory, patchy, provisional, imprecise, inadequate, incomplete, inexact, perfunctory, rough, scrappy, skimpy, superficial, undeveloped, vague; *opp* detailed

**skilful** adj able, accomplished, adept, adroit, clever, competent, consummate, deft, dexterous, efficient, expert, handy, masterful, masterly, nimble, practised, proficient, quick, skilled, trained

**skill** n ability, accomplishment, adeptness, adroitness, aptitude, artistry, cleverness, competence, craft, deftness, dexterity, efficiency, expertise, facility, finesse, flair, gift, knack, mastery, proficiency, prowess, quickness, talent, technique, workmanship

**skilled** *adj* able, accomplished, adept, adroit, clever, competent, consummate, deft, dexterous, efficient, experienced, expert, handy, masterful, masterly, nimble, practised, proficient, qualified, quick, skilful, trained; *opp* unskilled

**skim** *v* 1 coast, fly, glide, graze, plane, sail, skate, slide, soar. 2 flick through, flip through, glance at, leaf through, scan, skip

**skimp** *v* be economical with, be mean with, be sparing with, cut corners, economize, pinch, scrimp, save, stint

**skin** *n* 1 epidermis, fleece, fur, hide, pelt. 2 casing, coat, coating, covering, crust, exterior, film, husk, membrane, outside, peel, rind, shell, surface

**skin** *v* flay, pare, peel, shell, strip

**skip** *v* 1 bob, bound, caper, cavort, dance, frisk, gambol, hop, jump, leap, prance, romp, spring, trip. 2 avoid, bypass, forget, ignore, leave out, miss, miss out, omit, overlook, pass over, skim through

**skirmish** *n* affray, battle, brush, clash, combat, conflict, confrontation, contest, engagement, fight, fracas, fray, incident, mêlée, set-to, spat, tussle

**skirmish** *v* battle, clash, confront, contend, fight, tussle

**skirt** *v* avoid, border, bypass, circle, circumvent, dodge, evade, go round, pass round, sidestep, steer clear of

**sky** *n* air, atmosphere, blue, firmament, heavens, space, stratosphere

**slab** *n* block, chunk, hunk, lump, piece, slice, wedge, wodge *inf*

**slack** *adj* 1 baggy, drooping, droopy, limp, loose, sagging, saggy, soft, relaxed; *opp* tight. 2 careless, disorganized,

idle, inattentive, indolent, lax, lazy, neglectful, negligent, remiss, slapdash, slipshod, sloppy, undisciplined. 3 (business is slack) inactive, quiet, slow, sluggish; *opp* busy

**slack** *n* excess, leeway, play, room

**slacken** *v* 1 (a rope) droop, loosen, sag, soften, relax. 2 (pressure) abate, decrease, diminish, drop, ease off, lessen, loosen, moderate, reduce, relax, release

**slam** *v* 1 bang, crash, dash, fling, hurl, smash, throw, thump. 2 attack, blast *inf*, criticize, lambast, pillory, slate *inf*, vilify

**slander** *n* calumny, defamation, libel, misrepresentation, muck-raking, slur, smear

**slander** *v* blacken the name of, calumniate, defame, disparage, libel, malign, misrepresent, muck-rake, slur, smear, traduce, vilify

**slanderous** *adj* calumnious, damaging, defamatory, disparaging, false, libellous, malicious, scurrilous, untrue, vicious

**slant** *n* 1 angle, camber, diagonal, gradient, incline, list, pitch, rake, ramp, slope, tilt. 2 angle, approach, attitude, perspective, point of view, standpoint, take, view, viewpoint. 3 bias, distortion, emphasis, leaning, prejudice, twist, weight

**slant** *v* 1 be at an angle, be skewed, incline, lean, list, slope, tilt. 2 angle, bias, colour, distort, prejudice, skew, twist, weight

**slanting** *adj* angled, aslant, at an angle, diagonal, inclined, leaning, listing, oblique, shelving, skewed, sloping, tilted, tilting; *opp* straight

**slap** *v* clout, cuff, hit, smack,

spank, strike, whack

**slapdash** *adj* careless, clumsy, disorganized, hasty, hurried, inattentive, lax, messy, neglectful, negligent, remiss, slack, slipshod, sloppy, slovenly, undisciplined, untidy; *opp* careful

**slash** *n* cut, gash, hack, incision, laceration, rent, rip, slit

**slash** *v* 1 cut, gash, hack, knife, lacerate, rend, rip, score, slit. 2 (slash prices) cut, decrease, drop, lower, mark down, reduce

**slaughter** *n* bloodshed, butchery, carnage, extermination, killing, massacre, murder, slaying

**slaughter** *v* butcher, exterminate, kill, massacre, murder, slay

**slave** *n* drudge, serf, servant, skivvy, vassal

**slave** *v* drudge, labour, slog, sweat, toil, work your fingers to the bone

**slavery** *n* bondage, captivity, enslavement, serfdom, servitude, subjugation, thralldom

**slavish** *adj* 1 abject, cringing, deferential, fawning, grovelling, gushing, obsequious, servile, submissive, subservient, sycophantic. 2 (slavish imitation) close, strict, sycophantic, uncritical, unimaginative, unoriginal, unthinking

**slay** *v* assassinate, bump off *inf*, butcher, do away with *inf*, exterminate, get rid of *inf*, kill, massacre, murder, put to death, slaughter

**sleazy** *adj* cheap, disreputable, dirty, low, seedy, sordid, squalid, unwholesome

**sleek** *adj* gleaming, glossy, lustrous, satiny, shiny, silky, smooth, well-groomed

**sleep** *n* catnap, doze, forty winks *inf*, kip *inf*, nap, repose, rest, siesta, slumber, snooze

**sleep** *v* be asleep, catnap, doze, drop off *inf*, drowse, fall asleep, kip *inf*, nap, nod off *inf*, rest, slumber, snooze, snore, zizz *inf*

**sleepless** *adj* awake, conscious, insomniac, restless, wakeful, wide awake

**sleepy** *adj* dopey, drowsy, dull, heavy, lethargic, sluggish, somnolent, tired, torpid, weary

**slender** *adj* 1 fine, graceful, lean, narrow, slight, slim, svelte, sylph-like, willowy; *opp* fat. 2 (slender means) inadequate, insubstantial, insufficient, little, meagre, paltry, scanty, slight, small. 3 (a slender hope) faint, feeble, flimsy, fragile, frail, slight, slim, tenuous, thin, weak; *opp* strong

**slice** *n* layer, piece, portion, segment, share, shaving, sliver, wedge

**slice** *v* carve, cut, divide, segment

**slick** *adj* 1 glib, oily, plausible, polished, smarmy, smooth, specious, suave, unctuous. 2 (doing sth well) adroit, deft, dexterous, efficient, polished, skilful, smooth, streamlined, well-organized

**slide** *v* coast, glide, plane, skate, skid, skim, slip, slither, veer

**slight** *adj* 1 imperceptible, inconsequential, insignificant, meagre, minor, minute, modest, negligible, small, tiny; *opp* large. 2 delicate, frail, petite, slender, slim, small; *opp* big

**slight** *n* affront, discourtesy, disregard, disrespect, insult, neglect, rebuff, rudeness, snub

**slight** *v* affront, disdain, disregard, disrespect, ignore, insult, neglect, put down, rebuff, scorn, snub

**slightly** *adv* a bit, a little, moderately, somewhat, to a small extent

**slim** *adj* 1 fine, lean, narrow, slender, slight, svelte, sylph-like, trim, willowy; *opp* fat. 2 (slim hope) faint, feeble, flimsy, fragile, frail, remote, slight, slim, tenuous, thin, weak; *opp* strong

**slimy** *adj* 1 clammy, glutinous, greasy, mucous, muddy, oily, slippery, slithery, squidgy *inf*, squishy *inf*, viscous, wet. 2 (of a person) creepy *inf*, gushing, obsequious, oily, smarmy, smooth, sycophantic, unctuous

**sling** *v* cast, chuck *inf*, fling, heave, hurl, lob, pelt, pitch, throw, toss

**slink** *v* creep, prowl, skulk, slide, slip, sneak, steal

**slinky** *adj* clinging, close-fitting, sexy *inf*, sinuous, sleek

**slip** *v* 1 coast, glide, plane, skate, skid, skim, slide, slither. 2 creep, edge, slide, sneak, steal

**slip** *n* blunder, boob *inf*, bungle, error, failure, lapse, miscalculation, mistake, oversight, slip-up

**slippery** *adj* 1 glassy, greasy, icy, oily, perilous, slimy, slippy *inf*, skiddy *inf*, smooth, wet. 2 (of a person) crafty, cunning, devious, dishonest, evasive, shifty, sneaky, tricky, two-faced, unreliable, wily

**slit** *n* aperture, cleft, crack, cut, gash, hole, incision, opening, rent, slash, slot, split, tear, vent

**slit** *v* cut, cut open, gash, knife, lance, pierce, rip, slash, slice, tear

**slither** *v* creep, glide, slide, slink, slip, snake, undulate, worm

**slog** *n* 1 (hard work) effort, exertion, hard task, struggle. 2 (hard going) hike, trek, trudge. 3 (a hard hit) hit, slug *inf*, sock *inf*, stroke, wallop *inf*, whack *inf*

**slog** *v* 1 (hit sth) hit, hit for six *inf*, punch, slug, sock *inf*, strike, thump, wallop *inf*, whack. 2 (slog away at sth) labour, persevere, plod, plough, slave. 3 (slog through the mud) plod, tramp, trek, trudge

**slogan** *n* catchphrase, catchword, jingle, motto, saying

**slope** *n* angle, ascent, camber, descent, dip, drop, fall, gradient, incline, hill, mountain, pitch, ramp, rise, slant, tilt

**slope** *v* dip, drop away, fall, incline, lean, pitch, rise, slant, tilt, tip

**sloping** *adj* angled, diagonal, dipping, inclined, inclining, leaning, listing, oblique, slanted, slanting, tilting

**sloppy** *adj* 1 liquid, runny, sludgy, slushy, soggy, splashy, watery, wet; *opp* firm. 2 (of work) careless, clumsy, disorganized, hurried, lax, messy, slapdash, untidy, weak; *opp* careful. 3 (a sloppy film) mawkish, schmaltzy *inf*, sentimental, soppy *inf*, trite, wet *inf*

**slot** *n* 1 aperture, crack, gash, groove, hole, notch, opening, slit, vent. 2 opening, period, place, position, space, spot, time, vacancy

**slouch** *v* droop, hunch, loll, sag, slump, stoop

**slovenly** *adj* careless, dirty, dishevelled, disorderly, lax, loose, messy, negligent, slack, slapdash, slatternly, slipshod, sloppy *inf*, unmethodical, untidy; *opp* careful

**slow** *adj* 1 (slow movement) careful, cautious, creeping, dawdling, lazy, leaden, leisurely, measured, painstaking, ponderous, sluggish, snail-like, steady, unhurried, unwilling; *opp* fast. 2 (a slow death) gradual, lingering, long-drawn-out, prolonged, protracted; *opp* quick. 3 (a slow learner) backward, behind, late, retarded, with special needs. 4 dense, dim, dozy *inf*, dull, stupid

**slow** *v* decelerate, ease up *inf*, go slower, put the brakes on, reduce speed, slow down

**sluggish** *adj* drowsy, dull, heavy, inactive, inert, languid, lazy, lethargic, listless, slothful, slow, torpid, unresponsive; *opp* lively

**slump** *v* collapse, crash, drop, fall, go down, nosedive, plummet, plunge, sink, slip, subside

**slump** *n* collapse, crash, depression, devaluation, dip, downturn, drop, failure, fall, falling-off, low, nosedive, recession, trough; *opp* boom

**slur** *n* affront, aspersion, disgrace, insinuation, insult, libel, slander, slight, smear, stain, stigma

**sly** *adj* artful, crafty, cunning, deceitful, devious, foxy, furtive, mischievous, scheming, secret, secretive, shifty, shrewd, sneaky, stealthy, surreptitious, tricky, underhand, wily

**smack** *v* belt *inf*, clout, cuff, hit, pat, slap, spank, strike, swipe

**small** *adj* 1 baby *inf*, dinky *inf*, dwarf, little, microscopic, mini, miniature, minute, pocket-sized *inf*, teeny, teeny-weeny, tiny, wee, young; *opp* big. 2 (of a person) petite, pint-sized *inf*, puny, short, slender, slight, thin, undersized; *opp* big. 3 (a small problem) inconsequential, insignificant, minor, petty, trivial, unimportant; *opp* big. 4 (a small amount) inadequate, insufficient, meagre, mean, measly, scanty, stingy, unsatisfactory; *opp* large

**small-minded** *adj* bigoted, grudging, intolerant, mean, narrow-minded, petty, prejudiced, selfish, ungenerous

**smart** *adj* 1 chic, dapper, dashing *inf*, elegant, fashionable, neat, snazzy *inf*, spruce, stylish, tidy, well-dressed, well-groomed, well turned-out; *opp* scruffy. 2 (clever) astute, bright, clever, gifted, intelligent, quick, quick-witted, sharp

**smart** *v* burn, hurt, sting, throb, tingle

**smash** *n* accident, car crash, collision, crash, pile-up *inf*

**smash** *v* 1 break, crack, demolish, shatter. 2 (smash into sth) bash, bump, collide, crash, knock, pound, slam, strike

**smashing** *adj* brilliant, excellent, fabulous, first-class, great, marvellous, out of this world, sensational, super, terrific, wonderful; *opp* awful

**smattering** *n* bit, dash, small amount, sprinkling

**smear** *n* 1 blot, blotch, daub, mark, smudge, splotch, spot, streak. 2 (a smear on sb's name) blot, slur, stain, stigma

**smear** *v* 1 (smear sth with paint) bedaub, coat, cover, dirty, mark, soil, stain, streak. 2 (smear paint on sth) dab, daub, plaster, slap, smudge, wipe. 3 (smear sb's reputation) blacken, sully, tarnish, vilify

**smell** *n* 1 (the smell of roses) aroma, bouquet, fragrance, odour, perfume, redolence, scent. 2 (the smell of old socks) pong *inf*, reek, stench, stink, whiff

**smell** *v* 1 (be able to smell sth) get a

whiff of, scent, sniff out. **2** (sth smells)
hum *inf*, pong *inf*, reek, stink, whiff

**smelly** *adj* foul-smelling, high *inf*,
malodorous, pongy *sl*, rank, reeking,
stinking, whiffy *inf*

**smile** *n* beam, grin, laugh, smirk, sneer

**smile** *v* beam, grin, laugh, leer, simper,
smirk

**smirk** *v* grin, leer, look smug, simper,
sneer

**smitten** *adj* **1** (smitten with a disease)
affected, afflicted, laid low, plagued,
struck down, suffering. **2** (smitten with
sb) beguiled, bewitched, bowled over *inf*,
captivated, charmed, entranced,
infatuated, swept off your feet, taken

**smoke** *n* exhaust, fumes, pollution, smog,
steam, vapour

**smoke** *v* **1** (give off smoke) burn, emit
smoke, smoulder. **2** (smoke a cigarette)
have a cigarette, inhale, puff

**smooth** *adj* **1** even, flat, flush, horizontal,
level, plane, unwrinkled; *opp* bumpy.
**2** burnished, glossy, polished, satiny,
shiny, silken, silky, sleek, soft, velvety;
*opp* rough. **3** (smooth surface of a lake)
calm, glassy, mirrorlike, peaceful, still,
tranquil, unbroken, undisturbed,
unruffled. **4** (a smooth person) debonair,
glib, insincere, persuasive, slick, smarmy
*inf*, smug, suave, urbane. **5** (smooth
movements) comfortable, easy,
effortless, flowing, fluent, fluid, regular,
rhythmic, steady; *opp* jerky. **6** (smooth
sounds) agreeable, bland, mellow, mild,
pleasant, soft, soothing; *opp* harsh

**smooth** *v* brush, buff up, burnish,
comb, even out, file, flatten, iron,
level, plane, polish, press, press

down, roll out, sand down

**smother** *v* **1** (smother a person)
asphyxiate, choke, stifle, suffocate.
**2** (smother a sound) hide, keep back,
muffle, stifle, suppress. **3** (smother
flames) damp down, extinguish, put
out, stamp out

**smudge** *n* blotch, mark, smear, smut,
spot, streak

**smudge** *v* blur, dirty, mark, soil, smear,
streak

**smug** *adj* complacent, conceited, pleased
with yourself, priggish, self-important,
self-righteous, self-satisfied, superior

**snack** *n* bite, elevenses *inf*, light meal,
nibbles, refreshments

**snag** *n* catch, complication, disadvantage,
drawback, hitch, obstacle, problem, setback, stumbling-block

**snap** *n* **1** click, crack, crackle, pop.
**2** (a cold snap) interval, period, spell,
time. **3** (a holiday snap) photo,
photograph, picture, snapshot

**snap** *v* **1** break, come apart, crack,
fracture, give way, separate, split.
**2** (of a dog) bite, catch, nip, seize,
snatch. **3** (snap at sb) bark, flash, growl,
jump down sb's throat *inf*, retort, snarl,
speak sharply

**snare** *n* ambush, net, noose, trap

**snare** *v* capture, catch, ensnare, entrap,
net, seize, trap

**snatch** *n* (a snatch of a tune) bit,
fragment, part, piece, snippet

**snatch** *v* **1** catch, clutch, grab, grasp,
grip, pluck, pull, seize, take, win,
wrench. **2** abduct, hold to ransom,
kidnap, make off with, nab *inf*, steal,
take as a hostage

**sneak** n grass inf, informer, snitch inf, telltale

**sneak** v 1 (sneak through the bushes) cower, creep, lurk, pad, prowl, sidle, skulk, slink, stalk, steal. 2 (sneak sth in) slip, smuggle, spirit, whisk. 3 (sneak on sb) grass inf, inform against, report, shop sl, snitch inf, tell inf, tell tales

**sneaky** adj deceitful, furtive, mean, shady, shifty inf, sly, stealthy, surreptitious, treacherous, underhand

**sneer** v be contemptuous, be scornful, deride, hiss, jeer, laugh, mock, ridicule, scoff, smirk, snigger, taunt

**sniff** v breathe, breathe in, get a whiff of, inhale, scent, smell, snuffle

**snigger** v chuckle, giggle, laugh, sneer, titter

**snip** n bit, clipping, cutting, fragment, piece, scrap, shred, tatter

**snip** v clip, crop, cut, dock, nick, notch, prune, shave, trim

**snivel** v blubber, cry, grizzle, moan, sniff, sniffle, snuffle, sob, whimper, whine, whinge inf

**snobbish** adj arrogant, condescending, haughty, hoity-toity, patronizing, pompous, posh inf, proud, smug, snobby, snooty inf, stuck-up inf, superior, toffee-nosed inf

**snoop** v interfere, meddle, nose about inf, poke your nose in inf, pry, sneak, spy

**snub** n affront, insult, rebuff, slap in the face inf, slight

**snub** v be rude to, cut dead inf, give the cold shoulder to, humiliate, ignore, insult, rebuff, shun, slight, spurn

**snug** adj comfortable, comfy inf, cosy, intimate, sheltered, soft, warm

**snuggle** v cuddle, curl up, nestle, nuzzle

**soak** v 1 drench, saturate, wet through. 2 (soak sth) immerse, marinate, steep. 3 (soak into sth) infuse, penetrate, permeate

**soaking** adj drenched, dripping, saturated, soaked, soaked to the skin, sodden, sopping, waterlogged, wringing wet; opp dry

**soar** v 1 (of a bird) ascend, fly, hover, rise, take flight, take off. 2 (of prices) climb, escalate, go up, increase, rise, rocket, shoot up, spiral; opp plummet, tumble

**sob** v bawl, cry, gasp, howl, shed tears, snivel, weep

**sober** adj 1 abstinent, moderate, teetotal. 2 (sober clothing) dark, drab, dull, plain, restrained, sombre, subdued. 3 (a sober expression) grave, serious, solemn, thoughtful. 4 (a sober look at sth) calm, clear-headed, level-headed, rational, sensible

**sociable** adj affable, companionable, convivial, cordial, extroverted, friendly, gregarious, outgoing, social, warm, welcoming; opp unsociable

**social** adj 1 collective, communal, community, general, group, popular, public. 2 civilized, organized. 3 communicative, friendly, gregarious, outgoing, sociable; opp antisocial

**social** n do inf, gathering, get-together inf, party

**socialize** v be sociable, entertain, get together, go out, join in, mix

**society** n 1 civilization, community, culture. 2 mankind, people, the community, the public. 3 (club) association, circle, club, group, guild, league, union

**sodden** adj boggy, drenched, saturated, soaked, soggy, sopping, swampy, waterlogged; **opp** dry

**soft** adj 1 doughy, elastic, flexible, gelatinous, gooey inf, malleable, mushy, plastic, pliable, pulpy, spongy, springy, squashy, supple, tender, yielding; **opp** hard. 2 (a soft coat) downy, feathery, fleecy, fluffy, furry, silky, smooth, velvety; **opp** rough. 3 (soft light) diffuse, dim, faint, gentle, low, restful, subdued; **opp** harsh. 4 (soft sounds) dulcet, faint, gentle, hushed, inaudible, low, mellow, murmured, muted, quiet, soothing, subdued, whispered. 5 (soft colours) light, muted, pale, pastel; **opp** vivid. 6 (a soft breeze) balmy, gentle, light, mild, pleasant; **opp** strong. 7 (of a person) compassionate, easygoing, feeble, forgiving, gentle, kind, lenient, loving, sensitive, soft-hearted, soppy inf, sympathetic, tender-hearted, tolerant, weak. 8 (soft ground) boggy, marshy, muddy, swampy, waterlogged; **opp** firm

**soften** v alleviate, calm down, cushion, deaden, decrease, diminish, lower, make softer, moderate, muffle, quell, quieten, subdue, tone down, turn down

**soggy** adj boggy, sodden, soft, sopping, swampy, waterlogged, wet; **opp** dry

**soil** n clay, dirt, dust, earth, ground, loam, topsoil

**soil** v contaminate, dirty, foul, make dirty, muddy, pollute, smear, smudge, spatter, spot, stain, tarnish

**soldier** n commando, fighter, gunner, officer, paratrooper, private, serviceman, servicewoman, warrior

**sole** adj 1 (the sole survivor) lone, only, single, solitary. 2 (for your sole use) exclusive, individual

**solemn** adj 1 (looking solemn) earnest, grave, grim, long-faced, serious, sober, thoughtful, unsmiling. 2 (a solemn ceremony) ceremonial, ceremonious, dignified, formal, grand, holy, important, imposing, impressive, religious, stately. 3 (a solemn vow) genuine, honest, serious, sincere, wholehearted

**solicit** v (solicit advice) appeal for, ask for, request, seek

**solid** adj 1 compact, compressed, concrete, dense, firm, hard, impermeable, rigid, thick, unmoving. 2 durable, robust, sound, stable, strong, sturdy, substantial, well-made; **opp** flimsy. 3 (solid gold) genuine, pure, real, unalloyed, unmixed. 4 (a solid shape) cubic, rounded, spherical, three-dimensional; **opp** flat. 5 (solid support) complete, dependable, effective, reliable, stalwart, trustworthy, undivided, united, unwavering

**solidarity** n accord, camaraderie, cohesion, harmony, like-mindedness, stability, team spirit, unanimity, unity

**solidify** v become hard, clot, coagulate, congeal, crystallize, go hard, harden, jell, set, thicken; **opp** liquefy

**solitary** adj 1 (of a thing) alone, by itself, lone, one, single, sole. 2 (of a person) friendless, isolated, lonely, lonesome, unsociable. 3 (of a place) desolate, hidden, lonely, out-of-the-way, private, remote, secluded

**solitude** n isolation, loneliness, privacy,

remoteness, retirement, seclusion

**solo** *adj, adv* alone, by yourself, individually, on your own, unaccompanied

**soluble** *adj* (soluble in water) dispersing, dissolving, melting

**solution** *n* **1** answer, clarification, conclusion, explanation, key, result, solving, working out. **2** blend, compound, emulsion, infusion, mixture, solvent, suspension

**solve** *v* **1** (solve a mystery) clear up, explain, figure out, find the solution to, unravel. **2** (solve your problems) find the answer to, resolve, sort out. **3** (solve a clue) crack *inf*, decipher, interpret, puzzle out

**solvent** *adj* creditworthy, debt-free, in credit, in the black, solid, sound, viable

**sombre** *adj* black, bleak, cheerless, dark, dim, dismal, doleful, funereal, gloomy, joyless, melancholy, morose, mournful, sad, sepulchral

**song** *n* anthem, ballad, carol, ditty, hymn, lullaby, pop song, tune

**soon** *adv* any minute now *inf*, before long, before you know it *inf*, in a minute, in a moment, in a while, in the near future, in two shakes of a lamb's tail *inf*, quickly, shortly, straightaway

**soothe** *v* **1** alleviate, appease, assuage, calm, ease, relieve, soften. **2** (soothe a baby) calm, comfort, lull, pacify, quieten, settle

**sophisticated** *adj* **1** (of people) cool *inf*, cosmopolitan, cultivated, cultured, grown-up *inf*, mature, refined, suave, urbane, worldly, worldly wise; *opp* unsophisticated. **2** (of technology)

advanced, complex, complicated, elaborate, highly developed, intricate, involved; *opp* simple

**soppy** *adj* **1** (a soppy film) corny *inf*, mawkish, schmaltzy, sentimental, slushy *inf*. **2** (a soppy person) daft *inf*, foolish, overemotional, sentimental, silly, soft *inf*, wet

**sorcerer** *n* enchanter, enchantress, magician, sorceress, warlock, witch, wizard

**sorcery** *n* black magic, charms, incantations, magic, spells, voodoo, witchcraft, witchery, wizardry

**sordid** *adj* **1** dingy, dirty, filthy, foul, mean, miserable, seedy, shabby, sleazy, slovenly, squalid, ugly, unpleasant, vile, wretched. **2** corrupt, dishonourable, disreputable, immoral, mercenary, shabby *inf*, unethical

**sore** *adj* **1** aching, angry, bruised, burning, inflamed, irritated, painful, raw, red, sensitive, smarting, tender, wounded. **2** (feel sore about sth) aggrieved, annoyed, hurt, irritated, peeved *inf*, put out *inf*, resentful, upset

**sorrow** *n* anguish, dejection, desolation, disappointment, distress, grief, heartache, melancholy, misery, regret, sadness, tearfulness, unhappiness, woe, wretchedness; *opp* happiness, joy

**sorrowful** *adj* broken-hearted, dejected, grief-stricken, heartbroken, melancholy, miserable, sad, saddened, tearful, unhappy, upset, woebegone; *opp* happy

**sorry** *adj* **1** apologetic, ashamed, contrite, penitent, remorseful, repentant, shamefaced; *opp* unrepentant. **2** distressed, grieved, sad, sorrowful, unhappy, upset; **opp** glad. **3** (sorry for sb) compassionate, concerned, full of pity, moved, pitying, sympathetic; **opp** uncaring

**sort** n **1** brand, kind, make, type. **2** breed, family, kind, race, species, strain, type, variety. **3** category, class, classification, description, genre, kind, nature, style, type

**sort** v **1** (put things into groups) class, divide, grade, put in groups, rank, select. **2** (put things in order) arrange, catalogue, categorize, classify, group, put in order, systematize, tidy. **3** (sort papers) file, organize, tidy. **4** sort out (put in order) organize, tidy up. **5** sort out (sort out a problem) deal with, find a solution to, handle, resolve

**soul** n **1** being, body, creature, individual, mortal, person. **2** inner self, spirit, true being

**sound** adj **1** complete, entire, firm, fit, hale and hearty, healthy, in good health, in good shape, intact, perfect, unhurt, uninjured, whole. **2** (strong) robust, solid, strong, sturdy, substantial, tough, undamaged; **opp** flimsy. **3** (sound reasoning) convincing, correct, logical, plausible, proper, reasonable, right, sane, sensible, true, valid, wise

**sound** n bang, blare, crash, creak, cry, din, hoot, music, noise, scream, shout, squeak, thud, yelp, voice

**sound** v **1** be heard, echo, make a noise, resonate, resound, reverberate. **2** (you sound desperate) appear, look, seem. **3** (sound the words carefully) articulate, pronounce, say, utter, voice. **4** sound out canvass, examine, inquire

into, investigate, look into, probe, research, test

**soup** n bouillon, broth, consommé, stock

**sour** adj **1** (a sour taste) acid, bitter, lemony, pungent, sharp, tangy, tart, vinegary. **2** (sour milk) bad, curdled, off, rancid, turned; **opp** fresh. **3** (of a person) bad-tempered, bitter, cross, crotchety, discontented, grouchy inf, grumpy, irritable, jaundiced, nasty, unpleasant; **opp** pleasant

**source** n **1** author, beginning, cause, creator, origin, starting-point. **2** (source of a river) head, spring, start, well-head, well-spring

**souvenir** n keepsake, memento, memorabilia, relic, reminder

**sovereign** adj absolute, all-powerful, chief, dominant, highest, imperial, predominant, principal, royal, ruling, supreme, unlimited

**sovereign** n crowned head, emperor, empress, king, monarch, prince, princess, queen, ruler, tsar

**sow** v **1** (sow seeds) plant, scatter, strew. **2** (sow confusion) instigate, promote, spread

**space** n **1** emptiness, infinity, nothingness, vacuum, void. **2** (fired a rocket into space) outer space, the galaxy, the solar system, the stratosphere, the universe. **3** (need more space) capacity, elbow room inf, freedom, leeway, margin, room, scope, spaciousness. **4** (a large space) area, expanse, volume. **5** (gap) blank, empty space, gap, hole, opening

**spacious** adj ample, broad, capacious, comfortable, extensive, huge, large,

open, roomy, sizable, vast, wide;
*opp* small

**span** *n* distance, extent, length, reach,
spread, stretch, width

**span** *v* arch over, bridge, cover, cross,
extend across, go over, straddle, stretch
over, vault over

**spank** *v* belt, cuff, give a hiding to *inf*, put
over your knee, slap, smack, wallop

**spare** *adj* additional, emergency, extra,
free, in reserve, leftover, odd, remaining,
surplus, unoccupied, unused, unwanted

**spare** *v* 1 afford, do without, manage,
sacrifice. 2 (spare some change) donate,
give, provide. 3 (spare sb or sth) be
merciful, free, have mercy, let off *inf*,
pardon, release, reprieve, save

**sparing** *adj* careful, economical, frugal,
miserly, parsimonious, prudent, stingy
*inf*, thrifty, tight-fisted *inf*; *opp* lavish

**spark** *n* flare, flash, flicker, gleam, glint,
sparkle

**spark** *v* ignite, kindle, provoke, set off,
touch off, trigger

**sparkle** *v* 1 beam, flash, gleam, glint,
glisten, glitter, glow, shimmer, shine,
twinkle, wink. 2 bubble, effervesce, fizz

**sparse** *adj* light, meagre, scanty, scarce,
slight, thin

**spasm** *n* attack, bout, contraction,
convulsion, cramp, fit, jerk, outburst,
seizure, twitch

**spasmodic** *adj* convulsive, erratic, fitful,
intermittent, irregular, jerky, occasional,
periodic, sporadic

**spate** *n* deluge, flood, flow, rush, torrent

**spatter** *v* daub, pepper, shower, splash,
splatter, spray, sprinkle

**speak** *v* 1 argue, communicate, converse,

express yourself, give a lecture, have a
chat, have a word, hold forth, pipe up
*inf*, recite, say sth, talk, tell sth, use your
voice. 2 (speak Spanish) converse in,
pronounce, talk in. 3 **speak out** have
your say, make yourself heard, raise your
voice, sound off, speak up, speak your
mind

**speaker** *n* lecturer, orator, public speaker,
spokesperson

**spearhead** *v* initiate, launch, lead,
pioneer, set in motion

**special** *adj* 1 different, distinctive,
exceptional, extraordinary, noteworthy,
odd, out-of-the-ordinary, peculiar,
strange, unique, unmistakable, unusual;
*opp* ordinary. 2 (a special day) festive,
gala, important, memorable,
momentous, red-letter, significant,
unique, unusual; *opp* ordinary

**specialist** *n* authority, buff *inf*,
connoisseur, consultant, expert,
professional

**speciality** *n* claim to fame *inf*, field, forte,
gift, special skill, strength, strong point,
talent

**specialize** *v* be a specialist in, be best
at, concentrate on, focus on, have
a reputation for, have special
knowledge in

**species** *n* breed, class, genus, kind, sort,
type, variety

**specific** *adj* 1 definite, especial, exact,
individual, particular, special, specified.
2 (be specific about what you want)
definite, detailed, explicit, firm,
particular, precise, unambiguous,
unequivocal

**specification** *n* conditions, description,

details, instructions, particulars,
requirements

**specify** v define, detail, enumerate,
indicate, list, mention, name, set out,
spell out, state, stipulate

**specimen** n example, illustration,
instance, model, pattern, representative
sample, sample

**speck** n dot, fleck, smudge, speckle, spot

**speckled** adj dappled, dotted, flecked,
freckled, mottled, patchy, spotted,
stippled

**spectacle** n 1 display, event,
extravaganza, pageant, parade,
performance, scene, show, sight.
2 (make a spectacle of yourself)
curiosity, laughing-stock

**spectacular** adj beautiful, breathtaking,
daring, dazzling, dramatic, eye-catching,
impressive, magnificent, sensational,
striking

**spectator** n beholder, bystander,
eyewitness, observer, onlooker, viewer,
watcher, witness

**spectre** n apparition, ghost, phantom,
spirit, wraith

**speculate** v conjecture, consider,
hypothesize, make a guess, meditate,
muse, reflect, suppose, think, wonder

**speech** n 1 (make a speech) address,
discourse, lecture, monologue, oration,
sermon, soliloquy, talk. 2 (human
speech) communication, conversation,
dialogue, discussion, talk. 3 (way of
speaking) articulation, delivery, diction,
elocution, pronunciation, way of
speaking

**speechless** adj 1 dumb, inarticulate,
mum, mute, silent, struck dumb, tongue-

tied, wordless. 2 (too shocked to speak)
aghast, amazed, astounded, dazed,
dumbstruck, shocked, thunderstruck

**speed** n 1 briskness, haste, hurry,
quickness, rapidity, speediness, swiftness,
velocity. 2 pace, rate, tempo

**speed** v 1 flash, hurtle, race, streak, tear,
whizz, zoom. 2 (run) career, dash, fly,
gallop, hurry, race, run, rush, scamper,
sprint. 3 break the speed limit, exceed
the speed limit, go too fast. 4 speed up
accelerate, gather momentum, get
moving inf, hurry up, increase speed,
put on speed, put your foot down inf,
rush, step on it inf

**speedy** adj fast, hasty, hurried, immediate,
prompt, quick, rapid, swift

**spell** n 1 charm, enchantment,
incantation, magic formula, sorcery,
witchcraft. 2 (a spell of wintry weather)
interval, patch, period, time

**spellbound** adj bewitched, captivated,
charmed, enthralled, entranced,
fascinated, gripped, hooked inf,
mesmerized, overcome, rapt, riveted,
transported, under a spell

**spend** v 1 (spend money) fork out inf,
fritter away, pay out, shell out inf, splash
out inf, splurge inf, squander, use up,
waste. 2 (spend time) fill, occupy, pass,
while away

**sphere** n 1 ball, circle, globe, globule,
orb. 2 area, department, domain, field,
jurisdiction, province, realm, speciality,
subject, territory

**spherical** adj ball-shaped, globe-shaped,
globular, round

**spice** n 1 flavour, flavouring, kick inf,
piquancy, punch inf, relish, savour,

seasoning, spiciness. 2 (in life) colour, excitement, interest, zest, zing *inf*

**spicy** *adj* aromatic, flavoursome, fragrant, highly flavoured, hot, peppery, pungent, seasoned, sharp, well-seasoned; *opp* bland

**spike** *n* barb, nail, pin, point, prong, skewer, spine, stake

**spill** *v* 1 (spill a drink) knock over, overturn, slop, splash, tip over, upset. 2 (spill the contents of sth) drop, scatter, shed, upset. 3 (spill over) brim over, discharge, disgorge, overflow, pour, slop over, spill over, well over

**spin** *n* gyration, revolution, roll, rotation, turn, twist, whirl

**spin** *v* 1 circle, gyrate, pirouette, reel, revolve, rotate, swivel, turn, twirl, twist, wheel, whirl. 2 (your head spins) be giddy, go round, grow dizzy, reel, swim

**spine** *n* 1 backbone, spinal column, vertebrae. 2 barb, bristle, needle, quill, spike

**spine-chilling** *adj* bloodcurdling, creepy *inf*, eerie, frightening, hair-raising, horrifying, scary *inf*, spooky *inf*, terrifying

**spineless** *adj* cowardly, faint-hearted, feeble, gutless *inf*, lily-livered *inf*, soft *inf*, timid, weak, weak-willed, wimpish *inf*, yellow *inf*, yellow-bellied *inf*; *opp* courageous

**spiral** *adj* circular, coiled, corkscrew, helical, scrolled, twisting, winding

**spirit** *n* 1 apparition, ghost, phantom, poltergeist, spectre, vision. 2 (admire sb's spirit) attitude, bravery, courage, determination, enterprise, enthusiasm, guts *inf*, mettle, optimism, pluck, resolution, vigour, willpower

**spirited** *adj* animated, assertive, brave, daring, energetic, enthusiastic, gutsy *inf*, heroic, lively, passionate, vigorous

**spiritual** *adj* devotional, devout, divine, heavenly, holy, pure, religious, sacred

**spit** *n* dribble, drool, saliva, slaver, slobber, spittle

**spit** *v* dribble, hiss, salivate, slobber, splutter

**spite** *n* animosity, bitterness, envy, hate, hatred, ill-feeling, malice, maliciousness, pique, resentment, spitefulness, vindictiveness

**spiteful** *adj* barbed, catty *inf*, cruel, cutting, hurtful, ill-natured, malevolent, malicious, snide, venomous, vicious, vindictive

**splash** *n* 1 (splash of colour) burst, dash, patch, spattering, splodge, spot, streak. 2 (making a splash) impact, sensation. 3 (having a splash in the pool) dip, paddle, plunge, swim, wallow

**splash** *v* 1 (splash sb with water) shower, slop, slosh, spatter, splatter, spray, sprinkle, squirt, wash, wet. 2 (splash around) bathe, dabble, paddle, wallow. 3 (splash the news over all the papers) blazon, broadcast, headline, plaster, publicize, trumpet

**splendid** *adj* 1 admirable, awe-inspiring, glorious, grand, heroic, magnificent, outstanding, sublime, superb. 2 beautiful, costly, dazzling, elegant, fabulous, gorgeous, impressive, lavish, magnificent, opulent, rich, sumptuous. 3 beautiful, excellent, fantastic *inf*, fine, glorious, great *inf*, marvellous, super *inf*, wonderful

**splendour** *n* beauty, brightness,

brilliance, dazzle, glitter *inf*, grandeur, luxury, magnificence, pomp, radiance, richness, sumptuousness

**splice** *v* braid, entwine, intertwine, interweave, join, overlap, plait, tie together

**splinter** *n* chip, flake, fragment, needle, shard, shaving, sliver

**splinter** *v* break, chip, crack, fracture, shatter, smash, split

**split** *n* **1** breach, cleft, crack, division, fissure, gap, gash, opening, rip, slash, slit, tear. **2** (between people) break-up, difference of opinion, division, divorce, estrangement, rift, separation

**split** *v* **1** break, burst, crack, disintegrate, rip, separate, snap, splinter. **2** (split sth) bisect, break, chop, cleave, cut, divide, rip, separate, slash, slice, slit, tear (split the proceeds) distribute, divide, dole out, parcel out, share out. **3** (split into two) branch, diverge, divide, fork. **4 split up** break up, disband, divorce, go your separate ways, part, separate

**spoil** *v* **1** blemish, blight, damage, deface, destroy, disfigure, harm, impair, injure, mar, mess up, ruin, undermine, undo, upset, wreck. **2** (spoil sb) baby, coddle, cosset, indulge, make a fuss of, mollycoddle, overindulge, pamper. **3** (of food) addle, curdle, decay, go bad, go off *inf*, go sour, rot, turn

**sponsor** *n* backer, benefactor, patron, promoter, supporter

**sponsor** *v* back, finance, fund, promote, subsidize, support, underwrite

**spontaneous** *adj* automatic, impromptu, impulsive, instinctive, off-the-cuff, reflex, spur-of-the-moment,

unhesitating, unplanned, unrehearsed, voluntary; **opp** planned

**spooky** *adj* creepy, eerie, frightening, ghostly, hair-raising, scary, spine-chilling, supernatural, uncanny, unearthly, weird

**sporadic** *adj* erratic, every now and then, intermittent, irregular, occasional, on and off, patchy, periodic, random, scattered, spasmodic

**sport** *n* athletics, ball games, games, hunting, PE, physical activity, physical exercise, team games, water sports, winter sports

**sport** *v* carry, display, flaunt, show off, wear

**sporting** *adj* decent, fair, generous, gentlemanly, honourable; **opp** unsporting

**sportsman** *n* athlete, competitor, contestant, participant, player, sportswoman, team-member

**sporty** *adj* active, athletic, energetic, fit, healthy, muscular, outdoor

**spot** *n* **1** blackhead, freckle, mole, pimple, pock-mark, pustule, rash, whitehead, zit *inf*. **2** blob, blotch, dot, drop, fleck, mark, patch, speck, splash, stain. **3** area, location, place, position, site, situation. **4** bit, drop, little, smidgen, touch

**spot** *v* **1** catch sight of, glimpse, make out, notice, recognize, see. **2** mark, spatter, splash, stain

**spotless** *adj* **1** clean, gleaming, hygienic, immaculate, shining, spick and span, sterile; **opp** dirty. **2** (of sb's reputation) above reproach, faultless, flawless, squeaky-clean *inf*, unsullied, untarnished, whiter-than-white;

*opp* tarnished

**spotty** *adj* 1 blotchy, dappled, dotty, flecked, mottled, polka-dot, speckly, spotted. 2 acned, pimply

**spouse** *n* husband, missis *inf*, old man *inf*, other half *inf*, partner, wife

**spout** *v* 1 erupt, flow, gush, jet, pour, shoot, spew, spurt, squirt, stream. 2 expound, go on, harangue, hold forth, rabbit on *inf*, rant, rattle on *inf*

**sprawl** *v* 1 flop, languish, loll, lounge, recline, slouch, slump, spread out, stretch out. 2 be scattered, ramble, spill over, spread, straggle, tumble over

**spray** *n* 1 droplets, fountain, mist, shower, spatter. 2 aerosol, atomizer, pump-action spray, sprinkler, vaporizer

**spray** *v* mist, shower, spatter, splash, sprinkle, wet

**spread** *n* 1 (the spread of sth) advance, expansion, growth, increase, proliferation. 2 (span) expanse, extent, range, reach, span. 3 (in a newspaper) article, feature, piece, story. 4 (sth to put on bread) butter, conserve, jam, margarine, paste, pâté, preserve. 5 feast, meal

**spread** *v* 1 (open out) expand, extend, fan out, open out, stretch, unfold, unfurl. 2 (grow) broaden, develop, disperse, distribute, expand, get bigger, grow, increase, multiply, mushroom, proliferate, swell. 3 (reach) cover, extend, reach, sprawl, stretch. 4 (lay out) arrange, distribute, lay out, scatter. 5 (spread butter) apply, coat, cover with, plaster on *inf*, put on, rub over, smear on. 6 (spread news) advertise, broadcast, circulate, disseminate, give out, make

known, pass round, promulgate, publicize

**spree** *n* bender *inf*, binge, bout, day out, fling, junket *inf*, night out, splurge *inf*

**sprightly** *adj* active, agile, alert, brisk, chipper *inf*, energetic, jaunty, lively, nimble, perky *inf*, spry

**spring** *n* 1 bounce, bound, hop, jump, leap, vault. 2 elasticity, flexibility, springiness. 3 springtime. 4 geyser, spa, water source, well

**spring** *v* 1 bounce, bound, jump, leap, pounce, recoil, vault. 2 (spring from) come from, derive, emanate, originate, spring from, start, stem from. 3 (spring up) appear, develop, emerge, grow, mushroom, pop up, shoot up, spring up, sprout

**sprinkle** *v* dribble, drizzle, pepper, scatter, shower, spatter, spray, strew

**sprinkling** *n* dribble, dusting, few, handful, scattering, splash, trickle

**sprint** *v* charge, dash, hotfoot it *inf*, race, run, rush, tear

**sprout** *v* come into bud, come up, germinate, grow, put out shoots, shoot

**spur** *n* encouragement, impetus, incentive, inducement, motivation

**spur** *v* drive, encourage, give sb the incentive, goad, incite, motivate, pressurize, prod, prompt, stimulate, urge

**spurious** *adj* artificial, bogus, false, insincere, mock, phoney *inf*, pretended, pseudo, sham; *opp* genuine, real

**spurn** *v* give sb the cold-shoulder, rebuff, reject, repulse, shun, turn away; *opp* encourage

**spy** *n* agent, double agent, foreign agent, grass *inf*, informer, member of the secret service, mole *inf*, secret agent, snooper, undercover agent, 007 *inf*

**spy** v 1 catch sight of, discover, glimpse, notice, see, spot. 2 follow, gather intelligence, keep an eye on, keep under observation, trail, keep under surveillance, snoop *inf*, tail *inf*, watch

**squabble** n argument, difference of opinion, disagreement, fight, row, spat, tiff, wrangle

**squabble** v argue, bicker, fall out, fight, have a tiff, row, wrangle

**squalid** adj 1 deprived, dingy, dirty, filthy, foul, nasty, neglected, run-down, seedy, slovenly, wretched; *opp* smart. 2 corrupt, disreputable, indecent, shameful, sleazy, sordid

**squalor** n decay, deprivation, dilapidation, dirt, filth, neglect, seediness, wretchedness

**squander** v blow *inf*, fritter away, misuse, pour down the drain *inf*, splurge *inf*, throw away, waste

**square** adj 1 quadrilateral, rectangular, right-angled, true. 2 (of teams in a competition) equal, even, level-pegging, level. 3 (honest) above board, decent, fair, honest, on the level, straight

**squash** v 1 compress, crush, flatten, mash, pound, press, pulp, pulverize, squeeze. 2 (squash things in) cram, crowd, jam, pack, ram, squeeze, wedge

**squawk** v call, caw, croak, screech, shriek, squeak, squeal

**squeak** v cheep, cry, peep, pipe, scream, screech, shrill, squeal, yelp

**squeal** v cry, howl, scream, screech, shout, shriek, squawk, wail, yelp

**squeamish** adj delicate, faint, funny *inf*,

groggy *inf*, nauseated, queasy, sick

**squeeze** v 1 (press) clasp, compress, crush, grip, mash, nip, pinch, press, pulp, squash. 2 (squeeze things in) cram, crowd, force, jam, pack, ram, squash, stuff, wedge. 3 (squeeze sth to get out water) extract, press, twist, wring

**squirm** v fidget, flounder, thrash about, twist, wriggle, writhe

**squirt** v eject, gush, jet, shoot, shower, spew out, spray, spurt

**stab** v cut, gash, gore, jab, knife, pierce, run through, skewer, slash, spear, spike

**stability** n equilibrium, firmness, permanence, reliability, security, solidity, soundness, steadiness, strength, sturdiness; *opp* insecurity, shakiness, unsteadiness

**stabilize** v balance, keep steady, make stable, settle, steady

**stable** adj balanced, constant, established, fast, firm, lasting, on a firm footing, permanent, reliable, secure, solid, sound, steadfast, steady, sturdy, unchanging, unvarying, well-founded; *opp* shaky, unstable

**stack** n heap, hoard, mass, mound, mountain, pile, tower

**stack** v bank up, heap, load, pile up, pile, put, stow

**staff** n 1 baton, cane, crook, mace, sceptre, stave, stick, walking stick, wand. 2 crew, employees, members of staff, personnel, workers, workforce

**stage** n 1 (phase) juncture, lap, leg, level, phase, point, step. 2 (platform) dais, platform, podium, proscenium, rostrum. 3 (the stage) acting, footlights, repertory, show business, the boards, theatre

**stagger** v 1 career, lurch, pitch, reel, rock, roll, totter. 2 amaze, astound, flabbergast, gobsmack *inf*, overwhelm, shake, stun, surprise, take sb's breath away. 3 alternate, interlace, vary

**stagnant** *adj* brackish, foul, lethargic, sluggish, stale, standing, static, still; *opp* flowing, fresh

**stagnate** v decay, deteriorate, fester, go nowhere, become stagnant, languish, rot, vegetate

**staid** *adj* demure, fuddy-duddy *inf*, prim, proper, quiet, reserved, sedate, serious, solemn, stiff, strait-laced, stuffy *inf*, unadventurous; *opp* adventurous

**stain** n 1 blotch, discoloration, mark, spot. 2 colorant, colouring, dye, varnish

**stain** v 1 dirty, discolour, make dirty, mark, splash, spot. 2 blacken, damage, disgrace, spoil, taint, tarnish. 3 colour, dye, varnish

**stair** n escalator, flight of stairs, riser, rung, staircase, stairway, steps, tread

**stake** n 1 pole, post, rod, shaft, spike, stave, stick, support. 2 bet, money, wager. 3 claim, concern, interest, investment, share

**stake** v 1 brace, hold up, prop up, support. 2 bet, chance, gamble, risk, wager

**stale** *adj* 1 dry, hard, musty, off *inf*, old, past its sell-by-date, sour; *opp* fresh. 2 clichéd, dry-as-dust, dull, hackneyed, jaded, tedious, tired, worn-out; *opp* fresh, new

**stalk** v 1 follow, hound, hunt, pursue, shadow, tail, track, trail. 2 flounce, march, prance, stride, strut

**stall** n booth, kiosk, pitch, stand, table

**stall** v delay, drag your feet, hedge, hesitate, hold off, play for time, prevaricate, put off, stonewall

**stamina** n dynamism, endurance, energy, fortitude, go *inf*, guts *inf*, resilience, staying power, strength, vigour

**stammer** v fumble your words, hesitate, splutter, stumble, stutter, trip over your tongue

**stamp** n authorization, brand, die, impression, mark, print, seal

**stamp** v 1 (stamp on sth) crush underfoot, squash, step on, trample, tread on. 2 brand, emboss, impress, label, mark, mark, print. 3 stamp out abolish, destroy, eliminate, eradicate, exterminate, get rid of, put an end to, quash, suppress

**stampede** n charge, dash, headlong dash, rout, rush

**stance** n 1 angle, approach, attitude, line, position, stand, standpoint. 2 attitude, bearing, carriage, pose, posture

**stand** n 1 base, holder, pedestal, rack, support, tripod. 2 (stall) booth, kiosk, pitch, stall, table. 3 grandstand, terraces. 4 (take a stand) angle, approach, attitude, line, position, stance

**stand** v 1 (stand sth somewhere) erect, lean, place, position, put, set. 2 (stand up) get to your feet, get up, rise. 3 (be situated) be, be found at, be located, be situated, lie, sit. 4 (tolerate) abide, bear, cope with, endure, handle, put up with, stomach, take, tolerate, withstand

**standard** *adj* average, basic, normal, orthodox, regular, set, staple, typical, usual

**standard** n 1 benchmark, criterion, example, guideline, ideal, level, measure, model, norm, principle, quality, requirement, spec *inf*, specification, yardstick. 2 banner, colours, ensign, flag, pennant

**standardize** v bring into line, equalize, make consistent, regularize, regulate, systematize

**standpoint** n angle, approach, attitude, line, opinion, perspective, philosophy, point of view, position, school of thought, stance, stand, way of seeing things

**staple** adj basic, essential, key, main, normal, primary, standard, usual

**star** adj brilliant, leading, principal, prominent, well-known

**star** n 1 celebrity, film star, leading actor, leading light, name, personality, pop star, rock star, superstar. 2 celestial body. 3 asterisk

**star** v appear, feature, take the lead

**stare** v gape, gawp, gaze, glare, look, peer, scrutinize, watch

**stark** adj 1 (bleak) austere, barren, bleak, desolate, drab, grim, harsh, plain, severe. 2 (stark contrast) clear, glaring, obvious, sharp. 3 (stark terror) absolute, complete, downright, pure, sheer, total, unmitigated, utter

**start** n 1 beginning, birth, commencement, creation, dawn, early stages, foundation, inception, introduction, launch, onset, opening, origin, outset, root, source. 2 advantage, edge, head start, lead. 3 jerk, jump, spasm, wince

**start** v 1 (start doing sth) begin,

commence, get cracking *inf*, get down to it, get going, get the show on the road *inf*, kick off *inf*, make a start, set the ball rolling, set out, take the plunge. 2 (set sth up) create, establish, form, found, get off the ground, inaugurate, initiate, instigate, introduce, launch, open, pioneer, set up, start up, trigger. 3 (sth starts) appear, arise, begin, come into being, start up. 4 (start a journey) depart, get going, get the show on the road *inf*, get under way, hit the road *inf*, leave, push off *inf*, set off, set out. 5 (start a machine) activate, boot, get going, start up, switch on, turn on. 6 (jump) flinch, jerk, jump, jump out of your skin *inf*, shy away, wince

**startle** v alarm, frighten, give sb a fright, give sb a turn, make sb jump out of their skin, make sb jump, shock, surprise

**starvation** n famine, hunger, lack of food, malnutrition, undernourishment

**starve** v deprive of food, die of hunger, die of starvation, fast, go hungry, go on hunger strike, refuse food

**starving** adj could eat a horse *inf*, dying of hunger *inf*, famished, hungry, malnourished, ravenous, starved, undernourished

**state** n 1 circumstances, condition, mode, position, shape, situation, status. 2 (in a real state) chaos, condition, flap *inf*, flat spin *inf*, fluster, frame of mind, mess, mood, panic, plight, predicament, tizzy *inf*. 3 country, kingdom, land, nation, republic, territory. 4 (the state) civil authorities, establishment, government, parliament

**state** v affirm, announce, articulate,

assert, declare, express, proclaim, pronounce, put into words, say, specify, voice

**stately** adj ceremonial, dignified, formal, grand, imperial, imposing, magnificent, majestic, regal, royal

**statement** n account, announcement, assertion, bulletin, comment, communiqué, declaration, disclosure, explanation, press release, proclamation, report, testimony

**static** adj 1 (still) immobile, inert, motionless, stationary, still, unmoving; *opp* active, in motion. 2 (of pressure or costs) constant, fixed, frozen, level, stable, steady, unvarying; *opp* changeable, fluctuating, varying

**station** n 1 (for trains or buses) bus station, coach station, depot, interchange, railway station, stop, terminus. 2 (TV or radio station) channel, company, radio station, TV station, wavelength. 3 base, centre, depot, headquarters, post

**station** v install, locate, place, post, put, send, set, situate

**stationary** adj at a standstill, fixed, moored, motionless, parked, standing, static, still, stock-still, unmoving; *opp* moving

**statistics** n data, facts and figures, figures, numbers, records

**status** n 1 class, grade, importance, level, position, prestige, rank, standing. 2 condition, position, state

**staunch** adj faithful, firm, loyal, steadfast, strong, true, unswerving

**stay** n holiday, stop, stopover, vacation, visit

**stay** v 1 (wait) hang on, linger, remain, wait. 2 (persist) continue, go on, keep, last, persist, remain. 3 (stay with friends) be put up, crash *inf*, kip down *inf*, live, lodge, move in with, rent, sleep at, stop over, stop, visit

**steadfast** adj dependable, faithful, firm, loyal, reliable, stalwart, staunch, unswerving; *opp* fickle

**steady** adj 1 balanced, firm, safe, secure, solid, stable, still, sure; *opp* shaky, unstable, wobbly. 2 consistent, constant, continuous, even, non-stop, perpetual, regular, rhythmic, round-the-clock, unbroken, unfaltering, uniform, uninterrupted, unvarying. 3 (a steady climb) gentle, gradual; *opp* steep

**steady** v 1 balance, brace, hold steady, keep still, secure, stabilize, support. 2 calm, compose, control

**steal** v 1 burgle, embezzle, hijack, lift, misappropriate, nick *inf*, pilfer, pinch *inf*, pirate, poach, pocket, rob, shoplift, snatch, swipe *inf*, take, thieve, walk off with. 2 creep, glide, pussyfoot, slink, slip, sneak, tiptoe

**stealth** n cunning, furtiveness, secrecy, sleight of hand, slyness

**stealthy** adj clandestine, concealed, covert, cunning, furtive, inconspicuous, secretive, sly, sneaky, surreptitious, undercover

**steep** adj 1 abrupt, perpendicular, precipitous, sharp, sheer, sudden, vertical. 2 (of a price) excessive, extortionate, high, over the top *inf*, unreasonable

**steer** v 1 be at the wheel, be in the driving seat, direct, drive, guide, navigate, pilot. **2** (steer to the left of sth) direct, drive, go, head, turn, veer

**stem** *n* branch, shoot, stalk, trunk, twig

**stem** *v* check, contain, cut off, halt, staunch, stop

**step** *n* **1** footfall, footstep, gait, pace, print, stride, tramp, tread, walk. **2** (stair) doorstep, rung, stair, threshold, tread. **3** (stage) manoeuvre, measure, move, phase, procedure, stage. **4** level, point, position, rank

**step** *v* move, pace, stamp, stride, tramp, trample, tread, walk

**stereotype** *n* conventional idea, formula, model, mould, pattern

**stereotype** *v* label, pigeonhole, typecast

**sterile** *adj* **1** antiseptic, aseptic, clean, disinfected, germ-free, hygienic, pure, spotless, sterilized, uncontaminated. **2** barren, infertile, sterilized, unproductive; *opp* fruitful, productive. **3** fruitless, futile, pointless, unimaginative, unproductive, useless

**sterilize** *v* **1** clean, disinfect, make sterile. **2** castrate, give a man a vasectomy, make infertile, make sterile, neuter, spay

**stern** *adj* austere, cruel, forbidding, grave, grim, hard, harsh, serious, severe, sombre, strict

**stew** *n* casserole, goulash, hot-pot

**stick** *n* baton, branch, cane, crook, piece of wood, pole, rod, staff, stake, twig, walking stick, wand

**stick** *v* **1** (stick sth in) insert, jab, poke, push, stab, thrust. **2** (stick things together) attach, bond, cement, fasten, fix, fuse, glue, join, paste, secure, sellotape. **3** be unable to move, get bogged down, get clogged up, get stuck,

jam, seize up. **4** (stick sth somewhere) chuck, drop, dump, put. **5** (stick sth out) endure, linger, persist, remain, stay

**sticky** *adj* **1** adhesive, glutinous, gooey, gummed, self-adhesive, tacky, viscous. **2** clammy, close, humid, moist, muggy, oppressive, steamy, sultry. **3** (a sticky situation) awkward, delicate, difficult, embarrassing, tricky

**stiff** *adj* **1** arthritic, firm, hard, rheumatic, rigid, solid, solidified, taut, tense, unbending; *opp* bendy, supple. **2** challenging, determined, difficult, hard, resolute, rigorous, strict, strong, tough

**stiffen** *v* become stiff, brace, clot, coagulate, congeal, harden, gel, make rigid, reinforce, set, solidify, tense, thicken

**stifle** *v* **1** asphyxiate, choke, muffle, smother, suffocate. **2** check, control, crush, curb, keep back, quash, quell, repress, silence, suppress

**stigma** *n* blemish, blot, disgrace, dishonour, scar, shame, stain

**still** *adj* at rest, calm, flat, motionless, peaceful, quiet, restful, serene, silent, stagnant, static, stationary, tranquil, undisturbed, unmoving

**still** *v* calm, hush, lull, quieten, settle, soothe, subdue

**stilted** *adj* artificial, forced, laboured, stiff, unnatural, wooden; *opp* flowing, fluent, fluid, smooth

**stimulant** *n* anti-depressant, pick-me-up *inf*, restorative, tonic; *opp* depressant, downer *inf*

**stimulate** *v* animate, arouse, encourage, excite, fire up, foment, induce, inflame, instigate, invigorate, motivate, prompt, provoke, stir up, trigger; **opp** discourage

**stimulating** *adj* arousing, challenging, dynamic, exciting, exhilarating, inspiring, invigorating, motivating, stirring, thought-provoking; **opp** dull

**stimulus** *n* encouragement, goad, incentive, inducement, provocation, shot in the arm *inf*, spur

**sting** *v* 1 (of an insect) bite, hurt, nip, prick. 2 (hurt) burn, hurt, prickle, smart

**stink** *v* be high, hum *inf*, pong *inf*, reek, smell bad, smell

**stint** *n* session, share, shift, spell, stretch, time, turn

**stipulate** *v* demand, insist on, lay down, require, specify, state

**stir** *n* commotion, disturbance, excitement, flurry, furore, fuss, to-do, tumult, uproar

**stir** *v* 1 (with a spoon) agitate, blend, churn, mingle, mix. 2 (move) budge, come round, move, show signs of life, stir your stumps *inf*, wake up. 3 (stir feelings) arouse, excite, fire up, inflame, inspire, kindle, provoke, rouse, touch

**stirring** *adj* dramatic, electrifying, emotive, exciting, gripping, heady, invigorating, moving, rousing, spirited, thrilling

**stock** *n* 1 (merchandise) goods, merchandise, range, supply, variety, wares. 2 (reserve) cache, fund, hoard, reserve, reservoir, store, supply. 3 (family) ancestry, blood, descent, extraction, family, line, lineage, parentage, pedigree, race, strain. 4 (farm animals) animals, beasts, farm animals, livestock. 5 (of a gun)

handle, shaft, grip

**stock** *v* carry, deal in, handle, have available, have on sale, keep in stock, keep, sell, supply

**stock** *adj* 1 banal, clichéd, conventional, formulaic, hackneyed, ready, routine, set-piece, set, standard, traditional, trite; **opp** original. 2 average, basic, common, regular, standard; **opp** special

**stocky** *adj* chunky, dumpy, solid, squat, sturdy, thickset; **opp** slender

**stodgy** *adj* 1 (of food) filling, heavy, indigestible, solid, substantial, thick; **opp** light. 2 (of writing) dry, dull, heavy-going, stuffy, tedious, turgid, unimaginative; **opp** lively

**stoical** *adj* accepting, cool, dispassionate, impassive, imperturbable, long-suffering, phlegmatic, resigned, self-disciplined, unemotional

**stolid** *adj* bovine, impassive, slow, unemotional, unimaginative, unresponsive, wooden

**stomach** *n* 1 abdomen, belly, guts *inf*, insides *inf*, paunch, tummy. 2 (desire) appetite, desire, hunger, inclination, liking, taste

**stomach** *v* 1 abide, bear, endure, put up with, stand, take, tolerate. 2 digest, eat, swallow

**stone** *n* 1 boulder, pebble, rock. 2 gem, jewel, precious stone, rock *inf*, sparkler *inf*. 3 gravestone, headstone, memorial stone, monument, obelisk, tombstone. 4 (in fruit) pip, pit, seed

**stony** *adj* 1 gravelly, pebbly, rocky, shingly. 2 adamant, callous, hard, hardhearted, harsh, indifferent, pitiless, severe, unfeeling, unforgiving, unsympathetic. **3** blank, chilly, cold, expressionless, fixed, frigid, frosty, icy

**stoop** v **1** bend, bend down, bow, lean down. **2** be round-shouldered, hunch your shoulders. **3** (stoop to sth) condescend, deign, demean yourself, descend to, humble yourself, lower yourself to, resort to, sink to

**stop** n **1** cessation, conclusion, discontinuation, end, finish, halt, termination. **2** ban, bar, block, check, control, curb, hindrance, impediment. **3** break, pause, rest. **4** break, sojourn, stay, stop-off, stopover, visit. **5** depot, halt, station, terminal, terminus

**stop** v **1** (stop moving) come to a halt, come to a standstill, come to a stop, draw up, halt, pause, pull up, stop moving. **2** (stop sth happening) abolish, axe, ban, bring to an end, call off, crack down on, cut short, discontinue, end, finish, interrupt, nip in the bud, put a stop to, put down, quell, suppress, terminate, wind up. **3** (sth stops happening) be over, cease, come to an end, conclude, finish, pause, peter out. **4** (stop for lunch) break off, cease, desist, knock off *inf*, leave off, pack in *inf*, quit *inf*, refrain from. **5** (prevent) block, check, curb, foil, frustrate, hamper, hinder, hold back, impede, obstruct, prevent, repress, restrain, thwart. **6** (the police stop sb) arrest, capture, catch, detain, hold, intercept, seize. **7** (stop the flow of sth) block, bung up, plug, seal, stem, staunch, stop up. **8** (stop off somewhere) break your journey, lodge, put up, stay, stop off, stop over, visit

**stoppage** n **1** close, closure, halt, pause, interruption, shutdown, standstill, strike, walkout. **2** (money deducted) deduction, charge, subtraction

**store** n **1** cache, fund, hoard, provision, reserve, reservoir, stock, stockpile, supply. **2** depository, repository, storehouse, storeroom, warehouse. **3** chain store, department store, emporium, outlet, retail outlet, shop, supermarket, superstore

**store** v hoard, keep, lay down, lay in, preserve, put away, put by, reserve, save, set aside, squirrel away *inf*, stash *inf*, stockpile, stock up

**storey** n deck, floor, level

**storm** n **1** cyclone, gale, hurricane, tempest. **2** clamour, commotion, furore, outcry, row, rumpus, to-do *inf*, tumult, turmoil

**storm** v **1** attack, charge, make a raid on, rush, take by storm. **2** blow your top *inf*, bluster, complain, fly off the handle *inf*, fume, rage, rant, rave, scold, thunder

**stormy** adj blustery, gusty, rainy, squally, tempestuous, thundery, turbulent, wild, windy

**story** n **1** allegory, anecdote, fable, legend, myth, narrative, parable, romance, tale, yarn. **2** account, chronicle, history, record, report, saga. **3** (a news story) article, dispatch, feature, news item, piece, report. **4** plot, story-line. **5** falsehood, fib *inf*, lie, tall story, untruth, white lie

**stout** adj **1** big, beefy *inf*, burly, corpulent, fat, heavy, overweight, plump, portly, rotund, thickset, tubby; *opp* slender, slim. **2** robust, solid, strong, sturdy,

substantial, thick, tough; **opp** flimsy.
**3** brave, courageous, determined, firm, gallant, resolute, staunch, steadfast, tough, unswerving, valiant;
**opp** cowardly

**straight** adj **1** direct, unbending, unswerving. **2** aligned, erect, even, in line, level, square, symmetrical, true, upright. **3** in order, neat, orderly, organized, put to rights, shipshape, sorted out. **4** consecutive, in a row, one after another, on the trot inf, successive, unbroken, uninterrupted. **5** decent, fair, honest, honourable, right-minded, upright. **6** (straight talking) blunt, candid, direct, forthright, frank, honest, plain-speaking, sincere, straightforward. **7** (of alcoholic drinks) neat, pure, unadulterated, undiluted.
**8** conventional, orthodox

**straightaway** adv at once, immediately, instantly, now, pronto inf, right away, without delay

**straighten** v **1** make straight, neaten, put straight, tidy, unbend, uncurl, untwist. **2** straighten out clear up, disentangle, put in order, put right, resolve, settle, sort out

**straightforward** adj **1** blunt, candid, direct, forthright, frank, honest, plain-speaking, sincere. **2** easy, intelligible, simple, uncomplicated; **opp** complicated, difficult

**strain** n **1** tautness, tension. **2** sprain, wrench. **3** anxiety, burden, demands, pressure, stress, tension, worry.
**4** exertion, exhaustion, overwork.
**5** breed, species, variety

**strain** v **1** distend, draw tight, extend,

pull tight, stretch, tighten. **2** (a muscle) pull, rick, sprain, tear, twist, wrench. **3** (strain sb) be too much for, overtax, overwork, push to the limit, tax, tire, tire out, wear out, weary. **4** (strain to do sth) bend over backwards inf, do your utmost, drive yourself to the limit, exert yourself, give your all, knock yourself out inf, labour, make every effort, strive, struggle. **5** filter, purify, separate, sieve, sift

**strained** adj **1** artificial, awkward, embarrassed, false, forced, laboured, put-on, self-conscious, stiff, uncomfortable, unnatural, wooden. **2** drawn, stressed, tense, troubled, weary. **3** (of relations) hostile, tense, troubled, uneasy, under a strain

**strand** n **1** fibre, filament, thread. **2** lock, tress, wisp. **3** beach, coast, seashore, shore, waterfront

**stranded** adj **1** aground, beached, high-and-dry, stuck. **2** abandoned, forsaken, left high and dry, marooned, stuck, unable to leave

**strange** adj **1** abnormal, bizarre, curious, funny, mystifying, odd, peculiar, perplexing, puzzling, quaint, queer, remarkable, surreal. **2** eerie, grotesque, sinister, uncanny, weird. **3** (strange lands) alien, exotic, foreign, remote, unexplored, unknown. **4** (of a person) crazy, eccentric, funny, odd, unconventional, way out inf, zany

**stranger** n alien, foreigner, new arrival, newcomer, outsider, visitor

**strangle** v **1** asphyxiate, choke, garrotte, throttle. **2** check, curb, gag, repress, restrain, silence, stifle, suppress

**strap** n band, belt, leash, thong, tie

**strap** v bind, buckle, fasten, lash, secure, tie, truss

**stratagem** n dodge inf, manoeuvre, plan, plot, ploy, ruse, scheme, subterfuge, tactic, trick

**strategic** adj 1 calculated, deliberate, planned, politic, tactical. 2 critical, crucial, important, key, vital

**strategy** n approach, design, game plan, master plan, plan, plan of action, policy, programme

**stray** adj 1 abandoned, homeless, lost, wandering. 2 casual, chance, haphazard, isolated, odd, random

**stray** v 1 drift, meander, move aimlessly, ramble, range, roam, wander. 2 deviate, digress, err, get lost, go astray, go wrong, wander

**streak** n 1 band, bar, line, striation, strip, stripe. 2 mark, smear, smudge. 3 (mean streak) dash, element, touch, trace, vein. 4 (winning streak) period, run, series, stretch, time

**streak** v 1 mark with streaks, smear, smudge, striate. 2 dart, dash, flash, fly, gallop, hurtle, rush, speed, sprint, tear, whiz, zoom

**stream** n 1 beck, brook, burn, channel, creek Am, rill, rivulet, tributary, watercourse. 2 flow, gush, jet, rush, surge, torrent

**stream** v 1 cascade, course, flood, flow, gush, pour, run, spill, spout. 2 (of people) flood, pour, surge, swarm. 3 (in the wind) flap, float, flutter, swing

**streamlined** adj 1 aerodynamic, sleek, smooth. 2 efficient, organized, rationalized, slick, well-run

**street** n avenue, crescent, drive, lane, row, road, terrace

**strength** n 1 brawn, might, muscle, power, robustness, stamina, staying power, sturdiness, toughness, vigour. 2 effectiveness, efficacy, force, intensity, potency, power, validity, weight. 3 backbone inf, commitment, courage, determination, firmness, fortitude, grit, resolution, resolve, spirit, tenacity. 4 (strength of feeling) ardour, fervency, force, forcefulness, intensity, vehemence. 5 (the strengths of sth) advantage, asset, forte, strong point

**strengthen** v 1 (give more strength to) bolster, brace, buttress, consolidate, fortify, make stronger, prop up, reinforce, toughen. 2 (make sth more successful) boost, build up, encourage, make stronger, stiffen, support. 3 (sth strengthens) become strong, build up, gain strength, get stronger, grow stronger, heighten, intensify. 4 (strengthen a belief) authenticate, back up, bear out, confirm, corroborate, reinforce, substantiate, support. 5 (strengthen a person) build up, invigorate, make healthy, make strong, nourish, tone up, toughen up

**strenuous** adj 1 arduous, back-breaking, demanding, gruelling, hard, heavy, laborious, taxing, tiring, tough; opp easy, light. 2 active, determined, energetic, forceful, resolute, spirited, tenacious, vigorous, zealous

**stress** n 1 anxiety, pressure, strain, tension, worry. 2 difficulty, distress, trauma. 3 emphasis, importance, significance, weight. 4 accent, beat, emphasis

**stress** v 1 accentuate, dwell on, emphasize, harp on, lay stress on, point up, rub in, spotlight, underline.
2 accentuate, emphasize, place the accent on, put the stress on. 3 (stress sb) overtax, overwork, pressurize, push too far, subject to stress, subject to strain

**stressful** adj anxious, difficult, taxing, tiring, traumatic, worrying

**stretch** n 1 area, expanse, extent, spread, sweep, tract. 2 period, spell, stint, term, time

**stretch** v 1 distend, draw out, elongate, expand, extend, inflate, lengthen, pull out, pull taut, pull tight. 2 be elastic, be stretchy, enlarge, expand, get bigger, get loose. 3 extend, range, spread, unfold. 4 (stretch sb's mind) challenge, overtax, push to the limit, strain, tax. 5 **stretch out** (offer sth to sb) extend, hold out, offer, reach out. 6 **stretch out** (lie) lie down, lie flat, recline, sprawl

**strict** adj 1 authoritarian, firm, harsh, inflexible, rigid, severe, stern, stringent; *opp* lenient, soft. 2 accurate, close, exact, faithful, meticulous, precise, scrupulous, true. 3 absolute, complete, total, utter

**strident** adj discordant, grating, harsh, jarring, raucous, shrill

**strife** n animosity, bickering, conflict, contention, disagreement, discord, dissension, friction, hostility, quarrelling, wrangling

**strike** n 1 industrial action, stoppage, walkout. 2 assault, attack, bombardment

**strike** v 1 beat, clout *inf*, hit, punch, slap, smack, smite, sock *inf*, thump, wallop,

whack. 2 bang into, bump into, collide with, dash against, hit, run into, smash into. 3 (disaster strikes) affect, afflict, hit, reach, smite. 4 (attack sb) assault, attack, fall upon, launch an attack on, set upon, storm. 5 (strike a ball) drive, force, hit, impel, propel, swipe. 6 (strike a bargain) achieve, arrive at, attain, reach. 7 (go on strike) down tools, go on strike, mutiny, take industrial action, walk out. 8 (sth strikes you) appear, come to, dawn on, impress, occur to, seem

**striking** adj 1 arresting, dazzling, extraordinary, impressive, memorable, outstanding, splendid, stunning. 2 conspicuous, evident, noticeable, obvious, prominent, visible

**string** n 1 cord, line, rope, twine, yarn. 2 chain, sequence, series, succession. 3 column, file, line, row, queue, stream

**stringent** adj exacting, inflexible, rigid, rigorous, severe, strict, tight; *opp* loose

**strip** n band, bar, belt, piece, ribbon, shred, slip

**strip** v 1 disrobe, get undressed, strip off, take sb's clothes off, take your clothes off, undress, unclothe. 2 (strip sb of sth) confiscate, deprive, divest, take away. 3 (strip a place) clean out, clear out, empty, gut, loot, plunder, ransack, rob. 4 (strip sth off) pare, peel, peel off, remove, skin, take off

**striped** adj banded, barred, striated, stripy

**strive** v attempt, bend over backwards *inf*, do everything you can, do your utmost, endeavour, give it your best shot *inf*, labour, make a real effort, strain, struggle, toil, try, try your hardest.

**2** compete, contend, fight, grapple with, struggle

**stroke** n **1** blow, clout *inf*, hit, slap, smack, swipe, thump, wallop, whack. **2** achievement, coup, feat. **3** (pen stroke) flourish, line, mark, sweep. **4** (medical) apoplexy, cardiovascular accident, CVA, embolism, seizure, thrombosis

**stroke** v caress, fondle, massage, pet, run your hand over, rub, soothe

**stroll** n airing, amble, ramble, turn, walk

**stroll** v amble, dawdle, go for a stroll, go for a walk, ramble, saunter, stretch your legs, take a walk, wander

**strong** adj **1** athletic, brawny, burly, hardy, mighty, muscular, powerful, resilient, robust, rugged, strapping, sturdy, tough, vigorous. **2** hale and hearty, healthy, sound, vigorous, well. **3** brave, courageous, decisive, dependable, determined, firm, forceful, formidable, resolute, strong-minded, tough. **4** durable, hard-wearing, heavy, impenetrable, indestructible, long-lasting, solid, sturdy, tough, well-made, well-built. **5** (a strong supporter) dedicated, eager, enthusiastic, fervent, fierce, keen, loyal, passionate, staunch, steadfast, vehement, zealous. **6** (a strong argument) cogent, compelling, convincing, persuasive, plausible, powerful, valid, weighty. **7** (strong measures) draconian, drastic, extreme, firm, forceful, harsh, severe, tough. **8** (a strong light) bright, brilliant, dazzling, glaring, gleaming, intense, radiant, vivid. **9** (a strong flavour) full, highly flavoured, pungent, savoury, spicy, sharp, well-flavoured. **10** (a strong solution) concentrated, undiluted. **11** (strong drink) alcoholic, intoxicating

**structure** n **1** arrangement, configuration, conformation, constitution, design, form, formation, make-up, organization. **2** building, construction, edifice, erection, framework, pile

**structure** v arrange, build, construct, design, form, frame, organize, put together, shape

**struggle** n **1** brush, clash, conflict, contest, dust-up *inf*, encounter, fight, scrap, set-to *inf*, skirmish, tussle. **2** battle, difficulty, effort, fight, grind, hassle, labour, problem, trouble. **3** competition, contention, fight, rivalry

**struggle** v **1** bend over backwards *inf*, do everything you can, do your utmost, endeavour, give it your best shot *inf*, labour, make a real effort, strain, toil, try, try your hardest. **2** clash, compete, contend, fight, vie. **3** brawl, fight, grapple, scuffle, wrestle

**strut** v parade, swagger, walk proudly

**stubborn** adj **1** (of a person) adamant, defiant, determined, dogged, headstrong, inflexible, intractable, obdurate, obstinate, pig-headed, rigid, uncompromising, unreasonable, unyielding, wilful. **2** (of a stain) hard to get rid of, long-lasting, persistent, tenacious

**stuck** adj **1** bogged down, fast, fixed, immovable, rooted, unable to move. **2** fastened, fixed, glued. **3** at a loss, baffled, beaten, stumped, stymied *inf*, up against a brick wall *inf*

**student** n 1 pupil, scholar, undergraduate. 2 apprentice, learner, trainee

**studied** adj affected, artificial, calculated, conscious, contrived, deliberate, false, feigned, planned

**studious** adj 1 academic, attentive, bookish, earnest, hard-working, industrious, serious, scholarly, thoughtful. 2 assiduous, attentive, careful, diligent, meticulous, painstaking, thorough

**study** n 1 analysis, examination, inquiry, investigation, review, scrutiny, survey. 2 academic work, education, learning, lessons, reading, research, scholarship, schoolwork, swotting inf. 3 essay, paper, review

**study** v 1 analyse, consider, contemplate, enquire into, investigate, look into, research, survey, think about. 2 examine, inspect, look closely at, peruse, pore over, read carefully, scrutinize. 3 (study a subject) learn, learn about, major in Am, mug up on inf, read, read about, read up on, take a course in, take lessons in. 4 (study hard) burn the midnight oil inf, cram inf, mug up inf, read up on, revise, swot inf

**stuff** n 1 fabric, material, raw material, substance. 2 baggage, belongings, bits and pieces, effects, gear, goods and chattels, impedimenta, junk, kit, luggage, paraphernalia, possessions, things. 3 articles, bits and pieces, items, junk, objects, rubbish, things

**stuff** v 1 cram, crowd, fill, force, jam, load, pack, push, ram, shove, squeeze, stow, wedge. 2 fill, line, pack, pad

**stuffy** adj 1 airless, close, fuggy, muggy,

oppressive, stifling, suffocating, sultry. 2 conventional, dreary, dull, formal, fuddy-duddy inf, priggish, prim, sedate, staid, starchy, stiff, stodgy

**stumble** v 1 fall, flounder, lose your balance, lurch, reel, slip, stagger, trip. 2 blunder, falter, flounder, hesitate, stutter. 3 **stumble on** come across, discover, encounter, find, run across, turn up

**stun** v 1 astonish, astound, devastate, dumbfound, flabbergast inf, knock for six inf, overcome, overwhelm, shock, stagger. 2 daze, knock out, paralyse, stupefy

**stunning** adj 1 beautiful, brilliant, dazzling, fabulous, gorgeous, lovely, marvellous, ravishing, sensational, smashing inf, wonderful. 2 astonishing, extraordinary, impressive, incredible, remarkable, spectacular, splendid, striking, stupendous

**stunt** n act, deed, exploit, feat, trick

**stunted** adj diminutive, dwarf, dwarfish, little, small, tiny, undersized

**stupendous** adj 1 amazing, astounding, breathtaking, marvellous, overwhelming, phenomenal, prodigious, sensational, staggering, superb, wonderful. 2 colossal, enormous, gigantic, huge, massive, vast; opp tiny

**stupid** adj 1 (of a person) brainless, clueless, daft, dense, dim, foolish, gormless inf, gullible, half-witted, moronic, naïve, silly, simple, thick inf, unintelligent; opp clever, intelligent. 2 (of an idea) absurd, asinine, crack-brained, crazy, futile, half-baked, idiotic, ill-advised, inane, irrational, ludicrous, mindless, pointless, rash, senseless, silly, unwise; **opp** good, sensible

**stupidity** n 1 (of a person) brainlessness, foolishness, gullibility, lack of intelligence, naivety; **opp** intelligence. 2 (of an idea) absurdity, folly, foolishness, futility, idiocy, inanity, lunacy, madness, mindlessness, pointlessness, silliness; **opp** cleverness

**stupor** n coma, daze, oblivion, torpor, trance, unconsciousness

**sturdy** adj 1 (of a person) brawny, healthy, husky, muscular, powerful, powerfully built, robust, strapping, strong, tough, vigorous, well-built; **opp** slight. 2 (of an object) durable, solid, substantial, tough, well-made; **opp** delicate, flimsy

**stutter** v falter, hesitate, stammer, stumble

**style** n 1 (sb has style) dash, élan, elegance, flair, panache, polish, smartness, sophistication, stylishness. 2 approach, custom, habit, manner, method, way. 3 (a style of sth) design, kind, pattern, type, variety. 4 (fashion) cut, design, fashion, look, mode, pattern, shape, vogue. 5 (literary style) diction, language, mode of expression, sentence structure, wording. 6 (live in style) affluence, comfort, elegance, luxury

**style** v design, fashion, make, produce, tailor

**stylish** adj chic, classy inf, elegant, fashionable, modish, smart, snazzy inf, sophisticated, trendy; **opp** unfashionable

**subconscious** adj hidden, inner, intuitive, latent, repressed, subliminal; **opp** conscious

**subdue** v 1 conquer, crush, defeat, dominate, humble, master, overcome, overpower, quell, subjugate, tame, trample, vanquish. 2 (a feeling) check, control, curb, hold back, keep under control, repress, restrain, suppress. 3 mellow, moderate, quieten, restrain, tone down

**subdued** adj 1 chastened, crestfallen, dejected, down in the mouth, quiet, sad, serious, solemn; **opp** vivacious. 2 dim, hushed, low-key, muted, quiet, restrained, sober, soft, subtle, toned down, unobtrusive; **opp** bright, loud

**subject** n 1 affair, business, gist, issue, matter, point, question, subject matter, substance, theme, topic. 2 area of study, branch of knowledge, course, discipline, field. 3 (in an experiment) case, client, guinea-pig, participant, patient. 4 (of a country) citizen, national. 5 (of a king) liege, subordinate, underling, vassal

**subject** v expose to, lay open to, put through, submit to

**subjective** adj biased, emotional, individual, personal, prejudiced; **opp** objective

**subjugate** v beat down, break, bring to heel, bring sb to their knees, conquer, crush, defeat, enslave, gain ascendancy over, gain control over, gain mastery over, humble, overcome, quell, subdue, suppress, tame, vanquish

**sublime** adj awe-inspiring, exalted, excellent, exquisite, fine, ideal, lofty, magnificent, majestic, marvellous, out of this world inf, rarefied, refined, subtle, superb, superior, wonderful

**submerge** v 1 (sth submerges) dive,

go down, go under, plunge, sink; *opp* surface. **2 (submerge sth)** dip, dunk *inf*, engulf, immerse, plunge, sink

**submission** *n* **1** acquiescence, capitulation, compliance, surrender. **2 (submissive attitude)** boot-licking *inf*, deference, docility, meekness, obedience, passivity, self-effacement, servility, subjection, submissiveness, subservience, unassertiveness. **3 (a document submitted)** application, bid, paper, presentation, proposal, tender

**submissive** *adj* acquiescent, boot-licking *inf*, deferential, docile, grovelling, humble, masochistic, meek, obedient, passive, self-effacing, servile, subservient, unassertive; *opp* dominant

**submit** *v* **1** bend the knee, bow, capitulate, cede, concede, give in, give way, hoist the white flag, knuckle under, lay down your arms, succumb, surrender, yield; *opp* resist. **2 (submit a piece of work)** give in, hand in, present, put in, put forward, register, send in, surrender, tender

**subordinate** *adj* **1** inferior, lesser, junior, lower, lower-ranking; *opp* superior. **2** dependent, less important, low-priority, secondary, subsidiary

**subordinate** *n* assistant, deputy, inferior, junior, minion, underling; *opp* superior

**subscribe** *v* **1** enlist, enrol, join, register, sign up, take out a subscription. **2 subscribe to** (a magazine) buy, have sth delivered, take. **3 subscribe to** (a belief, principle) agree with, approve of, back, be in favour of, believe in, endorse, favour, hold, hold to, sign up to *inf*, support; *opp* oppose

**subscription** *n* **1** enrolment, membership, registration. **2 (money paid)** charge, contribution, dues, fee, subs *inf*

**subsequent** *adj* **1** consequent, ensuing, following, further, later, resulting, succeeding; *opp* preceding, prior. **2 subsequent to** after, as a result of, following, further to, in the wake of; *opp* prior to

**subside** *v* **1** cave in, collapse, crumble, fall down, settle, sink. **2** abate, calm down, die down, diminish, lessen, let up, quieten down, slacken off, peter out, recede

**subsidence** *n* collapse, crumbling, sinking

**subsidiary** *adj* additional, ancillary, auxiliary, less important, lesser, minor, secondary, subordinate, supplementary; *opp* main

**subsidize** *v* bail out, contribute to, finance, financially support, foot the bill for, fund, invest in, pay for, pick up the tab for *inf*, prop up *inf*, underwrite

**subsidy** *n* aid, contribution, financial support, finance, funding, grant, investment, loan

**substance** *n* chemical, gas, fluid, liquid, material, matter, mineral, ore, stuff *inf*

**substandard** *adj* below par, below standard, inadequate, mediocre, shoddy, unacceptable, unsatisfactory; *opp* satisfactory

**substantial** *adj* ample, considerable, extensive, great, large, important, marked, meaningful, notable, significant, sizable, valuable, weighty; *opp* insubstantial, negligible

**substantiate** v authenticate, back up, bear out, confirm, corroborate, demonstrate, establish, give substance to, illustrate, prove, support, uphold, validate

**substitute** n 1 replacement, stopgap, surrogate. 2 (person) deputy, locum, proxy, relief, reserve, stand-in, stopgap, surrogate, understudy

**substitute** v 1 exchange, replace, swap, switch. 2 **substitute for** cover for, deputize for, fill in for, hold the fort for inf, relieve, replace, stand in for, take over from, take the place of

**subtle** adj 1 complex, delicate, elusive, exquisite, fine, intricate, nice, nuanced, refined, sublime, understated; *opp* overstated. 2 adroit, artful, astute, clever, crafty, cunning, devious, diplomatic, discerning, discreet, discriminating, guileful, ingenious, perceptive, sensitive, shrewd, skilful, tactful, wily

**subtlety** n 1 complexity, delicacy, elusiveness, intricacy, nicety, nuance, refinement. 2 adroitness, artfulness, astuteness, cleverness, cunning, deviousness, diplomacy, discernment, discretion, ingenuity, guile, perceptiveness, sensitivity, shrewdness, skill, tact, tactfulness, wiles

**subtract** v deduct, knock off inf, remove, take away, take off; *opp* add

**suburbs** n dormitory towns, outlying areas, outskirts, periphery, satellite towns, sprawl, stockbroker belt inf, suburbia

**subversive** adj 1 avant-garde, challenging, mischievous, questioning,

radical, revolutionary. 2 corrupting, deceitful, destructive, disruptive, seditious, treasonable, underhand

**subvert** v corrupt, disrupt, pervert, sabotage, turn, undermine, vitiate, weaken

**succeed** v 1 achieve success, arrive inf, be successful, come up trumps inf, do well, flourish, get a result inf, get your name in lights inf, go from strength to strength, hit the jackpot inf, make good inf, make it inf, prosper, score inf, thrive, win, win through; *opp* fail. 2 (in doing or getting sth) accomplish, achieve, attain, be able, be successful, bring off, gain, manage, realize, win; *opp* fail. 3 (of a plan) be successful, come to fruition, do the trick inf, have the desired effect, turn out well, work, work out; *opp* fail. 4 (succeed sb in office) accede, be next in line, come after, come next, follow, follow in sb's footsteps, inherit, replace, take over, take sb's place; *opp* precede

**success** n 1 fame, fortune, fruition, mastery, prosperity, triumph, victory; *opp* failure. 2 accomplishment, achievement, attainment, gain, hit inf, triumph, victory, win; *opp* failure. 3 (a person) celebrity, somebody inf, star, VIP, winner; *opp* failure

**successful** adj 1 all-conquering, booming, flourishing, profitable, prosperous, rich, strong, thriving, top, triumphant, victorious. 2 (a successful attempt) effective, fruitful, lucky, lucrative, profitable, rewarding, victorious, winning; *opp* failed, unsuccessful

**succession** n 1 catalogue, chain,

continuation, course, list, litany, sequence, series. 2 (the succession to the throne) accession, descent, inheritance, line, lineage, order of precedence

**successive** adj consecutive, following, in succession, on the run, on the trot inf, one after the other, running, succeeding, unbroken, uninterrupted

**successor** n heir, inheritor, next in line, replacement; opp predecessor

**succinct** adj brief, clear, compact, concise, condensed, laconic, pithy, short, short and sweet inf, snappy, terse; opp long, wordy

**succulent** adj delicious, juicy, luscious, lush, ripe, sappy, tasty

**succumb** v capitulate, crumble, die, fall, fall victim, give up, give up the ghost inf, go under, submit, yield; opp survive

**sudden** adj 1 (quick) abrupt, hurried, instant, instantaneous, momentary, quick. 2 (unexpected) impromptu, impulsive, spontaneous, unexpected

**sue** v drag sb through the courts, have the law onto sb inf, proceed against, prosecute, serve a writ on, summons, take legal action against, take sb to court

**suffer** v 1 ache, ail, be in distress, be in pain, grieve, hurt inf, struggle, writhe. 2 (suffer from an illness) be a victim of, be affected by, be afflicted by, be cursed with, be troubled with, have. 3 (suffer hardship) bear, endure, experience, feel, go through, live through, put up with, sustain, undergo

**suffering** n affliction, agony, anguish, discomfort, distress, grief, hardship, harm, heartache, hurt, misery, pain, torment, torture

**suffice** v be sufficient, do, satisfy, serve

**sufficient** adj adequate, ample, decent, enough, plenty, satisfactory; opp insufficient

**suffocate** v asphyxiate, choke, smother, stifle, strangle, throttle

**suggest** v 1 advise, move, propose, recommend. 2 hint, imply, indicate, insinuate, intimate. 3 conjure up, connote, evoke, recall

**suggestion** n 1 idea, motion, plan, proposal, proposition. 2 hint, indication, intimation, remark, whisper

**suggestive** adj 1 evocative, indicative, reminiscent. 2 (sexually suggestive) bawdy, blue inf, improper, indelicate, indecent, lewd, ribald, rude, risqué, smutty, titillating

**suit** v 1 (of clothes) become, fit, flatter, go with, match, set off. 2 be suitable for, befit, conform to, please, satisfy

**suitable** adj acceptable, adequate, applicable, apposite, appropriate, apt, befitting, convenient, due, fit, fitting, opportune, pertinent, proper, relevant, right, satisfactory, to your liking; opp unsuitable

**suitor** n admirer, beau, swain

**sulk** v brood, fume, pout, seethe

**sulky** adj aloof, angry, bitter, brooding, broody, churlish, cross, fuming, gloomy, glum, grouchy inf, grumpy inf, in a huff inf, huffy inf, irascible, irritable, moody, morose, peeved inf, peevish, petulant, querulous, resentful, seething, sour, sullen, surly, truculent, uncommunicative, unco-operative, unhappy, unsociable, vexed; opp cheerful

**sullen** *adj* angry, ashen-faced, brooding, broody, cheerless, depressed, gloomy, hostile, moody, morose, obstinate, peeved *inf*, peevish, resentful, seething, sombre, sour, sulky, surly, tight-lipped, uncommunicative, unco-operative, unfriendly, unhappy, unsociable

**sultry** *adj* close, heavy, humid, muggy, oppressive, sticky, stifling, sweltering

**sum** *n* **1** addition, aggregate, tally, total. **2** (sum of money) amount, payment, quantity. **3** addition, calculation, division, multiplication, problem, subtraction

**summarize** *v* abridge, condense, encapsulate, outline, précis, put in a nutshell, round up, sum up

**summary** *n* abridgment, abstract, digest, outline, précis, résumé, round-up, rundown, synopsis

**summit** *n* **1** brow, crest, peak, pinnacle, top. **2** (of sb's career, achievements) acme, apex, consummation, crowning glory, height, peak, pinnacle, top, zenith; *opp* nadir

**summon** *v* beckon, bid, call, call for, call up, convene, convoke, invite, send for

**sumptuous** *adj* de luxe, glorious, gorgeous, grand, lavish, luxurious, magnificent, opulent, rich, splendid, superb; *opp* poor

**sundry** *adj* assorted, different, diverse, miscellaneous, odd, several, some, varied, various

**sunny** *adj* bright, brilliant, clear, cloudless, fine, glorious, radiant, summery, sunlit

**sunrise** *n* crack of dawn, dawn, day-break, first light; *opp* sunset

**sunset** *n* dusk, evening, gloaming *Scot*, sundown, twilight; *opp* sunrise

**superb** *adj* admirable, brilliant, excellent, exquisite, fabulous, fantastic, fine, first-class, first-rate, glorious, gorgeous, magnificent, marvellous, outstanding, splendid, sublime, superior, superlative, unrivalled, wonderful, world-class; *opp* awful, dreadful

**superficial** *adj* **1** (done quickly) casual, cursory, desultory, hasty, hurried, perfunctory, quick, rushed, sketchy, slapdash. **2** (without deep thought) facile, shallow, skin deep, silly, slight, trite, trivial; *opp* profound. **3** (on the surface) apparent, external, surface

**superfluous** *adj* excess, excessive, extra, left over, needless, redundant, remaining, residual, spare, surplus, unnecessary, unwanted

**superhuman** *adj* divine, god-like, heroic, miraculous, mythic, Olympian, supernatural; *opp* subhuman

**superior** *adj* **1** better, choice, classy *inf*, elegant, excellent, exclusive, fine, first-class, first-rate, high-quality, preferable, quality *inf*, refined, select, sophisticated, superlative, top, top-notch *inf*, up-market *inf*; *opp* inferior. **2** (in hierarchy) chief, commanding, higher, more important, outranking, ranking, senior; *opp* subordinate. **3** (of sb's character, attitude) arrogant, boastful, condescending, contemptuous, disdainful, élitist, haughty, high and mighty, lofty, paternalistic, patronizing, pretentious, scornful, self-important, smug, snobbish, snooty *inf*, stuck-up *inf*, supercilious

**superior** *n* boss, chief, commander, commanding officer, gaffer *inf*, guv *sl*, line manager; *opp* subordinate

**superlative** *adj* beyond compare, brilliant, excellent, fine, first-class, first-rate, glorious, great, incomparable, magnificent, marvellous, matchless, outstanding, peerless, perfect, second to none, superb, superior, tiptop *inf*, top-notch *inf*, unrivalled, unsurpassed, wonderful; *opp* awful, dreadful

**supernatural** *adj* eerie, ghostly, inexplicable, magical, miraculous, mysterious, mystic, occult, out of the ordinary, paranormal, phantom, preternatural, psychic, spectral, spiritual, strange but true, uncanny, unearthly, unexplained, unnatural, weird

**superstition** *n* belief, folklore, legend, myth, old wives' tale

**superstitious** *adj* credulous, irrational

**supervise** *v* administer, be in charge of, conduct, control, direct, govern, invigilate, keep an eye on, look after, manage, mind, monitor, organize, oversee, preside over, regulate, run, watch over

**supervision** *n* care, charge, control, direction, governance, invigilation, management, monitoring, organization, regulation, running, surveillance

**supervisor** *n* boss, controller, director, foreman, gaffer *inf*, governor, guardian, head, inspector, instructor, invigilator, leader, manager, manageress, monitor, organizer, overseer, prefect, regulator, teacher, timekeeper, trainer, tutor, warden

**supple** *adj* 1 bendy *inf*, elastic, flexible, malleable, plastic, pliable, pliant, soft, yielding; *opp* rigid. 2 (of a person) agile, double-jointed, graceful, lithe, nimble

**supplement** *n* 1 addendum, addition, add-on, appendix, continuation, extra, postscript. 2 (payment) bonus, excess, surcharge, top-up fee. 3 (to a newspaper) glossy *inf*, insert, magazine, pull-out, special issue

**supplement** *v* add to, augment, back up, bolster, boost, complement, enhance, extend, increase, reinforce, strengthen, support, top up

**supplementary** *adj* accompanying, added, additional, ancillary, auxiliary, backup, complementary, excess, extra, further, subsidiary, supporting, top-up

**supplier** *n* dealer, distributor, exporter, importer, merchant, provider, purveyor, retailer, seller, shopkeeper, source, trader, vendor, wholesaler

**supply** *n* 1 (the supply of goods) donation, delivery, distribution, export, provision, sale. 2 (a supply of sth) amount, cache, consignment, delivery, hoard, quantity, provision, ration, reserve, reservoir, stock, stockpile, store. 3 **supplies** (for soldiers, explorers) equipment, essentials, food, necessities, provisions, rations

**supply** *v* 1 (supply goods) contribute, deal in, deliver, distribute, donate, export, furnish, give, hand over, offer, procure, provide, purvey, retail, sell, trade in. 2 (supply a person) cater to, endow, equip, keep sb in sth

**support** *n* 1 aid, assistance, backing, backup, endorsement, help; *opp* opposition. 2 advocacy, agreement, approval, backing, endorsement, favour; *opp* opposition. **3** (financial) aid, assistance, backing, finance, funding, grant, investment, loan, maintenance, provision, relief, sponsorship, subsidy. **4** (an object giving support) brace, bracket, buttress, column, frame, mounting, pillar, prop, strut, truss

**support** v **1** aid, assist, back, back up, bolster, defend, endorse, get behind, give strength to, help, protect, reinforce, second, speak up for, stick up for; *opp* oppose. **2** advocate, agree with, approve of, back, be in favour of, believe in, endorse, favour, hold to, subscribe to; *opp* oppose. **3** (support a football team) cheer on, follow, get behind, root for, stick up for *inf*, worship *inf*. **4** (evidence that supports a theory) agree with, be consistent with, bear out, bolster, boost, buttress, confirm, corroborate, demonstrate, illustrate, prove, reinforce, strengthen, substantiate, underpin; *opp* contradict. **5** (financially) back, bail out, contribute to, donate to, finance, fund, invest in, keep, maintain, prop up *inf*, provide for, sponsor, subsidize, underwrite. **6** (physically) bear, carry, hold, hold up, keep in place, prop, prop up, shore up, withstand

**supporter** n **1** adherent, advocate, backer, believer, champion, defender, disciple, proponent, seconder, subscriber, voter; *opp* opponent. **2** (of a voluntary organization) benefactor, contributor, donor, friend, helper, member, patron, subscriber, volunteer. **3** (of a football team) cheerleader, devotee, fan, fanatic, follower. **4** (of a financial venture)

backer, benefactor, contributor, donor, funder, investor, patron, sponsor, subscriber, underwriter

**supportive** adj approving, caring, encouraging, helpful, reassuring, understanding, sympathetic

**suppose** v assume, conjecture, expect, guess, infer, presume, speculate, surmise, think

**supposition** n assumption, conjecture, hypothesis, guess, guesswork, presumption, speculation, theory

**suppress** v **1** beat down, bring to heel, conquer, crush, curb, defeat, destroy, eliminate, eradicate, extinguish, oppress, put down, quell, repress, snuff out, subdue, subjugate, terminate, vanquish, wipe out. **2** (suppress information) bury, censor, conceal, cover up, hide, keep back, keep secret, sit on *inf*; *opp* disclose. **3** (suppress feelings) conceal, control, hide, mask, repress, stifle; *opp* show

**suppression** n **1** conquest, defeat, destruction, elimination, eradication, extinction, oppression, repression, subjugation, termination. **2** concealment, secrecy; *opp* disclosure

**supremacy** n ascendancy, command, dominance, domination, dominion, hegemony, leadership, mastery, pre-eminence, sovereignty, superiority

**supreme** adj **1** absolute, best, consummate, excellent, exquisite, extreme, greatest, highest, perfect, pre-eminent, prime, ultimate. **2** most important, overriding, paramount, prime, uppermost

**sure** adj **1** certain, confident, in no doubt, positive; *opp* uncertain. **2** (be sure of getting sth) assured, certain, destined, guaranteed. **3** (a sure method of doing sth) infallible, reliable, trusty, unerring, unfailing

**surface** *n* **1** covering, crust, epidermis *tech*, exterior, face, skin, top, topsoil, upper layer. **2 on the surface** apparently, at first glance, on the face of it, outwardly, superficially, to the casual eye, to the untrained eye

**surface** *v* appear, break the surface, come to the surface, come up, emerge, rise; *opp* submerge

**surfeit** *n* excess, glut, overabundance, profusion, superfluity, surplus

**surge** *v* **1** (of water) gush, pour out, rush, stream. **2** (of the sea) billow, heave, rise, roll, swell, swirl. **3** (of a crowd) drive, force their way, move, press, push, rush. **4** (of emotions) grow, rise up, surge up, well up

**surly** *adj* bad-tempered, churlish, crusty *inf*, gruff, grumpy *inf*, hostile, ill-natured, irascible, irritable, rude, sulky, sullen, uncivil, unfriendly

**surmise** *v* assume, believe, conjecture, deduce, fancy, gather, guess, hypothesize, imagine, infer, judge, postulate, presume, speculate, suppose; *opp* know

**surpass** *v* beat, better, do better than, eclipse, exceed, leave behind, leave standing, outclass, outdo, outshine, outstrip, top

**surplus** *n* balance, excess, extra, glut, oversupply, remainder, residue, superfluity, surfeit; *opp* shortage

**surprise** *n* **1** (a feeling of surprise) amazement, astonishment, incredulity, wonder. **2** (be a complete surprise) bolt from the blue *inf*, bombshell, revelation, shock

**surprise** *v* **1** amaze, astonish, astound, bewilder, dumbfound, faze, flabbergast, nonplus, rock, take sb aback, take sb by surprise, shock, startle, stun, throw *inf*. **2** (surprise a burglar) burst in on, catch out, catch sb in the act, catch sb red-handed, detect, discover, spring upon, startle, take sb by surprise, take sb unawares

**surprised** *adj* amazed, astonished, astounded, bewildered, dumbfounded, fazed, flabbergasted, incredulous, nonplussed, shocked, speechless, staggered, startled, struck dumb, stunned, thrown *inf*, thunderstruck; *opp* unsurprised

**surprising** *adj* amazing, astonishing, astounding, bewildering, extraordinary, incredible, mind-blowing, remarkable, shocking, staggering, startling, unexpected, unusual; *opp* unsurprising

**surrender** *n* **1** capitulation, giving in, giving up, submission. **2** abandoning, giving up, handing over, relinquishment, waiving, yielding

**surrender** *v* **1** capitulate, concede, give in, give up, lay down your arms, submit, throw in the towel *inf*, yield; *opp* fight on. **2** (surrender sth) abandon, give up, hand over, part with, relinquish, waive, yield; *opp* keep

**surreptitious** *adj* clandestine, covert, crafty, furtive, hidden, secret, sly, shifty, sneaky, stealthy, underhand; *opp* open

**surround** *v* encircle, enclose, encompass, envelop, go round, girdle, ring, skirt

**surrounding** *adj* adjacent, adjoining,

bordering, nearby, neighbouring;
*opp* distant

**surroundings** n background,
environment, environs, location, milieu,
setting, vicinity

**surveillance** n inspection, observation,
reconnaissance, scrutiny, vigilance,
watch

**survey** n examination, inquiry,
inspection, overview, scrutiny, study

**survey** v 1 (survey the view)
contemplate, examine, inspect, look at,
observe, scan, scrutinize, view. 2 (survey
a building) appraise, do a survey of, map
out, measure, plan out, plot

**survive** v carry on, continue, endure,
keep going, last, live, live on, persist,
remain, subsist, succeed; *opp* fail

**susceptible** adj 1 (susceptible to sth)
disposed, given, inclined, liable, open,
predisposed, prone, subject, vulnerable;
*opp* resistant. 2 (susceptible teenagers)
gullible, impressionable, innocent,
sensitive, suggestible, vulnerable

**suspect** adj doubtful, dubious, iffy *inf*,
questionable, shady *inf*, suspicious;
*opp* trustworthy

**suspect** v 1 believe, conjecture, consider,
fancy, feel, guess, have a feeling, have a
hunch, imagine, suppose, surmise, think;
*opp* know. 2 (suspect sb) be sceptical
about, distrust, doubt, have doubts
about, have suspicions about, mistrust;
*opp* trust

**suspend** v 1 (suspend sth from the
ceiling) attach, dangle, hang, swing.
2 (suspend proceedings) adjourn, cut
short, defer, delay, discontinue, freeze,
interrupt, postpone, put off, put on ice,

put on the back burner, shelve;
*opp* continue

**suspense** n anticipation, anxiety,
apprehension, drama, expectancy,
expectation, not knowing, tension,
uncertainty, waiting

**suspicion** n 1 caution, distrust, doubt,
dubiousness, misgiving, mistrust,
wariness; *opp* trust. 2 (have a suspicion)
belief, feeling, funny feeling, hunch,
idea, impression, notion, supposition

**suspicious** adj 1 (a suspicious character)
dodgy *inf*, dubious, fishy *inf*, funny, shady
*inf*, shifty, suspect, unreliable,
untrustworthy; *opp* trustworthy.
2 (a suspicious husband) doubtful,
jealous, unbelieving; *opp* trusting

**sustain** v 1 continue, keep going, keep
up, maintain, prolong; *opp* lose.
2 (sustain the weight of sth) bear,
buttress, carry, keep up, prop, reinforce,
shore up, support

**sustained** adj constant, continuous, long-
term, nonstop, perpetual, prolonged,
steady; *opp* short-term

**swallow** v down *inf*, gulp, guzzle, wash
down

**swamp** n bog, fen, marsh, mire, mud,
quagmire

**swamp** v drench, flood, immerse,
submerge

**swampy** adj boggy, marshy, muddy, soggy,
spongy, waterlogged; *opp* dry

**swap, swop** v barter, exchange,
interchange, switch, trade

**swarm** n army, bevy, crowd, drove, flock,
herd, horde, mass, multitude, pack,
stream, throng

**swarm** v 1 (people swarm) cluster,

congregate, crowd, flock, gather, mass, stream, throng; **opp** trickle. 2 (swarming with people) be crowded with, be full of, be overrun with, bristle, crawl, seethe, teem

**sway** n authority, command, control, government, jurisdiction, power, rule, sovereignty

**sway** v 1 bend, incline, lean, lurch, oscillate, rock, swing, wave. 2 (sway sb's decision) affect, bias, change sb's mind, control, convert, govern, guide, induce, influence, persuade

**swear** v 1 blaspheme, curse, f and blind, use bad language. 2 (swear to do sth) avow, declare, give your word, promise, vouchsafe, vow

**swearing** n bad language, blasphemy, cursing, foul language

**swearword** n curse, expletive, four letter word inf, obscenity

**sweat** n (in a sweat) flap inf, fluster, fuss, lather inf, panic, state inf

**sweat** v 1 break out in a sweat, drip with sweat, glow, have a hot flush, perspire. 2 (sweat over sth) agonize, fret, lose sleep, panic, torture yourself, worry

**sweaty** adj clammy, damp, moist, perspiring, sticky, sweating; **opp** dry

**sweep** v 1 (sweep the floor) brush, clean, clear. 2 (sweep past) flounce, fly, glance, glide, sail, stride, tear, zoom

**sweeping** adj 1 (sweeping changes) across-the-board, all-embracing, all-inclusive, blanket, broad, comprehensive, extensive, far-ranging, far-reaching, global, wide, wide-ranging, universal; **opp** localized. 2 (a sweeping statement) exaggerated, indiscriminate,

overstated, superficial, unqualified, wholesale; **opp** considered

**sweet** adj 1 (sweet food) sugared, sugary, sweetened; **opp** savoury. 2 (a sweet child) agreeable, amiable, appealing, attractive, charming, cute, endearing, engaging, good-natured, likable, lovable, winning; **opp** disagreeable. 3 (a sweet smell) aromatic, balmy, fragrant, fresh, perfumed, pure; **opp** acrid

**sweeten** v add sugar to, honey, make sweeter, sugar

**sweetheart** n admirer, boyfriend, girlfriend, love, lover, suitor

**swell** n escalation, increase, rise, surge; **opp** reduction

**swell** v 1 balloon, billow, bloat, blow up, bulge, distend, enlarge, expand, extend, inflate; **opp** shrink. 2 (swell the population) add to, augment, boost, escalate, increase, raise; **opp** reduce

**swelling** n bulge, bump, enlargement, inflammation, lump, protrusion, protuberance, tumour

**swerve** v bend, deflect, deviate, diverge, career, dodge, sheer, shift, skew, swing, turn, veer, wander

**swift** adj brisk, fast, flying, hasty, hurried, nippy inf, prompt, quick, rapid, speedy; **opp** slow

**swim-suit** n bathing costume, swimming costume, swimwear

**swindle** v cheat, con inf, deceive, defraud, diddle inf, do inf, double-cross, dupe, fleece, pull a fast one, rip sb off inf, take sb for a ride, trick

**swindler** n cheat, con artist inf, con man inf, fraud, fraudster, shark inf

**swing** n change, fluctuation, shift, sway,

turnaround, variation

**swing** v 1 (swing from the ceiling) dangle, hang, suspend. 2 (swing from side to side) oscillate, rock, sway, veer, wave

**swirl** v churn, circulate, revolve, spin, turn, twirl, twist, whirl

**switch** n button, control, dial, knob, power-point

**switch** v 1 (switch brands) change, exchange, replace, substitute, swap, trade. 2 (switch direction) change, deflect, deviate, divert, redirect, reverse, turn

**swivel** v gyrate, pirouette, pivot, revolve, rotate, spin, swing, turn, twirl

**swollen** adj bloated, blown-up, bulging, distended, enlarged, inflamed, puffed-up, puffy

**swoop** v descend, dive, drop down, lunge, plunge, sweep down; **opp** rise

**syllabus** n course, curriculum, programme

**symbol** n badge, crest, emblem, insignia, logo, sign, token

**symbolic** adj 1 meaningful, significant; **opp** meaningless. 2 (symbolic of sth) allegorical, figurative, metaphorical, representative

**symbolize** v denote, indicate, mean, represent, signify, stand for, suggest

**symmetrical** adj balanced, even, proportional, regular; **opp** asymmetrical

**sympathetic** adj caring, compassionate, concerned, feeling, friendly, humane, interested, kind, responsive, supportive, understanding, warm; **opp** unsympathetic

**sympathize** v 1 agree, be on the same wavelength, empathize, identify, see eye to eye, understand. 2 be sorry for, commiserate, feel pity

**sympathizer** n advocate, ally, backer, partisan, supporter; **opp** opponent

**sympathy** n 1 caring, compassion, concern, friendliness, humanity, kindness, responsiveness, support, understanding; **opp** hostility. 2 (sympathy with sb's point of view) agreement, empathy, understanding; **opp** opposition

**symptom** n characteristic, evidence, indication, manifestation, sign, signal, warning, warning-sign

**synthesis** n amalgamation, blend, combination, compound, fusion, union

**synthetic** adj artificial, fake, man-made, manufactured, mock, simulated; **opp** natural

**system** n 1 (a filing system) arrangement, classification, network, set-up inf, structure. 2 (a system for dealing with complaints) approach, means, method, procedure, process, routine, scheme, technique, way

**systematic** adj efficient, logical, methodical, orderly, organized, precise, structured, well-organized; **opp** haphazard, random

**table** *n* 1 bench, breakfast bar, counter, desk, trestle, worktop.
2 (a mathematical table) chart, diagram, figure, graph, index, inventory, list, plan, register, roll, schedule

**table** *v* enter, move, propose, put forward, submit

**tablet** *n* capsule, drug, medication, medicine, pill

**taboo** *n* anathema, ban, prohibition, veto

**tacit** *adj* implicit, implied, inferred, taken for granted, understood, unexpressed, unspoken, unstated, unvoiced;
**opp** expressed

**taciturn** *adj* antisocial, quiet, reserved, reticent, uncommunicative, unforthcoming, unsociable, withdrawn;
**opp** chatty

**tack** *n* 1 drawing pin, nail, pin, staple.
2 (change tack) approach, course, direction, line, method, plan, policy, procedure, strategy, tactic, way

**tack** *v* 1 affix, attach, fasten, fix, nail, pin,
staple. 2 (tack cloth) sew, stitch

**tackle** *n* 1 (fishing tackle) apparatus, equipment, gear *inf*, kit, stuff *inf*, things *inf*, tools. 2 (in sport) block, challenge, grapple, interception

**tackle** *v* 1 (tackle a job) attempt, begin, have a go at *inf*, have a stab at *inf*, set about, take on, undertake. 2 (tackle a problem) confront, cope with, deal with, face up to, grapple with, handle, sort out. 3 (in sport) block, challenge, grapple with, intercept, take on

**tact** *n* care, delicacy, diplomacy, discretion, judgement, perception, savoir-faire, sensitivity, tactfulness;
**opp** tactlessness

**tactful** *adj* careful, delicate, diplomatic, discreet, perceptive, sensitive;
**opp** tactless

**tactic** *n* approach, course, line, manoeuvre, means, method, policy, procedure, scheme, strategy, tack, way

**tactical** *adj* clever, cunning, planned, shrewd, skilful, smart, strategic

**tactless** *adj* blundering, blunt, bungling, careless, clumsy, gauche, inconsiderate, indiscreet, insensitive, thoughtless, undiplomatic, unfeeling, unsubtle;
**opp** tactful

**tail** *n* back, brush, end, extremity, rear, train

**taint** *n* blemish, blot, defect, fault, flaw, smear, spot, stain, stigma

**taint** *v* adulterate, contaminate, corrupt, dirty, foul, infect, pollute, soil, spoil;
**opp** enrich

**take** *v* 1 (take sth from sb) get, grab, grasp, grip, obtain, receive, seize, snatch;
**opp** give. 2 (take sth to sb) carry, cart,

convey, ferry, transport. **3** (take sb to the door) accompany, escort, guide, lead, usher. **4** (buy or rent) buy, hire, lease, pay for, pick, purchase, rent, reserve, select. **5** (I can't take it any more) abide, bear, endure, put up with, stand, stomach, suffer, tolerate, undergo. **6** (take a pill) consume, drink, eat, swallow. **7** (take 3 from 10) deduct, subtract, take away; *opp* add. **8 take down** make a note of, minute, note, record, set down, transcribe, write. **9 take off** (run away) abscond, depart, disappear, go, go off *inf*, leave, run away, split *inf*. **10 take off** (clothing) remove, slip off, throw off; *opp* put on. **11 take on** employ, engage, enlist, enrol, hire, sign; *opp* dismiss. **12 take over** assume control, become leader, come to power, seize control, take command, usurp. **13 take up** adopt, become involved in, embark on, get into, start

**takeoff** *n* ascent, departure, launch, liftoff; *opp* landing

**take-over** *n* amalgamation, merger; *opp* sell-off

**takings** *n* earnings, income, profit, receipts, returns, revenue, yield; *opp* outgoings

**tale** *n* **1** fable, legend, myth, story, urban legend. **2** (a tale about sb's exploits) account, anecdote, report, story. **3** (tell tales) fabrication, falsehood, fib, lie, story *inf*, untruth, yarn *inf*; *opp* truth

**talent** *n* ability, aptitude, brilliance, capacity, expertise, flair, genius, gift, prowess

**talented** *adj* able, accomplished, brilliant, gifted, skilful

**talk** *n* **1** chat, chin-wag *inf*, chit-chat *inf*, conversation, gossip, natter. **2** conference, consultation, dialogue, discussion, negotiation, parley. **3** (give a talk) address, lecture, oration, presentation, sermon, speech

**talk** *v* **1** babble, chat, chatter, converse, gossip, have a conversation, natter, say, speak, tell, utter, verbalize. **2** confer, discuss, hold negotiations, negotiate, parley. **3** blab *inf*, confess, crack, inform, spill the beans *inf*, squeal *inf*, tell all

**talkative** *adj* chatty, communicative, effusive, expansive, garrulous, gossipy, long-winded, loquacious, open, verbose, vocal, wordy; *opp* taciturn

**tall** *adj* big, gangling, giant, high, lanky, lofty, soaring, towering

**tally** *n* addition, count, reckoning, record, score, sum, total

**tally** *v* **1** accord, agree, coincide, concur, conform, correspond, fit, harmonize, match up, square. **2** add up, calculate, compute, count, reckon, total, work out

**tame** *adj* **1** amenable, broken, disciplined, docile, domesticated, gentle, house-trained, manageable, obedient, submissive, tamed, tractable. **2** bland, boring, dull, feeble, flat, insipid, safe, uncontroversial, vapid, weak, wishy-washy *inf*

**tame** *v* break in, discipline, domesticate, house-train, master, pacify, subdue, train

**tamper** *v* adjust, alter, fiddle, interfere, meddle, mess, tinker

**tangible** *adj* actual, concrete, corporeal, definite, material, palpable, perceptible, physical, positive, real, solid, substantial, unmistakable

**tangle** n 1 coil, jumble, knot, mass, mat, mesh, mess, scramble, snarl, twist, web. 2 confusion, imbroglio, jumble, labyrinth, maze, mess, mix-up

**tangle** v catch, enmesh, ensnare, entangle, knot, scramble, snarl, trap, twist

**tangled** adj 1 caught, enmeshed, ensnared, entangled, jumbled, knotted, matted, scrambled, snarled, twisted. 2 complex, complicated, confused, jumbled, knotty, messy, mixed up, muddled, scrambled; *opp* simple

**tank** n 1 cistern, container, receptacle, reservoir, vat, vessel. 2 armoured car, combat vehicle

**tanned** adj bronzed, brown, sunburnt, suntanned, weather-beaten

**tantalize** v entice, fascinate, frustrate, keep sb on tenterhooks, lead sb on, make sb's mouth water, provoke, tease, tempt, titillate, torment

**tantrum** n display of temper, fit, outburst, paddy *inf*, storm

**tap** n 1 blow, knock, pat, rap, touch. 2 faucet *Am*, spigot, spout, stopcock, valve

**tap** v 1 drum, hit, knock, pat, rap, strike, touch. 2 bleed, drain, draw off, siphon off. 3 draw on, exploit, extract, make use of, milk, mine, use, utilize

**tape** n 1 band, binding, ribbon, strip. 2 audiotape, cassette, recording, tape-recording, video, videotape

**tape** v 1 bind, fasten, fix, seal, secure, stick. 2 record, tape-record, video, video-record

**target** n 1 aim, ambition, end, goal, hope, intention, mark, object, objective,

purpose. 2 (target of abuse, jokes) butt, object, prey, quarry, scapegoat, victim

**tariff** n 1 charges, menu, price list, rate, schedule. 2 duty, excise, levy, tax, toll

**tarnish** v 1 blacken, blemish, corrode, dirty, discolour, rust, soil, spoil, stain, taint. 2 (tarnish sb's reputation) blacken, blemish, blot, disgrace, dishonour, mar, ruin, spoil, stain, sully, taint

**tart** adj 1 acid, astringent, citrus, piquant, sharp, sour, tangy. 2 (tart remark) acid, astringent, biting, caustic, cutting, mordant, scathing, sharp, stinging, trenchant

**task** n activity, assignment, charge, chore, duty, enterprise, errand, exercise, job, mission, undertaking, work

**taste** n 1 flavour, relish, savour, smack, tang. 2 (have a taste of sth) bit, bite, dash, drop, morsel, mouthful, nibble, nip, sample, sip, swallow, touch. 3 (have a taste for sth) appetite, bent, desire, fondness, inclination, leaning, liking, love, partiality, penchant, predilection, preference, relish. 4 (good taste) class *inf*, cultivation, culture, discernment, discrimination, elegance, judgment, grace, polish, refinement, style, stylishness

**taste** v bite, nibble, sample, savour, sip, swallow, test, try

**tasteful** adj artistic, classy *inf*, cultivated, cultured, decorous, discerning, discriminating, elegant, graceful, in good taste, polished, refined, restrained, subtle, stylish, understated, well-judged; *opp* tasteless

**tasteless** adj 1 cheap, crude, flashy *inf*,

garish, gaudy, graceless, in bad taste, indecorous, inelegant, in poor taste, kitsch, loud, naff *sl*, tacky *inf*, tawdry, uncouth, undiscriminating, vulgar; *opp* tasteful. 2 (of food) bland, dull, flavourless, insipid, mild, uninteresting, vapid, watery; *opp* tasty

**tasty** *adj* appetizing, delectable, delicious, flavourful, flavoursome, luscious, mouth-watering, palatable, piquant, savoury, scrumptious *inf*, yummy *inf*; *opp* tasteless

**tattered** *adj* battered, frayed, ragged, raggedy, ripped, shredded, tatty, torn, worn out

**tatty** *adj* battered, frayed, old, ragged, raggedy, scruffy *inf*, shabby, shoddy, tattered, threadbare, worn

**taunt** *n* barb, catcall, dig, gibe, insult, jeer, sneer

**taunt** *v* deride, gibe, goad, insult, jeer, laugh at, make fun of, mock, poke fun at, revile, ridicule, sneer, tease, torment

**taut** *adj* firm, flexed, rigid, strained, stretched, tense, tight; *opp* slack

**tawdry** *adj* cheap, common, flashy *inf*, garish, gaudy, showy, tacky *inf*, tasteless, tatty, vulgar

**tax** *n* charge, due, duty, excise, imposition, levy, tariff, toll

**tax** *v* 1 assess, charge, exact, impose, levy, put duty on. 2 exhaust, make demands on, pressure, pressurize, push, strain, stretch, try, wear out

**teach** *v* advise, coach, direct, drill, educate, enlighten, give lessons, guide, impart, inculcate, instil, instruct, lecture, school, show, train, tutor

**teacher** *n* adviser, coach, don, educator, governess, guide, guru, instructor,

lecturer, master, mentor, mistress, pedagogue, professor, school-master, school-mistress, school-teacher, trainer, tutor

**team** *n* band, bunch, company, crew, gang, group, line-up, party, set, side, squad, troupe

**team up** *v* band together, co-operate, form an alliance, join, get together, unite, work together

**tear** *n* gash, hole, laceration, opening, rent, rip, rupture, scratch, slit, split

**tear** *v* claw, gash, gore, lacerate, mangle, pull apart, rend, rip, rupture, scratch, shred, split, sunder

**tearful** *adj* blubbering *inf*, crying, emotional, in tears, lachrymose, snivelling, sobbing, weeping, weepy *inf*

**tease** *v* bait, goad, laugh at, make fun of, mock, needle *inf*, pester, plague, poke fun at, provoke, pull sb's leg *inf*, rib *inf*, tantalize, taunt, torment, wind sb up *inf*

**technical** *adj* complicated, esoteric, expert, scientific, skilled, specialist, specialized, technological

**technique** *n* 1 course, manner, means, method, mode, procedure, system, way. 2 ability, art, artistry, craft, facility, knack, proficiency, skill, touch, workmanship

**technological** *adj* advanced, automated, computerized, electronic, high-tech *inf*, scientific

**tedious** *adj* banal, boring, drab, dreary, dull, endless, humdrum *inf*, laborious, long-drawn-out, long-winded, mind-numbing, monotonous, repetitive, prosaic, tiresome, uninteresting, vapid, wearisome; *opp* interesting

**tedium** *n* banality, boredom, drabness, dreariness, dullness, laboriousness, monotony, repetitiousness, routine, tediousness; *opp* interest

**teem with** *v* alive with, be full of, be infested with, be overrun with, brim with, crawl with, overflow with, seethe with, swarm with

**teenager** *n* adolescent, boy, girl, juvenile, minor, pubescent, young person, youth

**teetotaller** *n* abstainer, non-drinker

**telegram** *n* cable, telex, wire

**telephone** *n* blower *inf*, hand-set, mobile, phone

**telephone** *v* call, dial, get on the blower to *inf*, give sb a bell *inf*, give sb a buzz *inf*, give sb a call, give sb a ring, phone, ring

**televise** *v* broadcast, film, relay, send out, show, transmit

**television** *n* box *inf*, goggle-box *inf*, set, small screen, telly *inf*, tube *inf*, TV

**tell** *v* 1 (give information) advise, announce, communicate, describe, disclose, divulge, explain, express, impart, inform, let sb know, make known, mention, narrate, notify, recite, recount, relate, reveal, say, speak, state, utter. 2 (tell sb to do sth) bid, call upon, command, direct, enjoin, instruct, order, require. 3 (make known sth secret) blab *inf*, blow the whistle, give the game away, grass *sl*, inform, open your mouth *inf*, rat *inf*, snitch *inf*, spill the beans *inf*, squeal *sl*, talk, tell tales. 4 (tell what sth is) appreciate, calculate, comprehend, deduce, differentiate, discern, distinguish, identify, make out, notice, perceive, recognize, see

**telling** *adj* considerable, decisive,

effective, important, influential, marked, meaningful, potent, powerful, revealing, significant, sizeable, solid, striking, substantial, weighty

**temper** *n* 1 attitude, character, disposition, humour, make-up, mind, mood, nature, personality, temperament. 2 anger, annoyance, fury, hot-headedness, ill-humour, irascibility, irritability, paddy *inf*, passion, peevishness, petulance, rage, tantrum, wrath. 3 **lose your temper** blow up, blow your top *inf*, explode, flip *inf*, fly into a rage, fly off the handle *inf*, get angry, get mad *inf*, go crazy *inf*, go mad *inf*, go nuts *inf*, have a fit *inf*, hit the roof *inf*, lose your composure, lose your cool *inf*, see red

**temper** *v* allay, assuage, lessen, mitigate, moderate, modify, modulate, reduce, soften, soothe, tone down

**temperament** *n* attitude, character, constitution, disposition, humour, make-up, mind, mood, nature, personality, temper

**temperamental** *adj* capricious, changeable, emotional, erratic, excitable, fickle, highly strung, inconsistent, moody, sensitive, touchy, unpredictable, unreliable, volatile

**temperance** *n* abstemiousness, abstinence, continence, moderation, self-control, self-discipline, self-restraint, sobriety, teetotalism

**temperate** *adj* 1 (of weather) agreeable, balmy, clement, fair, mild, moderate, pleasant. 2 (of a person) abstemious, calm, continent, controlled, disciplined, moderate, reasonable, restrained, sensible, sober; *opp* wild

**tempest** *n* cyclone, gale, hurricane, storm, tornado, typhoon, whirlwind

**tempestuous** *adj* fierce, furious, heated, intense, passionate, stormy, tumultuous, turbulent, uncontrolled, violent, wild

**temple** *n* church, house of god, place of worship, sanctuary, shrine

**tempo** *n* beat, pace, rate, rhythm, pulse, speed, timing

**temporary** *adj* brief, ephemeral, fleeting, impermanent, interim, momentary, passing, provisional, short-lived, short-term, transient, transitory; *opp* permanent

**tempt** *v* allure, attract, bait, bribe, cajole, coax, dare, decoy, draw, entice, inveigle, invite, lure, persuade, provoke, seduce, tantalize, woo

**temptation** *n* allure, appeal, attraction, bait, bribe, decoy, draw, enticement, inducement, lure, provocation, pull, seduction, snare

**tempting** *adj* alluring, appetizing, attractive, enticing, inviting, mouth-watering, persuasive, seductive, tantalizing

**tenacious** *adj* adamant, determined, dogged, firm, fixed, immovable, inflexible, obstinate, persistent, resolute, set, single-minded, staunch, steadfast, strong, stubborn, unshakable, unswerving, unwavering, unyielding

**tenant** *n* inhabitant, leaseholder, lodger, occupant, occupier, resident

**tend** *v* **1** be disposed, be inclined, be liable, be prone, gravitate, have a tendency, incline, lean. **2** (look after) attend, care for, cultivate, guard, keep, look after, maintain, manage, minister to, nurse, protect, take care of, wait on, watch over

**tendency** *n* bent, bias, disposition, drift, inclination, leaning, partiality, penchant, predilection, predisposition, preference, proclivity, proneness, propensity, susceptibility, trend

**tender** *adj* **1** dainty, delicate, fragile, frail, sensitive, soft, vulnerable, weak; *opp* tough. **2** affectionate, amorous, caring, compassionate, concerned, emotional, fond, gentle, kind, loving, sentimental, solicitous, soft-hearted, sympathetic, tender-hearted, warm. **3** aching, bruised, inflamed, irritated, painful, raw, sensitive, smarting, sore, throbbing

**tenderness** *n* affection, caring, compassion, concern, fondness, gentleness, kindness, love, sentiment, solicitude, sympathy, warmth

**tense** *adj* **1** anxious, apprehensive, edgy, highly strung, jittery, jumpy, keyed-up *inf*, nervous, on edge, on tenterhooks, strained, stressed, twitchy *inf*, under pressure, uptight *inf*, worked up *inf*, worried; *opp* relaxed. **2** (a tense situation) exciting, fraught, nail-biting *inf*, nerve-racking, strained, stressful, worrying. **3** (keep a rope tense) firm, flexed, rigid, strained, stretched, taut, tight; *opp* slack

**tension** *n* **1** anxiety, apprehension, excitement, nervousness, pressure, stress, suspense, unease, worry. **2** (in a rope) firmness, pull, rigidity, strain, tautness, tightness

**tentative** *adj* cautious, diffident, doubtful, experimental, exploratory, faltering, hesitant, indecisive, indefinite, nervous, preliminary, provisional, shy, speculative, timid, uncertain, uncommitted, unsure, wavering; **opp** definite

**tenuous** adj doubtful, dubious, flimsy, fragile, insubstantial, shaky, sketchy, slender, slight, slim, uncertain; **opp** clear

**tepid** adj 1 hand-hot, lukewarm, warmish. 2 apathetic, cool, half-hearted, indifferent, lukewarm, unenthusiastic

**term** n 1 appellation, denomination, designation, epithet, expression, name, phrase, title, word. 2 duration, period, season, space, span, spell, time. 3 (in a school, college) course, semester, session

**term** v call, denominate, designate, dub, entitle, express, label, name, style, tag

**terminal** adj deadly, fatal, final, incurable, killing, lethal, mortal

**terminal** n 1 airport, depot, port, station, terminus. 2 keyboard, monitor, VDU inf, workstation

**terminate** v bring to an end, cease, conclude, cut off, end, discontinue, finish, interrupt, put an end to, put a stop to, stop, wind up; **opp** start

**terminology** n argot, cant, expressions, jargon, language, lexicon, nomenclature, phraseology, vocabulary, words

**terms** n 1 conditions, particulars, provisions, provisos, qualifications, specifications, stipulations. 2 charges, fee, payments, price, rates, schedule, tariff

**terrain** n country, ground, land, landscape, territory, topography, turf

**terrible** adj 1 abysmal, appalling, awful, bad, dire, dreadful, no good, poor,

rotten, rubbish inf, useless; **opp** brilliant, wonderful. 2 appalling, awful, dreadful, fearsome, frightful, ghastly, gruesome, harrowing, hateful, horrible, horrific, horrendous, horrifying, hideous, loathsome, nasty, nauseating, outrageous, revolting, shocking, unbearable, unspeakable, unthinkable, vile

**terrific** adj 1 amazing, brilliant, excellent, fabulous, fantastic, fine, good, great, marvellous, outstanding, superb, wonderful; **opp** awful, dreadful. 2 (a terrific noise) considerable, enormous, extraordinary, extreme, great, huge, tremendous, vast

**terrify** v alarm, frighten, horrify, make sb's blood run cold inf, make sb's hair stand on end inf, paralyze, petrify, scare sb to death, shock, terrorize

**terrifying** adj alarming, appalling, fearsome, frightening, frightful, horrendous, horrific, horrifying, petrifying

**territory** n area, country, county, district, enclave, land, neighbourhood, patch, precinct, province, region, space, state, terrain, zone

**terror** n alarm, dread, fear, fright, horror, panic, shock, trepidation

**terrorize** v browbeat, bully, coerce, frighten, intimidate, menace, oppress, persecute, scare, threaten, torment

**terse** adj 1 (a terse account) brief, concise, incisive, pithy, short, succinct, to the point; **opp** lengthy. 2 (a terse reply) abrupt, blunt, brusque, curt, short

**test** n analysis, appraisal, assessment, check, check-up inf, evaluation, exam, examination, investigation, questionnaire, quiz, research, trial

**test** v analyse, appraise, assess, check, evaluate, experiment, investigate, prove, put to the test, question, research, study, try, try out, verify

**testament** n attestation, demonstration, evidence, proof, testimony, witness

**testify** v 1 (testify in a court) be a witness, give evidence, state on oath. 2 (testify that you have done sth) affirm, assert, attest, avow, certify, declare, swear

**testimonial** n certificate, character reference, commendation, endorsement, recommendation, reference, tribute

**testimony** n affidavit, attestation, avowal, corroboration, evidence, protestation, statement, submission, sworn statement

**text** n 1 book, set book, textbook, work. 2 chapter, paragraph, passage, verse. 3 story, words, writing

**texture** n appearance, composition, consistency, feel, grain, quality, structure, surface, touch, weave

**thank** v offer thanks, say thank you, show appreciation, show gratitude

**thankful** adj appreciative, glad, grateful, happy, indebted, obliged, pleased, relieved

**thankless** adj (a thankless task) futile, unappreciated, unrecognized, unrewarded, unrewarding, useless, vain

**thanks** n acknowledgement, appreciation, credit, gratefulness, gratitude, recognition

**thaw** v defrost, de-ice, heat up, liquefy, melt, soften, warm, warm up

**theatre** n 1 acting, drama, dramatic art, show business, the stage. 2 auditorium, hall, playhouse

**theatrical** adj affected, artificial, dramatic, exaggerated, melodramatic, overdone, over the top inf, showy, stagy, unnatural

**theft** n burglary, embezzlement, fraud, larceny, pilfering, robbery, shoplifting, stealing, swindling, thieving

**theme** n argument, idea, matter, subject, text, topic

**theoretical** adj abstract, academic, hypothetical, notional, not practical, speculative, unproven, untested

**theorize** v conjecture, form a theory, guess, hypothesize, speculate, suppose

**theory** n argument, assumption, belief, conjecture, explanation, guess, hypothesis, notion, speculation, view

**therapeutic** adj beneficial, curing, good, healing, health-giving, helpful, medicinal, remedial

**therapist** n analyst, counsellor, healer

**therapy** n cure, healing, remedy, treatment

**thesis** n 1 argument, assertion, contention, hypothesis, idea, opinion, proposition, theory, view. 2 (write a thesis) composition, dissertation, essay, paper, treatise

**thick** adj 1 broad, bulky, chunky, deep, fat, large, solid, stout, wide; opp thin. 2 (a thick mixture) clotted, coagulated, concentrated, firm, dense, solid, sticky, stiff, viscous; opp thin. 3 (thick fog) dense, heavy, impenetrable, murky. 4 (a thick coat) heavy, padded, quilted, warm; opp thin. 5 (thick hair)

abundant, bushy, luxuriant, plentiful.
**6** (thick forest) close-packed, dense,
impassable, impenetrable. **7** (not clever)
brainless, dim *inf*, dozy *inf*, dull, obtuse,
slow, stupid, unintelligent; *opp* bright

**thicken** v cake, clot, coagulate,
condense, congeal, firm up, gel, set,
solidify

**thief** n bandit, burglar, cheat, embezzler,
highwayman, housebreaker, looter,
mugger, pickpocket, pirate, robber,
shoplifter, stealer, swindler

**thieving** adj dishonest, light-fingered

**thin** adj **1** (a thin line) fine, narrow.
**2** (thin material) delicate, diaphanous,
filmy, fine, flimsy, gauzy, gossamer, see-
through, sheer; *opp* thick. **3** (of a
person) bony, gaunt, lanky, lean, scraggy,
skinny, slender, slight, slim, svelte,
underweight, wiry; *opp* fat. **4** (a thin
mixture) dilute, diluted, runny, sloppy,
watery, weak

**thing** n **1** apparatus, article, device,
gadget, implement, instrument,
invention, item, machine, mechanism,
object, thingumajig, thingummy, tool,
utensil. **2** (a thing that happens) affair,
circumstance, deed, episode, event,
happening, incident, occurrence,
phenomenon, proceeding. **3** (a thing
you think) feeling, idea, notion, theory,
thought. **4** (a thing you do) act, action,
chore, exploit, job, responsibility, task,
undertaking. **5** (have a thing about
heights) (*inf*) aversion, dislike, fear,
fixation, hang-up *inf*, horror, mania,
neurosis, obsession, phobia,
preoccupation. **6** (have a thing about
chocolate) liking, love, partiality,
passion, penchant, weakness

**think** v **1** believe, be under the
impression, conclude, consider, feel,
guess *inf*, have an opinion, imagine,
judge, presume, reckon, suppose.
**2** (have time to think) brood, chew
things over, concentrate, day-dream,
deliberate, have a think, meditate, mull
things over, muse, ponder, rack your
brains, reflect, reminisce, worry. **3** (try
to think what might happen) anticipate,
envisage, expect, foresee, imagine, plan,
visualize, work out. **4 think over**
consider, contemplate, mull over,
ponder, weigh up. **5 think up** come up
with, concoct, create, devise, dream up,
imagine, improvise, invent

**thinker** n innovator, intellect, inventor,
philosopher, sage, scholar

**thinking** adj intelligent, logical,
philosophical, rational, reflective,
sensible, thoughtful

**thirst** n **1** dehydration, dryness,
thirstiness. **2** (a thirst for sth) appetite,
craving, desire, eagerness, hunger,
longing, yearning

**thirsty** adj **1** dehydrated, dry, gasping *inf*,
parched. **2** (wanting sth badly) avid,
eager, greedy, hankering, longing,
yearning

**thorn** n barb, needle, prickle, spike, spine

**thorny** adj **1** (with thorny stems) barbed,
pointed, prickly, sharp, spiky, spiny.
**2** (a thorny problem) awkward,
bothersome, complicated, difficult,
tough, troublesome, worrying;
*opp* simple

**thorough** adj **1** (a thorough
examination) careful, complete,

comprehensive, conscientious, deep, detailed, exhaustive, full, in-depth *inf*, intensive, methodical, meticulous, painstaking, scrupulous. 2 (a thorough waste of time) absolute, complete, downright, out-and-out, outright, perfect, sheer, thoroughgoing, total, unqualified, utter

**thoroughfare** *n* access, highway, motorway, passage, passageway, road, roadway, street, way

**thought** *n* 1 (require some thought) concentration, consideration, contemplation, deliberation, meditation, musing, reflection, rumination, thinking, worrying. 2 (have a thought) idea, notion, observation, opinion, plan. 3 (have thought for sb) compassion, concern, consideration, kindness, regard, sympathy, thoughtfulness

**thoughtful** *adj* 1 absorbed, contemplative, lost in thought, pensive, reflective, ruminative, serious, solemn, wistful, worried. 2 (a thoughtful person) attentive, caring, compassionate, considerate, helpful, kind, kindly, solicitous, unselfish

**thoughtless** *adj* 1 careless, foolish, ill-advised, irresponsible, mindless, rash, reckless, silly, stupid, unthinking, unwise. 2 cruel, impolite, inconsiderate, indiscreet, insensitive, rude, tactless, undiplomatic, unfeeling, unkind

**thrash** *v* 1 beat, belt *inf*, cane, flog, give sb a hiding, lash, punish, spank, whip. 2 (defeat) beat, defeat, hammer *sl*, lick *inf*, run rings round *inf*, trounce, wipe the floor with *inf*. 3 (thrash around in your bed) squirm, toss and turn,

twist, twitch, wriggle, writhe

**thread** *n* cotton, fibre, filament, hair, strand, yarn

**threadbare** *adj* frayed, holey, old, ragged, scruffy, shabby, tattered, tatty, used, worn, worn-out

**threat** *n* danger, foreboding, forewarning, hazard, menace, omen, portent, risk, warning

**threaten** *v* 1 endanger, imperil, jeopardize, put at risk, put in jeopardy. 2 (threaten sb) bully, intimidate, issue threats to, lean on *inf*, make threats to, pressurize, terrorize. 3 (black clouds threatening rain) forebode, foreshadow, forewarn of, give warning of, portend, warn of

**threatening** *adj* bullying, intimidatory, menacing, warning

**three** *n* threesome, triad, trinity, trio, triumvirate

**threshold** *n* 1 door, doorstep, doorway, entrance, entry, sill. 2 (on the threshold of sth) beginning, brink, opening, outset, start, verge

**thrift** *n* carefulness, economizing, economy, frugality, miserliness, penny-pinching, saving

**thrifty** *adj* careful, economical, economizing, frugal, mean, miserly, parsimonious, penny-pinching, prudent, sparing

**thrill** *n* 1 flutter, frisson, quiver, shudder, tingle, tremble, tremor, vibration. 2 delight, joy, pleasure. 3 buzz *inf*, kick *inf*

**thrill** *v* arouse, electrify, excite, stir, titillate

**thrilling** *adj* electrifying, exciting, gripping, hair-raising *inf*, riveting, rousing, sensational, stimulating, stirring

**thrive** v **1** be vigorous, bloom, do well, grow, shoot up. **2** develop, flourish, grow, increase, prosper, succeed

**thriving** adj **1** blooming, doing well, flourishing, growing, healthy, prolific. **2** booming, burgeoning, developing, growing, prospering, prosperous, successful, wealthy

**throb** v beat, palpitate, pound, pulsate, pulse, thump, vibrate

**throng** n crowd, flock, horde, host, mass, mob, multitude, swarm

**throttle** v asphyxiate, choke, smother, stifle, strangle, suffocate

**throw** n fling, heave, lob, shot, shy, toss

**throw** v **1** bowl, bung inf, cast, chuck inf, fling, heave, hurl, launch, lob, pitch, project, propel, shy, sling, toss. **2 throw away** (throw away the rubbish) bin inf, chuck out inf, discard, dispense with, dispose of, dump inf, jettison, reject, scrap, throw out. **3 throw away** (throw away your chance) blow inf, lose, squander, waste. **4 throw out** (throw out rubbish) bin inf, chuck out inf, discard, jettison, junk inf, scrap. **5 throw out** (throw sb out of their home) chuck out inf, evict, expel, kick out inf, turf out inf. **6 throw out** (throw out light) emit, give off, radiate, send out

**thrust** n **1** force, impetus, momentum, pressure. **2** drive, jab, lunge, poke, prod, push, shove, stab

**thrust** v drive, elbow, force, impel, jostle, lunge, plunge, poke, press, prod, push, shove, stab, urge

**thud** n bang, clunk, crash, smack, thump

**thud** v bang, clump, crash, knock,

smack, thump

**thug** n assassin, delinquent, gangster, heavy sl, hoodlum, hooligan, killer, murderer, ruffian, tough inf, troublemaker, vandal, yob

**thump** n bang, clunk, crash, knock, rap, slap, smack, thud

**thump** v **1** bang, batter, beat, clobber sl, crash, hit, knock, pound, punch, rap, smack, strike, thrash, thud, whack inf. **2** pound, pulse, throb

**thunder** n boom, booming, clap, crack, crash, roar, roaring, roll, rumble, rumbling

**thunder** v bellow, blast, boom, clap, crack, crash, peal, resound, reverberate, roar, rumble, shout, yell

**thwart** v check, defeat, foil, frustrate, hinder, impede, obstruct, oppose, outwit, prevent, stand in the way of, stop, stump

**ticket** n card, coupon, docket, label, pass, permit, slip, sticker, tab, tag, token, voucher

**tide** n course, current, drift, ebb, flow, stream, tidal flow, tidewater, tideway, undertow

**tidy** adj **1** (a tidy person) careful, house-proud, methodical, neat, organized, presentable, systematic, well-groomed; *opp* untidy. **2** (a tidy room) clean, in good order, shipshape, spick and span, spruce, trim, uncluttered, well-kept, well-ordered; *opp* untidy

**tie** n **1** catch, clip, cord, fastening, link. **2** (have no ties) bond, commitment, obligation, responsibility. **3** (in a game) dead heat, draw, stalemate. **4** (wear a tie) bow-tie, cravat, necktie

**tie** v **1** attach, bind, chain, connect,

couple, fasten, hitch, join, knot, lash, link, moor, rope, secure, splice, tether, tie up. **2** (in a game) be even, be equal, be level, be neck and neck, draw

**tier** *n* bank, file, layer, level, line, order, rank, row, storey

**tight** *adj* **1** fast, firm, fixed, rigid, secure, stiff, strained, stretched, taut, tense. **2** (a tight space) compact, constricted, cramped, inadequate, limited, restricted, small. **3** (a tight jumper) close-fitting, figure-hugging, snug, tight-fitting, too small; *opp* loose. **4** (a tight lid) airtight, impermeable, leak-proof, sealed, waterproof, watertight. **5** (not generous) mean, miserly, stingy, tight-fisted; *opp* generous. **6** (a tight match) close, even, well-matched

**tighten** *v* become tighter, close, close up, constrict, fasten, harden, make taut, make tight, narrow, pull tight, secure, squeeze, stiffen, stretch, tense

**tilt** *n* angle, inclination, incline, pitch, slant, slope

**tilt** *v* bank, heel over, incline, keel over, lean, list, slant, slope, tip

**timber** *n* beams, boards, firewood, forest, logs, planks, trees, tree trunks, wood

**time** *n* **1** (in the time of Henry VIII) age, days, epoch, era, period. **2** (do sth for a time) interval, period, spell, stretch, term, while. **3** (the right time to do sth) juncture, moment, occasion, opportunity, point. **4** (clap in time) beat, measure, metre, rhythm, tempo

**time** *v* **1** (time your arrival) choose a time for, fix a time for, plan, schedule, timetable. **2** (time how long sth takes) clock, count, measure

**timeless** *adj* ageless, deathless, endless, eternal, everlasting, immortal, lasting, permanent, unchanging, undying

**timely** *adj* appropriate, convenient, fitting, judicious, opportune, prompt, punctual, suitable, well-timed; *opp* untimely

**timetable** *n* agenda, calendar, diary, list, programme, rota, schedule

**timid** *adj* afraid, apprehensive, bashful, coy, fearful, nervous, scared, shy, spineless, unadventurous, wimpish *inf*; *opp* bold

**tingle** *n* **1** itch, pins and needles *inf*, prickling, stinging, tickle, tingling. **2** quiver, sensation, shiver, thrill, tremor

**tingle** *v* itch, prickle, sting, tickle

**tinker** *v* dabble, fiddle, meddle, mess about, play, potter, tamper, toy

**tint** *n* colour, colouring, dye, hue, shade, stain, tone, wash

**tint** *v* colour, dye, rinse, stain, wash

**tiny** *adj* diminutive, infinitesimal, insignificant, little, microscopic, mini *inf*, miniature, minute, negligible, small, teeny-weeny *inf*, wee; *opp* huge, large

**tip** *n* **1** (the end of sth) apex, cap, cover, crown, end, head, nib, peak, pinnacle, point, summit, top. **2** (rubbish tip) dump, refuse heap, rubbish heap. **3** (a useful tip) hint, piece of advice, pointer, recommendation, suggestion, tip-off. **4** (leave a tip) gift, gratuity, money, reward

**tip** *v* **1** capsize, incline, keel, lean, list, overturn, slant, spill, tilt, tip over, tip up, topple, upend, upset. **2** (tip sth somewhere) dump, empty, pour out, unload. **3** (tip sb) give a tip to, leave a tip for, reward

**tire** v 1 (tire sb) exhaust, overtire, take it out of *inf*, wear out, weary. 2 (feel tired) droop, flag, get tired. 3 (tire of sth) be fed up with *inf*, be sick of *inf*, be weary of, get bored with

**tired** adj dead on your feet *inf*, dog-tired *inf*, done in *inf*, drained, drowsy, exhausted, fatigued, shattered *inf*, sleepy, weary, worn out, zonked *sl*

**tireless** adj determined, dogged, energetic, industrious, unflagging, untiring, vigorous

**tiresome** adj annoying, boring, dull, exasperating, irritating, laborious, maddening, monotonous, tedious, troublesome, trying, wearing

**tiring** adj arduous, exacting, exhausting, fatiguing, strenuous, taxing, tough, wearying

**tissue** n 1 gauze, netting, webbing. 2 paper handkerchief. 3 tissue paper

**title** n 1 caption, credit, heading, headline, inscription, label, name. 2 designation, form of address, name, nickname, position, rank, status. 3 (title to sth) claim, entitlement, ownership, possession, privilege, right. 4 (win a title) championship, crown

**titled** adj aristocratic, noble, upper-class

**toast** n drink, salute, tribute

**toast** v 1 drink a toast to, drink the health of, drink to, raise your glass to, salute. 2 (toast sth under the grill) brown, crisp, cook, grill, heat, warm

**together** adv 1 (work together) closely, collectively, co-operatively, jointly, side by side. 2 (do sth together) all at once, at the same time, in chorus, in unison, simultaneously

**toil** n drudgery, effort, exertion, grind *inf*, hard work, industry, labour, slaving, work

**toil** v drudge, graft *inf*, keep at it *inf*, labour, push yourself, slave, slog, strive, struggle, sweat *inf*, work

**toilet** n bathroom, latrine, lavatory, loo *inf*, privy, urinal, washroom, WC

**token** adj nominal, notional, superficial, symbolic

**token** n 1 (a token of sth) demonstration, emblem, evidence, expression, indication, keepsake, mark, memento, proof, reminder, sign, symbol. 2 counter, coupon, disc, voucher

**tolerable** adj 1 acceptable, bearable, endurable; *opp* intolerable, unbearable. 2 acceptable, adequate, all right, average, fair, good enough, O.K. *inf*, not bad *inf*, satisfactory

**tolerance** n 1 acceptance, endurance, forbearance, fortitude, resilience, stamina, toughness. 2 fairness, forgiveness, indulgence, lenience, open-mindedness, patience, understanding

**tolerant** adj charitable, easygoing, forbearing, magnanimous, open-minded, patient, sympathetic, understanding, unprejudiced; *opp* intolerant

**tolerate** v accept, allow, bear, condone, countenance, endure, permit, put up with, sanction, stand, stomach, submit to, suffer, swallow, take, undergo

**toll** n 1 (pay a toll) charge, customs, dues, duty, fee, levy, payment, tariff, tax. 2 (a heavy toll) cost, damage, loss, penalty

**toll** v 1 chime, clang, knell, peal, ring,

sound, strike. **2** (toll the hour)
announce, call, herald, signal

**tomb** *n* burial chamber, catacomb, crypt,
grave, mausoleum, monument,
sepulchre, tombstone, vault

**tone** *n* **1** (of voice) accent, emphasis,
force, inflection, intonation,
modulation, phrasing, pitch, sound,
sound quality, stress, timbre, tone of
voice, volume. **2** (mood) air,
atmosphere, attitude, character, drift,
effect, feel, feeling, manner, mood,
note, quality, spirit, style, temper, vein.
**3** (colour) cast, colour, hue, shade, tint

**tone** *v* **1** blend, go, go well, harmonize,
match, suit. **2 tone down** dampen,
moderate, modulate, play down, reduce,
restrain, soften, subdue, temper

**tongue** *n* dialect, idiom, language, lingo
*inf*, parlance, patois, speech, talk,
vernacular

**tongue-tied** *adj* at a loss for words, dumb,
dumbfounded, dumbstruck, inarticulate,
mute, silent, speechless, struck dumb

**tonic** *n* boost, pick-me-up, refresher, shot
in the arm *inf*, stimulant

**tool** *n* aid, appliance, contrivance, device,
gadget, implement, instrument,
machine, utensil

**top** *adj* **1** (top score) best, high, highest,
maximum, most, winning. **2** (the top
step) highest, topmost, uppermost.
**3** (a top footballer) ace *inf*, fine, great,
top-notch *inf*. **4** (top people in society)
elite, important, influential, superior.
**5** (top quality) best, choicest, first,
finest, supreme

**top** *n* **1** apex, crest, crown, head, height,
highest point, peak, pinnacle, summit,

tip, vertex, zenith. **2** (top of a
container) cap, cork, cover, covering,
lid, stopper. **3** (top of the queue) head,
lead. **4** (piece of clothing) blouse,
jumper, shirt, sweater, sweat-shirt,
T-shirt

**top** *v* **1** (top the dish with tomatoes) coat,
complete, cover, decorate, finish,
garnish, spread. **2** (do better than sth or
sb) beat, do better than, eclipse, exceed,
excel, outdo, outstrip, surpass, transcend

**topic** *n* issue, matter, point, question,
subject, text, theme

**topical** *adj* contemporary, current, in the
news, recent, up-to-date

**topple** *v* **1** (topple sth) fell, knock down,
knock over, push over, tip over, upset.
**2** (sth topples) capsize, collapse, fall, fall
over, keel over, overbalance, overturn,
totter, tumble. **3** (topple a government)
bring down, oust, overthrow, overturn,
unseat

**torch** *n* brand, flashlight, lamp

**torment** *n* **1** agony, anguish, distress,
hell, misery, ordeal, pain, persecution,
suffering, torture, wretchedness.
**2** annoyance, bane, bother, curse, hassle
*inf*, irritation, nuisance, worry

**torment** *v* **1** afflict, cause pain to,
distress, harrow, hurt, pain, persecute,
plague, torture, victimize. **2** aggravate
*inf*, annoy, bother, harass, hassle *inf*,
irritate, nag, persecute, pester, provoke,
tease

**torn** *adj* **1** cut, lacerated, ragged, slit, split,
tattered. **2** (feel torn) in two minds *inf*,
split, uncertain, undecided, unsure,
wavering

**tornado** *n* cyclone, gale, hurricane,

squall, storm, tempest, twister *Am inf*,
typhoon, whirlwind

**torpid** *adj* apathetic, dull, heavy, inert,
languid, lethargic, listless, sleepy,
slothful, slow, slow-moving, sluggish

**torrent** *n* cascade, current, deluge,
downpour, flood, flow, gush, rush, spate,
stream, tide

**tortuous** *adj* circuitous, complicated,
convoluted, curling, curvy, indirect,
meandering, turning, twisted, twisting,
twisty, wandering, winding; *opp* direct

**torture** *n* abuse, agony, anguish, cruelty,
distress, hell, humiliation, martyrdom,
misery, pain, persecution, punishment,
suffering, torment

**torture** *v* 1 abuse, be cruel to, bully, cause
pain to, hurt, ill-treat, inflict pain on,
persecute, torment, victimize. 2 afflict,
agonize, distress, nag, plague, trouble,
worry

**toss** *n* 1 (a toss of the head) jerk, jiggle,
movement, shake. 2 (the toss of a coin)
flip, throw, tossing

**toss** *v* 1 chuck *inf*, fling, hurl, sling,
throw. 2 (ships being tossed by the
waves) bob, disturb, jolt, lurch, pitch,
plunge, rock, roll, shake. 3 (tossing and
turning) move restlessly, squirm, wriggle,
writhe, thrash, tumble. 4 (toss your
head) jerk, throw back. 5 (toss a
pancake) flip, throw, turn. 6 (toss a
coin) flick, flip, spin, throw

**total** *n* amount, answer, mass, sum, sum
total, totality, whole

**total** *v* 1 add up to, amount to, come to,
make, reach. 2 add up, calculate,
compute, count up, find the sum of,
reckon, tot up, work out

**totalitarian** *adj* absolute, authoritarian,
autocratic, despotic, dictatorial, fascist,
one-party, oppressive, tyrannical,
undemocratic

**totter** *v* be unsteady, dodder, falter, lurch,
quiver, reel, rock, shake, stagger,
stumble, sway, teeter, walk unsteadily,
wobble

**touch** *n* 1 blow, brush, caress, contact,
hit, pat, pressure, stroke, tap. 2 (a touch
of sth) bit, dash, drop, hint, jot, pinch,
smattering, speck, spot, suggestion, taste,
trace. 3 (do sth by touch) feel, feeling,
sense of touch, touching. 4 (sb's touch)
ability, artistry, capability, expertise,
flair, gift, knack, skill, technique, way

**touch** *v* 1 (touch sth) brush, caress, feel,
finger, fondle, handle, pat, push, rub,
stroke, tap. 2 (things touch) abut,
border, come into contact, come
together, converge, join, meet. 3 (touch
sb emotionally) affect, disturb, get to *inf*,
influence, make sad, move, soften, stir,
upset. 4 (don't touch) fiddle with,
interfere with, mess about with, move,
play with, toy with. 5 **touch up**
enhance, finish off, improve, patch up,
perfect, put the finishing touches to,
repair, retouch

**touching** *adj* affecting, emotional, heart-
rending, heart-warming, moving,
poignant, sad, stirring, tender, upsetting

**touchy** *adj* bad-tempered, cross, easily
offended, grouchy *inf*, grumpy,
hypersensitive, irritable, oversensitive,
quick-tempered, ratty *inf*, sensitive,
short-tempered, thin-skinned

**tough** *adj* 1 durable, firm, hard, hard-
wearing, indestructible, lasting, leathery,

rigid, rugged, solid, sound, stiff, stout, strong, sturdy, substantial, unbreakable, well-made; *opp* delicate, flimsy. **2** (a tough decision) difficult, hard, troublesome; *opp* easy. **3** (a tough climb) arduous, challenging, demanding, difficult, gruelling, hard, strenuous; *opp* gentle. **4** (tough meat) chewy, hard, gristly, leathery, rubbery, stringy; *opp* tender. **5** (of a person) hard, macho, rough, rowdy, strong, vicious, violent, wild. **6** (a tough life) grim, hard, harsh, rough, severe, strict; *opp* easy. **7** (be tough with sb) firm, merciless, severe, stern, strict, unbending, unsympathetic; *opp* lenient. **8** (that's tough) regrettable, too bad *inf*, unfortunate, unlucky

**tough** *n* brute, bully, heavy *sl*, hooligan, ruffian, thug

**tour** *n* excursion, jaunt, journey, outing, ride, trip

**tour** *v* explore, go round, go sightseeing, holiday in, journey through, travel round, visit

**tourist** *n* day-tripper, globe-trotter *inf*, holiday-maker, sightseer, traveller, tripper, visitor, voyager

**tournament** *n* championship, competition, contest, event, match, meeting, series

**tow** *v* drag, draw, haul, lug, pull, trail, tug

**tower** *n* **1** belfry, bell tower, column, minaret, obelisk, pillar, skyscraper, spire, steeple, turret. **2** castle, citadel, fort, fortress, keep, stronghold

**tower** *v* dominate, loom, mount, overlook, rear, rise, soar, stand out, stick up

**towering** *adj* **1** (very high) colossal,

gigantic, high, huge, lofty, sky-high, soaring. **2** (very intense) extreme, fiery, frenzied, intense, mighty, overpowering, terrible, vehement, violent

**town** *n* borough, city, settlement, township, village

**toxic** *adj* dangerous, deadly, harmful, lethal, noxious, poisonous

**toy** *n* game, plaything

**trace** *n* **1** evidence, indication, mark, record, relic, remnant, sign, survival, token, vestige. **2** (a trace of sth) bit, dash, drop, hint, iota, shadow, suggestion, touch, trifle, whiff. **3** footprint, mark, print, spoor, track, trail

**trace** *v* **1** detect, dig up, discover, find, get back, recover, retrieve, track down, turn up, uncover, unearth. **2** follow, pursue, track, track down, trail, tail. **3** (trace sth on paper) chart, copy, draw, go over, make a copy of, map, mark out, record, show, sketch

**track** *n* **1** footmark, footprint, footstep, mark, path, print, scent, spoor, trace, trail. **2** bridle path, bridleway, footpath, path, road, route, trail, way. **3** course, flight path, orbit, route, slipstream, trajectory, wake. **4** line, rail, rails, tramline. **5** circuit, dirt-track, racecourse, racetrack

**track** *v* chase, dog, follow, hound, pursue, shadow, stalk, tail, trace, trail

**tracks** *n* impressions, imprints, marks, wheelmarks

**tractable** *adj* amenable, compliant, controllable, docile, dutiful, manageable, obedient, submissive, tame, willing

**trade** n 1 barter, business, buying and selling, commerce, dealing, exchange, marketing, merchandising, trading, traffic, trafficking, transactions. 2 (learn a trade) business, calling, career, job, line of work, occupation, profession, skill. 3 (arrange a trade) deal, exchange, swap

**trade** v bargain, barter, buy and sell, deal, do business, exchange, market, peddle, traffic, swap, switch

**trader** n broker, buyer, dealer, merchant, retailer, salesman, seller, shopkeeper, supplier

**tradesman** n 1 merchant, retailer, seller, shopkeeper, storekeeper, supplier. 2 craftsman, skilled worker, workman

**tradition** n 1 belief, folklore. 2 custom, habit, institution, practice, rite, ritual, usage

**traditional** adj 1 conventional, customary, established, familiar, fixed, habitual, time-honoured, usual. 2 (traditional legends) folk, historic, old, oral, popular, unwritten

**traffic** n 1 cars, vehicles. 2 freight, movement of goods, movement of passengers, shipping, transport, transportation. 3 (traffic in drugs) barter, business, commerce, dealings, peddling, smuggling, trade, trading, trafficking

**traffic** v deal, do business, peddle, smuggle, trade

**tragedy** n 1 blow, calamity, catastrophe, disaster, misfortune, shock. 2 adversity, misfortune, sad events, sadness

**tragic** adj 1 appalling, awful, calamitous, catastrophic, dire, disastrous, dreadful, fatal, ill-fated, ill-starred, miserable, sad, shocking, unfortunate, unlucky; opp fortunate. 2 doleful, grief-stricken, hurt, pathetic, pitiful, sad, sorrowful, unhappy, woeful

**trail** n 1 evidence, footmarks, footprints, marks, scent, signs, slipstream, spoor, traces, wake. 2 path, pathway, road, route, track

**trail** v 1 (pull sth behind you) drag, draw, haul, pull, tow. 2 (hang down) dangle, drag, droop, hang, sweep. 3 (go after sb) chase, follow, pursue, shadow, stalk, tail, trace, track, track down. 4 (go along a surface) crawl, creep. 5 (go slowly) dawdle, drag, lag, linger, loiter, plod, straggle

**train** n 1 carriage, diesel, steam train. 2 caravan, column, convoy, line, file, procession. 3 (sth that follows) path, stream, wake, wash, tail, trail

**train** v 1 (train sb) coach, drill, educate, guide, indoctrinate, instruct, prepare, school, teach, tutor. 2 (train to do sth) learn, prepare, rehearse, study. 3 (train before a race) exercise, practise, work out. 4 (train a rifle on sb) aim, direct, level, point

**trainer** n coach, instructor, teacher, tutor

**training** n 1 exercise, practice, preparation. 2 discipline, education, guidance, instruction, schooling, teaching, upbringing

**trait** n attribute, characteristic, feature, idiosyncrasy, mannerism, peculiarity, quality, quirk

**traitor** n back-stabber, betrayer, deceiver, deserter, double-crosser, informer, Judas, renegade

**tramp** n bag lady, beggar, bum inf, dosser inf, down-and-out, drifter, homeless person, vagrant, wanderer

**tramp** v 1 (go for a walk) hike, march, ramble, roam, rove, stride, trek, walk. 2 (walk heavily) march, plod, stamp, stomp, stump, toil, traipse, trudge

**trample** v crush, flatten, squash, squish inf, stamp on, stand on, step on, tread on, walk on

**trance** n daze, dream, hypnotic state, rapture, reverie, semi-consciousness, spell, stupor

**tranquil** adj 1 calm, peaceful, placid, quiet, restful, serene, still, undisturbed. 2 (of a person) composed, cool, even-tempered, placid, serene, unemotional, unflappable

**tranquillity** n calm, calmness, composure, coolness, equanimity, peace, peacefulness, placidity, quiet, quietness, restfulness, serenity, stillness

**tranquillize** v calm, calm down, pacify, quieten, relax, sedate, settle, soothe

**tranquillizer** n barbiturate, downer inf, narcotic, sedative, Valium TM; opp stimulant

**transaction** n agreement, arrangement, deal, item, negotiation, purchase, sale, settlement

**transcend** v exceed, go beyond, leave behind, outdo, rise above, surpass, top

**transcribe** v copy, record, rewrite, transliterate, write out

**transfer** n 1 change, changeover, conveyance, delivery, move, relocation, transport, transmission. 2 change of ownership, conveyancing, handover, sale

**transfer** v 1 carry, change over, convey, ferry, move, relocate, transplant, transport. 2 give, hand over, pass on, pass over, sell

**transfix** v 1 fix, hold, hypnotize, mesmerize, paralyse, petrify, root to the spot. 2 impale, run through, skewer, spear, spike, stab

**transform** v alter, change, convert, make over, metamorphose, remodel, reshape, restructure, revolutionize

**transformation** n change, alteration, conversion, makeover, metamorphosis, remodelling, reshaping, restructuring, revolution, sea change, transition

**transgress** v 1 break the law, do wrong, misbehave, offend, sin; opp behave. 2 breach, break, contravene, defy, disobey, infringe, overstep, violate; opp abide by, keep, obey

**transgression** n 1 crime, disobedience, error, misbehaviour, misdemeanour, mistake, offence, sin, wrong, wrongdoing. 2 breach, contravention, infringement, violation

**transient** adj brief, ephemeral, fleeting, passing, short-lived, short, temporary, transitory; opp long-lasting, permanent

**transition** n change, conversion, development, evolution, progress, progression, shift, transformation

**transitional** adj 1 (a transitional government) caretaker, provisional, temporary. 2 change-over, changing, conversion, developing, developmental, evolutionary, evolving

**transitory** adj brief, ephemeral, fleeting, passing, short-lived, short, temporary, transient; opp long-lasting, permanent

**translate** v 1 decipher, decode, explain, interpret, paraphrase, transcribe. 2 alter, change, convert, rephrase, transform, turn

**transmission** n 1 broadcast, edition, programme, repeat, show, showing. 2 broadcasting, carriage, communication, despatch, dissemination, relaying, sending, shipment, spread, transfer, transport

**transmit** v broadcast, carry, convey, despatch, disseminate, emit, forward, mail, pass on, post, put on air, put out, relay, send, ship, spread, transfer, transport

**transparent** adj 1 blatant, clear, evident, obvious, open, patent, plain, plain as a pikestaff, unambiguous, unequivocal, unmistakable, visible; **opp** obscure. 2 clear, crystal-clear, glassy, see-through, sheer, translucent; **opp** cloudy, opaque

**transpire** v 1 arise, come about, happen, occur. 2 emerge, become apparent, become known, come to light

**transport** n carriage, conveyance, despatch, freight, haulage, movement, moving, shipment, shipping, transfer

**transport** v bring, carry, convey, fetch, move, shift, ship, take, transfer

**transpose** v 1 change, exchange, invert, reorder, reverse, swap, switch. 2 convert, rewrite

**trap** n ambush, booby-trap, pitfall, ploy, ruse, snare, trick

**trap** v block, catch, catch out, confine, corner, cut off, hold back, imprison, inveigle, lure, shut in, snare, trick, trip up

**trapped** adj blocked, caught, cornered, cut off, imprisoned, in a tight spot, locked in, shut in, snared, stuck, with your hands tied; **opp** free

**trappings** n accessories, apparatus, bits and pieces, extras, finery, frills, frippery, furbelows, gear inf, paraphernalia, things, trimmings

**trash** n 1 drivel, dross inf, hot air, nonsense, rot inf, rubbish, tripe inf, twaddle inf. 2 garbage, junk, litter, refuse, rubbish, waste,

**trashy** adj cheap, poor, shoddy, tacky, useless, worthless

**traumatic** adj difficult, distressing, frightening, harrowing, nerve-racking, painful, stressful, upsetting; **opp** easy

**travel** v backpack, cross, fly, go, go on a trip, go on holiday, holiday, journey, move, proceed, sail, tour, trek, visit, walk

**traveller** n backpacker, commuter, explorer, gypsy, holidaymaker, itinerant, migrant, nomad, passenger, pilgrim, Romany, tourist, tripper, visitor

**travelling** adj itinerant, migrant, migratory, mobile, nomadic, touring, wandering

**travesty** n caricature, distortion, farce, misrepresentation, mockery, parody, perversion, send-up, sham

**treacherous** adj 1 dangerous, dicey inf, hazardous, perilous, tricky, unsafe; **opp** safe. 2 deceitful, disloyal, double-crossing, double-dealing, faithless, false, unfaithful, untrustworthy; **opp** loyal

**treachery** n back-stabbing, betrayal, deceit, deception, disloyalty, double-dealing, duplicity, treason; **opp** loyalty

**tread** n footfall, footstep, step,

tramp, walk

**tread** v 1 go, march, pace, step, stride, tramp, walk. 2 crush underfoot, press, squash, stamp on, stand on, trample, walk on

**treason** n betrayal, disloyalty, high treason, rebellion, sedition, subversion, treachery

**treasure** n 1 booty, cache, gold, hoard, jewels, riches, treasure trove, valuables. 2 (a person) darling, gem, star

**treasure** v cherish, guard, idolize, love, prize, revere, value

**treat** n amusement, indulgence, luxury, outing, pleasure, present, surprise

**treat** v 1 consider, deal with, handle, manage, regard, tackle, think of, view. 2 (give treatment to) attend to, care for, cure, dress, give treatment to, minister to, nurse, tend. 3 (give sb a treat) buy sth for sb, entertain, give sb a treat, pay for, take sb out

**treatise** n article, dissertation, essay, monograph, paper, study, thesis, tract

**treatment** n 1 conduct, coverage, handling, management, usage, use. 2 care, cure, first aid, healing, medication, medicine, operation, prescription, remedy, surgery, therapy

**treaty** n agreement, alliance, concordat, contract, convention, deal, pact, protocol, settlement

**trek** n expedition, hike, journey, march, safari, slog inf, trip, walk

**trek** v backpack, hike, march, slog inf, traipse, travel, trudge, walk

**tremble** n judder, quaking, quiver, shaking, shiver, shudder, vibration, wobble

**tremble** v judder, quake, quiver, shake, shiver, shudder, vibrate, wobble

**tremendous** adj 1 ace inf, amazing, brilliant, excellent, fantastic, marvellous, sensational, superb, terrific, wonderful; opp awful, dire. 2 colossal, enormous, giant, gigantic, great, huge, massive, vast; opp minute, tiny

**tremor** n earthquake, judder, quake, quiver, shaking, shiver, tremble, trembling, vibration, wobble

**trench** n channel, ditch, furrow, hole, trough

**trend** n 1 bias, development, direction, inclination, movement, shift, tendency. 2 craze, fad inf, fashion, look, style, vogue

**trendy** adj all the rage, fashionable, in fashion, in vogue, latest, smart, stylish, up-to-date, up-to-the-minute

**trespass** v encroach, intrude

**trial** adj experimental, exploratory, pilot, probationary, provisional, test

**trial** n 1 case, court case, court martial, court proceedings, hearing, inquiry, lawsuit, legal action, legal proceedings, litigation, prosecution, tribunal. 2 (test) check, dry run inf, probation, test, test run, testing, trial period, trial run. 3 (hardship) adversity, difficulty, hardship, misery, nuisance, ordeal, pain inf, problem, suffering, tribulation, trouble, woe, worry

**tribe** n clan, ethnic group, family, group, people, race

**tribute** n accolade, acknowledgement, appreciation, compliment, honour, praise, recognition; opp criticism

**trick** n 1 cheat, con inf, deception, dodge,

hoax, leg-pull *inf*, ploy, practical joke, prank, ruse, scam *inf*, stunt, swindle.
**2** art, gift, knack, secret, skill, technique.
**3** conjuring, magic, sleight of hand

**trick** *v* cheat, con *inf*, deceive, diddle, double-cross, fool, pull a fast one *inf*, pull the wool over sb's eyes *inf*, swindle, take sb in

**trickery** *n* cheating, con *inf*, deceit, deception, dishonesty, double-dealing, duplicity, fraud, hoax, sleight-of-hand, swindle

**trickle** *n* dribble, drip, leak, leakage, seepage

**trickle** *v* dribble, drip, filter, leak, ooze, percolate, run, seep

**tricky** *adj* awkward, complicated, delicate, dicey *inf*, difficult, risky, sticky *inf*, touch-and-go; *opp* simple, straightforward

**trifle** *n* **1** bauble, irrelevance, knick-knack, nothing, rubbish, sth of little consequence, trinket, trivia, triviality.
**2** bit, drop, little bit, tad *inf*, touch

**trifle** *v* fiddle, fool, meddle, mess about *inf*, play, toy, treat lightly

**trifling** *adj* frivolous, inconsequential, insignificant, irrelevant, minor, negligible, paltry, petty, silly, trivial, unimportant, worthless; *opp* important, major

**trim** *adj* **1** neat, neat and tidy, orderly, smart, spick and span, tidy, well-groomed; *opp* untidy. **2** in good shape, shapely, slender, slim, willowy; *opp* fat, overweight

**trim** *v* **1** clip, cut, cut back, even up, lop, pare, peel, prune, shape, snip, tidy up.
**2** decorate, dress, garnish

**trimmings** *n* accompaniments, decorations, extras, garnish, ornaments, trappings

**trip** *n* business trip, day trip, excursion, expedition, holiday, journey, outing, ride, tour, visit

**trip** *v* fall, fall over sth, lose your footing, slip, stagger, stumble

**trite** *adj* banal, clichéd, dull, hackneyed, insincere, overused, stale, tired, unimaginative, uninteresting, uninspired, unoriginal, worn-out; *opp* original

**triumph** *n* **1** (a victory) achievement, coup, feat, sensation, success, victory, win. **2** (joy) elation, exultation, joy, jubilation, pride

**triumph** *v* carry the day, come out on top, come through, defeat, overcome, prevail, succeed, vanquish, win; *opp* fail, lose

**triumphant** *adj* **1** cock-a-hoop *inf*, elated, exultant, gleeful, joyful, joyous, jubilant, pleased, proud. **2** successful, victorious, winning

**trivia** *n* minutiae, rubbish, trifles, trivialities

**trivial** *adj* inconsequential, insignificant, minor, paltry, petty, trifling, unimportant, worthless; *opp* important

**troop** *n* band, bunch, company, contingent, crowd, flock, gang, group, horde, pack, squad, team, unit

**troop** *v* crowd, flock, go, march, stream, surge, swarm, trundle *inf*

**trophy** *n* award, cup, prize, shield

**tropical** *adj* hot, humid, steamy, sticky, sultry, sweltering, torrid

**trot** *n* jog, lope, run, scamper

**trot** v go, jog, run, scamper, scuttle, toddle, trundle

**trouble** n 1 (difficulty) affliction, anxiety, difficulty, hassle, heartache, misfortune, nuisance, problem, suffering, tribulation, worry. 2 (unrest) bother, commotion, discontent, disorder, disturbance, fighting, fuss, rioting, row, unrest; *opp* calm, peace. 3 (heart trouble) complaint, condition, defect, disorder, illness, problem

**trouble** v afflict, bother, concern, distress, disturb, plague, torment, upset, worry; *opp* reassure

**troublemaker** n agitator, hooligan, mischief-maker, rabble-rouser, rowdy, stirrer

**troublesome** adj 1 annoying, difficult, distressing, hard, irritating, problematic, tiresome, tricky, trying, upsetting, worrying; *opp* easy, straightforward. 2 (of a person) badly behaved, disobedient, disorderly, naughty, rowdy, undisciplined, unruly; *opp* obedient, placid, well-behaved

**trousers** n chinos *Am*, cords, denims, jeans, pants *Am*, ski-pants, slacks

**truant** n 1 absconder, absentee, dodger, runaway. 2 **play truant** be absent without leave, go AWOL, play hooky *inf*, skive off *inf*

**truce** n 1 armistice, cease-fire, cessation, let-up, pact, peace, respite, suspension of hostilities

**trudge** n haul, hike, march, slog *inf*, struggle, traipse, tramp, trek, walk

**trudge** v hike, march, plod, slog *inf*, stomp, struggle, traipse, tramp, trek, walk

**true** adj 1 (a true story) correct, factual, honest, legitimate, right, truthful, valid. 2 (genuine) actual, authentic, bona fide, genuine, proper, real. 3 (the true meaning) accurate, close, correct, exact, precise. 4 (loyal) constant, dedicated, dependable, devoted, faithful, firm, loyal, staunch, trustworthy

**trunk** n 1 (of a tree) main stem, stalk, stem. 2 box, case, chest, crate. 3 (of an animal) nose, snout. 4 body, torso

**trust** n 1 (faith) belief, confidence, expectation, faith, reliance. 2 (custody) care, charge, custody, guardianship, protection, responsibility, safekeeping

**trust** v 1 bank on, be sure of, count on, depend on, have confidence in, have faith in, put your faith in, rely on. 2 anticipate, assume, expect, hope, presume, suppose

**trusting** adj credulous, gullible, innocent, unquestioning, unsuspecting, unwary; *opp* sceptical, suspicious, wary

**trustworthy** adj dependable, honest, loyal, reliable, responsible, true; *opp* dishonest, unreliable

**trusty** adj dependable, faithful, loyal, reliable, staunch, trusted, trustworthy

**truth** n accuracy, authenticity, candour, correctness, fact, genuineness, honesty, legitimacy, reality, truthfulness, validity, veracity; *opp* falsehood, fallacy

**truthful** adj accurate, candid, correct, frank, honest, realistic, reliable, right, sincere, straight; *opp* deceitful

**try** n attempt, bash *inf*, effort, go, shot *inf*, stab *inf*

**try** v 1 aim, attempt, do your best, endeavour, have a go, have a stab at *inf*, make an attempt, make an effort, undertake. 2 (judge) adjudicate, hear, judge, put on trial. 3 (test) appraise, check out, evaluate, sample, test, trial, try out. 4 annoy, put to the test, strain, tax

**trying** *adj* annoying, arduous, demanding, difficult, exasperating, irritating, stressful, taxing, tiresome, tiring, tough; *opp* easy

**tub** *n* barrel, bath, butt, cask, container, jar, keg, pot

**tube** *n* conduit, cylinder, duct, hose, pipe, roll

**tug** *n* haul, heave, jerk, pluck, pull, wrench, yank

**tug** *v* drag, haul, heave, jerk, lug, pluck, pull, tow, wrench, yank

**tuition** *n* coaching, education, instruction, lessons, teaching, training, tutelage

**tumble** *n* 1 fall, somersault. 2 collapse, crash, drop, fall, nosedive, plunge, slump

**tumble** *v* 1 fall, fall over, lose your footing, overbalance, pitch, roll, somersault, topple. 2 (of prices or numbers) collapse, crash, dive, drop, fall, nosedive, plummet, plunge, slump; *opp* rise

**tumult** *n* bedlam, chaos, commotion, confusion, disorder, free-for-all, hubbub, hullabaloo, noise, pandemonium, racket, rumpus, turmoil, upheaval, uproar; *opp* calm, peace

**tumultuous** *adj* chaotic, confused, disorderly, frenzied, hectic, noisy, rowdy, stormy, turbulent, unruly, uproarious, wild; *opp* calm, peaceful

**tune** *n* ditty, melody, music, song

**tune** *v* adapt, adjust, pitch, regulate, set, suit

**tuneful** *adj* attractive, catchy, easy listening, easy on the ear, lilting, lyrical, melodic, melodious, musical, pleasant, sweet; *opp* discordant, harsh

**tuneless** *adj* atonal, discordant, dissonant, flat, harsh, monotonous, out of tune, unmusical; *opp* harmonious, melodic

**tunnel** *n* burrow, hole, passage, shaft, subway, underpass

**tunnel** *v* bore, burrow, dig, mine

**turbulent** *adj* confused, disorderly, in turmoil, rough, rowdy, seething, stormy, tempestuous, troubled, tumultuous, unruly, unsettled, unstable, violent, volatile, wild; *opp* calm, orderly, peaceful

**turf** *n* 1 grass, grassland, green, lawn, pitch. 2 clod, divot

**turgid** *adj* flowery, grand, highfalutin, ornate, pompous, pretentious, wordy; *opp* plain, simple

**turmoil** *n* bedlam, chaos, commotion, confusion, disorder, hubbub, pandemonium, tumult, turbulence, upheaval, uproar; *opp* calm, peace

**turn** *n* 1 (in a game or rota) go, move, period, round, shot, stint, try. 2 coil, cycle, loop, pirouette, revolution, roll, spin, twirl, twist. 3 (change of direction) angle, bend, change of direction, corner, curve, deviation, hairpin, junction, loop, swerve, turning, U-turn. 4 (events have taken a new turn) change, development, direction, drift, shift, tendency, trend, variation. 5 (a comedy turn) act, performance, performer, routine, set

**turn** v 1 (spin) circle, coil, curl, go round, gyrate, loop, pivot, revolve, roll, rotate, spin, spiral, swivel, twirl, wind. 2 bend, flip, fold, invert, reverse. 3 (change direction) change course, change direction, go, head, move, steer, swerve, swing round, veer, wheel. 4 (turn a corner) go round, negotiate, round, take. 5 (turn a hose on sb) aim, direct, point, train. 6 (change to) alter, become, change to, convert, get, go, mutate, transform. 7 **turn down** (reject) decline, refuse, reject, say no to, throw out, veto. 8 **turn down** (turn down the volume) decrease, lower, make softer, make quieter, muffle, mute, reduce, soften; *opp* turn up. 9 **turn off** (switch off) disconnect, put off, shut down, shut off, stop, switch off, turn out; *opp* start, switch on, turn on. 10 **turn off** (turn off the main road) leave, take a side road, take a turning, turn left, turn right; *opp* join. 11 **turn off** (put sb off) alienate, deter from, discourage, disgust, offend, put off, repel, sicken; *opp* attract. 12 **turn on** (switch on) activate, boot, get going, start, start up, switch on; *opp* stop, switch off, turn off. 13 **turn on** (depend on) dependent on, depend on, hang on, hinge on, rest on, revolve around. 14 **turn on** (attack) assault, attack, lay into, round on, set upon. 15 **turn on** (excite) attract, enthuse, excite, interest, stimulate, thrill; *opp* turn off. 16 **turn up** (arrive) appear, arrive, attend, come, get here, get there, put in an appearance, show up. 17 **turn up** (turn up the volume) amplify, increase, make louder, raise;

*opp* turn down . 18 **turn up** (discover) come across, dig up, discover, expose, find, uncover, unearth. 19 **turn up** (come to light) arise, be found, come to light, crop up, happen, occur, transpire. 20 **turn up** (turn up a hem) shorten, take up; *opp* lengthen, let down

**turning** n crossroads, exit, fork, junction, left turn, right turn, road, side road, turn, turn-off

**turning point** n change, crisis, crossroads, decisive moment, eleventh hour, juncture, key moment, moment of truth, point of no return, turn of the tide, watershed

**turnover** n business, flow, movement, output, production, profits, revenue, sales figures, takings, thoughput, receipts

**tutor** n coach, guru, instructor, lecturer, mentor, supervisor, teacher

**tutor** v coach, educate, instruct, lecture, supervise, teach, train

**twilight** n dusk, early evening, half-light, sundown, sunset, the end of the day

**twin** adj corresponding, dual, duplicate, identical, matching, symmetrical, twofold

**twin** n clone, counterpart, double, duplicate, match, mate, other half, pair, partner, spitting image, twin brother, twin sister

**twine** n cord, string, thread

**twine** v climb, coil, entwine, intertwine, snake, spiral, twist, weave, wind, worm, wrap

**twinkling** n flash, instant, jiffy, moment, second, split second, trice

**twirl** n coil, pirouette, revolution, rotation, spin, spiral, swirl, turn, twiddle, twist, whirl, whorl

**twirl** v coil, gyrate, pirouette, pivot, revolve, rotate, spin, spiral, turn, twiddle, twist, whirl, wind

**twist** n 1 coil, curl, screw, spin, spiral, swivel, turn, twiddle, twirl, wind, wring. 2 (bend) angle, bend, curve, hairpin, turn, zigzag. 3 (distortion) bend, buckle, contortion, distortion, kink, warp, wrinkle. 4 (turn of events) complication, development, oddity, quirk, revelation, slant, turn of events, variation

**twist** v 1 coil, corkscrew, curl, meander, screw, snake, spin, spiral, swivel, turn, twine, weave, wind, worm, wrap, wring, zigzag. 2 (contort) bend, buckle, contort, distort, kink, screw up, warp, wrinkle. 3 squirm, wriggle, writhe. 4 (twist your ankle) hurt, pull, rick, sprain, strain, turn, wrench. 5 (twist sb's words) change, distort, falsify, misinterpret, misquote, misrepresent, pervert, warp

**twisty** adj bendy, contorted, crooked, curving, meandering, rambling, serpentine, sinuous, snaking, tortuous, twisting, winding, zigzag

**twit** n clot, clown, dimwit inf, dingbat inf, dope inf, fool, idiot, nerd inf, nitwit inf, twerp inf, wally inf

**twitch** n 1 convulsion, jerk, jump, spasm, tic, tremor. 2 jerk, pull, tug, tweak, yank

**twitch** v 1 flutter, go into spasm, jerk, jump, shake, tremble. 2 jerk, pull, snatch, tug, tweak, yank

**two** n brace, couple, duet, duo, pair, twosome

**tycoon** n baron, businessperson, capitalist, entrepreneur, fat cat inf, financier, industrialist, magnate, millionaire, mogul, supremo, wheeler-dealer

**type** n 1 category, character, class, genre, group, kind, nature, order, sort, species, variety. 2 characters, font, fount, lettering, letters, print, text, typeface, words

**typical** adj 1 average, normal, ordinary, regular, routine, run-of-the-mill, usual; **opp** unusual. 2 archetypal, classic, conventional, model, orthodox, representative, quintessential, standard, stock; **opp** unusual. 3 characteristic, in character, normal, predictable, unsurprising, usual, to be expected; **opp** unusual

**typify** v be a good example of, characterize, epitomize, exemplify, personify, represent, sum up, symbolize

**tyrannical** adj authoritarian, autocratic, despotic, dictatorial, domineering, high-handed, oppressive, overbearing, severe, totalitarian, undemocratic, unjust

**tyranny** n 1 absolutism, authoritarianism, autocracy, despotism, dictatorship. 2 coercion, cruelty, harshness, oppression, severity

**tyrant** n 1 absolute ruler, authoritarian, autocrat, despot, dictator. 2 bully, martinet, oppressor, slave-driver

**ugly** *adj* 1 (of a person) not much to look at *inf*, plain, unattractive; *opp* good-looking. 2 (of a thing) grotesque, hideous, horrible, inelegant, misshapen, nasty, unprepossessing, unsightly. 3 (an ugly sight) disagreeable, distasteful, foul, frightful, hideous, horrible, monstrous, nasty, nauseating, obnoxious, offensive, repulsive, shocking, sickening, vile. 4 (an ugly situation) dangerous, menacing, nasty, ominous, sinister, threatening. 5 (an ugly mood) angry, hostile, sullen, surly

**ulterior** *adj* concealed, covert, hidden, private, secret, underlying, undisclosed; *opp* overt

**ultimate** *adj* 1 closing, concluding, eventual, extreme, final, last, terminal. 2 basic, fundamental, primary, root, underlying. 3 greatest, highest, paramount, supreme, unsurpassed

**umpire** *n* adjudicator, arbitrator, judge, ref *inf*, referee

**unabashed** *adj* blatant, bold, brazen, shameless, unconcerned, undismayed

**unable** *adj* 1 incapable, incompetent, ineffectual, not equal to, not up to, unfit, unqualified; *opp* able. 2 impotent, without the power to, not in a position to, powerless; *opp* able

**unabridged** *adj* complete, entire, full-length, unexpurgated, whole; *opp* abridged

**unacceptable** *adj* 1 inadequate, inadmissible, invalid, unsatisfactory; *opp* acceptable. 2 disagreeable, improper, inappropriate, intolerable, objectionable, obnoxious, offensive, taboo, undesirable, unpleasant, unsuitable

**unaccompanied** *adj* alone, by yourself, lone, on your own, solitary, solo, unescorted, unattended

**unaccustomed** *adj* 1 new, novel, out of the ordinary, special, unfamiliar, unusual; *opp* accustomed, usual. 2 **unaccustomed to** green, inexperienced, new to, not practised in, not used to, unfamiliar with, unversed in; *opp* accustomed to

**unafraid** *adj* bold, confident, daring, fearless, intrepid, undaunted; *opp* afraid

**unanimous** *adj* 1 collective, common, concerted, united. 2 agreed, at one, in complete agreement, like-minded, of one mind, united, with one voice

**unappetizing** *adj* flavourless, insipid, not very nice, off-putting *inf*, tasteless, unattractive, uninteresting, unpalatable, unpleasant, yucky *inf*; *opp* appetizing

**unapproachable** *adj* 1 aloof, chilly, cold, cool, detached, distant, frigid, remote, reserved, standoffish, unfriendly, unsociable, withdrawn; *opp* approachable. 2 inaccessible, out of reach, out of the way, remote; *opp* accessible.

**unarmed** *adj* defenceless, exposed, helpless, unprotected, vulnerable, weaponless; *opp* armed

**unassuming** *adj* diffident, humble, modest, natural, reticent, retiring, self-effacing, simple, unaffected, unassertive, unpretentious

**unattached** *adj* 1 available, footloose and fancy free, free, independent, on your own, single, unmarried, without a partner. 2 autonomous, independent, non-aligned. 3 detached, disconnected, loose; *opp* attached

**unattended** *adj* 1 abandoned, left alone, unguarded. 2 alone, by yourself, on your own, unaccompanied, unescorted

**unattractive** *adj* 1 (of a person) not much to look at *inf*, plain, ugly; *opp* attractive. 2 (of a thing) inelegant, unprepossessing, ugly, unsightly; *opp* attractive. 3 disagreeable, distasteful, foul, nasty, objectionable, off-putting *inf*, repellent, repulsive, unpleasant, vile. 4 dull, plain, uninteresting, uninviting; *opp* attractive

**unauthorized** *adj* illegal, illicit, irregular, unlawful, unlicensed, unofficial

**unavoidable** *adj* 1 bound to happen, certain, destined, fated, inescapable, inevitable, inexorable, predestined, sure, unalterable; *opp* avoidable. 2 compulsory, mandatory, necessary, obligatory

**unaware** *adj* ignorant, ill-informed,

oblivious, unconscious, uninformed, unknowing, unsuspecting; *opp* aware

**unbalanced** *adj* 1 asymmetrical, irregular, lopsided, out of balance, unstable, unsteady, wobbly; *opp* balanced. 2 crazy, demented, deranged, eccentric, insane, irrational, mad, mentally ill, off your head *inf*, off your trolley *inf*, out to lunch *inf*, unstable *inf*; *opp* sane. 3 biased, bigoted, one-sided, partial, prejudiced; *opp* balanced, fair

**unbearable** *adj* insufferable, intolerable, more than flesh and blood can stand *inf*, too much *inf*, unacceptable, unendurable

**unbelievable** *adj* beyond belief, far-fetched, implausible, impossible, improbably, inconceivable, incredible, preposterous; *opp* believable

**unbiased** *adj* disinterested, equitable, even-handed, fair, impartial, just, neutral, objective, unprejudiced; *opp* biased

**unbreakable** *adj* indestructible, shatter-proof, rugged, solid, tough, toughened

**uncalled-for** *adj* gratuitous, needless, undeserved, unjustified, unnecessary, unwarranted

**uncanny** *adj* 1 creepy *inf*, eerie, mysterious, queer, spooky *inf*, strange, supernatural, weird. 2 astonishing, astounding, extraordinary, incredible, remarkable, striking

**uncertain** *adj* 1 ambivalent, distrustful, doubtful, dubious, hesitant, indecisive, in two minds, not convinced, not sure, sceptical, tentative, unconvinced, undecided, unsure, vague, wavering; *opp* certain, sure. 2 chancy, dicey *inf*, dodgy *inf*, doubtful, iffy *inf*, in the balance, precarious, questionable, risky, unclear, undecided, unpredictable, up in the air. **3** changeable, erratic, fitful, inconstant, not dependable, unpredictable, unreliable, unsettled, variable

**uncertainty** *n* **1** ambivalence, confusion, distrust, doubt, hesitance, indecision, lack of confidence, perplexity, scepticism, vacillation, vagueness; *opp* certainty. **2** doubtfulness, unpredictability, unreliability. **3** doubt, misgiving, qualm

**uncharitable** *adj* censorious, hard, harsh, insensitive, intolerant, stern, unchristian, uncompromising, unforgiving, unkind, unsympathetic; *opp* charitable

**uncharted** *adj* not mapped, strange, undiscovered, unexplored, unfamiliar, unknown, unsurveyed

**uncivilized** *adj* **1** barbarian, barbaric, barbarous, primitive, savage, wild; *opp* civilized. **2** boorish, churlish, coarse, philistine, uncouth, uncultured, uncultivated, uneducated, unsophisticated

**unclean** *adj* **1** corrupt, defiled, lewd, licentious, sinful, unchaste; *opp* pure. **2** dirty, filthy, foul, impure, polluted, soiled, stained, tainted; *opp* clean

**unclear** *adj* **1** dim, blurred, faint, fuzzy, hazy, indistinct, out of focus, opaque; *opp* clear. **2** ambiguous, confused, garbled, imprecise, muddled, obscure, vague; *opp* clear. **3** not known, uncertain, unknown, unpredictable; *opp* clear

**uncomfortable** *adj* **1** cold, comfortless, cramped, hard, lumpy, painful, Spartan; *opp* comfortable. **2** anxious, awkward, edgy, embarrassed, ill-at-ease, nervous, self-conscious, troubled, worried; *opp* comfortable. **3** awkward, embarrassing, strained, unpleasant

**uncommon** *adj* **1** distinctive, exceptional, out of the ordinary, rare, special, strange, unusual. **2** few and far between *inf*, not common, rare, scarce, thin on the ground *inf*, unusual. **3** extraordinary, outstanding, remarkable, striking

**uncommunicative** *adj* **1** close, curt, secretive, short, silent, taciturn, tight-lipped, unforthcoming. **2** aloof, reserved, reticent, retiring, shy, standoffish, unsociable, withdrawn

**uncomplimentary** *adj* deprecatory, derogatory, disparaging, insulting, pejorative, rude, scathing, unfavourable, unflattering; *opp* complimentary

**uncompromising** *adj* firm, hard-line, implacable, inflexible, intransigent, obstinate, stiff-necked, strict, stubborn, unbending

**unconditional** *adj* absolute, categorical, complete, entire, full, outright, total, unlimited, unqualified, unreserved, unrestricted, wholehearted, with no strings attached *inf*

**unconnected** *adj* **1** detached, divided, independent, separate; *opp* connected. **2** disjointed, illogical, incoherent, irrelevant, rambling, unrelated

**unconscious** *adj* **1** comatose, dead to the world *inf*, in a coma, insensible, knocked out, out cold *inf*, out for the count *inf*, senseless; *opp* conscious. **2** ignorant, insensible, oblivious, unaware, unsuspecting. **3** accidental, inadvertent, unintended, unpremeditated, unwitting; *opp* deliberate. **4** automatic, instinctive, involuntary, reflex, spontaneous, unthinking. **5** repressed, subconscious, subliminal, suppressed; *opp* conscious

**uncontrollable** *adj* **1** incorrigible, out of control, recalcitrant, undisciplined, ungovernable, unmanageable, unruly, untameable, untamed, wild. **2** frantic, frenzied, furious, violent

**uncontrolled** *adj* **1** furious, rampant, riotous, undisciplined, untamed, wild. **2** unbridled, unchecked, uninhibited, unrestrained

**unconventional** *adj* **1** atypical, bizarre, different, idiosyncratic, irregular, odd, offbeat, peculiar, queer, strange, unorthodox, unusual, way-out *inf*, weird, zany; *opp* conventional. **2** bohemian, eccentric, independent, individual, unorthodox, wayward, zany; *opp* conventional. **3** futuristic, new, novel, original, progressive, revolutionary, unorthodox

**unconvincing** *adj* dubious, far-fetched, hard to believe, implausible, improbable, inconclusive, questionable, specious, unlikely; *opp* convincing

**unco-operative** *adj* lazy, not lifting a finger *inf*, obstinate, obstructive, recalcitrant, resistant, selfish, self-willed, unhelpful, unruly; *opp* co-operative, helpful

**unco-ordinated** *adj* all thumbs *inf*, awkward, blundering, bungling, clumsy, inept, lumbering, maladroit,

ungainly, ungraceful

**uncouth** *adj* bad-mannered, boorish, churlish, coarse, crude, loutish, rough, rude, uncivilized; *opp* polite

**uncover** *v* **1** bare, expose, lay bare, show, strip. **2** open, unwrap. **3** bring to light, detect, disclose, discover, reveal, unearth, unmask

**undecided** *adj* **1** indefinite, in the balance, not decided, not known, not settled, pending, uncertain, unresolved. **2** ambivalent, dithering, doubtful, hesitant, indecisive, in two minds, not convinced, uncertain, unsure

**undefined** *adj* **1** imprecise, indeterminate, unclear, unexplained, unspecified, vague. **2** blurry, formless, hazy, indefinite, nebulous, shadowy, vague

**undeniable** *adj* **1** certain, clear, evident, manifest, obvious. **2** indisputable, irrefutable, proven, sound, sure, unquestionable

**underclothes** *n* lingerie, smalls, undergarments, underwear, undies *inf*

**undercover** *adj* clandestine, concealed, covert, furtive, hidden, hush-hush *inf*, secret, stealthy, surreptitious

**undercurrent** *n* **1** feeling, hint, murmur, suggestion, tendency, undertone, vibes *inf*. **2** rip, rip tide, undertow

**underdog** *n* little fellow *inf*, loser, victim, weaker party

**underestimate** *v* **1** look down on, not appreciate, not do justice to, sell short *inf*, underrate, undervalue; *opp* overestimate. **2** (a cost or price) minimize, miscalculate, misjudge, set too low, undervalue

**undergo** v be subjected to, endure, experience, go through, submit to, suffer

**underground** adj 1 below ground, below the surface, buried, covered, subterranean sunken. 2 clandestine, concealed, covert, hidden, secret, surreptitious, undercover, unofficial. 3 alternative, revolutionary, subversive

**undergrowth** n brush, brushwood, ground cover, scrub

**underhand** adj crafty, crooked, deceitful, devious, dishonest, double-dealing, fraudulent, sly, sneaky, treacherous, unscrupulous

**underline** v 1 draw a line under, underscore. 2 accentuate, call attention to, emphasize, highlight, stress

**underlying** adj 1 basic, fundamental, intrinsic, primary, prime, root. 2 concealed, hidden, masked, veiled

**undermine** v 1 damage, impair, sabotage, sap, subvert, threaten, weaken. 2 burrow under, dig under, excavate, tunnel under. 3 erode, wear away

**underrate** v not appreciate, not do justice to, sell short inf, underestimate, undervalue; *opp* overrate

**understand** v 1 appreciate, apprehend, catch on inf, comprehend, cotton on inf, fathom, figure out, follow, get, get sb's drift inf, get the hang of inf, get the message inf, get the picture inf, get to the bottom of, grasp, interpret, see, take in, tumble to, twig inf, work out. 2 empathize with, feel compassion towards, know how sb feels, sympathize with. 3 assume, believe, conclude, gather, hear, learn, presume, suppose, think

**understanding** n 1 appreciation, apprehension, comprehension, grasp, interpretation. 2 acumen, awareness, discernment, insight, judgement, intelligence, knowledge, perceptiveness, percipience, sense, wisdom. 3 compassion, empathy, insight, kindness, sympathy, tolerance. 4 assumption, belief, conclusion, feeling, idea, perception, supposition, view. 5 arrangement, bargain, compact, contract, gentleman's agreement, pact. 6 consensus, fellow-feeling, harmony, sympathy

**understanding** adj compassionate, considerate, forgiving, kind, patient, perceptive, sensitive, sympathetic, tolerant

**understood** adj implicit, implied, inferred, tacit, unspoken, unstated

**undertake** v accept responsibility for, begin, embark on, give an undertaking, promise to do, set about, shoulder, start, tackle

**undertaking** n 1 affair, assignment, business, enterprise, operation, project, task, venture. 2 assurance, pledge, promise, vow, word

**undertone** n 1 low tone, low voice, murmur, whisper. 2 atmosphere, feeling, hint, suggestion, trace, undercurrent

**undervalue** v not appreciate, think too little of, underestimate, underrate

**underwear** n lingerie, smalls, underclothes, undergarments, undies inf

**underweight** adj all skin and bone inf, bony, emaciated, half-starved, scrawny, skinny, thin, undernourished; *opp* overweight

**underwrite** v 1 back, finance, fund, guarantee, insure, sponsor, subsidize, support. 2 agree to, approve, confirm, consent to, endorse, okay *inf*, ratify, sanction. 3 countersign, endorse, initial, sign

**undesirable** adj 1 disagreeable, disliked, nasty, unacceptable, unpleasant, unwanted. 2 disagreeable, nasty, objectionable, obnoxious, offensive, unattractive, unpleasant, unsavoury

**undisciplined** adj 1 anarchic, disobedient, disorderly, naughty, rebellious, uncontrollable, unmanageable, unruly, untrained, wild. 2 capricious, erratic, wilful. 3 chaotic, disorderly, disorganized, lax, uncontrolled, unsystematic

**undisputed** adj accepted, acknowledged, certain, indisputable, recognized, unchallenged, uncontested, undeniable, undoubted

**undistinguished** adj average, commonplace, everyday, indifferent, mediocre, nothing special *inf*, nothing to write home about *inf*, ordinary, unexceptional, unimpressive, unremarkable; *opp* special

**undo** v 1 detach, disconnect, disentangle, loosen, open, uncouple, unfasten, unlock, untie, unwrap. 2 annul, cancel, invalidate, nullify, quash, repeal, rescind, reverse, revoke, set aside. 3 defeat, destroy, overthrow, overturn, ruin, shatter, undermine, wreck

**undoing** n 1 collapse, defeat, destruction, disgrace, downfall, overthrow, reversal, ruin, shame. 2 blight, curse, misfortune, trouble, weakness

**undone** adj 1 detached, disconnected, free, loose, open, unbuttoned, uncoupled, unfastened, untied. 2 ignored, incomplete, left, neglected, not attended to, not done, omitted, outstanding, unfinished. 3 defeated, overthrown, ruined, shattered

**undoubted** adj 1 beyond doubt, certain, incontrovertible, indubitable, irrefutable, proved, proven, sure, undeniable, unquestionable. 2 certain, uncontested, undisputed

**undress** v 1 change, get changed, get undressed, peel off, strip, strip off, take your clothes off, tear your clothes off. 2 (undress sb) get sb undressed, strip, take sb's clothes off, tear sb's clothes off

**undue** adj disproportionate, excessive, extreme, inappropriate, inordinate, undeserved, unjustified, unnecessary, unreasonable, unwarranted

**unduly** adv disproportionately, excessively, inordinately, unnecessarily, unreasonably

**undying** adj constant, deathless, eternal, everlasting, immortal, perpetual, unceasing, without end

**unearth** v 1 bring to light, discover, expose, ferret out, find, reveal, uncover. 2 dig up, disinter, dredge up, excavate, exhume

**unearthly** adj 1 eerie, ghastly, ghostly, spooky *inf*, strange, uncanny, weird. 2 absurd, preposterous, ridiculous

**uneasy** adj 1 agitated, anxious, apprehensive, disturbed, edgy, jittery, nervous, on edge, perturbed, tense, troubled, twitchy, upset, worried. 2 awkward, insecure, precarious, strained, tense, uncomfortable, unstable

**uneconomic** adj inefficient, loss-making, uneconomical, unproductive, unprofitable, wasteful

**uneducated** adj ignorant, ill-informed, illiterate, lowbrow, non-academic, uncultivated, uninformed, unschooled, unskilled, untaught, untrained, untutored; **opp** educated

**unemotional** adj aloof, calm, cold, controlled, cool, deadpan, detached, dispassionate, distant, emotionless, expressionless, frigid, hard-nosed, heartless, icy, impassive, impersonal, indifferent, inscrutable, insensitive, passionless, phlegmatic, poker-faced, reserved, soulless, stoical, stolid, stony-faced, unconcerned, undemonstrative, unfeeling, unmoved, unresponsive, unruffled, unsentimental

**unemployed** adj idle, jobless, laid off, on the dole inf, out of a job, out of work, redundant, resting, signing on, unemployable, unoccupied; **opp** employed

**unending** adj ceaseless, constant, endless, eternal, everlasting, imperishable, incessant, never-ending, nonstop, perennial, permanent, perpetual, interminable, undying, unrelenting, unremitting, without end

**unequal** adj 1 asymmetrical, different, differing, disproportionate, dissimilar, uneven, unmatched, unvarying. 2 (of a society) class-ridden, hierarchical, inequitable, prejudiced, undemocratic, unfair, unjust; **opp** egalitarian

**unequalled** adj best, beyond compare, greatest, highest, incomparable, matchless, peerless, record, record-breaking, second to none, supreme, unbeaten, unique, unparalleled, unrivalled, unsurpassed

**unequivocal** adj absolute, certain, clear, definite, plain, unambiguous, unmistakable

**unethical** adj dishonest, dishonourable, unconscionable, unfair, unprincipled, unprofessional, unscrupulous, wrong; **opp** ethical

**uneven** adj 1 bumpy, jagged, lumpy, pitted, pockmarked, rough, rutted, undulating, up-and-down; **opp** even. 2 erratic, fitful, inconsistent, intermittent, irregular, spasmodic, up-and-down, variable, varying

**uneventful** adj boring, humdrum, ordinary, quiet, routine, unexciting, uninteresting; **opp** eventful

**unexceptional** adj average, indifferent, mediocre, middling, ordinary, regular, uneventful; **opp** exceptional

**unexpected** adj like a bolt from the blue, sudden, surprising, unannounced, unanticipated, unforeseen, unheralded, unpredicted; **opp** expected

**unfailing** adj absolute, constant, dependable, regular as clockwork, reliable, sure-fire inf

**unfair** adj 1 arbitrary, dishonest, sneaky inf, undeserved, unethical, unjust, unjustifiable, unmerited, unreasonable, wrong, wrongful; **opp** fair. 2 (favouring some people and not others) biased, discriminatory, inequitable, one-sided, partial, partisan, prejudiced, unbalanced, unequal, uneven; **opp** fair, just. 3 (victimizing sb) cruel, hard, harsh, unkind

**unfaithful** adj 1 adulterous, flighty, flirtatious, inconstant, philandering, promiscuous, two-timing; *opp* faithful. 2 deceitful, disloyal, double-crossing, double-dealing, faithless, false, perfidious, traitorous, treacherous; *opp* loyal

**unfashionable** adj behind the times, dated, dowdy, old-fashioned, out of date, out of fashion, out of favour, outdated, outmoded, square inf, unhip inf, unpopular; *opp* fashionable

**unfasten** v detach, free, loose, release, separate, unclip, uncouple, undo, unhitch, unhook, unlock, untie; *opp* fasten

**unfavourable** adj 1 (of circumstances) adverse, disadvantageous, inauspicious, unfortunate, unpromising. 2 (of comments, opinion) adverse, damning, critical, disapproving, hostile, negative; *opp* favourable

**unfeeling** adj callous, cold, cold-blooded, cold-hearted, cruel, emotionless, hard, impassive, indifferent, insensitive, hard-hearted, heartless, inhuman, inhumane, insensitive, pitiless, uncaring, unconcerned, unemotional, unmoved, unsentimental, unsympathetic; *opp* sympathetic

**unfit** adj 1 below par, ill, injured, out of shape inf, sick, stiff, unhealthy, unwell, weak; *opp* fit, healthy. 2 ill-adapted, ill-suited, inadequate, inappropriate, incapable, incompetent, unacceptable, unequipped, unsuitable, unsuited, unsatisfactory, useless

**unflinching** adj bold, brave, constant,

courageous, determined, nerveless, resolute, steadfast, steady, unflagging, unwavering

**unfold** v 1 extend, open out, spread out, straighten out, unfurl, unroll. 2 (of story, events) be revealed, become known, continue, develop, evolve, progress, take place, take shape

**unforeseen** adj sudden, surprising, unanticipated, unexpected, unplanned, unscheduled

**unfortunate** adj 1 hapless, ill-fated, ill-starred, luckless, out of luck, unlucky, unsuccessful. 2 annoying, deplorable, regrettable, infelicitous, lamentable, untimely

**unfounded** adj baseless, false, groundless, idle, invalid, unjustified, unproven, unsupported, untenable, untrue, without foundation

**unfriendly** adj aloof, antagonistic, churlish, cold, distant, hostile, impolite, rude, stand-offish inf, surly, unkind, unpleasant; *opp* friendly

**ungainly** adj awkward, clumsy, gangling, heavy-footed, hulking, lumbering, shambling, unco-ordinated; *opp* graceful

**ungodly** adj 1 blasphemous, corrupted, depraved, evil, heathen, profane, sacrilegious, sinful, unholy, wicked. 2 (at this ungodly hour) improper, inappropriate, indecent, uncivilized, unseemly

**ungrateful** adj churlish, discourteous, impolite, mercenary, rude, ungracious, unthankful; *opp* grateful

**unhappy** adj 1 depressed, disconsolate, distressed, downcast, downhearted, inconsolable, melancholy, miserable, sad; *opp* happy. **2** (unhappy about a decision) aggrieved, annoyed, discontented, disgruntled, dissatisfied, resentful; *opp* happy. **3** (of event, circumstances) deplorable, lamentable, regrettable, sad, tragic, unfortunate; *opp* fortunate

**unharmed** *adj* intact, safe, safe and sound, undamaged, unhurt, unscathed, untouched, whole

**unhealthy** *adj* **1** ailing, delicate, frail, ill, in poor health, infirm, invalid, sick, unfit, unwell, weak; *opp* healthy. **2** (unhealthy conditions) detrimental, harmful, insalubrious, insanitary, noxious, unwholesome

**unheard-of** *adj* inconceivable, original, unknown, unfamiliar, unimaginable, unimagined, unprecedented, without precedent

**unidentified** *adj* mysterious, nameless, unfamiliar, unknown, unnamed, unrecognized

**uniform** *adj* **1** common, comparable, consistent, equal, homogeneous, identical, invariable, same, similar, unified, universal. **2** (of speed, rate) constant, even, regular, same, smooth, unchanging, unvarying

**uniform** *n* costume, dress, livery, outfit, regalia, robes, suit

**uniformity** *n* consistency, evenness, homogeneity, monotony, regularity, sameness, similarity, unity

**unify** *v* amalgamate, bind, bring together, combine, fuse, harmonize, join, merge, unite

**unimaginable** *adj* beyond belief, fantastic, impossible, inconceivable,

incredible, unbelievable

**unimportant** *adj* insignificant, irrelevant, meaningless, minor, obscure, paltry, petty, secondary, trifling, trivial, two-bit *inf*, worthless; *opp* important

**uninhabited** *adj* barren, desert, deserted, empty, unoccupied, unpopulated, vacant; *opp* inhabited

**unintelligent** *adj* brainless *inf*, daft *inf*, dim *inf*, dozy *inf*, foolish, hare-brained *inf*, impractical, mindless, obtuse, senseless, silly, slow, slow-witted, stupid, thoughtless, unimaginative, unwise, witless; *opp* intelligent

**unintentional** *adj* accidental, casual, chance, coincidental, inadvertent, subconscious, unconscious, unintended; *opp* deliberate, intentional

**uninterested** *adj* apathetic, bored, distracted, fed up, incurious, indifferent, listless, tired, unconcerned; *opp* interested

**union** *n* **1** (act of coming together) amalgamation, association, combination, conjunction, fusion, intermingling, marriage, merger, unification, uniting. **2** (organization) alliance, association, brotherhood, coalition, confederacy, confederation, federation, fellowship, fraternity, guild, league, partnership, society

**unique** *adj* incomparable, inimitable, matchless, one of a kind, original, peerless, unequalled, unparalleled, unprecedented, unrepeatable, unrivalled

**unison** *n* **in unison** collectively, in agreement, in concert, in harmony, together, unanimously, with one accord, with one voice

**unit** n **1** agency, corps, department, detachment, detail, group, section, squad, task-force. **2** building block, component, constituent, element, item, member, module, part, piece

**unite** v **1** (unite things, groups) ally, amalgamate, associate, blend, bring together, combine, fuse, harmonize, join, link, marry, meld, merge, unify, wed; *opp* separate. **2** (people unite) ally, associate, band together, close ranks, collaborate, co-operate, come together, gang up, join forces, pool your resources, work together

**united** adj **1** (of people) agreed, at one, collaborative, collective, combined, concerted, co-operative, co-ordinated, in harmony, in unison, together, unanimous. **2** (of organizations) amalgamated, affiliated, allied, combined, in alliance, in association, unified

**unity** n **1** (within a structure, a text) agreement, coherence, cohesion, completeness, consistency, harmony, oneness, regularity, uniformity. **2** (within a group of people) accord, agreement, collaboration, concord, consensus, co-operation, harmony, like-mindedness, rapport, solidarity, sweetness and light *inf*, togetherness *inf*, unanimity; *opp* disunity

**universal** adj all-embracing, all-inclusive, common, comprehensive, constant, general, global, ubiquitous, uniform, unvarying, widespread

**universe** n cosmos, creation, ether, heavens, outer space, space, void

**unjust** adj immoral, indefensible, inequitable, undeserved, unequal, unfair, unjustifiable, unjustified, unmerited, wrong, wrongful; *opp* fair, just

**unjustifiable** adj excessive, illegitimate, indefensible, inexcusable, unacceptable, unconscionable, unforgivable, unjust, unjustified, unreasonable, unwarranted; *opp* justifiable

**unkind** adj beastly *inf*, callous, churlish, cruel, harsh, impolite, inconsiderate, insensitive, malevolent, malicious, mean, nasty *inf*, pitiless, rough, rude, sadistic, savage, severe, sharp, spiteful, uncaring, uncharitable, unchristian, unfair, unfriendly, unpleasant, unsympathetic, vicious; *opp* kind

**unknown** adj anonymous, mysterious, nameless, obscure, strange, uncharted, undiscovered, unexplored, unheard-of, unfamiliar, unidentified, unnamed, unrecognized, unspecified, unsung; *opp* famous, well-known

**unlawful** adj against the law, banned, criminal, forbidden, illegal, illicit, outlawed, prohibited, unauthorized, wrongful; *opp* legal

**unlike** prep **be unlike** be different from, be dissimilar to, bear no resemblance to, have nothing in common with

**unlikely** adj **1** (sth is unlikely to happen) doubtful, impossible, improbable, inconceivable. **2** (of a story) dubious, far-fetched, implausible, improbable, incredible, suspect, unbelievable, unconvincing; *opp* believable, convincing

**unlimited** adj boundless, endless, immeasurable, infinite, limitless, unbounded

**unload** v clear out, deposit, empty, remove, set down, take out, unpack

**unlock** v open, release, unbolt, unfasten; **opp** lock

**unloved** adj disliked, detested, emotionally deprived, forsaken, friendless, hated, jilted, loathed, neglected, rejected, shunned, starved of affection, uncared-for, unpopular, unwanted

**unlucky** adj down on your luck, hapless, ill-fated, ill-starred, luckless, out of luck, star-crossed, unfortunate, unhappy, unsuccessful; **opp** lucky

**unmarried** adj 1 bachelor, celibate, divorced, engaged, single, on the shelf inf, unattached, unwed, widowed; **opp** married. 2 (of a couple, partner) cohabiting, common-law, living in sin

**unmistakable** adj blatant, categorical, clear, conspicuous, glaring, indisputable, manifest, obvious, plain, striking, unambiguous, unequivocal

**unmitigated** adj absolute, complete, downright, out-and-out, thorough, total, unqualified, utter, veritable

**unmoved** adj aloof, cold, impassive, impervious, indifferent, stony-faced, unaffected, uncaring, unconcerned, unfeeling, unperturbed; **opp** moved

**unnatural** adj 1 (unnatural phenomena) abnormal, bizarre, extraordinary, paranormal, strange, supernatural; **opp** natural. 2 (of feelings, relationships) abnormal, against nature, deviant, perverted, unhealthy, unwholesome; **opp** natural, normal. 3 (of behaviour) affected, artificial, contrived, false, feigned, forced, insincere, mannered,

stagy, strained, studied; **opp** natural

**unnecessary** adj 1 dispensable, expendable, gratuitous, needless, pointless, redundant, superfluous, surplus to requirements, unwanted, useless; **opp** necessary. 2 excessive, gratuitous, inappropriate, injudicious, inopportune, out of place, uncalled-for, undesirable, unhelpful, unseasonable, unsuitable, untimely, untoward, unwelcome

**unnerve** v agitate, alarm, daunt, demoralize, deter, disconcert, discourage, dishearten, disquiet, frighten, fluster, perturb, put off, rattle inf, scare, shake, stop sb in their tracks, take aback, throw off balance, trouble, unman, unsettle, worry

**unobtrusive** adj discreet, low-key, low-profile, modest, self-effacing, unassuming, unnoticeable, unostentatious

**unoccupied** adj deserted, empty, uninhabited, unpopulated, vacant

**unofficial** adj casual, informal, unauthorized, unconfirmed, unsanctioned, wildcat; **opp** official

**unorthodox** adj abnormal, creative, different, irregular, noncomformist, non-standard, original, strange, unconventional, unusual; **opp** conventional, orthodox

**unpaid** adj amateur, free of charge, gratis, honorary, voluntary, volunteer; **opp** paid

**unpleasant** adj 1 bad, disagreeable, disgusting, distasteful, foul, nasty, nauseating, offensive, repellent, repugnant, unpalatable, unsavoury, unspeakable inf; **opp** pleasant.

**2** (of a person) bad-tempered, churlish, cruel, disagreeable, hostile, ill-natured, insulting, nasty, nauseating, obnoxious, offensive, repulsive, rude, surly, ugly, unattractive, unfriendly, unkind, unspeakable *inf*; **opp** nice

**unpopular** *adj* disliked, out of favour, unfashionable, unloved, unwanted, unwelcome; **opp** popular

**unpredictable** *adj* **1** chance, erratic, haphazard, in the balance, irregular, random, uncertain, unforeseeable, up in the air *inf*. **2** (of a person) capricious, enigmatic, erratic, fickle, full of surprises, inconsistent, mercurial, temperamental, unreliable, unstable, volatile

**unproductive** *adj* fruitless, futile, idle, ineffective, pointless, time-wasting, unprofitable, unrewarding, useless, vain, wasted, worthless; **opp** productive

**unravel** *v* disentangle, untangle, straighten out, unpick, untie

**unreal** *adj* **1** artificial, fabricated, false, fictitious, hypothetical, illusory, imaginary, imagined, invented, made-up, make-believe, non-existent, untrue; **opp** real. **2** (causing surprise, bewilderment) absurd, bizarre, paradoxical, strange, surreal, topsy-turvy, unnatural

**unrealistic** *adj* foolish, half-baked *inf*, impossible, impracticable, impractical, improbable, unreasonable, unworkable, wild; **opp** realistic

**unreasonable** *adj* **1** absurd, illogical, irrational, ludicrous, meaningless, nonsensical, senseless; **opp** reasonable. **2** (of demands, expectations, prices) disproportionate, excessive, exorbitant,

extortionate, extreme, inordinate, extravagant, outrageous, preposterous, steep, unconscionable, unfair; **opp** fair, reasonable. **3** (of a person) blinkered, cruel, harsh, inflexible, intolerant, obdurate, obstinate, opinionated, pig-headed *inf*, prejudiced, stubborn, unfair; **opp** reasonable

**unrelated** *adj* coincidental, disparate, independent, separate, unconnected; **opp** related

**unreliable** *adj* dubious, fallible, questionable, suspect, uncertain, unsafe, unsound, untrustworthy; **opp** reliable

**unrest** *n* agitation, discontent, discontentment, discord, dissatisfaction, dissension, dissent, protest, rebellion, rioting, strife, trouble, turmoil, violence; **opp** calm, peace

**unruly** *adj* badly behaved, disobedient, disorderly, insubordinate, misbehaving, mischievous, mutinous, naughty, obstreperous, rebellious, rowdy, uncontrollable, undisciplined, ungovernable, unmanageable, wayward, wild; **opp** quiet, well-behaved

**unsafe** *adj* **1** (of a person) at risk, in danger, insecure, unprotected, vulnerable; **opp** safe. **2** (of an activity, vehicle, equipment) dangerous, faulty, reckless, risky, unreliable, unsound; **opp** safe. **3** (of a criminal conviction) doubtful, dubious, questionable, unreliable, unsound, wrongful

**unsatisfactory** *adj* bad, disappointing, inadequate, poor, unacceptable, unfit, unsatisfying; **opp** satisfactory

**unsavoury** *adj* **1** disagreeable, distasteful, disgusting, gross, nasty, offensive, repellent, repulsive, unpleasant; *opp* pleasant. 2 (an unsavoury character) criminal, crooked, dodgy *inf*, doubtful, dubious, low-life, questionable, seedy, shady, sleazy *inf*, suspect, suspicious, underworld, untrustworthy

**unscrupulous** adj amoral, bad, corrupt, deceitful, devious, dishonest, evil, exploitative, immoral, ruthless, unconscionable, unethical, unprincipled, untrustworthy, wicked

**unsettle** v agitate, bother, confuse, discomfit, disconcert, disturb, make sb feel uncomfortable, perturb, rattle *inf*, ruffle, shake, throw, throw sb off balance, trouble, unnerve, upset, worry; *opp* reassure

**unsettled** adj 1 agitated, anxious, dissatisfied, edgy *inf*, fidgety, on edge, perturbed, restive, restless, shaken, rattled *inf*, tense, troubled, uneasy. 2 (of weather) changeable, rainy, showery, wet; *opp* settled

**unsightly** adj hideous, obtrusive, out of place, repulsive, ugly, unattractive, unpleasant; *opp* attractive

**unsound** adj defective, dodgy *inf*, doubtful, dubious, erroneous, fallacious, faulty, flawed, ill-founded, illogical, questionable, shaky, specious, spurious, uncertain, unreasonable, unreliable, unsafe, weak

**unspoiled** adj as good as new, conserved, in its natural state, intact, natural, perfect, preserved, unadulterated, unblemished, unchanged, undamaged, unimpaired, undefiled, untouched

**unspoken** adj implicit, implied, tacit, taken for granted, unarticulated,

undeclared, understood, unstated

**unstable** adj 1 (of a structure) flimsy, insecure, precarious, rickety, rocky, shaky, tottering, unsafe, unsteady, wobbly; *opp* stable. 2 (of a situation) changeable, erratic, fitful, fluctuating, inconsistent, shifting, unpredictable, variable, volatile; *opp* stable. 3 (of a person) capricious, irrational, temperamental, unbalanced, unhinged, unpredictable, unreliable; *opp* stable

**unsteady** adj 1 (of a structure) flimsy, insecure, precarious, rickety, rocky, shaky, tottering, unsafe, unstable, wobbly; *opp* steady. 2 (of sb's voice) changeable, erratic, fluctuating, inconstant, irregular, up and down, variable, wavering; *opp* steady

**unsuccessful** adj 1 failed, fruitless, futile, unprofitable, useless, vain; *opp* successful. 2 (in a game) beaten, defeated, hapless, losing, unlucky, vanquished; *opp* successful

**unsuitable** adj ill-chosen, ill-judged, inappropriate, inapt, incompatible, incongruous, out of keeping, out of place, unacceptable, unfitting, unsuited; *opp* suitable

**unsure** adj doubtful, dubious, hesitant, in two minds, irresolute, sceptical, suspicious, unconvinced, undecided, wavering; *opp* sure

**unsuspecting** adj credulous, green *inf*, gullible, naïve, off guard, trusting, unwary; *opp* sceptical

**untangle** v 1 (untangle a rope) disentangle, straighten, unravel; *opp* tangle. 2 (untangle a mystery) clear up, explain, solve, sort out

**unthinkable** adj 1 beyond the bounds of possibility, implausible, impossible, inconceivable; **opp** possible.
2 (unthinkable cruelty) incredible, outrageous, terrible, unbelievable, unimaginable

**untidy** adj cluttered, disorderly, in a mess, in a state, in disarray, jumbled, like a pig sty, littered, messy, rumpled; **opp** tidy

**untie** v disentangle, free, loosen, release, undo, unfasten, unhitch; **opp** fasten

**untimely** adj 1 (untimely death) early, premature. 2 (an untimely visit) ill-timed, inconvenient, inopportune; **opp** well-timed

**untold** adj 1 (untold damage) indescribable, inexpressible, unimaginable, unspeakable, unthinkable, unutterable. 2 (untold millions) countless, immeasurable, incalculable, innumerable, uncountable, uncounted

**untoward** adj improper, inappropriate, indecorous, unacceptable, unbecoming, unseemly, unsuitable; **opp** acceptable

**untrue** adj erroneous, fallacious, false, inaccurate, incorrect, mistaken, spurious, wrong; **opp** true

**untrustworthy** adj bent inf, crooked, deceitful, devious, dishonest, disloyal, shady inf, slippery inf, tricky, two-faced, undependable, unreliable; **opp** trustworthy

**unusual** adj abnormal, atypical, bizarre, curious, different inf, extraordinary, irregular, odd, out of the ordinary, queer, rare, remarkable, strange, surprising, uncommon, unexpected, unfamiliar, weird inf; **opp** normal, usual

**unwelcome** adj 1 (make sb feel unwelcome) excluded, rejected, uninvited, unwanted; **opp** welcome.
2 (an unwelcome intrusion) disagreeable, displeasing, unacceptable, undesirable, uninvited, unpleasant, unwanted; **opp** welcome

**unwell** adj ailing, groggy inf, ill, in poor health, not very well, off-colour, out of sorts, poorly, sick, sickly, under the weather; **opp** well

**unwieldy** adj 1 (of an object) bulky, cumbersome, hefty, hulking, massive, unmanoeuvrable. 2 (of a system) awkward, cumbersome, inconvenient, unmanageable; **opp** efficient

**unwilling** adj 1 (an unwilling helper) grudging, reluctant, resistant, uncooperative, unenthusiastic, unhelpful; **opp** willing. 2 (unwilling to do sth) averse, disinclined, indisposed, loath, slow; **opp** willing

**unwind** v 1 disentangle, slacken, uncoil, undo, unravel, unreel, unroll, untwist; **opp** wind. 2 (relax) chill out inf, relax, take it easy, wind down

**unwise** adj daft inf, foolhardy, foolish, ill-advised, ill-judged, improvident, imprudent, inadvisable, injudicious, irresponsible, rash, reckless, senseless, silly, stupid, thoughtless; **opp** wise

**unwitting** adj 1 innocent, unaware, unknowing, unsuspecting. 2 (an unwitting blunder) accidental, chance, inadvertent, involuntary, unintended, unintentional; **opp** intentional

**unworthy** adj base, contemptible, despicable, disgraceful, disreputable, reprehensible, shameful; **opp** worthy

**unyielding** adj adamant, firm, hardline, inflexible, intransigent, obstinate, pig-headed, resolute, rigid, steadfast, stubborn, tough, uncompromising; **opp** flexible

**upbringing** n breeding, cultivation, education, instruction, nurture, raising, rearing, training

**upgrade** v (upgrade sth) enhance, expand, improve, make better, refurbish; **opp** downgrade. 2 (upgrade sb) advance, elevate, promote, raise; **opp** downgrade

**upheaval** n chaos, commotion, confusion, difficulty, disorder, disruption, disturbance, revolution, to-do inf, turmoil, upset

**uphill** adj 1 (an uphill climb) ascending, climbing, rising, upward; **opp** downhill. 2 (an uphill struggle) arduous, difficult, exhausting, gruelling, hard, laborious, onerous, punishing, strenuous, taxing, tough; **opp** easy

**uphold** v advocate, back, champion, defend, encourage, endorse, maintain, stand by, stick up for inf, support; **opp** reject

**upkeep** n care, maintenance, repair, running, support

**uplifting** adj cheering, encouraging, feel-good, heartening, inspiring; **opp** depressing

**upper** n elevated, high, highest, superior, top, topmost, uppermost; **opp** lower

**upright** adj 1 erect, on end, perpendicular, straight, vertical; **opp** leaning. 2 decent, fair, good, honest, principled, respectable, righteous, straight inf, upstanding,

virtuous; **opp** dishonest

**uprising** n coup, coup d'état, disturbance, insurgence, insurrection, mutiny, rebellion, revolt, revolution, riot, rising

**uproar** n bedlam, chaos, commotion, hullaballoo inf, mayhem, outcry, pandemonium, riot, ructions inf, rumpus inf, tumult, turbulence, turmoil

**uproarious** adj 1 chaotic, boisterous, disorderly, loud, noisy, rowdy, riotous, tumultuous, turbulent, unruly, wild; **opp** calm. 2 (an uproarious show) hilarious, hysterical, rip-roaring, side-splitting

**upset** adj anxious, bothered, dismayed, distressed, disturbed, hurt, ruffled, saddened, shaken, troubled, worried

**upset** n 1 bother, dismay, distress, disturbance, hurt, sadness, worry. 2 (a stomach upset) complaint, disturbance, illness, sickness

**upset** v 1 (upset sb) bother, dismay, distress, disturb, hurt, ruffle, sadden, shake, trouble, worry. 2 (upset sb's plans) disrupt, disturb, hinder, interfere with, jeopardize, mess up, spoil. 3 (upset sth) overturn, tip over, topple, turn over, upend

**upshot** n conclusion, culmination, denouement, issue, outcome, result

**upside down** adj inverted, overturned, the wrong way up, topsy-turvy, upended, upturned

**upstanding** adj decent, fair, good, honest, principled, respectable, righteous, straight inf, upstanding, virtuous; **opp** dishonest

**upward** adj ascending, climbing, rising, uphill; **opp** downward

**urban** *adj* built-up, city, civic, inner-city, metropolitan, municipal, suburban, town; *opp* rural

**urge** *n* compulsion, desire, drive, hunger, impulse, itch, longing, need, thirst, wish, yearning

**urge** *v* **1** (urge sb to do sth) compel, drive, egg on *inf*, encourage, entreat, force, goad, impel, incite, induce, persuade, prompt, spur, stimulate. **2** (urge restraint) advise, advocate, back, counsel, endorse, recommend, suggest

**urgency** *n* haste, hurry, importance, necessity, need, seriousness, top priority

**urgent** *adj* compelling, crucial, high-priority, imperative, important, pressing, top-priority

**use** *n* **1** employment, exploitation, operation, usage, utilization. **2** (have several uses) application, function, purpose. **3** (be of no use) advantage, benefit, good, help, point, service, usefulness, value, worth

**use** *v* **1** employ, exploit, make use of, operate, ply, put into service, utilize, wield, work. **2** (use all of sth) consume, deplete, exhaust, expend, fritter away, get through, spend, waste

**used** *adj* cast-off, hand-me-down, nearly-new, second-hand, shop-soiled, worn; *opp* new

**useful** *adj* advantageous, beneficial, effective, fruitful, helpful, of help, of use, productive, profitable, rewarding, successful, valuable, worthwhile; *opp* useless

**useless** *adj* **1** fruitless, futile, hopeless, ineffective, of no help, of no use, pointless, unavailing, unproductive, unprofitable, unrewarding, unsuccessful, vain; *opp* useful. **2** (not good at sth) hopeless, inadequate, incapable, incompetent, inept, no good *inf*, poor, rubbish *inf*; *opp* talented

**usual** *adj* common, conventional, customary, established, expected, familiar, habitual, normal, ordinary, orthodox, regular, routine, set, standard, stock, traditional, typical; *opp* unusual

**utilize** *v* employ, have recourse to, make the most of, make use of, put to use, resort to, take advantage of, turn to, use

**utmost** *adj* extreme, greatest, highest, maximum, paramount, supreme

**utmost** *n* **1** (do sth to the utmost) extreme, greatest, highest, max *inf*, maximum. **2** (try your utmost) best, hardest

**utter** *adj* absolute, complete, downright, out-and-out, outright, perfect, sheer, total, unmitigated, unqualified

**utter** *v* articulate, come out with *inf*, express, put sth into words, say, speak, verbalize, vocalize, voice

**utterly** *adv* absolutely, completely, entirely, perfectly, thoroughly, totally

**vacancy** n job, opening, position, post, slot

**vacant** adj 1 (a vacant room) available, empty, free, idle, unfilled, unused; *opp* occupied. 2 (a vacant expression) absent-minded, blank, dreamy, faraway, inane, inattentive, vacuous; *opp* attentive

**vacate** v abandon, depart from, desert, evacuate, get out of, leave, quit, withdraw from

**vacuum** n emptiness, gap, nothingness, space, void

**vagabond** n beggar, bum Am inf, down-and-out, tramp, vagrant

**vagrant** n beggar, bum Am inf, down-and-out, tramp, vagabond

**vague** adj 1 (a vague image) blurred, dim, fuzzy, hazy, ill-defined, indistinct, misty, nebulous, obscure, out of focus, shadowy, unclear; *opp* clear. 2 (a vague answer) ambiguous, confused, doubtful, hazy, imprecise, inexact, loose, uncertain,

unclear, woolly inf; *opp* precise

**vain** adj 1 (of a person) arrogant, big-headed inf, boastful, cocky inf, conceited, egotistical, narcissistic, proud, self-admiring, swaggering; *opp* modest. 2 (a vain attempt) fruitless, futile, hopeless, ineffective, of no help, of no use, pointless, unavailing, unproductive, unprofitable, unrewarding, unsuccessful, useless; *opp* successful

**valiant** adj bold, brave, courageous, gallant, heroic, plucky inf, worthy; *opp* faint-hearted

**valid** adj acceptable, approved, authentic, authorized, bona fide, current, genuine, legitimate, official; *opp* invalid

**validate** v approve, authenticate, authorize, certify, endorse, legitimize, make valid, ratify, sanction; *opp* invalidate

**valley** n canyon, chasm, dale, dell, depression, glen, gorge, gully, hollow, ravine, vale; *opp* hill

**valuable** adj 1 costly, dear inf, expensive, irreplaceable, precious, priceless; *opp* worthless. 2 (valuable advice) advantageous, beneficial, helpful, of help, of use, useful, worthwhile; *opp* useless

**value** n 1 cost, price, rate, worth. 2 (the value of sb's advice) advantage, benefit, help, importance, merit, profit, use, usefulness, worth

**value** v 1 (value a house) assess, estimate, evaluate, price, put a figure on inf, rate. 2 (value sb's friendship) appreciate, cherish, hold dear, prize, respect, treasure

**vandal** *n* hooligan, looter, raider, ruffian, thug, trouble-maker

**vanish** *v* disappear, disperse, dissolve, dwindle, evaporate, fade, go away; *opp* appear

**vanity** *n* arrogance, big-headedness *inf*, boastfulness, cockiness *inf*, conceit, egotism, narcissism, pride, self-admiration; *opp* modesty

**vanquish** *v* beat, clobber *inf*, conquer, crush, defeat, lick *inf*, master, overcome, overpower, overthrow, put down, quash, quell, triumph over, wipe the floor with *inf*

**vapour** *n* fog, fumes, gas, haze, mist, smoke, steam

**variable** *adj* changeable, erratic, fickle, fitful, fluctuating, fluid, inconstant, shifting, unpredictable, unstable, unsteady, up and down *inf*, volatile, wavering; *opp* constant

**variation** *n* 1 (a variation from the norm) departure, deviation, difference, discrepancy, divergence, variant. 2 (every day without variation) alteration, change, modification

**varied** *adj* assorted, different, diverse, heterogeneous, miscellaneous, mixed, sundry, various

**variety** *n* 1 (enjoy variety) change, diversity, variation. 2 (a variety of different things) assortment, collection, combination, mixture, range. 3 (a variety of flower) brand, breed, category, class, classification, kind, make, sort, species, strain, type

**various** *adj* assorted, different, diverse, heterogeneous, miscellaneous, mixed, sundry, varied

**vary** *v* 1 (vary sth) adapt, adjust, alter, change, diversify, modify, transform. 2 (vary in quality) be different, differ

**vast** *adj* colossal, enormous, extensive, gigantic, great, huge, immense, infinite, limitless, mammoth, massive, monstrous, unlimited; *opp* tiny

**vault** *n* basement, cavern, cellar, crypt, repository

**vault** *v* bound, clear, hurdle, jump, leap, spring

**veer** *v* change course, change direction, dodge, sheer, shift, swerve, swing, turn

**vegetate** *v* go to seed *inf*, idle, languish, laze around, stagnate

**vegetation** *n* flora, foliage, greenery, growth, plant life, plants, undergrowth

**vehement** *adj* ardent, eager, earnest, enthusiastic, fervent, fierce, intense, keen, passionate, vigorous; *opp* half-hearted

**veil** *n* blanket, cloak, cover, covering, curtain, film, mantle, mask, screen, shade, shroud

**veil** *v* cloak, conceal, cover, disguise, hide, mask, obscure, screen, shroud

**vein** *n* 1 (in a lighter vein) humour, mode, mood, spirit, style, temper, tenor, tone. 2 (a vein of humour) dash, hint, strain, streak, thread. 3 (a vein of coal) bed, deposit, seam, stratum, streak, stripe

**vendetta** *n* conflict, feud, quarrel

**veneer** *n* 1 (a veneer of respectability) appearance, façade, front, guise, pretence, semblance, show. 2 (a veneer of lacquer) coating, covering, finish, surface

**venerable** *adj* esteemed, hallowed,

honoured, respected, venerated

**venerate** v adore, esteem, hero-worship, idolize, pay homage to, respect, revere, reverence, worship

**vengeance** n an eye for an eye, pay-back inf, reprisal, retaliation, retribution, revenge, tit for tat

**venom** n 1 poison, toxin. 2 acrimony, bitterness, grudge, hate, hatred, malevolence, malice, rancour, spite, viciousness, vindictiveness, virulence

**venomous** adj 1 deadly, noxious, poisonous, toxic. 2 acrimonious, bitter, grudging, malevolent, malicious, rancorous, savage, spiteful, vicious, vindictive, virulent

**vent** n aperture, cut, duct, flue, gap, hole, opening, orifice, outlet, passage, slit, slot, split

**vent** v air, articulate, emit, express, give vent to, let out, make known, pour out, utter, voice

**ventilate** v aerate, air, air-condition, freshen, oxygenate

**venture** n chance, endeavour, enterprise, experiment, gamble, project, risk, speculation, undertaking

**venture** v 1 bet, chance, dare, gamble, risk, speculate, stake, wager. 2 (venture an opinion) advance, dare, hazard, put forward, risk, volunteer

**venue** n location, place, setting

**verbal** adj oral, said, spoken, word-of-mouth

**verbose** adj garrulous, long-winded, loquacious, prolix, talkative, voluble, wordy; opp brief, concise

**verdict** n adjudication, assessment, conclusion, decision, finding,

judgment, opinion, ruling

**verge** n border, boundary, brink, edge, limit, lip, margin, side, threshold

**verge on** v approach, border on, come close, come near, tend towards

**verify** v affirm, attest, authenticate, check, confirm, corroborate, establish, prove, substantiate, support, testify to, validate, vouch for

**versatile** adj adaptable, all-round, flexible, handy, multi-purpose, resourceful, variable

**verse** n 1 canto, couplet, lines, stanza, strophe. 2 lyric, ode, poem, poetry, rhyme, sonnet

**version** n account, description, interpretation, portrayal, reading, rendering, rendition, report, translation

**vertical** adj erect, on end, perpendicular, standing, straight, upright; opp horizontal

**vertigo** n dizziness, giddiness, light-headedness, loss of balance

**very** adv awfully inf, decidedly, deeply, eminently, enormously, especially, exceedingly, extremely, greatly, highly, hugely, most, outstandingly, particularly, really, remarkably, to a great extent, terribly inf, truly, unbelievably, unusually, vastly

**vessel** n 1 boat, craft, ship. 2 container, pot, receptacle, tank, vat

**vet** v check out, examine, inspect, investigate, review, scan, scrutinize

**veteran** adj adept, experienced, expert, old, practised, seasoned

**veteran** n master, old hand, old soldier, past master, pro inf, trouper; opp novice

**veto** n ban, bar, block, boycott, embargo,

interdict, prohibition, refusal, rejection, thumbs down *inf*

**veto** *v* ban, bar, block, boycott, dismiss, forbid, prohibit, proscribe, refuse, reject, rule out, turn down, vote against; *opp* allow

**vex** *v* aggravate, annoy, bother, disturb, exasperate, get on sb's nerves *inf*, harass, hassle *inf*, infuriate, irk, irritate, plague, provoke, rile, torment, trouble, upset, worry, wind sb up *inf*

**viable** *adj* achievable, feasible, operable, possible, practicable, realistic, reasonable, sound, sustainable, usable, valid, workable; *opp* impossible

**vibrant** *adj* alive, animated, colourful, dynamic, electric, energetic, lively, sparkling, spirited, throbbing, vivacious, vivid; *opp* dull

**vibrate** *v* oscillate, pulsate, quiver, resonate, reverberate, shake, shiver, throb, tremble, wobble

**vibration** *n* oscillation, pulse, quivering, resonance, reverberation, shaking, shivering, throbbing, trembling, wave, wobble

**vice** *n* 1 badness, corruption, depravity, evil, immorality, iniquity, sin, turpitude, wickedness, wrongdoing; *opp* virtue. 2 bad habit, defect, failing, flaw, foible, imperfection, peccadillo, shortcoming, weakness; *opp* virtue

**vicinity** *n* area, district, environs, locale, locality, neighbourhood, proximity, region, territory, zone

**vicious** *adj* 1 atrocious, barbaric, barbarous, bloodthirsty, brutal, callous, cruel, diabolical, fiendish, foul, heinous, inhuman, merciless, monstrous, pitiless,

ruthless, sadistic, savage, vile, violent. 2 bitchy *inf*, catty, cruel, cutting, malicious, mean, nasty, poisonous, rancorous, savage, sharp, spiteful, venomous, vindictive, vitriolic; *opp* kind

**victim** *n* casualty, fatality, injured party, martyr, prey, scapegoat, sufferer, target

**victimize** *v* bully, discriminate against, exploit, intimidate, oppress, persecute, pick on, prey on, single out, take advantage of, terrorize, torment

**victor** *n* champion, conqueror, first, number one, prizewinner, vanquisher, winner

**victorious** *adj* champion, conquering, first, prizewinning, successful, top, triumphant, vanquishing, winning; *opp* defeated, vanquished

**victory** *n* conquest, mastery, success, triumph, win; *opp* defeat

**view** *n* 1 aspect, landscape, outlook, panorama, picture, prospect, scene, scenery, sight, vision, vista. 2 attitude, belief, conviction, feeling, idea, notion, opinion, perception, position, sentiment, thought

**view** *v* behold, check out *inf*, consider, contemplate, examine, eye, gaze at, inspect, look at, observe, regard, scan, survey, watch, witness

**viewer** *n* audience, observer, onlooker, spectator, watcher

**viewpoint** *n* angle, attitude, opinion, perception, perspective, point of view, position, slant, stance, standpoint

**vigilant** *adj* alert, attentive, careful, cautious, eagle-eyed, observant, on your guard, on your toes *inf*, sharp-eyed, unsleeping, wakeful, wary, watchful

**vigorous** adj active, animated, brisk, dynamic, effective, energetic, fit, flourishing, forceful, full-blooded, hale, hardy, healthy, hearty, intense, lively, lusty, potent, powerful, robust, sound, spirited, strong, sturdy, thriving, virile, vital

**vigour** n activity, animation, dash, dynamism, energy, fitness, force, forcefulness, gusto, health, heartiness, life, liveliness, power, robustness, soundness, spirit, stamina, strength, sturdiness, verve, virility, vitality

**vile** adj 1 bad, base, contemptible, debased, degenerate, depraved, despicable, detestable, evil, ignoble, immoral, impure, loathsome, low, perverted, shocking, sinful, ugly, vicious, wicked; **opp** good. 2 disgusting, foul, horrible, horrid, loathsome, nasty, nauseating, repellent, repugnant, repulsive, revolting, unpleasant, yucky inf; **opp** lovely

**villain** n baddy inf, criminal, crook inf, evil-doer, malefactor, miscreant, reprobate, rogue, ruffian, scoundrel, wretch, wrong-doer

**villainous** adj bad, base, corrupt, criminal, debased, dishonest, evil, fiendish, hateful, heinous, infamous, sinful, treacherous, vicious, vile, wicked

**vindicate** v confirm, corroborate, justify, prove sb right, substantiate, verify

**vindication** n confirmation, corroboration, justification, proof, substantiation, verification

**vindictive** adj avenging, bitter, malevolent, malicious, malignant,

rancorous, resentful, revengeful, spiteful, unforgiving, vengeful

**vintage** adj choice, classic, fine, good, high-quality, mature, mellowed, old, prime, quality, seasoned, select, superior, venerable

**violate** v 1 (violate a law) breach, break, contravene, defy, disobey, disregard, flout, ignore, infringe, transgress. 2 (violate sb) abuse, assault, attack, defile, desecrate, dishonour, force oneself upon, outrage, pollute, rape, ravish

**violation** n 1 (of a law) abuse, breach, breaking, contravention, defiance, disobedience, disregard, flouting, ignoring, infraction, infringement, offence, transgression. 2 (of a person) abuse, assault, attack, defilement, desecration, dishonouring, outrage, rape

**violence** n 1 aggression, assault, attack, bloodshed, brutality, fighting, ferocity, force, roughness, savagery. 2 (of feelings) passion, power, ferocity, force, forcefulness, intensity, power, strength, tempestuousness, vehemence, wildness

**violent** adj 1 aggressive, attacking, bellicose, belligerent, bloodthirsty, brutal, destructive, ferocious, fierce, hot-headed, hot-tempered, intemperate, savage, vicious, warlike. 2 passionate, powerful, fierce, fiery, forceful, intense, powerful, raging, strong, tempestuous, unbridled, uncontrollable, uncontrolled, unrestrained, vehement, wild

**VIP** n celebrity, dignitary, official, personality, star

**virgin** adj chaste, immaculate, inexperienced, maidenly, pure, uncorrupted, undefiled, untouched, vestal, virtuous

**virgin** n girl, maid, maiden

**virile** adj lusty, macho, male, manly, masculine, potent, red-blooded, rugged, strong, vigorous; **opp** effeminate

**virtue** n 1 goodness, honesty, honour, innocence, integrity, morality, probity, rectitude, righteousness, uprightness; **opp** vice. 2 advantage, asset, attribute, credit, good point, merit, quality, strength; **opp** weakness. 3 chastity, honour, innocence, purity, virginity; **opp** vice

**virtuoso** adj bravura, brilliant, dazzling, masterly, outstanding, stunning

**virtuoso** n artist, genius, maestro, master, prodigy

**virtuous** adj 1 blameless, decent, ethical, exemplary, good, honest, honourable, incorruptible, moral, principled, pure, righteous, upright, worthy. 2 chaste, innocent, maidenly, pure, uncorrupted, undefiled, untouched, vestal, virginal

**virulent** adj 1 dangerous, deadly, lethal, life-threatening, noxious, pernicious, poisonous, venomous. 2 acrimonious, bitter, hate-filled, hostile, malevolent, malicious, malignant, savage, vicious, vindictive

**visible** adj apparent, clear, conspicuous, detectable, discernible, distinct, distinguishable, evident, manifest, noticeable, observable, obvious, open, palpable, perceivable, plain, recognizable, unconcealed, undisguised, unmistakable; **opp** invisible

**vision** n 1 eyes, eyesight, perception, sight, view. 2 (sth imagined) apparition,

daydream, delusion, dream, fantasy, hallucination, illusion, image, mental image, mental picture. 3 (a person with vision) far-sightedness, foresight, imagination, insight, intuition, perception, perceptiveness, prescience, understanding

**visionary** adj farseeing, farsighted, futuristic, idealistic, imaginative, insightful, intuitive, perceptive, prescient, prophetic, Utopian

**visit** n call, stay, stopover, visitation

**visit** v call on, drop in on inf, go to see, look up inf, pay a call on, pay a visit to, pop in on inf, see, stay with, stop by

**visitor** n 1 caller, company, guest. 2 day-tripper, holiday-maker, pilgrim, sight-seer, tourist, traveller, tripper

**visual** adj 1 optic, optical. 2 discernible, observable, perceivable, perceptible, visible

**visualize** v conceive, dream up, envisage, have an image of, imagine, picture, think of

**vital** adj 1 basic, cardinal, critical, crucial, decisive, essential, fundamental, imperative, important, indispensable, key, mandatory, requisite, urgent; **opp** inessential. 2 alive, animated, dynamic, energetic, forceful, lively, sparkling, spirited, vigorous, vivacious; **opp** lifeless

**vitality** n animation, dynamism, energy, go inf, life, liveliness, sparkle, spirit, stamina, strength, vigour, vivacity, zest

**vitriolic** adj acerbic, acid, bitchy inf, bitter, caustic, cruel, hostile, malicious, poisonous, sardonic, savage, scathing, spiteful, venomous, vicious, vindictive, virulent, withering

**vivacious** *adj* alive, animated, bubbly, cheerful, ebullient, high-spirited, light-hearted, lively, sparkling, spirited, sprightly; *opp* dull

**vivid** *adj* **1** bright, brilliant, clear, colourful, dazzling, glowing, intense, rich, strong, vibrant; *opp* dull. **2** detailed, evocative, graphic, lifelike, memorable, powerful, realistic, stirring, striking

**vocabulary** *n* **1** lexicon, lexis, words. **2** dictionary, glossary, lexicon, phrasebook, word-list

**vocal** *adj* **1** oral, said, spoken, verbal, vocalized, voiced. **2** blunt, forthright, loud, noisy, outspoken, strident, vociferous

**vocation** *n* calling, career, employment, job, mission, niche, occupation, profession, role, work

**vociferous** *adj* blunt, forthright, insistent, loud, noisy, outspoken, strident, vehement, vocal

**vogue** *n* craze, fad, fashion, latest thing *inf*, in thing *inf*, mode, rage, style, taste, trend

**voice** *n* **1** accent, articulation, inflection, intonation, singing, speaking, speech, tone, utterance. **2** (the voice of the people) opinion, say, view, vote, will, wish

**voice** *v* air, articulate, assert, communicate, declare, divulge, enunciate, explain, express, give voice to, put into words, speak, tell, utter

**void** *n* blank, emptiness, gap, lacuna, nothingness, space, vacuum

**volatile** *adj* capricious, changeable,

erratic, explosive, fickle, flighty, inconstant, mercurial, moody, temperamental, unpredictable, unstable, unsteady, up and down *inf*, variable; *opp* stable

**volley** *n* barrage, battery, blast, bombardment, burst, discharge, explosion, fusillade, hail, salvo, shower

**volume** *n* **1** amount, body, bulk, capacity, dimensions, mass, quantity, size. **2** book, title, tome, treatise, work

**voluntary** *adj* elective, free, optional, non-compulsory, unforced; *opp* compulsory

**volunteer** *n* benefactor, helper, voluntary assistant

**volunteer** *v* be willing, offer, propose, put yourself forward, step forward

**voluptuous** *adj* **1** ample, buxom, curvaceous, curvy *inf*, plump, rounded, sexy, shapely, well-endowed. **2** carnal, hedonistic, luxurious, pleasure-seeking, self-indulgent, sensual

**vomit** *v* be sick, bring sth up, chuck *inf*, disgorge, heave *inf*, hurl *Am inf*, puke *inf*, regurgitate, retch, spew *inf*, throw up *inf*

**voracious** *adj* avid, devouring, eager, famished, gluttonous, greedy, hungry, insatiable, keen, ravenous

**vote** *n* **1** ballot, election, plebiscite, poll, referendum. **2** franchise, say, suffrage, voice

**vote** *v* cast your vote, choose, elect, have your say, nominate, opt, pick, return, select

**vouch for** *v* affirm, answer for, assert, attest to, bear witness, certify, confirm, endorse, guarantee, sponsor, uphold, validate, verify

**vow** *n* oath, pledge, promise, undertaking, word of honour

**vow** *v* affirm, declare, give your word, guarantee, pledge, promise, swear, take an oath

**voyage** *n* crossing, cruise, expedition, journey, passage, travels, trip

**vulgar** *adj* **1** coarse, common, crude, dirty, foul, gross, ill-bred, ill-mannered, impolite, improper, indecent, naughty, offensive, rude, uncouth, unseemly; *opp* polite. **2** flashy, gaudy, in bad taste, inelegant, nasty, showy, tasteless, tawdry; *opp* tasteful

**vulnerable** *adj* at risk, defenceless, easily hurt, exposed, helpless, open, powerless, sensitive, susceptible, tender, unguarded, unprotected, weak, wide open; *opp* strong

**wad** *n* ball, bundle, lump, mass, pad, plug, roll

**wade** *v* 1 paddle, splash. 2 (wade through sth) plough, work your way

**waffle** *n* evasiveness, padding, prattle, verbiage, wittering *inf*, wordiness

**waffle** *v* babble, blather *inf*, jabber, prattle, rabbit *inf*, ramble, witter *inf*

**waft** *v* 1 bear, carry, puff, transport. 2 be borne, be carried, drift, float, glide, travel

**wag** *v* 1 bob, flap, nod, waggle, wave, wiggle, wobble. 2 rock, shake, sway, swing, twitch, undulate, vibrate

**wage** *n* allowance, earnings, fee, income, pay, payment, pay packet, remuneration, salary, stipend, wages

**wager** *n* bet, flutter *inf*, gamble, stake

**wager** *v* bet, chance, gamble, lay odds, place a bet, punt, put money on, stake

**waggle** *n* shake, wag, wave, wiggle, wobble

**waggle** *v* flutter, oscillate, shake, sway, wag, wave, wiggle, wobble

**wail** *n* complaint, cry, howl, moan, sob

**wail** *v* bawl, caterwaul, cry, howl, lament, shriek, sob, weep

**wait** *n* delay, halt, hold-up, interval, pause, rest, stop

**wait** *v* 1 be patient, bide your time, delay, hang fire, hang on *inf*, hesitate, hold back, hold your horses *inf*, linger, pause, sit tight *inf*, stay, stop. 2 **wait on** attend to, minister to, serve

**waive** *v* forgo, give up, relinquish, renounce, sign away, surrender, yield

**wake** *v* 1 (wake sb) disturb, rouse, waken, wake up. 2 (sb wakes) get up, rise, stir, wake up

**wakeful** *adj* 1 restless, sleepless. 2 alert, attentive, observant, on the lookout, vigilant, wary, watchful

**waken** *v* awaken, stir, wake up

**walk** *n* 1 hike, promenade, ramble, stroll, trek. 2 (way of walking) gait, step, stride, way of walking. 3 (a tree-lined walk) alley, avenue, drive, footpath, lane, path, pavement

**walk** *v* 1 go by foot, go walking, hike, ramble. 2 amble, plod, saunter, stroll, traipse, tramp, troop, trudge. 3 (walk on the grass) stand, step, trample, tread. 4 **walk out** (leave) flounce out, get up and go, leave suddenly, storm out. 5 **walk out** (go on strike) down tools, go on strike, quit, stop work, strike, take industrial action. 6 **walk out on** abandon, desert, leave

**walker** *n* hiker, pedestrian, rambler

**walk-out** *n* industrial action, protest, stoppage, strike

**wall** *n* 1 panel, partition, room divider,

screen. **2** barricade, embankment, fortification, parapet, rampart

**wallet** *n* case, holder, pouch, purse

**wallow** *v* **1** (wallow in the mud) lie, roll, splash around, tumble, wade. **2** (wallow in emotions) bask, delight, enjoy, glory, indulge, luxuriate, revel, take delight

**wan** *adj* ashen, bloodless, colourless, pale, pasty, peaky, tired, washed out, waxen, white

**wand** *n* baton, rod, sprig, staff, stick, twig

**wander** *v* **1** cruise, drift, meander, ramble, range, roam, rove, saunter, stray, stroll, walk. **2** curve, wind, zigzag. **3** deviate, digress, drift, go off at a tangent, swerve, veer

**wane** *v* decrease, diminish, dwindle, ebb, fade, fail, grow less, lessen, shrink, subside, taper off, weaken; *opp* wax

**want** *n* **1** (sth wanted) craving, demand, desire, fancy, hankering, longing, need, requirement, thirst, wish. **2** (sth needed) absence, dearth, deficiency, insufficiency, lack, need, scarcity, shortage. **3** (living in want) destitution, famine, hunger, need, neediness, poverty; *opp* plenty, wealth

**want** *v* aspire to, covet, crave, desire, fancy, hanker after, like, long for, pine for, prefer, set your heart on *inf*, wish, yearn for. **2** (need sth) be in need of, be short of, call for, demand, lack, miss, need, require

**wanton** *adj* **1** (wanton destruction) gratuitous, malicious, motiveless, needless, pointless, senseless, spiteful, unjustified, unprovoked, wilful. **2** (having no morals) immoral, loose, promiscuous, shameless

**war** *n* **1** battle, campaign, conflict, crusade, fight, hostilities, military action. **2** combat, fighting, warfare

**ward** *n* **1** compartment, cubicle, room. **2** area, district, division, quarter, zone. **3** charge, dependant

**warden** *n* administrator, caretaker, curator, guard, guardian, janitor, keeper, supervisor, warder, watchman

**warder** *n* custodian, gaoler, guard, jailer, keeper, prison officer

**warehouse** *n* depository, depot, stockroom, store, storehouse

**wares** *n* goods, merchandise, produce, stock, stuff

**warfare** *n* armed conflict, combat, fighting, hostilities, strife

**warlike** *adj* aggressive, belligerent, combative, hostile, martial, militant, militaristic, warmongering, warring; *opp* peaceful

**warm** *adj* **1** (warm weather) balmy, hot, mild, pleasant, summery, sunny, temperate; *opp* cold. **2** (warm water) heated, lukewarm, tepid; *opp* cold. **3** (a warm embrace) effusive, emotional, enthusiastic, friendly, heartfelt, hearty, passionate, sincere; *opp* cold, cool. **4** (a warm nature) affectionate, caring, friendly, genial, happy, loving, warm-hearted; *opp* cold. **5** (a warm jumper) cosy, thick, woolly; *opp* thin

**warm** *v* heat, heat up, make warm, melt, reheat, thaw, thaw out, warm up; *opp* cool

**warmth** *n* **1** heat. **2** (warmth of feeling) affection, animation, ardour, eagerness, enthusiasm, fervour, heartiness, intensity, love, passion, sincerity, spirit, tenderness, zeal

**warn** v admonish, advise, alert, caution, counsel, forewarn, give notice, inform, let sb know, tell, tip off inf

**warning** n 1 advice, caution, forewarning, notice, notification, threat, tip, tip-off inf. 2 (a warning of what was to come) omen, portent, premonition, sign, signal, token

**warrant** n authority, authorization, document, licence, papers, permission, permit, sanction, written order

**warrant** v 1 affirm, assure, attest, certify, declare, endorse, guarantee, pledge, swear to, vouch for. 2 be a reason for, deserve, excuse, justify. 3 authorize, commission, empower, entitle, license, permit, sanction

**warrior** n fighter, soldier

**wary** adj alert, attentive, careful, cautious, distrustful, guarded, on the lookout, on your guard, prudent, suspicious, vigilant, watchful

**wash** n bath, clean, cleaning, rinse, scrub, shampoo, shower, washing

**wash** v 1 bath, bathe, clean, cleanse, flush, launder, moisten, mop, rinse, scrub, shampoo, shower, soap, sponge, swab, swill, wet, wipe. 2 (of waves) beat, break, dash, lap, splash

**washout** n débâcle, disappointment, disaster, failure, fiasco, flop inf

**waste** adj 1 extra, left over, superfluous, unusable, unused, unwanted, useless, worthless. 2 arid, bare, barren, bleak, derelict, desolate, empty, uncultivated, uninhabited, unproductive, wild

**waste** n 1 debris, dregs, dross, excess, garbage, junk, leavings, left-overs inf, litter, offcuts, refuse, remnants, rubbish, scrap, trash. 2 extravagance, loss, misuse, squandering, wastage, wastefulness. 3 (frozen wastes) desert, wasteland, wilderness

**waste** v 1 be wasteful with, blow inf, fritter away, misspend, misuse, splurge, squander, throw away, use up. 2 (wasting away) become emaciated, grow weak, waste away, weaken, wither

**wasteful** adj excessive, extravagant, lavish, needless, profligate, spendthrift, thriftless, uneconomical;
*opp* economical

**watch** n 1 chronometer, clock, digital watch, timepiece, wrist-watch.
2 (keep a watch) guard, lookout, surveillance, vigil

**watch** v 1 check out inf, eye, gaze at, look, note, observe, peer at, regard, see, stare at, view. 2 keep tabs on inf, keep watch on, spy on. 3 (watch what you're doing) attend to, be watchful, keep your eyes on, pay attention, take care.
4 (supervise sb) guard, keep an eye on, look after, mind, protect, supervise, take care of. 5 **watch out** be alert, be careful, be on your guard, be vigilant, be watchful, keep your eyes open, look out, mind out, take care

**watchful** adj alert, attentive, eagle-eyed, guarded, note, observant, sharp-eyed, suspicious, vigilant, wary, wide awake

**watchman** n caretaker, guard, lookout, security man, sentry

**water** v dampen, douse, drench, flood, hose, irrigate, moisten, saturate, soak, spray, sprinkle, wet

**waterfall** n cascade, cataract, falls

**waterproof** *adj* damp-proof, water-repellent, water-resistant, watertight, weatherproof

**watertight** *adj* sealed, sound, waterproof

**watery** *adj* **1** (like water) aqueous, fluid, liquid. **2** (too thin) dilute, diluted, runny, tasteless, thin, watered down, weak, wishy-washy *inf*. **3** (containing water) boggy, damp, moist, sodden, soggy, squelchy, waterlogged, wet. **4** (full of tears) moist, tear-filled, tearful, weepy, wet

**wave** *n* **1** (a wave of sth) current, flood, movement, outbreak, rush, stream, surge, tide, trend, upsurge. **2** (in the sea) billow, breaker, crest, ripple, roller, surf, swell, tidal wave. **3** (a wave of your hand) flourish, gesture, shake, sign, signal

**wave** *v* **1** (wave a stick) brandish, flourish, shake, swing, wag, waggle, wield. **2** (wave in the wind) billow, flap, flutter, ripple, stir, undulate. **3** (wave to sb) beckon, gesticulate, gesture, indicate, signal

**waver** *v* **1** be indecisive, be in two minds, dither, falter, hesitate, shilly-shally *inf*, vacillate. **2** become unsteady, flicker, fluctuate, quiver, reel, shake, sway, teeter, totter, tremble, undulate, vary, wave, weave, wobble

**wavy** *adj* **1** (wavy hair) curling, curly; *opp* straight. **2** (a wavy line) curving, curvy, squiggly, undulating, winding; *opp* straight

**wax** *v* broaden, develop, expand, get bigger, grow, increase, mount, rise, swell, widen; *opp* wane

**way** *n* **1** (way of doing sth) approach, manner, means, method, mode, plan, procedure, scheme, system, technique. **2** (the way to a place) access, avenue, channel, course, direction, lane, path, pathway, road, roadway, route, street, track, trail. **3** (sb's way) behaviour, conduct, custom, eccentricity, habit, manner, mannerism, nature, personality, routine, style, temperament, trait, wont. **4** (different in some ways) aspect, circumstance, detail, feature, particular, point, respect, sense

**waylay** *v* accost, ambush, attack, buttonhole, hold up, intercept, lie in wait for, pounce on, surprise

**weak** *adj* **1** anaemic, debilitated, decrepit, delicate, exhausted, faint, feeble, fragile, frail, infirm, puny, sickly, tender, tired, unsteady, wasted, weedy, worn out; *opp* strong. **2** breakable, brittle, fragile, inadequate, insubstantial, rickety, shaky, thin, unsafe; *opp* strong. **3** (a weak position) defenceless, exposed, open, unguarded, unprotected, vulnerable; *opp* strong. **4** (a weak ruler) cowardly, fearful, impotent, indecisive, ineffective, ineffectual, powerless, spineless, timid, unassertive; *opp* powerful. **5** (a weak sound) distant, dull, faint, low, muffled, quiet, small, soft; *opp* loud. **6** (a weak light) dim, fading, faint, poor, small; *opp* bright. **7** (a weak excuse) feeble, flimsy, hollow, lame, pathetic, unconvincing, unsatisfactory; *opp* good. **8** (a weak mixture) diluted, insipid, runny, tasteless, thin, thinned down, watery; *opp* strong

**weaken** *v* **1** (weaken sth) destroy, dilute, diminish, erode, exhaust, lessen, lower, make weaker, reduce, sap, soften, thin down, tire, undermine, water down, wear out. **2** (sth weakens) abate, become weaker, decline, decrease, dwindle, ease up, ebb, fade, flag, give in, give way, let up, tire, wane

**weakling** n coward, doormat inf, drip inf, mouse, sissy, weed inf, wet inf, wimp inf

**weakness** n **1** cowardliness, feebleness, frailty, impotence, powerlessness, spinelessness, vulnerability; *opp* strength. **2** Achilles' heel inf, defect, failing, fault, flaw, imperfection, shortcoming, weak point; *opp* strength. **3** (a weakness for sth) fondness, liking, partiality, penchant, soft spot, taste

**wealth** n **1** affluence, assets, capital, cash, funds, means, money, opulence, prosperity, resources, riches, treasure; *opp* poverty. **2** (a wealth of sth) abundance, bounty, fullness, mine, plenty, profusion, richness, store, treasury

**wealthy** adj affluent, comfortable, flush inf, loaded inf, prosperous, rich, well-heeled inf, well-off, well-to-do; *opp* poor

**weapon** n bomb, chemical weapon, firearm, gun, missile, nuclear weapon

**wear** n **1** (show signs of wear) damage, depreciation, erosion, friction, use. **2** (get more wear out of sth) mileage inf, use. **3** (leisure wear) attire, clothes, clothing, dress, garments, outfit

**wear** v **1** be clothed in, be dressed in, clothe yourself in, have on, put on, sport inf. **2** (wear glasses) have, need, use. **3** (wear away) become worn, corrode, damage, erode, fray, grind away, injure, mark, scuff, wash away, weaken, wear

away, wear out, wear thin. **4** wear off become weaker, decrease, diminish, fade, lose effect, peter out, subside, wane, weaken. **5** wear out deteriorate, fray, wear thin. **6** wear out (wear sb out) drain, exhaust, fatigue, sap, tire, weary

**wearing** adj draining, exasperating, exhausting, fatiguing, irksome, stressful, tiresome, tiring, wearisome

**wearisome** adj annoying, boring, bothersome, burdensome, dreary, dull, exhausting, fatiguing, monotonous, repetitive, tedious, trying

**weary** adj **1** dead on your feet inf, dog-tired inf, exhausted, fatigued, flagging, jet-lagged inf, shattered inf, sleepy, tired, worn out. **2** (weary of sth) bored, fed up, impatient, jaded, lethargic, listless, sick and tired inf

**weather** n climate, conditions, temperature, the elements

**weather** v **1** (come through sth successfully) brave, come through, endure, overcome, resist, surmount, survive, withstand. **2** (change because of the weather) be exposed, colour, erode, harden, toughen, wear

**weave** v **1** (weave threads) blend, braid, criss-cross, entwine, interlace, intermingle, intertwine, knit, merge, plait, sew, twist, unite. **2** (weave a web) build, construct, create, make, spin. **3** (weave between the cars) dodge, tack, wind your way, zigzag

**web** n cobweb, knot, lattice, mesh, net, network, tangle

**wedding** n marriage, nuptials, union

**wedge** n block, chock, chunk, lump, wodge inf

**wedge** v block, cram, crowd, force, jam, pack, squeeze, stick, stuff, thrust

**weep** v bawl, blubber, cry, lament, moan, mourn, shed tears, sob, wail, whimper

**weigh** v 1 (weigh sth) measure the weight of, put on the scales. 2 (weigh a certain amount) have a weight of, tip the scales at *inf*. 3 (weigh things up) assess, balance, compare, consider, contemplate, evaluate, judge, mull over, think about, think over, weigh up

**weight** n 1 (a heavy weight) burden, load. 2 (the weight of sth) density, heaviness, mass. 3 (what she says carries weight) authority, credibility, force, importance, influence, power, significance, value, worth. 4 (a weight off my mind) burden, load, strain, trouble, worry

**weighty** adj 1 burdensome, dense, heavy. 2 crucial, important, momentous, serious, substantial, vital; *opp* trivial. 3 burdensome, onerous, oppressive, stressful, troublesome

**weird** adj bizarre, creepy *inf*, eerie, funny, ghostly, grotesque, mysterious, odd, queer, spooky *inf*, strange, supernatural, uncanny, unearthly, unnatural, unusual, zany

**welcome** adj 1 (a welcome break) acceptable, agreeable, cheering, delightful, desirable, much-needed, pleasant, pleasurable, refreshing, wanted; *opp* unwelcome. 2 (make sb feel welcome) appreciated, wanted; *opp* unwelcome

**welcome** n greeting, hospitality, reception, salutation

**welcome** v 1 (welcome sb) give a welcome to, greet, meet, receive. 2 (welcome sth) accept, appreciate, be pleased by, like, want

**welfare** n comfort, good fortune, happiness, health, prosperity, success, well-being

**well** adj 1 (fit and well) fit, healthy, hearty, in good health, sound, strong, thriving; *opp* unwell. 2 (if all is well) all right, fine, O.K. *inf*, satisfactory

**well** n fount, fountain, pool, reservoir, shaft, source, spring, waterhole

**well** adv 1 (everything went well) nicely, pleasantly, satisfactorily, smoothly, successfully; *opp* badly. 2 (do sth well) ably, carefully, conscientiously, correctly, effectively, excellently, expertly, proficiently, properly, skilfully, thoroughly, with skill; *opp* badly. 3 (eat well) abundantly, amply, fully, heartily, sufficiently, very much. 4 (live well) comfortably, in comfort, prosperously. 5 (know sb well) deeply, fully, intimately, personally, thoroughly. 6 (treat sb well) civilly, fairly, generously, hospitably, kindly, nicely, politely; *opp* badly. 7 (speak well of sb) admiringly, favourably, glowingly, highly, warmly, with praise; *opp* ill

**well-balanced** adj balanced, elegant, graceful, harmonious, proportional, symmetrical, well-proportioned

**well-behaved** adj co-operative, disciplined, dutiful, good, hard-working, law-abiding, obedient, well-trained

**well-fed** adj 1 healthy, in good condition, well-nourished; *opp* malnourished. 2 chubby, fat, plump, podgy, stout; *opp* thin

**well-known** *adj* celebrated, eminent, familiar, famous, illustrious, notable, noted, notorious, popular, prominent, renowned, widely known; *opp* unknown

**well-off** *adj* 1 affluent, comfortable, prosperous, rich, wealthy, well-to-do; *opp* poor. 2 fortunate, lucky

**wet** *adj* 1 bedraggled, clammy, damp, dank, dewy, dripping, moist, saturated, soaking, sodden, soggy, sopping, waterlogged, watery, wet through, wringing wet; *opp* dry. 2 (of weather) drizzling, humid, pouring, raining, rainy, showery; *opp* dry. 3 (the paint is still wet) runny, sticky, tacky; *opp* dry

**wet** *v* dampen, dip, douse, drench, irrigate, moisten, put water on, saturate, soak, splash, spray, sprinkle

**wharf** *n* dock, jetty, landing stage, pier, quay

**wheel** *n* circle, disc, hoop, ring

**wheel** *v* 1 circle, go round, move in circles, pivot, revolve, rotate, spin, swerve, swing, swivel, turn, veer, whirl. 2 (wheel sth along) pull, push, trundle

**wheeze** *v* breathe noisily, cough, gasp, hiss, pant, puff, rasp, whistle

**whiff** *n* 1 aroma, blast, hint, odour, scent, smell, stink. 2 (a whiff of air) breath, gust, puff

**whim** *n* craze, desire, fancy, idea, impulse, notion, urge

**whimper** *n* cry, groan, moan, sob, whine

**whimper** *v* cry, grizzle *inf*, moan, sniffle, snivel, sob, weep, whine, whinge *inf*

**whimsical** *adj* bizarre, capricious, curious, fanciful, mischievous, odd, peculiar, playful, quaint, unusual

**whine** *n* cry, groan, moan, sob, wail, whimper

**whine** *v* bleat, complain, cry, fuss, gripe *inf*, grizzle *inf*, groan, grouch *inf*, grumble, moan, sob, wail, whimper, whinge *inf*

**whip** *n* birch, bull whip, cane, crop, horsewhip, lash, switch

**whip** *v* 1 beat, cane, flog, horsewhip, lash, tan *inf*, thrash. 2 (whip sth away) jerk, pull, snatch, yank. 3 (whip cream) beat, stir, whip up, whisk

**whirl** *n* confusion, daze, dither, flurry, muddle, spin

**whirl** *v* 1 circle, gyrate, pirouette, pivot, reel, revolve, roll, rotate, spin, swirl, turn, twist, wheel. 2 (my head starting to whirl) go round, reel, spin

**whirlwind** *n* hurricane, tornado, typhoon

**whisper** *n* low voice, murmur, quiet voice, undertone

**whisper** *v* breathe, murmur, mutter, say under your breath, speak softly, talk quietly

**white** *adj* 1 cream, ivory, off-white, snow-white. 2 (of sb's face) ashen, bloodless, pale, pallid, pasty, wan, white as a sheet. 3 (clean) bright, clean, immaculate, spotless

**whiten** *v* blanch, bleach, fade, lighten, make pale, make white

**whole** *adj* 1 complete, entire, full, solid, total, unabbreviated, unabridged, uncut. 2 flawless, good, in one piece, intact, perfect, sound, unbroken, undamaged, unharmed, unhurt, uninjured

**wholesale** *adj* broad, comprehensive, extensive, far-reaching, global, indiscriminate, mass, sweeping, universal, widespread

**wholesome** adj 1 beneficial, good, good for you, healthy, nourishing, nutritious, strengthening. 2 clean, decent, innocent, nice, pure, respectable, virtuous

**wicked** adj amoral, bad, blasphemous, corrupt, criminal, diabolical, dishonourable, evil, foul, immoral, malicious, mischievous, murderous, naughty, obscene, perverted, scandalous, shameful, sinful, unholy, unscrupulous, vicious, vile, villainous, violent, wrong; **opp** good

**wickedness** n evil, depravity, immorality, sin, sinfulness, villainy, wrong, wrongdoing; **opp** virtue

**wide** adj 1 ample, broad, expansive, full, large, roomy, spacious, vast, yawning. 2 all-embracing, broad, encyclopaedic, far-ranging, general, inclusive, wide-ranging. 3 dilated, extended, open, outspread, outstretched. 4 (wide of the mark) off-course, off-target

**widen** v broaden, dilate, enlarge, expand, extend, flare, make wider, open out, open wide, spread, stretch

**widespread** adj common, extensive, far-reaching, general, pervasive, popular, prevalent, rife, sweeping, universal

**width** n breadth, broadness, diameter, extent, girth, range, reach, scope, span, thickness, wideness

**wield** v 1 brandish, employ, flourish, swing, use, wave. 2 (wield power) command, exercise, exert, have, hold, possess

**wife** n bride, mate, partner, spouse

**wild** adj 1 (a wild animal) feral, ferocious, fierce, free, savage, unbroken, untamed; **opp** tame. 2 (wild country) desolate, godforsaken, natural, overgrown, remote, uncivilized, uncultivated, unpopulated, unsettled, waste; **opp** cultivated. 3 (wild behaviour) barbaric, boisterous, disorderly, excited, noisy, out of control, riotous, rough, rowdy, uncivilized, uncontrolled, undisciplined, unmanageable, unruly, violent; **opp** calm. 4 (drive sb wild) angry, berserk, crazy, delirious, demented, deranged, frantic, hysterical, incensed, mad, seething; **opp** calm. 5 (a wild guess) arbitrary, crazy, foolish, ill-considered, impulsive, inaccurate, random, reckless, silly, uninformed; **opp** sensible. 6 (of weather) blustery, rough, stormy, windy; **opp** calm. 7 (wild about sb) crazy inf, daft, mad inf, nuts inf, passionate, potty inf. 8 (a wild appearance) dishevelled, tousled, unkempt, untidy, wind-blown; **opp** neat

**wilderness** n desert, jungle, waste, wasteland, wilds

**wile** n 1 artfulness, cheating, craftiness, cunning, guile, slyness, trickery. 2 gambit, manoeuvre, ploy, ruse, stratagem, trick

**wilful** adj 1 determined, dogged, headstrong, inflexible, obstinate, perverse, pigheaded, self-willed, stubborn. 2 calculated, conscious, deliberate, intentional, premeditated

**will** n 1 (the will to succeed) determination, resolve, single-mindedness, willpower. 2 (do sth against sb's will) desire, wish. 3 (make a will) testament

**will** v (to will sth to happen) bid, cause, command, decree, effect, force, influence, order, persuade, wish

**willing** adj 1 (willing to do sth) happy, pleased, prepared, ready. 2 (a willing volunteer) co-operative, eager, enthusiastic, helpful, keen, obliging

**willpower** n commitment, determination, drive, nerve, purposefulness, resolution, resolve, self-control, self-discipline, strength of will, will

**wilt** v 1 (of flowers) become limp, droop, flop, sag, shrivel, wither. 2 (of courage) diminish, fade, fail, lessen, melt away, wane; *opp* grow

**wily** adj artful, clever, crafty, cunning, deceitful, furtive, scheming, shifty, shrewd, sly, tricky, underhand

**win** n conquest, success, triumph, victory

**win** v 1 be the winner, be victorious, come first, overcome, prevail, succeed, triumph. 2 (win sth) achieve, acquire, attain, catch, collect, earn, gain, get, pick up *inf*, receive, secure, walk away with *inf*

**wince** v blench, cower, cringe, draw back, flinch, grimace, quail, recoil, shrink, start

**wind** n 1 air, blast, breath, breeze, current, draught, gale, gust, hurricane, monsoon, squall, tornado, whirlwind, zephyr. 2 breath, puff *inf*, respiration

**wind** v 1 coil, curl, furl, loop, reel, roll, spiral, twine, twist, wrap, wreathe. 2 bend, curve, loop, meander, ramble, snake, turn, twist, zigzag

**windfall** n bonanza, godsend, jackpot, stroke of good luck

**winding** adj bending, circuitous, convoluted, crooked, curving, indirect, looping, meandering, rambling, roundabout, spiralling, twisting, wandering

**windy** adj blowy, blustery, breezy, draughty, fresh, gusting, gusty, squally, stormy, tempestuous, wild, windswept

**wing** n 1 (of a building) annex, extension. 2 (of a political party) branch, faction, group, grouping, section, side

**wink** v 1 bat, blink, flutter. 2 flash, gleam, glitter, sparkle, twinkle

**winner** n champ *inf*, champion, conquering hero, conqueror, prizewinner, title-holder, victor

**winning** adj 1 conquering, leading, successful, top, triumphant, unbeaten, victorious; *opp* losing. 2 (winning ways) alluring, attractive, beguiling, bewitching, captivating, charming, cute, delightful, disarming, endearing, lovely, sweet

**winnings** n booty, gains, proceeds, profits, spoils, takings

**wintry** adj arctic, biting, bleak, cheerless, chilly, cold, desolate, frozen, harsh, icy, snowy; *opp* summery

**wipe** v 1 brush, clean, dry, dust, mop, polish, rub, sponge, swab, wash. 2 **wipe out** annihilate, blot out, destroy, eradicate, erase, exterminate, obliterate

**wipe** n brush, clean, dust, rub, wash

**wiry** adj 1 (of a person) lean, muscular, sinewy, spare, strong, thin, tough. 2 (wiry hair) bristly, coarse, kinky, stiff

**wisdom** n cleverness, common sense, good sense, insight, intelligence, judgement, knowledge, learning, perception, sense, understanding

**wise** *adj* **1** (of a person) clever, deep-thinking, educated, experienced, fair, informed, intelligent, just, knowledgeable, perceptive, philosophical, well-informed, well-read; *opp* stupid. **2** (a wise choice) clever, diplomatic, good, logical, prudent, sensible, smart, thoughtful; *opp* unwise

**wish** *n* ambition, aspiration, craving, desire, fondness, hope, liking, longing, request, requirement, want, yearning

**wish** *v* **1** (wish for sth) covet, crave, desire, fancy, hanker after, hope for, hunger for, long for, need, set your heart on, thirst for, want, yearn for. **2** (if you wish) ask, bid, command, desire, direct, order, require, want. **3** (wish them Merry Christmas) bid

**wistful** *adj* disconsolate, dreaming, longing, melancholy, mournful, nostalgic, pensive, regretful, sad, yearning

**wit** *n* **1** banter, fun, funniness, humour, jokes, puns, quips, repartee, witticisms, wittiness, wordplay. **2** (a wit) comedian, comic, funny person, humorist, joker, wag. **3** (have the wit to do sth) common sense, intellect, intelligence, nous *inf*, sense, wisdom

**witch** *n* crone, enchantress, magician, sorceress

**witchcraft** *n* black magic, charms, enchantment, incantations, magic, sorcery, spells, the occult, voodoo, wizardry

**withdraw** *v* **1** cancel, extract, pull back, pull out, remove, retract, take back, take out. **2** (withdraw from the contest) back away, back down, back out, cry off *inf*, drop out, go, leave, pull out, quit, retire, retreat, run away

**withdrawal** *n* **1** extraction, removal. **2** departure, evacuation, exit, leaving, retreat

**withdrawn** *adj* aloof, detached, distant, introverted, private, quiet, reserved, shy, silent, taciturn, timid, uncommunicative, unsociable; *opp* outgoing

**wither** *v* decay, decline, die, disintegrate, droop, dry out, dry up, fade, go limp, languish, perish, shrink, shrivel, waste away, wilt

**withering** *adj* cruel, cutting, devastating, hurtful, scornful, wounding

**withhold** *v* check, control, curb, hide, hold back, keep, keep back, refuse, repress, reserve, retain, suppress

**withstand** *v* bear, brave, cope with, defy, endure, face, hold out against, put up with *inf*, resist, stand up to, survive, take, thwart, tolerate

**witness** *n* bystander, eyewitness, observer, onlooker, spectator, viewer, watcher

**witness** *v* behold, be present at, notice, observe, see, view, watch

**wits** *n* brains, common sense, ingenuity, intelligence, judgement, reason, sense, understanding

**witticism** *n* clever remark, crack *inf*, joke, one-liner, play on words, pun, quip, wisecrack *inf*, witty remark

**witty** *adj* amusing, brilliant, clever, comic, droll, facetious, funny, humorous, sarcastic

**wizard** *n* conjurer, enchanter, magician, sorcerer, warlock

**wobble** *v* be unsteady, quake, quaver, quiver, rock, see-saw, shake, stagger, sway, teeter, totter, tremble, vibrate, waver

**wobbly** *adj* 1 (a wobbly tooth) insecure, loose. 2 (a wobbly voice) quavering, shaking, shaky, trembling. 3 (feeling wobbly) rocky, teetering, tottering, unstable, unsteady

**woe** *n* affliction, anguish, despair, distress, grief, heartache, misery, misfortune, pain, sadness, sorrow, suffering, unhappiness

**woeful** *adj* 1 (unhappy) dismal, gloomy, miserable, mournful, remorseful, sad, sorrowful, sorry, unhappy; *opp* cheerful, happy. 2 heart-breaking, piteous, pitiful, sad, tragic, wretched. 3 (deplorable) abysmal, appalling, awful, deplorable, disgraceful, hopeless, miserable, poor, sorry, terrible; *opp* excellent

**woman** *n* female, girl, lady

**womanizer** *n* Casanova, Don Juan, ladies' man, philanderer

**womanly** *adj* female, feminine, ladylike, matronly, motherly

**wonder** *n* 1 amazement, astonishment, awe, fascination, reverence, surprise. 2 curiosity, marvel, miracle, mystery, phenomenon, sensation, sight, spectacle

**wonder** *v* ask yourself, conjecture, deliberate, ponder, puzzle, reflect, speculate, think. 2 be amazed, be flabbergasted, be surprised, marvel

**wonderful** *adj* brilliant, excellent, fantastic, great, incredible, magnificent, marvellous, outstanding, remarkable, sensational, smashing, stunning, superb, terrific; *opp* awful, dreadful

**woo** *v* 1 be after, chase, chat up *inf*, court, pursue, seduce. 2 attract, chase after, cosy up to *inf*, cultivate, find favour with, pursue, seek the support of

**wood** *n* 1 boards, chipboard, hardwood, lumber *Am*, planks, plywood, softwood, timber. 2 coppice, copse, forest, grove, jungle, orchard, rain forest, spinney, tree plantation, trees, woodland. 3 firewood, fuel, kindling, logs

**wooden** *adj* 1 made of wood, timber, wood. 2 awkward, clumsy, dead, deadpan, expressionless, flat, lifeless, stiff, stilted, unnatural; *opp* emotional, lively

**wool** *n* 1 coat, fleece, fur, hair. 2 fibre, yarn

**woolly** *adj* 1 curly, fleecy, fluffy, frizzy, furry, shaggy, soft, woollen. 2 confused, hazy, ill-defined, muddled, unclear, unfocused, unstructured, vague; *opp* crystal-clear

**word** *n* 1 expression, name, term. 2 (have a word with sb) chat, talk, discussion, conversation, brief exchange. 3 (news) comment, information, low-down *inf*, message, news, notice, remark, rumour, statement. 4 (give the word to go ahead) command, go-ahead, green light, order, signal. 5 (promise) guarantee, pledge, promise, undertaking, vow

**word** *v* couch, express, phrase, put, say, state

**wordy** *adj* discursive, long-winded, loquacious, never-ending, rambling, roundabout, verbose, waffly; *opp* brief, concise, succinct

**work** n 1 business, career, employment, field, job, line, livelihood, living, occupation, post, profession, trade. 2 (effort) donkey-work inf, drudgery, effort, elbow grease inf, exertion, graft inf, grind inf, hassle inf, slog inf, trouble. 3 (task) assignment, charge, chore, duty, housework, job, project, responsibility, task, undertaking. 4 (composition) book, composition, creation, oeuvre, opus, piece, production, writing

**work** v 1 be busy, be employed, beaver away, earn a living, go to work, have a job, labour, make an effort, slave, toil. 2 (the machine won't work) function, go, operate, perform, run. 3 (to work a machine) control, drive, handle, operate, use. 4 (the plan worked) be effective, have the desired effect, succeed, be successful, go according to plan. 5 (manoeuvre) ease, edge, guide, manoeuvre, push, wiggle. 6 (work loose, work free) become, get. 7 (arrange) accomplish, achieve, arrange, bring about, bring off, contrive, fix, produce, pull off, sort inf, swing it inf. 8 (work the soil) cultivate, dig, till. 9 **work out** (work out a sum or total) calculate, estimate, solve. 10 **work out** (the total works out at £600) add up to, amount to, be, come to, total. 11 **work out** (work out why sth happened) clear up, decide, figure out, puzzle out, resolve, solve, sort out, understand. 12 **work out** (work out a plan) construct, develop, devise, formulate, plan, put together. 13 **work out** (it worked out well/badly) develop, go, pan out inf, turn out. 14 **work out** (things didn't work out)

be successful, go as planned, go well, succeed, turn out well. 15 **work out** do exercises, exercise, get fit, train

**worker** n breadwinner, craftsperson, employee, labourer, member of staff, operative, staff, trader, troops inf, wage-earner, workaholic

**workforce** n crews, employees, labour force, labour pool, personnel, shop-floor, staff, team, troops inf

**workman** n labourer, tradesman, worker

**workmanship** n art, craft, craftsmanship, expertise, finish, handiwork, skill, work

**works** n 1 factory, foundry, industrial unit, mill, plant, workshop. 2 (of an author or musician) books, compositions, oeuvre, output, writings. 3 (good works) actions, acts, deeds. 4 (working parts) action, innards, insides, mechanism, working parts, workings. 5 **the works** the full treatment, the lot, the whole caboodle, the whole shebang.

**workshop** n 1 atelier, garage, industrial unit, production room, studio, workroom. 2 class, discussion group, practical session, seminar

**world** n 1 earth, globe, planet. 2 everybody, human race, humanity, international community, people, public, whole world. 3 (the academic world) domain, field, province, realm, sphere. 4 (the world of steam) age, days, era, life and times, period, time

**worldly** adj 1 earthly, material, materialistic, physical, secular, temporal, terrestrial; *opp* spiritual. 2 cosmopolitan, experienced, shrewd, smart, sophisticated, streetwise inf, worldly wise; *opp* naïve

**worldwide** *adj* global, international, transnational, ubiquitous, universal, widespread; *opp* local

**worn** *adj* decrepit, frayed, moth-eaten, old, ragged, scruffy, shabby, tattered, tatty *inf*, threadbare, tired, weary, worn-out; *opp* new

**worn-out** *adj* 1 all in *inf*, exhausted, fit to drop *inf*, shattered *inf*, tired out, weary. 2 broken-down, clapped out *inf*, decrepit, moth-eaten, on its last legs, shabby, tatty *inf*, threadbare, useless, wrecked

**worried** *adj* agitated, anxious, apprehensive, bothered, concerned, distraught, distressed, fearful, fretful, nervous, on edge, perturbed, stressed-out *inf*, tense, troubled, uneasy, uptight *inf*, worked-up; *opp* calm, laid-back *inf*, relaxed

**worry** *n* 1 (anxiety) agitation, anxiety, apprehension, bother, concern, disquiet, distress, nervousness, stress, tension, trouble, uneasiness. 2 (a problem) bother, burden, doubt, irritation, nuisance, pest, problem

**worry** *v* 1 (worry about sth) agonize, be agitated, be anxious, be concerned, bother, feel uneasy, fret, get worked up. 2 (sth/sb worries you) bother, concern, disturb, hassle, irritate, nag, pester, torment, trouble, unsettle, upset

**worsen** *v* 1 (get worse) decline, degenerate, deteriorate, get worse, go downhill, go from bad to worse; *opp* improve. 2 (make sth worse) aggravate, damage, exacerbate, make worse; *opp* improve

**worship** *n* deification, devotion, prayer, reverence, service, veneration

**worship** *v* 1 idolize, pray to, revere, venerate. 2 go to church, pray. 3 admire, adore, dote on, idolize, look up to, love, put on a pedestal

**worth** *n* 1 excellence, importance, merit, profit, significance, usefulness, value, virtue. 2 cost, price, value

**worthless** *adj* 1 futile, ineffective, insignificant, meaningless, not worth the paper it's written on, of no value, pointless, poor, rubbishy, useless, valueless; *opp* useful, valuable. 2 (good-for-nothing) despicable, good-for-nothing, useless, no-good *inf*

**worthwhile** *adj* advantageous, beneficial, constructive, fruitful, good, helpful, productive, profitable, rewarding, useful, valuable; *opp* useless

**worthy** *adj* commendable, deserving, excellent, good, honourable, laudable, praiseworthy, respectable

**wound** *n* 1 cut, gash, graze, injury, laceration, lesion, scar. 2 anguish, blow, damage, distress, grief, hurt, injury, scar, shock, trauma

**wound** *v* 1 cut, damage, harm, hurt, injure, lacerate, stab. 2 (distress) damage, distress, hurt, injure, offend, shock, traumatize

**wrangle** *n* argument, difference of opinion, disagreement, dispute, fight, quarrel, row, spat *inf*, squabble, tiff

**wrangle** *v* argue, bicker, disagree, fall out, fight, quarrel, row *inf*, squabble

**wrap** *v* 1 bind, cover, encase, enfold, envelop, fold, lag, muffle, package, shroud. 2 **wrap up** gift-wrap, package,

wrap. **3 wrap up** dress warmly, keep warm, muffle up, put warm things on.
**4 wrap up** bring to an end, close, conclude, finish off, round off, summarize, wind up. **5 wrap up** be quiet, pipe down, shut up. **6 wrapped up in** engrossed, hooked on, in another world, involved, obsessed, preoccupied

**wrath** n anger, annoyance, displeasure, fury, indignation, irritation, rage; *opp* delight, pleasure

**wreath** n 1 bouquet, floral tribute, tribute. 2 band, coronet, crown, garland

**wreathe** v coil, cover, encircle, envelop, festoon, smother, twist, wind, wrap

**wreck** n 1 (wreckage) mess, remains, ruin, ruins, shipwreck, wreckage, write-off. 2 (destruction) annihilation, destruction, devastation, loss, ruin, shattering, spoiling, wrecking

**wreck** v dash, demolish, destroy, devastate, play havoc with, put a spanner in the works *inf*, ruin, scupper *inf*, scuttle, smash, spoil, write off

**wreckage** n debris, pieces, remains, rubble

**wrench** v 1 jerk, pull, rip, tear, tug, twist, yank. 2 dislocate, pull, put out, rick, sprain, strain, twist

**wrestle** v contend with, fight, grapple, struggle, tussle

**wretch** n 1 down-and-out, miserable creature, poor soul, unfortunate. 2 louse *inf*, pig *inf*, rat *inf*, rogue

**wretched** adj 1 miserable, poor, sorry, unfortunate. 2 (bad) appalling, atrocious, bad, deplorable, grim, miserable, terrible; *opp* excellent, good, wonderful. 3 (unhappy) dejected,

depressed, distressed, down, downcast, gloomy, miserable, sad, unhappy; *opp* cheerful, happy

**wriggle** n squirm, twist, wiggle

**wriggle** v snake, squirm, twist, wiggle, worm, writhe

**wring** v 1 (wring out clothes) squeeze, twist. 2 (wring sb's hand) grasp, grip, press, pump, shake, squeeze. 3 (wring a confession from sb) exact, extract, force, wrest

**wrinkle** n crease, crinkle, crow's foot, fold, line, pucker

**wrinkle** v crease, crinkle, crumple, fold, pucker, ruck up, rumple; *opp* smooth

**writ** n court order, decree, injunction, instruction, order, summons

**write** v 1 (put in writing) jot down, note down, put down, put in writing, record, scrawl, scribble, sign. 2 (create) compile, compose, create, dash off, draft, draw up, pen, produce, put together.
3 (correspond) communicate, correspond, drop sb a line, write sb a letter. 4 **write off** cancel, discount, dismiss, disregard, forget about, wipe out. 5 **write off** (wreck) crash, destroy, smash up, total *Am*, wreck

**writer** n author, biographer, columnist, compiler, contributor, correspondent, creator, diarist, dramatist, editor, essayist, ghost-writer, hack, journalist, novelist, playwright, poet, scribbler, scriptwriter, wordsmith

**writhe** v flail, snake, squirm, thrash about, twist, worm, wriggle

**writing** n 1 article, book, composition, document, essay, letter, piece, publication, work. 2 calligraphy, hand,

handwriting, inscription, lettering,
letters, print, scribble, script, text

**wrong** *adj* 1 (incorrect) false, inaccurate,
incorrect, mistaken, untrue; *opp* correct,
right, true. 2 against the law, bad,
criminal, dishonest, evil, ill-advised,
illegal, illicit, ill-judged, immoral,
improper, inappropriate, misguided,
unacceptable, unethical, unfair,
unlawful, unsuitable, wicked; *opp* good,
legal, right. 3 (there's sth wrong with
this) amiss, awry, defective, faulty,
funny, out of order, strange

**wrong** *n* abuse, atrocity, bad deed, crime,
error, evil, immorality, iniquity,
injustice, mistake, offence, outrage, sin,
unfairness, wickedness, wrong-doing;
*opp* right

**wrongful** *adj* criminal, dishonourable,
illegal, improper, incorrect, unethical,
unfair, unjust, unjustified, unlawful,
unwarranted, wrong

**wry** *adj* caustic, cynical, derisive, ironic,
mocking, quizzical, sarcastic, sardonic,
twisted

**yard** *n* **1** area, back yard, compound, court, courtyard, enclosure, farmyard, garden, quadrangle. **2** dockyard, factory, steelyard, works, workshop

**yardstick** *n* benchmark, criterion, gauge, guide, measure, standard

**yarn** *n* **1** anecdote, story, tale, tall story. **2** fibre, silk, strand, thread, wool

**yawning** *adj* cavernous, deep, gaping, huge, massive, vast, wide

**yearly** *adj, adv* annual, annually, each year, every year, once a year, per annum, per year

**yearn** *v* covet, crave, desire, eat your heart out *inf*, hanker after, hunger for, long for, pine for, want

**yell** *n* bellow, cry, howl, roar, scream, screech, shout, whoop, yelp, yowl

**yell** *v* bawl, bellow, cry, howl, roar, scream, screech, shout, whoop, yelp, yowl

**yield** *n* crop, earnings, harvest, income, proceeds, profit, return, revenue

**yield** *v* **1** bear, bring in, earn, generate, pay, produce, provide, return. **2** accede, acquiesce, admit defeat, capitulate, comply, give in, give up, give way, relinquish, submit, surrender, throw in the towel *inf*; **opp** fight on, resist, stick to your guns

**young** *adj* adolescent, baby, fledgling, growing, immature, infant, junior, juvenile, new-born, new, teenage, youthful

**youth** *n* **1** adolescence, childhood, formative years, younger days. **2** (a young person) adolescent, lad, teenager, young man, young person. **3** (young people) children, kids *inf*, the young, the younger generation, young people

**youthful** *adj* childish, fresh, sprightly, well-preserved, young at heart, young-looking, young; **opp** old

**zoom** *v* bolt, career, charge, dash, flash, fly, gallop, hare, hurry, hurtle, run, rush, shoot, speed, tear, whiz, zip

**zany** *adj* absurd, crazy, daft *inf*, eccentric, mad, off the wall *inf*, wacky *inf*, wild

**zeal** *n* ardour, dedication, determination, enthusiasm, fanaticism, fervour, gusto, passion, vehemence, zest; *opp* apathy, lethargy

**zealous** *adj* ardent, dedicated, determined, devoted, enthusiastic, fanatical, fervent, passionate, vehement; *opp* apathetic, half-hearted, lethargic

**zenith** *n* climax, culmination, height, high point, peak, pinnacle, summit, top; *opp* nadir

**zero** *n* a duck, love, nil, nothing, nought, zilch *inf*

**zest** *n* 1 (enthusiasm) determination, enthusiasm, gusto, keenness, relish, zeal. 2 (spice) excitement, flavour, kick *inf*, spice, tang

**zone** *n* area, belt, district, locality, quarter, region, section, sector